International Arbitration Institute
Institut pour l'Arbitrage International

Precedent in International Arbitration

IAI Seminar
Paris – December 14, 2007

General Editor: Emmanuel Gaillard

Edited by Yas Banifatemi

J̶P
Juris Publishing, Inc.

Questions About This Publication

For assistance with shipments, billing or other customer service matters, please call our Customer Services Department at: 1-631-350-0200.

To obtain a copy of this book in the United States and Canada Call our Toll Free Order Line: 1-800-887-4064 or Fax: 1-631-351-5712

This book may be cited as:

IAI SERIES ON INTERNATIONAL ARBITRATION No. 5,
PRECEDENT IN INTERNATIONAL ARBITRATION
(Y. Banifatemi ed., 2008)

For any inquiry regarding these materials or the IAI, an organization created under the auspices of the Comité Français de l'Arbitrage (CFA), you may contact Nanou Leleu-Knobil (nleleuknobil@shearman.com).

Juris Publishing, Inc.
71 New Street
Huntington, New York 11743
USA
www.jurispub.com

PRECEDENT IN INTERNATIONAL ARBITRATION

TABLE OF CONTENTS

Foreword

Emmanuel Gaillard [*]

Whether the doctrine of precedent exists in international arbitration—irrespective of whether one refers to international commercial arbitration or international investment arbitration—is a question of increasing importance as arbitral awards are becoming more public and accessible to all the parties involved in international arbitration. Even though investment arbitration has taken centre stage in this debate as a result of the numerous investment arbitration awards that are publicly available, its importance should not be over-estimated. Investment arbitration and commercial arbitration are inter-dependent, and the questions surrounding the doctrine of precedent in international arbitration applies equally to both. Three points are important by way of introduction to the topic.

The *first* point concerns the relationship between arbitral precedent and arbitral jurisprudence. One may think that the latter is merely a continental law or civil law vision of precedent *per se*. In other words, 'precedent' is the common law way of talking about jurisprudence. But, in reality, in the context of this topic, one should think of precedent as more selective than jurisprudence. There is something collective about jurisprudence—a body of decisions—and more is required for such jurisprudence to become constant.

---

[*] Emmanuel Gaillard heads the International Arbitration Group of Shearman & Sterling LLP. He is also a Professor of Law at the University of Paris XII.

In jurisprudence there may be more diversity amongst decisions as jurisprudence may take many different directions before finally settling on a consistent interpretation. Jurisprudence *per se* is not necessarily monolithic. Jurisprudence may be reversed, but this implies the presence of a supreme jurisdiction, which does not exist in international arbitration. With respect to arbitral jurisprudence, often more scattered and less collective, one may not refer to a reversal of jurisprudence but of a slow deviation or of taking a different route.

Second, arbitral tribunals, as opposed to State courts, face certain specific issues when talking about precedent, or of arbitral jurisprudence. These issues arise both in investment arbitration and commercial arbitration. The first concerns knowledge of or access to precedent—*i.e.*, whether the arbitral award is public or confidential—and the second concerns consistency of awards. As jurisprudence is not systematically published in all States, there are countries in which one tries to identify precedent and collect it from an intuitive knowledge that such precedent does exist. The same may be said of arbitral case law.

When studying arbitral case law, one expects arbitral awards to diverge sharply on pertinent issues, as international arbitral tribunals are by definition dispersed and diverse. The rather consistent manner in which the law has developed in arbitral awards therefore comes as a surprise. Of course, there are exceptions to this line of consistent development, but when one compares arbitral precedent to judicial precedent, one finds that arbitral precedent might well be easier to determine and more consistent than judicial precedent. This is especially true of federal States, where precedent is shaped over numerous years by courts at various levels of the judiciary before a consistent line of authority is established.

Ultimately, this raises a question as to the sources of arbitration law. Is precedent a source of law? Do arbitral awards represent a binding authority or is it simply persuasive—a sort of downgraded source? These are all questions that will be addressed in this volume.

Thirdly, as a practitioner, one is tempted to think of arbitral decisions as having the value of precedent. Irrespective of whether one considers arbitral jurisprudence in the general sense to exist or not, one point is clear: precedent is part and parcel of our practical environment, and it is certain that arbitration practitioners invoke precedents in a natural and consistent manner to try and convince the arbitral tribunal of their argument. It is done spontaneously without even thinking of the theoretical aspect of the matter.

Of course, arbitration practitioners invoke decisions that support the argument they wish to convince the arbitral tribunal of in exactly the same way as arbitrators will refer to what other arbitrators have done before them whenever they have access to such arbitral precedents. Very often, this practice goes beyond the relevant applicable law of the dispute. It is almost second nature to invoke arbitral awards in support of one's argument, without even giving a second thought to the applicable law of the award that one is invoking.

These concerns are important, not only from a practical but also a theoretical standpoint. We therefore start this volume with Barton Legum's definitions of precedent in international arbitration.

Part I considers the question from the international commercial arbitration point of view, a field where confidential awards still largely prevails. Karl-Heinz Böckstiegel's introduction is followed by a reflection on the question whether there is a need for consistency in international commercial arbitration by François Perret. Alexis Mourre discusses the impact of confidentiality of international commercial arbitration awards, and, finally, Christopher Seppälä looks at the development of a case law in construction disputes relating to FIDIC contracts.

Part II of this volume deals with international investment arbitration. There is a tendency towards publication of investment arbitration awards, which changes the question at hand from whether arbitral jurisprudence can be said to exist, to the role of arbitral awards that are invoked in the course of arbitration proceedings. Prosper Weil gives a general overview of the topic, followed by James Crawford's consideration of the similarity of issues in disputes arising under the same or similarly drafted investment treaties. Judge Gilbert Guillaume reflects on the possibility that arbitral awards may be invoked as a source of law under Article 38 of the ICJ Statute and Thomas Wälde assesses the impact that publication of awards have in investment arbitration. Professor Gabrielle Kaufmann-Kohler concludes the discussion by reflecting on whether the search for consistency is a myth.

The Definitions of "Precedent" in International Arbitration

Barton Legum [*]

Defining "precedent" in a discussion of international arbitration is a daunting problem, for several reasons. First and foremost, because Professor Gabrielle Kaufmann-Kohler addressed the topic of precedent in international arbitration in her 2006 Freshfields lecture and, consistent with her reputation, explored the topic with such thoroughness and thoughtfulness it is difficult to think of anything more to say. [1]

Second, there is no single legal system or common set of legal principles applicable to international arbitration. The simple solution of taking a definition from a familiar common-law system like the United States is unsatisfactory.

---

[*]   Counsel, Debevoise & Plimpton LLP, Paris, France.

[1]   The lecture is published as Gabrielle Kaufmann-Kohler, *Arbitral Precedent: Dream, Necessity or Excuse? – The 2006 Freshfields Lecture*, 23(3) ARB. INT'L 357 (2007). There are a number of other remarkable contributions to the literature on the subject of precedent in international arbitration, including the following: Andrea K. Björklund, *Investment Treaty Arbitral Decisions as Jurisprudence Constante, in* INTERNATIONAL ECONOMIC LAW: THE STATE AND FUTURE OF THE DISCIPLINE 265 (C.B. Picker, I.D. Bunn and D.W. Arner eds., Hart Publishing, 2008); Tai-Heng Cheng, *Precedent and Control in Investment Treaty Arbitration*, 30 FORDHAM INT'L L.J. 1014 (2007); and the papers presented by Jan Paulsson, Anthony Sinclair and others at the British Institute of International and Comparative Law's 9th Investment Treaty Forum Public Conference on the topic of "The Emerging Jurisprudence of International Investment Law," held in London on September 14, 2007, *in* INVESTMENT TREATY LAW: CURRENT ISSUES III (A. Bjorklund, I. Laird, S. Ripinsky eds., British Institute of International and Comparative Law, forthcoming 2008)

Third, international arbitration assembles jurists from a wide variety of legal systems, many of which do not formally recognize judicial decisions to have precedential value. An appeal to general notions of what constitutes a precedent, successful though such an approach might with an audience composed of common lawyers, would be parochial and misplaced in this context.

Faced with a daunting problem such as this, I must resort for inspiration to one of the great problem-solvers of the 20th Century: Albert Einstein. In 1905, he published his *Theory of Special Relativity*, a document that has transformed the world. Einstein recounts that his inspiration for *Relativity* was an anomaly in traditional physics, exemplified by several trains departing a station at the same time.[2] A passenger on one train necessarily perceives the speed of another train as different from what a bystander on the platform or a passenger on a faster train see. Because each observer has a different speed relative to each other, each has a different perception of the speed of the others. Multiple, equally valid answers are possible to a seemingly simple question: how fast?

I propose to address the definition of precedent from the relative perspectives of the principal players in international arbitration: counsel for the parties; the arbitrators; and academic commentators and other members of the general public. I will

---

[2]   *See* WILLIAM R. EVERDELL, THE FIRST MODERNS 235 (University of Chicago Press, 1997) (Einstein's revelations on relativity were inspired by reflections on the traditional problem of the electrodynamics of moving bodies); *id.* at 236 (when Einstein "wrote a book to explain [relativity] to laypeople in 1916, he used a railroad car moving past an embankment" as the paradigm) (citing ALBERT EINSTEIN, RELATIVITY: THE SPECIAL AND THE GENERAL THEORY 9 (Robert W. Lawson trans., Crown Publishers, 15th ed. 1961) ("I stand at the window of a railway carriage which is traveling uniformly, and drop a stone on the embankment. . . . I see the stone descend in a straight line.")).

show that each of these perspectives is necessarily different. Each is valid on its own terms. I will attempt a synthesis with a view toward a unified definition of precedent in international arbitration.

I. COUNSEL'S PERSPECTIVE ON PRECEDENT

From counsel's perspective—and I see no difference here between counsel and the party counsel represents—the practical definition of precedent is clear:

> "a precedent is any decisional authority that is likely to affect the decision in the case at hand."

This is patently a results-oriented definition. But that is the nature of the mission of counsel—to attempt, zealously and using all legal means, to achieve the result in the client's interest. When, after months of waiting, an arbitration award arrives over the fax or email, neither counsel nor client immediately study the intricacies of the award's legal reasoning. The first thing they do is to turn to the dispositif, the operative part of the award, to find out who won and who lost. They of course do read carefully the award's reasoning, but this is secondary to the result.

An example may serve to drive this point home. In common-law systems that follow the principle of *stare decisis*, that of binding precedent and judge-made law, there is an established hierarchy of decisional authority. Typically the decisions of the supreme court have the greatest authority, those of the intermediate court of appeals second-greatest authority and those of other courts of first instance no legally binding authority at all.

In practice, a skillful advocate in such a system often ignores or even reverses the hierarchy. To a judge of first instance, a prior decision by that same judge may have greater persuasive force than a supreme court decision. If the judge herself accepted the principle of law in a prior case, she likely does not need to be persuaded of the proposition and will, being human, desire to be consistent from one case to another. Similarly, to a judge of first instance, a court of appeals decision applying a supreme court decision paradoxically has greater persuasive force than the supreme court decision itself—because it will likely contain more detail, and because the court of appeals' interpretation of that decision is what that court will likely consider authoritative in reviewing any decision of the court of first instance.

My point is that, even in a legal system with a highly formalized view of the role of precedent, in practice the definition that is followed is the practical one I have put forward. What counsel cites as "precedent" are the authorities that are most likely to persuade the judge or arbitrator to reach a result favorable to counsel's client.

II.   THE ARBITRATOR'S PERSPECTIVE ON PRECEDENT

A practically oriented approach leads to a similar definition of precedent from the arbitrator's perspective:

> "a precedent is any decisional authority that is likely to justify the award to the principal audience for that award."

This definition flows from the fact that, in almost every case, the arbitrators' decision as to the result will precede the exercise of writing up the reasons for that decision in an award. The decision is made in deliberations; the award is written later. This simple point of timing means that the arbitrators' analysis of whether or not to make reference to a precedent will inevitably take place in the context of justifying a decision already made.

Indeed, in certain respects the award-drafter's task resembles that of counsel: the ultimate position has been decided (in this case, by the tribunal rather than by the client); the task is to justify that position as persuasively and effectively as possible to the likely audience for the award.

Historically, the audience for an award in international arbitration has consisted of the parties to the case and the judges likely to entertain an action to enforce or annul the award. Of these, the principal audience was and remains that of the parties. After all, the parties are the ones paying the arbitrators to write the award. Drafting the award in a manner addressing the issues raised by the parties fulfils the arbitrators' contractual commitment to the parties. It also reduces the likelihood that the award will attacked in court. An award that persuades the parties of the correctness of its reasoning leaves little incentive for an annulment application.

In light of this, one would expect arbitrators to use precedent in an award where the parties have devoted such attention to a given precedent or line of precedent that discussion of it in the award is to be expected in the normal course of addressing the parties' contentions. Discussion of precedent on the arbitrators' own initiative is likely to follow in this traditional scenario where the arbitrators find the precedent to add materially to the persuasive force of the award's reasoning from the perspective of the parties or a reviewing court.

III. THE PUBLIC'S PERSPECTIVE ON PRECEDENT

A relatively recent development is the widespread publication of awards in investor-State arbitration and in sports arbitration. Because arbitration in each of these fields implicates questions of public interest, the traditional audience for awards has expanded to include a wide range of other players. In investment arbitration, the audience for awards includes Governments that are party to the treaty at issue or similar treaties; non-governmental and intergovernmental organizations interested in the public issues raised by such arbitrations; professors of international law and arbitration and other scholars writing or teaching about the field; members of the general public; colleagues who serve as arbitrators in investment cases; and, importantly, counsel specializing in the field who are a potential source of future arbitral appointments.

While it is difficult to generalize across such a broad and disparate group, I think it is fair to say that the majority of the interested public views investment arbitration as a system of administration of justice. And as is so for most such systems, the public expects that the system will generate results that are similar for broadly similar cases. A thief who steals a loaf of bread on one day should receive a sentence similar to that for a thief who stole a loaf on the day before. The public applies similar expectations to investment treaty arbitrations.

Thus, the focus, from the public's perspective, is not only whether the arbitrators have achieved justice in the case before them, but whether the *system* of arbitration has generated results that are just across the docket of cases handled by the system. The public is looking for a certain degree of consistency and coherence in approach to similar cases.

This focus requires a comparative approach, in which each new decision is considered in light of previous decisions in which broadly similar issues were raised. And this leads me to the definition of a precedent from the public's perspective:

> "a precedent is any decisional authority in which the factual and legal issues are sufficiently similar to the case at hand that the public reasonably expects the issues to be handled similarly."

IV. SYNTHESIS

Having demonstrated the different perspectives held by counsel, arbitrators and the general public, I will now attempt to identify a common thread that links each of these perspectives. Then, just as was done for Einstein's Theory of Relativity, I will attempt to test that common theorem against the available empirical data.

If one lines up the three definitions, a certain commonality immediately appears between the first two of the three:

Counsel's Perspective	A precedent is any decisional authority that is likely to affect the decision in the case at hand.
Arbitrator's Perspective	A precedent is any decisional authority that is likely to justify the arbitrators' decision to the principal audience for that decision
Public's Perspective	A precedent is any decisional authority in which the factual and legal issues are sufficiently similar to the case at hand that the public reasonably expects the issues to be handled similarly.

The commonality lies in the self-reinforcing circle of precedent from counsel's perspective and precedent from the arbitrator's perspective. Counsel tends to cite as precedent authorities that are likely to affect the arbitrators' decision; arbitrators tend to find useful as precedent authorities that justify their decision to the principal audience. The common thread is that what is important to arbitrators is what is important to counsel. What is a precedent to counsel should, therefore, correspond closely to what arbitrators consider to be a precedent.[3]

If this approach is correct, the working definition of a precedent in the international arbitration context might be as follows:

> "A precedent is any decisional authority that may reasonably serve to justify the arbitrators' decision to the principal audience for that decision."

The key here is that what is a precedent depends in significant part on the perceived audience for the award of the tribunal. Thus, in a field in which the traditional audience of the parties, their counsel and possible reviewing courts continues to hold sway, one would expect to see less reliance on precedent by arbitral tribunals. This is because, as noted, parties and their counsel tend to be more results-oriented and where a law other than the common law governs, precedent is less relevant to the award or review of the award. By contrast, in a field where the general public and its expectations of consistency and coherence form part of the perceived audience, one would expect to see greater reliance on precedent by arbitral tribunals.

The empirical evidence, as described by Professor Kaufmann-Kohler in her lecture, is broadly consistent with this approach. In the field of international commercial arbitration, where the model of the traditional, limited audience for arbitral awards holds sway in part because awards are not generally made

---

[3]   There is a small leap of logic here in that it is possible for a precedent to be persuasive to an arbitrator in arriving at the decision in the case, and yet not be viewed by the arbitrator to be useful in justifying the decision reflected in the award.

public, there tends to be relatively little reliance in awards on arbitral precedents.[4]

By contrast, Professor Kaufmann-Kohler notes that in the field of sports arbitration, there is a powerful institutional need to allow fair athletic competition through consistent and coherent arbitral treatment of alleged doping violations.[5] Sports arbitration awards are published and followed by an attentive public. After an initial period of lesser reliance on arbitral precedents, sports arbitration awards now demonstrate a degree of reliance on precedent approaching that of a legal system that recognizes binding precedent.[6]

Finally, in the field of investment arbitration there appears to be an increasing degree of reliance on precedents in arbitral awards. For this field, Professor Kaufmann-Kohler concludes that "there is a progressive emergence of rules through lines of consistent cases on certain issues, though there are still contradictory outcomes on others."[7] These results, I would submit, are broadly consistent with a field in which arbitrators are increasingly adapting their award-writing practices to an environment in which the general public—with its expectations of consistency and coherence—forms part of the relevant audience for the award.

---

[4]   Kaufmann-Kohler, *supra* note 1.

[5]   *Id.* at 376 ("As a result, there is a strong requirement of a level playing field and fairness to athletes, or in legal terms, equal treatment. In pragmatic terms, this requirement becomes strikingly obvious if one bears in mind that the athlete's performance on the playing field is measured by universal sports standards. The stopwatch is the same wherever and whenever a race takes place. The equality in front of the stopwatch must be replicated when it comes to the application of legal rules.").

[6]   *Id.* at 373 ("there is strong reliance on precedents in sports arbitration, which comes close to a true *stare decisis* doctrine").

[7]   *Id.*

Thus, I would suggest that there is empirical support for the theory that would define precedent in international arbitration as *any decisional authority that may reasonably serve to justify the arbitrators' decision to the principal audience for that decision.* I do not suggest that this empirical proof is as compelling as that for the *Theory of Relativity,* when the sun's gravitational effect on starlight was confirmed by observation during a solar eclipse.[8] But I'm no Einstein, after all.

---

[8] *See* EVERDELL, *supra* note 2 ("World celebrity [for Einstein] would come in 1919, when an eclipse provided astronomical proof of General Relativity.").

PART I

INTERNATIONAL COMMERCIAL ARBITRATION

Introductory Remarks

Karl-Heinz Böckstiegel [*]

May I first congratulate Emmanuel Gaillard for having taken the initiative in organising this conference on what is indeed a very topical issue. It was with pleasure that I accepted his kind invitation to chair this first of the two panels of the Conference. And the very large attendance I now see by eminent colleagues not only from Paris but from a number of other European cities confirms that the topic is considered by many as interesting and relevant for the theory and practice of international arbitration.

With the steadily growing number of arbitration cases all over the world and the awards resulting from them, parties, their lawyers and arbitrators also have a growing interest to receive information on earlier cases and resulting awards which may have dealt with similar factual or legal issues as in the case at hand.

The traditional confidentiality of arbitration, for many parties—be they enterprises or States—a major argument to choose arbitration as their preferred method of dispute settlement, on the other side has the effect of a lack of transparency of arbitral jurisprudence and the risk of an appearance of a lack of continuity and even arbitrariness of decisions of arbitrators in comparable cases. This is by no means a new problem and many steps have

---

[*] Professor Emeritus of International Business Law, University of Cologne (Germany); President, German Institution of Arbitration (DIS); Member of ICCA and ICC Arbitration Commission; President, LCIA (1993-1997); President, Iran-United States Claims Tribunal (1984-1988); Panel Chairman, United Nations Compensation Commission (UNCC) (1994-1996); President, German Association of International Law (1993-2006); President, International Law Association (2004-2006).

17

been taken to deal with it, such as publications of awards with the consent of the parties, at least publication of reports on cases after deleting the parties' names and other identifying characteristics, etc. Our topic of Precedent thus is closely connected with the topic of confidentiality, because the question of precedent can only arise in so far as information is available on earlier decisions. Therefore, for good reason, our second speaker, Alexis Mourre, will deal with the impact of confidentiality of awards.

But even if the parties, their lawyers and the arbitrators are aware of what other tribunals have decided on comparable factual and legal issues, the question still has to be answered whether and to which extent such earlier decisions are relevant or at least have to be taken into account by the tribunal deciding the present case. In order to answer this question, another question must first be answered, *i.e.*, whether there is a need for consistency in international commercial arbitration, which will be treated by our first speaker, Francois Perret. While I do not want to intrude into his topic, it would seem that the more one maintains the traditionally highly relevant need of confidentiality of commercial arbitration the more one must accept a potential of deviations from any need for consistency one might identify. You just cannot have both fully realized at the same time.

Our third speaker, Christopher Seppala, will take up the specific area of construction disputes relating to FIDIC contracts where it may seem particularly obvious that a maximum of consistency should be achieved and thus the issue of precedent may deserve a specific answer.

Since we have, after our session dealing with precedent in commercial arbitration, a further session dealing with investment arbitration, it may be useful to compare both fields and identify major common as well as major distinguishing qualifications with relevance to the topic of our Conference.

18

I.   MAJOR COMMON QUALIFICATIONS

A.   *No legally Binding Effect of Decisions*

Though the topic of this Conference identifies "precedent," it would seem obvious to me that, in the present context, we do not understand this term in the strict sense from the common law world. While State courts may indeed be bound by what other and specifically higher courts of the same jurisdiction have decided on an issue, neither in civil law jurisdictions nor in common law jurisdictions is it suggested that an arbitral tribunal is legally bound by the decision of another arbitral tribunal in an earlier case. "Exceptions" may be those few arbitral systems that provide for an appeal procedure against an award to another tribunal.

B.   *Primary Task: Decide the Case at Hand*

Though arbitral tribunals may indeed be well advised to take into account decisions of other tribunals on comparable factual or legal issues if they know of such other decisions, I feel strongly that one should stress that the primary function of an arbitral tribunal is to decide the specific case before it and on the relief sought by the parties in that dispute. Though I have been a university teacher for decades and appreciate the wish to develop general criteria for a field as important as commercial arbitration, I do not share the tendency I sometimes see when other professors and colleagues are acting as arbitrators and seem to extend their reasoning in an award far beyond what is relevant for the decision of the case in order to develop the law and jurisprudence in a direction they consider desirable. It is a tribunal's function to decide the case before it, no less but also no more.

C. Nobile Officium *to Take Earlier Decisions into Account*

On the other hand, I would consider it a *nobile officium* of all arbitrators, both in commercial and in investment cases, to take into account and consider the reasoning and conclusions of earlier tribunals they are aware of and which they consider relevant for the issues at stake in their present case in their own reasoning and conclusions. This does not mean that the tribunal is bound by such earlier considerations or decisions. But not only professional respect to other tribunals, but also the expectations of the parties and their lawyers who will often refer to such earlier decisions in their pleadings, require this as part of the mandate of the arbitral tribunal.

II. MAJOR DISTINGUISHING QUALIFICATIONS BETWEEN COMMERCIAL AND INVESTMENT ARBITRATION

A. *Applicable Law*

Regarding the applicable procedure, commercial arbitration will, as a rule, have to rely on the agreement of the parties, any institutional arbitration rules they may have chosen, and at least the mandatory rules of the national law of the seat of arbitration.

In investment arbitration, the procedure will, as a rule, have to rely on any specific agreements either between the parties of the dispute or between the home State of the investor and the host state. The latter will usually be public international law treaties such as bilateral investment treaties (BITs) or multilateral treaties such as the ICSID or NAFTA Conventions. In addition, arbitration rules may come into play which, depending on any choice in the submission to arbitration, may not only be those created for investment arbitrations in the context of public international law by ICSID or NAFTA, but also quite frequently in recent years the UNCITRAL Rules, or the arbitration rules of institutions created primarily for commercial arbitration such as the ICC, the LCIA or the Stockholm Institute.

Regarding the applicable substantive law, commercial arbitration will, as a rule, rely on a particular national law either expressly chosen by the contractual parties or determined according to specific provisions in arbitration rules such as Art. 17 of the ICC Rules. In our context there is no need to go into the well known question whether, in addition, non-national substantive rules may be applied under names such as *lex mercatoria* or transnational law.

In investment arbitration, as a rule, public international law will be the applicable substantive law, particularly treaties such as BITs and multilateral treaties such as the Vienna Convention on the Law of Treaties, as well as the other sources of international law identified in Art. 38 of the Statute of the International Court of Justice, with the support provided for the identification of customary international law by instruments such as the ILC's Articles on State Responsibility.

In addition, also in investment arbitration, domestic national law may have to be applied on the basis of specific provisions such as Art. 42 of the ICSID Convention, or in the context of an umbrella clause in a BIT.

B.   *Confidentiality*

In addition to my earlier remarks regarding the relevance of confidentiality for our topic, one has to realize that, in recent years, the practice between the two fields of arbitration has developed differently.

In commercial arbitration, confidentiality still seems to be the rule both as a priority of the parties and in the practical conduct of procedures, though an examination of many arbitration rules shows that little is said regarding confidentiality and nothing regarding sanctions in case of breach.

In investment arbitration, however, confidentiality seems to have become almost the exception in practice. This may be due to the demand of the national constituency in host States to make any dispute procedure transparent which concerns projects of public interest such as those of political or national economic relevance. Most awards in investment arbitration are nowadays published, either because the parties have agreed or because some leak occurred from unidentified persons involved in the dispute.

Let me illustrate this by examples from my own cases.

I still remember that in one of my ICSID cases, after we had refused access of the media to our hearing, a few days later, the transcript of the hearing and later also our award were available on the internet though the parties had not given their consent to publication.

In my most recent NAFTA case, consolidating claims of more than one hundred Canadian cattle farmers against the United States, the Parties had agreed that all procedural decisions and the award should be published and thus these were available on the website of the US State Department as soon as they were issued.

An example going much further is the *Softwood Lumber Case* which I am presently chairing and on which I can report, because the US and Canadian Governments as parties of the dispute have expressly agreed that, not only all procedural decisions and finally the award shall be published, but also that the hearing shall be open to the public. And indeed, more than a hundred observers attended the hearing we had in New York in December 2007.

C. *Similarity of Issues to be Decided*

In the context of discussing precedent, one also has to realize that—though every case has its own specific qualifications—investment arbitration may have a greater need for consistency of decisions, because the typical issues tend to be much more similar than in commercial arbitration cases. Issues such as the definition and interpretation of the terms "investment," "investor," "expropriation," "compensation" as well as MFN clauses and alleged umbrella clauses, will typically come up in many investment cases though differentiations may become necessary in the context of each particular treaty.

Such similarities will much less occur in commercial arbitration where the particular contract will normally be the primary source of the law between the parties, further particularized by the specific conduct of the parties, and only thereafter the provisions of a national substantive law which normally will contain few mandatory provisions of relevance. In this context, let me add that, in my own experience in decades of commercial arbitrations, I have found that the choice and identification of the applicable national law are given more prominence in legal writings as they become increasingly relevant in the practice of deciding a case where quite often only limited issues such as prescription or interest rates will depend on the applicable national law. Exceptions from this greater individualisation of commercial arbitration cases may be those where frequently used standard contracts lead to greater similarity of issues such as the FIDIC and other models in construction arbitration as well as standard forms used for insurance and maritime contracts.

These few considerations must suffice in order not to take too much time away from our distinguished speakers.

Is There a Need for Consistency in International Commercial Arbitration?

François Perret [*]

To set out the question is to answer it; obviously, the absence of conflicting decisions on the same issue is a requisite in view of ensuring the security of legal relationships. But how and to what extent can we achieve this goal in international arbitration? In other words, can we transpose the notion of precedent in the true sense of the word into arbitration? This is the question to be addressed herein. Precedent has been defined as a series of consistent decisions on a given question of law,[1] and that implies that their *ratio decidendi* is not limited to a specific dispute. In this regard, one should distinguish the decisions that enunciate a rule that may be applied to future cases of the same kind (*arrêts de principe*), from those in which the ruling does not extend beyond the specificity of the dispute at hand (*arrêts d'espèce*).[2]

Yet, it has been said that arbitral awards should only give a concrete and pragmatic solution to difficulties encountered by actors in international commerce, and thus do not have to contribute to the formation of the law which in any case is not the primary concern of such agents of the economic life.[3] These

---

[*] Emeritus Professor of Law, University of Geneva; Member of the Geneva Bar.

[1] B. STARCK, H. ROLAND, L. BOYER, INTRODUCTION AU DROIT ¶ 868, at 327 (Litec, 5th ed. 2000).

[2] *Id.* ¶ 872, at 328.

[3] Andrea Pinna, *Le concept de jurisprudence arbitrale et son application à la matière sportive*, Gaz. Pal., Oct. 15–17, 2006, at 23, 28; *see also* Guy

considerations would, in effect, limit the scope of any arbitral award to that of an *arrêt d'espèce* and consequently would tend to negate the existence of arbitral precedent. I do not share this opinion. While it is true that arbitrators must not loose sight of the main objective assigned to them, namely settling the dispute pending before them, it is equally true that in many cases the reasons for their decision are not limited to the application of a given legal rule on the circumstances at hand. Like an *arrêt de principe*, an arbitral award may give a solution to the legal issue at stake going beyond the contingency of the specific case and thus may be called upon to rule on disputes of the same kind. Already for this reason, the question of whether or not one can speak of precedent in arbitration is far from being deprived of interest. According to Philippe Fouchard, Emmanuel Gaillard and Berthold Goldman, the answer to that question depends upon the fulfillment of three criteria: first, the arbitral case law must be autonomous or independent from domestic legal orders; second, it must be consistent, and that means that it must present a certain degree of homogeneity; and lastly, it must be accessible to the public,[4] and that raises the issue of the confidential nature of arbitral awards, a topic to be addressed by Alexis Mourre,[5] reason for which I shall only discuss the first two conditions.

The first can only be met when the award is not subjected to any review by the domestic courts. This will not be the case when the arbitral tribunal is called upon to determine the regularity of its own constitution or its own jurisdiction, since these two

---

Horsmans, *Propos insolites sur l'efficacité arbitrale*, III LES CAHIERS DE L'ARBITRAGE 33 (2006).

[4] FOUCHARD GAILLARD GOLDMAN ON INTERNATIONAL COMMERCIAL ARBITRATION 183 *et seq.* (E. Gaillard & J. Savage eds., Kluwer, 1999).

[5] Alexis Mourre, *Precedent and Confidentiality in International Commercial Arbitration: The Case for the Publication of Arbitration Awards*, *infra* at 39.

questions may be brought before the domestic courts by means of an application to set aside the award. Because an arbitral award deciding either of these issues cannot escape the reach of domestic courts, it cannot be deemed autonomous with respect to the domestic legal order.[6]

Regarding the merits of the award, the situation is completely different as the domestic courts are only empowered to assess whether or not the award contravenes international public policy; in other words, a challenge of the award by way of an appeal in fact or in law is excluded in international arbitration, a principle which according to Fouchard Gaillard Goldman[7] is nevertheless insufficient for a finding of an autonomous character of the arbitral case law. Indeed and still according to Fouchard Gaillard Goldman, such case law should present specific features distinguishing it from the domestic jurisprudence. This condition would be fulfilled if the arbitrators rely on rules of law other than those applied by domestic judges—*i.e.*, an a-national or transnational body of rules such as the *lex mercatoria*. This opinion does not convince me for several reasons:

First, it would reduce the arbitral case law to the smallest share if one should adhere to this doctrine since, as pointed out by Yves Derains, the application of the *lex mercatoria* as a first choice of law is in practice rather unusual. This body of rules is most often relied on as a supplemental tool to solve ambiguities or fill in gaps of the applicable domestic law.[8] Second, one might wonder whether or not the *lex mercatoria* is the privilege of international arbitration.

---

[6]   FOUCHARD GAILLARD GOLDMAN, *supra* note 4, ¶ 376, at 184–85.

[7]   *Id.* ¶ 378, at 185–86; Yves Derains, *State Courts and Arbitrators*, *in* ARBITRATION IN THE NEXT DECADE 27, 32 (ICC Pub. No. 612, 1999).

[8]   Derains, *supra* note 7.

In this regard, I would point out that the *lex mercatoria* may be approached in two different ways; under the first doctrinal approach, promoted by Berthold Goldman, the *lex mercatoria* should represent an autonomous legal order, *i.e.*, an a-national one, called upon to intervene in the universal merchant society, and should comprise international trade usages, general principles of law, arbitration laws and rules, professional codification, standard form of contracts, customs and uncodified usages, and, lastly the practice of State courts and arbitral tribunals.[9]

Under a second doctrinal approach represented by Emmanuel Gaillard, the *lex mercatoria* is to be considered as a transnational law a body of general principles of law resulting from a comparative analysis of a plurality of domestic legal systems aimed to outline their points of conversion. For this reason, rather than speaking of *lex mercatoria*, Gaillard prefers to speak of transnational rules.[10]

However, irrespective of which understanding one might have of the *lex mercatoria*, in reality such concept is reduced to a few principles expressed in the form of legal adages, the most

---

[9] Berthold Goldman, *Frontières du droit et "lex mercatoria"*, 9 ARCHIVES DE PHILOSOPHIE DU DROIT 177 (1964); *Nouvelles réflexions sur la* Lex Mercatoria, *in* ETUDES DE DROIT INTERNATIONAL EN L'HONNEUR DE PIERRE LALIVE 241 (C. Dominicé, R. Patry and C. Reymond eds., Helbing & Lichtenhahn, 1993).

[10] Emmanuel Gaillard, *La distinction des principes généraux du droit et des usages du commerce international*, *in* ETUDES OFFERTES À PIERRE BELLET 203 (Litec, 1991); *Thirty Years of* Lex Mercatoria*: Towards the Discriminating Application of Transnational Rules*, *in* ICCA CONGRESS SERIES NO. 7, PLANNING EFFICIENT ARBITRATION PROCEEDINGS: THE LAW APPLICABLE IN INTERNATIONAL ARBITRATION 582 (A.J. van den Berg ed., Kluwer, 1996) (also published in French: *Trente ans de* Lex Mercatoria. *Pour une application sélective de la méthode des principes généraux du droit*, 122 J.D.I. 5 (1995)); *Transnational Law: A Legal System or a Method of Decision Making?*, 17(1) ARB. INT'L 59 (2001).

notable being *pacta sunt servanda, clausula rebus sic stantibus, exceptio non adimpleti contractus, non venire contra factum proprium* etc. These adages are deeply rooted within the various domestic legal systems through praetorian law.[11] Moreover, these adages constitute the mere implementation of a principle of a superior value, *i.e.*, the principle of good faith which is prevailing in most domestic laws.[12] Therefore, and in my opinion, one cannot see in the recourse to the *lex mercatoria* the autonomous character of the arbitral case law from that of the domestic Courts. The *Valenciana* decision rendered by the French Supreme Court supports this conclusion.[13] In this case, it was held that the sole arbitrator complied with his mission when applying the *lex mercatoria* as his award referred to "the group of rules of international commerce determined by practice and having received the sanction of national jurisprudences." In other words, under the cover of the *lex mercatoria*, the sole arbitrator had actually applied a body of rules whose existence had been duly recognized by domestic law and that led the Court to uphold the award.

It is true that Emmanuel Gaillard has sustained that the *lex mercatoria* is not a question of list or of content but one of method.[14] However, the comparative method recommended by Emmanuel Gaillard for determining a body of general principles of

---

[11] *See* JEAN-FRANCOIS POUDRET AND SÉBASTIEN BESSON, COMPARATIVE LAW OF INTERNATIONAL ARBITRATION ¶ 696, at 598 (S.V. Berti and A. Ponti trans., Sweet & Maxwell – Schulthess, 2nd ed. 2007).

[12] On the duty of good faith in international arbitration, see Pierre Mayer, *Le principe de bonne foi devant les arbitres du commerce international, in* ETUDES DE DROIT INTERNATIONAL EN L'HONNEUR DE PIERRE LALIVE 543 (C. Dominicé, R. Patry and C. Reymond eds., Helbing & Lichtenhahn, 1993).

[13] Cass. 1e civ., Oct. 22, 1991, Compania Valenciana de Cementos Portland v. Primary Coal Inc., 1992 REV. ARB. 457 (note by P. Lagarde); for an English translation, see 6(12) INT'L ARB. REP. B-1, B-4 (1991).

[14] Gaillard, *supra* note 10.

law is not unknown to States courts, or at least not to the Swiss State courts, which must have recourse to a comparative law approach when the domestic law applicable to the dispute does not provide an answer to the question at hand.[15]

On this matter, I shall also underscore the following: the codification of the law of contracts from an international as well as from a European point of view has been attained through such an approach—I am referring to the *"UNIDROIT Principles of International Commercial Contracts"* and to the *"Principles of European Contract Law."* Indeed, the creditor's duty to mitigate his damages,[16] as well as the parties' duty to enter into negotiations when the performance of a contract becomes excessively onerous because of change of circumstances fundamentally frustrating their initial engagement,[17] is the object of specific rules in both texts. Yet this duty is in effect a consequence of an application of the parties' broader obligation to act in accordance with the principle of good faith, a concept which is contained expressly or implicitly in the laws of all the civilized countries.[18] At this point, it must be emphasized that the UNIDROIT Principles and the Principles of

---

[15] NICOLAS ROUILLER, DROIT SUISSE DES OBLIGATIONS ET PRINCIPES DU DROIT EUROPÉEN DES CONTRATS 6–7 (Cedidac, 2007), and the doctrine cited by this author.

[16] Principles of European Contract Law, Article 9:505.

[17] *Id.*, Article 6:111.

[18] On the creditor's duty under Swiss law to mitigate damages in accordance with the duty of good faith, see Pascal Pichonnaz, *Le devoir du lésé de diminuer son dommage*, *in* LA FIXATION DE L'INDEMNITÉ 109 (F. Werro ed., Staempfli, 2004). It should be here noted that according to Berthold Goldman (*Nouvelles réflexions sur la* Lex Mercatoria, *supra* note 9), no such duty exists under French law so that it can only be imposed upon the creditor by the application of the *lex mercatoria*, a questionable opinion. On the same question, see JÉRÔME ORTSCHEIDT, LA RÉPARATION DU DOMMAGE DANS L'ARBITRAGE COMMERCIAL INTERNATIONAL ¶ 230, at 113 (Dalloz, 2001), who sustained that the creditor's obligation to mitigate his damages is one of the most well established principles in arbitral case law.

European Contract Law can be invoked not only when the parties have agreed to apply the *lex mercatoria* to their dispute, but also in the event that the applicable domestic law does not contain a rule capable of solving the legal issue at stake.[19] Thus—and inasmuch as this codification of a transnational law of contract is relevant not only for international arbitrators, but also for domestic judges— one must admit that the general principles of law which constitute the basis of such codification are not the exclusive domain of the international arbitrators. Besides, one might reasonably wonder if the prohibition of any review by the State courts of the merits of an arbitral award, save its contradiction to public policy, is not by itself sufficient to recognize the autonomous character of arbitral case law in regard to any given domestic legal system. If, as it has been argued by Fouchard Gaillard Goldman, this autonomy must lead to a certain independence of arbitral case law with respect to that of the State courts, this criterion would appear to be fulfilled provided, however, that arbitral case law does not constitute a slavish imitation of State courts' decisions. Put it differently, this criterion should be met so long as the arbitrator does not behave as an *"arbitre singe,"* conduct that has been rightly criticized by Serge Lazareff.[20]

---

[19]   Principles of European Contract Law, Article 1:101(4).

[20]   Serge Lazareff, *L'arbitre singe ou comment assassiner l'arbitrage*, *in* GLOBAL REFLECTIONS ON INTERNATIONAL LAW, COMMERCE AND DISPUTE RESOLUTION. LIBER AMICORUM IN HONOUR OF ROBERT BRINER 477 (eds. ICC Publishing, 2005). In this respect, the following should be underscored: even though in a recent case (Swiss Fed. Trib., June 13, 2007, X. v. Réseau hospitalier fribourgeois, ATF 133 III 462), the Federal Tribunal has ruled that the reception in Swiss law of the theory of the loss of an opportunity was rather problematic, nevertheless an arbitral tribunal applying Swiss law could invoke this theory, all the more so as Swiss doctrine is in favour of it. *See* in this regard Luc Thévenoz, *La perte d'une chance et sa réparation*, *in* QUELQUES QUESTIONS FONDAMENTALES DU DROIT DE LA RESPONSABILITÉ CIVILE : ACTUALITÉS ET PERSPECTIVES 237 (F. Werro ed., Staempfli, 2002); and CHRISTOPH MÜLLER, LA PERTE D'UNE CHANCE − ETUDE COMPARATIVE EN VUE DE SON

31

I shall now discuss the second condition that must be satisfied in order to be able to admit the existence of an arbitral case law, *i.e.*, that of its homogeneity. Can this condition be fulfilled even though arbitral tribunals are not organized hierarchically? It is true that, in the absence of a superior jurisdiction, an arbitral award has no binding authority over future awards that have to decide on the same legal issue. Within domestic legal systems, the same question is to be raised, however, in slightly different terms; even though in civil law systems the principle of *stare decisis* is unknown, so that, as a rule, a judge which has not yet decided on a given issue is not bound by previous decisions on the same issue, nevertheless, as a result of the so called *loi d'imitation* in French law, lower courts, fearing censure, will most often adhere to the rulings of higher courts.[21] In other words, a decision rendered by the higher court will have at least a *de facto* binding authority over lower courts although this is far from being an absolute principle. Indeed, in the Swiss legal system, the cantonal courts may proceed to re-examining a point of law already decided by the Federal Tribunal,[22] and their possible diverging decisions will be reversed by the Federal Tribunal only if they are arbitrary,[23] *i.e.*, they are not founded on serious and objective grounds.

INDEMNISATION EN DROIT SUISSE, NOTAMMENT DANS LA RESPONSABILITÉ MÉDICALE (Staempfli, 2002).

[21] STARCK, ROLAND, BOYER, *supra* note 1, ¶ 881, at 331; *see also* Christian Larroumet, *A propos de la jurisprudence arbitrale*, Gaz. Pal., Dec. 14, 2006, at 5.

[22] Geneva Court of Justice, May 28, 1945, Bälher & Cie v. de Coulanges, ATF 71 I 229; Zurich *Kassationsgericht*, Sept. 25, 1947, Iten v. Zurkirchen, ATF 73 I 188; Liestal *Präsident des Bezirksgerichtes*, Dec. 14, 1960, Hupfen & Söhne v. Senn & Co., ATF 86 I 269.

[23] Swiss Fed. Trib., Oct. 28, 1988, F. v. R. & R. AG, ATF 114 II 353; Swiss Fed. Trib., Feb. 22, 1994, B. SA v. L. SA, ATF 120 II 214; Swiss Fed. Trib., Jan. 22, 1996, ATF 122 III 36. *See also* ARTHUR MEIER-HAYOZ, BERNER

This having been said, the lack of any binding authority of arbitral awards cannot, in my opinion, negate the existence of an arbitral case law in the true sense of the term. True, and to the extent that State case law constitutes a source of law to be put on equal footing with statutory law, which is indeed a controversial point,[24] one must agree with Christian Larroumet that arbitral precedents cannot by themselves create rules of law.[25] Nonetheless, if a succession of arbitral awards is consistent on a given point of law, those decisions shall undoubtedly exert a persuasive authority on arbitrators called upon to decide on the same issue.[26]

Of course this persuasive authority does not guarantee continuity of future awards, as an arbitral tribunal seized on the same issue may not follow the solution adopted by previous awards. According to Andrea Pinna, this argument is by itself sufficient to deny the concept of precedent in arbitration[27] This opinion is not convincing already because in any judicial systems, the change of a given trend of case law is always possible. Therefore one should recognize the existence of arbitral case law under the same conditions that apply to State courts, *i.e.*, when the solution adopted by a certain number of decisions on a given legal question present a continuous homogeneity.

KOMMENTAR – KOMMENTAR ZUM SCHWEIZERISCHEN PRIVATRECHT, Article 1, ¶ 492 and MAX BAUMANN, DAVID DÜRR, VIKTOR LIEBER, ARNOLD MARTI, BERNHARD SCHNYDER, ZÜRCHER KOMMENTAR – KOMMENTAR ZUM SCHWEIZERISCHES ZIVILGESETZBUCH, Article 1, ¶¶ 605 *et seq.* (Schulthess, 1998).

[24] FRANÇOIS TERRÉ, INTRODUCTION GÉNÉRALE AU DROIT ¶ 284, at 281–82 (Dalloz, 6th ed. 2003).

[25] Larroumet, *supra* note 21.

[26] *Id.*

[27] Pinna, *supra* note 3.

We must therefore ask ourselves what is the basis for such homogeneity. The fact that arbitral awards have been rendered under the auspices of an arbitral institution such as the ICC, as it has been suggested,[28] does not play any part in this respect since the ICC when reviewing an award, is not empowered to see to it that the solution adopted by various arbitral awards deciding on a same issue are uniform.[29]

The reason must be sought elsewhere. For the purpose of deciding on international commercial disputes, particularly on contractual disputes, arbitrators are not in a *terra incognita* but in a legal environment which, because it is familiar to them, may constitute a common ground for their decision.[30] It is therefore not surprising at all to note the homogeneous character of arbitral awards deciding on the same point of law, and that is, in my opinion, sufficient to admit the existence of arbitral case law, even if this homogeneity is not guaranteed in the future. In this regard, I shall refer to five arbitral awards which have all been decided in the same way on a rather controversial issue of substantive Italian law, despite the fact that none of these awards had been published at the time they were rendered. In these five cases, the arbitrators had to decide on the issue of the legal treatment of a guarantee entered into by the seller of shares of stock in regard to the economic consistency of the patrimony of the target company; such guarantee could be analyzed either as a promise of the quality of the object of the sale within the meaning of Article 1497 of the Italian Civil Code ("CCI"), or as a *sui generis* guarantee falling

---

[28] FOUCHARD GAILLARD GOLDMAN, *supra* note 4, ¶ 381, at 187.

[29] This is so true that arbitral tribunals have drawn different conclusions as to whether a party not having paid its share of the advance on arbitration costs can be ordered to reimburse the other party that paid those costs on behalf of the defaulting party. *See* Matthew Secomb, *Awards and Orders Dealing with the Advance on Costs in ICC Arbitration: Theoritical Questions and Practical Problems*, 14(1) ICC BULL. 63 (2003).

[30] FOUCHARD GAILLARD GOLDMAN, *supra* note 4, ¶ 382, at 187.

34

outside the legal regime of the sale of goods of Articles 1470 *et seq.* of the same Code. At its core, this question amounted to a decision whether or not the patrimony of the target company was part of the subject matter of the sale along with all the rights accruing to the quality of shareholder. In the affirmative, Article 1495 CCI would have to be applied; it should here be noted that this article—in its paragraph 1—obliges the buyer to give notice to the seller of any violation of the said guarantee within 8 days, under the penalty of forfeiture of its rights, whilst according to its paragraph 3 the period to start legal action is limited to one year. It should be further noted that the first of these deadlines is not mandatory and thus can be contractually extended whereas the second is mandatory according to Article 2936(3) CCI. Now, in the negative, *i.e.*, if the subject matter of the sale agreement does not include the patrimony of the target company, the breach of the guarantee would fall within the scope of the ordinary regime of obligations which is governed by Articles 1218 *et seq.* CCI.

The various decisions of the Italian *Corte di Cassassione* on this matter are somehow contradictory, although a decision rendered by the First Section of this Court in 2004,[31] *i.e.*, at a time the fifth arbitral tribunal had not yet issued its award, resolved that issue in applying Article 1495 CCI. Notwithstanding this decision, the arbitrators in the aforesaid award did not behave like an *"arbitre-singe"* and in line with the four previous awards, ruled that the patrimony of the target company was not a part of the object of the sale. In short, the guarantee regarding the economic consistency of the patrimony of the target company was treated as an autonomous guarantee governed by the ordinary regime of obligations so that a claim under the guarantee would not be time barred if submitted within the period of ten years fixed by Article 2946 CCI—the one year contemplated by Article 1495(3) CCI not

---

[31] Italian Supreme Court, 1st Civil Section, Feb. 20, 2004, No. 3370, Emilio Giacomelli, Maria Domenica Mottini v. Fin. Recos S.r.l.

being applicable. In their ruling on this issue, these five arbitral tribunals relied not only on the prevailing Italian doctrine on that matter,[32] but also, and above all, on the consistent contractual practice inspired by the business warranties and indemnity clauses of the Anglo-American law.[33] Furthermore, it should be noted that in the case decided by the fifth award, the parties had agreed to fix a time limit exceeding one year within which the buyer had to give notice of the non-conformity of the guarantee, an extension which, as stated before, was possible according to Aritcle 1495(1) CCI. It would thus have been contrary to the intent of the parties as interpreted in light of the principle of good faith, to rule that the period of limitation as per Article 1495(3) CCI had elapsed even though the deadline imposed upon the buyer to give notice to the seller of the violation of the guarantee had not yet expired.

I consider these five arbitral awards as the best illustration of the existence of an arbitral case law on this issue, as pointed out by Franco Bonelli in a recent article containing extracts from those

---

[32] *See* Sergio Erede, *Durata delle guaranzie e conseguenze della loro violazione, in* ACQUISIZIONI DI SOCIETÀ E DI PACCHETTI AZIONARI DI RIFERIMENTO 199 (F. Bonelli and M. De Andrè eds., Giuffrè, 1990); and more recently Franco Bonelli, *Acquisizioni di società e di pacchetti azionari di riferimento: le garanzie del venditore,* 21.2 DIRITTO DEL COMMERCIO INTERNAZIONALE 293, 312 *et seq.* (2007).

[33] Erede, *supra* note 32. In Swiss law, see Pierre Wessner, *La vente portant sur la totalité ou la majorité des actions d'une société anonyme : la garantie en raison des défauts de la chose, in* MÉLANGES PIERRE ENGEL 459 (Payot, 1989); Silvio Venturi, *Commentaire – Article 197, in* COMMENTAIRE ROMAND. CODE DES OBLIGATIONS I, at 1065, ¶¶ 19 *et seq.*, at 1070 *et seq.* (L. Thévenoz and F. Werro eds., Helbing & Lichtenhahn, 2003). *See also* Swiss Fed. Trib., June 27, 1996, ATF 122 III 426, 1998 JdT 171: in this decision, the Federal Tribunal held that an independent guarantee must relate to some future events, such as future profits, and not to qualities already existing at the time of sale. In the latter case, the guarantee would be subject to the law of sales and to the one-year statute of limitations under Article 210 of the Swiss *Code des Obligations*, a period which, different to Italian law, may be extended if the seller offered a longer guarantee.

awards.[34] If a sixth arbitral tribunal is ever called upon to decide on the same question, it should, in my opinion, follow the precedent set by the aforementioned awards which undoubtedly have persuasive authority considering the continuous homogeneity of their rulings. Indeed, and contrary to the First Section of the *Corte di Cassassione*, this arbitral case law adheres in every aspect to the practices of international commerce which no arbitral tribunal should ignore. In the event that this precedent could lead the United Sections of the *Corte di Cassassione* to decide in the same sense, then, and this will be my conclusion, it shall contribute to the formation of a *"jurisprudence tout court"* in the field of the law of international commerce.[35]

---

[34] Bonelli, *supra* note 32.

[35] *See* in that sense PIERRE TERCIER AND CHRISTIAN ROTEN, LA RECHERCHE ET LA RÉDACTION JURIDIQUES ¶ 525, at 111 (Schulthess, 5th ed. 2007).

Precedent and Confidentiality in International Commercial Arbitration

The Case for the Publication of Arbitral Awards

Alexis Mourre [*]

The case for the publication of arbitration awards was made twenty-five years ago by Julian D.M. Lew.[1] The conclusion reached by the author was that:

> [t]he publication of arbitration awards would . . . identify the real advantages of arbitration: specialist and expert arbitrators operating on the international level. The development of an arbitral case law would give to arbitration a greater certainty than that presently existing, with respect to the probable attitude of the arbitrators, and would facilitate the commercial world's knowledge and acceptance of the *lex mercatoria*. This would almost certainly obviate many recurring problems presented to arbitrators and would influence the negotiating attitudes and commercial decisions of businessmen. Above all, the systematic publication of arbitration awards would show that not only is arbitration an alternative to national courts as a system of dispute settlement, but it would prove conclusively that arbitration is

---

[*]   Partner, Castaldi Mourre & Partners.

[1]   Julian D.M. Lew, *The case for the publication of arbitration awards*, in THE ART OF ARBITRATION – ESSAYS ON INTERNATIONAL ARBITRATION – LIBER AMICORUM PIETER SANDERS 12 SEPTEMBER 1912–1982, at 223 (J.C. Schultsz and A.J. van den Berg eds., Kluwer, 1982).

the most appropriate forum in which to resolve disputes arising out of international commerce.[2]

Julian Lew's opinion identifies many different and important benefits of the publication of awards, including legal certainty and predictability, permitting international arbitrators to seek guidance in past cases, and facilitating the development and acceptance of the *lex mercatoria*, even though this is still a fertile ground for debate. Is the case made by Julian Lew twenty-five years ago still valid today? At the core of the issue is the difficult question of precedent in international commercial arbitration, the answer to which depends on different philosophical concepts of arbitration as a means of dispute resolution. Do international arbitrators apply the law chosen by the parties in the same way a national court would do? Or is international arbitration a free-standing system of international justice relying on a body of legal rules of its own? Are international arbitrators only concerned with the case before them, or do they feel compelled to adhere to past arbitral solutions for the sake of consistency? In sum, is arbitral jurisprudence anything more than a dream or an excuse?

One point in respect to which almost all authors seem to agree is that the term "precedent" should be qualified as far as arbitration is concerned. As Professor Gabrielle Kauffmann-Kohler noted in her *2006 Freshfields Lecture*,[3] the concept of precedent has a precise legal significance as far as court litigation is concerned, which is the legally binding effect of past decisions in a given legal system. Yet, the same concept can also be taken from another quite different perspective, namely the notion of *persuasive precedent*. Persuasive precedent, rather than precedent

---

[2]   *Id.* at 232.

[3]   Gabrielle Kaufmann-Kohler, *Arbitral Precedent: Dream, Necessity or Excuse? – The 2006 Freshfields Lecture*, 23(3) ARB. INT'L 357 (2007).

in the meaning of the doctrine of *stare decisis*,[4] is the concept that can be applied to arbitration.[5] Persuasive precedent can be defined as the *de facto* tendency for an international arbitrator to accept what has been consistently decided in a significant number of past arbitral decisions. It would therefore be misguided to describe the concept of precedent in arbitration from the same perspective as that applied to courts. The jurisprudence of state courts present characteristics of homogeneity in a hierarchical system that arbitral case law does not and cannot have. Yet, international commercial arbitration produces decisions. These decisions are not the product of a given municipal judicial system: they are autonomous decisions issued by tribunals which have no forum and which are not rooted in the judicial system of the seat of the arbitration.[6] These decisions are referred to by other arbitrators, and they may in certain cases persuade a future tribunal to adhere to previous solutions. Arbitral precedent is no more and no less than this capacity of past arbitration awards to convince future tribunals to adhere to the solution they embody. The proper question should

---

[4]   The *stare decisis* doctrine finds its origin in the Latin maxim *stare decisis et non quieta movere* (to stand by things decided and not to disturb settled points).

[5]   *Supra* note 3, at 358. It is worth noting, however, that the doctrine of *stare decisis* has evolved in Common law countries, effectively permitting greater flexibility, while civil law countries have also evolved towards a sort of *de facto stare decisis*.

[6]   *See* the recent decision of the French Supreme Court in Cass. 1e civ., June 29, 2007, PT Putrabali Adyamulia v. Rena Holding, 2007 REV. ARB. 507 (note by E. Gaillard); 134 J.D.I. 1236 (2007) (note by T. Clay); Petites affiches, No. 192, Chron. 20 (2007) (note by M. de Boisséson); for an English translation, see XXXII Y.B. COM. ARB. 299 (2007) and the definition of the international arbitration award as an "international decision of justice."

therefore not be whether arbitral precedent exists, but how and when it operates.[7]

The persuasiveness of past arbitration awards implies to a certain extent that international arbitrators see themselves as part of a group of international adjudicators, whose role and *raison d'être* is to fulfil the particular needs of the international business community, and who think of arbitration as a free-standing and autonomous system of international justice. If the idea of such a free-standing system of international justice is accepted, it is perfectly understandable that international arbitrators try to be as consistent as possible with past decisions of other international tribunals. Such effort of consistency is not driven by any structural homogeneity of arbitration as a dispute resolution system, or by any hierarchical structure. There is no such homogeneity or hierarchy in international arbitration. The driving force of arbitral precedent is rather the arbitrators' desire to meet the parties' legitimate expectation that their dispute will be resolved by international adjudicators according to internationally accepted procedures and from an international perspective. That is to say: resolved in a way that is not a mere imitation of what municipal judges would do. The idea that opting for arbitration as an international means of resolving business disputes implies that arbitrators will make their decisions in a manner which is—at least to a certain extent—different from that of courts, not only as regards procedure, but also as to the perspective adopted for the resolution of substantive legal issues that are certainly controversial, deserves a discussion that is not within the scope of

---

[7]   This paper will not deal with the issue of precedent in investment arbitration, sports arbitration or domain name arbitration. Neither shall it deal with the Iran-US Claims Tribunal nor with other treaty-based special forms of international adjudication. In this respect, see Kaufmann-Kohler, *supra* note 3. In respect of precedent in sports arbitration, see Andrea Pinna, *Le concept de jurisprudence arbitrale et son application à la matière sportive*, Gaz. Pal., Oct. 15–17, 2006, at 23.

this presentation. Yet, one cannot accept the dynamics of arbitral precedent as a tool for consistency and as a rule-making instrument without accepting also the specificity of arbitration, not only as regards procedure, but also the way tribunals deal with substantive issues. On the other hand, arbitration cannot be thought of as a truly autonomous system of justice without accepting the role and existence of arbitral precedent. Precedent in arbitration and arbitral autonomy are two closely intertwined concepts.

Analyzing the precedential effect of arbitral awards is fraught with difficulties. When preparing her *Freshfields Lecture*, Professor Kauffmann-Kohler studied several hundred awards to determine if and how arbitral tribunals rely on previous awards. The conclusion was that "arbitrators do what they want with past cases and . . . there is no clear practice in this field."[8] Yet, arbitral case law is a reality in practice, albeit an imperfect one. Past solutions have some impact on the thinking of arbitrators having to resolve future cases, even though the past decisions may not be referred to in their awards. The real issue is therefore not whether awards have a precedential effect, but how such effect operates in practice. The quality of the reasoning of a particular award may of course play a role in the thinking of future tribunals. Yet, I submit that good reasoning is not the driving factor of arbitral precedent. Precedent in international arbitration is not—or is not only—the product of the intrinsic qualities of one or more particularly well-reasoned awards. It is not, either, the product of the arbitrators' own will, although some show a certain tendency to include *obiter dicta* in their awards.[9] Arbitral precedent is a pure *phénomène*

---

[8] Kaufmann-Kohler, *supra* note 3, at 362.

[9] Stated in a more nuanced manner, see Klaus Peter Berger, *The International Arbitrators' Application of Precedents*, 9(4) J. INT'L ARB. 5, 19 (1992): "[t]his growing practice reveals that international arbitration is gradually developing into a self-contained judicial system in which the different judicial bodies, even though usually created on an *ad hoc* basis and becoming *functus officio* once their task is accomplished, regard themselves as having precedential

d'entraînement. And it is all the more difficult to define since most of the time it is difficult to analyze the exact role that reference to past cases played in the arbitral tribunal's reasoning. While an arbitral tribunal might refer to a given solution adopted in one or two particularly well-reasoned awards as a mere illustration of its reasoning, the same solution will, if adopted in similar terms by five, six or more awards rendered in comparable cases, have not only an illustrative value but also a compelling effect.[10] This is not to say that consistent solutions given in a line of awards will *always* be perceived as binding in future cases. Their relevance will of course depend on the rules of law applicable to the case. From this perspective, procedural issues should be distinguished from questions of substance.

As far as issues of procedure are concerned, it is beyond doubt that solutions adopted in past arbitration awards are likely to be considered as precedent by arbitrators. The *Dow Chemical* award is well known:

> [t]he decisions of these [arbitral] tribunals progressively create caselaw which should be taken into account, because it draws conclusions from economic reality and conforms to the needs of international commerce, to which rules specific

---

authority, their rulings having a significance that goes well beyond the individual case for which they were originally created by the parties."

[10] We do not believe that institutional awards have greater precedential effect than *ad hoc* awards. What matters is, in fact, the similarity of decisions adopted in different cases, whether institutional or *ad hoc*. Moreover, arbitral institutions do not exercise any control on the merits of the solutions adopted by arbitrators. Even when institutions have a closed list of arbitrators, such lists do not create *in se* and *per se* an *esprit de corps*. *Contra, see* Rolf A. Schütze, *The Precedential Effect of Arbitration Decisions*, 11(3) J. INT'L ARB 69, 71 (1994): "the precedential effect of the arbitration decisions of institutional arbitration tribunals is very different to that of decisions of *ad hoc* arbitration tribunals."

to international arbitration, themselves successively elaborated should respond.[11]

The *Dow Chemical* award related to an issue of arbitral jurisdiction over a group of companies. Since then, the same solution has been adopted not only by subsequent arbitral awards,[12] but also by national courts.[13] Decisions on procedural issues or questions of arbitral jurisdiction are the natural ground for the emergence of arbitral jurisprudence because arbitral tribunals have the first say on these issues and, arbitral tribunals having no forum, they will generally not resolve them by reference to any particular national law. A similar conclusion may be drawn as far as issues of applicable law are concerned,[14] as it is generally recognized that, in the absence of a choice of law provision in the arbitration agreement, arbitral tribunals can resolve the dispute by referring to

---

[11]   ICC Case No. 4131, Dow Chemical France v. Isover Saint Gobain, Sept. 23, 1982 Interim Award, IX Y.B. COM. ARB. 131, 136 (1984); CA Paris, Oct. 21, 1983, Isover-Saint-Gobain v. Dow Chemical France, 1984 REV. ARB. 98 (note by A. Chapelle).

[12]   ICC Case No. 5721, European company v. American and Egyptian parties, 1990 Award, 117 J.D.I. 1020 (1990) (observations by Y. Derains); ICC Case No. 5730, 1988 Award, 117 J.D.I 1029 (1990) (observations by Y. Derains); ICC Case No. 6519, French Group of Companies v. English company, 1991 Award, 118 J.D.I 1065 (1991) (observations by Y. Derains); ICC Case No. 6673, Licensor v. Licensee, 1992 Award, 119 J.D.I 992 (1992) (observations by D. Hascher); ICC Case No. 7155, Norwegian Company v. Three French Companies, 1993 Award, 123 J.D.I 1037 (1996) (observations by J.-J. Arnaldez).

[13]   CA Paris, Oct. 21, 1983, *supra* note 11; CA Paris, Nov. 30, 1988, Korsnas Marma v. Durand-Auzias, 1989 REV. ARB. 691 (note by P.-Y. Tschanz).

[14]   August 23, 1958 Arbitral Award in the dispute between the Government of Saudi Arabia and the Arabian American Oil Company (ARAMCO), 27 INT'L L. REP. 117 (1963); for a French translation, see 1963 REV. CRIT. DIP 272, 305; Henri Batiffol, *La sentence Aramco et le droit international privé*, 1964 REV. CRIT. DIP 647.

the rules of law they believe to be appropriate.[15] As far as issues of substance are concerned, reference to arbitral precedents is possible when, absent a choice-of-law provision in the arbitration agreement, the arbitral tribunal decides to apply transnational principles, trade usages, or the *lex mercatoria.* The scope of this paper is certainly not to address the much-debated issue of the existence, role and content of *lex mercatoria.* But if non-national rules of law are to play any role in the adjudication of international trade disputes, arbitral precedents cannot but be an important source—albeit non-exclusive—of the same. Even where a choice of law has been made, arbitral precedents may play a role in the resolution of the dispute. Two situations should be borne in mind in this respect. The first is when a particular legal issue has not yet been settled under the particular applicable law. One example could be the specific performance of contractual obligations: in some jurisdictions, in particular where inspired by the French civil code, it is not clearly settled by case law whether specific performance is an adequate remedy. Another example is the pay-if-paid or pay-when-paid clauses in construction sub-contracts, as there are few court decisions regarding the validity and interpretation of these clauses, in particular as to whether they should be considered a term or a condition.[16] Second the

---

[15] Article VII of the European Convention on International Commercial Arbitration, done at Geneva on April 21, 1961, 349 U.N.T.S. 374 (1963–1964); Art. 28 of the 1985 UNCITRAL Model Law on International Commercial Arbitration (available at www.uncitral.org); Art. 1496 of the French New Code of Civil Procedure (available in French at www.legifrance.gouv.fr); Art. 17 of the 1998 ICC Rules of Arbitration (available at www.iccwbo.org/court).

[16] Section 113 of the U.K. Housing Grants, Construction and Regeneration Act 1996 provides that: "(1) A provision making payment under a construction contract conditional on the payer receiving payment from a third person is ineffective, unless that third person, or any other person payment by whom is under the contract (directly or indirectly) a condition of payment by that third person, is insolvent." Yet, although frequent in practice, many jurisdictions do not address the regime of these clauses. *See* Franco Bonelli and Stefano Rellini, *Effetti della clausola* if and when*: una rassegna ragionata della*

construction of *hardship* clauses, which are unknown in many systems of law, is also a proper ground for the application of arbitral precedent. The same can, to a certain extent, be said for *force majeure* provisions and for clauses excluding or limiting liability.[17] International conventions providing for substantive rules of law are also a natural area in which arbitral jurisprudence may be applied, particularly when said conventions, like the CISG, are characteristically detached from national laws for purposes of interpretation.[18] Finally, as Professor François Perret noted in his presentation with respect to an issue of interpretation of Italian law rules on the obligation of the seller of shares, there are situations in which courts' case law is unclear or contradictory.[19] The assumption that reference to arbitral precedents would not be conceivable with respect to substantive issues in presence of a choice of law clause is therefore incorrect. Arbitral jurisprudence may be a source of legal rules in a number of different fields,

---

giurisprudenza italiana e internazionale, 11.2 DIRITTO DEL COMMERCIO INTERNAZIONALE 239 (1997).

[17] MARCEL FONTAINE AND FILIP DE LY, DROIT DES CONTRATS INTERNATIONAUX 388 and 391 (Bruylant, 2nd ed. 2003); Emmanuel Jolivet, *Les clauses limitatives et élusives de responsabilité dans l'arbitrage CCI*, III LES CAHIERS DE L'ARBITRAGE 254 (2006).

[18] Article 7 of the United Nations Convention on Contracts for the International Sale of Goods (1980) (available at www.uncitral.org): "(1) In the interpretation of this Convention, regard is to be had to its international character and to the need to promote uniformity in its application and the observance of good faith in international trade. (2) Questions concerning matters governed by this Convention which are not expressly settled in it are to be settled in conformity with the general principles on which it is based or, in the absence of such principles, in conformity with the law applicable by virtue of the rules of private international law."

[19] *See* his contribution in this publication, *Is There a Need for Consistency in International Commercial Arbitration?*, *supra* at 25.

including with respect to issues of substantive law and when a national law is applicable to the dispute.[20]

The concept of arbitral precedent naturally raises the issue of the availability of arbitration awards. The fundamental importance of a publication of arbitration awards derives from the fact that, in absence of a doctrine of *stare decisis* in arbitration, arbitral precedent will only operate if identical solutions are repeated in a number of different cases. Precedent in arbitration is, from that perspective, a rule-making mechanism comparable to that of trade usages. For a rule-making mechanism to operate, arbitration awards must be available in sufficient quantity to permit the emergence of trends and the distinction of lines of identical or similar solutions. In other words, in order for past awards to be perceived as binding, there needs to be something close to what has been defined as *path dependency*[21] for state courts, *i.e.*, the accumulation of identical or similar solutions able to generate a phenomenon of imitation. As Professor Christian Larroumet correctly points out:

> . . . the persuasiveness,—which supposes an exemplary value and, by consequence, a judgment on the value of a particular decision,—often needs to be combined with quantity. As far as a decision on an important issue by the highest national courts, the European Court of Human Rights or the European Court of Justice are concerned, and as far as such decision have been expected to settle the law on such issues, it can be considered this particular decision

---

[20] *Contra see* Yves Derains, *State Courts and Arbitrators*, in ARBITRATION IN THE NEXT DECADE 27, 32 (ICC Pub. No. 612, 1999): "arbitration case law may develop only when arbitrators do not apply a national law . . . ."

[21] For a definition of the concept in the context of court litigation, see Andrea Pinna, *La spécificité de la jurisprudence arbitrale*, 16 JUSLETTER 7 (Oct. 2006).

is authoritative and has precedential value. Conversely, lower court decisions can obviously not have the same authority. Precedential value can only be given to a consistent line of decisions. The same applies to arbitral awards . . . . For arbitral awards to have precedential effect, it is therefore necessary that awards be known and available.[22]

The main condition for arbitration awards to have precedential effect is therefore that such awards be known and accessible in sufficient quantity; in other words, that they be *systematically* published.[23] To assess whether the system of international arbitration has reached a level of maturity sufficient to generate a case law of its own, it is necessary to study whether and how arbitration awards are published (I) and whether principles such as the privacy and confidentiality stand in the way of systematic publication (II).

---

[22] Christian Larroumet, *A propos de la jurisprudence arbitrale*, Gaz. Pal., Dec. 14, 2006, at 5 (author's translation) (". . . l'autorité, qui suppose la valeur exemplaire et, par conséquent, un jugement de valeur porté sur la décision, doit souvent être combinée avec le nombre. Lorsqu'il s'agit d'une décision de la formation la plus haute d'une Cour suprême nationale ou bien de la Cour européenne des droits de l'homme ou de la Cour de justice des communautés européennes sur une question importante et que l'on attendait cette décision pour que l'état du droit soit fixé, on peut considérer que cette seule décision fait autorité et a valeur d'exemple. En revanche, lorsqu'il s'agit d'une décision d'une juridiction inférieure, il est évident que la même autorité ne saurait lui être attachée. L'autorité ne pourrait être attachée qu'à un ensemble de décisions dans le même sens. Il en irait exactement de même des sentences arbitrales. . . . Pour que l'autorité nécessaire à la construction d'une jurisprudence soit reconnue à des sentences arbitrales, il faut, bien entendu, que ces sentences soient connue et puissent être consultées.")

[23] On the publication of arbitration awards, see Emmanuel Jolivet, *Access to Information and Awards*, 22(2) ARB. INT'L 265, 272 (2006).

I. ARBITRAL PRECEDENT AND THE PUBLICATION OF ARBITRATION AWARDS

Whoever tries to study arbitral precedent may draw the conclusion that there is no use of arbitral precedent in awards, or at least not in a systematic manner. A survey of awards relating to the CISG—which is certainly, for the reasons analyzed above, a proper ground for the use of arbitral precedent—showed that:

> [o]ut of 500 cases, only about 100 were available in sufficient detail to make a finding possible, and out of these, only six referred to past awards.[24]

Another study by Professor Kauffmann-Kohler, relating to published ICC awards, was no more successful, as only 15% of 190 awards reviewed cited other arbitration awards, mostly with regard to matters of jurisdiction, procedure, and applicable law.[25] The conclusion thus might seem to be that international commercial arbitrators do not feel the need to refer to arbitral precedents—at least not as far as issues of substantive law are concerned—and that past cases have no rule-making role in international commercial arbitration. A possible explanation for this could be that, in commercial arbitration, disputes are essentially fact and contract driven, and that arbitrators enjoy broad discretion in determining and applying the law governing the merits. It is also often submitted that, as far as the *lex mercatoria* and transnational rules are concerned, principles such as *pacta sunt servanda, rebus sic stantibus, non venire contra factum proprium,* etc. are generally embodied in national laws and international treatises, so that arbitrators do not need to resort to arbitral

---

[24] Kaufmann-Kohler, *supra* note 3, at 362.

[25] *Id. See also* Jan Paulsson, *La Lex Mercatoria dans l'arbitrage C.C.I.,* 1990 REV. ARB. 55, 80.

precedents to reason their awards thereto.[26] These arguments are certainly part of the reason why arbitral awards seem to contain so few references to precedents. Yet, it would, in our opinion, be incorrect to conclude that arbitral precedents play no significant role in commercial arbitration. While general principles such as *pacta sunt servanda* and good faith are most of the time embodied in national laws and international treatises, this is not always true for all transnational and non-national principles. The principle *non venire contra factum proprium*, for example, owes much to jurisprudence and scholarly writings.[27] International conventions such as the CISG should be construed and applied on the basis of international standards. When applying non-national rules of law, such as the UNIDROIT principles, arbitrators naturally tend to look into arbitral precedents, as it would be paradoxical to construe non national rules on the basis of national principles of law. As far as trade usages are concerned, past arbitration awards, if available in sufficient quantity, could certainly reveal the existence of consistently applied commercial practices in certain areas of business, and, from that standpoint, one may conclude that arbitral precedent can play a rule-making role. As regards municipal laws, there are many issues lacking clear court precedent. It should finally not be overlooked, as explained by Professor Perret in his presentation, that courts' case law may be contradictory or unclear on many questions. There is, therefore, no doubt that arbitral precedent has a role to play in international arbitration. From a

---

[26]   *See* François Perret, *supra* note 19; Kauffmann-Kohler, *supra* note 3, at 364 and 376.

[27]   *See* Giovanni Marini, *Italian Report on Protecting Legitimate Expectations and Estoppel, in* LA CONFIANCE LÉGITIME ET L'*ESTOPPEL* – DROIT PRIVÉ COMPARÉ ET EUROPÉEN VOL. 4, at 295 (B. Fauvarque-Cosson ed., Société de législation comparée, 2007); Gianluca Sicchiero, *L'interpretazione del contratto ed il principio* nemo contra factum proprium venire potest, *in* CONTRATTO E IMPRESA 507 (CEDAM, 2003); FESTI FIORENZO, IL DIVIETO DI "VENIRE CONTRO IL FATTO PROPRIO" (Giuffrè, 2007).

more general perspective, it is certainly advisable that arbitration achieve greater consistency. If arbitration is to remain, according to the sacramental formula, the *mode commun de règlement des différends du commerce international*, it needs to provide the business community with greater predictability of the possible outcome of trade disputes. In turn, better knowledge of arbitral jurisprudence would allow the business community to have a clearer idea of the realities and advantages of arbitration. This is, of course, not to say that arbitrators should be deprived of their discretion in the resolution of each particular case.[28] But such discretion in assessing the facts and determining the appropriate rules of law is in no way incompatible with the availability of a body of arbitral precedents upon which tribunals could rely if appropriate.

Yet, and although a precise study remains to be done on the question, it would appear from a superficial survey of published arbitration awards that arbitrators rarely rely on arbitral precedents. As stated above, few ICC awards refer to arbitral precedents in dealing with substantive questions, including when tribunals have to deal with international instruments such as the CISG. Chistopher Seppala showed in his presentation how rare reference is made to past cases in FIDIC arbitration,[29] yet, FIDIC arbitration

---

[28] In some instances arbitral tribunals do refer to past cases by stressing that they do not feel bound by the solutions adopted thereto; *see* Pinna, *supra* note 21. An example is the January 29, 2004 Decision on Jurisdiction in SGS Société Générale de Surveillance S.A. v. Republic of the Philippines (ICSID Case No. ARB/02/6), 8 ICSID REP. 518, 545 (2005): "in the Tribunal's view, although different tribunals constituted under the ICSID system should in general seek to act consistently with each other . . . , there is no doctrine of precedent in international law, if by precedent is meant a rule of the binding effect of a single decision." For an author positing that the lack of arbitral precedent would reinforce the discretion of arbitral tribunals, see Guy Horsmans, *Propos insolites sur l'efficacité arbitrale*, III LES CAHIERS DE L'ARBITRAGE 33 (2006).

[29] *See* his contribution in this publication, *infra* at 67.

would be a perfect ground for the application of arbitral precedents because FIDIC contracts are a creation of business practice and disputes in this field are almost always resolved by arbitral tribunals. In addition, a closer look at those few arbitral awards which do rely on past cases would probably show that such references are mainly illustrative and used to reinforce a demonstration based on other elements, such as national law, treatises, or scholarly writings. Still, as shown by the five arbitration awards mentioned in his presentation by Professor Perret,[30] arbitral precedent is a reality, and it is likely that such reality has greater importance in practice than a statistical study would reveal. Why is reliance on arbitral precedents then not a more frequent occurrence? In our view the reason can be found in the lack of transparency of commercial arbitration as a dispute resolution system. How can an arbitral tribunal ever conclude that consistent past arbitration awards express a rule of law or a usage when the overwhelming majority of arbitration awards are unknown? It is certainly true that not all courts' decisions themselves are uniformly available. Many courts select the cases they wish to be released to the public, and this is in particular true for Supreme courts. It is nonetheless fair to say that the proportion of court decisions which are made available to the public through publications in official bulletins, legal publications and on the internet is quite representative of the overall jurisprudence of a given judicial system. The same cannot be said of arbitration. Save for a very limited number of exceptions, almost no *ad hoc* awards are published, whereas such awards probably represent a very consistent share—if not the majority—of the total volume of arbitration decisions rendered each year in the world. Arbitral institutions are therefore the exclusive—or almost exclusive— source of published arbitration awards. Yet, only a small minority of arbitral institutions does publish awards. Moreover, amongst those institutions which publish arbitration awards, the ICC

---

[30] Perret, *supra* note 19.

certainly represents the overwhelmingly dominant source of information, the only other institutions having a publication policy being the Stockholm Chamber of Commerce and the CEPANI. The Stockholm Chamber publishes awards in its quarterly Stockholm International Arbitration Review, and a collection of published awards has been made available in a recently edited volume,[31] covering 24 awards rendered between 1999 and 2003. If one considers that about 690 awards have been rendered during the same period of time by that institution, the figure gives an idea of how limited and therefore unreliable the information available to arbitrators is. As for the ICC, that institution publishes awards in a number of different publications, including the ICC Court Bulletin, issued twice a year, once a year in the *Yearbook Commercial Arbitration* and the *Journal du Droit International (Clunet)*, and twice a year in *Les Cahiers de l'Arbitrage (Gazette du Palais)*. The ICC, in addition, publishes some awards in Spanish and Russian.[32] Yet, as systematic as this publication policy may be, it only covers a small minority of the total volume of ICC awards rendered each year, as the following statistic shows. Considering that, since 1974, the ICC has registered roughly 13,000 new cases and has, to date, 1,200 pending cases, and that about 50% of registered cases are withdrawn for various reasons,[33] the conclusion is that since 1974 about 6,000 ICC awards have been rendered. Yet, during the same period of time, only about 700 awards have been published by the ICC in a form or another. The conclusion is therefore, allowing of course for a certain margin of

---

[31]   SCC ARBITRAL AWARDS 1999–2004 (S. Jarvin and A. Magnusson eds., JurisNet, 2006).

[32]   *See* the *Revista de Derecho Internacional y del Mercosur* published twice a month in Spanish, Portuguese and English; and in Russian, the quarterly journal *Mezhdunarodny Kommerchesky Arbitrazh* published in cooperation with Kluwer.

[33]   Information kindly provided by the ICC Court of Arbitration.

error, that those arbitral institutions having a publication policy make less than 15% of their published awards available to the public, which *in se* and *per se* could be considered as a relevant figure. But if we consider that the majority of arbitral institutions (including important international institutions such as the ICDR or the LCIA) do not have a publication policy, the conclusion is that only a very small minority of institutional awards are published. And if we recall that almost no *ad hoc* awards are published, the reality is that the immense majority of awards remain unpublished.

It is of course true that an important part of rendered awards may not be of any interest, as they only settle issues of fact. Likewise, decisions rendered in commodity arbitrations or *in ex aequo et bono* (*amiable composition*) do not present any interest to the issue of setting a precedent. Without a doubt, however, the volume of published cases is not representative of the global reality of international arbitration. Awards are published randomly, depending on whether they have been rendered under the aegis of one of the institutions having a publication policy. In addition, the availability of information depends on the editorial policy of these arbitral institutions. This is of course not to say that such policy would lack sufficient academic standards. Quite the contrary, institutions such as the ICC meet high academic standards in selecting and commenting on awards for publication. The issue is however not *how* arbitration awards are selected for publication, but whether there should at all be any such selection, except for awards that are manifestly without any public interest. Publications that are driven by the desire to treat certain specific issues of general interest that the editor has sought to cover will not, because of the subjectivity of the editor's policy and the limited range of issues covered, allow for the creation of a database sufficient to treat a wider range of questions. Additionally, awards are frequently published in the form of summaries or as extracts, which frequently happens to be insufficient to make a finding possible.

Should awards be published with the names of the arbitrators? Most of the times, they are not. Yet, unlike court decisions, knowing the arbitrators' identity may be relevant to the effect of a proper understanding of the decision's reasoning. Judges are part of a hierarchical and unified judicial body, so that their decisions are more the product of the judicial system to which they belong than their individual creation: what matters is more the circuit, the court or particular section of the court which issued a decision. Conversely, awards are rendered by individuals selected for their personal credentials and reputation, who have no forum and whose decisions are not subject to the control of any superior court. Such individuals have frequently published extensively, and expressed opinions regarding to the issues addressed in their awards. Knowing who they are can therefore be important information for a proper understanding of their findings. Moreover, the high reputation of certain arbitrators may enhance the value of an award in the eyes of their peers. Of course, publication of awards with the names of the members of the arbitral tribunal could have negative effects, such as the multiplication of *obiter dicta* by arbitrators desiring to promote their own "jurisprudence." It could also dissuade arbitrators from taking bold positions. Yet, the example of investment arbitration, where awards are made public with the names of the members of the tribunal, shows that these inconveniencies, as real as they might be, do not outweigh the advantages of putting complete, unabridged information at the disposition of parties and arbitrators.

How could mass publication of complete, unabridged awards be achieved? An excellent model could certainly be the CLOUT database. CLOUT[34] is an information system based on a

---

[34] Case Law On UNCITRAL Texts.

1988 UNCITRAL decision,[35] established for collecting and disseminating information on court decisions and arbitral awards relating to conventions and model laws that have emanated from the work of the Commission. The scope and purpose of such system, as explained by the UNCITRAL user guide, is:

> to promote international awareness of such legal texts elaborated or adopted by the Commission, to enable judges, arbitrators, lawyers, parties to commercial transactions and other interested persons to take decisions and awards relating to those texts into account in dealing with matters within their responsibilities and to promote the uniform interpretation and application of those texts.[36]

Why could a similar system not be instituted to promote the international awareness of arbitral precedent in commercial arbitration? A new database with that precise scope could easily be organised under the aegis of the UNCITRAL, with the same successful system than that which has been used for CLOUT. Awards could be submitted to the Secretariat, which would then ensure that the names of the parties and any non relevant or secret information be deleted, exactly in the same way as this is done for published decisions of the European Commission in the field of mergers. The Secretariat would also ensure that there is no opposition from the parties to their award being available online a certain period of time after it was rendered. Such a system would allow the progressive constitution of a wide database which, provided an efficient index and search system is available, would

---

[35] *See* Report of the United Nations Commission on International Trade Law on the work of its twenty-first session (New York, 11–20 Apr. 1988), Doc. A/43/17 (available at www.uncitral.org).

[36] United Nations Commission on International Trade Law, Case Law on UNCITRAL Texts (CLOUT), User Guide, Doc. A/CN.9/SER.C/GUIDE/1/Rev.1, Feb. 4, 2000, at 2 (available at www.uncitral.org).

constitute the necessary basis of the elaboration of a true system of arbitral precedent.

II.   IS CONFIDENTIALITY A VALID OBJECTION TO THE PUBLICATION OF ARBITRATION AWARDS?

It may, however, be argued that the systematic publication of complete, unabridged awards would be contrary to the privacy and confidentiality of arbitration. The argument is in our opinion not decisive. In fact, not all arbitration rules provide that awards may not be published without the consent of the parties and, even under these rules, such consent may easily be given. Moreover, in *ad hoc* arbitrations or institutional arbitrations which rules do not provide for such a requirement, the existence of a general principle of confidentiality preventing the publication of awards is highly debatable. Finally, the existence of a principle of confidentiality of the arbitration would not necessarily imply the confidentiality of the arbitration award itself once it has been rendered.

Many arbitration rules provide that arbitration awards should not be published without the consent of the parties. This is the case of the UNCITRAL Rules at Article 32(5).[37] A similar rule is contained in Article 43(3) of the Swiss Rules,[38] in Articles 27(4) and 34 of the ICDR Rules,[39] in Article 30.3 of the LCIA Rules,[40] in

---

[37]   Article 32(5) of the UNCITRAL Arbitration Rules provides that "[t]he award may be made public only with the consent of both parties."

[38]   Article 43(3) of the Swiss Rules of International Arbitration provides that "[a]n award may be published, whether in its entirety or in the form of excerpts or a summary, only under the following conditions: . . . (c) No party objects to such publication within the time-limit fixed for that purpose by the Chambers."

[39]   Article 27(4) of the International Arbitration Rules of the International Centre for Dispute Resolution provides that "[a]n award may be made public

Articles 75 and 76 of the WIPO Rules,[41] and in Article 29(5) of the Inter-American Commercial Arbitration Commission.[42] A similar provision can also be included in the arbitration agreement itself, or in the Terms of Reference. In the presence of such a provision, parties must consent prior to any publication. This does not mean, of course, that publication will in practice be impossible. In fact, such rules do not in general provide that consent should be given in written form. Implied consent after proper notice to the parties

---

only with the consent of all parties or as required by law." According to Article 34 of the same Rules, "[c]onfidential information disclosed during the proceedings by the parties or by witnesses shall not be divulged by an arbitrator or by the administrator. Except as provided in Article 27, unless otherwise agreed by the parties, or required by applicable law, the members of the tribunal and the administrator shall keep confidential all matters relating to the arbitration or the award."

[40]   Article 30.3 of the LCIA Rules states that "[t]he LCIA Court does not publish any award or any part of an award without the prior written consent of all parties and the Arbitral Tribunal."

[41]   Article 75 of the WIPO Arbitration Rules provide that "[t]he award shall be treated as confidential by the parties and may only be disclosed to a third party if and to the extent that: (i) the parties consent; or (ii) it falls into the public domain as a result of an action before a national court or other competent authority; or (iii) it must be disclosed in order to comply with a legal requirement imposed on a party or in order to establish or protect a party's legal rights against a third party." Article 76 states that: "(a) Unless the parties agree otherwise, the Center and the arbitrator shall maintain the confidentiality of the arbitration, the award and, to the extent that they describe information that is not in the public domain, any documentary or other evidence disclosed during the arbitration, except to the extent necessary in connection with a court action relating to the award, or as otherwise required by law. (b) Notwithstanding paragraph (a), the Center may include information concerning the arbitration in any aggregate statistical data that it publishes concerning its activities, provided that such information does not enable the parties or the particular circumstances of the dispute to be identified."

[42]   Article 29(5) of the Rules of Procedure of the Inter-American Commercial Arbitration Commission holds that "[t]he award may be made public only with the consent of both parties."

may therefore be sufficient to the effect of permitting the publication of the award. The only exceptions to such possibility would be with respect to awards rendered under the aegis of the LCIA and Swiss rules, for Articles 30.3 of the LCIA Rules[43] and 43(1) of the Swiss rules[44] require the parties' written consent prior to publication of an award.[45] Certain precautions should in any case be taken prior to any publication of an arbitration award. Clearly, an award should not be published if the parties are still litigating. A certain period of time should also have elapsed after the award was rendered (the ICC practice of waiting at least three years before publishing an award seems healthy). In addition, any potentially confidential or secret information contained in an award which is not necessary to understand the decision should be redacted even if the award is to be published in its entirety. This certainly includes the names of the parties involved in the arbitration, the names of third parties, as well as—unless necessary to the understanding of the award, such as data relating to market shares and turnover in antitrust cases—most of the economic and financial information contained in the award.

---

[43] *Supra* note 40.

[44] According to Article 43.1: "Unless the parties expressly agree in writing to the contrary, the parties undertake as a general principle to keep confidential all awards and orders as well as all materials submitted by another party in the framework of the arbitral proceedings not otherwise in the public domain, save and to the extent that a disclosure may be required of a party by a legal duty, to protect or pursue a legal right or to enforce or challenge an award in legal proceedings before a judicial authority. This undertaking also applies to the arbitrators, the tribunal-appointed experts, the secretary of the arbitral tribunal and the Chambers."

[45] For the opposite approach, see Article 41 of the Rules of Arbitration of Tokyo Maritime Arbitration Commission (TOMAC) of the Japan Shipping Exchange, Inc.: "The award given by the Tribunal may be published unless both parties beforehand communicate their objections." *See also* Kenji Tashiro, *Quest for a Rational and Proper Method for the Publication of Arbitral Awards*, 9(2) J. INT'L ARB. 97, 103 (1992).

In absence of a provision expressly requiring the parties' consent to publish the award, the issue is whether a rule to that effect can be deduced from an express or implied rule of confidentiality applicable to the arbitration. As noted by J.-F. Poudret and S. Besson,[46] most arbitration statutes do not expressly provide for a general principle of confidentiality.[47] Arbitration statutes may provide for rules applicable to the protection of business secrets, or the secrecy of deliberations (as Article 1469 of the French New Code of Civil Procedure), but they do not embody a general rule preventing the publication of arbitration awards. As to arbitration rules, those which do not provide for specific rules applying to the publication of awards do not either, in general, contemplate a general principle of confidentiality. The ICC Rules refer, in Article 20.7, to the protection of business secrets and, in Article 21.3, to the privacy of the hearings. The Rules of arbitration of the Vienna Chamber also refer only to the protection of business secrets.[48] These provisions would not, in and of

---

[46] JEAN-FRANCOIS POUDRET AND SÉBASTIEN BESSON, COMPARATIVE LAW OF INTERNATIONAL ARBITRATION 315 (S.V. Berti and A. Ponti trans., Sweet & Maxwell – Schulthess, 2nd ed. 2007).

[47] With limited exceptions, such as the New Zealand Arbitration Act 1996, which provides in Article 14 that disclosure of information relating to arbitral proceedings and awards are prohibited: "(1) Subject to subsection (2), an arbitration agreement, unless otherwise agreed by the parties, is deemed to provide that the parties shall not publish, disclose, or communicate any information relating to arbitral proceedings under the agreement or to an award made in those proceedings. (2) Nothing in subsection (1) prevents the publication, disclosure, or communication of information referred to in that subsection – (a) If the publication, disclosure, or communication is contemplated by this Act; or (b) To a professional or other adviser of any of the parties."

[48] Article 7(4) of the Vienna Rules of Arbitration provides that "[t]he arbitrators must perform their duties in complete independence and impartiality, to the best of their ability, and are not subject to any directives in that respect. They are bound to secrecy in respect of all matters coming to their notice in the course of their duties."

themselves, stand in the way of the publication of awards, provided, as mentioned above, that certain precautions are taken. Certain authors have however argued that arbitration is subject to an *implied* general principle of confidentiality. Such an implied principle of confidentiality is arguably a necessary consequence of the parties' consent to arbitrate,[49] either as part of *lex mercatoria*,[50] or as a transnational rule of international arbitration.[51]

Yet, the fact that most arbitration statutes do not embody such a general principle of confidentiality could be seen as an indication that there is no such general principle. Quite the contrary, the solutions adopted with respect to confidentiality are very different from one jurisdiction to another. In fact, far from expressing a general acknowledgement of the implied confidentiality of arbitration, case law seems to state the opposite in many jurisdictions. While English courts have upheld the existence of a general principle of confidentiality,[52] in Australia, the *High Court* repealed the idea that the parties could be bound by a duty of confidentiality absent an express agreement to that effect.[53] In the United States, a district court seems to have

---

[49]   Emmanuel Gaillard, *Le principe de confidentialité de l'arbitrage commercial international*, Dalloz, Chron. 153 (1987); THOMAS CLAY, L'ARBITRE 595 (Dalloz, 2001); Phillipe Cavalieros, *La confidentialité de l'arbitrage*, III LES CAHIERS DE L'ARBITRAGE 56 (2006); Eric Loquin, *Les obligations de confidentialité dans l'arbitrage*, 2006 REV. ARB. 323.

[50]   Cavalieros, *id.*

[51]   Gaillard, *supra* note 49.

[52]   Ali Shipping Corp. v. Shipyard Trogir, [1998] 2 All E.R. 136; *see also* Dolling-Baker v. Merrett, [1990] 1 W.L.R. 1205; Hassneh Insurance Co. of Israel and others v. Steuart J. Mew, [1993] 2 Lloyd's Rep. 243 (QB).

[53]   Esso Australia resources Ltd. v. Plowman, [1995] 128 A.L.R. 391; Coppée-Lavalin SA/NV v. Ken-Ren Chemicals and Fertilizers Limited, 1995 REV. ARB. 513 (note by D. Kapeliuk-Klinger).

decided likewise.[54] In Sweden, the unauthorised publication of an award led the Supreme Court to decide that, absent an express provision to that effect, the submission of a dispute to arbitration does not imply any duty of confidentiality.[55] Interestingly, the Swedish court held that, by submitting to the arbitration rules of the United Nations Economic Commission for Europe, which includes a provision to the effect that all arbitration hearings are confidential and held *in camera*, the parties did not automatically accept a general duty of confidentiality. The court did, of course, not deny that arbitrating commercial disputes implies a *certain degree* of confidentiality; yet, the parties' duty to preserve confidentiality was balanced according to the underlying interests at stake. In other words, there is no principle of secrecy *in se* and *per se* and the existence of an implied duty of confidentiality does not necessarily imply that *any* information relating to the arbitration should be kept secret. The principle according to which hearings are held *in camera* is, for example, justified by the parties' desire to protect the serenity of the debates. The confidentiality of the documents produced in the arbitration is justified by the need to preserve business secrets, etc. From that perspective, one could wonder what the rationale would be for preventing the publication of an award years after it was rendered if the names of the parties and any potentially secret or confidential information has been removed. A recent decision of the Paris Court of Appeal endorsed the view that any implied duty of confidentiality should be justified by the protection of a legitimate interest. The case related to the production before the Court of Appeal of accounts obtained during the arbitration, and the court denied the claim for damages on the basis that a party seeking

---

[54]   United States of America v. Panhandle Eastern Corp., 118 F.R.D. 346 (D. Del. 1988), quoted by Loquin, *supra* note 49, at 327, note 8.

[55]   Supreme Court of Sweden, Oct. 27, 2000, Bulgarian Foreign Trade Bank Ltd. v. A.I. Trade Finance Inc., 2001 REV. ARB. 821 (note by S. Jarvin and G. Reid).

damages for breach of the confidentiality of arbitration has the duty to provide explanations as to the existence and scope of such purported principle of confidentiality.[56] This is obviously not tantamount to denying that arbitration is to a certain degree confidential, but means that any duty of secrecy should be balanced and proportioned. As rightly noted by J.-F. Poudret and S. Besson:

> there is no uniform conception of confidentiality in arbitration. The notion varies with the situations and functions which it is supposed to cover and does not even apply equally to all participants in arbitral proceedings.[57]

Positing that arbitration is *la chose des parties* and that the award belongs to the litigants is clearly not sufficient justification to prevent its publication. An award is not only the ultimate product of the parties' arbitration agreement. It is not solely a private document. It is also a judicial decision which may, to a

---

[56]   CA Paris, Jan. 22, 2004, National Company for Fishing and Marketing "Nafimco" v. Foster Wheeler Trading Company, 2004 REV. ARB. 647, 656–57 (note by E. Loquin).   In an earlier case, the Paris Court of Appeal had acknowledged that "it is in the nature of arbitration to ensure that the dispute is resolved in a confidential manner" (CA Paris, Feb. 18, 1986, Aïta v. Ojjeh, 1986 REV. ARB. 583) (note by G. Flécheux)).   Yet, in this case, the violation of confidentiality was accompanied by a clear will to harm the other party's interest, by suing such party in a jurisdiction which was manifestly deprived of jurisdiction.   The same observation applies to the case in which the Paris Tribunal of Commerce held a party liable for having made certain information available to the press, which led to a drop in the value of the listed shares of the plaintiff (Trib. Com. Paris, Feb. 22, 1999, Publicis v. True North, 2003 REV. ARB. 189).

[57]   POUDRET & BESSON, *supra* note 46, at 316 citing to Gregory Reid, *Confidentiality - an Algorithm*, 2000(1) STOCKHOLM ARB. REP. 53; *see also* Jan Paulsson and Nigel Rawding, *The trouble with confidentiality*, 5(1) ICC BULL. 48 (1994): "a general obligation of confidentiality cannot be said to exist *de lege lata* in international arbitration."

certain extent, affect the public, and in which the business community at large has an interest. There are many instances in which disclosure of information relating to arbitration is required and permitted. Statutes applicable to listed companies may require the parties to publish financial information.[58] In the *Esso* case,[59] one of the parties was compelled by the Australian Ministry of Energy to produce certain information. Disclosure of the award will be also necessary for the purpose of enforcement proceedings. A party may find itself obliged to produce the award to defend a claim, or to protect its interest or image.[60] These are cases in which a counterbalancing interest mandates disclosure rather than secrecy. Likewise, the public interest in the development of arbitral case law, in the enhancement of the quality of arbitration, and in providing transparency and predictability to the business community overrides the principle of confidentiality as far as the publication of arbitration awards is concerned.

---

[58]   *See* Fabrice Fages, *La confidentialité de l'arbitrage à l'épreuve de la transparence financière*, 2003 REV. ARB. 5, 13.

[59]   *Supra* note 53.

[60]   *Hassneh Insurance, supra* note 52.

The Development of a Case Law in Construction Disputes Relating to FIDIC Contracts

Christopher R. Seppälä [*]

I. INTRODUCTION

As I did not choose the topic of my talk, I can only speculate about why, in the context of this conference dealing with "Precedent in International Arbitration," it might have been proposed. The reasons would appear to have included the following:

1.   It is well established that construction contracts often give rise to disputes—they are endemic to construction;

2.   The contracts published by the *Fédération Internationale des Ingénieurs-Conseils* (the International Federation of Consulting Engineers), commonly known as "FIDIC," are perhaps the best known and most widely used standard forms of international construction contract;

3.   Since the first FIDIC standard form of construction contract was published in 1957, more than fifty years ago, they have provided for the final settlement of disputes under the Rules of Arbitration of the International Chamber of Commerce (the "ICC"); and

[*]   Partner, White & Case LLP, Paris. The author gratefully acknowledges the research assistance of Michael Jaskierowicz, *stagiaire* (trainee) with White & Case LLP, Paris, in the preparation of this paper.

4.   While international arbitral awards are not regularly or systematically reported, it is well known that a substantial number of ICC arbitrations have involved FIDIC contracts.

For these reasons, one may, very understandably, be led to suppose that if ever there was an area where an arbitration case law should have developed, it would be in relation to the FIDIC contracts.

But what are the facts? How many arbitral awards dealing with the various standard forms of FIDIC contract have been published? How many of the awards that deal with a FIDIC contract interpret that standard form in a way that can be of subsequent value as precedent? Can it be said that a case law relating to FIDIC contracts, made up of arbitral awards, has developed and is given weight by arbitral tribunals in their awards?

II.   AWARDS INTERPRETING FIDIC CONTRACTS

It is very difficult to know the exact number of arbitral awards that have been published dealing with the FIDIC contracts as, like other international arbitral awards, they are not published regularly or systematically in any single place. On the contrary, such awards are dispersed in different legal journals and books, published in different countries and, sometimes, even in different languages.

Moreover, often the award itself is not published but only an extract, a digest or a summary is provided. When extracts, digests or summaries are published, there is no way of being sure of their accuracy. If they have been translated into another language as well, this can only enhance the risk of error.

This being said, based on a review of the following sources:

1.   collections of ICC awards (4 volumes) (1974-2000);

2.   International Council for Commercial Arbitration – Yearbook Commercial Arbitration (1976-2007);

3.   ICC International Court of Arbitration Bulletin (issues of June 1991 and May and November 1998);

4.   The International Construction Law Review (1983-2007); and

5.   other sources (*e.g.*, the ASA Bulletin, Mealey's International Arbitration Report, etc.);

only about 40 arbitral awards interpreting FIDIC contracts were found.   Of these, only about 5 cited to prior awards interpreting FIDIC contracts.

40 awards is not a lot, especially when it is appreciated that they relate not to one, but to two quite different forms of FIDIC contract as well as to different editions of these two forms.   The two forms and their respective editions are, as follows:

FIDIC Form of Contract	Editions
Conditions of Contract for Works of Civil Engineering Construction (the **"Red Book"**)	1st (1957) 2nd (1969) 3rd (1977) 4th (1987)
Conditions of Contract for Electrical & Mechanical Conditions (the **"Yellow Book"**)	1st (1963) 2nd (1980) 3rd (1987)

Moreover, most of the awards dealt, in whole or in part, with one issue, namely, whether a party had complied with Clause 67 ("Settlement of Disputes – Arbitration") of the FIDIC Red Book, which provided for a "time bar" or time limit within which to preserve the right to arbitrate.

All of the published awards relate to FIDIC contracts which have been published between 1957 and 1987. Since 1987, there have, of course, been new editions of the FIDIC contracts—in fact, an entire new suite of construction contracts was published in 1999—but, to the author's knowledge, no form of FIDIC contract published after 1987 has been the subject of a published arbitral award.

Thus, if by case law relating to FIDIC contracts one is referring exclusively to published arbitral awards, there is really not very much available. Moreover, what exists is unlikely to be very helpful in interpreting the current FIDIC forms of contract, as the current forms published in 1999 constitute not merely new editions of their predecessors but entirely new documents, with a new structure and clause numbering system.

However, Barton Legum has at this conference—quite rightly—defined precedent in international arbitration broadly as "any decisional authority" that may help to provide a reasoned basis for an arbitrator's decision.[1] Applying this broad definition of "precedent," which would include national court decisions, there is, in fact, quite a lot of useful precedent, as well as commentary, relating to FIDIC contracts which may be examined.

---

[1] *See* Barton Legum, *The Definitions of "Precedent" in International Arbitration, supra* at 5.

III. OTHER PRECEDENTS RELATING TO FIDIC CONTRACTS: ENGLISH AND OTHER COMMON LAW COURT PRECEDENTS

As is well known, the first few editions of the FIDIC Red Book were closely modeled on the English ICE (Institution of Civil Engineers) Conditions of Contract and the official and authentic text of the FIDIC contracts has always been the version in the English language. Furthermore, as a practical matter, the FIDIC contracts have always been drafted, and are still drafted, primarily by English engineers. It is, therefore, appropriate to look to English and other common law court precedents to develop an understanding of the FIDIC contracts, their contract procedures and terminology.

English and other common law precedent is relevant in two ways:

1.   for a better understanding of the legal principles and contract procedures embodied in the FIDIC contracts (*e.g.*, the role of the independent engineer as an intermediary between the parties or the procedure for variations), and

2.   for a better understanding of the intention of the language of the FIDIC contracts.[2]

It is, therefore, not surprising that the main published commentaries, in book form, on the FIDIC contracts, are by British lawyers and engineers, and that they refer primarily to English case law precedent and hardly ever to an arbitral award. As an illustration, the following is a table setting out the main published

---

[2]   English court decisions dealing with issues relevant to FIDIC contracts have been published, notably, in *Building Law Reports* in England, whose index volumes reference the "FIDIC Contract" and indicate the cases which are relevant to particular clauses.

commentaries on the FIDIC Red Book and the precedent (court decisions or awards) that they cite to:

Author	Title (and Year)	English and Other Court Cases
I.N. Duncan Wallace[3]	THE INTERNATIONAL CIVIL ENGINEERING CONTRACT (1974, 1980)	**63** (no awards cited)
E.C. Corbett[4]	FIDIC 4TH – A PRACTICAL LEGAL GUIDE (1991)	**76** (one award cited)
Nael Bunni[5]	THE FIDIC FORMS OF CONTRACT (2005)	**154** (no award cited)
J. Glover & S. Hughes[6]	UNDERSTANDING THE NEW FIDIC RED BOOK: A CLAUSE BY CLAUSE COMMENTARY (2006)	**111** (no award cited)

---

[3] I.N. DUNCAN WALLACE, THE INTERNATIONAL CIVIL ENGINEERING CONTRACT (Sweet & Maxwell, 1974); I.N. DUNCAN WALLACE, THE INTERNATIONAL CIVIL ENGINEERING CONTRACT: FIRST SUPPLEMENT (Sweet & Maxwell, 1980).

[4] EDWARD C. CORBETT, FIDIC 4TH – A PRACTICAL LEGAL GUIDE (Sweet & Maxwell, 1980).

[5] NAEL BUNNI, THE FIDIC FORMS OF CONTRACT (Blackwell Publishing, 4th ed. 2005).

[6] JEREMY GLOVER AND SIMON HUGHES, UNDERSTANDING THE NEW FIDIC RED BOOK (intro. by C. Thomas, Sweet & Maxwell, 2006).

One may regret that one must have recourse primarily to legal authority from one system of law—that of the common law world—for interpreting what purports to be an international standard form of contract. Indeed, a retired English judge, His Honour Judge Humphrey Lloyd, QC, in his book review of the last book listed above, stated that:

> A legal commentary on the FIDIC Red Book should not be mainly confined to UK law.[7]

But, for the historic and linguistic reasons mentioned above, users seem to have little choice, at least, until there exists a much wider use of the FIDIC contracts internationally or a more developed and sophisticated system of contract law at the international level, except to refer to precedent from the common law world.

IV. USE OF NATIONAL COURT PRECEDENT FROM A DEVELOPED SYSTEM OF LAW TO FILL "GAPS" IN GOVERNING LAW

In the author's experience, an issue of precedent which often arises in relation to FIDIC and other international construction contracts is the following:

An international construction contract typically relates to a large and/or complex project to be carried out at a site in a developing country for an employer residing in that country (the contractor being usually from a developed country). The employer

---

[7] Humphrey Lloyd, *Book Review (Understanding the New FIDIC Red Book: A Clause-by-Clause Commentary. By Jeremy Glover and Simon Hugues. London: Thompson Sweet & Maxwell, 2006)*, 24 INT'L CONSTR. L. REV. 503, 505 (2007).

will normally require that the contract be governed by the law of its country, which is also logical as the site will usually be located there. But, typically, there lies the problem because, invariably, the law of that country and, specifically its contract law or law of obligations, which will be the law of principal relevance to the interpretation of the contract, will also be developing—it will likely contain "gaps"—and not provide clear or precise answers to many of the legal issues to which large, complex construction projects can give rise.

On the other hand, the construction contract issues to which such projects typically give rise will often have been analyzed in depth and addressed by courts or legislatures in, for example, the developed countries of Western Europe or the U.S. In those countries, there is often no difficulty in finding answers to those issues.

The author will present below four illustrations of this problem, two taken from actual ICC cases (the first resulting in an award and the second of which was settled before an award) and two taken from international construction disputes which were settled before any arbitration began. In doing so, the author has had necessarily to simplify certain of the facts in these cases so that they can be presented briefly.

The **first example** was a case where the governing law was that of an Arab country with an undeveloped law.

The dispute related to a project to build a town consisting of 3,000 housing units and related utilities and infrastructure on a green field (undeveloped) site in the Arab country concerned. The employer had let the works out to three different contractors under three different main construction contracts (commonly known, at least in the United States, as "multi-prime" construction contracts), as follows:

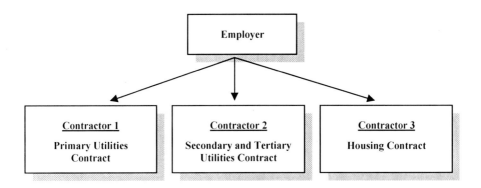

However, although it might be considered normal practice for the programs or schedules for the works under each of these contracts to be carefully integrated with each other, nothing was specified in any of these contracts or elsewhere on this subject.

This gave rise to the following question: what duty, if any, does an employer owe to its various prime or main contractors in the case of a multi-prime construction project, where no provision is made for coordination of the performance of work under those contracts by the employer?

The Arab law concerned did not address the issue. It provided only that a party must perform a contract in good faith, and provided some rudimentary examples of how this duty should be interpreted by reference mainly to the treatise on civil law of Dr. Al-Sanhouri, the eminent Egyptian legal scholar. It gave no meaningful guidance about how this duty or principle should be construed and applied in the case of a multi-prime construction contract situation.

The absence of law in this area heightened the risk, naturally, that the ICC arbitral tribunal, whose members were not construction specialists, could apply this duty or principle erroneously or inappropriately.

To limit this risk, we, as counsel to the contractor, undertook some research in comparative law and discovered that the law relating to the rights and duties of owners and contractors in multi-prime construction contract situations, though not much developed in Europe (*e.g.*, in England or France), is highly developed in the United States.[8] While U.S. law does not refer to or apply the doctrine that a contract be performed in good faith as did the law of the Arab country (like, indeed, the law of civil law countries generally), the duties which U.S. law imposed on owners in multi-prime contract situations appeared to us to be entirely consonant with this principle.

But what was especially useful and illuminating was that U.S. case law provided precise guidance as to how—consistent, it seemed to us (and to our Arab counsel), with the obligation to perform a contract in good faith, as provided for by the relevant Arab law—an owner should be conducting himself towards his contractors in a multi-prime contract situation. The U.S. case law made clear that even where nothing is specified in the relevant construction contracts, where an owner has entered into multiple prime construction contracts whose performance can impact the performance of others, the owner has an implied affirmative duty to coordinate those contracts and to limit the risk that performance under one will or may prevent or hinder performance under another.

The arbitral tribunal, which consisted of two Arab lawyers (including one from the country of the governing law concerned) and one English barrister, a Queen's Counsel (the Chairman), expressed relief at the hearing that concrete expression had been found as to how the principle that a contract must be performed in

---

[8] For an excellent, though not recent, article on this subject, see John B. Tieder, Jr., *The Duty to Schedule and Co-Ordinate on Multi-Prime Contractor Projects—The United States Experience*, 3(2) INT'L CONSTR. L. REV. 97 (1986).

good faith, as provided for by the relevant Arab governing law, might be applied to the conduct of an owner in a multi-prime contract situation. In fact, we found one U.S. case presenting almost identical facts to our case, which the tribunal said they found very helpful.[9]

Not only did the tribunal adopt the solution that there had been a violation, in this case, of the principle that a contract be performed in good faith (consistent with U.S. law that there had been a breach of contract), the tribunal cited to passages from the relevant U.S. cases in its award, as follows:

> This conception was also confirmed by American law. Thus, it was held that an employer has an implicit duty to co-ordinate the various contractors in order to prevent unreasonable delays in the project (Born v. Malloy, 381 N.E. 2d. 52, 55 (1978)).

> According to the American courts, the employer's inaction in the face of unnecessary and unreasonable delays by one of the contractors would ordinarily evidence that the employer breached its implied duty to co-ordinate (Broadway Maintenance Corp. v. Rutgers, 90 N.J. 253 (1982)).[10] [Emphasis added]

The **second example** concerns a case where the governing law was that of the former People's Republic of Congo (the "**PRC**").

This ICC arbitration, which had its seat in Paris, involved a subcontract for the construction of a road in the PRC. The subcontract contained (like many subcontracts) a clause providing, in essence, that the subcontractor would be paid only if and when,

---

[9]   Paccon, Inc. v. United States, 399 F.2d. 162 (Ct. Cl. 1968).

[10]   ICC Case Nos. 3790/3902/4050/4051/4054 (joined cases), 1984 Final award, at 179 (unpublished).

or as and when, the main contractor was paid by the employer. The employer had effectively gone bankrupt and, thus, the main issue in the case was whether the main contractor was entitled to maintain, based on such "if and when" or "paid when paid" clause (as they are commonly called) in the subcontract, that it was relieved of having ever to pay the subcontractor anything more as it would never be paid by the employer who was bankrupt. To put the issue another way, was the "if and when" or "pay when paid" clause to be interpreted as establishing a condition precedent to the main contractor's obligation to pay the subcontractor (as the main contractor argued) or did such clause only regulate the time for payment, and thus not relieve the main contractor from having ultimately to pay the subcontractor (as the subcontractor argued)?

As there was no law, or very little law, in the PRC to show how such clause was to be interpreted and very little relevant law in France or Belgium from which PRC law may be said, in some measure, to derive (or to which it may be related), both parties in the arbitration cited extensively to the wealth of U.S. case law on the issue of how the particular "if and when" or "pay when paid" clause at issue was to be interpreted (that is, whether it establishes a condition to payment or regulates only the time for payment).[11] While U.S. cases are themselves divided on the question, they contain a great deal of useful analysis which the parties (and later an arbitral tribunal) could draw on for guidance. Thus, this is an example of a case where (as in the case of the first example) resort was made by both parties to case law from a different family of law from that of the governing law (as the same family of law of the governing law contained very little relevant precedent).

---

[11]   As such clauses are in wide-spread use in the United States, there are literally hundreds, if not thousands, of reported U.S. federal court and state court decisions interpreting such clauses.

While this dispute settled before there was an award, there is no doubt that the arbitral tribunal would have been expected to take account of the analysis in such case law when determining, in their award, how PRC law should apply to the issue.[12]

The **third example** involves a case where the governing law was that of former Zaire.

In this case, when drafting a price escalation clause for a public works contract with a foreign contractor, the Zairian public owner (or its consultant) had evidently neglected to take account of the effect of devaluations / re-evaluations of the currencies in which the cost indices in the price escalation clause were denominated (the indices were denominated in three different currencies, as the construction site lay in three different countries). During the performance of the contract, the currency of Zaire was devalued 500 per cent which, as the labor index was denominated in the currency of Zaire and the currencies in which the other indices were denominated did not change in value, had a sudden distorting effect on the operation of the clause, causing an aberrational 50% increase in the contract price from about US$ 50 million to US$ 75 million.

This gave rise to the question of whether, based on a literal and strict application of the price escalation clause, the contractor was entitled to the increased price, as the contractor claimed.

The contract was, as mentioned earlier, governed by the law of Zaire and, as in the previous two examples mentioned, the law of Zaire provided no clear answer to this question.

---

[12] ICC Case No. 6158. In presenting comparative law to an arbitral tribunal, an important tactical consideration will be the composition of the arbitral tribunal, as the nationality and legal backgrounds of its members will bear on how receptive it is likely to be to the particular national law or laws being presented.

Based on a brief review of English law (which was certainly irrelevant, but which is nevertheless widely referred to in the case of international construction contracts because they are often based on English forms, as indicated above), it appeared that, under English law, price escalation clauses are ordinarily enforced strictly as they are written and the employer would have been entitled to no relief. The employer would have had to pay the additional amount resulting from strict application of the price escalation clause.

But the law of the former Zaire is derived from Belgian law and, in the case of an administrative (public works) contract, as was the case here, Belgian law or, more precisely, French law to which a Belgian court would look, would provide relief. Under French administrative law, it was (and doubtless still is) well established that if a price escalation clause in an administrative contract gives rise to a result which the parties could not reasonably have intended, then, under the theory of *imprévision*, the court is empowered to adjust the result obtained from a literal application of the price escalation clause to a result which the parties could reasonably have intended.[13] Very arguably, this principle should apply to a public works contract in the former Zaire.

At all events, the solution permitted the parties to overcome the difficulty which derived from the aberrational effect of their price escalation clause and, despite the magnitude of the contractor's claim (US$ 25 million), the case settled without the need for arbitration.

The **fourth example** involved a case where the governing law was that of India.

---

[13] For information on this subject, see ANDRÉ DE LAUBADÈRE, FRANCK MODERNE AND PIERRE DELVOLVÉ, TRAITÉ DES CONTRATS ADMINISTRATIFS, Vol. 2, ¶ 1365 (LGDJ, 1984).

This case involved a dispute between an Indian owner and a foreign contractor who was building a hydro-electric plant for the owner in India. In the course of constructing the tunnels for such plant, the contractor encountered severe adverse geological conditions which would make it extremely difficult, if not impossible, as a practical matter (in terms of cost and time), for the contractor to complete the hydro-electric plant. This gave rise to the issue of whether the contractor could be released or discharged from the contract, which (as mentioned) was governed by Indian law, by virtue of the common law—and Indian law—doctrine of frustration.

The issue was analyzed extensively under Indian law. While India had (and perhaps still does) its own Contract Act 1872 and doctrine of frustration (provided for in Section 56 of that Act), and there are a number of reported Indian cases applying the doctrine of frustration, nevertheless, fairly extensive use was made also (including by Indian counsel) of well known English cases where the doctrine of frustration has been applied to construction contracts, such as *Davis Contractors v. Fareham U.D.C.*[14]

While the dispute ultimately settled, this case illustrates again the use of case law from a country with a developed system of law in order better to analyze the issues and/or reinforce the solutions provided for by the law of the country that is expressed to govern an international construction contract.

In each of the above four cases (except perhaps the last one), the local governing law—which was relatively undeveloped—had not addressed the specific question at issue. On the other hand, in each of these cases, the questions involved were classic or typical construction law issues, which had been analyzed

---

[14]   Davis Contractors v. Fareham Urban District Council, [1956] A.C. 696.

in courts in the United States, France and England, which had come up with well reasoned and sensible solutions.

In the author's view, where there are gaps in a governing law, that is developing, the analysis and solutions that courts in developed legal systems can provide should not be disregarded. On the contrary, to the extent that they are in harmony with the governing law and provide good solutions, they should be considered by international arbitral tribunals. By virtue of their multi-national composition and international character, international arbitral tribunals are better qualified, and should be more receptive, than national courts, to look to comparative law for solutions.

V.   CONCLUSION

In the case of countries with developing legal systems, international legal principles, such as the excellent UNIDROIT Principles 2004, may certainly be useful in filling "gaps" in the relevant national law, where this is appropriate and not inconsistent with such law. But because they are necessarily of a relatively high level of generality and are not addressed specifically to construction contracts, their practical utility may be limited in the case of a construction dispute.

Moreover, the legal issues that arise in international construction disputes (such as those relating to multi-prime construction contracts, "pay when paid" and price escalation clauses and difficulties a contractor may experience in performing the works, referred to above) are often no different from the very same issues that arise in a domestic context and, thus, do not (like some other issues) call for a specifically "international" solution when they arise in international arbitration.[15] The very same issues will often have arisen and been addressed in domestic construction law, at least in countries with developed legal systems, and therefore there is no reason—provided that this is compatible with the relevant governing law—that they should not be dealt with in the same way in the case of an international dispute.

Therefore, when a "gap" is found in the law governing an international construction contract, a party's counsel may be well advised, in addition to investigating such legal principles of the governing law as may be relevant (for there are always likely to be some, and these must always be respected), to search for relevant court precedent or legal principles in the law of an appropriate developed legal system (which will usually be within the same family of law as the governing law, if not the law of the country, if any, from which the governing law is derived). Thus,

(1)   if the governing law is that of a civil law country, and its legal system has historic links to France or Belgium, one may want to begin research with the standard works of, *e.g.*:

(a)   de Laubadère, Moderne & Delvolvé (administrative contracts)[16] or Jacques Montmerle (private contracts) in France,[17] or

(b)   Maurice-André Flamme in Belgium, or

---

[15]   The need for an "international" solution (as opposed to one provided by a country's domestic law) is a commonly invoked rationale for the development of *lex mercatoria*. *See* ALAN REDFERN AND MARTIN HUNTER WITH NIGEL BLACKABY AND CONSTANTINE PARTASIDES, LAW AND PRACTICE OF INTERNATIONAL ARBITRATION 109 (Sweet & Maxwell, 4th ed. 2004).

[16]   DE LAUBADÈRE, MODERNE AND DELVOLVÉ, *supra* note 13.

[17]   JACQUES MONTMERLE, ALBERT CASTON, MARC CABOUCHE, LAURENT DE GABRIELLI AND MICHEL HUET, PASSATION ET EXÉCUTION DES MARCHÉS DE TRAVAUX PRIVÉS (Le Moniteur, 5th ed. 2006).

(2)   if the governing law is that of a <u>common law</u> country, and its legal system has historic links to England, one may want to begin research with the standard works of, *e.g.*, *Hudson's Building and Engineering Contracts*[18] and *Keating On Construction Contracts*[19] in England. The works of Mr. Justin Sweet[20] and *Bruner & O'Connor on Construction Law*[21] in the United States might also be consulted.

Provided it is compatible with the governing law and can be justified as reflecting how a court of the country of the governing law would likely decide the question if it were submitted to it, then a court decision on similar facts, or a relevant legal principle, from a developed system of law may help to provide a better grounded, more precise and convincing means of filling a "gap" than an attempt to do so by resorting merely to the general principles of the governing law and then attempting to reason from there. In short, why re-invent the wheel, given the wealth of analysis and wisdom that judicious use of comparative law can provide?

Under this proposal, arbitrators are not to disregard the governing law, as Lord Asquith reportedly did in his 1951 award in the well known *Petroleum Development Ltd. v. The Sheikh of Abu Dhabi* case.[22] On the contrary, they must faithfully apply the

---

[18]   HUDSON'S BUILDING AND ENGINEERING CONTRACTS (I.D. Wallace ed., Sweet & Maxwell, 11th ed. 2003).

[19]   KEATING ON CONSTRUCTION CONTRACTS (V. Ramsey and S. Furst eds., Sweet & Maxwell, 8th ed. 2006).

[20]   JUSTIN SWEET AND JONATHAN J. SWEET, SWEET ON CONSTRUCTION INDUSTRY CONTRACTS: MAJOR AIA DOCUMENTS (Aspen Publishers, 4th ed. 2007).

[21]   PHILLIP L. BRUNER AND PATRICK J. O'CONNOR, BRUNER & O'CONNOR ON CONSTRUCTION LAW (Thomson West, 2002).

[22]   In the Matter of an Arbitration between Petroleum Dev. (Trucial Coast) Ltd. and the Sheikh of Abu Dhabi, Award, Aug. 28, 1951, 1 INT'L & COMP. L.Q. 247 (1952). In that case, Lord Asquith disregarded the law of Abu Dhabi

relevant legal principles, to the extent they may exist, of the governing law.

But, where there is a gap, they should also take account of the best reasoning and experience from any other relevant legal system or systems and, specifically, a developed system within the same family of law as the governing law (if not the law of the country, if any, from which the governing law is derived), so long as, and to the extent that, that reasoning and experience is wholly compatible with the governing law. At the least, where there is a gap, the solutions, reasoning and experience of a relevant developed system of law can point the arbitrators in the right direction, even if they might prefer not to refer to such other system of law in their award.

In conclusion, counsel (especially, as arbitrators depend upon them) and arbitrators should make more use—but judicious use, for it must always be the governing law that is finally applied—of the immense resources of comparative law when considering a governing law that is developing.[23] As a practical matter, a limitation on their ability or willingness to do so may be

---

which was referred to in the contract as not sufficiently sophisticated to provide a solution to the relevant dispute and applied instead English law insofar as it reflected universal legal principles. *See* FOUCHARD GAILLARD GOLDMAN ON INTERNATIONAL COMMERCIAL ARBITRATION 842–45 (E. Gaillard & J. Savage eds., Kluwer, 1999).

[23]   Note that often the problem, as a practical matter, is not merely that the law is developing but that what law may exist is poorly reported—when reported at all—or difficult to access for various reasons. This is a familiar problem to lawyers working with the laws of developing countries. Indeed, it is the subject of an express provision of the 1999 FIDIC Red Book, Sub-Clause 2.2, providing: "The Employer shall (where he is in a position to do so) provide reasonable assistance to the Contractor at the request of the Contractor: (a) by obtaining copies of the Laws of the Country [defined as the country where the site is located] which are relevant to the Contract but are not readily available . . . ."

their insufficient knowledge or familiarity with foreign and comparative law. But with the steady increase in world trade and the concomitant increase in the number of lawyers (at least practising international arbitration) who are qualified in two or more (ideally, common law and civil law) jurisdictions, this should, hopefully, be becoming less of a problem.

Comments and Discussion

Jean-Louis Delvolvé–. I would like to turn to our friend Barton Legum. I like the reference to the train of relativity of Einstein (1905) where there are three people—the Counsel, the Arbitrator and the Judge—but I think on the train there is also the user, the client whose point of view does count, because he is the main beneficiary of what is going to happen. But the client wants to achieve his aim, *i.e.*, he wants to have the award which is going to give him a result which he likes, which makes sure that he wins, and an award which is enforceable in a country.

Now I will go on to turn to Emmanuel Gaillard and to François Perret. The reference which is made to the idea that there is an arbitral case law only if it is autonomous and independent from control by State courts; but, in fact, it is State courts which are going to be able to say whether an award can be enforced or not. So my question is very simple: when the arbitrator or the counsel looks at case law, do they not have to point to the weight or the authority of the arbitral precedent, or the arbitral jurisprudence after it has been confronted with the judge, either the judge of the country where the award was rendered or the judge of the country where the award will be enforced? Does a precedent have the same value depending on whether it has gone through the scrutiny of either one or the other court?

Claude Reymond–. My question picks up on the question which has just been raised by Jean-Louis Delvolvé and also the remarks by François Perret. It seems to me that in history—and unfortunately we have come to an age where we think more about the past of arbitration—the consistency of arbitration case law and reference to precedent have mostly manifested themselves with respect to the development of arbitration law.

And I am thinking of the situation forty years back. There was a time when the autonomy of the arbitration clause was not self-evident; an ICCA Congress had to be organized to actually defend that new bold idea. Then, little by little, thanks to the dialog that took place—that is why I do not totally agree with the excellent presentation made by François Perret—a dialog started between arbitrators among themselves, between the arbitrators and courts, and finally between the courts and the legislators; and that is how arbitration law, as we know it today, developed.

And I would just like to remind you of the importance of that dialog and the fact that in our experience—and here it is a common experience with Karl-Heinz Böckstiegel—there is an award which is often quoted which relates to the scope of an arbitral tribunal's powers and the scope of the obligations of a State which has signed an international convention. These are questions of arbitration law; but I do not want to minimize, of course, the importance of State case law and arbitral case law in other fields, because for an arbitrator it is very fortunate to be able to say that other arbitrators dealing with the same subject matter have rendered the same type of award as him.

Bassam Onaissi–. I would like to submit two thoughts to the speakers and to the audience concerning the paucity of references to case law. Now, first of all, in State case law, is there a request for predictability, for consistency, for coherence? Or is it also a request—that is lacking in arbitration—for equality, *i.e.*, each citizen has the right to get the same decision, if that person is in a same situation as a person who has had his case judged previously. That is the principle of equal treatment which is at the basis of democratic States, and which does not pertain to arbitration.

The second thought is that arbitration law is, of course, fact based, because the legal forms which we enjoy as legal experts in a specific law give rise to a number of refinements as decisions are known, whereas for the facts—if we state that for arbitrators the only law is the one chosen by the parties, *i.e.*, the contract which will prevail in any case, the question is, as was stated by a Greek philosopher: "You never bathe in the same waters twice".

Emmanuel Gaillard–. On the statistical approach to case law and the need to publish the awards—an issue which was raised by Alexis Mourre—to complete the picture, it would also be interesting to have a statistical approach of what is interesting in domestic case law. If you take the 10% of published ICC decisions, Alexis finds that it is not very much and it sounds like an insignificant number; on the contrary, you can feel it is a lot and it is fairly revealing, because the arbitrators deal with the matters that are submitted to them; there are a number of cases which are very interesting to the parties but they have no interest whatsoever as precedent (because the claim had a 45-day delay or one party was too late in carrying out the contract, etc.). Thus, the 10% are perhaps statistically significant and I would apply the theory of relativity to those figures.

And I found a very interesting example in what François Perret was saying, that is the relative value—there we go, we come back to relativity—for an arbitrator of a State precedent relating to the law applicable to the contract in question—he mentioned Italian law—as compared to the persuasive value of arbitral precedents applying the same law. We had, on one side, the Italian Supreme Court and, on the other, a corpus of arbitral decisions which seemed more consistent to the last arbitral tribunal. You see that the arbitrators attached a lot of importance to arbitral precedents.

Barton Legum–. I agree, I think, with each of one of the comments that is been made so far. One point that I would like to pick up on is the notion of consistency in the abstract—that every decision involving similar facts should receive the same result. While, as a matter principle that is, I think, an ideal perhaps we should all aspire to, it is worth bearing in mind that that is an ideal that no system of justice that I am aware of has ever been able to attain. In the United States, which does have a system of precedent, you typically have very different decisions from dozens of Courts of First Instance and many Courts of Appeals that exist for years before the Supreme Court eventually gets around to addressing it and resolving the inconsistency—if ever. And the other thing I would note that is the profession of many of us in this room is 'lawyer' and we would not really be able to justify the fees that we charge our clients if every client with the same facts was entitled to exactly the same result. The reality is that advocacy does matter, that how the case is presented does matter and therefore, as we all know, it is inevitable, and desirable from the client's point of view that the result may be different from one case to another.

François Perret–. Maître Delvolvé, was your question the following one: when an arbitral tribunal has a precedent, must it inform the parties before judging?

I think that the French jurisprudence did decide the matter in the sense that it is not necessary to do so; but if the arbitration has is seat in Switzerland, I would be very careful because the Federal Tribunal is very protective of the rights of each party to be heard.

With respect to Claude Reymond's comment, I agree with you. At the beginning, it was all about arbitration law, but now I have doubts. There are new question arising which are submitted to arbitral tribunals and which give rise to divergent awards. I am talking about, for example, the violation by one party of its obligation to pay its advance on costs. Some arbitral tribunals say it is a material obligation, that the party has to be condemned, while others say 'well, no, maybe we can find a way out of this.' So that is a problem which must be solved because you cannot have divergent decisions, inconsistent decision especially as they were rendered in Geneva—you have two divergent arbitral awards rendered in Geneva. That is where the ICC does not examine the discrepancies.

Part II

International Investment
Arbitration

Introductory Remarks

Prosper Weil [*]

The question whether and to what extent judicial decisions constitute a source of law and, therefore, a binding authority upon tribunals, is, as we all know, a difficult and controversial one.

There are competing sociological imperatives at play: the need for continuity of jurisprudence, which is to say stability in the rules of law, without which there can be no predictibility, weighs against the need for the evolution of such rules of law, responsive to an ever changing political, sociological, and economic climate. Permanence and stability serve certain purposes; flexibility and evolution serve others.

This dilemma, to which various domestic laws give different responses, is aggravated in the international context.

This observation is certainly true of inter-state jurisdictions. We are all aware of the Statute of the International Court of Justice's cautious approach to recognising jurisprudence as a source of international law: according to the well-known Article 38, the Court shall apply "subject to the provisions of Article 59, judicial decisions . . . as subsidiary means for the determination of rules of law"—which establishes a double protection: not only are judicial decisions a "subsidiary" source of law, but, even within this limitation, they only rise to the level of source of law "subject to the provisions of Article 59."

---

[*]   Emeritus Professor of Law, University of Panthéon-Assas (Paris II).

Yet, Article 59 provides, "[t]he decision of the Court has no binding force except between the parties and in respect of that particular case"—which theoretically undermines the recognition of judicial decisions as a source of law.

Setting aside inter-state jurisdictions, this difficulty is no less real when one deals with the jurisdiction of arbitral tribunals over disputes between States and private foreign investors. Nonetheless, we all know the zeal with which lawyers scrutinize arbitral awards hoping to discover the enunciation of some rules or principles on which they can base future arguments. We also know the great care arbitrators take to avoid articulating principles that could haunt them in future disputes in which they have been named arbitrator or counsel.

It is this debate, among others, that will be confronted herein, beginning with Professor James Crawford's discussion of the *Similarity of issues in disputes arising under the same or similarly drafted investment treaties.*

Similarity of Issues in Disputes Arising under the Same or Similarly Drafted Investment Treaties

James Crawford [*]

It is tempting in the time available to give a simple and short answer to the question. When investment treaties are drafted in exactly the same way they should be interpreted in the same way, when they are drafted in different terms they should be interpreted differently. But perhaps some further elaboration is in order.

Two points of principle confront us in the field of investment arbitration when it comes to what Emmanuel Gaillard has called the problem of precedent. The first is that the investment treaties which provide the source of jurisdiction and in most cases also the basis of claim, are, in principle, bilateral treaties concluded between different States at different times with, one supposes, the intention of those States as the primary factor to be taken into account. As is well known, there are over two thousand of these bilateral treaties.

It follows from that fact alone that the decisions reached by the tribunals sitting under these treaties, however we analyze them (whether as real international tribunals, or as derivative international tribunals, or as hybrids), are only binding on the parties and only in respect of the particular case. There is no

[*] Whewell Professor of International Law, University of Cambridge; Barrister, Matrix Chambers.

express statement to the effect of Article 59 of the Statute of the International Court of Justice.[1] But it is inherent in the situation.

Moreover, some of the devices which the International Court has available to it which conduce to at least some consistency in its jurisprudence[2] do not exist. For example, there is no equivalent of Article 63 of the Statute[3] in relation to investment arbitration; there is no possibility of intervention. There is no possibility, in most cases, that the States themselves will provide guidance as to the interpretation of the treaty. There is a notable exception to that, the provision for authoritative interpretation by the Free Trade Commission under the NAFTA,[4] a provision which has nonetheless caused the hackles to rise of certain investment arbitrators who do not like their freedom of action being interfered with even by the States Parties to the Treaty and even under an express provision of the Treaty.[5] But as is so

---

[1] Article 59 of the Statute of the International Court of Justice provides: "The decision of the Court has no binding force except between the parties and in respect of that particular case."

[2] As to which see MOHAMED SHAHABUDDEEN, PRECEDENT IN THE WORLD COURT 29 (Cambridge University Press, 1996).

[3] Article 63 of the Statute of the International Court of Justice provides: "1. Whenever the construction of a convention to which states other than those concerned in the case are parties is in question, the Registrar shall notify all such states forthwith. 2. Every state so notified has the right to intervene in the proceedings; but if it uses this right, the construction given by the judgment will be equally binding upon it."

[4] Article 2001(1) of the North American Free Trade Agreement (NAFTA) provides for the establishment of the Free Trade Commission, comprising "cabinet-level representatives of the Parties or their designees." Pursuant to Article 2001(2)(c), the work of the Commission is defined to include the resolution of disputes that may arise regarding the interpretation or application of the Agreement.

[5] See Pope & Talbot Inc. v. Canada (UNCITRAL (NAFTA) Arbitration), Award in respect of Damages, May 31, 2002, 7 ICSID REP. 148, 152–54 (2002); and contrast the more nuanced approach of the Tribunal in Mondev International

often the case with investment arbitration, the exception proves the rule.

So we have the fact that the arbitral decision itself, consistent with principle stated in Article 59 of the Statute,[6] is only binding on the parties and the fact that these bilateral investment treaties are themselves fractions of international law made between two States. You put those two principles together and you have what an English poet described as a "wilderness of single instances."[7] No doubt it is too much to say, looking at the large field of investment arbitration decisions published in the last twenty years that they are a "wilderness of single instances." But it is certainly possible to say that there are major discrepancies within the jurisprudence and the practical problem we face is what to do about this.

The first point to note on that subject is that arbitrators themselves are anxious for guidance, and you see this by their tendency to refer to the same sources of general international law with a view to deciding the case before them. For example, we see endless reference to the general principles of interpretation in the Vienna Convention on the Law of Treaties, as if they solved the problems. We see multiple references to the *Chorzów Factory* case as if that solved the problems. But the Permanent Court in *Chorzów Factory* itself distinguished between the principles of quantification of damages applicable in inter-state matters and those applicable in cases between States and private parties;[8] of

---

Ltd. v. United States of America (ICSID Case No. ARB(AF)/99/2), Award, Oct. 11, 2002, 6 ICSID REP. 192, 217–26 (2004).

[6]   *See supra* note 1.

[7]   Alfred, Lord Tennyson, *Aylmer's Field* (1864).

[8]   Case concerning the Factory at Chorzów (Germany v. Poland), Judgment No. 13 of Sept. 13, 1928, 1928 P.C.I.J., Series A, No. 17, at 27–28.

course *Chorzów* fell in the first category not the second. So it is not particularly helpful.

Then you see endless reference, and perhaps undue deference, to the ILC Articles on State Responsibility. These are referred to even in relation to issues to which the ILC Articles do not in terms apply. For example the ILC Articles Part II, dealing with remedies, have no application to investment arbitration: the Articles are only applicable to cases between States. Now it is true that it is possible to apply some of those principles by analogy as the Tribunal did (and as the Annulment Committee approved) in *MTD v. Chile* in relation to Article 39 of the ILC Articles.[9] Even with respect to provisions of the ILC Articles which are in principle applicable, there is a tendency to apply them beyond the terms of the ILC's text. For example, the rules of attribution, in Part I of the ILC Articles, which are applicable to treaty claims by private parties, are sometimes relied on to interpret the scope of jurisdictional clauses, or to determine the scope of umbrella clauses. But they have nothing to do with the scope of contractual responsibility under the applicable law of a contract. They are concerned with the attribution to the State of conduct of organs and other bodies in respect of breaches of international obligations. That is a different question.

So what should tribunals—and annulment committees—do? I would make three points.

The first concerns the specificity of texts. Let us respect the text, apply that text, and not try to develop theories of text which go beyond its own terms. We see striking examples of the tendency to do the contrary in the interpretation of umbrella

---

[9] MTD Equity Sdn Bhd. & MTD Chile S.A. v. Republic of Chile (ICSID Case No. ARB/01/7), Decision on Annulment, Mar. 21, 2007, available at http://ita.law.uvic.ca.

clauses. The three leading cases on umbrella clauses involved clauses that were differently formulated, yet the discussion that is revolved around them has tended to ignore the differences in those texts. In *Salini v. Jordan*, the relevant clause was not really an umbrella clause at all, a point which the Tribunal, if I may say so, got completely correct.[10] In *SGS v. Pakistan* there was a very peculiarly worded "perpetual guarantee."[11] In *SGS v. Philippines* again the clause was different, and, I would say, clearer.[12]

The second point to make is that when people talk about precedent they often posit a unitary doctrine which does not in truth exist. In particular the term "precedent" conjures up the so-called Anglo-American doctrine of precedent. There is no Anglo-American doctrine of precedent. Precedent is specific to the legal system within which it arises and exists to perform particular

---

[10] Salini Costruttori S.p.A. and Italstrade S.p.A. v. Hashemite Kingdom of Jordan (ICSID Case No. ARB/02/13), Decision on Jurisdiction, Nov. 29, 2004, 44 I.L.M. 569, ¶¶ 120–30 (2005). The relevant clause, Article 2(4) of the Jordan-Italy BIT of July 21, 1999 read as follows: "Each Contracting Party shall create and maintain its territory a legal framework apt to guarantee to investors the continuity of legal treatment, including the compliance, in good faith, of all undertakings assumed with regard to each specific investor." The Claimant had argued that this provision (taken together with Article 2(5) and Article 11(2) of the BIT), amounted to an umbrella clause.

[11] SGS Société Générale de Surveillance S.A. v. Islamic Republic of Pakistan (ICSID Case No. ARB/01/13), Decision on Objections to Jurisdiction, Aug. 6, 2003, 8 ICSID REP. 406, 416, 418, 424, 427, 442, 446 (2005).

[12] SGS Société Générale de Surveillance S.A. v. Republic of the Philippines (ICSID Case No. ARB/02/6), Decision on Objections to Jurisdiction, Jan. 29, 2004, 8 ICSID REP. 518, 544, 550 (2005). In SGS v. Phillipines, *id.* at 550, the umbrella clause in the Philippines-Switzerland BIT, Article X(2), stipulated: "Each Contracting Party shall observe any obligation it has assumed with regard to specific investments in its territory by investors of the other Contracting Party." The clause in the Pakistan-Switzerland BIT in SGS v. Pakistan, *supra* note 11 at 416, provided that: "Either Contracting Party shall constantly guarantee the observance of the commitments it has entered into with respect to the investments of the investors of the other Contracting Party."

functions of that system. The doctrine of precedent in the English legal system is a doctrine of the centralization of authority. It seeks to prevent lower courts going off on frolics of their own, and centralizes law-making authority in the highest court. That the Court of Appeal is bound by its own previous decisions is a proposition about the authority of the House of Lords and only incidentally a proposition about the authority of the Court of Appeal.[13] Compare this with the United States. There is a single common law in England and Wales, there is no federal common law in the United States. And the Supreme Court is itself, of course, not an adherent to the doctrine of the single precedent.

A more sensible approach which this common lawyer finds is the principle of *jurisprudence constante*—the general sense of the way decisions should be made in relation to similarly formulated provisions. But the problem is that we do not have a *jurisprudence constante* in relation to core issues of investment arbitrations at present. We do not have a *jurisprudence constante* on fair and equitable treatment, though one is perhaps starting to emerge. We do not have a *jurisprudence constante* in relation to the role of legitimate expectations.[14] We do not have a *jurisprudence constante* in the relationship between quantification of breaches of the fair and equitable treatment standard and that of the standard for expropriation: the two tend to be conflated. And we do not have a *jurisprudence constante* in relation to umbrella

---

[13] *See generally* RUPERT CROSS AND J.W. HARRIS, PRECEDENT IN ENGLISH LAW (Clarendon Press, 4th ed. 1991), especially at 3–7 (preliminary statement), 19–20 (contrast with USA), 108–19 (the Court of Appeal).

[14] *See, e.g.*, Técnicas Medioambientales TECMED S.A. v. United Mexican States (ICSID Case No. ARB(AF)/00/2), Award, May 29, 2003, 43 I.L.M. 133 (2004); International Thunderbird Gaming Corporation v. United Mexican States (UNCITRAL (NAFTA) Arbitration), Award, Jan. 26, 2006, available at http://ita.law.uvic.ca; MTD Equity Sdn Bhd. & MTD Chile S.A. v. Republic of Chile (ICSID Case No. ARB/01/7), Award, May 25, 2004, 12 ICSID REP. 3 (2007); and Decision on Annulment, Mar. 21, 2007, *supra* note 9.

clauses specifically, or more generally the relation between treaty and contract.[15]

The only way we are going to get it—this is my third elementary piece of guidance—is for arbitrators to pay decent regard to the opinions of other investment arbitrators. Let us pay decent regard to what other people say. One may have to disagree, but if so it is better to say one is disagreeing and to make it clear why, than simply to ignore contrary decisions, as has happened in a number of cases. Let us address the underlying arguments for and against particular propositions. I have mentioned some of the areas of disagreement: let us hope that the strategies of unification which international law has, which are quite different from the strategies of unification of the common law, may in time prevail.

---

[15]   In relation to umbrella clauses, *see, e.g.*, SGS v. Pakistan, *supra* note 11; SGS v. Philippines, *supra* note 12; CMS Gas Transmission Company v. Argentine Republic (ICSID Case No. ARB/01/8), Decision of the *ad hoc* committee on the application for annulment of the Argentine Republic, Sept. 25, 2007, 46 I.L.M. 1136 (2007); El Paso Energy International Company v. Argentine Republic (ICSID Case No. ARB/03/15), Decision on Jurisdiction, Apr. 27, 2006, 21 ICSID REV. 488 (2006); and Eureko BV v. Republic of Poland (*Ad hoc* Arbitration), Partial Award, Aug. 19, 2005, 12 ICSID REP. 331 (2005).   For the treaty/contract distinction, *see, e.g.*, Zachary Douglas, *The Hybrid Foundations of Investment Treaty Arbitration*, 74 BRITISH Y.B. INT'L L. 151 (2003); CAMPBELL MCLACHLAN, LAURENCE SHORE, MATTHEW WEINIGER, INTERNATIONAL INVESTMENT ARBITRATION: SUBSTANTIVE PRINCIPLES (Oxford University Press, 2007); Compañía de Aguas del Aconquija S.A. and Compagnie Générale des Eaux (Vivendi Universal) v. Argentine Republic (ICSID Case No. ARB/97/3), Award, Nov. 21, 2000, 5 ICSID REP. 299 (2002), and Decision on Annulment, July 3, 2002, 6 ICSID REP. 340 (2004).

Can Arbitral Awards Constitute a Source of International Law under Article 38 of the Statute of the International Court of Justice?

Gilbert Guillaume [*]

I was asked to answer the question whether arbitral awards may be considered as a source of international law in accordance with Article 38 of the Statute of the International Court of Justice.

Firstly, we must remind ourselves of the text of the Statute, which provides that the International Court of Justice,

> "whose function is to decide in accordance with international law such disputes as are submitted to it, shall apply:
>
> (a) international conventions, whether general or particular, establishing rules expressly recognized by the contesting states;
>
> (b) international custom, as evidence of a general practice accepted as law;
>
> (c) the general principles of law recognized by civilized nations;
>
> (d) subject to the provisions of Article 59, judicial decisions and the teachings of the most highly qualified publicists of the various nations, as subsidiary means for the determination of rules of law."

---

[*] Member of the Permanent Court of Arbitration, Former President of the International Court of Justice.

Two preliminary comments should be made in light of this text:

1) The list provided by Article 38 is not exhaustive. In fact, several sources of international law that are important today are not mentioned, such as unilateral acts of States and the acts of the international organizations, both of which are taken into consideration by the Court in its judgments and advisory opinions.[1]

2) The general principles of law mentioned in Article 38 sub-paragraph (c) should not be confused with the general principles of Public International Law.

While general principles of Public International Law are enshrined in international custom, and for advocates of *jus cogens*, may even be considered as "peremptory norms of international law," general principles of law are common to national legal systems and transposable to Public International Law. It is difficult to draw up a list of general principles of law as it manifests in case law. However, the principle of good faith, the *nemo auditur* legal doctrine, as well as fundamental rules of tort law seem to belong to the latter category.[2]

Arbitral awards as such are not covered by the sub-paragraphs (a) to (c) of Article 38. Therefore we should focus our attention on sub-paragraph (d), which deals with judicial decisions. This provision applies, in the first place, subject to Article 59 of the Statute of the International Court of Justice, which provides

---

[1] *See, e.g.,* PATRICK DAILLIER AND ALAIN PELLET, DROIT INTERNATIONAL PUBLIC 113 (LGDJ, 7th ed. 2002); THE STATUTE OF THE INTERNATIONAL COURT OF JUSTICE: A COMMENTARY ¶¶ 74 *et seq.* (A. Zimmermann, C. Tomuschat and K. Oellers-Frahm eds., Oxford University Press, 2006).

[2] *See, e.g.,* DAILLIER AND PELLET, *supra* note 1, at 225–27; THE STATUTE OF THE INTERNATIONAL COURT OF JUSTICE, *supra* note 1, ¶¶ 249 *et seq.*

that "[t]he decision of the Court has no binding force except between the parties and in respect of that particular case." Thus, the Court's judgments are only binding *rationae personae* and *rationae materiae* within this double limitation (relating to the parties to the dispute and the specific circumstances of the case in which it was rendered). Stated differently, Public International Law does not attach binding value to precedents. It ignores the doctrine of "*stare decisis*." A judicial decision, even issued by the International Court of Justice, is not, as such, a source of international law.[3]

Still, as provided by Article 38(d), judicial decisions are a "subsidiary means for the determination of rules of law." Recognizing this role means in reality that, while settling disputes, a judge applies and interprets a rule of law. He is not compelled to follow the same solution that justified the decision he had previously made, but he will be inclined to do so in order to ensure legal certainty through "consistency with its own past case law."[4]

From this perspective, the Court has expressly pointed out that if "[t]here can be no question of holding [a State party to the dispute] to decisions reached by the Court in previous cases", "[t]he real question is whether, in this case, there is cause not to follow the reasoning and conclusions of earlier cases."[5] In fact, as is often mentioned in the opinions of authors, the Court frequently

---

[3] DAILLIER AND PELLET, *supra* note 1, at 259 and 547; THE STATUTE OF THE INTERNATIONAL COURT OF JUSTICE, *supra* note 1, ¶¶ 26–27, 45–48.

[4] *See* the Joint Declaration of Vice-President Ranjeva, Judges Guillaume, Higgins, Kooijmans, Al-Khasawneh, Buergenthal and Elaraby in the various cases concerning Legality of Use of Force, Preliminary Objections, Judgment of Dec. 15, 2004, 2004 I.C.J. REPORTS 330, 476, 621, 766, 912, 1061, 1208, 1353.

[5] Case concerning the Land and Maritime Boundary between Cameroon and Nigeria (Cameroon v. Nigeria), Judgment of June 11, 1998, 1998 I.C.J. REPORTS 275, 292.

cites to its earlier judgments, as well as to those of the Permanent Court of International Justice.[6]

In light of these essential reminders, how should one position arbitral awards in relation to Article 38(d) of the Statute? Firstly, we observe that arbitral awards are not mentioned in the text as a means to determine rules of law. Article 38(d) only refers to judicial decisions. Could this term be interpreted broadly to cover arbitral awards as well? Academic authors have taken conflicting positions to this question. Max Sorensen is hesitant[7]. While Sir Humphrey Waldock considers that Article 38 should be interpreted broadly[8], Julio Barberis[9] and Alain Pellet[10] hold the opposite opinion.

In practice, the question does not seem to be of great importance since, arbitral awards form, in any event and independent from Article 38(d), a subsidiary means for the determination of rules of law, as recognized by the International Court of Justice.

For a long time, the Court has shown certain reluctance in this regard. For example, in the *Case concerning the Barcelona Traction* in 1970, the Court held:

---

[6] *See, e.g.*, MOHAMMED SHAHABUDDEEN, PRECEDENT IN THE WORLD COURT (Cambridge University Press, 1996).

[7] MAX SØRENSEN, LES SOURCES DU DROIT INTERNATIONAL: ÉTUDE SUR LA JURISPRUDENCE DE LE COUR PERMANENTE DE JUSTICE INTERNATIONALE 162 (Einar Munksgaard, 1946).

[8] Humphrey Waldock, *General Course on Public International Law*, in COLLECTED COURSES OF THE HAGUE ACADEMY OF INTERNATIONAL LAW, Vol. 106-II, Year 1962, at 88 and 92.

[9] Julio A. Barberis, *La jurisprudencia internacional como fuente de derecho de gentes según la Corte de La Haya*, 1971 ZEITSCHRIFT FÜR AUSLÄNDISCHES ÖFFENTLICHES RECHT AND VÖLKERRECHT 641, 643.

[10] DAILLIER AND PELLET, *supra* note 1, ¶¶ 259–60.

The Parties have . . . relied on the general arbitral jurisprudence which has accumulated in the last half-century. However, in most cases the decisions cited rested upon the terms of instruments establishing the jurisdiction of the tribunal or claims commission and determining what rights might enjoy protection; they cannot therefore give rise to generalization going beyond the special circumstances of each case.[11]

The ICJ, as well as the Permanent Court of International Justice, nevertheless made general reference to their previous decisions on several occasions,[12] as well as to decisions of arbitral tribunals,[13] to international arbitrators[14] or to international jurisprudence.[15]

However, for a long time, the Court did not make reference to any specific arbitral awards. Later, two awards found its favor. The first was the award in the *Alabama* case, which generally recognizes, according to the Court, the principle that every tribunal has "the right to decide as to its own jurisdiction."[16] The second

---

[11]   Case concerning the Barcelona Traction, Light and Power Company, Limited (Belgium v. Spain), Judgment of Feb. 5, 1970, 1970 I.C.J. REPORTS 3, especially ¶ 63, at 40.

[12]   The Case of the S.S. "Lotus" (France v. Turkey), Judgment No. 9 of Sept. 7, 1927, 1927 P.C.I.J., Series A, No. 10, at 26.

[13]   Case concerning the Factory at Chorzów (Germany v. Poland), Judgment No. 13 of Sept. 13, 1928, 1928 P.C.I.J., Series A, No. 17, at 47.

[14]   Nottebohm Case (Liechtenstein v. Guatemala), Judgment of Apr. 6, 1955, 1955 I.C.J. REPORTS 4, 21 and 22.

[15]   The Corfu Channel Case (United Kingdom of Great Britain and Northern Ireland v. Albania), Judgment of Apr. 9, 1949, 1949 I.C.J. REPORTS 4, 18; Constitution of the Maritime Safety Committee of the Inter-Governmental Maritime Consultative Organization, Advisory Opinion of June 8, 1960, 1960 I.C.J. REPORTS 150, 169.

[16]   Nottebohm Case (Liechtenstein v. Guatemala), Judgment of Nov. 18, 1953, 1953 I.C.J. REPORTS 111, 119; Case concerning the Arbitral Award of 31

award concerned the determination of the maritime boundary between France and United Kingdom in the Iroise Sea in 1977 that combined all the different delimitation methods of continental shelf boundaries found in the Geneva Conventions of 1958 and in the Convention adopted in Montego Bay in 1982 in one concise definition.[17]

In recent years, with the delimitation of boundaries, for example, in the Gulf of Fonseca,[18] the Kasikili/Sedudu Island,[19] between Qatar and Bahrain,[20] between Malaysia and Indonesia,[21]

July 1989 (Guinea-Bissau v. Senegal), Judgment of Nov. 12, 1991, 1991 I.C.J. REPORTS 53, 68–69.

[17] Case concerning the Continental shelf (Tunisia/Libyan Arab Jamahiriya), Judgment of Feb. 24, 1982, 1982 I.C.J. REPORTS 18, 57 and 79; Case concerning Delimitation of the Maritime Boundary in the Gulf of Maine Area (Canada/United States of America), Judgment of Oct. 12, 1984, 1984 I.C.J. REPORTS 246, 284, 302 and 324; Case concerning Maritime Delimitation in the Area between Greenland and Jan Mayen (Denmark v. Norway), Judgment of June 14, 1993, 1993 I.C.J. REPORTS 38, 58, 62, 68, etc.

[18] Case concerning the Land, Island and Maritime Frontier Dispute (El Salvador v. Honduras: Nicaragua intervening), Judgment of Sept. 11, 1992, 1992 I.C.J. REPORTS 351: the Judgment refers, in paragraph 28 (at 380), to the 1933 award issued by Chief Justice Charles Evans Hughes in the case concerning the Honduras borders between Guatemala and Honduras, and, in paragraph 391 (at 351), to the 1910 arbitral award of the Permanent Court of Arbitration in the *North Atlantic Coast Fisheries* case.

[19] Case concerning Kasikili/Sedudu Island (Botswana/Namibia), Judgment of Dec. 13, 1999, 1999 I.C.J. REPORTS 1045: the Judgment refers, in paragraph 20 (at 1060), to the 1994 arbitral award in the *Laguna del desierto* case, in paragraph 30 (at 1064), to the 1966 arbitral award in the *Rio Palena* arbitration and, in paragraph 33 (at 1064), to the 1933 arbitral award in the case concerning the Honduras borders between Guatemala and Honduras.

[20] Case concerning Maritime Delimitation and Territorial Questions between Qatar and Bahrain (Qatar v. Bahrain), Judgment of Mar. 16, 2001, 2001 I.C.J. REPORTS 40: the Judgment refers, in paragraph 100 (at 70), to Max Huber's award in the *Island of Palmas* case and, in paragraph 117 (at 77), to the award in the *Dubai/Sharjah Border* arbitration.

and finally between Cameroun and Nigeria,[22] the number of these references have multiplied in the jurisprudence of the Court.

Thus, for the Court, there is no doubt. There are some arbitral awards which merits mention as establishing rules of law.

Two observations should be made which may limit the significance of this statement.

In the first place, arbitral awards that have been mentioned by the Court have always been rendered in intergovernmental disputes. The Court has never made reference to arbitral awards issued in other domains, such as commercial arbitration or investment arbitration.

Moreover, the Court seems to rely on a few selected arbitral awards. Thus, while some awards are cited repeatedly, others are simply mentioned and some are completely ignored.

Arbitral precedents, just like judicial precedents, do not carry equal weight. Moreover, they form jurisprudence determining rules of law in accordance with Article 38(d) of the Statute only if specific conditions are met. In this regard, I can do no better than to recall what Louis Renault, then legal consultant to French Ministry of Foreign Affairs and future Nobel Peace Prize winner, stated in 1904:

---

[21] Case concerning Sovereignty over Pulau Ligitan and Pulau Sipadan (Indonesia/Malaysia), Judgment of Dec. 17, 2002, 2002 I.C.J. REPORTS 625: the Judgment mentions at paragraph 135 (at 682) the arbitral award rendered in the *Palena* case.

[22] Case concerning the Land and Maritime Boundary between Cameroon and Nigeria (Cameroon v. Nigeria: Equatorial Guinea intervening), Judgment of Oct. 10, 2002, 2002 I.C.J. REPORTS 303, 415: paragraph 222 cites to the *Rann of Kutch* arbitral award and *Beagle Channel* arbitration.

> In law, it is true that the authority of *res judicata* is limited; but in reality, who could deny the impact of the precedents? I do not mean that outside the scope of the dispute giving rise to a decision, arbitral awards do not carry any weight. They certainly do. However, a different tribunal, dealing with completely different claims involving new points, composed of judges of different nationalities, could reasonably take that into consideration. When a controversial question has been decided in a same way by a number of arbitral tribunals, one realizes what authority will be attached to a solution given several times in total independence by highly qualified judges of various nations . . . . The solution will enter then into the body of international law . . . .[23]

It is under these conditions, as emphasized by Louis Renault, that arbitral awards, even if it cannot be considered as a source of law, are nevertheless, in accordance with Article 38(d), a "subsidiary means for the determination of rules of law," as stated by the International Court of Justice with regard to inter-state judgments. The situation might be the same for arbitral jurisprudence, both in commercial and investment domains, if or when it attains a sufficient degree of publicity and consistency.

---

[23] A. DE LAPRADELLE AND N. POLITIS, RECUEIL DES ARBITRAGES INTERNATIONAUX, TOME PREMIER 1798-1855 (A. Pedone, 1905), Foreword by Louis Renault at VII ("En droit, il est vrai que la chose jugée n'a qu'une autorité toute relative; mais en fait, qui pourrait nier l'influence des précédents? Je ne veux pas dire qu'en dehors du litige qu'elles auront terminé, les sentences arbitrales n'auront aucune valeur. Elles en auront une certainement, mais un tribunal nouveau, composé d'éléments tout différents, de juges d'autres nationalités, pourra, en toute liberté, en tenir tel compte que de raison. Lorsqu'une question controversée aura été tranchée de la même façon par plusieurs tribunaux d'arbitrage, on comprend quelle autorité aura une solution donnée à diverses reprises dans des conditions de complète indépendance par des juges d'une grande valeur appartenant à divers pays. . . . Elle entrera dans le corps du droit international . . . .").

Confidential Awards as Precedent in Arbitration

Dynamics and Implication of Award Publication

Thomas Wälde [*]

I.   INTRODUCTION, QUESTION & CONTEXT

I have been asked to provide a comment on the question of the extent to which confidential awards can serve as (persuasive) precedent in arbitration. I will not deal with the issue of precedent in arbitration *per se*. In essence, I consider that, at least in investment arbitration, individual awards merit attention and discussion while a reasonably "settled jurisprudence" (also referred to as "*jurisprudence constante*" or "*staendige Rechtsprechung*") creates considerable authority for subsequent tribunals. Awards should, for reasons of legitimate expectation and legal certainty and consistency, not deviate from established jurisprudence, except if there are significant new arguments and only with careful and detailed reasoning. The question posed to me, however, is if such respect and attention (or the capacity to create or rather contribute to "*jurisprudence constante*") also apply to arbitral awards that are confidential, *i.e.*, which, while available to one party in the arbitration and perhaps informally circulating in collegial networks, have not been published in one of the hard-paper or electronic publications available.[1]

---

[*]   Professor of Law, University of Dundee.

[1]   Investment awards are by now primarily published electronically, particularly on the following websites: icsid.worldbank.org; ita.law.uvic.ca;

113

I need to explain what is meant by "precedent" in international arbitration.[2] On the lowest or "softest" level, it is the suggestion to the tribunal that other experts have dealt with similar issues and that their experience and wisdom might serve as a good illustration of how to solve the issue facing the tribunal. On the

---

www.investmentclaims.com; www.transnational-dispute-management.com (for which I serve as editor). Some awards are also published on governmental websites (in particular of the three NAFTA countries). While previously the main source of published awards was academic journals, such as International Legal Materials, the ICSID Reports, the ICSID Journal (Foreign Investment Law Review) and major international arbitration journals, the trend is shifting towards full publication on websites rather than in these hard-copy academic and professional journals.

²   See, in particular, Gabrielle Kaufmann-Kohler, *Arbitral Precedent: Dream, Necessity or Excuse? – The 2006 Freshfields Lecture*, 23(3) ARB. INT'L 357 (2007); Jan Paulsson, *International Arbitration and the Generation of Legal Norms: Treaty Arbitration and International law*, in ICCA CONGRESS SERIES NO. 13, INTERNATIONAL ARBITRATION 2006: BACK TO BASICS? 879 (A.J. van den Berg ed., Kluwer, 2007), also available at 3(5) TDM (Dec. 2006); Pierre Duprey, *Do Arbitral Awards Constitute Precedents? Should Commercial Arbitration Be Distinguished in this Regard from Arbitration Based on Investment Treaties*, in IAI INTERNATIONAL ARBITRATION SERIES NO. 3, TOWARDS A UNIFORM INTERNATIONAL ARBITRATION LAW? 251 (A.V. Schlaepfer, P. Pinsolle, L. Degos eds., Juris Publishing, 2005); *see also* Saipem S.p.A. v. The People's Republic of Bangladesh (ICSID Case No. ARB/05/07), Decision on Jurisdiction and Recommendation on Provisional Measures, Mar. 21, 2007, 22(4) INT'L ARB. REP. B-4 (2007), also available at http://ita.uvic.edu, ¶ 67: "The Tribunal considers that it is not bound by previous decisions. At the same time, it is of the opinion that it must pay due consideration to earlier decisions of international tribunals. It believes that, subject to compelling contrary grounds, it has a duty to adopt solutions established in a series of consistent cases. It also believes that, subject to the specifics of a given treaty and of the circumstances of the actual case, it has a duty to seek to contribute to the harmonious development of investment law and thereby to meet the legitimate expectations of the community of States and investors towards certainty of the rule of law."; and International Thunderbird Gaming Corporation v. United Mexican States (UNCITRAL (NAFTA) Arbitration), Separate Opinion of Thomas Wälde, Jan. 26, 2006, ¶ 15 (available at http://ita.law.uvic.ca).

next level, as "persuasive precedent," is the idea that, by analogy to domestic courts (in common and civil law systems) and to international courts (ECJ, ICJ, WTO), special respect is owed to expert "colleagues" acting in a quasi-judicial capacity. That gives previous decisions more weight than would simply be owed to an "expert legal opinion." At most, it would probably require, in case of reliance, citation and, in case of disagreement, an explicit reasoning (sanctionable possibly under ICSID annulment rules for inadequate reasoning). On the third and highest level, cumulative arbitral jurisprudence in the field of investment arbitration could be said to crystallise into "settled jurisprudence" ("*staendige rechtsprechung*" or "*jurisprudence constante*"). It would create a high level of continuity, consistency and frequency which would mean that such jurisprudence constitutes the applicable "law" and deviation is only possible in rare circumstances, *e.g.*, "distinction", possibly sanctionable as "manifest excess of powers"—perhaps under ICSID annulment practice—, or "manifest error of law" if this is available under national arbitral award challenge rules.

The starting point of the discussion has to be that throughout legal history, in particular in common law systems where the rule of precedent is more formalised than in civil law countries,[3] precedent is closely linked to publication. The

---

[3]   The difference in legal practice between common and civil law systems is much less than is often made out. In common law countries, the rule of precedent is softened by the practice of distinguishing cases from each other. Depending on the criteria for comparison used, distinguishability is influenced not only by objective standards but also by more subjective judgment. In civil law countries (where distinguishability is employed too, albeit perhaps in a less formal way), the decisions of higher courts tend to be followed by lower courts as they otherwise are subject to successful appeal. There are often more formal rules of precedent and judicial consistency among the highest courts (*e.g.*, with "grand chambers" having to determine different opinions held by individual chambers). "*Jurisprudence constante,*" or "*Staendige Rechtsprechung,*" by the leading courts is seen as an authoritative interpretation of the law with which lower courts are expected to conform. The way to breach "settled

reporting of English court decisions started in the 14th century provides the foundation for a formal theory of precedent. This is first a practical issue: without reporting it is difficult to know of relevant cases and use them for persuasion of the court. It is, second and on a more general level, also a matter of theory and principle: cases that are not public, will not only be known to a much smaller group of litigation professionals, but they also lack an essential quality, that of exposure to the forces of transparency, *i.e.*, critical discussion by the relevant professional communities (primarily judges, advocates and then academics and the journalistic media). In such debate, not just the quality of the reasoning, but also the quality of the practical and policy judgment issues involved, as well as the wider ramifications of the decision, comparison with similar situations and issues of consistency versus contradiction are likely to emerge over time in a more reliable and extensive way than simply in the judgment and its reasoning. Cases that may appear persuasive at first may, in the wider context, be revealed by professional and academic debate as outliers rather than as indicators of a trend covered by the consensus of those who count.

The link between publication and precedent is thus a strong one but not necessarily an absolute requirement—in all circumstances the link is a peremptory one. Judgments (as legal rules) are not always public. In legal systems without sufficient resources and a strong adherence to the concept of a "rule of law,"[4] legal rules and judgments are often not public. They are part of the

---

jurisprudence" is as a rule by arguing that a new case can be distinguished, in significant aspects, from established jurisprudence. On the much greater similarity, in substance, between civil and common law systems, see Carl Baudenbacher, *Some Remarks on the Method of Civil Law*, 34 TEXAS INT'L L.J. 333 (1999).

[4] BRIAN Z. TAMANAHA, ON THE RULE OF LAW: HISTORY, POLITICS, THEORY (Cambridge University Press, 2004); F.A. HAYEK, THE POLITICAL IDEAL OF THE RULE OF LAW (Cairo, 1955).

prerogatives and privileges of "those in the know." They will be raised when convenient and kept confidential when inconvenient. Progress towards at least formal conceptions of the "rule of law" (understood largely as information on the law which is sufficient enough to allow people to predict the impact of rules) requires— throughout legal history and at present in countries in transition and developing countries—that, first, the formal, written legal rules become easily available at least to professionals and later to the public at large and, second, that the way the legal rules are applied by courts and administrative bodies becomes equally easily available. Many modern economic treaties thus include an obligation of "transparency," largely meaning the obligation to publish legal rules.[5] The more such rules (and their application by courts and tribunals) become public, the more open ("democratic"), balanced and predictable the adjudicatory process, the more effective the "rule of law" and the less there are special privileges for those "in the know" and those with the power to use or withhold relevant information. Legal history, now including both commercial and investment arbitration, is thus characterised by an increased publishing of legal rules, judgments and other matters relating to the adjudicatory process. Without such openness, the process will have imbalances that will reduce its perceived fairness and thus, its acceptability and effectiveness.

If, in a specific arbitration, a party submits an award which is otherwise not public, one could view this less as an argument about a precedent to be followed because of its widespread acceptance for reasons of legal certainty, but rather as an example of how three "experts" have solved a similar question. Citing such a confidential award has some similarities with an expert opinion submitted by a party or produced at the request of the tribunal. But there are important differences: an expert opinion will as a rule

---

[5]   UNTACD, TRANSPARENCY, UNCTAD Series on Issues in International Investment Agreements (2004), available at www.unctad.org.

only be considered by the tribunal if the other party has had a chance to cross-examine the expert witness. Opinions by experts without cross-examination, or at least the availability of the expert for cross-examination, will generally have little or no value.

Perhaps one can then compare the submission of a confidential award to the submission of an academic article as awards are frequently submitted as annexes to a party's briefs. However, there are still differences. If an academic or professional article is submitted, the submitting party wishes to rely on the authority or persuasiveness of the reasoning of the author, usually to highlight a point made by the author that favours its case. That is comparable to the submission of a confidential award. But there is a significant difference in that the article in question will be public, *i.e.*, it has usually gone through some form of moderate to intensive quality control by the publishers. It is also an intellectual product which the author has felt confident enough to publish and thus to expose to professional and academic criticism where his or her reputation is at stake. Finally, by its publication it has been exposed to the critical view of the relevant professional and academic communities which have had the opportunity to form a view (held informally or expressed in other writings) about the persuasiveness of the published author's conclusion. While not tested by cross-examination, publication of an article involves other tests of the solidity and plausibility of its conclusions.

All these characteristics are missing in the case of a confidential award. Furthermore, the confidential award may be just part of a series of other (related or unrelated) awards which may reinforce or contradict the submitted award's conclusion. Neither the tribunal nor the other party may be aware of the fact that the award submitted is just one part of a larger puzzle selected by the submitting party with its tactical preferences in mind. Its relative persuasiveness in such situations rests on the superior "intelligence" of the submitting party in locating a favourable award through its informal networks. If obtained confidentially and submitted selectively, the submission may, in effect, deceive both the tribunal and the opposing party over the "state of play" behind the veils of arbitral confidentiality.

We need also to be aware of the various levels of confidentiality and their implication. There does not seem to be a rule in international law that "confidential materials" are, *per se*, excluded from consideration by international courts and tribunals, *e.g.*, confidential materials relevant to the interpretation of a treaty.[6] There are materials that are confidential simply because their owners or authors keep them secret and which, in one way or another, comes into the possession of the submitting party. There is, however, a second level of confidentiality where the submitting party or its agents (or a third party on which they rely) have obtained the confidential materials illegally, *e.g.*, through breach of a confidentiality contract or, even worse, by theft or illegal

---

[6]   H. Lauterpacht, *Some Observations on Preparatory Work in the Interpretation of Treaties*, 48 HARV. L. REV. 549 (1934-1935); note that this is in the context of discussing confidential "*travaux*" material relevant for the operation of Art. 32 of the Vienna Convention on Treaties. But, according to W. Michael Reisman and Eric E. Freedman in *The Plaintiff's Dilemma: Illegally obtained evidence and admissibility in International Adjudication*, 76 AM. J. INT'L L. 737, 743 (1982), the ICJ repeatedly declined admission of materials on the history of certain articles of the Versailles Treaty because they were confidential and not been provided to the Court with the consent of the parties. Reisman also refers to two other cases where evidence relating to confidential negotiations for a treaty was refused admissibility. There is a difference, though, between using confidential materials regarding the negotiations of a treaty and using a confidential award. The former is only a supplemental method of identifying the common intention of the drafters while the confidential award comes with at least some claim of at least persuasive precedent as having been generated in a judicial setting by one or three formally appointed arbitrators after an extensive adversary procedure testing the positions of both parties.

intrusion into private property.[7] Comparative procedural and arbitral law seems to be open to both an absolute prohibitive approach as well as a less prohibitive approach. Even the Methanex tribunal's rejection of evidence obtained illegally through snooping in garbage bins was hedged by a statement that this evidence was not very significant[8] leaving open the possibility that in case of truly significant evidence an illegal acquisition might not lead automatically to the qualification of such evidence as inadmissible.

Finally, there is the possibility of grading the illegality (from modest breaches of minor rules to very serious offences under criminal law, for example obtaining evidence through torture). In the case of arbitral awards, illegality is likely to be based mostly on breaches of confidentiality agreements or procedural rules imposing confidentiality on the direct participants in the arbitration process, though one could also visualise more serious offences such as obtaining at least a reference to a confidential award through methods of espionage such as eavesdropping and other forms of surveillance.[9]

For all these questions, the criterion of "publication" is key. I will therefore in the following part examine the question of what

---

[7] *See* Methanex Corporation v. United States of America (NAFTA (UNCITRAL) Arbitration), Aug. 3, 2005 Final Award, ¶¶ 53–54, considering evidence that was obtained illegally inadmissible (available at http://ita.law.uvic.ca). This is the "fruit of the poisonous tree" doctrine which originated mainly from criminal law, *i.e.*, where greater protection of the accused is warranted than may be the case for a party in an investment or commercial dispute. *See also* Reisman and Freedman, *supra* note 6.

[8] *See* Methanex Corportation v. United States of America, *supra* note 7, ¶ 56.

[9] *See*, for example, Gulf Petro Trading Co. v. Nigerian National Petroleum Corp., 512 F.3d 742 (5th Cir. 2008); cf. note by J. Price, for TDM (2008, forthcoming), available at www.transnational-dispute-management.com).

is "publication" for arbitral awards, as well as the "dynamics" of publication, *i.e.*, why and how arbitral awards rendered in non-public proceedings tend to become public, in particular in investment disputes.

II. PUBLICATION OF ARBITRAL AWARDS

For the precedent effect, as non-formal and rather persuasive they are, to operate, it would seem that awards must be "public," *i.e.*, not obtained secretly and provided to the tribunal, but available in the public domain.

Just to recapitulate: awards in the public domain come closest in character to national or international judgments by courts. They require, as a measure of rule of law, transparency, *i.e.*, general publication. After publication they are not only easily known or knowable to all parties, including *amici*, in advance—allowing them to prepare their case and regulate their behaviour accordingly, rather than being surprised in the proceedings—but they are also exposed to professional, academic and politically critical debate which allows for their reasoning to be tested. A "secret award" unearthed surreptitiously does not stand up to these tests.

A. *So What is "Publication"?*

In legal history, publication seems, as a rule, to have been started by private actors, *e.g.*, notes written up by lawyers for subsequent use and reference in their own cases and then later shared with others.[10] That is not so different from the practice in

---

[10] T. Ellis Lewis, *The History of Judicial Precedent*, 48 L.Q. REV. 230 (1932).

most major international arbitration firms where awards, even confidential awards are apparently kept, used and discussed, not only by the litigators in a particular case but also by their colleagues in the international arbitration department. Some lawyers subsequently devoted considerable time and effort to collecting information on judgments from others, as possession and access would have given them an advantage in competition for clients. Later, they started to publish this information, probably mainly for the professional reputation developed in this way, but also, probably in a more limited way, for the income generated thereby. That again is not very different from the situation today where private websites are probably mainly intended to develop the professional and academic good-will of the lawyers investing considerable time and effort to its maintenance, with "transparency" an additional, more ideological than practical, objective. But, as so often, it is the "invisible hand" of self-interest which drives the inexorable march of legal history towards greater transparency and accompanying critical discussion.

Official publication is usually the last step. It is intended to assure that a technically correct version of the judgment is available—*i.e.*, unadulterated by private authors' edits and publishers that may (at some point in time) perhaps have been carried out for the purpose of saving space or for ulterior tactical motives. That seems again to be paralleled in investment arbitration with official publication of awards, for example on the websites of the major NAFTA and occasionally other governments. However, given that these awards are politically sensitive in domestic politics, the result of an adversarial process where the publishing government is a party to the dispute and which may be significant for future cases where the government will act as a respondent, one should not automatically assume full objectivity of such official—*i.e.*, governmental—reporting. Greater objectivity, for example, is likely to be achieved by reporting such as on the World Bank's ICSID website or academic reporting, *i.e.*, the still paper based International Law Reports (I.L.R.), ICSID Reports, International Legal Materials or other fully or partially academic websites.[11] National courts in developed countries or international courts (including the ICJ, ECJ, WTO dispute panels and Appeal Board) as a rule now publish judgments on their websites. There is a trend to publish at least excerpts of or commentary on international arbitral awards by the ICC, the LCIA or the SCC.[12]

Today we increasingly have the ICSID practice of publication unless the parties object. This could be called "official" publication. We now also have seemingly selective publication of SCC awards, sometimes by other arbitral institutions. The ICC through Clunet and the ICA Yearbooks provides selective and sanitised publication. Investment awards are at present most comprehensively published on http://www.investmentclaims.com,[13] free service on http://ita.law.uvic.ca and subscription-based on http://www.transnational-dispute-management.com. They have also been published for quite a while in the International Law Reports, the ICSID Reports, International Arbitration and sometimes fully or with excerpts in other arbitration and international law journals, as well as international economic law journals.

These publication services, in particular the website based services unencumbered by considerations of space, focus primarily

---

[11] *See, e.g.*, http://ita.law.uvic.ca; http://www.investmentclaims.com; and http://www.transnational-dispute-management.com.

[12] *See* Kaufmann-Kohler, *supra* note 2. *See also* J.P. Commission, *Precedent in Investment Treaty Arbitration: The Empirical Backing*, 4(5) TDM (Sept. 2007), available at www.transnational-dispute-management.com; and Emannuel Jolivet, *Access to Information and Awards*, 22(2) ARB. INT'L 265 (2006).

[13] Now published with a premium service by Oxford University Press.

on jurisdictional decisions (sometimes called awards) and the final decisions on the merits (awards). NAFTA governments and the website services publishing about NAFTA cases usually also publish government memorials, procedural orders issued by the tribunals, and *amicus* briefs. There is, however, no guarantee that all documentation in a case is published and there is likely to be some documentation considered confidential by one of the parties, in particular the government party, that will as a rule not become public.

Expert opinions—both the increasingly used legal expert opinions, primarily on international (investment) law, and quantum expert opinions containing frequently controversial valuations—are generally not public. The reasons for this limitation are not clear. Presumably, they contain information and assessments that are considered by at least one of the parties as either confidential or too sensitive, even after the definitive end of an arbitration proceeding. Expert opinions can play a decisive role in an arbitration. Their absence from publication (even though they are referred to in the parties' memorials and at times the tribunals' decisions) does therefore affect the proper appreciation of an award. For example, if an authoritative expert proposes one legal theory in one case for his appointing party, but an inconsistent one in another case, that should reduce his or her credibility and thus authority for persuading a tribunal. Such inconsistencies, however, cannot easily be identified if the expert opinions are not public. The web-based services will tend to publish anything they get hold of and which they consider sufficiently of material interest to their readers, *i.e.*, the professional and academic community.

If awards are published in widely available and reputed sources, even ones with a reasonable subscription fee, they should be considered as "published", similar to national and international court reports, and thus exposed to international debate and to the knowledge of the professional community. They should not be considered as published if it would take an inordinate effort and expense to access them, *e.g.*, in special studies or services available to a few corporate subscribers at a fee that makes regular access impractical. Similarly, one needs to distinguish awards which are formally published from awards which are "widely known" within a select group of major arbitration law firms, usually because one firm was involved in a case and informal trading on a reciprocal or collegial basis takes place. Such "known" but not "published" awards are essentially a barrier to entry into the relevant discourse to professionals and academics outside a narrow magic circle of "those in the know." They add to the informational strategic asset power of the major arbitration firms but are not "owned" by the wider professional and academic communities. "Publication" of awards is thus also part of a trend which Professor José Alvarez described as "democratization" of the field of international investment law.[14]

B.   *Dynamics of Publication: Why are Awards Published?*

We need to understand why awards get into the public domain, in particular if the arbitration procedure is confidential, as is still the rule in traditional commercial arbitration. As always, the self-interest of the various players in publicising (or keeping secret) is combined with more lofty, or philosophical and policy-oriented attitudes. Interests and attitudes in commercial arbitration are widely carried over into investment arbitration. At times respondent States do not want their dirty linen displayed in public, questions of corruption, of abuse of government power, of woefully ineffectual administration and coordination or of helplessness in the face of fraud often turn up in investment disputes. They add little that is favourable to the image of a

---

[14]   José E. Alvarez, *The Democratization of the Invisible College*, ASIL Newsletter (Nov. 2007), available at www.asil.org.

government at home or abroad. Similarly, investors' conduct under the glare of the adversarial process may prove less attractive or less competent than they would like to project to the world at large. So there is, or at least can be, as in commercial arbitration, an interest in confidentiality. It is often suggested that there is "proprietary" or commercially valuable secret information at issue, though I have not really seen such a case in reality.

On the other hand, there can also be a counter-interest by the parties—the principals in investment disputes—in bringing the dispute out into the open. The threat of seeing embarrassing details of governmental and corporate conduct disclosed can add leverage against a recalcitrant party. If NGOs are involved, directly through *amicus* briefs or indirectly in support of and in association with governments as is the normal case, they will have an interest in a public "show trial" to highlight their agenda and role. There may be actual or alleged regulatory reasons both for governments and companies (*e.g.*, disclosure under securities market regulations or "freedom of information" rules) to disclose details of arbitration, though such reasons can also be a pretext for using disclosure for tactical reasons.

The strongest self-interest in "transparency"—defined as the far-reaching practice of placing the details of investment disputes into the public domain—is less that of the <u>principals,</u> but rather that of the agents. While supposedly tightly controlled and funded by the parties and oriented exclusively to the interest of their clients, in reality <u>agents</u> have and pursue their own interests. It is in the self-interest of law firms to widely publicise their involvement in investment cases. Such involvement is easier to publicise than in commercial arbitration, which is often more technical, has less public interest value and, from a regulatory and client interest perspective, is truly more confidential. Emerging law firms wish to develop their arbitration profile through investment arbitration and established firms wish in particular to emphasise their "winning record." Nothing is more appealing to prospective clients than a law firm that has a convincing and extensive record of winning controversial cases. It is not surprising therefore that the newsletters, client briefings and websites of many leading and ambitious law firms publicise, in identified, identifiable or indirect terms, their role in the successful representation either for the claimant or the respondent in investment disputes. If awards "leak" to the public websites, then the publicity engendered would seem to be most favourable to the law firm's team that have counseled a successful party. But even the law firm acting for the losing side will often not be opposed to publicity as it, at least, confirms that they have a significant activity in the field.

Arbitrators, in particular from a commercial arbitration tradition, are least likely to leak a confidential award. But even they have little interest in having their role kept secret since involvement in a significant investment dispute can only add to their reputation and appointability except if the award's quality is clearly substandard, something that can occur easily with commercial arbitrators not attuned to the critical quality control discussions that now regularly follows when an award enters into the public domain. Protestations about confidentiality can ring hollow if an award of substandard quality is unexpectedly published and then subject to widespread and legitimate criticism. Arbitrators, theoretically, could pursue publication of awards without their authorisation as copyright breaches.[15] But it is unlikely that, without strong encouragement and financial support by both parties, members of a tribunal would want to be seen

---

[15] Since the parties pay for arbitration, they could require, as part of a specific agreement with the arbitrators, that copyright to the award be transferred to them. That, however, is not the current practice. It would give the parties, possibly more often interested in confidentiality than the arbitrators, a more effective remedy against publication.

acting contrary to the dominant trend towards transparency by relying on an intellectual property right that, so far, seems to have almost never been exercised.[16]

The pursuit of real or perceived self-interest by the various players (and numerous associated players which can be "subagents" of "agents" of "principals") takes place in an overall atmosphere where "transparency" is widely, and I believe largely correctly, perceived as the dominant trend in investment arbitration. I will not discuss the often repeated arguments in favor of more transparency in detail, but in essence, the typically greater public interest and involvement of a State acting in its regulatory and sovereign capacity, is seen at present as a strong enough justification to overcome the traditional commercial arbitration confidentiality (which mirrors traditions of secrecy of government affairs, still largely upheld in non-Western authoritarian systems).[17] With transparency widely acknowledged as a newly

---

[16] There may be a case or two where this issue has arisen, cf. OGEMID discussion between 2004 and 2006.

[17] Howard Mann and IISD have made themselves frequent advocates of "transparency" of investment arbitration against the conventions or rules of arbitral confidentiality; but see also Jan Paulsson, *Avoiding Unintended Consequences*, *in* APPEALS MECHANISM IN INTERNATIONAL INVESTMENT DISPUTES 241 (K.P. Sauvant ed., Oxford University Press, 2008); Biwater Gauff (Tanzania) Limited v. United Republic of Tanzania (ICSID Case No. ARB/05/22), Procedural Order No. 3, Sept. 29, 2006 (available on http://ita.law.uvic.ca), ¶ 114: "Without doubt, there is now a marked tendency towards transparency in treaty arbitration." The tribunal noted that in the absence of a specific confidentiality obligation, there is no general rule imposing either a general duty of confidentiality or transparency in ICSID arbitration; CHRISTOPH H. SCHREUER, THE ICSID CONVENTION: A COMMENTARY 822–23 (Cambridge University Press, 2001), where Prof. Schreuer suggests that the parties may not only disclose an award, but also their memorials. One should, however, question, at least from a copyright perspective, if they are at liberty to disclose the other party's memorials or expert reports; Stewart Boyd and V.V. Veeder, *Le développement du droit anglais de l'arbitrage depuis la loi de 1979*,

emerging principle of investment arbitration, it is much harder to apply formally available legal rules against publications copyright, confidentiality agreements,[18] implied confidentiality obligations or confidentiality obligations included in arbitration rules.[19] This trend is more marked as investment arbitration is seen less as a subcategory of commercial arbitration (from where most of the procedure, conventions and arbitrators come from) but rather as a particular form of international law adjudication, with similarities with international courts (such as the ICJ, the ECJ and WTO dispute panels[20] or the ECHR). International "public law" adjudication is, like domestic administrative law litigation, largely in the public domain. So as the "pull" from the "public law" perspective of investment arbitration increases, so does the distance from the culture of commercial arbitration.

This push to the view that investment disputes are or should be in the public domain is very much supported by NGOs and academic communities. NGOs need to seek a visible role and confidential arbitration does not provide a forum for them, but the

---

1991 REV. ARB. 209, 256; Monique Pongracic-Speier, *Confidentiality and the Public Interest Exception*, 3(2) J. WORLD INV. 231 (2002).

[18] One could examine if publication of an investment award can be subsumed under the concept of "tortious interference" with confidentiality agreements signed between parties and possibly implied into the relationship of the parties with counsel and arbitrators' under the procedural rules applicable including a confidentiality commitment. The most effective confidentiality obligation is usually the one which is, and remains, linked to benefits to the parties, *e.g.*, outstanding obligations by respondent to pay compensation to claimant, perhaps in future tranches.

[19] *See* Joyiyoti Misra and Roman Jordans, *Confidentiality in International Arbitration: An Introspection of the Public Interest Exception*, 23(1) J. INT'L ARB. 39 (2006).

[20] Note the argument of Debra P. Steger, *The Rule of Law or the Rule of Lawyers?*, 3(5) J. WORLD INV. 769 (2002), suggesting that confidentiality rules and conventions in WTO dispute settlement are obsolete and rather hark to the earlier era of diplomatic negotiations.

more public investment arbitration, and the more opportunities for participation in direct or indirect ways, the more their search for a publicly visible role is satisfied. The academic community in international investment law has grown from a few professors, usually all-purpose public international law scholars with a side-interest in investment protection, to a quite substantial community producing an ever greater number of dissertations, articles, and books. They, naturally, need "food" for their intellectual work processes and international investment law without publicly available awards would choke off supply to them. The same applies for international agencies UNCTAD and OECD in particular who can argue more easily for extended and continued mandates if there is material to obtain, investigate, classify, discuss and present to their constituencies. That trend has not left the arbitral institutions untouched. ICSID is publishing (presumably with some persuasion directed at the parties) more and more arbitral awards on its website. The Stockholm Chamber of Commerce, in particular with its new publication, has followed by relaxing the traditionally quite strict confidentiality approach towards publication by discussion of awards which are either identified or only thinly disguised.

In light of these developments, control over confidentiality has weakened, both in attitudinal and legal terms. Pursuit of theoretically available remedies based on copyright or confidentiality obligations (with an often unclear reach) is more difficult and a practice of "benign appropriation" has developed and will be harder to constrain the more it is established and *de facto* accepted. Non-pursuit thus enhances non-compliance and weakens the potential strength of subsequent enforcement. Without an effective remedy or actor ready to enforce the rules which may remain, such rules become emptied of legal strength and in the end risk failing into disuse. The fact that awards get "leaked," *i.e.*, provided discreetly, to publishers illustrates how difficult it is to enforce confidentiality rules in practice. As with every "leaking" to the press, there is a large group of participants in investment arbitration, with links to intermediate players in particular within and between the main law firms, that one might expect to be the source of the award.

These considerations may help to explain why arbitral awards in investment disputes are increasingly published, with or without cooperation from the parties. What we do not know is how many awards remain truly confidential. UNCTAD, supported by Mr. Peterson's ITN newsletters[21] has been trying to develop a fuller picture of awards not (yet) in the public domain. A review of the ICSID and ITA websites allows one to identify some awards that were rendered but have not gone into the public domain. Very little seems to be known at present (at least to me) about non-public treaty-based investment awards made in the context of ICC, LCIA or SCC arbitration otherwise, and even less is known about awards that may have been rendered under the rules of regional arbitration centres (*e.g.*, in particular Cairo, Kuala Lumpur, Singapore, Hong Kong).[22] It is, however, awards that are rendered in *ad hoc* arbitration, based in particular on the UNCITRAL Rules that often offers the least public information. It is possible that the current interest in investment disputes brings at least the existence of many of such disputes to light by references in the press, governmental, corporate or law firm press releases or corporate disclosure so that at least the very fact of an investment dispute would be by and large captured. Challenges before domestic courts or ICSID annulment proceedings will also at times reveal the award, at times its main (and for the challenge or annulment relevant) facts and reasoning or at least the existence of a dispute.

---

[21] Available at www.iisd.org, and www.unctad.org. *See also* the current list of ECT disputes on www.encharter.org.

[22] *See, e.g.*, Walid Ben Hamida, *The First Arab Investment Court Decision*, 7(4) J. WORLD INV. & TRADE 699 (2006).

One can not exclude that where both parties truly and seriously wish to keep an arbitration secret, they succeed. There can be strong institutional and strategic reasons for keeping awards confidential, *e.g.*, to facilitate compliance, facilitating an on-going relationship which can get easily disturbed if an award—with its record of wrongdoing and exaggerated party claims—becomes known. Some institutions may even maintain (or even return to) confidentiality as a special competitive advantage. That applies equally to governments (not wanting to see dirty linen aired in public) and to companies (commercial secrecy, managerial misconduct). One would expect that Asian institutions will rather be in favour of secrecy than transparency as there is a difference of political and societal culture—and less investigative journalism.

These speculative observations as to non-public investment awards are of some relevance for the precedent question: if it should turn out that a substantial number of investment awards are not public, would the confidential awards then loose some claim to fame with respect to providing material for precedent? Should the "precedent effect", mainly in terms of contributing towards a "settled caselaw", depend on how many awards are "in the light" and how many are "in the shadow"?[23] It is true that the aggregate authoritative character of awards thought to form settled case-law is more questionable if they should only represent a minor percentage of all awards. But statistics suggest[24] that a majority, perhaps even a quite large majority, of awards now enter into the public domain. What is more, the fact that the remaining confidential awards may, or may not, adopt different positions

---

[23] I refer here to Mackie Messer's song in Bertolt Brecht's Three-Penny Opera.

[24] For example by Unctad; Luke Peterson for his ITN-newsletter, available at www.iisd.org. *See also* R.E. Walck and L.A. Ahee, *Investment Arbitration Update (As of December 31 2007)*, TDM (Feb. 2008), available at www.transnational-dispute-management.com.

should not count so much. Being out of the public domain and out of public awareness and debate, their contribution to the formation of precedent in other words arbitral caselaw is largely irrelevant. Awards that are not public, as those rendered in commercial arbitration still largely are, can not, and should not, be credited with any significant effect. It might be different if all non-public awards resolutely adopted rules absolutely contrary to those which are public, perhaps because confidentiality would allow or prompt an approach different from one triggered by exposure to public visibility. In that case, it would be harder to establish settled practice also in the sense of established customary law (*e.g.*, under Art. 38 (1)(d) of the ICJ Statute). But there is no indication that "confidential" awards adopt a fundamentally different approach from the one adopted in awards where the tribunals are conscious of public accountability for their result and reasoning. The only indication we have is that awards not envisaged for public knowledge tend to have shallow or non-existent reasoning as contrasted with public awards which tend to increasingly conform with the style of reasoning expected from international courts.

To sum up: we have a clear trend towards an "international public law" style of awards. As this trend imposes itself, the emergence of settled arbitral caselaw (irrespective of small drafting differences in the underlying treaty material) becomes possible, perhaps not in the clarity and consistency that is possible in hierarchically organised national and international judicial bodies working with uniform legal material but, as informed observers will acknowledge, subject to a universal logic of law and lawyers to work towards consistency as a feature of the rule of law.

III. PROCEDURAL QUESTIONS, ADVOCACY AND ARBITRAL APPROACHES RELATING TO "CONFIDENTIAL" AWARDS

What should a tribunal do when a party submits a confidential award? Parties and counsel want to use an informational advantage when possible. So having a confidential award, or an award that will be, but is not, as yet public, can offer an irresistible tactical opportunity. That is particularly so if:

- The award's results of reasoning is favourable to the submitting party's legal theory;

- There is no settled arbitral caselaw or, in particular, if there is no other precedent in terms of a comparable issue determined by a tribunal available; or

- The confidential award has a persuasive reasoning which, more over and more importantly, is carried by arbitrators with authority, reputation and perhaps links with those on the tribunal.

Should a tribunal accept the submission of such a confidential award? I would counsel considerable caution and recommend a restrictive approach without taking at this time an absolute position. If the reasoning is persuasive, there is no reason why the interested party cannot adopt the same reasoning: referring to the authority and reputation of the tribunal for the confidential award is not necessary. Moreover, the party in possession of the confidential award enjoys other significant advantages. It will know more about the case, the way it developed, perhaps even the submissions and expert opinions put forward in that case. It may know of contradictory awards and challenges but it will naturally only select and submit what appears favourable to its position. The submitting party is unlikely to disclose (if it can) and the tribunal is unlikely to be aware if the confidential award was based on weak and unequal advocacy, dubious expertise, questionable evidence or various other factors which may influence a tribunal's decision (in particular one which does not fear the exposure of its reasoning to public accountability).

A restrictive approach is even more advisable if there are indications that there is no consent by the parties owning the award or if use of the award indicates the breach of a confidentiality commitment. In line with some (but not universal) precedent by international courts,[25] illegally obtained evidence should be either excluded or treated with the greatest caution.

That is very different from seeking persuasive support from a "public award." Such award is in the public eye, its quality is likely to be higher, in particular if the tribunal expected it to be published. More will be known about the background and context, and critical peer debate may have shown implications of the award that were not presented to or known by the tribunal at the time the award was rendered. The presumption of relative persuasive authority should therefore always be in favour of publicly available, and against confidential awards.

There are other more mundane practical questions with respect to the submission of awards. It is current practice to require counsel to provide all arbitrators with a full set of "authorities" with all relevant arbitral awards to which reference is made. With availability of almost all "public" awards on the internet, should it not be sufficient if counsel simply refers to such awards (and where to find them) or, at most, provides a copy of the relevant passages cited?

My last question is: when should a tribunal assume a decision constitutes "settled caselaw"? It is hard to define this in

---

[25] *Supra* note 6.

purely quantitative terms. As Jan Paulsson has repeatedly pointed out,[26] individual awards have, and should have, different authority, depending on the quality of reasoning and of the work by the advocates and perhaps the reputation of the arbitrators. Since there is no hierarchical order in international investment arbitration as, for example, within the European Court of Justice, the WTO dispute resolution bodies, or national courts, an arbitral award gains currency less on its position in a hierarchical order but rather by its intrinsic persuasive strength. That may as well apply to the ICSID annulment committees for, as Paulsson points out,[27] they, as appointees of the World Bank administration, do not have the legitimacy that comes from being appointed by the parties themselves. That does not mean that a numeric count is without virtue: a subtly reasoned decision by a brilliant academic running counter to all other arbitral practice which is depreciated as mediocre and pedestrian has in its favour the weight of consistency, predictability and its creation of legitimate expectations with treaty users. In case of doubt, tribunals should obey established practice rather than arrogate for themselves the prerogative of genius. Throughout the history of law and its acceptance, it is the logic of certainty, of alignment with established practice and, in particular, in form and reasoning, a very slow speed of progression appealing to tradition and convention, that have informed judicial practice and its acceptance.

---

[26] Most recently in Paulsson, *Avoiding Unintended Consequences*, *supra* note 17.

[27] *Id.* at 262.

Is Consistency a Myth?

Gabrielle Kaufmann-Kohler [*]

This contribution addresses whether consistency in investment arbitration is a myth.[1] The term myth has many meanings, from an ancient story dealing with supernatural beings to a popular belief associated with a person. There come to mind the Myth of Don Juan, the Myth of Sisyphus, or the Myth of the Noble Savage. These types of myths are not the ones discussed here. Indeed, there is another meaning that appears more topical.

---

[*] Professor, Geneva University; Partner, Lévy Kaufmann-Kohler. The author thanks James Fry and Dr. Thomas Schultz, respectively research fellow and postdoc at Geneva University Law School, whose work is funded by the Swiss National Science Foundation, for their assistance in carrying out the research and finalizing the footnotes for this article. She also thanks Aurélia Antonietti, associate with Lévy Kaufmann-Kohler, for similar assistance.

[1] On consistency in investment arbitration, see also Gabrielle Kaufmann-Kohler, *Arbitral Precedent: Dream, Necessity or Excuse? – The 2006 Freshfields Lecture*, 23(3) ARB. INT'L 357 (2007); Jeffery P. Commission, *Precedents in Investment Treaty Arbitration: a Citation Analysis of a Developing Jurisprudence*, 24 J. INT'L ARB. 129 (2007); Christoph Schreuer and Matthew Weiniger, *Conversations Across Cases – Is there a Doctrine of Precedent in Investment Arbitration?*, in THE OXFORD HANDBOOK ON INTERNATIONAL INVESTMENT LAW (P. Muchlinski, F. Ortino, C. Schreuer eds., Oxford University Press, forthcoming 2008), available at http://www.univie.ac. at/intlaw/conv_across_90.pdf; Andrea K. Björklund, *Investment Treaty Arbitral Decisions as Jurisprudence Constante*, in INTERNATIONAL ECONOMIC LAW: THE STATE AND FUTURE OF THE DISCIPLINE 265 (C.B. Picker, I.D. Bunn and D.W. Arner eds., Hart Publishing, 2008); Tai-Heng Cheng, *Precedent and Control in Investment Treaty Arbitration*, 30 FORDHAM INT'L L.J. 1014 (2007); Jan Paulsson, *International Arbitration and the Generation of Legal Norms: Treaty Arbitration and International Law*, in ICCA CONGRESS SERIES No. 13, INTERNATIONAL ARBITRATION 2006: BACK TO BASICS? 879 (A.J. van den Berg ed., Kluwer, 2007).

It deals with a fiction, especially one based on an ideological belief, or, in other words, a belief that does not correspond to reality. This certainly is the meaning of myth that applies here.

Consistency is easier to define. Consistency addresses a logical coherence among things or a uniformity of successive results.

This article will address whether consistency is a myth by asking three subquestions: First, do we have consistency? In other words, is there uniformity of results in investment arbitration today? Second, do we need consistency? More specifically, is there a need for logical coherence among arbitral decisions? Third, if we need consistency, what are the means likely to promote consistency?

I.   DO WE HAVE CONSISTENCY?

The answer to this first question is twofold: yes and no. It can be illustrated with four examples, two yes examples and two no examples.

A.   *First Yes Example: The Distinction between Treaty and Contract Claims*

There is consistency on the distinction between treaty and contract claims. The distinction initially was touched upon in certain cases,[2] and was first clearly spelled out in the *Vivendi*

---

[2]   Lanco International, Inc. v. Argentine Republic (ICSID Case No. ARB/97/6), Preliminary Decision on Jurisdiction, Dec. 8, 1998, 40 I.L.M. 457 (2001). All ICSID decisions and/or awards mentioned herein are available on the ICSID website, unless otherwise specified.

annulment decision.[3] Since then, it has been repeated and applied in numerous decisions or awards.[4]

---

[3]   Compañia de Aguas del Aconquija S.A. and Compagnie Générale des Eaux (Vivendi Universal) v. Argentine Republic (ICSID Case No. ARB/97/3), Decision on Annulment, July 3, 2002, ¶ 96.

[4]   Salini Costruttori S.p.A. and Italstrade S.p.A. v. Kingdom of Morocco (ICSID Case No. ARB/00/4), Decision on Jurisdiction, July 23, 2001, ¶ 61, [French original] 129 J.D.I. 196 (2002); English translation of French original in 6 ICSID REP. 400 (2004); Consortium R.F.C.C. v. Kingdom of Morocco (ICSID Case No. ARB/00/6), Award, Dec. 22, 2003, ¶ 41 [French original]; SGS Société Générale de Surveillance S.A. v. Islamic Republic of Pakistan (ICSID Case No. ARB/01/13), Decision on Objections to Jurisdiction, Aug. 6, 2003, ¶ 161; Azurix Corp. v. Argentine Republic (ICSID Case No. ARB/01/12), Decision on Jurisdiction, Dec. 8, 2003, ¶ 76; Joy Mining Machinery Limited v. Arab Republic of Egypt (ICSID Case No. ARB/03/11), Award, Aug. 6, 2004, ¶ 81; Impregilo S.p.A. v. Islamic Republic of Pakistan (ICSID Case No. ARB/03/3), Decision on Jurisdiction, Apr. 22, 2005, ¶¶ 214–15; CMS Gas Transmission Company v. Argentine Republic (ICSID Case No. ARB/01/8), Award, May 12, 2005, ¶ 300; Bayindir Insaat Turizm Ticaret Ve Sanayi A.S. v. Islamic Republic of Pakistan (ICSID Case No. ARB/03/29), Decision on Jurisdiction, Nov. 14, 2005, ¶¶ 166–67; BP America Production Company and others v. Argentine Republic (ICSID Case No. ARB/04/8), Decision on Jurisdiction, July 27, 2006, ¶ 91, available at http://ita.law.uvic.ca/documents/ PanAmericanBPJurisdiction-eng.pdf; Pan American Energy LLC and BP Argentina Exploration Company v. Argentine Republic (ICSID Case No. ARB/03/13), Decision on Jurisdiction, July 27, 2006, ¶ 91, available at http://ita.law.uvic.ca/documents/PanAmericanBPJurisdiction-eng.pdf; Siemens A.G. v. Argentine Republic (ICSID Case No. ARB/02/08), Award, Feb. 6, 2007, ¶¶ 247 et seq., available at http://ita.law.uvic.ca/documents/Siemens-Argentina-Award.pdf; Compañia de Aguas del Aconquija S.A. and Compagnie Générale des Eaux (Vivendi Universal) v. Argentine Republic (ICSID Case No. ARB/97/3), Award, Aug. 20, 2007, ¶ 7.3.10, available at http://ita.law.uvic.ca/ documents/VivendiAwardEnglish.pdf; Noble Energy Inc. and Machala Power Cía. Ltd. v. Republic of Ecuador and Consejo Nacional de Electricidad (ICSID Case No. ARB/05/12), Decision on Jurisdiction, Mar. 5, 2008, ¶¶ 205–06, available at http://ita.law.uvic.ca/documents/Noblev.EcuadorJurisdiction.pdf.

SGS v. Philippines may be read differently,[5] but the difference may be due to the interference of the umbrella clause more than to a divergence from the treaty-contract claim distinction. In other words, a true *jurisprudence constante* has evolved, and it is ironic that it was precisely called for by *SGS Philippines*. Whether the distinction is a good or a bad one is a different question. The fact is that it is well-settled.

B.   Second Yes Example: Fair and Equitable Treatment

Since the *Neer* case in 1927,[6] there has been an evolution towards more demanding requirements imposed on the host State in the context of fair and equitable treatment. It is true that arbitral tribunals pay great attention to treaty language and facts. However, beyond these case-driven factors, there is a clear emergence of standards on at least three aspects:

•   Arbitral tribunals have abandoned the view that unfair and inequitable treatment requires bad faith—an evolution that started with *Mondev*,[7] and was followed by a number of other cases;[8]

---

[5]   SGS Société Générale de Surveillance S.A. v. Republic of the Philippines (ICSID Case No. ARB/02/6), Decision on Jurisdiction, Jan. 29, 2004, ¶ 134.

[6]   Neer Case (United States v. Mexico), 4 U.N.R.I.A.A. 60 (Gen. Cl. Comm'n 1926).

[7]   Mondev International Ltd. v. United States of America (ICSID Case No. ARB(AF)/99/2), Award, Oct. 11, 2002, ¶ 166, 42 I.L.M. 85 (2003), 6 ICSID Rep. 192 (2004), 125 I.L.R. 110 (2004).

[8]   Técnicas Medioambientales Tecmed, S.A. v. United Mexican States (ICSID Case No. ARB(AF)/00/2), Award, May 29, 2003, ¶ 153; The Loewen Group, Inc. and Raymond L. Loewen v. United States of America (ICSID Case No. ARB(AF)/98/3), Award, June 26, 2003, ¶ 302, 42 I.L.M. 811 (2003), 7 ICSID Rep. 442 (2005); CMS Gas Transmission Company v. Argentine

• Tribunals emphasize the need for a stable legal and business framework. This first was mentioned in *Metalclad*,[9] and thereafter repeatedly stressed by *MTD* and others;[10] and

• Tribunals give weight to legitimate and reasonable expectations of the investors.[11]

So much for inconsistent results.

Republic, *supra* note 4, ¶ 280; Azurix Corp. v. Argentine Republic (ICSID Case No. ARB/01/12), Award, July 14, 2006, ¶¶ 368 *et seq.*; PSEG Global et al. v. Republic of Turkey (ICSID Case No. ARB/02/5), Award, Jan. 19, 2007, ¶ 246; Enron Corporation and Ponderosa Assets, L.P. v. Argentine Republic (ICSID Case No. ARB/01/3), Award, May 22, 2007, ¶ 263, available at http://ita.law.uvic.ca /documents/Enron-Award.pdf.

[9] Metalclad Corporation v. United Mexican States (ICSID Case No. ARB(AF)/97/1), Award, Aug. 30, 2000, ¶ 99.

[10] MTD Equity Sdn. Bhd. and MTD Chile S.A. v. Republic of Chile (ICSID Case No. ARB/01/7), Award, May 25, 2004, ¶ 205; CME Czech Republic B.V. v. Czech Republic (UNCITRAL), Partial Award, Sept. 13, 2001, ¶ 611, available at http://ita.law.uvic.ca/documents/CME-2001PartialAward.pdf; CMS Gas Transmission Company v. Argentine Republic, *supra* note 4, ¶¶ 274 *et seq.*; LG&E Capital Corp. and LG&E International Inc. v. Argentine Republic (ICSID Case No. ARB/02/1), Decision on Liability, Oct. 3, 2006, ¶¶ 125 *et seq.*; PSEG Global et al. v. Republic of Turkey, *supra* note 8, ¶¶ 250 *et seq.*

[11] *See, e.g.*, Técnicas Medioambientales Tecmed, S.A. v. United Mexican States, *supra* note 8, ¶ 154; Eureko B.V. v. Republic of Poland (UNCITRAL), Partial Award, Aug. 19, 2005, ¶ 232, available at http://ita.law.uvic.ca/ documents/Eureko-PartialAwardandDissentingOpinion.pdf; Saluka Investments BV (The Netherlands) v. Czech Republic, Partial Award, Mar. 17, 2006, ¶ 302, available at http://ita.law.uvic.ca/documents/Saluka-PartialawardFinal.pdf; International Thunderbird Gaming Corporation v. United Mexican States (UNCITRAL (NAFTA) Arbitration), Award, Jan. 26, 2006, ¶ 147, available at http://ita.law.uvic.ca/documents/ThunderbirdAward.pdf; Azurix Corp. v. Argentine Republic, *supra* note 8, ¶ 372; Enron Corporation and Ponderosa Assets, L.P. v. Argentine Republic, *supra* note 8, ¶ 262.

C.   First No Example: The Umbrella Clause

In this area, the original discrepancy, which was clearly illustrated by the two *SGS* cases,[12] resided between decisions that deemed the umbrella clause to elevate contract claims to treaty claims,[13] and others that denied such effect.[14] Looking at more recent cases, the problem appears to have shifted somewhat towards the question of whether the umbrella clause encompasses only obligations entered into by the state in a sovereign capacity or whether it also covers commercial obligations.[15] Be this as it may, the controversy remains.

D.   Second No Example: State of Necessity

The defense of state of necessity has arisen recently in the Argentinean cases, the question being whether Argentina was entitled to take the measures it took during the crisis on the

---

[12]   SGS Société Générale de Surveillance S.A. v. Islamic Republic of Pakistan, *supra* note 4 and SGS Société Générale de Surveillance S.A. v. Republic of the Philippines, *supra* note 5.

[13]   CMS Gas Transmission Company v. Argentine Republic, *supra* note 4, ¶¶ 299 *et seq.*; Eureko B.V. v. Republic of Poland (UNCITRAL), *supra* note 11, ¶ 53; LG&E Capital Corp. and LG&E International Inc. v. Argentine Republic, *supra* note 10, ¶¶ 170–71; Siemens A.G. v. Argentine Republic, *supra* note 4, ¶¶ 204 *et seq.*

[14]   Joy Mining Machinery Limited v. Arab Republic of Egypt, *supra* note 4, ¶ 81; El Paso Energy International Company v. Argentine Republic (ICSID Case No. ARB/03/15), Decision on Jurisdiction, Apr. 27, 2006, ¶ 70; Pan American Energy LLC and BP Argentina Exploration Company v. Argentine Republic, *supra* note 4, ¶¶ 105 *et seq.*; CMS Gas Transmission Company v. Argentine Republic (ICSID Case No. ARB/01/8), Decision of the *ad hoc* committee on the application for annulment of the Argentine Republic, Sept. 25, 2007, ¶ 95.

[15]   Enron Corporation and Ponderosa Assets, L.P. v. Argentine Republic, *supra* note 8, ¶ 274; Sempra Energy International v. Argentine Republic (ICSID Case No. ARB/02/16), Award, Sept. 28, 2007, ¶¶ 310 *et seq.*

grounds of necessity. So far, there are four decisions against,[16] and one in favor of,[17] resorting to a state of necessity. However, this is a misleading statistic because three of the cases that refused to apply a state of necessity were presided over by the same chairman. The actual result is, thus, more balanced than it appears. In this context, one should also mention the decision of the annulment committee in *CMS*,[18] which adds methodological directions but no answer to the issue of principle. In short, cases so far have yielded clearly inconsistent results on this issue.

II.   DO WE NEED CONSISTENCY?

The preceding section shows that we have consistency on some issues and that we do not on others. That leads to the second question: do we need consistency?

When answering the second question, one should not ignore that some solutions are treaty- or fact-specific. One should not ignore the likelihood that a degree of inconsistency is inherent in any legal system and is not intolerable.[19] Beyond these

---

[16]   CMS Gas Transmission Company v. Argentine Republic, *supra* note 4, ¶¶ 324 *et seq.*; Enron Corporation and Ponderosa Assets, L.P. v. Argentine Republic, *supra* note 8, ¶¶ 307 *et seq.*; Sempra Energy International v. Argentine Republic, *supra* note 15, ¶¶ 346 *et seq.*; BG Group Plc. v. Argentine Republic (UNCITRAL), Final Award, Dec. 24, 2007, available at http://ita.law.uvic.ca/documents/BG-award_000.pdf.

[17]   LG&E Capital Corp. and LG&E International Inc. v. Argentine Republic, *supra* note 10, ¶¶ 339 *et seq.*

[18]   CMS Gas Transmission Company v. Argentine Republic, *supra* note 14, ¶ 95.

[19]   MATTHEW H. KRAMER, OBJECTIVITY AND THE RULE OF LAW 128–29 (Cambridge University Press, 2007) ("There is a qualitative difference between a system of governance whose norms are replete with contradictions and a system of governance whose norms contain few or no contradictions. Only the

143

observations, the question is whether on the same legal issues we need the same answers.

This leads one to reflect on the relationship between the law and the practice of following precedents. Legal theory tells us that the rule of law is only the rule of law if it is consistently applied so as to be predictable.[20] It also teaches us that decision-makers have an obligation—whether moral or legal is not relevant here—to strive for consistency and predictability and thus to follow precedents.[21]

This obligation is not the same under all circumstances and in all fields. The scope of the obligation depends on the stage of

---

latter is a legal system."). *See also* I. Laird and Rebecca Askew, *Finality versus Consistency: Does Investor-State Arbitration Need an Appellate System?*, 7(2) J. APP. PRAC. & PROCESS 285, 298 (2005); Susan D. Franck, *The Legitimacy Crisis in Investment Treaty Arbitration: Privatizing Public International Law Through Inconsistent Decisions*, 73 FORDHAM L. REV. 1521, 1613 (2005) (noting how "a minor degree of inconsistency may be useful, as it permits a challenge to the fundamental principles of the system and fosters the considered evolution of law . . . ."); Susan D. Franck, *The Nature and Enforcement of Investor Rights Under Investment Treaties: Do Investment Treaties Have a Bright Future?*, 12 U.C. DAVIS J. INT'L L. & POL'Y 47, 68 (2005) (discussing the benefits of inconsistency).

[20] LON L. FULLER, THE MORALITY OF LAW 33, 38–39 (New Haven, rev. ed. 1969); KRAMER, *supra* note 19, at 109 *et seq.*; MATTHEW H. KRAMER, IN DEFENSE OF LEGAL POSITIVISM: LAW WITHOUT TRIMMINGS 142–46 (Oxford University Press, 1999); MICHEL VAN DE KERCHOVE AND FRANÇOIS OST, LEGAL SYSTEM BETWEEN ORDER AND DISORDER 135 (I. Stewart trans., Clarendon Press, 1994). *See also* Kaufmann-Kohler, *supra* note 1, at 373 *et seq.*

[21] FULLER, *supra* note 20, at 42–43; KRAMER, *supra* note 19, at 143; Jacques Chevallier, *L'ordre juridique*, *in* LE DROIT EN PROCÈS 7–8 and 11–14 (PUF, 1983); BRIAN Z. TAMANAHA, ON THE RULE OF LAW: HISTORY, POLITICS, THEORY 122–26 (Cambridge University Press, 2004); Richard H. Fallon, *"The Rule of Law" as a Concept in Constitutional Discourse*, 97 COLUM. L. REV. 1, 3 (1997); JOHN LOCKE, THE SECOND TREATISE ON CIVIL GOVERNMENT Chap. 9, Sec. 124 (1690). *See also* Kaufmann-Kohler, *supra* note 1, at 373 *et seq.*

development of the law.[22] In essence, the less developed the law is, the more important the role of the dispute resolver will be with respect to the creation of the rule.[23] Indeed, rules cannot emerge without consistency.[24]

Obviously, investment law is in its early stages of development and thus requires consistency. In sum, the answer to the second question is that we need consistency for the sake of the development of the rule of law.

III. HOW TO ACHIEVE CONSISTENCY?

If we need consistency but lack it, at least in part, then the question arises how to achieve it for that part which is lacking. One possibility might be to simply wait for consistency to emerge with time in the hope that "good awards will chase the bad [ones],"[25] knowing that rule creation is not linear and that the road to consistency necessarily has dead-ends and u-turns. However, there is a significant risk that simply waiting for consistency to emerge will not produce the results hoped for because certain fundamental disagreements will remain.

In the same vein, another view points to the *esprit de corps* of the arbitrators as a unifying force.[26] With the explosion of the

---

[22]   Norberto Bobbio, *Ancora sulle norme primarie e norme secondarie*, 59 RIVISTA DI FILOSOFIA 35, 51 (1968) (translated into French as *Nouvelles réflexions sur les normes primaires et secondaires*, *in* LA RÈGLE DE DROIT 104 (C. Perelman ed., Bruylant, 1971)). *See also* Kaufmann-Kohler, *supra* note 1, at 373 *et seq.*

[23]   Bobbio, *supra* note 22, at 51–52.

[24]   TAMANAHA, *supra* note 21, at 96 *et seq.*

[25]   Paulsson, *supra* note 1, at 889.

[26]   Commission, *supra* note 1, at 136 *et seq.*

number of cases, with the increasing diversity of arbitrators, it is not certain that the *esprit de corps* will do away with genuine disagreements on legal issues.[27]

If waiting and hoping is insufficient, are there other ways of improving consistency? The following possible ways come to mind. First, because of the limitation of the grounds available, the annulment mechanism cannot play a major role in bringing about consistency.[28] Second, the possibility of creating an appeal mechanism has been discarded so far, for the better because its drawbacks seem to outweigh its advantages.[29]

Another solution lies in today's topic: precedent. For precedents to foster consistency, tribunals would have to systematically rely on a consistent line of cases and depart from it only for compelling reasons. This would amount to a principle of

---

[27] For instance, the decision of the *ad hoc* committee in CMS, *supra* note 14, is certainly not a testimony to *esprit de corps*.

[28] The CMS *ad hoc* Committee for instance said so expressly: "Both parties recognize that an *ad hoc* committee is not a court of appeal and that its competence extends only to annulment based on one or other of the grounds expressly set out in Article 52 of the ICSID Convention." (*supra* note 14, ¶ 43). *See also id.*, ¶ 136 (asserting that "the Committee cannot simply substitute its own view of the law . . . for those of the Tribunal.").

[29] Gabrielle Kaufmann-Kohler, *In Search of Transparency and Consistency: ICSID Reform Proposal*, 2(5) TDM 5 (2005). *See also* Laird and Askew, *supra* note 19, at 300 (noting how appellate review is not likely to be a panacea to all inconsistency problems, as the main problem arising from the Lauder arbitration cases was that these were not consolidated, not that they were not reviewed by an appellate body); Jan Paulsson, *Avoiding Unintended Consequences*, in APPEALS MECHANISM IN INTERNATIONAL INVESTMENT DISPUTES 241, 242, 262 (K.P. Sauvant ed., Oxford University Press, 2008) (mentioning how proposals for a universal appellate mechanism are unrealistic); Hans Smit, *Note, Dispute Resolution in Patent Pooling Arrangements: The Arbitration Solution*, 16 AM. REV. INT'L ARB. 547, 548–59 (2005) (noting how appellate review by *ad hoc* tribunals might just add another layer of inconsistency to international arbitration).

stare decisis applied not to a single case but to a line of cases, or *jurisprudence constante*. Over time, that practice could develop, as Thomas Wälde have suggested,[30] into customary international law, implying a well-established practice and an *opinio juris*. Reasonable minds may differ on whether such a doctrine of precedent may work in a decentralized mode of regulation with *ad hoc* tribunals and no supervising institution binding them together. If one has serious doubts, one could consider instituting a system of preliminary rulings along the lines of Article 234 of the EC Treaty.[31] Such a creation would require a strong political will and careful crafting. This option does not appear likely in the short or medium term. Hence, precedent remains the main tool to promote efficiency.

In conclusion, one may answer the question posed at the outset as follows: Consistency is not a myth. Consistency is a reality and a necessary objective at the same time.

---

[30] International Thunderbird Gaming Corporation v. United Mexican States (UNCITRAL (NAFTA) Arbitration), Separate Opinion of Thomas Wälde, Jan. 26, 2006, ¶ 16, available at http://ita.law.uvic.ca/documents/ThunderbirdSeparateOpinion.pdf.

[31] For more details, see Gabrielle Kaufmann-Kohler, *Annulment of ICSID Awards in Contract and Treaty Arbitrations: Are there Differences?*, *in* IAI INTERNATIONAL ARBITRATION SERIES NO. 1, ANNULMENT OF ICSID AWARDS 189 (E. Gaillard & Y. Banifatemi eds., Juris Publishing, 2004). *See also* Schreuer and Weiniger, *supra* note 1, at 17–18.

Comments and Discussion

Brigitte Stern–. To go back to this concept of *jurisprudence constante* by James Crawford and Gabrielle Kaufmann-Kohler, I note that there are fields where we are certain that there is a *jurisprudence constante*, others that we are practically sure that there is not and others where we do not know.

I heard James Crawford say that on fair and equitable treatment there is no *jurisprudence constante* and Gabrielle Kaufmann-Kohler says the contrary. So we already have a problem here. What might be of interest is to see which fields, where a *jurisprudence constante* appeared very fast—Gabrielle mentioned a few—and to wonder why this is the case in some fields and not in others.

Let me take two examples where a *jurisprudence constante* appeared very fast.

Arbitration without privity. First decision: 1988 SPP. It was accepted that a State could unilaterally give its consent under a law—in that case, Egyptian law. 2nd decision: 1990 AALP, same position for bilateral treaties. Finally, in 1994, in Tradex Hellas, it was said 'oh well it goes without saying; there is not even any need to discuss it.' Thus, in 6 years, so really rapidly, jurisprudence has been established.

Same thing, and this is even more interesting, with respect to acceptance of *amicus curiae*. Here, there is a thinking process which should be launched on cross-fertilization of the various fields of economic international law. We know that *amicus curiae* was first accepted in WTO proceedings, in the *Shrimp-turtle case*. Then Nafta, and then finally, ICSID in the 2 *Aguas de Argentina* and *Aguas de Santa Fe* cases where Gabrielle Kaufmann-Kohler was President.

This *jurisprudence constante* soon became a source of law, not a source of law *per se* but because it was adopted by the new ICSID Rules. So it is interesting to see the role of jurisprudence in the evolution of law.

And last comment: Why is there a *jurisprudence constante* in certain fields? I think that when there is a *jurisprudence constante* it is because it reflects the needs of the arbitration community and when it is not the case it is because there are still conflicts of interests. These conflicts should be solved and we should find a balance between the interests of investors and those of States.

Yannick Radi–. My first question is addressed to President Guillaume. Given the enormous amount of bilateral treaties, one might wonder about the emergence of a customary law in this field, at least with respect to certain provisions of the BITs, I would like to ask, if one admits that there is some consistency—and this goes beyond the problem of the relationship between treaty and custom—, could a uniform arbitral practice play a role in the emergence of customary law? Could that become a general practice?

My second question has to do with consistency. Appeal— could we not introduce an appellate mechanism which would give greater consistency of arbitral practice? What do you think?

James Crawford–. To respond to the first question: "why does coherence emerge in some fields and not in others?" First of all I think it is a mistake to say that there is a single problem with the fair and equitable treatment standard, or there is a single problem with treaty/contract standard. I mean, I entirely agree that we have moved beyond the *Neer* standard in relation to fair and equitable treatment. That particular problem may have been resolved but there are a number of others about the margin of appreciation and so on, and which I think are not resolved. That is a cluster of problems and some of them are being sorted out. Similarly treaty and contract, I think there are some issues that have been resolved—certainly the arbitration without privity has been resolved, although the crucial test for arbitration without privity is what would happen if national courts had to deal with that problem in reviewing BIT decisions outside the framework of ICSID. We have crossed that threshold now with the court decision in *Occidental*, and I think that is now safe. But it shows that there is a process of dialogue, which, actually, international lawyers should not be too surprised about, because that is how we developed the customary international law of State immunity and customary international law on various other things—by taking time about it and by talking to each other and by being frank about our disagreements.

Gilbert Guillaume–. To answer the questions that was put to me personally, I think that the day that jurisprudence in the field of commercial arbitration or investment arbitration has reached sufficient publicity and consistency, I do not see why the ICJ should not recognize it as a subsidiary means for the determination of rules of law.

This being said, the Court—like any other tribunal—deals only with the issues that are submitted to it in the fields it is seized of; so, these problems would first have to be presented to it.

Yas Banifatemi–. I have two questions to all the members of the panel.

The first one has to do with the impact of the publication of awards. We have all seen in the past few years the multiplication of the publication of awards and the fact that published awards are longer and longer, more and more detailed, citing more and more sources, whether they be jurisprudential, doctrinal, etc.

My question is to all of you as arbitrators: Could the impact of this publication be that arbitrators, beyond the drafting for the parties, also bear in mind the public that is going to read such decisions, be it either other parties in other cases or, for NAFTA-type decisions, the public at large and NGOs?

My second question has to do with the very concept of precedent. I wanted to know whether we all agree on the fact that there is no precedent in investment law in the sense of binding decisions. Do we agree that, in the case of an ICSID decision annulled by an *ad hoc* committee and resubmitted by the parties to a second tribunal, the second tribunal is not bound by the *ad hoc* committee decision and may in fact decide exactly in the same way as the first tribunal with respect to the issues that are submitted to it and to the arguments of the parties?

Prosper Weil–. Should we not—and this sounds maybe as a silly question—establish a distinction between two aspects of the source of international law, sources of law? There are those awards that are a source of law, insofar as they have authority, they were rendered by prestigious arbitrators, they are well drafted, they are convincing and they inspire the follow-up in the future, other awards. And, on the other side, the formal source, in other words, what has been decided in the award is, within certain limitations, *res judicata* and bind the arbitrators in the future. It is not quite the same thing and I am not convinced that we should not establish a distinction between these two sides of the problem "Are arbitral awards a source of international law?" This is a question that I am just raising. I do not have the answer but it was prompted by the various speeches.

Thomas Wälde–. On Yas Banifatemi's question, I think you can see a very clear distinction between the commercial arbitration tradition and what I would call the modern international investment law tradition.

If you compare Stockholm Chamber awards, or "unsettled" awards, to the extent they become public, they are written for the parties and the arbitrator will tell you 'it is of no concern to me, the wider public; this is for the parties; I am not here to make law'. But then if you compare this with ICSID awards, you will see very different. There is much more pressure, there is the transparency, the publicity, the critique, and simply the wish of arbitrators not to be regarded as, kind of, not very competent. In that competition which is very strong in arbitration, the awards tend to be typically not as such a long discussion of the facts—which is typical for commercial arbitration awards—, but they go much more into law. You could probably do a statistical analysis, facts versus the law, you would see probably that in commercial arbitration awards, facts are multiple of the law, where it is different in investment arbitration. So there is a cultural, generational change. Arbitrators who write a 'commercial arbitration award' in investment dispute and suddenly see themselves exposed to unexpected criticism, either disappear or they change their ways.

The other thing I think which was mentioned is the annulment committee incoherence. I think the ICSID annulment committee construction is highly dysfunctional and produces enormous lack of coherence. If there is reform, there are many issues to be reformed. I am currently working for Columbia University on a study on this. I think that something needs to be done about the ICSID annulment committee.

First, I think it is wrong to mix up appointments to the annulment committee with appointments to arbitration. This is incestuous; it leads also to all sorts of jealousies and sympathies, which should not have a place in a proper system of justice.

Another point, I think, is that the annulment committee needs a coherent, almost a permanent judiciary, like the WTO appeals body. My impression is, and to my mind the expertise you look for is the expertise, experienced arbitration judges in countries with challenge, enforcement experience. I could think of who to my mind in France should be on that committee. My impression is that in ICSID these thoughts are not as alien and new, and that they might actually think about them as well, but the annulment committee system is dysfunctional and needs reform.

The other thing is that it also needs a very strong focus on the task at hand and avoiding *obiter dicta* which cause at the moment a lot of grief and confusion, but that again is a result that there is no uniform style of annulment committee decision which has evolved.

Gilbert Guillaume–. I totally disagree with what has just been said but that is quite legitimate in a discussion panel.

I would just like to answer the question which was raised earlier on about whether in an *ad hoc* committee the members address just the parties or have a wider audience.

I think that, because of the nature of the ICSID system, it might be useful for an *ad hoc* committee, when it is faced with an award which it is not competent to annul, to point out mistakes which might have been made, not for the benefit of the parties but for the benefit of future arbitral tribunals so that they can also read the decision of the *ad hoc* committee and think about the questions raised.

Michael Schneider–. I was very struck by the difference of position between the proponents of traditional public international law and what Thomas Wälde called modern investment law, with the reluctance you showed as to the power to go beyond the specific decision, and the theory that Gabrielle Kaufmann-Kohler, who is the spokesman on behalf of the whole community, gave to us saying 'our reference is the development of the rule of law and that type of objectives'. But who do you think you are? I mean you have been appointed by two parties in the context of a bilateral treaty and it is to go beyond your role to take on the role of wanting to develop international law and to have responsibility that goes beyond the parties that have appointed you, beyond the framework of the case you are dealing with. So, there is that tendency—maybe I am exaggerating what Gabrielle Kaufmann-Kohler was saying—but the tendency exists and I think we have to go back to the specific responsibility within the dispute.

There is also the problem with reference to precedent as an expression. There is a manifold way in which a judge or an arbitrator can refer back to what has been decided elsewhere. In the framework of a treaty, for example if you apply the Vienna Convention on the Sales of Goods, you apply the decisions of another State because it is in the framework of the same treaty or as the Federal Tribunal because another foreign judge has had a bright idea. So I think we have to open up the concept of reference, and I think Barton Legum did that.

Walid Ben Hamida–. I have a question about the publication of awards and decisions. So I would like to give you a number of events. I would like to ask explanations from the panel, notably Professor Wälde, because I cannot find any logic.

First phenomenon: in investment law, the principle is publication, but there are a number of awards which are not published. If you look at ICSID, five awards are not published. There is a sort of 'iron curtain,' they are inaccessible. Why? I am intrigued by the fact that only those awards have not been published.

Second phenomenon: sometimes within ICSID there is publication, but publication of extracts only. For example, an award of 110 pages, only 11 are published.

Other phenomenon: late publication. Publication can happen 10 years later and there again extracts sometimes. Those extracts are invoked in a pending case and quoted in a recent decision.

Fourth phenomenon: publication of the decision on annulment of the award, but no publication of the award itself. I do not understand why.

And, finally, with regard to NAFTA, Professor Wälde said it was a model of transparency: you publish everything, you publish pleadings, you publish awards and *amicus* of NGOs. But in the case of Glamis against the United States, the United States was opposed to the publication of legal opinions.

Antonio Crivellaro–. I would like to bring an optimistic note. We forgot that thanks to the theory of precedent, jurisprudence has come to a solution which is now well balanced and consolidated with respect to the definition of an investment. In the first cases referred to ICSID arbitration, there were major uncertainties. There was a clear division and we did not know exactly what operations were covered by the concept of investment or not. If you look at decisions from 2000 to 2006, they all refer back to precedents to see whether an operation was covered by the definition or not within the Convention and within investment bilateral treaties. So that is a theory of precedent which has functioned well. In another field it has not functioned that well, but that is more delicate. I am referring to the Most Favored Nation clause, the MFN clause. There again, on that point, jurisprudence is still split and we have to wait as Gabrielle Kaufmann-Kohler was saying. But I am optimistic. I am sure that we will find a solution there also. We have to look at the difference between treaty claims and contract claims. I am not sure that we have achieved consistency in that field but uncertainties are much reduced compared to just 5 or 6 years ago when jurisprudence was very uncertain and I know all about it personally. And in the risky situations we started several cases.

And another note of optimism. I was very surprised to know from Thomas Wälde that he was wondering where that secret information comes from. I thought until last night that it was from you, from your own website OGEMID which is a source of precious information, lots of information! I receive 10 to 20 messages a day and I am sure that your website will become, as President Guillaume said, a subsidiary source of law.

ANNEXES

ANNEX 1

International Centre for Settlement of Investment Disputes
Washington, D.C.

In the proceedings between

AES Corporation
(Claimant)

And

The Argentine Republic
(Respondent)

ICSID Case No. ARB/02/17

DECISION ON JURISDICTION

Members of the Tribunal
Professor Pierre-Marie Dupuy, President
Professor Karl-Heinz Böckstiegel, Arbitrator
Professor Domingo Bello Janeiro, Arbitrator

Secretary of the Tribunal
Mr. Gonzalo Flores

Representing the Claimant
Messrs. David M. Lindsey and
James M. Hosking
Clifford Chance U.S. LLP
New York, NY

Representing the Respondent
Procurador del Tesoro de la Nación
Argentina
Dr. Osvaldo César Guglielmino
Procuración del Tesoro de la Nación
Argentina
Buenos Aires
República Argentina

Date of Decision: April 26, 2005

I. Procedure

1. On November 5, 2002, the International Centre for Settlement of Investment Disputes ("ICSID" or "the Centre") received a Request for Arbitration against the Argentine Republic ("the Respondent" or "Argentina") from the AES Corporation ("the Claimant" or "AES"), a company incorporated in the State of Delaware, with headquarters in Arlington, Virginia, United States of America. The Request concerns AES' investment in eight electricity generation companies and three major electricity distribution companies in Argentina, and Argentina's alleged refusal to apply previously agreed tariff calculation and adjustment mechanisms.

2. In its request, AES invoked the provisions of the 1991 Treaty between the United States of America and the Argentine Republic Concerning the Reciprocal Encouragement and Protection of Investment (the "Argentina–US Bilateral Investment Treaty" or the "BIT").[1]

3. On November 6, 2002, the Centre, in accordance with Rule 5 of the ICSID Rules of Procedure for the Institution of Conciliation and Arbitration Proceedings (Institution Rules), acknowledged receipt and transmitted a copy of the request to the Argentine Republic and to the Argentine Embassy in Washington D.C.

4. On December 19, 2002, the Secretary-General of the Centre registered the request, pursuant to Article 36(3) of the Convention on the Settlement of Investment Disputes between States and Nationals of other States (the "ICSID Convention" or "the Convention"). On the same date, the Secretary-General, in accordance with Institution Rule 7, notified the parties of the registration of the request and invited them to proceed, as soon as possible, to constitute an Arbitral Tribunal.

5. Pursuant to the parties' agreement, the Tribunal in this case would comprise one arbitrator appointed by the Claimant, one arbitrator appointed by the Respondent, and a third, presiding, arbitrator, to be appointed by the Secretary-General of ICSID.

6. On February 18, 2003, the Claimant appointed Professor Karl-Heinz Böckstiegel, a German national, as an arbitrator. On April 3, 2003, Argentina

---

[1]   Treaty between the United States of America and the Argentine Republic Concerning the Reciprocal Encouragement and Protection of Investment, done in Washington, D.C. on November 14, 1991, in force since October 20, 1994.

appointed Professor Domingo Bello Janeiro, a national of the Kingdom of Spain, as an arbitrator.

7. With the agreement of both parties, the Secretary-General of ICSID appointed Professor Pierre-Marie Dupuy, a French national, as the President of the Arbitral Tribunal. On June 3, 2003, the Acting Secretary-General, in accordance with Rule 6(1) of the Rules of Procedure for Arbitration Proceedings (Arbitration Rules), notified the parties that all three arbitrators had accepted their appointments and that the Tribunal was therefore deemed to have been constituted on that date. On the same date, pursuant to ICSID Administrative and Financial Regulation 25, the parties were informed that Mr. Gonzalo Flores, Senior Counsel, ICSID, would serve as Secretary of the Arbitral Tribunal.

8. The first session of the Tribunal with the parties was held on July 8, 2003, at the seat of the Centre in Washington, D.C. During the session the parties expressed their agreement that the Tribunal had been properly constituted in accordance with the relevant provisions of the ICSID Convention and the ICSID Arbitration Rules and that they did not have any objections in this respect.

9. During the first session the parties agreed on a number of procedural matters reflected in written minutes signed by the President and the Secretary of the Tribunal. The Tribunal, after consultation with the parties, fixed the following schedule for the written phase of the proceedings: The Claimant would file a memorial on the merits within forty five (45) to ninety (90) days from the date of the first session; the Respondent would file a counter memorial on the merits within ninety (90) days from its receipt of the Claimant's memorial; the Claimant would file a reply within sixty (60) days from its receipt of the counter memorial; and the Respondent would file a rejoinder within sixty (60)days from its receipt of the Claimant's reply.

10. During the first session it was noted that consideration of eventual objections to jurisdiction from the Argentine Republic would be premature. It was thus agreed to leave the matter open for further discussion in due course.

11. On October 7, 2003, the Claimant filed its Memorial on the Merits with accompanying documentation. On December 31, 2003 Argentina filed a Memorial with objections to jurisdiction.

12. By letter of January 12, 2004, the Tribunal confirmed the suspension of the proceedings on the merits in accordance with ICSID Arbitration Rule 41(3), and invited the parties to file their views on a schedule for their presentations on jurisdiction. Both parties submitted their views on January 16, 2004, with the Claimant also requesting the Tribunal to join the questions of jurisdiction raised by Argentina to the merits of the dispute. Argentina, upon invitation of the Tribunal, filed a response to the Claimant's request on January 27, 2004.

13. On February 18, 2004, the Tribunal, having carefully considered the positions of the parties, confirmed the suspension of the proceedings on the merits and fixed the following timetable for the filing of the parties' submissions on the question of jurisdiction: the Claimant would file a counter memorial on jurisdiction within thirty (30) days from the date of the Tribunal's decision; the Respondent would file a reply on jurisdiction within thirty (30) days from its receipt of the Claimant's counter memorial; and the Claimant would file a rejoinder on jurisdiction within thirty (30) days from its receipt of the Respondent's reply. The Tribunal would thereafter, decide, whether oral arguments on the question of jurisdiction would be necessary, and, if so, fix a date for a hearing on jurisdiction.

14. In accordance with the timetable fixed by the Tribunal, the Claimant filed its Counter-Memorial on Jurisdiction on February 20, 2004. Argentina filed its Reply on Jurisdiction on March 26, 2004 and the Claimant filed its Rejoinder on Jurisdiction on April 26, 2004.

15. By letter of May 13, 2004, the Tribunal informed the parties its desire to hold a hearing on jurisdiction and proposed dates for such hearing. The hearing was held, with the agreement of the parties, on October 23 and 24, 2004 in Paris, France. Messrs. David M. Lindsay, James H. Hosking and Stephen Kantor and Ms. Andrea Goldbarg, from the law firm of Clifford Chance US LLP and Mr. Mark Sandy, from the AES Corporation, attended the hearing on behalf of the Claimant. Ms. Luz Moglia, Ms. María Soledad Vallejos Meana and Mr. Ignacio Torterola, from the Procuración del Tesoro de la Nación Argentina, attended the hearing on behalf of the Respondent. During the hearing Messrs. Lindsay and Hosking and Ms. Goldbarg addressed the Tribunal on behalf of the AES Corporation. Mr. Torterola, Ms. Moglia and Ms. Vallejos Meana addressed the Tribunal on behalf of the Argentine Republic. The Tribunal posed questions to the parties, as provided in Rule 32(3) of the Arbitration Rules.

16. The Tribunal has deliberated and considered thoroughly the parties' written submissions on the question of jurisdiction and the oral arguments delivered in the course of the October 23, 24, 2004 hearing. As indicated in paragraphs 12 and 13 above, the consideration of the merits has been suspended until the issue of the Centre's jurisdiction and the Tribunal's competence has been decided by the Tribunal. Having considered the basic facts of the dispute, the ICSID Convention and the 1991 Argentina–US BIT, as well as the written and oral arguments of the parties' representatives, the Tribunal has reached the following decision on the question of jurisdiction.

II. Opening Considerations

A. Relevance of other ICSID Arbitral Tribunal's Decisions on Jurisdiction

17. Prior to establishing its position with regard to the five objections made by the Argentine Republic to its jurisdiction, the Tribunal shall address some preliminary considerations made by both parties in their respective argumentations. All of them were raised in relation with an opinion expressed by the Claimant in its Counter-Memorial on Jurisdiction.[2] In reaction to the objections filed by Argentina to the jurisdiction of this Tribunal, AES argued that:

> "Each of Argentina's five objections are based on similar
> or identical arguments presented by it in other factually
> similar arbitrations in which Argentina is the respondent.
> In every instance, the same arguments have either been
> rejected or the corresponding ICSID tribunal has decided
> to join this objection to the merits."

18. In its Counter-Memorial, AES further referred to several ICSID tribunal decisions on jurisdiction, including the *Vivendi* decisions I[3] and II[4], together with the *CMS*[5] and the *Azurix* decisions on jurisdiction[6]. Later, and in particular during the hearing, AES further referred to other decisions which, in the meantime, had become available, such as the *LG&E v. Argentina*[7], the *ENRON v. Argentina*[8] and the *SIEMENS A.G. v. Argentina*[9] decisions on jurisdiction.

---

[2] See The AES Corporation Counter-Memorial on Jurisdiction, February 20, 2004 at 8-12, §§ 18-30.

[3] *Compañía de Aguas del Aconquija S.A. & Compagnie Générale des Eaux v. Argentine Republic*, ICSID Case N° ARB/97/3, Award, November 21, 2000, 40 I.L.M. 426 (2001). Also available at http://www.worldbank.org/icsid/cases/ada_AwardoftheTribunal.pdf.

[4] Ibid., Decision on Annulment, July 3, 2002, 41 I.L.M. 1135 (2002). Also available at http://www.worldbank.org/icsid/cases/vivendi_annul.pdf.

[5] *CMS Gas Transmission Company. v. Argentine Republic*, ICSID Case N° ARB/01/8, Decision on Jurisdiction, July 17, 2003, 42 I.L.M. 788 (2003).

[6] *Azurix Corp. v. Argentine Republic*, ICSID Case N° ARB/01/12, Decision on Jurisdiction, December 8, 2003, 43 I.L.M. 262 (2004).

[7] *LG&E Energy Corp.,LG&E Capital Corp. and LG&E International, Inc v. Argentine Republic*, ICSID Case N° ARB/02/1, Decision on Jurisdiction, April 30, 2004.

[8] *Enron Corporation and Ponderosa Assets, L.P. v. Argentine Republic*, ICSID Case N° ARB/01/3, Decision of Jurisdiction (Ancillary Claim), August 2, 2004.

The argument made by the Claimant on the basis of these decisions, treated more or less as if they were precedents, tends to say that Argentina's objections to the jurisdiction of this Tribunal are moot if not even useless since these tribunals have already determined the answer to be given to identical or similar objections to jurisdiction.

19. In response, Argentina raises a series of issues. They deal respectively with the legal basis for the jurisdiction of the Tribunal and with the way in which, according to the Respondent, the Tribunal should interpret them for determining whether it has or has not jurisdiction on this case. These arguments must indeed be considered in relation with the delimitation of the task of the Tribunal at this stage of the proceedings.

20. After having recalled that the jurisdiction of ICSID arbitral tribunals is based upon the ICSID Convention (Art. 25), in conjunction with the bilateral treaty for the protection of investments in force between Argentina and the national State of the foreign investor, Respondent insists upon the specificity of each bilateral agreement as compared to others. Argentina says in particular that:

> "Each bilateral Treaty for the protection of investments has a different and defined scope of application. It is not a uniform text"[10].

21. Argentina further contends that:

> "The consent granted by signatory States of bilateral treaties shall not be extended by means of presumptions and analogies, or by attempting to turn the *lex specialis* into *lex general* (sic)."[11]

22. In addition, Argentina states that:

> "The reading of some awards may lead to believe that the tribunal has forgotten that it is acting in a sphere ruled by a *lex specialis* where generalizations are not usually wrong, but, what is worst, are illegitimate. Repeating decisions taken in other cases, without making the factual and legal distinctions, may constitute an excess of power

---

[9]   *Siemens A.G. v. Argentine Republic*, ICSID Case N° ARB/02/8, Decision on Jurisdiction of August 3, 2004.

[10]   See Argentine Republic's Reply on Jurisdiction, April 2, 2004 at 2-3, § 9.

[11]   Ibid. at 8, § 27.

and may affect the integrity of the international system for the protection of investments".[12]

23. For this Tribunal, Argentina is right to insist on the limits imposed on it as on any other arbitral ICSID tribunal. The provisions of Article 25 of the ICSID Convention together with fundamental principles of public international law dictate, among others, that the Tribunal respects:

a) the autonomy of the will of the Parties to the ICSID Convention as well as that of the Parties to the pertinent bilateral treaty on the protection of investments;

b) the rule according to which *"specialia generalibus derogant"*, from which it derives that treaty obligations prevail over rules of customary international law under the condition that the latter are not of a peremptory character;

c) the fact that the extent of the jurisdiction of each tribunal is determined by the combination of the pertinent provisions of two *"leges specialia"*: on the one hand, the ICSID Convention and, on the other hand, the BIT in force between the two concerned States; as the case may be, the arbitration clause in contracts between the private investor and the State or its emanation may also interfere with the two previous ones for determination of the scope of the tribunal's jurisdiction.

d) the rule according to which each decision or award delivered by an ICSID Tribunal is only binding on the parties to the dispute settled by this decision or award.[13] There is so far no rule of precedent in general international law; nor is there any within the specific ICSID system for the settlement of disputes between one State party to the Convention and the National of another State Party. This was in particular illustrated by diverging positions respectively taken by two ICSID tribunals on issues dealing with the interpretation of arguably similar language in two different BITs.[14] As rightly stated by the Tribunal in SGS v. Philippines:

> "...although different tribunals constituted under the ICSID system should in general seek to act consistently with each other, in the end it must be for each tribunal to exercise its competence in accordance with the applicable law, which will

---

[12] Ibid.

[13] Article 53 of the ICSID Convention.

[14] *SGS Société Genérale de Surveillance S.A. v. Islamic Republic of Pakistan*, ICSID Case N° ARB/01/13 and *SGS Société Genérale de Surveillance S.A v. Republic of the Philippines*, ICSID Case N° ARB/02/6.

by definition be different for each BIT and each Respondent State."[15]

The same position was echoed by the *ENRON* Tribunal on jurisdiction:

"The Tribunal agrees with the view expressed by the Argentine Republic in the hearing on jurisdiction held in respect of this dispute, to the effect that the decisions of ICSID tribunals are not binding precedents and that every case must be examined in the light of its own circumstances."[16]

24. The present Tribunal indeed agrees with Argentina that each BIT has its own identity; its very terms should consequently be carefully analyzed for determining the exact scope of consent expressed by its two Parties.

25. This is in particular the case if one considers that striking similarities in the wording of many BITs often dissimulate real differences in the definition of some key concepts, as it may be the case, in particular, for the determination of "investments" or for the precise definition of rights and obligations for each party.

26. From the above derive at least two consequences: the *first* is that the findings of law made by one ICSID tribunal in one case in consideration, among others, of the terms of a determined BIT, are not necessarily relevant for other ICSID tribunals, which were constituted for other cases; the *second* is that, although Argentina had already submitted similar objections to the jurisdiction of other tribunals prior to those raised in the present case before this Tribunal, Argentina has a valid and legitimate right to raise the objections it has chosen for opposing the jurisdiction of this Tribunal. According to Article 41(2) of the ICSID Convention:

"Any objection by a party to the dispute that that dispute is not within the jurisdiction of the Centre, or for other reasons is not within the competence of the Tribunal, shall be considered by the Tribunal which shall determine whether to deal with it as a preliminary question or to join it to the merits of the dispute."

---

[15] *SGS Société Genérale de Surveillance S.A v. Republic of the Philippines*, ICSID Case N° ARB/02/6, Decision of the Tribunal on Objections to Jurisdiction, January 29, 2004, available at http://www.worldbank.org/icsid/cases/SGSvPhil-final.pdf.

[16] *ENRON v. Argentina*, Decision on Jurisdiction (Ancillary Claim), August 2, 2004, at 8, § 25.

27. Under the benefit of the foregoing observations, the Tribunal would nevertheless reject the excessive assertion which would consist in pretending that, due to the specificity of each case and the identity of each decision on jurisdiction or award, absolutely no consideration might be given to other decisions on jurisdiction or awards delivered by other tribunals in similar cases.

28. In particular, if the basis of jurisdiction for these other tribunals and/or the underlying legal dispute in analysis present either a high level of similarity or, even more, an identity with those met in the present case, this Tribunal does not consider that it is barred, as a matter of principle, from considering the position taken or the opinion expressed by these other tribunals.

29. In that respect, it should be noted that the US-Argentina BIT, in conjunction with the ICSID Convention, provides the very same basis for the jurisdiction in this case and in some previous ones, as, in particular, those in which Argentina faced or is still facing a dispute with *ENRON Corp.*, *CMS*, *AZURIX Corp*, or *LG&E and others*; in each and every of these cases the tribunals respectively constituted have already delivered their decisions on jurisdiction.

30. An identity of the basis of jurisdiction of these tribunals, even when it meets with very similar if not even identical facts at the origin of the disputes, does not suffice to apply systematically to the present case positions or solutions already adopted in these cases. Each tribunal remains sovereign and may retain, as it is confirmed by ICSID practice, a different solution for resolving the same problem; but decisions on jurisdiction dealing with the same or very similar issues may at least indicate some lines of reasoning of real interest; this Tribunal may consider them in order to compare its own position with those already adopted by its predecessors and, if it shares the views already expressed by one or more of these tribunals on a specific point of law, it is free to adopt the same solution.

31. One may even find situations in which, although seized on the basis of another BIT as combined with the pertinent provisions of the ICSID Convention, a tribunal has set a point of law which, in essence, is or will be met in other cases whatever the specificities of each dispute may be. Such precedents may also be rightly considered, at least as a matter of comparison and, if so considered by the Tribunal, of inspiration.

32. The same may be said for the interpretation given by a precedent decision or award to some relevant facts which are basically at the origin of two or several different disputes, keeping carefully in mind the actual specificities still featuring each case. If the present Tribunal concurs with the analysis and interpretation of these facts as they generated certain special consequences for

the parties to this case as well as for those of another case, it may consider this earlier interpretation as relevant.

33. From a more general point of view, one can hardly deny that the institutional dimension of the control mechanisms provided for under the ICSID Convention might well be a factor, in the longer term, for contributing to the development of a common legal opinion or *jurisprudence constante*, to resolve some difficult legal issues discussed in many cases, inasmuch as these issues share the same substantial features.

B.   The Law Applicable for this Tribunal's Jurisdiction.

34. There seems to be a substantial agreement among the parties as to the identification of the law applicable by this Tribunal to assess whether it has jurisdiction in the present case.

35. The requirements for ICSID jurisdiction are set forth in Article 25 of the ICSID Convention, which provides as follows:

> "(1)   The jurisdiction of the Centre shall extend to any legal dispute arising directly out of an investment between a Contracting State (or any constituent subdivision or agency of a Contracting State designated to the Centre by that State) and a national of another Contracting State, which the parties to the dispute consent in writing to submit to the Centre. When the parties have given their consent, no party may withdraw its consent unilaterally.
>
> (2)   'National of another Contracting State' means :
> (…)
>
> b) any juridical person which had the nationality of a Contracting State other than the State party to the dispute on the date on which the parties consented to submit such dispute to conciliation or arbitration and any juridical person which had the nationality of the Contracting State party to the dispute on that date and which, because of foreign control, the parties have agreed should be treated as a national of another Contracting State for the purposes of this Convention."

36. In addition to the jurisdictional requirements under the ICSID Convention, Article VII of the US-Argentina BIT requires the following before an arbitration may be brought:

"1. For the purpose of this Article, an investment dispute is a dispute between a Party and a national or company of the other Party arising out of or relating to (a) an investment agreement between that Party and such national or company; (b) an investment authorization granted by the Party's foreign investment authority (if any such authorization exists) to such national or company; or (c) an alleged breach of any right conferred or created by this Treaty with respect to an investment.
2. In the event of an investment dispute, the parties to the dispute should initially seek a resolution through consultation and negotiation. If the dispute cannot be settled amicably, the national or company concerned may choose to submit the dispute for resolution (…)
c) in accordance with the terms of paragraph 3.

3. a) Provided that the national or company concerned has not submitted the dispute for resolution under paragraph 2 (a) and (b) and that six months have elapsed from the date on which the dispute arose, the national or company concerned may choose to consent in writing to the submission of the dispute for settlement by binding arbitration :
    i.)   to the International Centre for the Settlement of Investment Disputes ("Centre") established by the Convention on the Settlement of Investment Disputes between States and Nationals of other States, done at Washington, March 16, 1965 ('ICSID Convention'), provided that the Party is a party to such convention."

37. It is in the light of these provisions that the objections raised to the jurisdiction of this Tribunal by Argentina will be hereafter considered.

38. As rightly asserted by Argentina, the BIT establishes in which conditions and events Respondent consented to the ICSID jurisdiction. Article 25 of the ICSID Convention, in turn, provides the requirements for jurisdiction.[17].

39. Although some of the views expressed by the parties concern aspects relating to the merits of the dispute, the Tribunal, at this stage, has only to decide on the issue of jurisdiction.

---

[17]   See Argentina's Reply on Jurisdiction, April 2nd, 2004, at 17, § 61.

III. Objections to Jurisdiction.

A. First objection: absence of a legal dispute.

40. Argentina's first objection to jurisdiction is based on the purported absence of a legal dispute. This objection deals basically with the definition of what is to be understood under "legal dispute" in the sense in which it is used by Article 25 (1) of the ICSID Convention. This is an issue that has been abundantly considered by a number of commentators.[18]

41. AES for its part answers by asserting first, that it is "the proper claimant"[19] and second, that there is a legal dispute[20]. From this second point of view, AES rebuffs in particular the way in which Respondent tends to interpret and use in its own argumentation the Methanex decision.[21]

42. The Tribunal considers that only the second out of the two points made by Claimant in response to Argentina's arguments is at this stage appropriate. The issue of whether a parent company can bring claims for the losses it has suffered as a result of its investment in a host State whether or not that investment is made in or through a subsidiary, discussed by AES in its Counter-Memorial on Jurisdiction,[22] shall be considered later in this decision, in relation with the fourth objection to jurisdiction articulated by Argentina.

43. The Tribunal wants to stress that in the present case there are, in substance, two elements to be met for a dispute to be considered as a *legal* one in conformity with the requirement set forth in Article 25 (1) of the ICSID Convention. The first deals with the intrinsic definition of what is a legal

---

[18] See for instance Amerasinghe, CF, The Jurisdiction of the International Centre for the Settlement of Investment Disputes, p. 170-172; R. Kovar, La compétence du Centre International pour le règlement des différends relatifs aux investissements, in Investissements Etrangers et Arbitrage entre Etats et Personnes Privées, La Convention B.I.R.D. du 18 mars 1965 (Centre de Recherche sur le Droit des Marchés et des Investissements Internationaux de la Faculté de Droit et des Sciences Economiques de Dijon, ed. 25 (1969), p. 29; G.R. Delaume, La Convention pour le règlement des différends relatifs aux investissements entre Etats et ressortissants d'autres Etats, 93 Journal du droit international, 26, 35 (1966); Ch. Schreuer, The ICSID Convention: A Commentary, Cambridge Univ. Press, 2001, 103-106.

[19] See AES Counter-Memorial on Jurisdiction at 13, §§ 33-40.

[20] Ibid. at 16, §§ 41-47.

[21] Methanex Corporation v. United States of America, NAFTA/UNCITRAL Arbitration Proceedings, Preliminary Award on Jurisdiction of August 7, 2002. Respondent's Memorial on Jurisdiction, Exhibit ALRA2.

[22] At 13, §§ 33-40.

dispute; the second deals with the inherent logic which presided over the creation of ICSID.

a. In general terms, as it is also more generally the case in international law, and according to the definition recalled by the International Court of Justice in the Case concerning East Timor, a dispute in the legal sense is:

> "a disagreement on a point of law or fact, a conflict of legal views or interests between parties"[23]

b. Within the specific context of the ICSID Convention, as rightly commented by Professor Ch. Schreuer with regard to Article 25 (1):

> "It is submitted that the disagreement between the parties must also have some practical relevance to their relationship and must not be purely theoretical. It is not the task of the Centre to clarify legal questions *in abstracto*."[24]

44. The Tribunal consequently considers that the true test of jurisdiction consists in determining

(a) whether, in its claim, AES raises some *legal* issues in relation with a concrete situation, and

(b) if the Tribunal's determination of the answer to be given to these issues would have some practical and concrete consequences.

It is enough, here, to state that, considering the very features of AES' claims the Tribunal be also *prima facie* convinced that AES' interest may have not only been "merely affected" but hurt.

45. Yet, on the basis of the elements already brought by the Memorial filed by AES together with a number of supporting evidence, AES' claim seems *prima facie* a substantial one. It deals with a series of legal issues which manifest an evident disagreement among the parties.

46. AES declares to have invested 1 billion US dollars in the sector of electricity in Argentina; AES alleges to be in control of 6 generators and 3

---

[23] 1995 ICJ Reports 89, § 99 with reference to earlier cases.
[24] Ch. Schreuer, The ICSID Convention, op.cit. at 102, § 36.

distributors of electricity in Argentina; AES invokes the breach by Argentina of articles II(2)(a), II(2)(b), II(2)(c) and IV(1) of the Treaty binding upon Argentina and the United States of America on the protection of investments.[25] It is precisely the substantial interest constituted by the importance of AES investment that the Claimant argues to have been affected by a determined Argentine legislation. AES depicts in particular some Argentine legislation including the Executive Decree N° 570/01, the National Emergency Law N° 25.561 and posterior decrees of application as being at the origin of the breach by Argentina of its international obligations. AES further provided the Tribunal with a detailed estimation of the cost of damages produced to its investment in Argentina by the enforcement of this legislation. Claimant has also articulated a documented claim for compensation.

47. All these elements are *prima facie* convincing evidence for considering that the AES' claims involve a legal dispute in the terms of Article 25 of the ICSID Convention, therefore falling within the ICSID jurisdiction.

B. Second Objection: the legal dispute does not arise directly out of an investment.

48. Article 25 (1) of the ICSID Convention not only retains that the jurisdiction of the Centre shall extend to any legal dispute. It also says that such a legal dispute must arise "*directly* out of an investment". On the basis of this supplementary condition, a second objection to jurisdiction was raised by Argentina. This objection is that the measures alleged by AES are not specifically related to AES investments. They were measures of general bearing, which aimed at restoring the economy of the country at the national level; they did not target AES in particular.

49. According to Argentina, AES must "demonstrate a direct, proximate and immediate causation between the measure and its alleged investment."[26]

50. AES response to this is that "it is sufficient that AES has made a *prima facie* showing that the measures instituted by Argentina directly affected its investments."[27] In relation with this point, AES further refutes the interpretation and use made by Argentina of the *Methanex* decision.[28]

---

[25] See The AES Corporation Memorial on the Merits, October 6, 2003, at 84, §§ 218-376.

[26] Argentina's Memorial on Jurisdiction, at 16, § 43.

[27] AES' Counter-Memorial on Jurisdiction, at 18, §§ 50-53.

[28] Ibid., §§ 54-58.

51. In connection with these allegations, the Tribunal notes that the factual and legal elements at the origin of the present dispute are basically the same as those considered by other tribunals which, at the same time, share the same sources of jurisdiction (ICSID Convention and US-Argentina BIT). So was it, among others, in the *CMS*, the *Azurix* and the *ENRON* cases.

52. It is then of real interest to look at the way in which these tribunals considered the measures reputed by claimants to be at the origin of the damage directly produced on their respective investments.

53. In particular, the Argentinean legislation which brought to an end the regime of convertibility and parity of the Argentine peso with the United States dollar[29] is, due to its concrete consequences on the interests of claimants invested in Argentina prior to December 2001, at the source of the respective claims filed before ICSID in the cases already mentioned above.

54. In the decision on jurisdiction issued by the ICSID Tribunal in the *CMS* case, in particular, the Tribunal referred to the legislation referred to above in paragraph 53 and said pertinently that it should make:

> "a clear distinction between measures of a general economic nature, particularly in the context of the economic and financial emergency discussed above, and measures specifically directed to the investment's operation."[30]

55. The same tribunal further observed:

> "What is brought under the jurisdiction of the Centre is not the general measures in themselves but the extent to which they may violate those specific commitments."[31]

56. In the present case, the situation seems *prima facie* to be the same. At this stage, the Tribunal notes that AES' claims are not broadly based on Argentina's general economic policies. Their ground is provided by the fact that the regulatory and legal framework AES relied upon in making its investments was dismantled by the Argentinean legislative measures here at stake. It is, in particular, Argentina's alleged refusal to apply a previously agreed tariff calculation and adjustment regime which is at the core of AES' claims. It is also the impact of the legislative and regulatory measures taken by Argentina which

---

[29] National Emergency Act N°25.561 in particular.
[30] *CMS*, Decision on Jurisdiction, at § 25.
[31] Ibid. at § 27.

is reputed by the Claimant to have breached the commitment made to it by the host State through the US-Argentina BIT.

57. This Tribunal shares consequently the views earlier expressed by the Tribunal in the *CMS* decision on jurisdiction. What is at stake in the present case, as it was in the *CMS* one, are not the measures of a general economic nature taken by Argentina in 2001 and 2002 but their specific negative impact on the investments made by AES. As a sovereign State, the Argentine Republic had a right to adopt its economic policies; but this does not mean that the foreign investors under a system of guarantee and protection could be deprived of their respective rights under the instruments providing them with these guarantees and protection. Without anticipating, at this stage, on the consideration of the issue, whether this delicate balance between the respective rights of the host State and those of the investor were respected in substance, the present Tribunal states that it has jurisdiction for considering this issue.

58. It should be further noted that reliance by Respondent on the *Methanex* case is inaccurate. As stated above, and in conformity with what has been strongly asserted from the outset by Argentina itself, one should take each agreement on its term and avoid drawing out of other treaties which are *not* applicable to this case, any conclusion neglecting the substantial difference of terminology, scope and meaning existing between these instruments.

59. Now, it is well known that *Methanex* relied on the NAFTA. In that multilateral treaty, only binding upon the United States, Canada and Mexico, the definition of "investors" and of "investments" used in Chapter 11 (Investment) is quite specific in terms and substance. This definition is all the way narrower than the definition of "investment" provided by Article VII(1) of the US-Argentina BIT. The latter states that "an investment dispute is a dispute…arising out of or relating to (a) an investment agreement between the Party and such national or company;…or (c) an alleged breach of any right conferred or created by this Treaty with respect to an investment". This definition is much larger than the one at stake in *Methanex*, since NAFTA Article 1101(1) provides that Chapter 11 "applies to measures adopted or maintained by a Party to: a) investors of another Party [or] b) investments of investors of another Party in the territory of a Party." It should be stressed that the element of "directness" under NAFTA Chapter 11 deals with the way in which the measures at stake affect the investor or the investment. The measure must directly affect the investment. "Directness" in ICSID Convention (Art. 25) is something different.

60. As to the interpretation of the terms "any legal dispute arising directly out of an investment" used in Article 25 of the ICSID Convention, it is well established by commentators relying on constant practice that it should not be

given a restrictive interpretation.[32] Under this provision, directness has to do with the relationship between the dispute and the investment rather than between the measure and the investment.

61. As a result, in the light both of Article VII of the US-Argentina BIT and of the interpretation to be given to Article 25 (1) of the ICSID Convention this Tribunal rejects the second objection to its jurisdiction raised by Argentina.

C. Third objection : AES' Claim is not Ripe.

62. Argentina contends that, due to ongoing negotiations still taking place between AES' local subsidiaries and Argentine authorities, either at the national or at the local level, AES has prematurely brought its claim before ICSID. In relation with this assertion, Respondent further argues that the damages claimed in the electricity generation companies are not quantifiable.

63. AES reacts by asserting first that "any 'negotiations' by distribution companies do not strip ICSID of jurisdiction"[33] and that, in fact, no real progress has been made with the renegotiation process in Argentina (sic at the October 23-24, 2004 hearing). AES also argues that electricity generation damages are quantifiable and recoverable.[34]

64. In respect to the first aspect of Argentina's objection, according to which ongoing negotiations would prevent the claim from being legitimately filed, the Tribunal recalls what it has already said with regard to the basis and scope of its jurisdiction. This basis, as insisted upon by Argentina itself in its Memorial on Jurisdiction, is predominantly defined by the specific instruments binding upon the Argentine Republic i.e. the BIT and the ICSID Convention. This does not mean that the Tribunal could not apply, as the case may be, any customary rule of international law which it would consider compatible with the pertinent provisions of these two "*leges specialia*."

65. The Tribunal recognizes that a negotiation process, being a diplomatic or political means of settlement of disputes and not a judicial one, presents some specific features. Consequently, negotiation should not be assimilated to *judicial* remedies. Still, there is no rule relevant in this procedure, either in the ICSID Convention or in the US-Argentina BIT, which would subordinate recourse to the ICSID system of settlement to any "prior exhaustion of local negotiations."

---

[32] See in particular Ch. Schreuer, op.cit.supra at 116, § 71, quoting *Holiday Inns v. Morocco*, ICSID Case N° ARB/72/. See also the *Amco* and *Kaiser Bauxite v. Jamaica* cases, as referred to by Ch. Schreuer at 119-120, § 76.

[33] AES' Counter-Memorial on Jurisdiction, at 23 §§ 60-67.

[34] Ibid. §§ 68-69.

66. In its Memorial on Jurisdiction, the Argentine Republic did not rely on any specific or general source of international law for supporting its argument. Argentina only referred to the case law of the US Supreme Court,[35] which, as such, is irrelevant for the present case. There is no need here for having recourse to any "general principle of law" as mentioned in Article 38 of the Statute of the International Court of Justice. It is enough to concentrate on the two treaties mentioned above, the US-Argentina BIT and the ICSID Convention.

67. In the US-Argentina BIT, Article VII (2) provides:

> "In the event of an investment dispute, the parties to the dispute should initially seek a resolution through consultation and negotiation. If the dispute cannot be settled amicably, the national or company concerned may choose to submit the dispute for resolution (…)"

68. In the present case, the Tribunal notes that it is only following the established fact that the parties had been unable to resolve the dispute within six month that AES filed its Request for Arbitration with ICSID; and it did so pursuant to Article VII(3) of the US-Argentina BIT.[36]

69. As for Article 25 of the ICSID Convention, the Tribunal reiterates that there is no rule according to which a "legal dispute" should only be brought to ICSID subject to prior exhaustion of local remedies, including negotiations between the investor and the authorities of the host State. On the contrary, the ICSID system has been established on the basis of a reversed rule of exhaustion of local remedies. Under Article 26 of the Convention, for entering into play, exhaustion of local remedies shall be expressly required as a condition of the consent of one party to arbitration under the Convention. Absent this requirement, exhaustion of local remedies cannot be a precondition for an ICSID Tribunal to have jurisdiction. What is only needed is that the claimant prima facie demonstrates that there is a "legal dispute arising directly out of an investment between a Contracting State (…) and a national of another Contracting State" and that both disputing parties have consented in writing to dispute settlement through ICSID arbitration. The conditions set forth in Article 25 of the ICSID Convention are cumulative but do not give room for further conditions.

70. International practice confirms the interpretation given above. Without even considering here the numerous decisions that rejected recourse to local judicial remedies as a condition for jurisdiction, no ICSID Tribunal so far has

---

[35] Argentina's Memorial on Jurisdiction, op.cit.supra, at § 48. Abbott Laboratories v. Gardner, 387 US 136 (1967).
[36] See Request for Arbitration dated November 5, 2002.

subordinated its jurisdiction to the demonstration of prior ending of negotiations between the parties to the dispute. On the contrary, confronted with a very similar argument by Argentina, the Tribunal in *CMS* declared that:

> "... it is not for the Tribunal to rule on the perspectives of the negotiation process or on what TGN might do in respect of its shareholders, as these are matters between Argentina and TGN or between TGN and its shareholders."[37]

71. In the present case, equally, negotiations are reputed to go on in particular between two distributors, EDELAP and EDEN on the one side, the Argentinean authorities, respectively at the federal and at the local level, on the other side. But, even if the taking into account of such negotiations were relevant, it is impossible for this Tribunal to assess whether there is any reasonable prospect for any settlement to be reached at one stage or the other throughout negotiations.

72. With respect to the second aspect of the objection raised by Respondent, which consists in saying that the damages claimed by AES in relation with electricity generation are not quantifiable, the Tribunal recalls that AES has provided the Tribunal on December 2003 with an expert report on damages. This document sets out in detail the quantification of AES' claim as it relates to electricity generation.[38]

73. Furthermore, as rightly stated by the *Azurix* tribunal:

> "the question before the Tribunal at this stage is whether it has jurisdiction; whether the Claimant can prove loss is a matter to be considered as part of the merits."[39]

74. This Tribunal shares this view and finds accordingly no ground for accepting the third objection raised by Argentina to its jurisdiction.

D. Fourth Objection: AES is not the investor.

75. The Argentine Republic argues that AES has failed to prove its status as an investor for the purposes of the US-Argentina BIT. According to Argentina:

> "a) in view that the BIT with USA includes no specific provision on the applicable law, pursuant to article 42 of

---

[37] *CMS*, Decision on Jurisdiction at § 86.

[38] See AES' Counter-Memorial on Jurisdiction at § 67, referring to LECG Report at 91-92.

[39] Azurix Decision on Jurisdiction, at § 101.

the ICSID Convention the law of the State that is a party to the dispute should apply, including its international private law rules and those international law rules that may be applicable, b) therefore, the determination of the rules applicable to the nationality of the parties under the BIT with USA shall be judged by the Argentine international private law, c) consequently, AES should have proven its lawful creation. This is so pursuant to Argentine international private law."[40]

76. AES answers by saying that it has efficiently proven to be a US corporate citizen[41] as well as it has demonstrated that it owns and controls the AES' entities by providing the Tribunal with sworn witness statements by top managers from AES and its subsidiaries.[42]

77. For the Tribunal, the Respondent's position does not start from the right assumption as to the law applicable to the determination of the nationality of the private investor. First, as rightly contended by Claimant, the clear terms of the US-Argentina BIT, which define a company, should be taken into account. Pursuant to Article I(1)(b) of this treaty:

"Company' of a Party means any kind of corporation, company, association, state enterprise, or other organization, legally constituted under the laws and regulations of a Party or political subdivision thereof whether or not organized for pecuniary gain, and whether privately or governmentally owned."

78. *Second*, Argentina wrongly considers that Article 42 of the ICSID Convention is applicable to this issue of nationality. This is not correct. As rightly pointed out by Professor Ch. Schreuer:

"[An] issue that is not governed by the rule of Art. 42 is the nationality of the investor. The nationality of a natural person is determined primarily by the law of the State whose nationality is claimed (...). The nationality of a juridical person is determined by the criteria of incorporation or seat of the company in question subject to pertinent agreements, treaties and legislation."[43]

---

[40] See the Argentine Republic Reply on Jurisdiction § 88.
[41] AES' Counter-Memorial on Jurisdiction, §§ 71-76.
[42] Ibid. §§ 77-80.
[43] Ch. Schreuer, The ICSID Convention: A Commentary, p.cit.supra, at 554-555, § 5.

79. The same author indicates also that:

> "During the Convention's preparatory work, it was generally acknowledged that nationality would be determined by reference to the law of the State whose nationality is claimed subject, where appropriate, to the applicable rules of international law (History, Vol. II, pp. 67, 286, 321, 448, 580, 705, 839)."[44]

80. In the present case, the Tribunal is satisfied that AES, already at the stage of its Request for Arbitration, has indicated, and convincingly proved, to be incorporated in the State of Delaware with headquarters in Arlington, Virginia (USA). This was in particular evidenced by the production of a certificate signed by Mr. Leith Mann, AES' Assistant Secretary, attaching a true copy of AES' Certificate of Incorporation authenticated by Delaware's Secretary of State, in conformity with Delaware legislation. Mr. Mann also confirmed that at the time the Request for Arbitration was submitted the Certificate had not subsequently been modified and remained in force.[45].

81. Still under the same fourth objection, Argentina contends that AES has not "proven to have acquired the shares that allegedly give it a majority interest in the [operation] companies" because the evidence "appear[s] exclusively on information issued by claimant" rather than being "proven in a certifying way". Respondent further stated that:

> "Ownership of or control over national are merely claimed and appear exclusively on information issued by claimant. For the purpose of determining the jurisdiction, AES should have proven in a certifying way the above mentioned requirements."[46]

82. The Tribunal takes note of the fact that the Argentine Republic does not really seem to substantially challenge that AES actually became the majority shareholder of the operating companies. Neither does Argentina raise some doubts as to the true ownership or control by AES of the companies concerned. Argentina's argument remains basically of a formal or procedural nature. What is questioned by Respondent is "the probative value" of the material submitted by Claimant for evidencing its control as a majority shareholder of the said companies.[47] This material consists of a sworn witness statement by Mr. Robert

---

[44]   Ibid. at 267, § 430.
[45]   AES' Request for Arbitration at § 2 and Exhibit B.
[46]   Argentina's Reply on Jurisdiction, at 22-23, § 90.
[47]   Argentina's Reply on Jurisdiction, at § 94.

Venerus (Vice-President, AES Business Development Group) together with other witness statements by other managers in particular of EDELAP, EDEN and EDES, or AES Andes Generation Assets.[48] These witness statements refer to corporate charts showing in detail the ownership structure of each of the AES' operating companies.[49] In addition, AES provides a summary of the percentage it owns in each of the subsidiaries.[50] In its Rejoinder on Jurisdiction, AES recognized that there had been a minor miscalculation in percentage ownership and further filed an erratum, which substantially did not alter the fact that AES is the majority shareholder in each and every one of the companies concerned.[51]

83. It is consequently for the Tribunal to appreciate whether it is satisfied at this stage that the material and information provided by AES is accurate for evidencing its ownership and control of all the companies concerned. In this respect, the Tribunal notes that production of expert and witnesses reports is common practice in international arbitration. In consideration of this practice, the Tribunal itself, at its first session, had specifically requested that Claimant file such documentary evidence.[52] This is in conformity with Arbitration Rule 34, which states that the Tribunal shall be the judge of the "admissibility of any evidence adduced and of its probative value."[53]

84. Without excluding the possibility of requiring Claimant, later in the course of proceedings, to produce further evidence of ownership and control of its subsidiaries in Argentina, pursuant to Rule 34 mentioned above as well as to Article 1 of the Protocol of the US-Argentina BIT, the Tribunal considers that it was so far sufficiently informed and has no reason to consider in essence the kind of material produced by AES in this respect to be inaccurate.

85. As a further related issue, the Tribunal wants to raise briefly the question of the actual protection of shareholders and that of their *jus standi* before an ICSID Tribunal.

86. Without any need to look at the actual evolution of general international law on this matter, which, as such, was convincingly analyzed by the Tribunal in *CMS*,[54] it suffice here to recall that the very terms in which the US-Argentina

---

[48] See AES' Counter-Memorial on Jurisdiction, at 30, § 78-80.

[49] See witness statements of Messrs. Banderet, Pujals, Giorgio, Dutrey.

[50] AES' Memorial on the Merits, Exhibit 52.

[51] AES' Rejoinder on Jurisdiction of, April 26, 2004 at § 55.

[52] Summary Minutes of the First Session of the Tribunal, Washington D.C, July 8, 2003.

[53] See ICSID Basic Documents, ICSID/15, January 1985 at 77.

[54] See *CMS* Decision on jurisdiction, at §§ 43-48, 49-56, 57-65.

BIT defines an "investment" provide a solid ground for recognizing AES' legal interest as a claimant for alleged losses suffered as a result of its investment in Argentina.

87. As stated in Article I(1)(a) of the BIT, a claim may be filed in relation to an "investment" as it consists in:

> "...every kind of investment in the territory of one Party owned or controlled directly or indirectly by nationals or companies of the other Party..."

88. This definition is a very wide one and it makes no doubt that AES' economic involvement in the concerned companies generating and distributing electricity in Argentina falls under the definition provided by this provision of the BIT. This involvement equally satisfies the requirements for recognizing an international investment. They realize contribution in capital over a reasonably lengthy period of time for the economic development of the host State, an operation AES has accepted to share the inherent risks which it presents.

89. The Tribunal meets the views expressed on the same basis by other ICSID tribunals dealing with the same BIT; in particular tribunals' decisions on jurisdiction, respectively, in the *Lanco*[55], the *CMS*[56] and the *Azurix* cases[57]. AES' *jus standi* in the present case is not subject to doubt, not only, as seen earlier, because AES has a legal dispute with the Argentine Republic but also because AES is the proper claimant.

E. Fifth Objection: Forum Selection Clause Precludes ICSID Arbitration

90. According to Argentina, the "Argentine Companies AES claims to control have executed national forum selection clauses, with express waiver of all other authority and jurisdiction. That circumstance prevents this arbitration from proceeding."[58]

91. Claimant first observes that Argentina makes reference only to the concession contracts and related documents pertaining to some entities (EDES, EDELAP, Alicurá and Hidroeléctrica San Juan) but to none of the other AES Entities.[59] AES also relies on the case law of recent ICSID tribunals which

---

[55] Lanco International, Inc.v. Argentine Republic, ICSID Case N° ARB/97/6, Preliminary Decision Jurisdiction of the Arbitral Tribunal, December 18, 1998, printed at 40 I.L.M. 457 at §10 (2001).
[56] *CMS* Decision on Jurisdiction at § 68.
[57] *Azurix* Decision on Jurisdiction at § 74.
[58] Argentina' Memorial on Jurisdiction at § 65.
[59] AES' Counter-Memorial on Jurisdiction at § 82.

rejected the same argument in several other ICSID arbitrations in which Argentina is the respondent as well as in some other cases involving other countries[60]. AES contends that, as a national of the US, it is entitled to have Argentina's breach of international law determined by this Tribunal, as is expressly contemplated by the US-Argentina BIT.[61]

92. As a matter of fact, Argentina's argumentation is inaccurate inasmuch as it establishes confusion between two distinct legal orders: the international and the national one. What is at stake is an alleged breach of Argentina's obligations in international law as set out in the US-Argentina BIT, of which AES, as a national company of the United States, may seek immediate reparation through the special ICSID system of settlement of disputes; this is in exception to the classical and ordinary means provided under general international law by the display of diplomatic protection exercise by the national State of the company alleging to have suffered damage.

93. As for them, the Entities concerned have consented to a forum selection clause electing Administrative Argentine law and exclusive jurisdiction of Argentine administrative tribunals in the concession contracts and related documents. But this exclusivity only plays within the Argentinean legal order, for matters in relation with the execution of these concession contracts. They do not preclude AES from exercising its rights as resulting, within the international legal order from two international treaties, namely the US-Argentina BIT and the ICSID Convention.

94. In other terms, the present Tribunal has jurisdiction over any alleged breach by Argentina of its obligations under the US-Argentina BIT. As such, it has no jurisdiction over any breach of the concession contracts binding upon the companies controlled by AES and the Argentine public authorities under administrative Argentine law, unless such breach would at the same time result in a violation by the host State of its obligations towards the US private investors under the BIT.

95. The Tribunal concurs with a position already adopted by previous tribunals confronted with the same argument raised by Argentina. In *CMS*, the Tribunal took note of the decisions already rendered in *Lanco*, *Vivendi* I and *Vivendi II*, which had rejected the very same argument. It said:

> "The Tribunal shares the views expressed in those
> precedents. It therefore holds that the clauses in the
> License or its Terms referring certain kinds of disputes to

---

[60]   Ibid. § 83ff.
[61]   Ibid. at § 90.

the local courts of the Argentine Republic are not a bar to the assertion of jurisdiction by an ICSID tribunal under the [US-Argentina BIT], as the functions of these various instruments are different."[62]

96. Further to this decision, the Azurix Tribunal maintained the same analysis. It also rejected the Argentinean argument in the following terms:

"The tribunals in the cases cited concluded that such forum selection clauses did not exclude their jurisdiction because the subject-matter of any proceeding before the domestic courts under the contractual agreements in question and the dispute before the ICSID tribunal was different and therefore the forum selection clauses did not apply. This reasoning applies equally to the waiver of jurisdiction clause in this case."[63]

97. The present Tribunal cannot but share the views already expressed by these tribunals, dealing with the same argument, repeated again and again by Argentina. In particular, this Tribunal wants to stress that the comparison raised by Respondent in its Reply on Jurisdiction[64] between the waiver of jurisdiction met in this case and the famous "Calvo Clause" is inaccurate.

98. This is so simply because this very clause only made sense by reference to the general international law rule of diplomatic protection; the "Calvo Clause" was in essence a clause by which private persons mistakenly pretended to renounce to a right which in law did not belong to them but to their national State: the right for this State to exercise in favor of its nationals its diplomatic protection.

99. Since under the ICSID system of settlement of disputes, exercise of diplomatic protection is per *definition* put aside, it is irrelevant to compare it with a clause the rationale of which is inseparable from diplomatic protection. As a consequence, the Tribunal cannot but reject Argentina's fifth objection.

---

[62] *CMS* Decision on Jurisdiction at § 76.
[63] *Azurix* Decision on Jurisdiction at § 79.
[64] Argentina's Reply on Jurisdiction at § 144-155.

IV. Conclusion.

100.   For the reasons stated above the Tribunal decides that the present dispute is within the jurisdiction of the Centre and the competence of the Tribunal. The Tribunal has, accordingly, made the necessary Order for the continuation of the procedure pursuant to Arbitration Rule 41(4).

Prof. Pierre-Marie Dupuy

President

[signature]

Prof. Karl-Heinz Böckstiegel

Arbitrator

[signature]

Prof. Domingo Bello-Janeiro

Arbitrador

[signature]

ANNEX 2

International Centre for Settlement

of Investment Disputes

SAIPEM S.p.A.

CLAIMANT

v.

THE PEOPLE'S REPUBLIC OF BANGLADESH

RESPONDENT

ICSID Case No. ARB/05/07

DECISION ON JURISDICTION

AND RECOMMENDATION ON PROVISIONAL MEASURES

Rendered by an Arbitral Tribunal composed of:

Prof. Gabrielle Kaufmann-Kohler, President

Prof. Christoph H. Schreuer, Arbitrator

Sir Philip Otton, Arbitrator

Mrs. Martina Polasek, Secretary to the Arbitral Tribunal

TABLE OF CONTENTS

TABLE OF ABBREVIATIONS

Arbitration Rules ICSID Rules of Procedure for Arbitration Proceedings

BIT	Bilateral investment treaty; specifically "Agreement Between the Government of the Republic of Italy and the Government of the People's Republic of Bangladesh on the Promotion and Protection of Investments" of 20 March 1990
C-Mem.	Bangladesh's Counter-Memorial on the objections to jurisdiction and the merits of 14 May 2006
Contract	of 14 February 1990
Exh. C-	Claimant [Saipem]'s Exhibits
Exh. R-	Respondent [Bangladesh]'s Exhibits
ICSID	International Centre for Settlement of Investment Disputes
ICSID Convention	Convention on the Settlement of Investment Disputes between States and Nationals of other States
IDA	International Development Association
Mem.	Saipem's Statement of Claim of 20 February 2006
RA or Request	Saipem's Request for Arbitration of 5 October 2004
Rejoinder J.	Saipem's Rejoinder on Objections to Jurisdiction dated 14 September 2006
Reply J.	Bangladesh's Reply on Jurisdiction dated 18 August 2006
Response J.	Saipem's Reply [Response] on Objections to Jurisdiction of 14 July 2006
Tr. J. [I/II] [page:line]	Transcript of the hearing on jurisdiction [day one/day two]

190

I.   FACTS RELEVANT TO JURISDICTION

1.   This chapter summarizes the factual background of this arbitration insofar as it is necessary to rule on Bangladesh's objections to jurisdiction.

1.   THE PARTIES

1.1   The Claimant

2.   The Claimant, Saipem S.p.A ("Saipem" or the "Claimant"), is a company incorporated and existing under the laws of Italy. Its principal office is situated at Via Martiri di Cefalonia, 67, 20097 San Donato Milanese, Milan, Italy.

3.   The Claimant is represented in this arbitration by Professors Antonio Crivellaro and Luca Radicati di Brozolo and Mr. Andrea Carta Mantiglia, BONELLI EREDE PAPPALARDO, Via Barozzi 1, 20122 Milan, Italy.

1.2   The Respondent

4.   The Respondent is the People's Republic of Bangladesh ("Bangladesh" or the "Respondent").

5.   The Respondent is represented in this arbitration by Messrs. Ajmalul Hossain QC, Mejbahur Rahman and Syed A Hossain, A. HOSSSAIN & ASSOCIATES LAW OFFICES, 3/B Outer Circular Road, Maghbazar, Dhaka-1217, Bangladesh.

2.   THE PROJECT AND THE DISPUTE

2.1   The pipeline contract

6.   The Bangladesh Oil Gas and Mineral Corporation (Petrobangla) is a State entity established under the Bangladesh Oil, Gas and Mineral Corporation Ordinance of 1985 as amended by the Bangladesh Oil, Gas and Mineral Corporation Act of 1989.

7.   On 14 February 1990, Saipem and Petrobangla entered into a contract to build a pipeline of 409 km to carry condensate and gas in various locations of the north east of Bangladesh (the "Contract"). The contract price amounted to USD 34,796,140 and BDT 415,664,200. The project was sponsored by the World Bank and financed to a large extent by the International Development Association (IDA).

191

8.   Clause 1.2.5 of the Contract afforded Petrobangla the right to retain 10% of each progress payment due to Saipem as Retention Money up to an amount equivalent to 5% of the total contract price, *i.e.*, USD 1,739,807 plus BDT 20,783,210 (the "Retention Money"). The Retention Money was to be released to Saipem in two tranches, half of it not later than 30 days from the issuance of the Final Taking Over Certificate by Petrobangla, and the remaining half not later than 30 days from the issuance of the Final Acceptance Certificate by Petrobangla.

9.   The same Clause 1.2.5 of the Contract provided that Petrobangla could release the second half of the Retention Money prior to the Final Acceptance Certificate against a Warranty Bond of equal value from a bank acceptable to Petrobangla (the "Warranty Bond").

10.   The Contract was governed by the laws of Bangladesh and contained the following arbitration clause:

> If any dispute, question or difference should arise between the parties to this Contract with regard to rights and obligations hereunder which cannot be settled amicably, such dispute, question or difference shall be finally settled under the Rules of Conciliation and Arbitration of the International Chamber of Commerce by three arbitrators, one to be nominated by each party and the third arbitrator shall be appointed by the two arbitrators in accordance with the said Rules and if the arbitrators are unable to do so, the third arbitrator shall be appointed by the Court of Arbitration of the International Chamber of Commerce under the said Rules. The venue of the arbitration shall be Dhaka, Bangladesh. The procedure in arbitration shall be in English.
> (Exh. C-4)

2.2   The origin of the present dispute

11.   Pursuant to Article 1.1.14 of the Contract, the project was to be completed by 30 April 1991. It was, however, significantly delayed due to problems with the local population which rebelled against the project. On 29 May 1991, Saipem and Petrobangla, with the approval

of the World Bank, agreed to extend the completion date by one year, *i.e.*, to 30 April 1992.

12. The project was completed and the pipeline taken over by Petrobangla with effect from 14 June 1992. Petrobangla issued the certificate of final taking over on 17 June 1992. Shortly thereafter, Petrobangla returned the first half of the Retention Money.

13. The second half of the Retention Money was to be released by Petrobangla against a warranty bond of the same amount, *i.e.*, USD 869,903.50 and BDT 10,391,605.00.

14. The warranty bond was provided on behalf of Saipem on 27 June 1992 (warranty Bond No. PG/USD/12/92 issued by Banque Indosuez; the "Warranty Bond"). Petrobangla agreed that such bond would be released no later than 30 days from the issuance of the certificate of final acceptance (see C-Mem, p. 26).

15. On 18 April 1993, Petrobangla sent an "extend or pay letter" in the following terms:

> The validity of the captioned guarantee which was extended by you vide your letter No. CRDT/AU.-PG-12/92-551/93 dated 04-05-93, will expire on 30-06-93.
> We have requested the Contractor to extend the validity of the said guarantee for further period up to 31-12-93 before its expiry.
> If the Contractor does not give any extension of the validity of this guarantee before its expiry date i.e. 30-06-93, you will treat this letter as our encashment notice against the subject guarantee and in that event you will effect payment to us by a Demand-Draft drawn in favour of the Project Implementation Unit, Petrobangla.
> (Exh. R-67)

16. It is undisputed that Petrobangla did not repay the Retention Money even though the Warranty Bond had been issued. The parties disagree on whether the letter to "extend or pay" just quoted constitutes a call on the Warranty Bond and whether Petrobangla initiated an action to obtain and eventually obtained payment under the Warranty Bond.

17. A dispute arose between the parties with respect to Petrobangla's failure (i) to pay the additional costs allegedly agreed, together with the

extension of time as well as other compensations and (ii) to return the Warranty Bond and the balance of the Retention Money.

2.3   The ICC Arbitration

18.   According to the dispute resolution procedure set forth in the Contract, Saipem referred this dispute to ICC arbitration by filing a request for arbitration on 7 June 1993.

19.   An arbitral tribunal composed of Dr. Werner Melis (Chairman), Prof. Riccardo Luzzatto and Prof. Ian Brownlie, QC, was constituted on 4 May 1994 (the "ICC Arbitral Tribunal").

20.   On 27 November 1995, the ICC Arbitral Tribunal issued an award on jurisdiction dismissing Petrobangla's challenge to its jurisdiction (Exh. C-7). It then addressed the merits of the case.

21.   In substance, Saipem claimed compensation in excess of USD 11 million (USD 7,579,445 and BDT 123,350,330) and the return of the Warranty Bond. Petrobangla opposed these claims and raised several counterclaims in the total amount of USD 10,577,941.98.

22.   After the exchange of the written submissions in the ICC Arbitration, a witness hearing was held on 22-27 July 1997 in Dhaka. During the hearing, the ICC Arbitral Tribunal rejected several procedural motions made by Petrobangla, in particular (i) a request to strike from the record the statement of a witness produced by Saipem who could not attend the hearing, (ii) a request that all witnesses to be heard during the hearing be allowed to stay in the hearing room, (iii) a request that a letter from Petrobangla which was not on record be filed during the cross-examination of a witness, (iv) a request to strike from the record a "draft aide-mémoire" of the World Bank and certain unilaterally prepared calculations of costs, and (v) a request for written transcripts to be made of the tape recordings of the hearing.

23.   In August 1997, Petrobangla wrote to the ICC Arbitral Tribunal to request information regarding Saipem's insurance policy and claims. The ICC Arbitral Tribunal issued an order that Saipem's refusal to submit the requested documents would be assessed at a later stage of the proceedings, when appropriate.

24.   On 16 November 1997, Petrobangla filed an action seeking the revocation of the ICC Arbitral Tribunal's authority in the First Court of

the Subordinate Judge of Dhaka (Exh. R-83)[1]. The action was based on the arbitrators' alleged misconduct and breach of the parties' procedural rights when rejecting Petrobangla's procedural motions during the hearing of 22-27 July 1997[2].

25. On 17 November 1997, Petrobangla seized the High Court of Dhaka of an application requesting a decision "to stay all further proceedings of the Arbitration Case No. 7934/CK pending before the arbitral tribunal and/or to restrain the opposite party and/or the tribunal by and from proceeding further with the said arbitration" (Exh. C-10.2).

26. On 24 November 1997, the Supreme Court of Bangladesh issued an injunction restraining Saipem from proceeding with the ICC Arbitration (Exh. C-10.3)[3]:

> [Saipem] is hereby restrained by an order of ad-interim injunction from proceeding with the said

---

[1] On 23 June 1999, Saipem filed an application for "rejection of the application" on the merits (Exh. R-85), which was refused by an order dated 5 September 1999 (Exh. R-87). Saipem did not appeal from this order in the High Court Division of the Supreme Court.

[2] Petrobangla also sought an interim injunction pending the hearing of its application, which was dismissed by the Court by an order dated 16 November 1997 (Exh. C-10.1). On 17 November 1997, Petrobangla filed an appeal from this order (Exh. C-10.2). By a judgment dated 2 May 1999, the High Court allowed Petrobangla's appeal, set aside the order dated 16 November 1997 of the lower court, and granted the interim injunction in respect of the proceedings of the ICC Tribunal (Exh. C-10.5). On 30 June 1999, Saipem appealed from this judgment in the Appellate Division of the Supreme Court and requested a stay of the operation of the Judgment of the High Court Division. The Appellate Division granted the stay and extended it by two separate orders dated 4 and 18 July 1999 until 22 July 1999. After having heard both parties, on 25 July 1999 the Appellate Division rendered a judgment upholding the High Court decision of 2 May 1999.

[3] Saipem appealed against the judicial stay of the arbitration on the ground that the Bangladeshi courts had no jurisdiction to decide on Petrobangla's petition regarding the alleged misconduct of the proceedings by the arbitrators. Specifically, Saipem submitted that the ICC Arbitration Rules elected by the parties provided for an exclusive mechanism for disqualification of the arbitrators and that such an election had to be taken into consideration according to Section V of the Bangladeshi Arbitration Act of 1940. Pursuant to this provision, "the authority of an appointed arbitrator is irrevocable except with the leave of the court, unless a contrary intention is expressed in the arbitration agreement".

> arbitration case No. 7934CK for a period of 8
> (eight) weeks from date.
> (Exh. C-10.3, p. 2)

27.   Several other decisions confirmed and maintained the stay of the arbitration, including a decision of the High Court Division of the Supreme Court of Bangladesh handed down on 23 March 1998 (Exh. C-10.4).

28.   On 19 September 1999, Saipem filed a written objection to Petrobangla's action seeking the revocation of the ICC Arbitral Tribunal's authority (Exh. R-88).

29.   On 5 April 2000, the First Court of the Subordinate Judge of Dhaka issued a decision revoking the authority of the ICC Arbitral Tribunal on the following grounds:

> In view of the submission of the lawyers for the parties and perusal of the documents filed by both sides I hold that the Arbitral Tribunal has conducted the arbitration proceedings improperly by refusing to determine the question of the admissibility of evidence and the exclusion of certain documents from the record as well as by its failure to direct that information regarding insurance be provided. Moreover, the Tribunal has manifestly been in disregard of the law and as such the Tribunal committed misconduct. Therefore, in the above circumstances, it appears to me that there is a likelihood of miscarriage of justice.
> (Exh. C-11, as quoted in Mem., p. 21, para. 92)

30.   It is common ground that Saipem has not appealed this decision.

31.   On 30 April 2001, the ICC Arbitral Tribunal decided to resume the proceedings on the ground that the challenge or replacement of the arbitrators in an ICC arbitration falls within the exclusive jurisdiction of the ICC Court and not of the Bangladeshi courts. It thus held that the revocation of the authority of the ICC Arbitral Tribunal by the Bangladeshi courts was contrary to the general principles governing international arbitration (Exh. C-8).

32.   On 9 May 2001, Petrobangla brought an action before the First Court of
        the Subordinate Judge of Dhaka to set aside the ICC Arbitral Tribunal's
        order of 30 April resuming the arbitration (Exh. C-12).

33.   On 24 May 2001, Petrobangla filed a request for a declaration that the
        ICC Arbitration was unlawful on the ground that the authority of the
        ICC Arbitral Tribunal was revoked by the decision of the Subordinate
        Judge of 5 April 2000. It also applied for an interim and a permanent
        injunction. On the same day, the court refused to grant the interim
        injunction. On 27 May 2001, Petrobangla filed an appeal before the
        High Court Division of the Supreme Court against this refusal. On the
        same date, the High Court Division issued an injunction restraining
        Saipem from pursuing the ICC Arbitration[4]. This decision was
        confirmed by the High Court Division on 23 October 2001, 16 January
        2002 and 15 July 2002.

34.   On 9 May 2003, the ICC Arbitral Tribunal rendered an award holding
        that Petrobangla had breached its contractual obligations by not paying
        the compensation for time extension and additional works and ordered
        Petrobangla to pay to Saipem the total amount of USD 6,148,770.80
        plus EUR 110,995.92 (which included the Retention Money which
        remained unpaid) plus interest at 3.375% from 7 June 1993. It also
        ordered Petrobangla to return the Warranty Bond to Saipem (the "ICC
        Award"; Exh. C-6).

35.   On 19 July 2003, Petrobangla filed an application before the High
        Court Division of the Supreme Court of Bangladesh under Sections
        42(2) and 43 of the Arbitration Act 2001 to set aside the ICC Award
        (Exhibit C-13).

36.   On 21 April 2004, the High Court Division of the Supreme Court of
        Bangladesh denied Petrobangla's application to set aside the Award as
        it was "misconceived and incompetent inasmuch as there is no Award
        in the eye of the law, which can be set aside" (Exh. C-21, p. 11). In the
        most relevant passage, the High Court Division decision reads as
        follows:

> [...] On a perusal of materials on record and
> particularly Annexure-"D" that is the judgment
> passed by the learned Subordinate Judge, First
> Court, in Arbitration Miscellaneous Case No. 49
> of 1997, it appears that the authority of the

---

[4]   Saipem did not appear before the Court and the case is still pending.

Arbitral Tribunal to proceed with the Arbitration Case No. 7934/CK/AER/ACS/MS has been revoked on 5.4.2000. Therefore the Arbitral Tribunal proceeded with the said arbitration case most illegally and without jurisdiction after the pronouncement of the judgment of Arbitration Miscellaneous Case No. 49 of 1997. Moreover, the Arbitral Tribunal was injuncted upon by the High Court Division not to proceed with the said arbitration case any further but in spite of that the Tribunal proceeded with the Arbitration Case and ultimately declared their Award on 9.5.2003. [...]

The applicable law of the agreement was set out in clause 1.1.1a of the agreement in the following terms: "1.1.1a The contract shall be governed and construed with reference to the law in force in Bangladesh...". Thus it is clear the Bangladesh Court has jurisdiction to entertain a suit/proceeding if initiated by a party to the Contract. Therefore, the judgment passed by the First Subordinate Judge in Arbitration Miscellaneous Case No. 49 of 1997 and the injunction order dated 2.5.1999 passed by this Court in the Miscellaneous Appeal No. 25 of 1997 were binding upon the Arbitral Tribunal [...]

It is, thus, clear and obvious that the Award dated 9.5.2003 passed by the Arbitral Tribunal in Arbitration Case No. 7934/CK/AER/ACS/MS is a nullity in the eye of the law and this Award can not be treated as an Award in the eye of the law as it is clearly illegal and without jurisdiction inasmuch as the authority of the Tribunal was revoked as back as on 5.4.2000 by a competent Court of Bangladesh. [...]

A non-existent award can neither be set aside nor can it be enforced.

(Exh. C-21, p. 11).

2.4 Related litigation

37. On 4 October 1992, at the request of a subcontractor of Saipem, a court in Bangladesh issued an injunction restraining payments by Petrobangla to Saipem. The injunction was lifted on 31 May 1993.

38. On 17 June 1993, Saipem obtained an injunction from the courts in Milan prohibiting Banque Indosuez Italy (the bank which had issued the Warranty Bond) to pay out on the Warranty Bond to Banque Indosuez Pakistan (the correspondent bank in Pakistan). This injunction was confirmed on 19 July 1993 and subsequently affirmed by the Court of Appeal of Milan on 12 August 1993[5].

39. Being exposed to the risk of a call on the Warranty Bond, on 12 February 1994, Banque Indosuez Pakistan filed an action before the Court of the 4th Sub-Judge of Dhaka for a declaration that no payment should be made in favor of Petrobangla under the Warranty Bond until the injunction of the court of Milan was vacated. According to the Court's order sheet, a further hearing was set on 4 June 2006. This action was still pending at the time of the hearing on jurisdiction in this arbitration. Saipem is not a party to it (Tr. I 53:14-21).

2.5 The BIT

40. The present proceedings are brought on the basis of the "Agreement Between the Government of the Republic of Italy and the Government of the People's Republic of Bangladesh on the Promotion and Protection of Investments" of 20 March 1990 (the "BIT"), which entered into force on 20 September 1994 (Exh. C-1).

41. Specifically, Saipem relies upon Article 5 of the BIT, pursuant to which investments under the Treaty may not be subject to expropriation or measures equivalent to expropriation without immediate, full, and effective compensation.

II. PROCEDURAL HISTORY

1. INITIAL PHASE

42. On 5 October 2004, Saipem filed a Request for Arbitration (the "Request" or "RA") with the International Centre for Settlement of

---

[5] The action on the merits, which was initiated to maintain the injunction was still pending at the time of the hearing on jurisdiction in this arbitration (Tr. 2: II 63:22-64:3).

Investment Disputes ("ICSID" or the "Centre"), accompanied by 17 exhibits (Exh. C-1 to 17). In its Request, Saipem invoked the provisions of the BIT and sought the following relief:

> *6.1   Claim for Declaratory Decisions*
> The Claimant requests that the Arbitral Tribunal declare that:
> -   Bangladesh has expropriated Claimant of its investment without paying compensation;
> -   Bangladesh has breached its international obligations under the BIT.
>
> *6.2   Monetary Claims*
> The Claimant requests that the Arbitral Tribunal award it complete compensation for all the damages and losses it suffered as a result of Bangladesh's breaches of its obligations.
> As the Claimant will substantiate at the proper stage of the proceedings, the loss suffered by the Claimant amounts to at least US$ 12,500,000.00, plus interest at the proper rate.
> The Claimant also requests that the Arbitral Tribunal order Bangladesh to return or extinguish the Warranty Bond.
>
> *6.3   Interim Relief*
> In light of Bangladesh's bad faith attempts to draw upon the Warranty Bond, the Claimant requests that the Tribunal issue a provisional order pursuant to Article 47 of the Convention ordering Respondent to refrain from pursuing - and to prevent Petrobangla from pursuing - any payment demand based on this Bond until the outcome of the present arbitration.
>
> *6.4   The Costs of the Present Arbitration*
> The Claimant requests that the Arbitral Tribunal order Respondent to reimburse Claimant for all the costs incurred and to be incurred by it in connection with the present arbitration, including legal fees.
> (RA, pp. 27-28, paras. 121-126, footnote omitted)

43.   On 12 October 2004, the Centre, in accordance with Rule 5 of the ICSID Rules of Procedure for the Institution of Conciliation and

Arbitration Proceedings (the "Institution Rules"), transmitted a copy of the RA to Bangladesh.

44.   After a protracted exchange of correspondence (during which the Claimant filed additional exhibits to the Request – Exh. C-18 to 21) between the parties and the Centre, on 27 April 2005, the Secretary-General of the Centre registered Saipem's Request, pursuant to Article 36(3) of the Convention on the Settlement of Investment Disputes between States and Nationals of other States (the "ICSID Convention" or "the Convention"). On the same date, in accordance with Institution Rule 7, the Secretary-General notified the parties of the registration of the Request and invited them to proceed, as soon as possible, to constitute an Arbitral Tribunal.

45.   The parties agreed on a Tribunal composed of three arbitrators with one arbitrator each to be appointed by the parties and the presiding arbitrator to be jointly nominated by the two party-appointed arbitrators. On 27 June 2005, Saipem appointed Prof. Christoph Schreuer, a national of Austria. On 4 July 2005, Bangladesh appointed Sir Philip Otton, a national of the United Kingdom. On 21 July 2005, the Secretariat informed the parties that the co-arbitrators had agreed to appoint Prof. Gabrielle Kaufmann-Kohler, a national of Switzerland, as the President of the Tribunal.

46.   On 22 August 2005, the Secretary-General of ICSID, in accordance with Rule 6(1) of the ICSID Rules of Procedure for Arbitration Proceedings (the "Arbitration Rules"), notified the parties that all three arbitrators had accepted their appointment and that the Tribunal was therefore deemed to be constituted and the proceedings to have begun on that date. The same letter informed the parties that Mrs. Eloïse M. Obadia, ICSID Counsel, would serve as Secretary to the Tribunal. Mrs. Obadia was subsequently replaced as the Secretary of the Tribunal by Mrs. Martina Polasek, ICSID Counsel.

47.   By decision of 11 October 2005, Sir Philip Otton and Prof. Gabrielle Kaufmann-Kohler dismissed Bangladesh's Proposal for Disqualification of Prof. Christoph Schreuer concluding that the latter met the requirement of independence and impartiality, or, in the words of Article 14(1) of the ICSID Convention, that he had the ability to "exercise independent judgment".

48.   On 1 December 2005, the Tribunal held a preliminary session in London. At the outset of the session, the parties expressed agreement that the Tribunal had been duly constituted (Arbitration Rule 6) and

stated that they had no objections in this respect. The remainder of the procedural issues on the agenda of the session were discussed and agreed upon, including a procedural calendar. An audio recording of the session was later distributed to the parties. Minutes were drafted, signed by the President and the Secretary of the Tribunal, and sent to the parties on 13 January 2006.

2. THE WRITTEN PHASE ON JURISDICTION

49. In accordance with the timetable agreed upon during the preliminary session, on 20 February 2006, Saipem submitted its Statement of Claim (Mem.) accompanied by two volumes of exhibits (Exh. C-21 to Exh. C-84). Saipem did not append any witness statement or expert opinion.

50. Following a short extension, on 14 May 2006, Bangladesh submitted its Counter-Memorial on the objections to jurisdiction and the merits (C-Mem.) accompanied by five volumes of exhibits (Exh. R-1 to R-113) and four witness statements (WS of Messrs. Mohammed Quamruzzaman, Abdul Monsur Md. Azad, Salahuddin Ahmad and Abdur Razzaq). Mr. Razzaq's WS introduced a legal opinion on issues of Bangladeshi law, which was accompanied by ten annexes.

51. In accordance with the timetable agreed upon during the preliminary session, on 14 July 2006, Saipem submitted its Response on Objections to Jurisdiction (Response J.) accompanied by one volume of exhibits (Exhibits C-85 to C-99). Saipem did not append any witness statement or expert opinion.

52. On 26 July 2006, the Tribunal held a telephone conference with counsel for the parties to deal with the organization of the hearing on jurisdiction.

53. In line with the extension of time allowed by the Tribunal, on 18 August 2006, Bangladesh submitted its Reply on Jurisdiction (Reply J.)[6].

54. On 14 September 2006, within the extension of time allowed by the Tribunal, Saipem submitted its Rejoinder on Objections to Jurisdiction (Rejoinder J.) accompanied by one volume of exhibits (Exhibits C-100 to C-101), without witness statements or expert opinions.

---

[6]   In the cover letter, Bangladesh announced that a Supplemental WS by Mr. Razzaq would be filed "over the week-end".

3. THE HEARING ON JURISDICTION

55. The Arbitral Tribunal held the hearing on jurisdiction from 21 to 22 September 2006 in London. In addition to the Members of the Tribunal and the Secretary, the following persons attended the jurisdictional hearing:

(i) On behalf of Saipem:
- Prof. Antonio Crivellaro, Bonelli Erede Pappalardo
- Prof. Luca Radicati di Brozolo, Bonelli Erede Pappalardo
- Mr. Andrea Carta Mantiglia, Bonelli Erede Pappalardo
- Mr. Alexander Backovic, Bonelli Erede Pappalardo
- Mr. Francesco del Giudice, Saipem

(ii) On behalf of Bangladesh:
- Mr. Ajmalul Hossain, QC, A Hossain & Associates Law Offices
- Mr. Sameer Sattar, A Hossain & Associates Law Offices
- Mr. Syed Afzal Hossain, A Hossain & Associates Law Offices
- Mr. Syed Ahrarul Hossain, A Hossain & Associates Law Offices

56. During the jurisdictional hearing, the Tribunal heard witness evidence from Messrs. Abdul Monsour Azad, Salahuddin Ahmad, Abdul Razzaq and Mohammed Quamruzzaman.

57. Mr. Hossain presented oral argument on behalf of Bangladesh and Messrs. Crivellaro, Radicati di Brozolo and Carta Mantiglia addressed the Tribunal on behalf of Saipem.

58. The jurisdictional hearing was tape-recorded, a *verbatim* transcript was taken and delivered to the parties (Tr. J. J.).

* * *

59. It was agreed at the close of the jurisdictional hearing that the Tribunal would issue a reasoned decision on the preliminary question of jurisdiction. If the decision were negative, the Tribunal would render an award terminating the arbitration. If the decision were affirmative, the Tribunal would render a decision asserting jurisdiction and issue an order with directions for the continuation of the procedure pursuant to Arbitration Rule 41(4).

60. The Tribunal has deliberated and thoroughly considered the parties' written submissions on jurisdiction and the oral arguments presented in the course of the jurisdictional hearing. In the following sections, it

will first summarize the parties' positions (III), analyze them (IV), and then reach a conclusion on jurisdiction (V).

III. PARTIES' POSITIONS

1. SAIPEM'S POSITION

61. In its written and oral submissions, Saipem has put forward the following five main contentions:

(i) Petrobangla has resorted to the local courts which colluded with the State entity to sabotage the ICC Arbitration and deny the foreign investor's right to arbitrate under the Contract and obtain satisfaction of its claims;

(ii) By referring to the ICC Arbitration Rules, the parties validly excluded the authority of the courts of the seat of the arbitration;

(iii) The Contract constitutes an investment under the BIT;

(iv) Immaterial rights can be subject to expropriation;

(v) Saipem's right to arbitrate and more specifically its right that disputes with Petrobangla be settled by arbitration is a contractual right or, in the words of Article 1(e) of the BIT, a "right accruing by law or by contract" having an economic value;

(vi) The actions of Petrobangla and of the courts of Bangladesh can be attributed to the Republic of Bangladesh.

62. On the basis of these contentions, Saipem requests the Tribunal to:

(i) find that the conditions for its jurisdiction in the present case are satisfied and accordingly reject the Respondent's objections and declare itself to have jurisdiction in respect of the Claimant's claim; and

(ii) issue a provisional measure recommending that Bangladesh refrain from calling on the Warranty Bond and return it to the Claimant together with the Retention Money without further delay. (Rejoinder, p. 28, para. 107)

2. BANGLADESH'S POSITION

63. In its written and oral submissions, Bangladesh has raised the following five main arguments:

(i) Saipem did not make an investment within the meaning of the BIT;

(ii) Since the seat of the ICC Arbitration was Dhaka, the courts of Bangladesh had jurisdiction to revoke the authority of the ICC Arbitral Tribunal;

(iii) In Art. 5(1)(1) of the BIT, Bangladesh has expressly excluded consent in respect of "judgments or orders issued by Courts or Tribunals having jurisdiction";

(iv) Saipem elected not to lodge an appeal to a higher court. It has thus deprived Bangladesh of the opportunity to rectify the alleged wrongdoings of its lower courts in connection with the ICC Arbitration;

(v) By agreeing on ICC Arbitration in Dakha, Saipem accepted any potential failure to enforce an ICC award in its favour in Bangladesh as a calculated business risk.

64. In reliance on these arguments, Bangladesh invites the Tribunal to:

> Make findings [...] that the Tribunal lacks jurisdiction to hear this case.
>
> If the Tribunal does not wish to go into the evidence on jurisdictional facts at this stage, it should still decline jurisdiction on the basis that the Claimant has not discharged its prima facie burden of proof.
>
> Dismiss the claim in its entirety and [...] make a declaration to that effect and make an award of costs in favour of the Respondent on a full indemnity basis.
>
> (Reply J., pp. 19-20)

IV. ANALYSIS

1. INTRODUCTORY MATTERS

65. Before turning to the issues to be resolved, the Tribunal wishes to address certain preliminary matters, *i.e.*, the relevance of prior ICSID decisions (a), the law applicable to the Tribunal's jurisdiction (b), and certain uncontroversial matters (c).

1.1 The relevance of previous ICSID decisions or awards

66. In support of their positions, both parties relied on previous ICSID decisions or awards, either to conclude that the same solution should be adopted in the present case or in an effort to explain why this Tribunal should depart from that solution.

67.   The Tribunal considers that it is not bound by previous decisions[7]. At the same time, it is of the opinion that it must pay due consideration to earlier decisions of international tribunals. It believes that, subject to compelling contrary grounds, it has a duty to adopt solutions established in a series of consistent cases. It also believes that, subject to the specifics of a given treaty and of the circumstances of the actual case, it has a duty to seek to contribute to the harmonious development of investment law and thereby to meet the legitimate expectations of the community of States and investors towards certainty of the rule of law[8].

1.2   The rules governing the Tribunal's jurisdiction

68.   The Tribunal's jurisdiction is contingent upon the provisions of the BIT and of the ICSID Convention. The law applicable to the merits of the dispute does not govern jurisdiction.

69.   The relevant provision of the ICSID Convention is Article 25(1), which reads as follows:

> The jurisdiction of the Centre shall extend to any legal dispute arising directly out of an investment between a Contracting State (or any constituent subdivision or agency of a Contracting State designated to the Centre by that State) and a national of another Contracting State, which the parties to the dispute consent in writing to submit to the Centre. When the parties have given their consent, no party may withdraw its consent unilaterally.

70.   The relevant provision of the BIT is Article 9, which provides for ICSID arbitration in the following terms:

> 1. Any disputes arising between a Contracting Party and the investors of the other, relating to compensation for expropriation, nationalization, requisition or similar measures including

---

[7]   *See e.g., AES Corporation v. the Argentine Republic,* ICSID Case No. ARB/02/17, Decision on jurisdiction of 13 July 2005, paras. 30-32; available at http://www.investmentclaims.com/decisions/AES-Argentina_Jurisdiction.pdf.

[8]   On the precedential value of ICSID decisions, *see* Gabrielle Kaufmann-Kohler, Arbitral Precedent: Dream, Necessity or Excuse?, Freshfields lecture 2006, publication forthcoming in Arbitration International 2007.

disputes relating to the amount of the relevant payments shall be settled amicably, as far as possible.

2. In the event that such a dispute cannot be settled amicably within six months of the date of a written application, the investor in question may submit the dispute, at his discretion for settlement to: [...]

c) the "International Centre for the Settlement of Investment Disputes", for the application of the arbitration procedures provided by the Washington Convention of 18th March 1965 on the "Settlement of Investment Disputes between States and Nationals of other States", whenever, or as soon as both Contracting Parties have validly acceded to it.

1.3   Uncontroversial matters

71.   There is no dispute as to the competence of this Tribunal to decide on the jurisdictional challenges brought by Bangladesh pursuant to Article 41 of the ICSID Convention.

72.   It is further undisputed that four conditions must be met for the Tribunal to uphold jurisdiction under Article 25 of the ICSID Convention, *i.e.*, (i) the dispute must be between a Contracting State and a national of another Contracting State, (ii) the dispute must be a legal dispute (iii) it must arise directly from an investment, and (iv) the parties must have expressed their consent to ICSID arbitration in writing.

73.   With respect to the first requirement just referred to, the Tribunal notes that, at the hearing, Bangladesh has abandoned its jurisdictional objection *ratione personae* pursuant to which Saipem was not a private investor (Tr. J. II 31:12-13). The Tribunal further notes that the parties to the dispute are a State (Bangladesh) and an Italian company (Saipem), and that both Bangladesh and Italy are Contracting States within the meaning of Article 25(1) of the ICSID Convention. It thus deems the first requirement met.

74.   With respect to the fourth requirement, Saipem relies upon (i) the consent of Bangladesh to arbitration contained in the BIT combined with (ii) its own consent embodied in the Request. According to a now "well established practice, it is clear that the coincidence of these two

forms of consent can constitute 'consent in writing' within the meaning of Article 25(1) of the ICSID Convention [...] if the dispute falls within the scope of the BIT."[9] This is not disputed by Bangladesh.

75.   Bangladesh's objections concern the scope of its consent under the BIT as well as the second and the third requirements referred to above.

1.4   Bangladesh's objections

76.   Bangladesh has objected to the jurisdiction of the Tribunal and/or to the admissibility of Saipem's claim upon the following main grounds:

(i)   There is no real legal dispute between the parties (Tr. J. 2:II 23:9-20).

(ii)   Saipem has not made an investment within Article 1(1) of the BIT.

(iii)   Bangladesh's consent to arbitration does not cover disputes arising out of the acts of its courts pursuant to Article 5(1) of the BIT (Reply J., p. 15, paras. 3.14-3.16).

(iv)   The alleged breaches of the Treaty "have not crossed the necessary threshold for establishing that the actions were that of the state of Bangladesh in the exercise of its sovereign authority" (Reply J., p. 16, at para. 31.8).

(v)   Saipem's claim constitutes an abuse of process (C-Mem para. 4.40 et seq.; Tr. J. II 34:9 et seq.).

77.   While recognising that there may be an overlap between some of the objections to the jurisdiction of the Tribunal and some of the objections to the admissibility of the claims[10], the Tribunal will distinguish between jurisdictional objections under Article 25 of the ICSID Convention (see below 4), jurisdictional objections under the BIT (see below 5), and objections to the admissibility of Saipem's claims (see below 6). As preliminary matters, the Tribunal will discuss the law applicable to its jurisdiction (see below 2) and the relevant standard for establishing jurisdiction (see below 3).

---

[9]   *Impregilo S.p.A. v. Islamic Republic of Pakistan*, ICSID Case No. ARB/03/3, Decision on Jurisdiction of 22 April 2005, para. 108; available at http://www.worldbank.org/icsid/cases/impregilo-decision.pdf.

[10]   See also *Consortium Groupement L.E.S.I. - DIPENTA v. République Algérienne Démocratique et Populaire*, Award of 10 January 2005, p. 12 at para. 2, where the Tribunal stresses that the distinction has no practical bearing in ICSID proceedings; available at http://www.worldbank.org/icsid/cases/lesi-sentence-fr.pdf.

2.   LAW APPLICABLE TO JURISDICTION

78.   It is not challenged that the interpretation of the ICSID Convention and of the BIT is governed by international law (Reply J., p. 12, para. 3.2).

79.   At the hearing, Bangladesh withdrew the argument that the words "in conformity with the laws and regulations of the latter" at the end of the first paragraph of Article 1(1) of the BIT, impose the application of national law. Bangladesh accepts that the words relate to the mode, not to the definition of the investment (Tr. J. II 20:1-2)[11].

80.   The parties are, however, in disagreement on the question whether the BIT refers to Bangladeshi law "in respect of the definition and construction of the word 'investment'" (Reply J., p. 12, paras. 3.2 and 3.4).

81.   According to Bangladesh, the fact that the BIT's definition of investment uses the word 'property' and not 'assets' as in other bilateral investment treaties implies a reference to Bangladeshi law. In support of this assertion, Bangladesh submits that the word 'property' was chosen because it is a notion well known in Bangladesh (Reply J., pp. 13-14, para. 3.8), thus suggesting that the word 'property' must be interpreted according to its ordinary meaning in Bangladeshi law. That meaning is allegedly "more specific and narrower than the word 'assets'" (Reply J., p. 14, para. 3.9).

82.   The Tribunal notes that Bangladesh has indeed entered into other bilateral investment treaties in which the definition of 'investment'

---

11   For the sake of completeness, the Tribunal wishes to note that the phrase "in conformity with the laws and regulations [of the host State]" following the "investment" in Article 1(1) does not limit the definition of investment under the BIT to investment within the laws and regulations of Bangladesh. Indeed, as convincingly held by the tribunal in *Salini v. Morocco*, such a "provision [*i.e.*, the requirement of conformity with local laws] refers to the validity of the investment and not to its definition" (*Salini. v. Morocco*, [*supra* Fn. 22] para. 46. *See* also *PSEG* et al. *v. Turkey*, Decision on Jurisdiction, 4 June 2004, paras. 109, 116-120, available at http://www.investmentciaims.com/decisions/PSEG-Turkey-Jurisdiction-4Jun2004.pdf; *L.E.S.I. - Dipenta v. Algeria* [*supra* Fn. 10]; *Plama v. Bulgaria*, Decision on Jurisdiction, 8 February 2005, 44 ILM 721 (2005) paras. 126-131; *Bayindir v. Pakistan*, Decision on Jurisdiction, 14 November 2005, paras. 105-110, available at http://www.investmentclaims.com/decisions/Bayindir-Pakistan-Jurisdiction.pdf.

refs to the concept of 'asset'[12]. However, in the absence of any indication that the contracting states intended to refer to 'property' as a notion of Bangladeshi law[13], the Tribunal cannot depart from the general rule that treaties are to be interpreted by reference to international law. It is thus not prepared to consider that the term "investment" in Article 1(1) of the BIT is defined according to the law of the host State.

3. TEST FOR ESTABLISHING JURISDICTION

3.1 The onus of establishing jurisdiction

83. In accordance with accepted international practice (and generally also with national practice), a party bears the burden of proving the facts it asserts. For instance, an ICSID tribunal held that the Claimant had to satisfy the burden of proof required at the jurisdictional phase and make a *prima facie* showing of Treaty breaches[14].

---

[12] *See*, in particular, the Bangladesh-UK BIT, the Bangladesh-Japan BIT, and the Belgo-Luxemburg-Bangladesh BIT mentioned in Mr. Razzaq's supplemental WS.

[13] *See*, in a different context, the clear intent of the parties resulting from *travaux prépararatoires* in *Inceysa Vallisoletana S.L. v. El Salvador*, ICSID Case No. ARB/03/26, Award of 2 August 2006, paras. 190 *et seq.*; available at http://www.investmentclaims.com/decisions/InceysaVallisoletana-ElSalvador-Award.pdf.

[14] *Impregilo v. Pakistan* [*supra* Fn. 9], para. 79. On the *prima facie* test for purposes of jurisdiction, see among others *UPS v. Canada*, Decision on Jurisdiction, 22 November 2002, paras. 33-37; *Siemens v. Argentina*, Decision on Jurisdiction, 3 August 2004, para. 180, available at http://www.investmentclaims.com/decisions/Siemens-Argentina-Jurisdiction-3Aug2004-Eng.pdf; *Plama v. Bulgaria* [Fn. 11], paras. 118-120, 132; *Bayindir v. Pakistan* [Fn. 11] paras. 185-200; *El Paso v. Argentina*, Decision on Jurisdiction, 27 April 2006, paras. 40-45, 109, available at http://www.investmentclaims.com/decisions/El_Paso_Energy-Argentina-Jurisdictional_Decision.pdf; *Jan de Nul v. Egypt*, Decision on Jurisdiction, 16 June 2006, paras. 69-71, available at http://www.investmentclaims.com/decisions/Jan_de_Nul-Egypt-Jurisdictional_Award.pdf; *Telenor v. Hungary*, Award, 13 September 2006, paras. 34, 53, 68, 80, available at http://www.investmentclaims.com/decisions/Telenor_Mobile-Hungary-Award-13-09-06.pdf.

3.2   The relevant standard

84.   In their respective submissions (*see* in particular Reply J., pp. 8-9), the parties referred to the decisions in *Impregilo* and *Bayindir*. In particular, reference was made to the following test stated in *Impregilo*:

> [T]he Tribunal has considered whether the facts as alleged by the Claimant in this case, *if* established, are capable of coming within those provisions of the BIT which have been invoked.[15]

85.   The Tribunal agrees with this test, which is in line with the one proposed by Judge Higgins in her dissenting opinion in *Oil Platforms*[16]. The test strikes a fair balance between a more demanding standard which would imply examining the merits at the jurisdictional stage, and a lighter standard which would rest entirely on the Claimant's characterization of its claims.

86.   The Tribunal must now determine whether the claims "fall within the scope of the BIT, assuming *pro tem* that they may be sustained on the facts"[17]. In other words, the Tribunal should be satisfied that, if the facts alleged by Saipem ultimately prove true, they would be capable of constituting a violation of Article 5 of the BIT. In this respect, the Tribunal agrees with the observation in *United Parcel Service v. Government of Canada* that "the reference to the facts alleged being 'capable' of constituting a violation of the invoked obligations, as opposed to their 'falling within' the provisions, may be of little or no consequence.[18]

87.   At the hearing, Bangladesh agreed with this approach:

> If we look at paragraph 16 of the rejoinder, it is stated that it is unanimously recognised that in the jurisdictional phase issues of merits are relevant only insofar as they are necessary to

---

15   *Impregilo v. Pakistan* [*supra* Fn. 9], para. 254, emphasis in the original.
16   *Case concerning Oil Platforms* (*Islamic Republic of Iran v. United States of America*), I.C.J. Reports 1996, II, p. 803, 810, at paras. 16-17.
17   *Impregilo v. Pakistan* [*supra* Fn. 9], para. 263.
18   *United Parcel Service v. Government of Canada* [NAFTA], Decision on Jurisdiction, 22 November 200, para. 36; available at http://www.investmentclaims.com/decisions/UPS-Canada-Jurisdiction-22Nov2002.pdf.

> enable the court or the tribunal to ascertain
> whether the claims brought before it fall within
> its personal subject matter jurisdiction.
> [...] With respect, we agree. We submit that that
> is the way that you should approach your task.
> (Tr. J. 2: II 7:18-25)

88.   In spite of this statement, Bangladesh submitted that Saipem's case is
        not supported by appropriate evidence nor is it sufficiently defined.
        Specifically, Bangladesh alleges that Saipem must establish the
        following elements: (i) the existence of an investment, (ii) the
        occurrence of an act of expropriation, and (iii) the threshold for treaty
        claims (Rejoinder J., p. 11). Bangladesh referred to a definition of the
        Permanent Court of International Justice (PCIJ) and to another one of
        the International Court of Justice (ICJ) and submitted that the facts
        relevant to assert jurisdiction must be proven.

89.   In particular, Bangladesh referred to the PCIJ decision in *Mavromatis*[19].
        It also relied on the following passages of the ICJ decision between
        Spain and Canada in the *Fisheries Jurisdiction Case*:

> There is no doubt that it is for the Applicant, in
> its Application, to present to the Court the
> dispute with which it wishes to seise the Court
> and to set out the claims which it is submitting to
> it. [...]
> In order to identify its task in any proceedings
> instituted by one State against another, the Court
> must begin by examining the Application.
> However, it may happen that uncertainties or
> disagreements arise with regard to the real
> subject of the dispute with which the Court has
> been seised, or to the exact nature of the claims
> submitted to it. In such cases the Court cannot
> be restricted to a consideration of the terms of
> the Application alone nor, more generally, can it

---

[19]   Judgment No. 2 of the PCIJ *The Mavromatis Palestine Concessions*, 30 August
        1924, Fifth (Ordinary) Session, Publications of the Permanent Court of
        International Justice Series A No.2; Collection of Judgments, A.W. Sijthoff's
        Publishing Company, Leyden, pp. 12-16; also available at http://www.icj-
        cij.org/cijwww/cdecisions/ccpij/serie_A/A_02/06_Mavrommatis_en_Palestine
        _Arret.pdf. After having carefully considered this decision, the Tribunal was
        unable to discern the relevance of this decision in the present case.

regard itself as bound by the claims of the Applicant.

Even in proceedings instituted by Special Agreement, the Court has determined for itself, having examined all of the relevant instruments, what was the subject of the dispute brought before it, in circumstances where the parties could not agree on how it should be characterized [...].

It is for the Court itself, while giving particular attention to the formulation of the dispute chosen by the Applicant, to determine on an objective basis the dispute dividing the parties, by examining the position of both Parties [...] The Court's jurisprudence shows that the Court will not confine itself to the formulation by the Applicant when determining the subject of the dispute.

The Court will itself determine the real dispute that has been submitted to it [...]. It will base itself not only on the Application and final submissions, but on diplomatic exchanges, public statements and other pertinent evidence [...].

In so doing, the Court will distinguish between the dispute itself and arguments used by the parties to sustain their respective submissions on the dispute [...].

The Court points out that the establishment or otherwise of jurisdiction is not a matter for the parties but for the Court itself. Although a party seeking to assert a fact must bear the burden of proving it, this has no relevance for the establishment of the Court's jurisdiction, which is a "question of law to be resolved in the light of the relevant facts".

That being so, there is no burden of proof to be discharged in the matter of jurisdiction. Rather, it is for the Court to determine from all the facts and taking into account all the arguments advanced by the Parties, "whether the force of

> the arguments militating in favour of jurisdiction is preponderant, and to 'ascertain whether an intention on the part of the Parties exists to confer jurisdiction upon it'[20].

90. The Tribunal fails to see how these decisions could be interpreted as justifying a different approach than the one referred to above and described by the tribunal in *Impregilo*. That said, it is undisputable that the Tribunal determines its jurisdiction without being bound by the arguments of the parties.

91. To summarize, the Tribunal's task is to determine the meaning and scope of the provisions upon which Saipem relies to assert jurisdiction and to assess whether the facts alleged by Saipem fall within those provisions or would be capable, if proven, of constituting breaches of the treaty obligations involved. In performing this task, the Tribunal will apply a *prima facie* standard, both to the determination of the meaning and scope of the relevant BIT provisions and to the assessment whether the facts alleged may constitute breaches of these provisions. In doing so, the Tribunal will assess whether Saipem's case is reasonably arguable on its face. If the result is affirmative, jurisdiction will be established, but the existence of breaches will remain to be litigated on the merits.

4.   JURISDICTIONAL OBJECTIONS UNDER ARTICLE 25(1) OF THE ICSID CONVENTION

92. With respect to Article 25(1) of the ICSID Convention, Bangladesh objected that there is no legal dispute (a), that Saipem did not make an investment (b) and that the dispute does not arise directly out of the investment (c).

4.1   Is the dispute a legal dispute under Article 25(1) of the ICSID Convention?

93. At the hearing, Bangladesh submitted that the existence of a legal dispute within the meaning of Article 25(1) of the ICSID Convention presupposes the "existence of a cause of action" (Tr. J. II, 15-17). In the present case, according to Bangladesh, "there is no valid cause of

---

[20]   International Court of Justice, Judgment of 4 December 1998, *Fisheries Jurisdiction Case (Spain v. Canada)*, available at http://www.icj-cij.org/icjwww/idocket/iec/iecjudgment(s)/iec_ijudgment_981204.htm, paras. 29-32 and 37-38, citations omitted.

action because the ingredients of such a cause of action are not supported by any or any proper evidence [and] are not sufficiently clearly defined in the formulation of the claim" (Tr. J. II 22:10-13).

94. Specifically, Bangladesh referred to the articulation of Saipem's claim in para. 13 of the Reply J. as repeated in para. 28 of the Rejoinder J., which reads as follows:

> As is clearly set out in the Statement of Claim, the Claimant's claim relates to the expropriation by Bangladesh of (i) its right to arbitration of its disputes with Petrobangla; (ii) the right to payment of the amounts due under the Contract as ascertained in the ICC Award; (iii) the rights arising under the ICC Award, including the right to obtain its recognition and enforcement in Bangladesh and abroad; and therefore (iv) the residual value of its investment in Bangladesh at the time of the ICC Award, consisting of its credits under the Contract. All these matters are facets of the same issue. The focus of the Claimant's case is that its right to payment under the Contract as ascertained by, and incorporated in the ICC Award has been expropriated by the unlawful decisions of the Bangladeshi courts that revoked the authority of the ICC arbitrators and declared the ICC Award null and void, thus precluding its enforcement in Bangladesh or elsewhere. The net result of all this was, obviously, to deprive the Claimant of the compensation for [the expropriation of] its investment.
> (Rejoinder J., p. 8)

95. In the Tribunal's Opinion, the dispute before it is a legal dispute as it involves a disagreement about legal rights or obligations. Or, to use the words of the Report of the Executive Directors of the World Bank on the Convention, the present dispute is legal in nature because it deals with "the existence or scope of [Claimants'] legal rights" and with the

nature and extent of the relief to be granted to the Claimants as a result of the Respondent's alleged violation of those legal rights[21].

96. The Tribunal fails to see how the alleged lack of clarity of Saipem's claim could change that conclusion. It will examine whether the claim is supported by evidence when discussing the substantiation of the claim (*see* below at 5).

97. The determination whether the rights asserted by Saipem do exist must await the proceedings on the merits. Subject to determining whether Saipem made an investment within the meaning of Article 25 of the ICSID Convention, which will be discussed below, the Tribunal holds that the assertion of such rights has given rise to a legal dispute which falls within the scope of the jurisdiction of the Centre as set forth in Article 25(1) of the ICSID Convention.

4.2 Has Saipem made an investment under Article 25 of the ICSID Convention?

98. In its relevant part, Article 25(1) of the ICSID Convention provides that "[t]he jurisdiction of the Centre shall extend to any legal dispute arising directly out of an investment".

99. To determine whether Saipem has made an investment within the meaning of Article 25 of the ICSID Convention, the Tribunal will apply the well-known criteria developed by ICSID tribunals in similar cases, which are known as the "Salini test". According to such test, the notion of investment implies the presence of the following elements:

(a) a contribution of money or other assets of economic value, (b) a certain duration, (c) an element of risk, and (d) a contribution to the host State's development[22].

---

[21]   *See* Report of the Executive Directors on the Convention on the Settlement of Investment Disputes Between States and Nationals of Other States; International Bank for Reconstruction and Development, 18 March 1965, para. 26; available at http://www.worldbank.org/icsid/basicdoc/partB-section05.htm#03.

[22]   *Salini Costruttori S.p.A and Italstrade S.p.A. v. Kingdom of Morocco*, ICSID Case No. ARB/00/4, Decision on Jurisdiction of 23 July 2001, 42 ILM, 2003, *passim*. The need for the last element is sometimes put in doubt, (*L.E.S.I. - DIPENTA v. République Algérienne Démocratique et Populaire*, Decision on jurisdiction of 12 July 2006, para. 72.)

100. Referring to several decisions implementing this test[23], Saipem submitted that the Contract was an investment, since "Saipem invested substantial technical, financial and human resources in the project, which gave a substantial contribution to Bangladesh's economic development, and it assumed risks for a significant duration (the performance phase lasted two and a half years)" (Response J., p. 8, para. 35).

101. Bangladesh does not dispute the fact that Saipem made a significant contribution in terms of both technical and human resources. Nor does Bangladesh dispute that these resources contributed to its economic development. Bangladesh's objection relates to the duration of the project. While it agrees that two years are generally considered as a sufficient period of time under the Salini test, Bangladesh insists on the fact that the period during which works were actually performed was less than one year (Tr. J. II 84:10 *et seq.*).

102. The Tribunal cannot follow this line of argument. Bangladesh did not put forward any particular reason why the actual duration of the work should be considered as the applicable criterion, nor did it point to any authority supporting that position. The time of the project during which the works are interrupted or suspended entails risks that may even be higher than those incurred while the works are being performed.

103. As a further line of argument, Bangladesh mainly disputed the existence of an investment on the ground that throughout the project Saipem never "was a net creditor vis-à-vis Petrobangla in respect of the Pipeline Contract having actually put its own money into the project" (C-Mem., p. 61). At the hearing, Bangladesh relied upon the following *dictum* of the Tribunal in *Soabi v. Senegal*[24]:

> The Tribunal observes finally that the object of the general undertaking was limited to construction of a building to be paid for by the client as work progressed and could thus not be said to be an agreement concerning investments. Disputes arising thereunder could therefore not

---

23   L.E.S.I. - Dipenta v. Algeria [Fn. 10], paras. 13-15; Impregilo v. Pakistan [Fn. 9]; Bayindir v. Pakistan [Fn. 11] paras. 104-138, Jan de Nul N. V. v. Egypt [Fn. 14].

24   *Société Ouest Africaine des Bétons Industriels (SOABI) v. Senegal*, ICSID Case No. ARB82/1, Award of 25 February 1988, 2 ICSID Reports 190 at para. 219.

be investment disputes, as required by Article 25
of the ICSID Convention.
(quoted in Tr. J. II 83:18-22 by reference to
BISHOP/CRAWFORD/REISMAN, p. 368)

104. Saipem refuted this objection with the argument that "[i]n construction
and similar contracts it is often the case that the foreign investor
receives a part of the funds – by way of advances or partial payments –
from the host State prior to completion of the project" and that this fact
"has never been given any relevance in past case law which has
characterized this type of contract as an investment". More generally,
Saipem submits that "[t]he source of the funds whereby the investor
funded the works is not of itself relevant" to the Salini test for
determining whether there is an investment (*see* also Tr. J. II 59:2-7).

105. In this debate, the Tribunal identifies two distinct issues, one about the
origin of the funds and one about the commercial risk incurred by the
investor.

106. With respect to the first one, it is true that the host State may impose a
requirement that an amount of capital in foreign currency be imported
into the country[25]. However, in the absence of such a requirement,
investments made by foreign investors from local funds or from loans
raised in the host State are treated in the same manner as investments
funded with imported capital. In other words, the origin of the funds is
irrelevant. This results from the drafting history of the ICSID
Convention and is confirmed by several arbitral decisions relating to
BITs.

107. During the elaboration of the Convention, an argument was made that
the nationality of the investment was more important than the one of
the investor. The Chairman, Dr. Broches, answered that he did not see
how the Convention could make a distinction based on the origin of
funds (History of the Convention, Vol. II, pp. 261, paras. 397-398). As
a consequence, the idea of looking to the origin of funds was
abandoned.

108. Cases do not consider the origin of the funds either. As an illustration
in lieu of several others[26] one may refer to *Wena Hotels v. Egypt*, where

---

25   *See Amco v. Indonesia*, Award, 20 November 1984, 1 ICSID Reports 413,
     paras. 481-489.
26   *See Tradex v. Albania*, Award, 29 April 1999, 5 ICSID Reports 70, at paras.
     105, 108-111; *Olguín v. Paraguay*, Award, 26 July 2001, 6 ICSID Reports 164,

both the Tribunal and the *ad hoc* Committee found the alleged origin of the funds from other investors who were not entitled to benefit from the applicable BIT irrelevant[27].

109.   Bangladesh's argument appears to refer more to the second issue identified above, *i.e.*, to the fact that the investor did not incur any commercial risk because it received an advance payment. The Tribunal cannot agree with this argument. In the present case, the undisputed stopping of the works which took place in 1991 and the necessity to renegotiate the completion date constitute examples of inherent risks in long-term contracts. Moreover, the contractual mechanism providing for Retention Money created an obvious risk for Saipem, which in fact materialised.

110.   Finally, the Tribunal wishes to emphasize that for the purpose of determining whether there is an investment under Article 25 of the ICSID Convention, it will consider the entire operation[28]. In the present case, the entire or overall operation includes the Contract, the construction itself, the Retention Money, the warranty and the related ICC Arbitration.

111.   Applying the Salini test to this comprehensive operation, the Tribunal comes to the conclusion that Saipem has made an investment within the meaning of Article 25 of the ICSID Convention.

4.3   Does the dispute arise directly out of the investment?

112.   Bangladesh claims that a dispute arising out of the ICC Award is not a dispute arising directly from the original investment, *i.e.*, from the Contract (Tr. J. 2: II 28:21-29:2):

>   any rights arising out of the contractual dispute
>   [...] would not survive an award.   So, if the

---

         at para. 66, Fn. 9. *See* also *Tokios Tokeles* v. *Ukraine*, Decision on Jurisdiction, 29 April 2004, at para. 80, available at http://www.investmentclaims.com/decisionslTokios-Ukraine-Jurisdiction-29 Apr2004.pdf.

[27]   *Wena Hotels v. Egypt*, Award, 8 December 2000, 41 ILM 896 (2002) at para. 126, Decision on Annulment, 28 January 2002, 41 ILM 933 (2002) at para. 54.

[28]   *See*, from the very beginning of ICSID practice, *Holiday Inns v. Morocco*, Decision of jurisdiction of 12 May 1974, reported in Pierre Lalive, The First World Bank Arbitration (Holiday Inns v. Morocco) – Some Legal Problems, British Yearbook of International Law 1980, p. 159.

award is a valid award, those rights would be
replaced by rights arising out of the award itself.

113. This argument refers to the requirement of Article 25(1) of the ICSID
Convention that the dispute "aris[e] directly out of an investment". The
Tribunal agrees with Bangladesh that the rights arising out of the ICC
Award arise only *indirectly* from the investment. Indeed, the opposite
view would mean that the Award itself does constitute an investment
under Article 25(1) of the ICSID Convention, which the Tribunal is not
prepared to accept.

114. However, as already mentioned, the notion of investment pursuant to
Article 25 of the ICSID must be understood as covering all the
elements of the operation, that is not only the ICC Arbitration, but also
inter alia the Contract, the construction itself and the Retention Money
(*see* above No. 110). Hence, in accordance with previous case law[29],
the Tribunal holds that the present dispute arises directly out of the
overall investment.

* * *

115. Finally, the Tribunal notes Bangladesh's point "that Article 26 of the
Washington Convention does not allow that these proceedings be run
[...] accept[ing] the findings from the ICC Tribunal and us[ing] that for
[this Tribunal's] findings" (Tr. II, 82:15-18). To the extent that this
may be interpreted as a jurisdictional objection, the Tribunal stresses
that it is not requested to "accept and use" the ICC Tribunal's findings.
It is requested to review whether the ICC Award was frustrated
contrary to the protection provided in the BIT.

5. JURISDICTIONAL OBJECTIONS UNDER THE BIT

116. It is undisputed that the jurisdiction of the Tribunal under the BIT is
limited to the scope of the dispute resolution clause contained in Article
9 of the BIT. Under the heading "Settlement of Disputes between
Investors and the Contracting Parties", this provision states:

> 1. Any disputes arising between a Contracting
> Party and the investors of the other, <u>relating
> to compensation for expropriation,
> nationalization, requisition or similar</u>

---

[29] *See*, for instance, *CSOB v. The Slovak Republic* (ICSID Case No. ARB/97/4),
Decision on Jurisdiction of 24 May 1999, ICSID Review 1999, p. 275.

measures, including disputes relating to the amount of the relevant payments shall be settled amicably, as far as possible.

2. In the event that such a dispute cannot be settled amicably within six months of the date of a written application. The investor in question may submit the dispute, at his discretion, for settlement to:

a) the Contracting Party's Court, at all instances, having territorial jurisdiction;

b) an ad hoc Arbitration Tribunal, in accordance with the Arbitration Rules of the "UN Commission on International Trade Law" (UNCITRAL),

c) the "International Centre for the Settlement of Investment Disputes" for the application of the arbitration procedure provided by the Washington Convention of 18th March 1965 on the "Settlement of Investment Disputes between States and nationals of other States", whenever, or as soon as both Contracting Parties have validly acceded to it.

(Emphasis added)

117. This provision implicitly refers to Article 5 of the BIT, which speaks of expropriation of "investments". Under the heading "Nationalization or Expropriation", this provision reads in pertinent part as follows:

1. (1) The investments to which this Agreement relates shall not be subject to any measure which might limit permanently or temporarily their joined rights of ownership, possession, control or enjoyment, save where specifically provided by law and by judgments or orders issued by Courts or Tribunals having jurisdiction.

(2) Investments of investors of one of the Contracting Parties shall not be directly or indirectly nationalized, expropriated, requisitioned or subjected to any measures

having similar effects in the territory of the other Contracting Party, except for public purposes, or national interest, against immediate full and effective compensation, and on condition that these measures are taken on a non-discriminatory basis and in conformity with all legal provisions and procedures.

118.   In turn, investments are defined in Article 1(1) of the BIT as follows:

[1.]   The term "investment" shall be construed to mean any kind of property invested before or after the entry into force of this Agreement by a natural or legal person being a national of one Contracting Party in the territory of the other in conformity with the laws and regulations of the latter.

Without limiting the generality of the foregoing, the term "investment" comprises:

a)   movable and immovable property, and any other rights in rem including, insofar as they may be used for investment purposes, real guarantees on other property;

b)   shares, debentures, equity holdings and any other negotiable instrument or document of credit, as well as Government and public securities in general;

c)   credit for sums of money or any right for pledges or services having an economic value connected with investments, as well as reinvested income as defined in paragraph 5 hereafter; [...]

e)   any right of a financial nature accruing by law or by contract and any licence, concession or franchise issued in accordance with current provisions governing the exercise of business activities, including prospecting for, cultivating, extracting and exploiting natural resources.

5.1   Has Saipem made an investment under Article 1(1) of the BIT?

119.   It is common ground between the parties that the Tribunal's jurisdiction is conditioned upon Saipem having made an investment within the meaning of the BIT (RA, p. 27, para. 118).

120.   As already mentioned, the Tribunal is not prepared to consider that the term "investment" in Article 1(1) of the BIT is defined according to the law of the host State (*see* above IV, B). Accordingly, the question is whether Saipem made an investment within the meaning of Article 1(1) of the BIT, without reference to the law of Bangladesh.

5.1.1   The general definition of investment in Article 1(1) of the BIT

121.   Article 1(1) of the BIT gives a general definition of investment as "any kind of property". On its face, this general definition is very broad[30].

122.   In the light of the conclusion reached above according to which Saipem made an investment within the meaning of Article 25 of the ICSID Convention, the Tribunal fails to see how the operation at issue could not be considered as a "kind of property" protected by the BIT.

123.   At the hearing, Bangladesh modified its argumentation on the law governing the term 'property' which was referred to earlier (see above No. 81) as follows:

> We do not say directly that Bangladesh law must apply to determine the meaning, we do not say that; but we say you get some help from the fact that this [i.e. "property"] is a concept well known in Bangladesh and it is probably the reason why this has happened.
> (Tr. J. II 18-22-25)[31]

124.   The Tribunal is not convinced by this amended argument either. To discard it, it suffices to imagine that the term 'property' (or its

---

[30]   The terms "any kind of property" correspond to "every kind of asset", which is generally acknowledged as *"[p]ossibly the broadest [...] general definition"* contained in a BIT (*see* Noah RUBINS, International Investment, Political Risk and Dispute Resolution, 2005, p. 291).

[31]   In its last written submission, Bangladesh already put forward a similar argument: "the types of property said to be included in the list must be considered in the light of the word 'property' itself" and of its alleged narrow meaning under Bangladeshi law (Reply J., p. 14, para. 3.10).

translation in Italian) could have a specific meaning under Italian law. If one were to follow Bangladesh's approach, this would lead to a different interpretation and thus a different scope of protection under the BIT depending on the country in which the investment is made. This cannot be the meaning of the BIT.

5.1.2 A "credit for sums of money" within Article 1(1)(c) of the BIT

125. It is Saipem's primary case that the Contract is an investment as defined in Article 1(1) of the BIT and that "the rights accruing from the ICC Award fall squarely within the notion of 'credit for sums of money [...] connected with investments' set out in Article 1(1)(c) of the BIT" (Response J., p. 10, para. 46).

126. Bangladesh objects that "[t]hese words would normally include bank deposits or book debts on a running account" (Rejoinder J., p. 14, para. 3.11). This may well be so. However, in their ordinary meaning, the words 'credit for sums of money' also cover rights under an award ordering a party to pay an amount of money: the prevailing party undoubtedly has a credit for a sum of money in the amount of the award.

127. This said, the rights embodied in the ICC Award were not created by the Award, but arise out of the Contract. The ICC Award crystallized the parties' rights and obligations under the original contract. It can thus be left open whether the Award itself qualifies as an investment, since the contract rights which are crystallized by the Award constitute an investment within Article 1(1)(c) of the BIT.

128. Having reached this conclusion, the Tribunal does not need to make a final ruling on Saipem's additional argument that the arbitration agreement contained in the Contract constitutes a "right of a financial nature accruing by law or by contract" within Article 1(1)(e) of the BIT (Tr. J. II 58:20-23).

5.2 Are the facts alleged by Saipem capable of constituting an expropriation under Article 5 of the BIT?

129. According to Saipem, its case is based on Petrobangla's alleged unlawful disruption of the ICC Arbitration, on the alleged interference by the domestic courts with the Arbitration, and on the *de facto* annulment of the ICC Award. These acts allegedly deprived Saipem of the sums awarded to it by the ICC Award, and thus amount to an illegal

expropriation in breach of Article 5 of the BIT (Response J., p. 4, para. 15). At the hearing, Saipem further submitted that a State's disavowal of its undertaking to arbitrate a contractual dispute may have a "confiscatory effect" (Tr. J. II, 50:16-23[32]) and summarized its case as follows:

> [T]he claims which are brought before the tribunal are a claim for expropriation in violation of Article 5 of the BIT. It is an expropriation which has resulted from a complex behaviour of the whole state, which reneged on its obligations to enforce the arbitration award and to respect the proper conduct of the arbitration proceedings [...].
> (Tr. J. II 52:12-18)

130. Saipem brings a claim for expropriation and the BIT provides for ICSID jurisdiction in case of expropriation. Bangladesh does not claim that the ICC Award and/or the rights determined by the Award are not capable of being expropriated. Rightly so, as it is widely accepted under general international law that immaterial rights can be the subject of expropriation[33]. Moreover, as the European Court of Human Rights unequivocally held, rights under judicial decisions are protected property that can be the object of an expropriation:

> In order to determine whether the applicants had a "possession" for the purposes of Article 1 of Protocol No. 1 (P1-1), the Court must ascertain whether judgment no. 13910/79 of the Athens Court of First Instance and the arbitration award had given rise to a debt in their favour that was sufficiently established to be enforceable. [...] [T]he arbitration award, which clearly recognised the State's liability up to a maximum of specified amounts in three different currencies [...].

---

32   Referring to the developments in Saipem's letter to ICSID of 5 April 2005

33   *See* for instance *Phillips Petroleum Iran v. Islamic Republic of Iran et National Iranian Oil Company*, Iran-US Claims Tribunal, Case No. 39, Chamber Two, Award No. 425-39-2 of 29 June 1989, Yearbook of Commercial Arbitration, Vol. XVI (1991), pp. 298-321, para. 75.

> According to its wording, the award was final
> and binding; it did not require any further
> enforcement measure and no ordinary or special
> appeal lay against it [...]. Under Greek legislation
> arbitration awards have the force of final
> decisions and are deemed to be enforceable. The
> grounds for appealing against them are
> exhaustively listed in Article 897 of the Code of
> Civil Procedure [...]; no provision is made for an
> appeal on the merits.
>
> At the moment when Law no. 1701/1987 was
> passed the arbitration award of 27 February 1984
> therefore conferred on the applicants a right in
> the sums awarded. Admittedly, that right was
> revocable, since the award could still be
> annulled, but the ordinary courts had by then
> already twice held - at first instance and on
> appeal - that there was no ground for such
> annulment. Accordingly, in the Court's view,
> that right constituted a "possession" within the
> meaning of Article 1 of Protocol No.1 (P1-1)[34].

131. A further question relates not to the object, but to the subject or the
author of the expropriation. Indeed, more often than not the
expropriation results from an act of the executive power. By contrast,
Saipem submitted at the hearing that the acts of a court, *i.e.* of the
judiciary power, can effect an expropriation:

> It is undeniable [...] that the interference by a
> State (including by the action of its courts) with
> an arbitration agreement with a foreign national
> constitutes a violation of international law. [...]
> [i]f such interference has the effect of
> confiscating the foreign national's investment as
> it does in the present case, it also constitutes an
> expropriation under the BIT and international
> law.

---

[34] *Stran Greek Refineries and Stratis Andreadis v. Greece* – 13427/87 [1994] ECHR 48 (9
December 1994), paras. 59-62, cross-references omitted; also available at
http://worldlii.org/eu/cases/ECHR/1994/48.html. *See* also *Brumarescu v. Romania*
Source: Human Rights Case Digest, Volume 10, Numbers 10-12, 1999, pp. 237-241,
also available at http://worldlii.org/eu/cases/ECHR/1999/105.html.

This is perfectly demonstrated in a very recent publication by Judge Schwebel dealing with the confiscatory effects of the interference by State courts with arbitration. Judge Schwebel makes it quite clear that "[t]he contractual right of an alien to arbitration of disputes arising under a contract to which it is party is a valuable right, which often is of importance to the very conclusion of the contract." Therefore, any "[v]itiation of that right" through court interference "attracts the international responsibility of the State of which the issuing court is an organ". Judge Schwebel refers to anti-suit injunctions, but this statement clearly applies more broadly to all court interference, including that of the Bangladeshi courts in the present case, the effect of which is obviously identical. Such interference constitutes a "ground of violation of customary international law", and more specifically of

> "the principle that a State is not entitled to take the property or contractual rights of an alien within its jurisdiction by actions that are arbitrary, tortious and confiscatory" [Emphasis added].

(Saipem's letter of 24 March 2005 submitted at the hearing, with the agreement of Bangladesh [Tr. J. II 88:8-13], as Exh. C-102[35])

132. Irrespective of whether Judge Schwebel's opinion can be applied in the present context, the Tribunal considers that there is no reason why a judicial act could not result in an expropriation. Nothing in the BIT indicates such a limitation. Moreover, Bangladesh did not cite any decision supporting the opposite view. Quite to the contrary, the Tribunal notes that the European Court of Human Rights had no hesitation to hold that court decisions can amount to an expropriation[36].

---

[35] Referring to S. M. Schwebel, Anti-Suit Injunctions in International Arbitration: An Overview, in Anti-Suit Injunctions in International Arbitration (E. Gaillard, editor), IAI (International Arbitration Institute) Series on International Arbitration, no. 2, Juris Publishing, 2004, p. 13.

[36] *Allard v. Sweden*, no. 35179/97 (Sect. 4) (bil.), ECHR 2003-VII – (24.6.03), available at http://worldlii.org/eu/cases/ECHR/2003/310.html.

Indeed, this is at least implicitly conceded by Bangladesh when it insists on the fact that consent to jurisdiction over the purported expropriation by acts of the judiciary is excluded by Article 5.1 of the BIT (Tr. J. II, 33:6-9; *see* section 5.3 below).

133. For these reasons, the Tribunal considers that the facts alleged by Saipem would be capable of constituting an expropriation under Article 5 of the BIT if they were established.

134. For the sake of clarity it should be added that whether or not Petrobangla and the courts of Bangladesh actually breached the guarantees of the BIT is a question to be determined with the merits of the dispute. On the merits, Saipem will have to produce evidence and legal arguments to establish the alleged breach and Bangladesh will have the right to challenge such evidence and legal arguments.

5.3 Did Bangladesh consent to ICSID arbitration for claims based on decisions by its courts?

135. Bangladesh further asserts that even if *quod non* the Contract and the ICC Award were to qualify as investment, Saipem's claims would not fall within the scope of Bangladesh's consent to ICSID arbitration:

> Since Saipem claims that its right to the ICC Award has been affected by the judicial acts in Bangladesh, as a matter of interpretation of the BIT, such rights cannot have any protection under Art. 5(1)(1) of the BIT. Bangladesh has expressly excluded consent in respect of *"judgments or orders issued by Courts or Tribunals having jurisdiction"*.
> (C-Mem, p. 53, para. 4.11)

136. According to Saipem, interpreting the last phrase of this provision as an exclusion of the consent to arbitrate with respect to judicial acts would result in negating the protection which the BIT grants investors. It stresses that "in almost all instances expropriations occur as a result of actions which directly or indirectly derive from an action contemplated in a law or a judgment" and that accepting the Respondent's position would render the State's actions immune from the rules of the BIT (Rejoinder J., pp. 21-22, para. 86).

137. In the Tribunal's opinion, Article 5(1)(1) *in fine*, which was quoted above (*see* above No. 117) cannot be understood as creating immunity in favour of the judiciary power. This provision merely affirms the

principle that, "in order to escape being considered an internationally wrongful act, a State measure limiting or excluding an investor's rights of ownership, control or enjoyment can only be considered legal if it has been adopted by law or by a judicial decision" (Response J. p. 17, paras. 74-75, see also Tr. J. II, 61:10-12).

138. Under these circumstances, the Tribunal does not have to make a ruling at this stage *on* whether in the present instance the courts of Bangladesh "ha[d] jurisdiction" within the meaning of Article 5(1)(1) *in fine* of the BIT.

5.4 Are Saipem's treaty claims in reality contract claims?

139. *In* its Counter-Memorial, Bangladesh submitted that Saipem's "claim is in reality a contractual claim dressed up as a treaty claim" (C-Mem., p. 14, para. 1.43).

140. Saipem opposes this submission with the following argument:

> The focus of the Claimant's case is that its right to payment under the Contract as ascertained by, and incorporated in, the ICC Award has been expropriated by the unlawful decisions of the Bangladeshi courts that revoked the authority of the ICC arbitrators and declared the ICC Award null and void, thus precluding its enforcement in Bangladesh or elsewhere. The net result of all this was, obviously, to deprive the Claimant of the compensation for its investment.
> (Response J., p. 3, para. 13)

141. In the Tribunal's view, the essence of Saipem's case is that the courts of Bangladesh acted in violation of the New York Convention and in an "illegal, arbitrary and idiosyncratic" manner amounting to a violation of the protection afforded to foreign investors under Article 5 of the BIT. Saipem does not request relief under the Contract; it does not raise contract claims over which the Tribunal would have no jurisdiction.

142. Whether Saipem's treaty claim is well-founded is a different issue which will be decided when dealing with the merits of the dispute. For instance, it is not for the Tribunal to rule at this stage on Bangladesh's submission that "the Claimant is in essence asserting that the Bangladeshi court acted in a way to deny it justice" and that such a breach of international law presupposes the exhaustion of local

remedies (Reply J., pp. 17-18, para. 12), or on the allegation that the courts of Bangladesh actually breached the New York Convention or other principles of international law. These are matters which will have to be reviewed during the merits phase of this arbitration.

5.5   Are the disputed actions attributable to Bangladesh?

143.   Saipem submits that the expropriation was caused by the combined actions of Petrobangla and the courts of Bangladesh. Bangladesh does not dispute that the courts are "part of the State" (Tr. J. II 32:6) and, thus, that their actions are attributable to Bangladesh. Indeed, this cannot be seriously challenged in light of previous ICSID cases[37]. Hence, the only disputed question is whether Petrobangla's acts can be attributed to Bangladesh.

144.   According to the test set forth above (*see* above No. 84 *et seq.*), it is not for the Tribunal at the jurisdictional stage to examine whether the acts complained of give rise to the State's responsibility, except if it were manifest that the entity involved had no link whatsoever with the State. This is plainly not the case in the present dispute.

145.   In fact, at first sight at least, Petrobangla appears to be part of the State under Bangladeshi law. Indeed, upon a specific question from the Tribunal at the hearing, Mr. Razzaq confirmed that "Petrobangla is a statutory public authority" within the meaning of the Constitution of Bangladesh and is thus "included in the definition of the state, the same as Parliament" (Tr. J. I 166:19-20 [Razzaq]).

146.   In this context and still at first sight, the Tribunal fails to see the relevance of Bangladesh's emphasis on the fact that Petrobangla, as a part of the State, "has its own legal personality" (Tr. J. I 61:20-21 [Razzaq]) distinct and allegedly independent from the Government of Bangladesh (Tr. J. I. 60:1 *et seq.*; 66:20-21 [Razzaq]). In any event, these circumstances do not imply that Petrobangla has no link whatsoever with the State.

---

[37]   *See*, for instance, *The Loewen Group Inc. and Raymond L. Loewen v. United States of America*, ICSID Case No. ARB(AF)/98/3, Decision on Jurisdiction of 5 January 2001, paras. 39 *et seq.*, also available at http://www.investmentclaims.com/decisions/Loewen-US-Jurisdiction-5Jan2001.pdf; *Waste Management Inc. v. United Mexican States*, ICSID No. ARB(AF)/00/3, Award of 30 April 2004, available at http://www.investmentclaims.com/decisions/WasteMgmt¬Mexico-2-FinalAward-30Apr2004. pdf.

147.   Similarly, the allegation that Petrobangla's actions were "not acts of the State in a sovereign capacity" (Tr. J. II 31:21-22) and that Petrobangla acted in front of the courts of Bangladesh "as a contracting party which feared bias of the arbitrators they were facing at the time" (Tr. J. II 31:25-32:1) does not make a difference at this jurisdictional stage.

148.   When assessing the merits of the dispute, the Tribunal will rule on the issue of attribution under international law, especially by reference to the Articles on State Responsibility as adopted in 2001 by the International Law Commission and as commended to the attention of Governments by the UN General Assembly in Resolution 56/83 of 12 December 2001 (the ILC Articles) as a codification of customary international law.   The Tribunal will in particular consider the following provisions:

- Art. 4 of the ILC Articles which codifies the well-established rule that the conduct of any State organ, according to the internal law of the State, shall be considered an act of that State under international law.   This rule addresses the attribution of acts of so-called *de jure* organs which are empowered to act for the State within the limits of their competence.
- Art. 5 of the ILC Articles which goes on to attribute to a State the conduct of a person or entity which is not a *de jure* organ but which is empowered by the law of that State to exercise elements of governmental authority provided that person or entity is acting in that capacity in the particular instance.
- Art. 8 of the ILC Articles which states that the conduct of a person or group of persons acting under the instructions of or under the direction or control of the State shall be considered an act of that State under international law.

149.   At this jurisdictional stage, there is no indication that either the courts of Bangladesh or Petrobangla could manifestly not qualify as state organs at least *de facto*.

6.   OJECTIONS RELATED TO THE ADMISSIBILITY OF SAIPEM'S CLAIM

6.1   Does the requirement to exhaust local remedies apply?

150.   It is Bangladesh's submission that Saipem did not exhaust all the local remedies available against the court decisions issued in relation to the arbitration, in particular the decision to revoke the arbitrators' authority (*see* in particular Tr. J. II 32:11 *et seq.*).   Moreover, Bangladesh submits that there is no evidence before the Tribunal that it would have

been futile for Saipem to take such further judicial steps (Tr. J. II 32:22 *et seq.*).

151.   To the extent that this submission is regarded as a bar to the admissibility of the claim and/or to the jurisdiction of the Tribunal (Reply J., para. 3.25), the Tribunal cannot follow it. Article 26 of the ICSID Convention dispenses with the requirement to exhaust local remedies. It is true that such requirement does apply to claims based on denial of justice, but this is not a matter of the claim's admissibility but a substantive requirement[38]. As a matter of principle, exhaustion of local remedies does not apply in expropriation law[39]. Since Saipem's claim is brought on the ground of expropriation, there appears to be no ground to deny jurisdiction for the reason that Saipem did not exhaust the judicial remedies available in Bangladesh.

152.   That said, it is true that in the present case the alleged expropriating authority is a judicial body. This raises the question whether an analogy should be made between expropriation and denial of justice when it comes to exhaustion of local remedies. Bangladesh actually argues that Saipem "is in essence asserting that the Bangladeshi courts acted in a way to deny it justice" (Reply J., p. 17, para. 3.21).

153.   Whether the requirement of exhaustion of local remedies may be applicable by analogy to an expropriation by the acts of a court and whether, in the affirmative, the available remedies were effective are questions to be addressed with the merits of the dispute. The relevant test for jurisdictional purposes requires that the facts alleged may constitute a breach of Article 5 of the BIT. Saipem's contention that the courts of Bangladesh expropriated its investment and that the available remedies were futile meets this test. If they were proven, they may constitute breaches of Article 5 of the BIT.

6.2   Does Saipem's claim constitute an abuse of process?

154.   Bangladesh's second objection concerning admissibility is that Saipem's claim constitutes an abuse of process as it seeks in substance to "enforce an invalid ICC award using the ICSID jurisdiction" (Tr. J. II, 34:17-23). More specifically, according to Bangladesh:

---

[38]   Jan Paulsson, Denial of Justice in International Law, pp. 100 *et seq.* (2005). See also *The Loewen Group, Inc, and Raymond Loewen* v. *United States of America*, Award, 26 June 2003, para. 153, 42 ILM 811, 836 (2003).

[39]   *Generation Ukraine, Inc.* v. *Ukraine*, Award, 16 September 2003, paras. 20.30 and 20.33.

Saipem is asking the ICSID tribunal to rubberstamp the ICC award, thereby converting it into an ICSID award, in order to bypass the correct method of enforcement of an ICC award. Saipem is thereby trying to take advantage of:

(1)   the more favourable means of enforcement of an ICSID award;

(2)   trying to have a second attempt at enforcing the ICC award;

(3)   trying to mutate the Dhaka-ICC arbitration mechanism into a delocalised one to avoid any potential domestic Bangladesh annulment proceedings.

It is submitted that this would constitute an abuse of the ICSID Convention, the Arbitration Act 1940 of Bangladesh and the express will of the parties. In addition, this would be an abuse of the process of this Tribunal as the arbitral tribunal's duty is to adjudicate upon all issues before it for itself.

Further, ICSID is not an appeals facility: the appropriate appeals mechanism against the Bangladesh judgment was an appeal to the next court within the Bangladesh court hierarchy. This was not done on the express choice and election of Saipem.

(C-Mem., p. 59, references omitted)

155.   In the Tribunal's opinion, the present proceedings are not aimed at enforcing an award which is inexistent according to the courts of Bangladesh. The Tribunal understands Saipem's case to claim that Bangladesh has frustrated its rights by unlawfully interfering in the arbitration process. The fact that the indemnity claimed in this arbitration matches the amounts awarded in the ICC arbitration at least to some extent, does not mean in and of itself that this Tribunal would "enforce" the ICC Award in the event of a treaty breach. To avoid any ambiguity, the Tribunal stresses that Saipem's claim does not deal with the courts' regular exercise of their power to rule over annulment or setting aside proceedings of an award rendered within their jurisdiction. It deals with the court's alleged wrongful interference.

156.   Finally, Bangladesh invokes "an abuse of process [...] because this whole claim goes against party autonomy" (Tr. J. II, 34:17). In substance, Bangladesh insists that, by choosing a seat of the arbitration in Dhaka, Saipem has accepted the supervisory powers of the local courts and thus assumed the risk of such courts interfering. It argues that a determination by this Tribunal not recognizing the nullity of the ICC Award would be contrary to party autonomy.

157.   In the Tribunal's opinion, it is true that the choice of Dhaka as seat of the arbitration implied the acceptance of the jurisdiction of the local courts in aid and control of the ICC Arbitration and the acceptance of the related litigation risk (Tr. J. II 27:18-19). It is also true that – contrary to Saipem's submissions (Tr. J. II, 36:25-37:2) – the latter was not compelled to accept that risk (Tr. J. II 76:1 *et seq.*).

158.   But this is not the question here. By accepting jurisdiction, this Tribunal does not institute itself as control body over the ICC Arbitration, nor as enforcement court, nor as supranational appellate body for local court decisions. This Tribunal is a treaty judge. It is called upon to rule exclusively on treaty breaches, whatever the context in which such treaty breaches arise.

7.   COSTS

159.   Having concluded that it has jurisdiction over the present dispute, the Tribunal reserves all questions concerning the costs and expenses of the Tribunal and of the parties for subsequent determination.

160.   This being said, the Tribunal has taken due note of Bangladesh's complaint that Saipem did not provide all the copies of the cited authorities thus creating additional costs for Bangladesh (Tr. J. II 1:11 *et seq.*).

V.   DECISION ON JURISDICTION

161.   For the reasons set forth above, the Tribunal:

a)   Holds that the present dispute is within the jurisdiction of the Centre and the competence of the Tribunal;

b)   Dismisses all of the Respondent's objections to the admissibility of the claims, the jurisdiction of ICSID, and the competence of this Tribunal;

c)   By virtue of Rule 41(4) of the Arbitration Rules will make the necessary order for the continuation of the proceedings on the merits;

d)   Reserves all questions concerning the costs and expenses of the Tribunal and of the parties for subsequent determination.

VI.   DETERMINATION ON PROVISIONAL MEASURES

1.   RELEVANT FACTS AND SAIPEM'S REQUEST

162.   It is common ground that Petrobangla did not repay the Retention Money after the issuance of the Warranty Bond.

163.   In the Request for Arbitration and Statement of Claim, Saipem asked for provisional measures aiming at restraining Bangladesh and at preventing Petrobangla from pursuing any payment demand based on the Warranty Bond until the outcome of the present arbitration (*see* above No. 62).

164.   The parties subsequently agreed to the Tribunal's proposal that a decision be deferred until after the submission of the Counter-Memorial.

165.   Pointing out that Bangladesh acknowledged that "it should have released the Retention Money against Receipt of the Bond" (C-Mem., p. 27, para. 33), Saipem submitted that "the natural follow-up of [this statement] would have been that the Respondent formally state its intention not to seek payment of, and to return, the Bond and to return the Retention Money and to take all the necessary steps needed to end the litigation in Bangladesh and in Italy relating to the Bond". It then invited Bangladesh to "provide a formal declaration to this effect by June 30, 2006" (Response J., p. 31, para. 141). Saipem confirmed by letter of 31 May 2006 that its request for provisional measures was thus suspended.

166.   During the telephone conference held on 26 July 2006, the parties and the Tribunal agreed as follows in respect of Saipem's request for provisional measures:

> The parties can further address the question of the Claimant's request for interim relief in their respective briefs and at the hearing. The Tribunal will decide this issue after the hearing.
> (PO#2, Section VII)

167.   In its Reply on Jurisdiction, Bangladesh submitted *inter alia* that the Tribunal lacked jurisdiction to order any interim relief, since the

Retention Money and the Warranty Bond were "contractual breaches not amounting to a BIT claim" (Reply J., p. 19, para. 4.4).

168.   In its Rejoinder on Jurisdiction, Saipem reiterated the request formulated in the Request for Arbitration and asked the Tribunal to

> issue a provisional measure recommending that Bangladesh refrain from calling on the Warranty Bond and return it to the Claimant together with the Retention Money without further delay. (Rejoinder, p. 28, para. 107(ii))

169.   At the end of the hearing, Saipem amended its original request for provisional measures as follows:

> Claimant respectfully submits the following requests for provisional measures under Article 47 of the ICSID Convention and Rule 39 of the ICSID Rules:
> - to recommend that the Respondent cause (i) the return of the Bond to Claimant for cancellation and (ii) the immediate termination of the litigation pending in Bangladesh against former Banque Indosuez; in the subordinate, to cause the suspension of said litigation and to prevent or avoid encashment of the Bond by Petrobangla until final adjudication of these proceedings;
> - to recommend that the Respondent cause the Retention Money, in the amount of USD 869,903 plus Taka 10,391,605 plus interest at the rate of 3.375% per annum from 17 June 1992 to be paid to Claimant right away; in the subordinate, to recommend that the Retention Money be put in an escrow account in the name of ICSID or another neutral party with instructions that payment thereunder be made upon issuance of the ICSID award adjudicating in favour of Claimant.

2.   RELEVANT PROVISIONS

170.   Provisional measures are governed by the ICSID Convention and the ICSID Arbitration Rules.

171.   Article 47 of the ICSID Convention reads as follows:

> Except as the parties otherwise agree, the Tribunal may, if it considers that the circumstances so require, recommend any provisional measures which should be taken to preserve the respective interests of either party.

172.   Rule 39 of the ICSID Arbitration Rules provides in relevant part as follows:

> (1) At any time during the proceedings a party may request that provisional measures for the preservation of its rights be recommended by the Tribunal. The request shall specify the rights to be preserved, the measures the recommendation of which is requested, and the circumstances that require such measures.
>
> (2) The Tribunal shall give priority to the consideration of a request made pursuant to paragraph (1).
>
> (3) The Tribunal may also recommend provisional measures on its own initiative or recommend measures other than those specified in a request. It may at any time modify or revoke its recommendations.

3.   TRIBUNAL'S POWER TO RECOMMEND PROVISIONAL MEASURES

173.   Having concluded that it has jurisdiction to hear the present dispute, there can be no doubt that this Tribunal has the power to recommend provisional measures.

4.   RELEVANT STANDARD

174.   It is generally acknowledged that, by providing that the Tribunal may recommend any provisional measures "if it considers that the circumstances so require", Article 47 of the ICSID Convention requires that the requested measure be both necessary and urgent.

175.   Following *Pey Casado*, *Maffezini* and *CSOB*, the Tribunal considers that under Article 47 of the Convention a tribunal enjoys broad discretion when ruling on provisional measures, but should not

237

recommend provisional measures lightly and should weigh the parties' divergent interests in the light of all the circumstances of the case[40].

5. **PARTIES' POSITIONS**

176. In support of its request, Saipem puts forward the following main arguments:

(i) By sabotaging the ICC Arbitration and by rendering the ICC Award unenforceable, Bangladesh has deprived Saipem of its right to the Retention Money and to the restitution of the Warranty Bond which were both awarded by the ICC Award.

(ii) Saipem is thus exposed to the risk of a call under the Bond (which was declared inadmissible by the ICC Tribunal) which would lead to a further expropriation.

(iii) Bangladesh's actions in relation to the Bond and to the Retention Money are therefore in themselves direct breaches of the prohibition on expropriation.

177. Given that the proceedings in Italy and Bangladesh are still pending, Saipem claims to face the risk

> that if Petrobangla succeeds in the action in Bangladesh, the Bangladesh bank will have to pay and the Bangladesh bank obviously will ask the Italian bank to be paid by the Italian bank

---

[40] "[...] provisional measures authorized by Article 47 of the ICSID Convention and Rule 39 of the Arbitration Rules-provisions which contain no indication or exact statement in this regard-can be extremely diverse and are left to the appreciation of each Arbitration Tribunal." *Victor Pey Casado and President Allende Foundation v. Republic of Chile* (ICSID Case No. ARB/98/25), Decision on Provisional Measures (25 September 2001), para. 15, English translation of French and Spanish originals in 6 ICSID Reports 375 (2004), "The imposition of provisional measures is an extraordinary measure which should not be granted lightly by the Arbitral Tribunal" and that the party requesting the measures "has the burden to demonstrate why the Tribunal should grant its application" (*Emilio Agustín Maffezini v. Kingdom of Spain* (ICSID Case No. ARB/97/7), Decision on Request for Provisional Measures (October 28, 1999), p. 3, para. 10) and in *CSOB* that "the provisional measures envisaged under Article 47 of the ICSID Convention are not exceptional measures in the sense that they require more than a showing that they are necessary to preserve the rights of the parties" (*Ceskoslovenska Obchodni Banka, A.S. v. The Slovak Republic* (ICSID Case No. ARB/97/4), Procedural Order No. 3 (November 5, 1998), p. 2)

and the Italian bank will ask Saipem in the
current proceedings already instituted in Italy to
be paid the amount of money.
(Tr. J. II 62:17-21).

178.   In its Reply on Jurisdiction, Bangladesh submits in substance that its
        admissions on the Retention Money and on the Warranty Bond were
        based on an analysis of the parties' obligations under the Contract and
        have thus no bearing in an action for violation of the BIT (Reply J., p.
        19, para. 19). Moreover, Bangladesh claims that it never called upon
        the Warranty Bond.

6.   TRIBUNAL'S DETERMINATION

179.   Bangladesh's argument that its admissions on the Retention Money
        have no bearing in an action for violation of the BIT overlooks the fact
        that the ICC Award disposed of the Retention Money and of the
        Warranty Bond and that the claims in this treaty arbitration relate at
        least in part to the ICC Award.

180.   Similarly, Bangladesh's assertion that Petrobangla never requested the
        payment of the Bond is difficult to reconcile with the content of the
        "extend or pay" letter of 18 April 1993 and with the fact that such a
        payment remains an issue in the pending litigation in Bangladesh.

181.   Moreover, at the hearing Saipem convincingly showed that there is a
        risk that it may be required to pay to the Italian bank the amount that
        the Bangladeshi bank may have to pay to Petrobangla.

182.   Hence, in view of the pending litigation in Bangladesh, the Tribunal
        considers that there is both necessity and urgency. This finding is
        reinforced by the facts that, apart from denying that it called the
        Warranty Bond, Bangladesh does not contest Saipem's contentions and
        that there is a risk of irreparable harm if Saipem has to pay the amount
        of the Warranty Bond.

7.   CONCLUSION

183.   Considering that under the current circumstances there is a risk that
        Petrobangla may draw on the Warranty Bond while keeping the
        Retention Money, that Bangladesh admitted that either the Retention
        Money should have been released or the Warranty Bond returned, and
        taking into account the parties' respective interests, the Tribunal is of
        the opinion that Bangladesh should take the necessary steps to ensure
        that Petrobangla does not proceed to encash the Warranty Bond.

184. Such a recommendation strikes a fair balance between the parties' interests. Saipem is protected from the risk of being required to effect payment to the Italian bank; Petrobangla is protected from the risks that are inherent in Saipem's requests to return the Warranty Bond for cancellation and to terminate or suspend immediately the litigation pending in Bangladesh.

185. By contrast, the Tribunal is of the opinion that Saipem's second request, *i.e.* the request for the return of the Retention Money, must be dismissed. Indeed, it is difficult to see how an immediate payment is necessary and urgent today. While the Tribunal is prepared to recommend measures preventing an increase of the harm allegedly suffered by one of the parties, the Tribunal is not inclined to recommend measures guaranteeing an award in favour of Saipem. Indeed, as correctly put by Bangladesh, this could be viewed as a *de facto* enforcement of part of the ICC Award.

8. RECOMMENDATION

On the basis of the reasons set forth above, the Tribunal hereby recommends that Bangladesh take the steps necessary to ensure that Petrobangla refrain from encashing the Warranty Bond No. PG/USD/12/92 issued by Banque Indosuez.

Done on March 21, 2007,

signed   *signed*

_____   _____

      Prof. Christoph Schreuer
      Sir Philip Otton

          signed

         _____

    Prof. Gabrielle Kaufmann-Kohler

ANNEX 3

Centre International pour le Règlement des Différends relatifs aux Investissements

CIRDI

Washington D.C.

dans la procédure

VICTOR PEY CASADO ET FONDATION « PRESIDENTE ALLENDE »
(Parties demanderesses)

contre

REPUBLIQUE DU CHILI
(Partie défenderesse)

Aff. CIRDI N° ARB/98/2

SENTENCE ARBITRALE

Membres du Tribunal
M. le Professeur Pierre Lalive, Président
Maître Mohammed Chemloul, Arbitre
M. le Professeur Emmanuel Gaillard, Arbitre

Secrétaires du Tribunal
Mme Gabriela Alvarez-Avila / Mme Eloïse Obadia

Date d'envoi aux parties : 8 mai 2008

CONSEILS

Pour les demanderesses :

Dr. Juan E. Garcés, Cabinet Garcés y Prada, Abogados, Madrid, Espagne,

avec la coopération de :

Me Carole Malinvaud et Me Alexandra Muñoz, Cabinet Gide, Loyrette, Nouel, Paris, France,

Me Samuel Buffone, Cabinet Ropes & Grey, Washington D.C., Etats-Unis, et

M. William W. Park, Professeur de Droit, Boston University, Etats-Unis.

Pour la défenderesse :

M. Eduardo Escalona Vásquez – Chef de la Division juridique, Ministère de l'économie, du développement et de la reconstruction, République du Chili,

M. Eduardo Bobadilla Brinkmann, M. Nicolás Muñoz Montes et M. Diego Rioseco Antezana – Programme de défense des arbitrages relatifs aux investissements étrangers, Ministère de l'économie, du développement et de la reconstruction, République du Chili,

M. Jorge Carey Tagle et M. Gonzalo Fernández Ruiz, Carey & Cía. Ltda. Abogados, Santiago du Chili, République du Chili,

M. Paolo Di Rosa, Arnold & Porter LLP, Washington D.C., Etats-Unis.

TABLE DES MATIERES

243

I.   INTRODUCTION

1.   Le présent litige oppose deux parties demanderesses, M. Pey Casado, se présentant comme ressortissant espagnol, et la Fondation espagnole Président Allende, d'une part, et la République du Chili, défenderesse (et partie demanderesse à l'exception d'incompétence) d'autre part.

2.   L'instance a été introduite par les parties demanderesses sur le fondement de la Convention de Washington de 1965 pour le

Règlement des Différends relatifs aux Investissements entre Etats et Ressortissants d'autres Etats (ci-après la « *Convention CIRDI* »), ratifiée par le Chili le 24 septembre 1991 et par l'Espagne le 18 août 1994, et de l'Accord entre le Royaume d'Espagne et la République du Chili pour la Protection et la Promotion Réciproque des Investissements, signé le 2 octobre 1991 et entré en vigueur le 29 mars 1994 (ci-après « *l'API Espagne-Chili* » ou « *l'API* »).

3.   Le litige concerne essentiellement les conséquences de la confiscation, par le Gouvernement chilien, des biens des sociétés Consortium Publicitaire et Périodique S.A. (ci-après « *CPP S.A.* ») et Entreprise Périodique Clarin Ltda (ci-après « *EPC Ltda* ») dont les demanderesses se prétendent propriétaires. Les faits de la cause feront l'objet plus loin d'un résumé sommaire et résulteront ensuite de l'exposé et de la discussion des thèses respectives des parties.

II.   PROCEDURE

4.   Le litige a donné lieu entre les parties à une procédure arbitrale exceptionnellement longue et complexe, en deux langues, le français et l'espagnol, procédure dont les principales étapes peuvent être résumées comme suit :

5.   Le 2 octobre 1997, M. Pey Casado a donné son consentement à l'arbitrage CIRDI (à l'exclusion de ce qui concernait un litige spécifique relatif à une rotative, qui sera désignée dans la présente sentence comme la rotative Goss) et le 6 octobre 1997, la Fondation Président Allende a consenti à l'arbitrage.[1]

6.   Le 3 novembre 1997, les deux demanderesses ont déposé auprès du Centre International pour le Règlement des Différends Relatifs aux Investissements (ci-après « *le Centre* » ou « *le CIRDI* ») une requête d'arbitrage contre la République du Chili. Cette requête d'arbitrage tendait à ce que :

> « *le Centre...*
> *- reconnaisse l'introduction de la présente demande d'arbitrage avec ses cinq copies, l'identification des Parties, ainsi que la preuve de la date de leur consentement à l'arbitrage, la production de l'information requise relative aux matières formant l'objet du différend de nature juridique découlant directement de la confiscation d'un investissement*

---

[1]   Annexes 10 et 2, respectivement, de la requête d'arbitrage du 3 novembre 1997.

> *étranger, accompagnés du droit d'enregistrement de la demande,*
> *- consente à en effectuer l'enregistrement, et après qu'elle ait été pleinement étayée,*
> *- déclare illégitime et contraire au Droit International la saisie et la confiscation de l'investissement réalisé par le citoyen espagnol, Monsieur Victor Pey Casado,*
> *- condamne la République du Chili à payer des dommages et intérêts pour un montant minimum de US$ 500,822,969, ainsi qu'au payement des intérêts à partir de la date de la sentence arbitrale, des honoraires et frais d'arbitrage, des honoraires professionnels,*
> *- y adjoigne toute autre condamnation que le Centre estimerait juste et équitable ».[2]*

7. Le 6 novembre 1997, le Centre a accusé réception de la requête d'arbitrage et, conformément à l'article 36 (1) de la Convention CIRDI, a transmis une copie de la requête à la République du Chili.

8. Le 20 avril 1998, le Secrétaire général du CIRDI, en dépit de l'opposition de la République du Chili, a procédé à l'enregistrement de la requête d'arbitrage conformément à l'article 36 (3) de la Convention CIRDI et a notifié cet enregistrement le même jour aux parties.

9. Le 14 septembre 1998, le Tribunal arbitral a été constitué, conformément à l'article 37 (2)(b) de la Convention CIRDI, de Monsieur le Juge Mohammed Bedjaoui, désigné par les parties demanderesses, de M. Jorge Witker Velásquez, désigné par la défenderesse, et de Monsieur le Juge Francisco Rezek, appelé à la présidence du Tribunal, désigné par le Président du Conseil administratif. Le 18 novembre 1998, l'Ambassadeur Galo Leoro Franco (Équateur) a été appelé à remplacer l'Arbitre Witker Velásquez qui avait donné sa démission le 21 octobre 1998. Conformément à l'article 25 du Règlement administratif et financier, M. Gonzalo Flores a été nommé secrétaire du Tribunal.

10. Le 1er février 1999, la défenderesse a communiqué au Secrétaire général du CIRDI une lettre objectant à la compétence du Centre et du Tribunal arbitral et sollicitant ce dernier de fixer des délais pour le dépôt par les parties des écritures relatives aux objections préliminaires à la compétence.

11. Le Tribunal a tenu sa première session avec les parties le 2 février 1999 au siège de la Banque mondiale à Washington, D.C. Un

---

[2] Requête d'arbitrage du 3 novembre 1997, p. 10.

calendrier a été fixé pour le dépôt d'écritures par les parties et, le 23 mars 1999, les demanderesses ont déposé un mémoire (daté du 17 mars), demandant au Tribunal arbitral de :

> « [déclarer] illégitime, contraire au Droit, nulle et de nul effet ab initio la saisie par un acte de force, la confiscation des biens, droits et crédits, de C.C.P. S.A. et de E.P.C. Ltée, ainsi que la dissolution de C.P.P. S.A. et de E.P.C. Ltée,
>
> - [condamner] l'Etat défendeur à indemniser en conséquence la Partie demanderesse eu égard à la totalité des biens confisqués, aux dommages et préjudices causés par les actes illégaux de force et de confiscation desdits biens, droits et crédits ainsi que de dissolution desdites Sociétés, y compris le lucrum cessans, et les intérêts capitalisés compensatoires à partir de la date de l'acte de force - le 11 septembre 1973- jusqu'à la date de la Sentence - et ce pour un montant minimum estimé provisoirement à la date du 11 septembre 1999, sauf erreur ou omission, à US\$ 515,193,400, auquel s'ajoute le dommage moral estimé selon les termes spécifiés au point 4.6.6.2 du présent Mémoire ;
>
> - [condamner] l'État défendeur à payer à la Demanderesse des intérêts moratoires calculés selon les mêmes termes que les intérêts compensatoires ou, subsidiairement, selon ce qui aura été fixé par le Tribunal à sa discrétion - à partir de la date de la Sentence et jusqu'à son accomplissement intégral ; et
>
> - [condamner] l'État défendeur à payer les frais de la procédure d'arbitrage, y compris les frais et honoraires des Membres du Tribunal, les frais pour l'utilisation des installations du CIRDI, les frais de traduction, ainsi que les frais et honoraires professionnels de la présente Partie, des avocats, experts, et autres personnes appelées à comparaître devant le Tribunal, ou subsidiairement, les frais de procédure de la présente Partie,
>
> - et à payer les sommes conformes à toutes autres condamnations que le Tribunal estimerait justes et équitables,
>
> - et ordonner l'exécution provisoire de la Sentence à intervenir. »[3]

---

[3]   Mémoire des demanderesses du 17 mars 1999, pp. 86-87.

12. Le 20 juillet 1999, la défenderesse a déposé un mémoire d'incompétence, affirmant notamment que :

> *« 1) Monsieur Pey Casado a la nationalité chilienne ;*
> *2) l'Accord pour la Protection et le Développement Réciproque des Investissements (A.P.P.I.) invoqué n'a pas d'effet rétroactif et ne peut donc pas s'appliquer pour résoudre des situations établies avant son entrée en vigueur ;*
> *3) Les actifs réclamés ne constituent pas un investissement étranger ;*
> *4) La Fondation « Président Allende » n'a pas soutenu les consultations amiables exigées dans ledit Accord ;*
> *5) Les Réclamants (Parties demanderesses) ont opté pour la juridiction chilienne en renonçant par conséquent, à la juridiction internationale ; et finalement,*
> *6) L'Etat du Chili n'a jamais donné son consentement pour que cette controverse puisse être soumise à la connaissance d'un Tribunal du CIRDI ».*[4]

13. La défenderesse concluait en demandant au Tribunal de déclarer que le différend *« excède manifestement la compétence du Centre »* et était hors de la juridiction de ce dernier et qu'il n'existait pas de motif plausible justifiant la présente instance, d'où résultait notamment que les parties demanderesses devaient être condamnées aux dépens.[5]

14. Le 13 septembre 1999, la défenderesse a déposé une requête de mesures provisoires aux fins de voir garantir la solvabilité des parties demanderesses pour couvrir le cas échéant les frais et dépens découlant de la procédure arbitrale.

15. Le 6 octobre 1999, les demanderesses ont déposé une *« réponse au mémoire soutenant l'incompétence »* (datée du 18 septembre 1999), demandant au Tribunal arbitral de :

> *« [Rejeter] intégralement la question de compétence soulevée par la République du Chili,*
> *[Déclarer] pleinement dans le champ de sa juridiction le fait de connaître et de juger le différend juridique qui lui est posé ; et*

---

[4] Mémoire d'incompétence de la défenderesse du 20 juillet 1999, p. 155.
[5] Mémoire d'incompétence de la défenderesse du 20 juillet 1999, p. 156.

> *[Disposer]* la poursuite de la procédure, avec la condamnation aux frais de cet incident ».[6]

16. Le 3 janvier 2000, la défenderesse a déposé son « *mémoire en réplique sur l'incompétence* » (daté du 27 décembre 1999), reprenant les conclusions 1 à 6 précitées de son écriture du 20 juillet 1999, et concluant que :

> « *7) les tentatives de Monsieur Pey Casado de se dépouiller de la nationalité chilienne afin d'accéder à un Tribunal qui autrement lui aurait été interdit, ainsi que le transfert de 90% de ses prétendus droits à une fondation espagnole dans le but évident de rattacher la controverse à un élément étranger, constitue le plus clair exemple de fraude à la loi* ».[7]

17. Dans les mêmes écritures, la défenderesse a demandé au Tribunal arbitral de décliner sa compétence. Elle a déclaré en outre que le Gouvernement du Chili « *ne conteste pas qu'il doive payer une indemnisation pour les biens confisqués, raison pour laquelle il a édicté une loi spéciale. Dans le cas spécifique de la confiscation des actifs appartenant aux Consorcio Publicitario y Periodístico S.A. et à la Empresa Periodística Clarín Ltda, l'État du Chili paiera l'indemnisation correspondante à ses propriétaires légitimes, conformément à une procédure qui se trouve actuellement bien avancée au bénéfice des affectés* ».[8]

18. Le 11 février 2000, les demanderesses ont déposé une « *réplique à la réponse soumise par la République du Chili au Contre-Mémoire réfutant le Déclinatoire de Compétence* » (datée du 7 février 2000), dans laquelle elles ont demandé au Tribunal de rejeter les objections de la défenderesse et de constater sa compétence pour connaître du présent litige.[9]

19. Du 3 au 5 mai 2000, le Tribunal arbitral a tenu des audiences sur la question de sa compétence à Washington DC.

20. A la suite de la démission du Juge Francisco Rezek, Président du Tribunal arbitral (survenue le 16 mars 2001 et effective dès le 13 mars), le Professeur Pierre Lalive (Suisse) a été nommé le 11 avril 2001 Président du Tribunal arbitral, lequel a été ainsi reconstitué (le Juge M. Bedjaoui et l'Ambassadeur G. Leoro Franco demeurant en

---

[6] Réponse au mémoire soutenant l'incompétence soumis par la défenderesse du 18 septembre 1999, p. 143.

[7] Mémoire en réplique sur l'incompétence du 27 décembre 1999, p. 162.

[8] *Id.*, p. 163.

[9] Réplique à la réponse soumise par la République du Chili au contre-mémoire réfutant le déclinatoire de compétence, du 7 février 2000, p. 35.

leur qualité d'arbitres désignés respectivement par les parties). La procédure a repris. Le Secrétaire général du CIRDI a désigné Madame Gabriela Alvarez Avila comme Secrétaire du Tribunal en remplacement de M. Flores, ce dernier ayant entre-temps cessé temporairement ses fonctions au CIRDI.

21. Le 23 avril 2001, les demanderesses ont déposé une requête de mesures provisoires tendant à la suspension de la Décision ministérielle n°43 du Chili, datée du 28 avril 2000.

22. À la suite d'une audience tenue à Genève le 21 juin 2001, le Tribunal arbitral a rendu, le 25 septembre 2001, une décision sur les mesures provisoires sollicitées par les parties.[10]

23. Le 26 septembre 2001, le Tribunal arbitral a rendu une ordonnance de procédure datée du 25 septembre 2001 concernant la production de documents et l'organisation d'audiences sur la question de compétence.[11] Les parties ont déposé des notes et observations. Les demanderesses ont, en outre, déposé une requête tendant à la production de nouvelles pièces. Les 29 et 30 octobre 2001, le Tribunal a tenu une audience sur la question de la compétence, après quoi les parties ont déposé un résumé de leur argumentation orale.

24. Le 8 mai 2002, le Tribunal arbitral, en application de l'article 41 de la Convention CIRDI, a décidé à l'unanimité « *de joindre au fond les exceptions d'incompétence soulevées par la République du Chili* », réservant la suite de la procédure.[12]

25. Le 10 mai 2002, le Tribunal a rendu une ordonnance de procédure établissant un calendrier pour le dépôt des écritures des parties et fixant la date des audiences sur la compétence et le fond.[13] Ce calendrier a été modifié par la suite par les ordonnances de procédure n°6-2002 du 9 juillet 2002, n°8-2002 du 20 août 2002 et n°11-2002 du 12 décembre 2002.

---

[10] Soit celles demandées par la défenderesse dans son mémoire d'incompétence et le 13 septembre 1999 « tendant à obtenir une garantie suffisante pour couvrir les dépens auxquelles les Parties demanderesses pourraient éventuellement être condamnées » et les mesures sollicitées par les demanderesses le 23 avril 2001. Cette décision a été publiée dans la revue du CIRDI (16 ICSID Review – Foreign Investment Law Journal 567 (2001) pour la version en langue française et 16 ICSID Review – Foreign Investment Law Journal 603 (2001) pour la version en langue espagnole).

[11] Ordonnance de procédure n°4-2001.

[12] Décision du 8 mai 2002, p. 51.

[13] Ordonnance de procédure n°5-2002.

26. Le 16 septembre 2002, les demanderesses ont déposé leur mémoire sur la compétence[14] et le fond[15] daté du 11 septembre 2002, concluant à ce que le Tribunal décide notamment que :

> *« - L'Investissement réalisé a été conforme à l'Accord API et à la législation chilienne,*
> *- Monsieur Pey Casado satisfait les critères de nationalité prévus par la Convention de Washington,*
> *- la Fondation Espagnole est habilitée à agir ».*[16]

27. Confirmant leurs conclusions précédentes du 17 mars 1999, les demanderesses ont conclu en demandant que la défenderesse soit condamnée :

> *« - à indemniser en conséquence les parties demanderesses eu égard à la totalité de leurs dommages et préjudices ainsi causés, y compris le* lucrum cessans, *à partir de la date de l'acte de force - le 11 septembre 1973 - jusqu'à la date de la Sentence - et ce pour un montant minimum estimé provisoirement à la date du 11 septembre 2002, sauf erreur ou omission, à US$ 397,347,287 auxquels s'ajoutent les dommages moraux et non patrimoniaux infligés à Monsieur Victor Pey Casado selon l'estimation que le Tribunal jugera opportune,*
> *- à payer aux Demanderesses des intérêts moratoires à partir de la date du 11 septembre 2002 et jusqu'à son exécution intégrale ».*[17]

28. Le 8 octobre 2002, la défenderesse a déposé une requête tendant à ce que soient séparées les questions de responsabilité de celles des dommages et intérêts. Le Tribunal arbitral, par une ordonnance de procédure n°9-2002 du 3 décembre 2002, a rejeté cette requête.

29. Le 4 novembre 2002, les demanderesses ont déposé une demande complémentaire « relative à la compensation des dommages découlant de la saisie par les autorités chiliennes des presses Goss, confisquées par le Décret Suprême n°165 du 10 février 1975, que les parties demanderesses soumettent au Tribunal arbitral en conformité notamment de la clause de la nation la plus favorisée de l'API entre l'Espagne et le Chili, du 2 octobre 1991, qui lui permet d'invoquer

---

[14] Exposé complémentaire sur la compétence du Tribunal arbitral du 11 septembre 2002.

[15] Exposé complémentaire sur le fond de l'affaire du 11 septembre 2002.

[16] Exposé complémentaire sur la compétence du Tribunal arbitral du 11 septembre 2002, p. 179.

[17] Exposé complémentaire sur le fond de l'affaire du 11 septembre 2002, pp. 152-153.

également l'API conclu entre la Suisse et la République du Chili le 24 septembre 1999. »[18]

30. Le 3 février 2003, la défenderesse a déposé un contre-mémoire sur le fond et la compétence, dans lequel il était demandé au Tribunal arbitral :

> « *1) De rejeter l'action introduite devant le CIRDI par Monsieur Pey et la Fondation Président Allende pour défaut de compétence du Tribunal ;*
> *2) Au cas où le Tribunal se déclarerait compétent de déclarer la République du Chili non responsable et de rejeter l'action ;*
> *3) Au cas où le Tribunal se déclarerait compétent et qu'il déciderait que la République du Chili est responsable, de restreindre le montant des dommages-intérêts conformément à ce qui a été exposé dans le présent Mémoire et dans le Rapport de l'expert, Monsieur Kaczmarek, et*
> *4) D'ordonner le paiement par les Demanderesses des frais encourus par la République du Chili dans le cadre de la présente procédure d'arbitrage ».*[19]

31. Le 3 mars 2003, les demanderesses ont déposé leur réplique sur le fond et la compétence, datée du 23 février 2003, qui reprenait dans leur intégralité leurs demandes précédentes.[20] Le 4 avril 2003, la défenderesse a déposé sa duplique sur le fond et la compétence, reprenant notamment sa requête du 3 février 2003.[21]

32. Enfin, du 5 au 7 mai 2003, le Tribunal arbitral a tenu des audiences orales à Washington D.C. au cours desquelles les parties ont exposé et développé leurs points de vue respectifs, ont répondu à diverses questions du Tribunal arbitral, et confirmé leurs écritures.[22]

33. A la fin de l'audience du 7 mai 2003, le Président a précisé que le Tribunal se réservait, après avoir étudié l'ensemble des écritures, des documents et des plaidoiries respectives, de demander au besoin des compléments d'information, raison pour laquelle la procédure ne devait pas encore être considérée comme « *close* ».[23]

---

[18] Demande complémentaire des demanderesses du 4 novembre 2002.
[19] Contre-mémoire de la défenderesse du 3 février 2003, p. 414.
[20] Réplique des demanderesses au contre-mémoire de la défenderesse, du 23 février 2003, p. 254.
[21] Réplique de la défenderesse du 4 avril 2003, p. 65-69.
[22] Transcription de l'audience du 5 au 7 mai 2003 à Washington D.C.
[23] Au sens de l'article 46 du règlement d'arbitrage CIRDI ; v. la transcription de l'audience du 5 au 7 mai 2003, p. 625.

34.   Au cours de l'été 2005, le Président rédigea un projet partiel de décision sur la compétence, dont il soumit le 3 juin le texte, confidentiel, aux autres membres du Tribunal pour une délibération prévue à New York le 19 septembre 2005.

35.   Par lettre du 23 août 2005, la République du Chili a demandé la récusation des trois membres du Tribunal arbitral, dont l'un (l'Ambassadeur Galo Leoro Franco, de nationalité équatorienne) donna sa démission par lettre du 26 août 2005, au motif qu'il aurait perdu la confiance de la partie l'ayant désigné. A la suite de cette démission, le Chili a retiré par écrit sa requête de récusation concernant ce dernier. La démission de Monsieur Leoro Franco, à la veille de la délibération du Tribunal fixée avec son accord, n'étant justifiée au regard d'aucun des motifs prévus aux articles 56 (3) de la Convention CIRDI et 8 (2) du Règlement d'arbitrage, elle n'a pas été acceptée par les deux autres membres du Tribunal arbitral, et le Président du Conseil administratif a été appelé à pourvoir à la vacance ainsi créée. C'est ce qu'il a fait en désignant M. Emmanuel Gaillard, professeur de droit et avocat à Paris.

36.   Il est apparu par la suite, notamment après un entretien accordé par M. Robert Dañino, alors Secrétaire général du CIRDI, à une importante délégation chilienne sur la demande de cette dernière, que la récusation demandée par le défendeur à la veille de la délibération prévue par le Tribunal arbitral était motivée en réalité par la connaissance du projet de décision partielle proposé par le Président, projet interne que l'Arbitre Leoro Franco avait cru pouvoir communiquer à la partie qui l'avait désigné, au mépris de l'obligation, incontestée, de la confidentialité des documents de travail du Tribunal et du secret des délibérations.

37.   L'existence de cette violation n'est pas contestée, mais au contraire reconnue par la défenderesse. Le doute subsiste seulement sur la question de savoir qui en a pris l'initiative mais il n'incombe pas au présent Tribunal arbitral de se prononcer à ce sujet, malgré les protestations et demandes présentées au CIRDI par les demanderesses.

38.   En ce qui concerne les récusations formées par la défenderesse contre les deux arbitres restants, elles étaient fondées, quant à Monsieur Bedjaoui, sur sa qualité de Ministre des Affaires étrangères de la République algérienne et, quant au Président, sur de prétendues lenteurs de la procédure arbitrale et des craintes alléguées concernant son état de santé (article 57 et 14 de la Convention CIRDI).

39.   Le Président du Conseil administratif, compétent en la matière,[24] a préféré (peut-être compte tenu de l'entretien accordé à ce sujet à l'une des parties par le Secrétaire général du CIRDI alors en exercice) s'en rapporter aux recommandations du Secrétaire général de la Cour permanente d'arbitrage à La Haye. Il en est résulté le rejet de la récusation du Président mais en même temps l'admission de la récusation de Monsieur Bedjaoui. Celui-ci a été remplacé par un avocat algérien choisi par les demanderesses, Me Mohammed Chemloul.

40.   Le Tribunal arbitral dûment reconstitué,[25] s'est réuni à Genève en juillet 2006 pour une première session de travail et a adopté un calendrier préliminaire, tenant compte du temps nécessaire aux deux nouveaux arbitres pour étudier un volumineux dossier.

41.   Après des échanges de vues avec les parties, en août et septembre 2006, quant à l'opportunité et au sujet d'une nouvelle audience, le Tribunal a pris diverses décisions procédurales.

42.   Tout d'abord, il a estimé « désirable, vu la composition renouvelée du Tribunal arbitral et l'article 12 du Règlement, d'offrir aux deux parties la faculté de s'exprimer <u>oralement</u> - une réouverture de la procédure écrite étant <u>exclue</u> - sur un certain nombre de points ».[26]

43.   Enfin, il s'est « préoccupé des conséquences possibles de l'inégalité procédurale insolite résultant du fait que l'une des Parties, et non l'autre, a eu connaissance du projet de sentence préparé par le Président et destiné à une délibération qui devait avoir lieu à New York en septembre 2005 ». Il a donc décidé de communiquer officiellement ce projet, à titre de document de travail, « afin de préserver les principes supérieurs de l'égalité des parties et du respect du contradictoire », étant entendu que « cette communication ne préjuge en rien l'issue du délibéré à venir ».[27]

44.   Le 2 octobre 2006, le Tribunal a communiqué les questions sur lesquelles devait porter l'exposé oral éventuellement souhaité par les parties lors d'une prochaine audience.

45.   Par ordonnance de procédure n°13 du 24 octobre 2006, le Tribunal arbitral a fixé au 15 et 16 janvier 2007 la tenue de ladite audience, prévue à Paris dans les locaux de la Banque mondiale.

46.   Par une lettre-mémoire du 8 novembre 2006, la défenderesse a demandé au Tribunal de « reconsidérer sa décision de ne pas autoriser une quelconque soumission écrite » et de « limiter l'ordre

---

24   V. l'article 58 de la Convention CIRDI.
25   Cf. lettre du 14 juillet 2006 du Secrétariat du CIRDI.
26   Lettre aux parties du 13 septembre 2006.
27   *Id.*

du jour de l'audience aux seules questions communiquées aux Parties le 2 octobre 2006 ».

47. Dans une lettre complémentaire du 17 novembre 2006, les conseils de la défenderesse ont repris et développé des arguments analogues et critiqué le contenu et la forme de l'ordonnance de procédure n°13/2006.

48. Par ordonnance de procédure n°14/2006, le Tribunal arbitral a rejeté les conclusions de la défenderesse et maintenu les termes de l'ordonnance n°13, non sans relever un certain nombre de malentendus et erreurs commis par cette partie dans ses communications précédentes, en particulier quant à la confidentialité et au secret des délibérations.

49. Par lettre du 15 décembre 2006, la République du Chili a énoncé et récapitulé ses diverses objections à certains des considérants contenus dans les ordonnances de procédure n°13 et n°14.

50. Les audiences fixées par le Tribunal arbitral se sont déroulées comme prévu, sans incident, les 15 et 16 janvier 2007 à Paris, au siège de la Banque mondiale. Une transcription en espagnol et en français des exposés respectifs des questions posées par le Tribunal et des réponses données, a été remise comme convenu aux parties.

51. Par lettre du 18 juillet 2007, le Tribunal arbitral a invité les parties à lui communiquer les documents qui lui permettraient de prendre connaissance des montants précis alloués aux bénéficiaires de la Décision n°43 adoptée par le Ministère chilien des biens nationaux le 28 avril 2000, invitation à laquelle les demanderesses ont répondu par une lettre en date du 19 juillet 2007. En l'absence de réponse de la part de la défenderesse, le Tribunal arbitral, par une lettre en date du 3 octobre 2007, a réitéré son invitation à la défenderesse de se prononcer, si elle le souhaitait, sur la position des demanderesses concernant les montants alloués aux bénéficiaires de la Décision n°43. La défenderesse a répondu à cette invitation par lettre du 18 octobre 2007, concernant laquelle les demanderesses ont formulé des remarques supplémentaires dans une lettre en date du 29 octobre 2007. La défenderesse, elle, a formulé des commentaires additionnels par lettre reçue le 9 novembre 2007 (mais erronément datée du 18 octobre 2007).

52. Par lettre du 24 août 2007, la défenderesse a envoyé au Tribunal arbitral copies de deux décisions récentes rendues dans des affaires CIRDI, demandant que le Tribunal arbitral les considère lors de ses délibérations. Les demanderesses, par lettre en date du 31 août 2007, ont demandé que le Tribunal arbitral « *rejette ces documents des débats en ce qu'ils ont été communiqués hors délai, en violation de la règle qui avait été édictée par le Tribunal selon laquelle aucune*

pièce ne pourrait plus être communiquée par les Parties sauf demande expresse du tribunal. » Le Tribunal arbitral a décidé, à l'unanimité, de confirmer sa décision antérieure d'exclure la réouverture de la procédure écrite. Par lettre du 3 octobre 2007, il a informé les parties, qu'il « *s'est tenu et se tient bien entendu au courant des développements ' jurisprudentiels ' ou doctrinaux survenus depuis la dernière audience, de janvier 2007, et [qu'il] estime dès lors superflu et inopportun d'autoriser de nouvelles productions ou commentaires.* »

53.   Finalement, par une autre lettre en date du 3 octobre 2007, le Tribunal arbitral a invité les parties à communiquer le montant de leurs coûts et dépens, en ce compris les honoraires de conseils et autres frais exposés dans le présent arbitrage, accompagné de justificatifs. Les parties ont répondu à cette invitation par leurs lettres du 23 octobre 2007 (pour les demanderesses) et du 3 novembre 2007 (pour la défenderesse), adressées par le Secrétariat au Tribunal arbitral simultanément le 5 novembre 2007. Les demanderesses ont formulé des commentaires supplémentaires concernant les coûts et dépens par lettre en date du 7 novembre 2007, ainsi que l'a fait la défenderesse par lettre en date du 20 novembre 2007.

54.   Sur le plan procédural, il y a lieu de noter que Mme Eloïse Obadia a été désignée comme Secrétaire du Tribunal en remplacement de Mme Alvarez-Avila à partir du 27 août 2007. En outre, le Tribunal arbitral a déclaré l'instance close le 31 janvier 2008, en application de l'article 38 du Règlement d'arbitrage. Du fait du dépôt tardif des traductions en français de certaines correspondances et documents produits par la défenderesse avant la clôture de l'instance, le Tribunal s'est vu dans l'obligation de proroger de 30 jours le délai de 60 jours prévu à l'article 46 du Règlement d'arbitrage pour rédiger et signer la sentence.

III.   EXPOSE DES FAITS

55.   Le présent litige présente en somme deux chronologies distinctes de faits pertinents ;   la première concerne les faits relatifs aux investissements prétendument faits par les demanderesses, notamment l'achat des sociétés CPP S.A. et ECP Ltda, ainsi qu'aux développements menant à la confiscation de ces biens ; la deuxième concerne les faits sur la base desquels le Tribunal arbitral doit décider la question de la nationalité des parties demanderesses. Il convient, dans un souci de clarté, de résumer ces deux chronologies de faits séparément.

A. Les faits concernant l'investissement et la confiscation des biens en question

56. En résumant les faits concernant l'investissement allégué par les demanderesses, il convient d'abord de rappeler brièvement le cadre légal s'appliquant aux investissements au Chili dans les années 1960.

57. Le 30 mars 1960,[28] le décret chilien no 258 crée un statut de l'investissement et concerne « les personnes qui apportent dans le pays de nouveaux capitaux, provenant de l'extérieur, dans le but d'initier, fortifier, élargir, améliorer ou rénover les activités productrices ». Il est précisé que lesdites opérations concernant « les apports auxquels fait référence le présent Décret ayant force de loi pourront seulement entrer : a) en devises et en crédits dûment qualifiés ». Ce statut prévoit que le Président de l'État peut accorder diverses franchises aux investissements qui en respecteraient les dispositions.

58. Le 24 mai 1961, le Traité de Montevideo entre en vigueur au Chili de par le Décret no 269 ainsi qu'un Décret n°1272-1961, approuvé le 7 septembre 1961.[29]

59. Le 3 août 1967, est créé le CPP S.A. avec un capital initial de 200'000 escudos, représenté par 40'000 actions. M. Dario Sainte-Marie est propriétaire de 93% des actions.[30]

60. Le 4 septembre 1967 est approuvée la Loi 16643 qui restreint, dans certains secteurs de l'économie chilienne, dont la presse, la possibilité des investissements étrangers. L'article 5 de ladite loi prévoit que les journaux doivent être la propriété de ressortissants chiliens ou d'une société dont la propriété doit être en mains chiliennes pour au moins 85%, sous peine d'amendes administratives.

61. Le 9 mai 1968, la société CPP S.A. acquiert les 95,5% du capital de la société EPC Ltda, société éditrice du journal « El Clarin » fondée par M. Sainte-Marie en 1955. Le Directeur de ce journal est M. Sainte-Marie. Il est assisté depuis 1957-1958 et, en particulier, en 1969-1970 par son ami, l'entrepreneur M. Pey Casado.[31]

62. Le 30 juillet 1969, a-t-il été allégué, l'Accord de Carthagène entre en vigueur au Chili de par le Décret n°428. L'année suivante, le

---

[28] Publié le 4 avril 1960.
[29] Publié au Journal officiel le 11 novembre 1961.
[30] La décision du 8 mai 2002, p. 9 mentionne cependant un pourcentage de 99%, en raison semble-t-il d'une erreur de transcription.
[31] A ce sujet v. la déclaration de M. Pey Casado devant le Tribunal arbitral, en mai 2003, transcription de l'audience du 5 mai 2003, p. 149.

31 décembre 1970, la Commission de Carthagène approuve un
« *régime commun de traitement (consenti) aux capitaux étrangers et
concernant les marques, brevets, licences et droits d'exploitation* »
ou « *Décision 24* », dont il est allégué par la défenderesse qu'il est
entré en vigueur au Chili par « *Décret en réitération* » (« *Decreto de
insistencia* ») n°488, du 30 juin 1971, en dérogation au Décret n°258
de 1960.[32] Quant aux parties demanderesses, elles ont allégué que ce
régime commun de traitement (consenti) aux capitaux étrangers
n'avait pas été appliqué au Chili, en tout cas avant le 11 septembre
1973, et que l'investissement de M. Pey Casado était régi par les
dispositions du Décret-loi 258/1960.[33]

63.   Il est allégué que M. Sainte-Marie, en 1972, pour « *des raisons
strictement personnelles* » et semble-t-il d'ordre familial[34] a décidé
de vendre la société CPP S.A. à son ami M. Pey Casado, lequel,
depuis bien des années, 1957-58[35] l'avait assisté en tant que
collaborateur et conseiller technique, notamment pour le
développement et l'orientation de l'entreprise et était devenu « *son
collaborateur le plus étroit* », le vendeur souhaitait en effet « *quitter
le pays pour toujours et de façon totale* ». C'est la raison pour
laquelle, selon M. Pey Casado, le « *mécanisme de transfert de
l'entreprise* » se serait déroulé de façon rapide et moins formelle
qu'il est d'usage sur le plan commercial.[36]

64.   Le 29 mars 1972, une somme de USD 500'000 a été transférée d'une
banque tchécoslovaque par l'intermédiaire d'un compte de la
Manufacturers Trust Co. à Londres[37] à un compte de M. Sainte-Marie
auprès de la Banco Hispano Americano de Madrid où elle est
parvenue le 4 avril 1972. Le 30 mars de la même année, M. Pey
Casado est devenu directeur de la société CPP S.A. et le 6 avril 1972
il aurait reçu de M. Sainte-Marie, 25'500 actions de la société CPP
S.A. (avec leurs bordereaux de transfert signés en blanc).

65.   Le 13 mai 1972, M. Pey Casado et M. Sainte-Marie ont signé un
accord (à Estoril au Portugal), considéré par les demanderesses
comme la conclusion finale de la vente de la société CPP S.A.[38] La

---

32   V. contre-mémoire de la défenderesse du 3 février 2003, p. 165.
33   V., par exemple, exposé complémentaire sur la compétence du Tribunal
     arbitral du 11 septembre 2002, p. 55.
34   Transcription de l'audience du 5 mai 2003, p.150.
35   *Id*, p. 149.
36   *Id.*, p. 151.
37   Annexe 21 à la requête d'arbitrage, du 3 novembre 1997.
38   V., par exemple la chronologie fournie par les demanderesses dans leur
     exposé complémentaire sur la compétence du Tribunal arbitral du 11
     septembre 2002, pp. 15-23.

défenderesse considère, elle, que cet accord ne remplirait pas les conditions formelles d'un transfert de propriété.[39]

66.   Dans la seconde moitié de 1972 diverses opérations eurent lieu, concernant les actions de la société. Le 14 juillet 1972, M. Sainte-Marie transféra un certain nombre d'actions à M. González et le 6 septembre 1972 d'autres actions à M. Venegas. Selon les demanderesses, les actions de MM. González et Venegas auraient été remises à M. Pey Casado avec leurs bordereaux de transfert signés en blanc à l'attention de M. Pey Casado. Ce dernier se serait servi de ces bordereaux de transfert signés en blanc reçus par lui le 6 avril pour faire établir des actions nouvelles au nom de MM. González et Venegas qui, simultanément, lui auraient remis les originaux de ces actions (avec les bordereaux de transfert correspondants signés en blanc par eux).[40]

67.   Le 23 septembre 1972, M. Sainte-Marie a remis à M. Pey Casado, devant un notaire, une procuration donnant à ce dernier tous pouvoirs sur le nom du journal Clarin ainsi que sur 4,5% des actions de la société EPC Ltda.

68.   Le 2 octobre 1972, par un acte unilatéral signé à Genève, M. Pey Casado aurait donné sa conclusion définitive au contrat de vente avec M. Sainte-Marie.[41] Le 3 octobre 1972, le vendeur M. Sainte-Marie a reçu la somme de USD 780'000, en plusieurs versements d'une « Bank für Handel und Effekten ».[42] Selon la défenderesse, pour qui M. Pey Casado aurait agi dans ces diverses transactions comme mandataire plutôt qu'en son nom propre, ladite somme aurait été versée sur le compte de M. Pey Casado par un virement provenant du Banco Nacional de Cuba, le 26 septembre 1972, un jour après l'ouverture du compte par M. Pey Casado.[43]

69.   Le 18 octobre 1972, M. Sainte-Marie a transféré des actions à M. Venegas et à M. Carrasco, les deux paquets d'actions étant remis à M. Pey Casado « avec leurs bordereaux de transfert signés en blanc ».[44] Le 12 décembre 1972, les statuts de la société EPC Ltda ont été modifiés, la société passant sous le contrôle effectif total de la société CPP S.A.

[39]   V., par exemple, contre-mémoire de la défenderesse du 3 février 2003, pp. 291 et ss.

[40]   V., par exemple, exposé complémentaire sur la compétence du Tribunal arbitral, du 11 septembre 2002, pp. 17-18. Annexes 7 et 8 au mémoire des demanderesses du 17 mars 1999.

[41]   Annexe C-66.

[42]   V., par exemple, exposé complémentaire sur la compétence du Tribunal arbitral du 11 septembre 2002, p. 19.

[43]   V. contre-mémoire de la défenderesse du 3 février 2003, pp. 85-86.

[44]   Annexe 4 au mémoire des demanderesses du 17 mars 1999, et annexe C-161.

70. Le 11 septembre 1973, le Président Allende est renversé par un coup d'Etat militaire qui prend le contrôle du Chili. Les forces armées pénètrent dans les bureaux du Journal Clarin où elles arrêtent le directeur[45] et un certain nombre de personnes et séquestrent les locaux et les biens.[46]

71. Le 14 septembre 1973, M. Pey Casado se réfugie à l'Ambassade du Venezuela à Santiago. Le 27 octobre 1973, il quitte le Chili.

72. Sur le terrain des confiscations dont se plaignent les demanderesses, il y a lieu de signaler que, le 21 octobre 1974, le Décret-exempté chilien n°276, applique le Décret n°77 aux sociétés CPP S.A. et EPC Ltda. La situation « *patrimoniale* » de M. Pey Casado et d'autres personnes y est examinée.

73. Selon la défenderesse, un décret n°600 du 13 juillet 1974 a établi un « *statut des investissements étrangers* », lequel, avec le décret n°746 du 9 novembre 1974, confirmerait que la Décision n°24 de la Commission de Carthagène avait été appliquée au Chili.[47] Par la suite, le 10 février 1975, un décret n°165 prononce la dissolution des sociétés CPP S.A. et EPC Ltda et le transfert de leurs biens à l'Etat. Un décret n°580 du 24 avril 1975 applique le décret 77 à M. Pey Casado et confisque un bâtiment propriété de la société EPC Ltda. Ces textes, avec un Décret n°1200 du 25 novembre 1977, prononcent ou confirment la confiscation de « *tous les biens meubles et immeubles, droits et actions appartenant au dit M. Pey Casado* ».

74. Selon les demanderesses, M. Pey Casado continuait à être interdit d'entrée au Chili ; il n'aurait pas reçu notification de ces mesures et ni les sociétés CPP S.A. et EPC Ltda ni M. Pey Casado n'auraient été représentés dans ces procédures.

75. En septembre de l'année 1975, les autorités fiscales chiliennes ont introduit des poursuites pénales pour fraude fiscale présumée contre M. Pey Casado et d'autres personnes. M. Pey Casado n'aurait pas reçu notification de la plainte ni n'aurait été représenté dans la procédure judiciaire.[48] Depuis le 11 décembre 1975, le Directeur national des impôts internes ne lui aurait imputé aucune infraction.[49] Le 1er septembre 1976, le juge l'avait déclaré « *rebelle* ».[50] Dans ce procès, les autorités chiliennes n'auraient reproché à M. Pey Casado

---

45   V. la déclaration judiciaire de M. Manuel Alberto Gamboa Soto, Directeur du quotidien Clarin, du 11 septembre 1973, annexe C-47.

46   Décret no 93 du 20 octobre 1973, annexe 3 au mémoire des demanderesses, du 17 mars 1999.

47   V. son préambule et l'article 19-1.

48   Annexe D-19.

49   Annexes C-189 et C-191.

50   Annexe C-197.

aucune infraction au décret-loi n°258/1960,[51] non plus qu'au décret n°482/1971 ou à la Décision n°24, ou encore au décret-loi n°1272/1961 portant contrôle des changes.[52]

76. On notera que, après la chute du régime militaire Pinochet, les décrets n°276, 580 et 1200 ont été déclarés nuls et de nul effet.

77. Sur le terrain des démarches tendant à une indemnisation, il y a lieu de noter que le 1er février 1995, M. Pey Casado a saisi la Huitième Chambre criminelle de Santiago d'une demande en restitution de la société CPP S.A. et des documents y-relatifs, demande qui fit l'objet d'une décision favorable le 29 mai 1995, « *compte tenu de la valeur probante des antécédents* ».[53]

78. En 1995 les demanderesses saisirent le Président de la République (le 6 septembre 1995) ainsi que la Première Chambre civile de Santiago (le 4 octobre 1995) d'une demande en restitution ou en compensation pour la perte de la rotative Goss. Cette requête, que M. Pey Casado a réitérée le 10 janvier 1996 auprès du Président de la République[54], fut contestée le 17 avril 1996 par le Conseil national de Défense en tant que représentant du Chili devant le tribunal civil, pour défaut de qualité pour agir *(locus standi)*. Cela au motif que M. Pey Casado n'était pas propriétaire et donc pas légitimé à agir : premièrement, du fait que « *le Demandeur a confondu sa qualité de propriétaire de 99% du capital social de l'Entreprise périodique Clarín Ltda avec la qualité du titulaire du droit de pleine propriété sur les biens de cette dernière* » ; deuxièmement et subsidiairement, du fait « *de la validité du Décret suprême n°165, de 1975, du Ministère de l'Intérieur* » portant confiscation de CPP S.A. et d'EPC Ltda.[55] Néanmoins, le Tribunal civil accepta de considérer la demande comme recevable en se fondant sur six questions préliminaires.

79. Le 20 novembre 1995, le ministère des biens nationaux informe M. Pey Casado que la loi d'indemnisation qui permettra de traiter les situations comparables à celle de M. Pey Casado n'a pas encore été promulguée.[56] Le 25 juin 1998, c'est-à-dire huit mois après le dépôt de la requête d'arbitrage dans la présente instance le 3 novembre 1997, est promulguée la loi n°19.568 relative à la restitution ou indemnisation pour biens confisqués et acquis par l'Etat. Les parties demanderesses vont cependant informer le Ministre des biens nationaux par lettre du 24 juin 1999 de leur décision de ne pas

---

[51] Annexe C-111.
[52] Annexe C-112.
[53] Annexe 21 à la requête d'arbitrage du 3 novembre 1997.
[54] V. requête d'arbitrage du 3 novembre 1997, p. 8 et annexe 23 à la requête d'arbitrage du 3 novembre 1997.
[55] Annexe C-181.
[56] Annexe 23 à la requête d'arbitrage du 3 novembre 1997.

recourir à la loi n°19.568, du fait de la requête d'arbitrage introduite en 1997 et de la clause d'option irrévocable (*fork-in-the-road*) contenue dans l'API Espagne-Chili.[57]

80. Le 28 avril 2000, le Ministère des biens nationaux adopta la Décision n°43, décision considérée par les demanderesses comme une nouvelle confiscation ou une nouvelle manifestation de la confiscation de leurs droits découlant de l'investissement (après celles du 10 février 1975, 24 avril 1975 et 25 novembre 1977).[58] Cette décision a été prise alors que le présent arbitrage était déjà pendant.

B. Les faits concernant la nationalité de M. Pey Casado et de la Fondation Allende

81. M. Pey Casado est né en 1915 de parents espagnols en Espagne, d'où il a émigré en 1939, après la chute de la République, pour s'établir au Chili, pays dans lequel il a vécu jusqu'en 1973, date à laquelle a eu lieu, le 11 septembre, le coup d'Etat militaire dirigé par le Général Pinochet.

82. En 1947, il a été enregistré au Consulat espagnol de Santiago comme résidant permanent au Chili.

83. Le 24 mai 1958, l'Espagne et le Chili ont signé une Convention sur la double nationalité, convention qui permet aux ressortissants de l'un des États contractants d'acquérir la nationalité de l'autre, sans perdre sa nationalité d'origine. C'est en application de ladite Convention que M. Pey Casado a sollicité et obtenu la nationalité chilienne, par un Decreto supremo n°8054 du 11 décembre 1958.

84. Le 11 septembre 1973, le Président Allende est renversé par un coup d'Etat militaire qui prend le contrôle du Chili. Le 14 septembre 1973, M. Pey Casado se réfugie à l'Ambassade du Venezuela à Santiago. Le 27 octobre 1973, après s'être vu refuser, selon lui, un passeport par les autorités chiliennes, M. Pey Casado quitte le Chili, à l'aide d'un sauf-conduit des autorités. Selon les demanderesses, c'est à cette époque que M. Pey Casado aurait été *de facto* privé de sa nationalité.

85. Selon la défenderesse, en novembre 1973, M. Pey Casado, aurait voyagé au Pérou avec le passeport chilien n°014078, délivré le 2 octobre 1967, et le 23 novembre 1973 il aurait signé une procuration au bénéfice de son frère, en s'identifiant à l'aide de ce passeport

---

[57] Lettre des demanderesses au Ministre des biens nationaux du 24 juin 1999 (annexe C-32).

[58] V. par exemple la transcription de l'audience du 5 mai 2003, p. 175-179 (Me Malinvaud).

chilien et d'une carte d'identité nationale chilienne.[59] Selon M. Pey Casado, il aurait fait ce voyage avec un passeport d'urgence du Venezuela, le passeport chilien étant périmé depuis le 12 décembre 1971.

86. Le 8 novembre 1973 est pris le Décret-loi n°77 par les autorités militaires chiliennes, décret qui, selon les demanderesses, aurait servi de base à la réglementation du Décret-suprême n°1726 du 3 décembre 1973 pour justifier la confiscation des propriétés de M. Pey Casado pendant que celui-ci était interdit d'entrer librement au Chili et sans que personne au Chili ne soit chargé de sa représentation, de sa défense et de ses intérêts dans ses entreprises de presse.[60]

87. Le 8 janvier 1974, les autorités vénézuéliennes délivrent un passeport d'urgence à M. Pey Casado ainsi que, le 28 janvier, une carte d'identité pour les « *étrangers de passage (transeúnte)* ».[61] Le 9 janvier 1974, le Consulat d'Espagne à Caracas accorde à M. Pey Casado un visa pour l'Espagne, valable pour trois mois, que M. Pey Casado utilise le 31 mai 1974 pour se rendre en Espagne.

88. Selon la défenderesse, M. Pey Casado aurait, entre le 8 janvier et le 11 juin 1974, accompli, à partir du Pérou, divers voyages en Colombie, en Allemagne, aux États-Unis, avec trois passeports différents.[62] M. Pey Casado a nié avoir fait ces voyages et avoir disposé d'autres documents de voyage que les passeports d'urgence délivrés par le Venezuela.[63] La défenderesse a reconnu au cours de l'audience du 6 mai 2003 « *qu'il y a peut-être des erreurs dans ces documents* [relatifs aux déplacements de M. Pey Casado] ; *nous ne le contestons pas* ».[64]

89. Le 4 juin 1974, M. Pey Casado se fait enregistrer à la Municipalité de Madrid et reçoit une carte nationale d'identité espagnole et un passeport espagnol. Selon la défenderesse, M. Pey Casado aurait omis de se faire enregistrer dans le registre de l'état civil espagnol, comme cela aurait été nécessaire, à son avis, selon la Convention hispano-chilienne sur la double nationalité, s'il avait voulu modifier sa nationalité « *effective* ».

---

[59] Contre-mémoire de la défenderesse du 3 février 2003, pp. 21-22 ; réplique de la défenderesse du 4 avril 2003, pp. 14-15.

[60] En effet, il n'est pas contesté par la défenderesse que M. Pey Casado n'est retourné au Chili qu'en 1989.

[61] Annexes C-48 et C-253.

[62] V., par exemple, mémoire en réplique sur l'incompétence du 27 décembre 1999, pp. 48-49.

[63] Transcription de l'audience du 5 mai 2003, pp. 46-52, 239-240 ; transcription de l'audience du 7 mai 2003, pp. 499, 518.

[64] Transcription de l'audience du 7 mai 2003, p. 425.

90. Le 11 juin 1974, M. Pey Casado reçoit un passeport espagnol à Madrid, valable jusqu'au 10 juin 1979. Au cours de 1974, il se fait enregistrer au Consulat d'Espagne à Caracas et, le 28 janvier 1975, reçoit une carte d'identité de résident de la part du Venezuela.

91. Le 24 mai 1977, il est enregistré au Consulat d'Espagne à Lima, dont il recevra divers passeports : le 25 juin 1979 (passeport valable jusqu'au 24 juin 1984) et le 16 janvier 1984 (passeport valable jusqu'au 15 janvier 1989).

92. Le 14 juin 1984, le Ministère chilien de l'Intérieur a approuvé un décret n°597 portant règlement concernant les étrangers. Selon la défenderesse, ce texte confère tous pouvoirs à ce ministère pour déterminer la nationalité étrangère en cas de doute.[65] C'est à ce ministère que M. Pey Casado a adressé, le 10 décembre <u>1996</u>, une communication par laquelle il lui a fait savoir qu'il n'avait pas la qualité de bénéficiaire de la Convention sur la double nationalité depuis 1974.[66]

93. Le 17 novembre 1988, M. Pey Casado a reçu un passeport du Consulat d'Espagne à Caracas (valable jusqu'au 16 novembre 1993) et le 18 janvier 1989, il a renouvelé auprès du même Consulat d'Espagne sa carte nationale d'identité espagnole.

94. Selon la défenderesse, le frère de M. Pey Casado, prétendant agir comme son représentant, aurait déclaré les 25 mars et 12 avril 1989 que M. Pey Casado était un ressortissant chilien.[67] Et toujours selon la défenderesse, M. Pey Casado aurait agi dans les actes constitutifs de la Fondation en tant que double national, jusqu'en 1997.[68]

95. A la suite de l'échec du Général Pinochet lors du plébiscite du 5 octobre 1988, M. Pey Casado s'est rendu au Chili le 4 mai 1989 pour la première fois depuis 1973. Selon les demanderesses, il s'agissait d'une visite en qualité de touriste désireux de s'informer de la situation de ses biens, et notamment de ses actions dans la société CPP S.A.[69]

96. Selon le Département de contrôle des frontières du Chili (Ministère de l'Intérieur), M. Pey Casado serait entré au Chili le 4 mai 1989 « *en qualité de touriste espagnol* », avec son passeport espagnol.[70] Et c'est en cette même qualité que, le 22 mai 1989 (c'est à dire 18 jours

---

[65] Contre-mémoire de la défenderesse du 3 février 2003, pp. 226-227.
[66] Annexe C-21. V. réponse au mémoire soutenant l'incompétence soumis par la défenderesse, du 18 septembre 1999, p. 61.
[67] Contre-mémoire de la défenderesse du 3 février 2003, p. 29.
[68] Contre-mémoire de la défenderesse du 3 février 2003, p. 28.
[69] Réponse au mémoire soutenant l'incompétence soumis par la défenderesse, du 18 septembre 1999, pp. 73-74.
[70] Annexe 9 au mémoire en réplique sur l'incompétence du 27 décembre 1999.

après son entrée) il aurait quitté le Chili ; serait rentré au Chili (le 25 mai 1989) puis qu'il en serait sorti et rentré ensuite, à plusieurs reprises, toujours avec son passeport espagnol, jusqu'en novembre 1990.

97. Selon la défenderesse, M. Pey Casado aurait repris alors sa résidence au Chili et, le 6 octobre 1989, aurait comparu devant un notaire de Miami, pour donner tout pouvoir à M. Juan Garcés de créer la Fondation Président Allende, s'identifiant alors comme double national hispano-chilien.[71]

98. C'est le 16 janvier 1990 que, à la suite d'un pouvoir donné par M. Pey Casado le 6 octobre 1989, la « *Fundacíon Presidente Allende* » a été créée selon le droit espagnol et avec son siège en Espagne. Dans l'acte de constitution, M. Pey Casado est identifié comme double national chilien et espagnol.[72] Le 6 février 1990, M. Pey Casado, s'identifiant avec un passeport espagnol, a comparu par-devant un notaire à Miami et a passé un contrat de cession irrévocable, d'une part, et d'acceptation de la cession, d'autre part, portant sur le « *patrimoine, les titres, droits et crédits de toute nature découlant des contrats privés d'achat et vente que le cédant a passé en 1972 avec M. Dario Sainte-Marie Soruco, par lesquels ce dernier a vendu, et M. Victor Pey Casado a acheté cent pour cent des actions de CPP SA et d'EPC Ltée.* ».[73] C'est le 27 avril 1990 que la Fondation Allende a été enregistrée comme une institution charitable auprès du Ministère espagnol de la Culture.

99. Presque six mois après, le 18 octobre 1990, M. Pey Casado est entré de nouveau au Chili avec son passeport espagnol. Par la suite, le 5 janvier 1991, M. Pey Casado a demandé et reçu une carte d'identité chilienne.[74]

100. Le 20 février 1991, M. Pey Casado, se trouvant alors au Chili, a constaté qu'il avait perdu son passeport espagnol n°13.008, délivré le 17 novembre 1988 et expirant le 16 novembre 1993.[75] Il a alors sollicité et obtenu un passeport des autorités chiliennes. L'article 1er du Décret n°676, du 15 février 1966 portant approbation du règlement des passeports disposait que les <u>étrangers</u> pouvaient demander un passeport chilien dans des cas exceptionnels.[76] Le

---

[71] V. contre-mémoire de la défenderesse du 3 février 2003, pp. 27-28.

[72] Annexe 22 au contre-mémoire de la défenderesse du 3 février 2003. V. aussi mémoire d'incompétence de la défenderesse du 20 juillet 1999, p. 33.

[73] Annexe 18 du mémoire de demanderesses du 17 mars 1999.

[74] Réplique des demanderesses au contre-mémoire de la défenderesse, du 23 février 2003, pp. 177-178.

[75] Annexe C-48.

[76] Annexe 15 à l'avis de droit de M. Nogueira, produit par la défenderesse au soutien du contre-mémoire de la défenderesse, du 3 février 2003, version

Décret n°1.010, du 5 septembre 1989 « *portant approbation du Règlement des passeports ordinaires et des documents de voyages et titres de voyage pour étrangers* » autorisait leur délivrance à des ressortissants <u>étrangers</u> pour sortir du pays.[77]

101. Les autorités chiliennes ont constaté que M. Pey Casado s'est servi de ce passeport chilien pour entrer au Chili seulement deux fois, le 22 août 1991 et le 6 novembre 1994, mais non après qu'il eut voyagé en Espagne en mai 1997 et que les autorités espagnoles lui eurent délivré le passeport n°027703339-B le 28 mai 1997, expirant le 2 mai 2007.[78] Ce fait paraît corroborer les déclarations de M. Pey Casado à cet égard devant le Tribunal arbitral.[79] Avec ce passeport chilien M. Pey Casado s'est rendu, selon la défenderesse, aux USA le 5 juillet 1991.[80]

102. Il y a lieu de rappeler à ce stade que c'est le 25 janvier 1991 que le Chili a signé la Convention CIRDI, entrée en vigueur le 24 octobre 1991 et que la même Convention a été signée le 21 mars 1994 par l'Espagne, avec entrée en vigueur le 17 septembre 1994. Le 2 octobre 1991, le Chili et l'Espagne ont signé l'API Espagne-Chili, entré en vigueur le 29 mars 1994.

103. Selon la défenderesse, à partir du 20 février 1991, date de sa demande de passeport, M. Pey Casado s'est présenté à diverses reprises comme ressortissant chilien, et il a sollicité l'assistance du Chili en tant que tel à son retour au pays. C'est ainsi que, par exemple, le 17 février 1992, il s'est inscrit dans les registres électoraux à Vitacura, que le 25 mai 1992, il a sollicité les avantages prévus pour les ressortissants et les personnes qui avaient possédé la nationalité chilienne revenus au pays, auprès de la « *Oficina nacional de retorno* »[81], et que le 1er août 1992, il a signé un contrat de travail avec son frère, dans lequel il s'identifie comme Chilien. En outre, en août 1992, il se serait identifié à plusieurs reprises à l'aide de sa carte

---

[77] française dans l'annexe C-260, traduction dans la demande incidente des demanderesses du 23 février 2003, p. 38.
V. les articles 3(b) et 11 de l'annexe 16 à l'avis de droit de M. Nogueira, produit par la défenderesse au soutien du contre-mémoire de la défenderesse du 3 février 2003, version française dans l'annexe C-260.

[78] Annexe 9 et 10 au mémoire en réplique sur l'incompétence du 27 décembre 1999 et annexe C-48.

[79] Pendant les audiences des 29 octobre 2001 et 7 mai 2003; transcription de l'audience du 7 mai 2003, pp. 622-623.

[80] Contre-mémoire de la défenderesse du 3 février 2003, p. 32.

[81] L'article 1er de la loi n°18.994, du 14 août 1990, sur le retour des exilés au Chili (v. pp. 32-34 du contre-mémoire de la défenderesse du 3 février 2003), accorde les bénéfices de cette loi à « *tous les exilés qui ont ou ont eu la nationalité chilienne* » ; annexe 31 au contre-mémoire de la défenderesse du 3 février 2003, version française dans l'annexe C-259.

d'identité nationale chilienne.[82] Le 17 juillet 1993, il s'est inscrit dans le registre électoral de la Reina (un fait admis par les demanderesses qui font valoir cependant que les lettres (CH) relatives à la nationalité n'auraient pas été écrites par M. Pey Casado).[83] Le Chili a soumis divers autres documents appuyant la thèse selon laquelle M. Pey Casado s'est présenté lui-même (entre 1991 et janvier 1997) comme Chilien, avec une carte chilienne d'identité ou avec un domicile chilien.

104. Le 23 octobre 1994, M. Pey Casado s'est rendu en Bolivie avec un passeport chilien. Selon la défenderesse, il aurait utilisé le même passeport au cours d'un autre voyage en Bolivie le 6 novembre 1994 et en Espagne à travers les États-Unis le 21 mai 1997.[84]

105. Le 29 mai 1996, le Conseil de M. Pey Casado avait adressé une communication au Ministre espagnol des Affaires Étrangères, dans laquelle il a déclaré « qu'en application des instructions expresses de son mandant », il invoquait l'API Espagne-Chili.[85]

106. Le 10 décembre 1996, M. Pey Casado avait informé le Département chilien d'immigration qu'il avait sa résidence en Espagne depuis 1974 et qu'il n'entendait pas se prévaloir de la Convention hispano-chilienne sur la double nationalité.[86] Il s'agirait, selon la demanderesse, du premier acte invoqué comme étant une « renonciation » à la nationalité chilienne.[87] Le 19 décembre 1996, la Municipalité de Madrid a confirmé la résidence de M. Pey Casado en Espagne.[88]

107. Le 7 janvier 1997, M. Pey Casado aurait prié le consulat d'Espagne à Santiago de « mettre le registre en accord avec la réalité, dans l'hypothèse où le registre pertinent du Consulat n'attesterait pas » qu'il « n'avait pas recours aux bénéfices et aux avantages de la Convention sur la double nationalité », et « qu'il était domicilié en Espagne depuis le début de 1974 ».[89] Le 5 février 1997, le Consulat espagnol à Santiago a rayé le nom de M. Pey Casado du registre des

---

[82]   V. contre-mémoire de la défenderesse du 3 février 2003, pp. 26 et ss.
[83]   V. réponse au mémoire soutenant l'incompétence soumis par la défenderesse, du 18 septembre 1999, pp. 74-75 ; exposé complémentaire sur la compétence du Tribunal arbitral du 11 septembre 2002, p. 113.
[84]   V. mémoire en réplique sur l'incompétence du 27 décembre 1999, pp. 48-49.
[85]   Annexe C-20.
[86]   Annexe C-21 ; v. réponse au mémoire soutenant l'incompétence soumis par la défenderesse, du 18 septembre 1999, p. 61.
[87]   V. réponse au mémoire soutenant l'incompétence soumis par la défenderesse, du 18 septembre 1999, pp. 61-62
[88]   Annexe 8 à la requête d'arbitrage du 3 novembre 1997.
[89]   Annexe C-22.

ressortissants espagnols résidant au Chili. Le 28 mai 1997, M. Pey Casado a reçu à Madrid un passeport espagnol.

108. Le 16 septembre 1997, M. Pey Casado a procédé, auprès du Consulat d'Espagne à Mendoza (Argentine) à une déclaration officielle renonçant expressément et solennellement à la nationalité chilienne « *au cas où serait requise par l'Administration chilienne une renonciation formelle* ».[90]

109. Le 2 octobre 1997, M. Pey Casado a donné son consentement à l'arbitrage CIRDI en en excluant ce qui concerne la rotative Goss (question soumise aux autorités judiciaires chiliennes en octobre 1995). Le 6 octobre 1997, la Fondation Président Allende a exprimé son consentement à l'arbitrage mais en excluant également ce qui concerne la rotative Goss.

110. Le 6 novembre 1997, M. Pey Casado a saisi le Registre civil central (*Registro Civil Central*) d'une demande tendant à constater qu'il avait établi sa résidence à Madrid en juin 1974, demande transcrite dans le Registro Civil Central Uno de Madrid le 20 novembre 1997 par son secrétaire.[91]

111. Le 7 novembre 1997, on l'a vu, M. Pey Casado a déposé sa requête d'arbitrage contre la République du Chili et, le 18 mars 1998, le Chili a déclaré s'opposer à l'enregistrement de cette requête. Celle-ci a néanmoins été enregistrée par le Secrétaire général du CIRDI le 20 avril 1998.

112. Le 24 avril 1998, le Ministère espagnol des affaires étrangères a été saisi par le Dr Garcés, représentant de M. Pey Casado,[92] à l'effet de vérifier si « *la communication à la Partie chilienne de la renonciation formelle de M. Victor Pey Casado à bénéficier de la Convention sur la double nationalité* », avait bien été faite, à l'effet de confirmer aux autorités chiliennes que « *depuis le 4 juin 1974, il possède exclusivement la nationalité espagnole* ». La lettre concernant cette demande a été transmise le 10 juillet 1998 aux autorités chiliennes, par l'intermédiaire du Consulat d'Espagne à Santiago, et communiquée le 24 juillet 1998 par la Direction des affaires consulaires du Ministère chilien des affaires étrangères au registre chilien de l'état civil, où un officier public a constaté, le 4 août 1998, la renonciation par M. Pey Casado à sa nationalité

---

[90]   Annexe C-40.
[91]   Annexe C-10.
[92]   Annexe C-24.

chilienne et à son statut étranger et a fait inscrire sur sa fiche signalétique que M. Pey Casado était « *étranger* ».[93]

113. C'est dans ce contexte de fait que l'on examinera successivement la compétence du Centre et du Tribunal pour connaître de la demande de Monsieur Pey Casado (IV) et, la compétence du Centre et du Tribunal pour connaître de la demande de la Fondation Allende (V) avant d'aborder les questions de recevabilité et de fond du dossier.

IV. COMPETENCE DU CENTRE ET DU TRIBUNAL POUR CONNAITRE DE LA DEMANDE DE M. PEY CASADO

114. La première question à examiner, compte tenu des positions respectives des parties et notamment de l'exception d'incompétence soulevée par la défenderesse, est celle de la compétence du CIRDI et du Tribunal arbitral quant à la première partie demanderesse, M. Pey Casado.

115. L'article 25 de la Convention CIRDI fixe les conditions de compétence du Centre dans les termes suivants :

> « *(1) La compétence du Centre s'étend aux différends d'ordre juridique entre un Etat contractant (ou telle collectivité publique ou tel organisme dépendant de lui qu'il désigne au Centre) et le ressortissant d'un autre Etat contractant qui sont en relation directe avec un investissement et que les parties ont consenti par écrit à soumettre au Centre. Lorsque les parties ont donné leur consentement, aucune d'elles ne peut le retirer unilatéralement.*
> *(2) « Ressortissant d'un autre Etat contractant » signifie :*
> *(a) toute personne physique qui possède la nationalité d'un Etat contractant autre que l'Etat partie au différend à la date à laquelle les parties ont consenti à soumettre le différend à la conciliation ou à l'arbitrage ainsi qu'à la date à laquelle la requête a été enregistrée conformément à l'article 28, alinéa (3), ou à l'article 36, alinéa (3), à l'exclusion de toute personne qui, à l'une ou à l'autre de ces dates, possède*

---

[93] V. le décret n°597 du 14 juin 1984 - Règlement concernant les Étrangers - qui confère au Ministère de l'intérieur, selon la défenderesse, le pouvoir pour déterminer la nationalité étrangère en cas de doute ; annexe 17 de l'avis du Professeur Humberto Nogueira sur la nationalité en droit chilien, produit avec le contre-mémoire de la défenderesse du 3 février 2003.

> *également la nationalité de l'Etat contractant partie au différend ;*
>
> *(b) toute personne morale qui possède la nationalité d'un Etat contractant autre que l'Etat partie au différend à la date à laquelle les parties ont consenti à soumettre le différend à la conciliation ou à l'arbitrage et toute personne morale qui possède la nationalité de l'Etat contractant partie au différend à la même date et que les parties sont convenues, aux fins de la présente Convention, de considérer comme ressortissant d'un autre Etat contractant en raison du contrôle exercé sur elle par des intérêts étrangers ».*

116.   Pour que le Centre et le Tribunal soient compétents pour connaître de la demande de M. Pey Casado, la partie demanderesse doit justifier de l'existence d'un différend d'ordre juridique, du fait que ce différend oppose un Etat contractant et le ressortissant d'un autre Etat contractant, du fait que ce différend est en relation directe avec un investissement et du fait que les parties ont consenti par écrit à soumettre le différend au Centre.

117.   La condition relative à l'existence d'un différend d'ordre juridique et celle relative à la qualité d'Etat contractant de la défenderesse ne font l'objet d'aucune contestation de la part de la défenderesse.   En revanche, les parties sont en profond désaccord sur la condition d'investissement, sur la condition relative à la nationalité de l'investisseur et sur le fait que M. Pey Casado puisse être considéré seulement comme le ressortissant d'un autre Etat contractant, ainsi que sur la condition de consentement de l'Etat contractant que la partie demanderesse estime avoir été donnée par la conclusion de l'API Espagne-Chili.

118.   Les parties ont longuement débattu des conditions d'investissement et de nationalité sans toujours spécifier très clairement si les développements consacrés à ces questions concernent la condition d'investissement ou de nationalité au sens de la Convention CIRDI ou la condition d'investissement ou de nationalité au sens de l'API Espagne-Chili.   La condition relative à l'existence d'un investissement et la condition relative à la nationalité de la partie demanderesse ne s'apprécient pas nécessairement de la même manière pour les besoins de la satisfaction des exigences de la Convention CIRDI et pour ceux de l'API. Le présent Tribunal prendra soin, en conséquence, de distinguer ces deux sujets. Si les conditions d'application de l'API Espagne-Chili ne sont pas satisfaites, notamment les conditions d'investissement et la condition de nationalité au sens de ce texte, c'est, aux fins de l'application de la Convention CIRDI, le consentement de l'Etat à l'arbitrage qui ferait défaut, celui-ci étant exclusivement recherché dans l'API. C'est la

raison pour laquelle les conditions d'investissement et de nationalité au sens de la Convention CIRDI seront examinées en tant que telles et les conditions d'investissement et de nationalité au sens de l'API à l'occasion des développements consacrés à la vérification de l'existence du consentement à l'arbitrage de l'Etat défendeur.

119. Avant de procéder à l'examen de ces conditions, le Tribunal tient à préciser qu'il n'est pas lié par les décisions et les sentences CIRDI rendues antérieurement. Le présent Tribunal estime toutefois qu'il se doit de prendre en considération les décisions des tribunaux internationaux et de s'inspirer, en l'absence de justification impérieuse en sens contraire, des solutions résultant d'une jurisprudence arbitrale établie. Tout en tenant compte des particularités du traité applicable et des faits de l'espèce, le Tribunal estime aussi devoir s'efforcer de contribuer au développement harmonieux du droit des investissements et, ce faisant, de satisfaire à l'attente légitime de la communauté des Etats et des investisseurs quant à la prévisibilité du droit en la matière.[94]

120. Par ailleurs, il n'est pas superflu de rappeler que le Tribunal arbitral n'est pas tenu de discuter et trancher chacune des très nombreuses questions de fait ou de droit qui ont été soulevées et analysées par les parties au cours de la procédure exceptionnellement longue résumée plus haut mais qu'il suffit, sur le terrain de la compétence, que fasse défaut l'une des conditions requises pour que le Tribunal arbitral se déclare incompétent et s'abstienne dès lors de se prononcer sur toute autre question portant sur le fond du litige.

A. La condition d'investissement au sens de la Convention CIRDI

121. Le Tribunal rappellera les positions des parties sur la condition d'investissement au sens de la Convention CIRDI avant d'exposer les conclusions auxquelles il est parvenu à ce sujet.

1. Position des parties

a) Position de la défenderesse

122. Après avoir concédé que la notion d'investissement n'était pas définie par la Convention CIRDI, la défenderesse s'est essentiellement efforcée de démontrer qu'il n'existait aucun investissement de la part de M. Pey Casado et que la condition d'investissement posée par l'article 25 de la Convention n'était donc pas satisfaite.

---

[94]   V. en ce sens, *Saipem S.p.A. c. République populaire du Bangladesh*, affaire CIRDI n°ARB/05/07, décision sur la compétence et recommandation sur les mesures provisoires du 21 mars 2007, para. 67.

123. La défenderesse s'attache à prouver, dans de longs développements, que M. Pey Casado n'a jamais été propriétaire des titres de la société CPP S.A. qui elle-même possédait 99%[95] du capital de la société EPC Ltda.[96] Elle conteste aussi bien la véracité des faits exposés par la partie demanderesse que la légalité de l'acquisition des actions de CPP S.A. par M. Pey Casado, dans l'hypothèse où la vente des titres aurait eu lieu.

124. Elle insiste sur ce qu'elle estime être les incohérences de la chronologie présentée par la demanderesse sur l'achat des titres de CPP S.A. par M. Pey Casado telle que la décrivent les demanderesses et avance une version des faits relatifs au transfert des actions de CPP S.A. en 1972 substantiellement différente de celle des demanderesses.

125. Au début de l'année 1972, M. Sainte Marie aurait été détenteur de 93% du capital de la société CPP S.A., soit de 37.200 actions, et non de 100% des titres comme l'affirment les demanderesses. Le 14 juillet 1972, M. Darío Sainte Marie aurait cédé 20.000 titres à M. Emilio González González et n'aurait ainsi plus détenu que 17.200 titres, soit 43% du capital de la société CPP S.A. Il serait donc impossible, d'après la défenderesse, que M. Pey Casado ait reçu 25.200 actions de M. Darío Sainte Marie le 6 avril 1972 comme le prétendent pour la première fois les demanderesses dans leur exposé complémentaire sur la compétence du 11 septembre 2002 (p. 17). La défenderesse ajoute que les demanderesses affirmaient dans leurs mémoires antérieurs avoir acquis les 40.000 actions sans plus de précision et qu'elles n'offrent toujours pas de preuve au soutien de leurs prétentions.

126. Le 14 août 1972, M. Darío Sainte-Marie aurait acheté les actions appartenant à MM. Osvaldo Sainte-Marie, Pablo Sainte-Marie, Juan Kaiser Labbé et à Mme Juana Labbé Venegas, qui représentent 7% du capital de CPP S.A., et se serait trouvé en possession de 20.000 titres, l'autre moitié du capital étant entre les mains de M. González.[97] Les demanderesses ne pouvaient donc pas non plus être

---

95   V. contre-mémoire de la défenderesse du 3 février 2003, p. 56, l'acte authentique rédigé devant M. Patricio Zaldívar, notaire public, le 2 février 1972 (annexe 9 du rapport Sandoval) et l'acte authentique rédigé devant M. Alfredo Astaburuaga Gálvez le 27 novembre 1972 (annexe 10 du rapport Sandoval).

96   V. par ex. v. pp. 276-363 de la transcription de l'audience du 6 mai 2003 ; v. également le contre-mémoire de la défenderesse du 3 février 2003, pp. 284-364.

97   V. contre-mémoire de la défenderesse du 3 février 2003, p. 64-66 et annexe 16 au rapport Sandoval. Au vu du rapport de la surintendance des sociétés anonymes du 2 avril 1974 (annexe 16 au rapport Sandoval), la défenderesse ajoute qu'il est impossible que « *M. Pey [ait donné] cours à des demandes*

en possession de ces titres au mois d'avril 1972, contrairement à ce qu'elles affirment.

127. Le 6 septembre 1972, M. Darío Sainte-Marie aurait cédé 5.200 actions de la société à M. Jorge Venegas, ne conservant plus à ce stade que 14.800 actions. Le 18 octobre 1972, M. Darío Sainte-Marie aurait d'une part cédé à M. Jorge Venegas 1.200 titres supplémentaires et d'autre part 1.600 autres titres de CPP S.A. à M. Ramón Carrasco. Selon la défenderesse, il s'agirait là des dernières cessions de titres de CPP S.A. au vu des documents fournis. Ainsi, en octobre 1972, les actionnaires de la société CPP S.A. auraient été MM. Darío Sainte-Marie, Emilio González, Jorge Venegas et Ramón Carrasco.

128. La défenderesse considère par ailleurs que les Protocoles d'Estoril et le Document de Genève, que les demanderesses présentent comme les contrats de vente des titres de CPP S.A., ne se réfèrent à aucun moment à la vente des titres en question.

129. Les Protocoles d'Estoril ne pourraient, selon elle, être considérés comme un « *contrat de vente* » puisqu'au lieu d'être désignés de la sorte, ils portent l'intitulé « *obligations à ce qui avait déjà été fait et accepté par les parties* ». La défenderesse estime que « *le document d'Estoril n'identifie à aucun moment M. Pey comme ' l'acquéreur ' des actions citées dans la clause E* » et que « *M. Pey semble avoir agi comme agent fiduciaire de M. Darío Sainte-Marie et de tierces personnes dans les supposées transactions des documents d'Estoril et de Genève* ». Elle cite à cet effet les clauses A, E et F du Protocole d'Estoril et souligne que la clause E indique que 50% des actions de CPP S.A. seront remises à M. Pey Casado, sans dire à quel titre ni en quelle qualité M. Pey Casado reçoit les titres. Elle attire également l'attention du Tribunal sur le fait que les clauses A et F se réfèrent toutes deux à la remise d'une lettre de change à M. Pey Casado, ce qui confirmerait son rôle d'intermédiaire.[98]

---

de transfert signées par « *MM. [Osvaldo et Pablo] Sainte-Marie, Kaiser et Labbé* » *en faveur de M. González González, et que le 14 août de la même année - un mois après exactement - les mêmes* « *MM. Sainte-Marie, Kaiser et Labbé* » *[aient émis] des demandes de transferts concernant les mêmes actions en faveur de M. Darío Sainte-Marie* » (v. contre-mémoire de la défenderesse du 3 février 2003, p. 306).

[98] V. contre-mémoire de la défenderesse du 3 février 2003, pp. 296. La défenderesse insiste sur le fait que MM. González, Venegas et Carrasco ont tous trois indiqué dans des déclarations devant la Huitième Chambre du Tribunal correctionnel que M. Pey Casado avait agi comme le représentant de M. Sainte Marie (contre-mémoire de la défenderesse du 3 février 2003, pp. 310-311). La défenderesse se fonde également sur la déclaration de M. Osvaldo Sainte Marie devant la même juridiction (annexe 145 au contre-

130. La défenderesse insiste par ailleurs sur le fait que les Protocoles d'Estoril manquent de clarté et souligne que si des actions ont été remises par M. Sainte Marie à M. Pey Casado, vraisemblablement en qualité de dépositaire, il ne s'agit pas des 25.200 actions évoquées par les demanderesses puisque le document se réfère à 50% des actions de CPP S.A. Le document ne contient aucune référence aux 40.000 actions de CPP S.A., ni à leur vente et mentionne un dépôt de 250.000 USD ainsi qu'un dépôt antérieur 500.000 USD, sans plus de précisions.

131. Le Document de Genève ne constituerait pas un contrat mais une déclaration unilatérale, M. Sainte Marie ne l'ayant du reste pas signé ; ce document ne pourrait être qualifié de cession ou de vente et correspondrait en réalité à « *un dépôt de garantie* » de 12.000 actions de la société CPP S.A., reçues de M. Sainte Marie par M. Pey Casado, que ce dernier conservera sans les céder ou les transférer à quiconque tant que les conditions fixées dans ce document ne sont pas satisfaites. Rien n'indiquant que les conditions posées ont été

---

mémoire) qui, selon elle, corroborerait les déclarations de MM González, Venegas et Carrasco.

La défenderesse considère en outre que le rôle d'intermédiaire de M. Pey Casado est confirmé par l'existence du mandat, octroyé par M. Sainte Marie à M. Pey le 6 avril 1972, afin que ce dernier procède à la vente de 50% du capital d'EPC Ltda détenu par M. Sainte Marie (v. contre-mémoire de la défenderesse du 3 février 2003, p. 305 et annexe 146 au contre-mémoire). Elle évoque également un second mandat octroyé par M. Sainte Marie à M. Pey le 29 septembre 1972 et autorisant M. Pey à vendre, au nom de M. Sainte Marie, les 4,5% du capital d'EPC Ltda que celui-ci détient encore (v. contre-mémoire de la défenderesse du 3 février 2003, p. 314 et annexe 140 au contre-mémoire). Selon la défenderesse, ces mandats ne peuvent en aucun cas être interprétés comme des cessions de titres à M. Pey Casado (v. contre-mémoire de la défenderesse du 3 février 2003, p. 316).

La défenderesse ajoute que M. Sainte Marie possédait 4,5% du capital d'EPC Ltda depuis février 1972, le reste étant détenu par CPP S.A. (v. contre-mémoire de la défenderesse du 3 février 2003, p. 57 et annexe 9 au rapport Sandoval). Le 27 novembre 1972, M. Sainte Marie aurait cédé 3,5% de ses titres à CPP S.A. et 1% à M. Carrasco (v. contre-mémoire de la défenderesse du 3 février 2003, pp. 57-58 et annexe 10 au rapport Sandoval). La défenderesse qualifie d'incohérente la version des faits exposée par les demanderesses selon laquelle M. Pey aurait pu transférer 50% des droits sociaux détenus par M. Sainte Marie à CPP S.A. en avril 1972 et par la suite, le 27 novembre 1972, transférer à nouveau les 4,5% de titres de M. Sainte Marie à CPP S.A., à l'exception d'un pourcent cédé à M. Carrasco (v. contre-mémoire de la défenderesse du 3 février 2003, p. 315). Selon la défenderesse, M. Pey Casado aurait eu pour seule tâche d'agir au nom de M. Sainte Marie et de procéder à la vente de ses titres dans EPC Ltda à CPP S.A. d'un part et à M. Carrasco d'autre part (v. annexe 10 au rapport Sandoval).

remplies, les 12.000 titres seraient restés en la possession de M. Sainte Marie. Le document n'aurait de sens que si M. Pey Casado avait agi comme intermédiaire ou mandataire.

132. Lors de l'audience du 6 mai 2003, la défenderesse a conclu que le droit applicable à ces documents importait peu. Quel qu'il soit, le droit applicable ne pourrait permettre de considérer qu'il existe en l'espèce un contrat de vente entre M. Pey Casado et M. Sainte Marie.

133. Même si les Protocoles d'Estoril et le Document de Genève devaient être considérés comme un contrat de vente des actions de la société CPP S.A., aucun des documents produits ne décrit M. Pey Casado comme l'acquéreur des 40.000 actions de la société CPP S.A. Les Protocoles d'Estoril et le Document de Genève ne font référence qu'à 32.000 actions en tout. A supposer même que 25.200 actions aient été reçues par M. Pey Casado en avril 1972, on atteindrait le nombre de 37.200 et non de 40.000 actions. Pour l'Etat défendeur, les demanderesses n'ont prouvé à aucun moment la remise de 14.800 actions en octobre à Genève et ce chiffre n'apparaît nulle part dans le Document de Genève rédigé par M. Pey Casado. En toute hypothèse, M. Sainte Marie n'a pu vendre les 40.000 actions à M. Pey Casado. M. Sainte Marie n'aurait jamais été le propriétaire de l'intégralité des titres puisque la législation de l'époque l'interdisait.[99]

134. La défenderesse conteste également que les demanderesses puissent justifier de la propriété des actions sur le fondement des titres et des transferts signés en blanc qu'elles ont soumis au Tribunal. Outre les incohérences chronologiques, la défenderesse souligne que parmi les titres que M. Pey Casado prétend avoir reçu de M. Sainte Marie en avril 1972, aucun n'est enregistré au nom d'Osvaldo et Pablo Sainte-Marie, Juan Kaiser et Juana Labbé, contrairement aux prétentions des demanderesses ;[100] les titres litigieux sont en réalité inscrits au nom des actionnaires qui figurent dans les documents de la Surintendance

---

[99] La défenderesse soutient que le droit chilien exigeait à l'époque la présence d'au moins deux actionnaires dans le capital d'une société anonyme, sous peine de dissolution de la société (v. contre-mémoire de la défenderesse du 3 février 2003, p. 70). Le délai de 30 jours évoqué par les demanderesses ne remettrait pas en cause l'automaticité et l'immédiateté de la dissolution ; il serait simplement destiné à permettre au conseil d'administration de la société de prendre les mesures administratives nécessaires (v. la transcription de l'audience du 7 mai 2003, pp. 548-552 (Me Di Rosa).

[100] La défenderesse se réfère à l'exposé complémentaire des demanderesses sur la compétence Tribunal arbitral du 11 septembre 2002, p. 17.

des sociétés anonymes, soient MM. Darío Sainte-Marie, Emilio González, Jorge Venegas et Ramón Carrasco.[101]

135. De même, les transferts signés en blanc ne pourraient être les véritables transferts qui ont été utilisés à l'époque car un formulaire de transfert devrait être signé par le cédant et le cessionnaire, puis soumis pour approbation au « *Directoire* » et inscrit au Registre des actionnaires pour enfin ne plus laisser « *aucune trace* », le formulaire de transfert n'ayant plus d'utilité. En l'espèce, les formulaires de transfert produits par les demanderesses ne sont signés que par le cédant et non par le prétendu cessionnaire dont le nom n'apparaît pas davantage. Ces exigences n'auraient pu échapper à M. Pey Casado qui, en tant que président du conseil d'administration de CPP S.A., s'était occupé des procédures d'approbation des cessions d'actions à MM. González, Venegas et Carrasco et aurait eu tout le temps de procéder aux démarches nécessaires en sa faveur s'il l'avait souhaité.

136. La défenderesse insiste également sur le caractère, à son avis, « *mystérieux* » des transferts de fonds réalisés par M. Pey Casado pour prétendument effectuer l'achat des titres de CPP S.A. pour la somme totale de 1,28 million USD. Pour ce qui est du premier virement de 500.000 USD, M. Pey Casado, qui n'aurait pas produit de contrat de vente, n'aurait pas davantage prouvé qu'il est titulaire des comptes ouverts dans les banques *Zivnostenska Banka, N.C.* et Manufacturers Trust Co. par lequel les fonds ont transité. De même, l'origine des fonds resterait indéterminée. Rien ne permettrait non plus d'établir un lien entre ce virement et les Protocoles d'Estoril qui désignent M. Pey Casado comme le dépositaire d'un certain nombre d'actions. Quant au montant restant de 780.000 USD, la défenderesse s'étonne de ce qu'il ait été transféré d'abord d'un compte domicilié au *Banco nacional* de Cuba, dont M. Pey Casado ne prouve pas qu'il est titulaire, vers un compte ouvert la veille par M. Pey Casado à la *Bank für Handel und Effekten*, puis sept jours plus tard sur un compte de M. Sainte Marie à Madrid. La défenderesse fait valoir que les demanderesses s'abstiennent de révéler l'origine des fonds transférés depuis le *Banco nacional* de Cuba ; le compte ouvert auprès de la *Bank für Handel und Effekten* n'aurait servi que de compte de transit, ce qui suggérerait que M. Pey Casado a agi comme intermédiaire.

137. Elle ajoute que parmi les éléments de cette somme de 780.000 USD, l'ordre de paiement de 10.000 USD que M. Pey Casado prétend avoir

---

[101] V. contre-mémoire de la défenderesse du 3 février 2003, p. 79. Le fait pour la défenderesse de ne pas produire le registre des actionnaires serait sans pertinence puisque les propres registres de la surintendance des sociétés anonymes auraient la même valeur probante que le registre des actionnaires de la société (v. réplique de la défenderesse du 4 avril 2003, pp. 53-55).

effectué au profit de M. Sainte Marie ne comporte aucun destinataire et ne serait donc pas une preuve de paiement. Il n'y aurait pas davantage de preuve de l'existence de la lettre de change de 20.000 USD dans la documentation produite par les demanderesses.

138. La défenderesse soutient que la version des faits avancée par les demanderesses serait également contredite par les déclarations faites en 1975 par MM. González, Venegas et Carrasco qui indiquent avoir conservé leurs titres jusqu'à ce qu'ils confient un mandat spécial à M. Pey Casado et le chargent ainsi de revendre leurs actions dans le courant de l'année 1973. Ces déclarations ont été faites pour les besoins de la procédure introduite devant la Huitième Chambre du Tribunal correctionnel de Santiago le 3 septembre 1975 contre M. Darío Sainte-Marie Soruco, M. Osvaldo Sainte-Marie Soruco, M. Ramón Carrasco Peña, M. Víctor Pey Casado, M. José Emilio González Gonzàlez et M. Jorge Venegas Venegas, ainsi qu'à l'encontre des comptables de CPP S.A. et de EPC Ltda, M. Alfonso Bruce Bañados et M. Juan Biggs Gómez. L'enquête ouverte visait à déterminer si les sociétés CPP S.A. et EPC Ltda et les personnes citées se sont rendues coupables de certains délits fiscaux et si les acheteurs de ces sociétés agissaient en tant que « prête-noms » pour le Président Allende soupçonné d'en être le véritable propriétaire.[102]

139. La défenderesse relève que « dans le contexte de l'investigation de la plainte pour évasion fiscale, MM. Venegas, González et Carrasco se sont livrés à des déclarations, en 1974 et 1975, dans lesquelles ils affirment être propriétaires des actions de CPP S.A. ; les avoir acquises sur le conseil du Président Allende mais en leur nom et avec leur argent personnel ; que quelques mois après l'achat et pour diverses raisons (telles que, entre autres, de graves problèmes de conflits de travail au sein de CPP S.A.), ils avaient décidé de vendre les actions et, à cet effet, ils avaient remis des transferts signés en blanc à M. Pey Casado pour qu'il vendre les actions en leur nom ; que la vente n'a pas eu lieu puisqu'ils n'ont pas obtenu d'argent pour ces actions et, qu'en définitive, il n'y a eu aucun transfert. Par conséquent, ils sont restés propriétaires des actions qui n'ont donc pas été cédées à des tiers ou à M. Pey Casado. M. Osvaldo Sainte-Marie déclare également, et fait référence aux acquisitions d'actions par MM. Venegas, González et Carrasco ».[103] Le fait que MM. Venegas, González et Carrasco aient été, selon elle, « complètement relaxés » au terme de la procédure, à une époque où les tribunaux avaient intérêt à plaire au pouvoir en place, montrerait que « ces

---

[102] V. contre-mémoire de la défenderesse du 3 février 2003, p. 103 et la plainte en annexe 85 au contre-mémoire.

[103] V. contre-mémoire de la défenderesse du 3 février 2003, p. 105 et les déclarations des intéressés en annexe 87 au contre-mémoire.

*personnes ont bien été les propriétaires légitimes des actions de CPP
S.A., et qu'ils n'ont pas agi en qualité de prête-noms pour le compte
du Président Allende ou de qui que ce soit d'autre ».*[104]

140. Cela expliquerait que M. Pey Casado se soit retrouvé en possession
des titres et des formulaires de transfert en blanc mais qu'à aucun
moment MM. González, Venegas et Carrasco n'aient affirmé que M.
Pey Casado fût le véritable propriétaire des titres de CPP S.A. Par
ailleurs, le nom de M. Pey Casado n'apparaîtrait dans aucun
document de la société censé consigner sa qualité de propriétaire des
actions de CPP S.A.

141. Dans le but d'établir que M. Pey Casado n'a jamais été propriétaire
des actions de CPP S.A., la défenderesse se fonde également sur les
« *décharges* » formulées en décembre 1974 par MM. Jorge Venegas
et Emilio González visant à ne plus se voir appliquer les dispositions
du *decreto exento* n°276 du 21 octobre 1974. Ce décret prévoyait
entre autres « *la mise en observation* » du patrimoine des intéressés,
ce qui revenait à en imposer la confiscation provisoire jusqu'à ce
qu'une demande de « *décharge* » soit déposée pour en obtenir la
restitution. Les déclarations à décharge de MM. Jorge Venegas et
Emilio González démontreraient qu'ils étaient propriétaires de 6.400
et 20.000 titres de CPP S.A. respectivement et que ce sont les seuls
biens de leur patrimoine pour lesquels ils n'ont pas demandé la levée
de la confiscation.[105]

142. La défenderesse produit de la déclaration de M. Jorge Venegas du 20
novembre 2002 dans laquelle M. Venegas affirme qu'il a acquis ses
actions auprès de M. Sainte Marie par l'intermédiaire de M. Pey
Casado et que ce dernier aurait aussi agi en cette qualité dans la vente
des 20.000 actions à M. Emilio González. Cette version des faits est
confirmée par la déclaration de M. Ovalle, avocat que MM. Venegas
et González aurait consulté lorsqu'ils craignaient pour leur vie du fait
de leur qualité d'actionnaire de CPP S.A. M. Ovalle affirme leur
avoir suggéré de proposer aux autorités de l'époque la cession de

---

[104]   V. contre-mémoire de la défenderesse du 3 février 2003, pp. 107 et les
décisions de la Huitième Chambre du Tribunal correctionnel de Santiago et
de la Cour d'appel de Santiago en annexes 88 à 90 au contre-mémoire.

[105]   V. contre-mémoire de la défenderesse du 3 février 2003, pp. 96-98, pp. 321-
324 et annexes 81 et 82 au contre-mémoire. La défenderesse soutient que
MM. Jorge Venegas et Emilio González avaient l'intention de céder leurs
titres à une fondation. L'argument selon lequel les déclarations de MM.
Venegas et González, datées du 23 décembre 1974, auraient fait l'objet d'une
falsification au prétexte que le décret n°165 du 10 février 1975 n'y fait pas
référence, contrairement au décret n°580 du 24 avril 1975, serait infondé.
L'explication réside dans le fait que MM. Venegas et González auraient
déposé leurs décharges au-delà du délai légal, « *de manière intempestive* »
(v. réplique de la défenderesse du 4 avril 2003, pp. 49-54 et spéc. p. 53).

leurs titres à une fondation à caractère scientifique. C'est l'entrée en vigueur du *decreto exento* n°276 qui aurait par la suite conduit MM. Venegas et González a présenté des déclarations de décharge, ce dont prend acte le décret suprême n°580 en déclarant le *decreto exento* n°276 sans effet à leur égard.[106]

143. Les déclarations des autorités chiliennes en 1975 dont se prévalent les demanderesses pour affirmer que l'Etat défendeur a reconnu la qualité d'acquéreur et de propriétaire de M. Pey Casado seraient sans pertinence. Selon la défenderesse, ces déclarations « *sont sans doute issues de conclusions motivées davantage par des facteurs politiques et idéologiques que par des considérations de fait et de droit* ». Les juridictions chiliennes, qui seules auraient le pouvoir de se prononcer sur la propriété des actions litigieuses, auraient rejeté les thèses des autorités chiliennes telles qu'elles ont été exposées dans le mémorandum du 3 février 1975. Le procès devant la Huitième Chambre du Tribunal correctionnel de Santiago aurait même permis d'établir la validité des contrats d'achat d'actions par MM. Carrasco, González et Venegas et de reconnaître la propriété des actions de CPP S.A. à ces mêmes personnes.

144. Le fait que le testament de M. Sainte Marie du 28 mars 1979 et l'inventaire de ses biens réalisé par ses héritiers en décembre 1983 ne fassent aucune mention des actions des sociétés CPP S.A. ne pourrait par ailleurs constituer une preuve de l'achat des actions en question par M. Pey Casado. Il en irait de même du testament de M. González qui ne contient pas de référence aux actions de CPP S.A. Quant à M. Carrasco, la défenderesse affirme qu'il serait mort intestat et s'il avait effectivement rédigé un testament sans mention relative aux actions litigieuses, cela n'aurait été d'aucun secours pour les demanderesses car cette prétendue omission ne peut être une preuve de propriété pour M. Pey Casado.

145. La défenderesse fait valoir également que la restitution des titres et des formulaires de transfert en blanc par la Huitième Chambre à M. Pey Casado ne prouve en rien la qualité de propriétaire de ce dernier. A l'appui de cet argument, elle indique tout d'abord que la question de la propriété des actions de CPP S.A. n'a pas été traitée en 1975 à l'occasion de la procédure intentée par les services fiscaux chiliens. La requête présentée par M. Pey Casado vise seulement à obtenir la restitution de documents et non une décision se prononçant sur la

---

[106] La défenderesse explique que le décret suprême n°580 du 24 avril 1975 déclare sans effet le *decreto exento* n°276 du Ministère de l'intérieur en ce qui concerne MM. Jorge Venegas et Emilio González qui ont pu, selon la défenderesse, disposer librement de leurs biens à partir de la date d'entrée en vigueur du décret suprême n°580 (v. contre-mémoire de la défenderesse du 3 février 2003, p. 93).

propriété des actions. La Huitième Chambre du Tribunal correctionnel n'a signifié l'existence de la demande de M. Pey Casado qu'au service des impôts internes qui n'a pas réagi à cette signification. Le tribunal correctionnel n'a signifié la demande à aucune autre personne ni aucune autre institution, y compris MM. Venegas, González et Carrasco, les « *véritables intéressés* ». On ne pouvait par ailleurs s'attendre à ce que ces personnes, que la défenderesse prétend être les véritables propriétaires des actions, ne cherchent à s'informer de l'issue de cette procédure. Le tribunal n'a pas non plus établi le contrôle des actions mais a pourtant ordonné leur restitution. Selon la défenderesse, la décision du tribunal ne pourrait être interprétée ni comme déterminant la propriété des actions ni comme une reconnaissance par l'Etat défendeur sur ce point.

146. La défenderesse soutient également que « même dans l'hypothèse où MM. Darío Sainte Marie et Pey seraient effectivement convenus de la vente des actions de la société CPP S.A., cet accord aurait été en soi insuffisant pour effectuer le transfert du contrôle concernant les actions en question en faveur de M. Pey ». Le contrat de vente des actions devrait être distingué du « transfert du contrôle des actions concernées » qui exige la satisfaction d'un certain nombre de conditions dont l'inscription au registre des actionnaires de la société. En l'espèce, les demanderesses n'auraient pas accompli les formalités imposées par le droit chilien sous peine de nullité.

147. Selon la défenderesse, les demanderesses prétendent à tort que « le droit applicable au moyen d'acquisition du contrôle sur les actions de sociétés anonymes constituées au Chili serait le Code civil portugais (lieu où aurait été conclu le contrat d'achat-vente) ; le droit du canton de Genève (« lieu ou le contrat a été achevé et signé » et où aurait été payé le prix convenu) ; et/ou le Code de commerce espagnol (« droit du lieu de résidence du vendeur ») » en application du principe locus regit actum. Selon la défenderesse, l'application de cette règle concernerait certes la formation, les effets et l'interprétation du contrat mais n'exempterait pas du respect des formalités de cession d'actions en droit chilien.

148. La défenderesse fait valoir que ces formalités sont celles que prévoyait en 1972 le Code de commerce. Celles-ci prévaudraient sur celles du Code civil chilien invoquées par les demanderesses et pourtant inapplicables à la cession d'actions nominatives de sociétés anonymes.

149. La défenderesse prétend également que l'état du droit en chilien en 1972 ne permettrait pas l'émission d'actions au porteur. La réglementation en vigueur à partir de 1970, plus particulièrement l'article 451 du code de commerce et l'article 37 du règlement sur les

sociétés anonymes, n'autoriseraient plus que les actions nominatives et exige que leur transfert s'effectue par le biais d'une inscription au registre des actionnaires. La doctrine comme la jurisprudence confirmeraient le fait que la validité d'une cession d'actions nominatives dépend de son inscription au registre des actionnaires, cette dernière ne pouvant être analysée comme une simple mesure de publicité.

150. La défenderesse en conclut qu'il était impossible en 1972 de procéder à l'acquisition d'actions nominatives par l'obtention de transferts signés en blanc. Les documents produits par les demanderesses ne satisferaient aucune des formalités imposées par la réglementation en vigueur et notamment l'article 37 du règlement sur les sociétés anonymes qui exige entre autres choses la signature du cédant et du cessionnaire devant deux témoins. Les « *transferts en blanc* » ne constitueraient pas en eux-mêmes des titres de propriété et ne feraient pas davantage partie des modes de cession prévus la législation chilienne de l'époque qui ne prévoyait pas d'exception aux conditions de validité du transfert d'actions nominatives. Il ne s'agirait pas non plus d'une coutume qui, en toute hypothèse, ne serait appliquée que dans le silence de la loi et dont les demanderesses n'auraient pas prouvé l'existence.

151. La défenderesse insiste enfin sur le fait qu'aucune demande de transfert d'actions au nom et au profit de M. Pey Casado n'a été transmise au conseil d'administration comme l'exige l'article 37 du règlement sur les sociétés anonymes, règle reprise par ailleurs dans les statuts de CPP S.A. depuis le 30 mars 1972. Il n'existerait pas non plus d'inscription au registre des actionnaires au nom de M. Pey Casado, ainsi que le révèle la liste des actionnaires dressée dans les rapports de la surintendance des sociétés anonymes. L'argument selon lequel M. Pey Casado n'aurait pas eu le loisir d'effectuer les formalités nécessaires du fait des événements de septembre 1973 n'est pas crédible car, selon la défenderesse, M. Pey Casado avait tout le temps d'y procéder avant. Enfin, si vraiment un transfert d'actions avait été effectué au profit de M. Pey Casado, la société aurait émis de nouveaux titres au nom de l'intéressé, ce qui ne s'est jamais produit.

b) Position des demanderesses

152. Selon les demanderesses, M. Pey Casado aurait fait l'acquisition des sociétés CPP S.A. et EPC Ltda au mois d'octobre 1972 et serait ainsi devenu titulaire d'un investissement au sens de la Convention CIRDI. Dans ses notes de plaidoirie relatives aux audiences des 29 et 30 octobre 2001, la partie demanderesse a soutenu que l'investissement en cause satisfaisait la condition posée par la Convention CIRDI dans la mesure où la Convention ne fournit pas de

283

définition de la notion d'investissement et n'exige pas le transfert physique de fonds sur le territoire de l'Etat contractant.[107]

153. Comme la défenderesse, les demanderesses ont consacré la majeure partie de leurs développements sur la condition d'investissement au sens de la Convention CIRDI à démontrer que M. Pey Casado était bien l'acquéreur et le propriétaire véritable des actions de CPP S.A.

154. Les demanderesses retracent ainsi dans leurs écritures ce qu'elles considèrent être la chronologie de l'acquisition des actions des sociétés CPP S.A. et EPC Ltda. Elles affirment ainsi que M. Pey Casado aurait versé à M. Darío Sainte Marie, alors propriétaire de l'intégralité du capital de CPP S.A., la somme de 500.000 USD le 29 mars 1972, au moyen d'un virement de la banque Manufacturers Trust Co. de Londres sur le compte bancaire de M. Darío Sainte Marie à Madrid. Le contrat signé à Estoril le 13 mai 1972 (les Protocoles d'Estoril) comporterait également la preuve de ce paiement en se référant au dépôt antérieur de 500.000 USD.

155. C'est en contrepartie de ce premier versement que M. Pey Casado aurait été nommé à la présidence du conseil d'administration de la société CPP S.A. et pris « *le contrôle effectif des entreprises* [CPP S.A. et EPC Ltda] ». Pour compléter cette contrepartie, M. Sainte Marie aurait, d'une part, mis à la libre disposition de M. Pey Casado 50% de ses participations dans la société EPC Ltda et, d'autre part, remis en mains propres à M. Pey Casado 25.200 actions de la société CPP S.A. avec leurs « *bordereaux de transfert signés en blanc* ».[108] M. Pey Casado a lui-même expliqué devant le Tribunal qu'il envisageait de s'associer avec des personnes proches du monde politique et journalistique de manière à pouvoir se consacrer également à ses autres activités. Dans cette perspective, M. Pey Casado aurait proposé à M. González un paquet de 20.000 actions de la société CPP S.A., tout en conservant les titres et les bordereaux en blanc jusqu'à ce la situation politique et économique permette de déterminer le prix des actions. M. Pey Casado aurait procédé de façon identique avec MM. Venegas et Carrasco, réalisant ainsi une « *transaction d'usage commun* ». Il par ailleurs précisé que MM. Venegas et González ne se sont à aucun moment trouvés en

---

[107] V. notes de plaidoirie des demanderesses relatives aux audiences des 29 et 30 octobre 2001, pp. 63-64. Les demanderesses invoquent la sentence rendue dans l'affaire *Fedax* au soutien de leur argument.

[108] V. exposé complémentaire sur la compétence du Tribunal arbitral du 11 septembre 2002, p. 17. Les demanderesses précisent que les 25.200 titres remis sont enregistrés au nom de Darío, Osvaldo et Pablo Sainte-Marie, Juan Kaiser et Juana Labbé et se fondent sur les annexes C-109, C-113 (témoignage d'Osvaldo Sainte Marie, frère de Darío Sainte Marie) et C-43 (p. 2).

possession des titres et des bordereaux de transfert, contrairement à ce qu'a pu affirmer la défenderesse.

156. Le 13 mai 1972, M. Pey Casado et M. Sainte Marie seraient convenus de la somme de 1,28 million USD pour la vente de l'intégralité des 40.000 actions de la société CPP S.A. Les Protocoles d'Estoril, présentées par les demanderesses comme le contrat de vente des actions de CPP S.A., prendrait acte dans son article A d'un premier versement de 500.000 USD. Il offrirait par ailleurs à l'acheteur deux options : soit le versement, à deux reprises, de la somme de 250.000 USD (article A) et celui d'une rente viagère, soit deux versements de 500.000 USD et 280.000 USD (article F). C'est en combinant l'article A et l'article F que l'on parviendrait au prix de 1.280.000 USD effectivement payé par M. Pey Casado.

157. Le 23 septembre 1972, M. Sainte Marie aurait signé par devant notaire à Zürich un second pouvoir en faveur de M. Pey Casado, lui conférant la libre disposition de la marque *Clarín* et des dernières actions que M. Sainte-Marie possédait dans EPC Ltda, soit 4.5% du capital.[109]

158. Les demanderesses affirment également que le contrat conclu à Estoril a été « *parachevé* » à Genève le 2 octobre 1972.[110] A cette même date, « *étaient passées les écritures modificatives des Statuts de CPP S.A. et en assurant le contrôle effectif à celui qui, le lendemain, allait être mis en possession des actions et des transferts des actions dûment signés* ». Le 3 octobre 1972, M. Pey Casado a ainsi reçu des mains de M. Sainte Marie 14.800 actions de CPP S.A. avec les transferts signés en blanc qui correspondent à ces actions. M. Pey Casado ayant choisi d'exercer l'option de rachat de la rente viagère prévue dans les Protocoles d'Estoril, M. Darío Sainte Marie

---

[109] V. exposé complémentaire sur la compétence du Tribunal arbitral du 11 septembre 2002, p. 18 et annexe C-80. M. Pey aurait procédé à la cession de ces 4,5% du capital d'EPC Ltda à CPP S.A. le 27 novembre 2007, à l'exception d'une action vendue à M. Carrasco (v. exposé complémentaire sur la compétence du Tribunal arbitral, du 11 septembre 2002, p. 18 et annexe C-68). La société CPP S.A. serait ainsi devenue actionnaire à 99% de la société EPC Ltda. C'est ce qu'a expliqué M. Pey Casado lors de l'audience du 5 mai 2003 : « *Comme déjà je disposais de la majorité des actions du Consortium j'ai utilisé ce pouvoir pour transférer la participation de M. Sainte Marie dans la société limitée au Consortium, je le répète, dont j'étais déjà l'actionnaire majoritaire. Dans le but d'éviter l'extinction de la société limitée, vu que selon la loi du Chili tout le patrimoine ne peut pas résider en une seule personne, j'ai décidé dans un accord commun avec M. Ramon Carrasco qu'il apparaisse nominalement avec 1 pour cent de la société limitée* » (transcription de l'audience du 5 mai 2003, p. 152).

[110] V. exposé complémentaire sur la compétence du Tribunal arbitral du 11 septembre 2002, p. 19 et annexe C-66 (« *document de Genève* »).

aurait pour sa part reçu la somme de 780.000 USD par les moyens de paiement suivants :

- un premier virement de 500.000 USD d'un compte bancaire de M. Pey Casado à l'ordre de M. Sainte Marie ;
- un second virement de 250.000 USD d'un compte bancaire de M. Pey Casado vers un compte bancaire de M. Sainte Marie à la Citibank de Genève ;
- un ordre de paiement pour un montant de 10.000 USD depuis un compte bancaire de M. Pey Casado, remis en mains propres à M. Sainte Marie par M. Pey Casado le 3 octobre 1972 ;
- une lettre de change pour un montant de 20.000 USD, remise par M. Pey Casado à M. Sainte Marie, à la même date.

159. Les demanderesses en concluent que M. Pey Casado a bien fait l'acquisition des 40.000 titres[111] de la société CPP S.A. auprès de M. Sainte Marie pour la somme de 1,28 million USD. Les autorités chiliennes l'auraient du reste confirmé en ne mettant pas en question la validité du transfert de propriété au moyen de bordereaux de transfert signés en blanc intervenu au profit de M. Pey Casado.

160. Les demanderesses estiment même que les autorités chiliennes ont reconnu à plusieurs reprises que M. Pey Casado avait fait l'acquisition des titres de CPP S.A. Il leur serait désormais impossible de revenir sur cette position et de mettre en avant des arguments en ce sens contraire.

161. La combinaison du décret n°165 de 1965, complété par le décret n°580 de 1975, avec le décret n°1200 de 1977 montrerait que M. Pey Casado était considéré comme le propriétaire de la société CPP S.A.[112] Les demanderesses insistent sur le fait que le Ministère de l'intérieur a rendu public, à peine quelques jours avant l'adoption du décret n°165, un mémorandum dans lequel il est conclu que « [...]

---

[111]   Les demanderesses indiquent que le capital social de CPP S.A. a toujours été de 40.000 actions, l'émission de 1.040.000 actions libérées approuvée par le Directoire en décembre 1972 n'ayant pas été effectuée (v. exposé complémentaire sur la compétence du Tribunal arbitral du 11 septembre 2002, p. 21 et communication n°01500 de la surintendance des valeurs et des assurances du Chili du 5 mai 1995 en annexe C-79).

[112]   V. réplique des demanderesses au contre-mémoire de la défenderesse du 23 février 2003, pp. 42-43. Le décret suprême n°16 du 8 janvier 1979 le confirmerait en indiquant que l'interdiction faite à M. Pey de disposer de ses biens ne s'applique pas aux biens relatifs à la société Socomer. *A contrario*, l'interdiction s'appliquerait à tous les autres biens de M. Pey et donc aux actions de CPP S.A. (v. réplique des demanderesses au contre-mémoire de la défenderesse, du 23 février 2003, pp. 42-43).

c'est ce dernier [M. Pey] *qui a acheté le consortium publicitaire et périodique S.A., et l'entreprise périodique Clarín* [...] ».[113]

162. Les éléments de la procédure pour infraction à la législation fiscale introduite en 1975 par le directeur du service des impôts internes viendraient corroborer cette conclusion. Les demanderesses invoquent ainsi le rapport d'expertise des inspecteurs des impôts remis à la Huitième Chambre du Tribunal correctionnel le 26 novembre 1975 qui conclut que M. Pey Casado est bien l'acquéreur de la société CPP S.A. : « *encore que les transferts d'actions aient été effectués aux personnes indiquées dans les paragraphes précédents [MM. Venegas, González et Carrasco], ces dernières n'ont pas reçu les titres, ayant signé à leur tour des bordereaux de transfert en blanc en faveur de Víctor Pey Casado, qui du 30 Mars au 6 Décembre 1972 était président du Directoire de la Société, d'où l'on déduit que ce doit être ce dernier qui a acheté le Consortium Publicitaire et Périodique S.A.* ».[114]

163. Les demanderesses estiment en outre que MM. Venegas, González et Carrasco n'ont pas été condamnés dans cette procédure car ils n'ont produit « *aucun antécédent, titre ni cause d'aucune sorte de nature à fonder l'achat de la moindre action de CPP S.A.* » et en l'absence d'un acte imposable (la prétendue acquisition d'actions de CPP S.A.), le juge chilien ne pouvait leur reprocher de ne pas avoir payé d'impôt.[115] Cela expliquerait pourquoi la Huitième Chambre du Tribunal correctionnel a accepté de restituer à M. Pey Casado les titres de CPP S.A. après avoir demandé « *que soit démontrée préalablement la pleine propriété des actions dont la restitution est demandée* ».[116] En ordonnant la restitution des titres de CPP S.A. à M. Pey Casado le 29 mai 1995, la justice chilienne aurait elle aussi confirmé que M. Pey Casado en était le seul et véritable propriétaire,

---

[113] V. exposé complémentaire sur le fond de l'affaire du 11 septembre 2002, pp. 41-42 et annexe C-8. V. également la transcription de l'audience du 5 mai 2003, pp. 59-65 (Me Garcés) et le rapport du Conseil de défense de l'Etat au Ministre de l'intérieur cité par Me Garcés en date du 16 octobre 1974 : « *Des antécédents qui s'y rattachent, il résulterait que c'est Víctor Pey qui a acheté le Consortium et la société limitée étant donné qu'il a effectué les paiements correspondants au moyen de US 780 000 dollars [...] à part les 500 000 dollars que Sainte Marie avait reçus auparavant* » (transcription de l'audience du 5 mai 2003, p. 65).

[114] V. rapport d'expertise des inspecteurs des impôts remis à la Huitième Chambre du Tribunal correctionnel le 26 novembre 1975, p. 5 (annexe C-43).

[115] Exposé complémentaire sur le fond de l'affaire du 11 septembre 2002, p. 47. M. Pey a quant à lui été déclaré en rébellion (v. *ibid.*, p. 48 et annexe C-197).

[116] Exposé complémentaire sur le fond de l'affaire du 11 septembre 2002, p. 49, pp. 51-52 et annexe 21 à la requête d'arbitrage, du 3 novembre 1997.

M. Pey Casado ayant indiqué au tribunal que la restitution des titres devait lui permettre « *d'entreprendre des actions destinées à attaquer les prétendues expropriations* ». Afin de contourner la reconnaissance judiciaire des droits de propriété de M. Pey Casado, la défenderesse s'emploie aujourd'hui à critiquer le bien-fondé de la décision du juge chilien.

164. Les demanderesses ajoutent que le Conseil de défense de l'Etat du Chili aurait également reconnu la qualité de propriétaire de M. Pey Casado sur la totalité des actions de CPP S.A. dans la procédure relative à la restitution de la rotative Goss. Enfin, le gouvernement chilien aurait lui-même reconnu la qualité d'actionnaire de M. Pey Casado en se référant en 1997 à « *la réalisation des opérations commerciales destinées à acquérir le patrimoine dont la confiscation fait l'objet de votre réclamation* ».[117]

165. La défenderesse ayant ainsi reconnu à plusieurs occasions que M. Pey Casado était propriétaire des titres de CPP S.A., l'argument selon lequel M. Pey Casado devrait être qualifié de « *simple mandataire* » de M. Sainte Marie ou de MM. Venegas et González serait totalement infondé. Les demanderesses résument leur position sur ce point dans les termes suivants :

> « • *la seule personne [M. Pey Casado] qui a passé contrat, entièrement rempli les conditions à la satisfaction du vendeur pour un montant de 1.280.000$, reçu et conservé la totalité des titres d'actions, dirigé seul les entreprises à partir du départ de M. Darío Sainte-Marie en avril 1972, qui a été proclamé l'acquéreur à la lumière de toutes les enquêtes diligentées par l'Etat du Chili, en a subi la confiscation, ne peut pas être un simple ' mandataire ' successif des uns ou des autres ;*
> • *des personnes qui n'ont passé aucun contrat [MM. Venegas et González], prétendent avoir acheté des parts de l'entreprise pour des sommes qui situeraient la valeur totale de l'entreprise entre 4.000 et 5.000 $ U.S. Or elles ne peuvent attester le paiement du moindre centime, ne peuvent démontrer avoir été en possession d'aucun titre d'actions à aucun moment. De plus, elles ont été reconnues par l'Etat du Chili à l'époque comme n'ayant pu être acquéreurs, et n'ont jamais subi de confiscations. Comment dans ces conditions pourraient-elles être les propriétaires,*

---

[117] Exposé complémentaire sur le fond de l'affaire du 11 septembre 2002, p. 56.

> *conjointement à la personne qui a vendu toutes ses actions à M. Pey ? »*[118]

166. Après avoir rappelé que MM. Venegas, González et Carrasco n'ont pas apporté la preuve de ce qu'ils avaient acheté les actions de la société CPP S.A. et n'ont fourni notamment aucune preuve de paiement, les demanderesses contestent l'authenticité et la crédibilité des déclarations de décharge de MM. Venegas et González du 23 novembre 1974. Les prétendues décharges, à supposer qu'il s'agisse des véritables décharges déposées par ces personnes auprès des autorités de l'époque,[119] montreraient essentiellement « *la collusion* »[120] entre ces derniers et les autorités chiliennes. La lecture de leurs déclarations révèlerait qu'ils ne peuvent fournir la moindre preuve de leur achat, ce qui expliquerait pourquoi ils ont pu être qualifiés de « *prête-noms* » et pourquoi ils acceptent l'un et l'autre le maintien de l'interdiction frappant les actions de CPP S.A. tout en demandant la levée de cette interdiction sur tous leurs autres biens.

167. Les demanderesses voient par ailleurs une autre preuve de la propriété de M. Pey Casado sur les actions de CPP S.A. dans le testament que M. Sainte Marie a passé par-devant notaire à Madrid, le 28 mars 1979, et qui ne fait aucune mention, dans l'inventaire des biens de M. Sainte Marie, de CPP S.A. ni d'EPC Ltda. Il en irait de même des testaments de MM. González et Carrasco qui ne contiennent aucune référence aux actions litigieuses.

168. Dans le but de démontrer la validité de l'acquisition réalisée par M. Pey Casado, les demanderesses soutiennent que le mode

---

[118] Réplique des demanderesses au contre-mémoire de la défenderesse, du 23 février 2003, p. 33.

[119] Les demanderesses soutiennent qu'il ne s'agit pas réellement de décharges et reproche à l'Etat défendeur de s'être livré à une « *distorsion-falsification manifeste touchant le cœur de la question de la propriété* » (v. réplique des demanderesses au contre-mémoire de la défenderesse, du 23 février 2003, p. 80). Les demanderesses insistent sur le fait que le décret n°165 du 10 février 1975 ne se réfère qu'aux décharges de MM. Osvaldo Sainte Marie et Marion Osses et ne fait aucune mention des prétendues décharges de MM. Venegas et González dont la défenderesse affirme qu'elles datent du 23 décembre 1974 (v. réplique des demanderesses au contre-mémoire de la défenderesse, du 23 février 2003, p. 81).

[120] V. réplique des demanderesses au contre-mémoire de la défenderesse, du 23 février 2003, p. 82. Les demanderesses ajoutent que les prétendus témoignages de MM. Venegas et Ovalle, recueillis les 20 et 18 novembre 2002, ne sont guère crédibles d'autant qu'ils sont contredits par les propres déclarations de MM. Venegas et González de novembre 1975 devant la huitième Chambre du Tribunal correctionnel de Santiago (v. réplique des demanderesses au contre-mémoire de la défenderesse, du 23 février 2003, p. 100).

d'interprétation du contrat de vente retenu par la défenderesse est totalement inadapté. La lecture effectuée par la défenderesse ferait abstraction du contexte dans lequel les Protocoles d'Estoril et le Document de Genève ont été conclus et ne tiendraient aucun compte de la relation de confiance unissant M. Pey Casado et M. Sainte Marie. Or, ce sont précisément les rapports intimes qu'entretenaient les deux parties au contrat et la rapidité avec laquelle la décision de vendre a été prise qui expliqueraient la formulation et la structure du contrat. L'analyse avancée par la défenderesse, qui fait de M. Pey Casado un mandataire ou un intermédiaire remplissant les obligations fixées dans un contrat de dépôt, serait donc inexacte.

169. Les demanderesses ont également procédé à l'exposé du droit applicable au contrat de vente des titres de CPP S.A. et ont résumé leur position au cours de l'audience du 5 mai 2003. S'agissant de la forme des contrats, il conviendrait d'appliquer la règle *locus regit actum*. Les deux contrats dont disposent les demanderesses ayant été conclus respectivement à Estoril et à Genève, le droit portugais et le droit suisse leur seraient applicables et tous deux respecteraient le principe de liberté de forme des contrats. Pour ce qui concerne le fond du contrat, la règle de conflit portugaise désignerait la loi du lieu de résidence habituelle du débiteur de la prestation caractéristique, en l'espèce, la loi espagnole. La règle de conflit suisse désignerait également la loi de la résidence habituelle du débiteur de la prestation caractéristique. Le droit espagnol applicable ne comporterait qu'une seule exigence de fond, celle du contrat de vente et donc d'un accord sur la chose et sur le prix, conditions qui seraient réunies en l'espèce. La cession d'actions ainsi réalisée ne produirait ses effets au Chili qu'à la condition que soient satisfaites les exigences posées par le Code civil chilien, qui pour la tradition d'une action requiert la simple remise du titre. Les demanderesses précisent que les contrats ont bien été exécutés, l'acheteur ayant effectué un paiement de 1,28 million USD et le vendeur ayant remis les titres et les bordereaux de transfert en blanc correspondants.

170. Les demanderesses ont examiné plus particulièrement le « régime juridique de la transmission des actions sociales nominatives » et soutiennent que « selon le régime légal en vigueur en Espagne, au Portugal, en Suisse et au Chili les actions nominatives 1. étaient transférables sans acquiescement préalable de la société émettrice. En ce cas l'auteur du transfert devait se borner à notifier à cette dernière la cession, afin qu'elle soit inscrite au Livre-Registre des actionnaires aux fins de relation éventuelle avec la Société, et de publicité à l'égard des tiers ; 2. leur transfert par acte juridique pouvait avoir lieu par la remise du titre endossé à l'acquéreur. En l'espèce cela a pris la forme d'une variante de cet endossement avec la remise du

titre original à l'acquéreur joint à une lettre signée de « transfert des actions » (traspaso de acciones). »[121]

171. Elles précisent également dans leurs écritures que l'inscription d'une personne au livre-registre des actionnaires d'une SA, mesure de publicité à l'égard de la société et des tiers, requiert au préalable la démonstration de la qualité de propriétaire des actions. La preuve requise serait constituée par les titres et les bordereaux de transfert correspondants. Selon les demanderesses, la remise par le cédant au cessionnaire du bordereau de transfert des actions signé par la personne au nom de qui figurent les actions[122] « *constitue de façon coutumière, et reconnue par la jurisprudence, un droit d'accès à la publicité* » du statut d'actionnaire. Les demanderesses concluent que « *la coutume et la jurisprudence reconnaissent ainsi que le détenteur légitime du bordereau de transfert dispose du droit de désigner l'attributaire des actions en ne faisant pas figurer immédiatement le nom du cessionnaire dans l'emplacement réservé à cet effet sur le bordereau* ». Le cessionnaire aurait dès lors le choix entre deux solutions : faire figurer son nom sur le bordereau de transfert, le signer, le présenter à l'inscription au registre pour archivage des titres et des bordereaux de transfert et remise des nouveaux titres émis au nom de l'intéressé ; ou laisser le transfert en blanc et, « *le cas échéant, [...] le remettre, avec le titre d'actions correspondant, à un cessionnaire à venir, retransmettant ainsi successivement la subrogation initiale, jusqu'à ce qu'un propriétaire souhaite effectuer une nouvelle inscription* ».[123]

172. Les demanderesses ajoutent que l'utilisation des titres accompagnés de transferts signés en blanc pour acquérir le capital d'une société est un « *procédé habituel, courant, banal qui se pratique depuis toujours*

---

[121] Exposé complémentaire sur la compétence du Tribunal arbitral du 11 septembre 2002, pp. 38-39. Les demanderesses jugent sans pertinence l'argumentation développée par la défenderesse sur les actions au porteur au motif que « *rien n'apparente les pratiques utilisées à l'usage ' titres au porteur ', puisque, les titres des actions sont nominatifs et que l'usage des bordereaux de transfert correspondants implique qu'ils soient remplis nominalement, par qui en dispose légitimement, avec signature nominale du titulaire des actions corrélatives* » (v. réplique des demanderesses au contre-mémoire de la défenderesse, du 23 février 2003, p. 42).

[122] Selon les demanderesses, cette personne peut être « *le cédant ou la dernière personne à avoir été inscrite pour ces actions au Registre des Actionnaires* » (exposé complémentaire sur le fond de l'affaire du 11 septembre 2002, p. 13).

[123] Exposé complémentaire sur le fond de l'affaire du 11 septembre 2002, pp. 13-14.

et partout », qui « *ne présente pas la plus petite trace d'illégalité.* »[124]

173. Víctor Pey Casado s'est exprimé devant le Tribunal pour confirmer l'existence de la pratique coutumière décrite par les demanderesses. M. Pey Casado a ainsi indiqué que « *nous avons convenu d'un procédé simple et facile, en usage courant dans les couloirs de la Bourse de Santiago : consigner les titres des actions, et les transferts signés en blanc de celles-ci, dans les formulaires dont disposait la Bourse des Valeurs de Santiago à cet effet* ».[125]

174. L'examen de la jurisprudence pertinente permettrait, selon les demanderesses, de tirer les conclusions suivantes :

> « *La qualité de propriétaire d'actions d'une S.A. ne peut être attestée que par l'ensemble d'éléments suivants :*
> *a) Le titre constitutif de la mutation de la propriété de ces actions (par exemple, un contrat d'achat et vente dont les conditions ont été reunies),*
> *b) La possession effective et légitime des titres de propriété desdites actions (titres des actions avec, le cas échéant, le(s) bordereau(x) de transfert correspondant(s) signé(s) par le ou leurs(s) titulaire(s) figurant au Livre-Registre des Actionnaires).*
> *Le Livre-Registre des Actionnaires quant à lui permet seulement*
> *d'attester – sous réserve de données opposables en sens contraire – l'identité de la personne dont*
> *a) les prises de position et échanges peuvent être acceptés par la Société en relation avec les actions,*
> *b) les dettes envers des tiers de bonne foi peuvent entraîner la mise en cause des actions* ».[126]

175. En conséquence, Víctor Pey Casado devrait être considéré comme le seul et véritable propriétaire des actions de CPP S.A., lui qui détient les titres et les bordereaux de transfert signés en blanc.

176. Les demanderesses relèvent en outre que l'Etat défendeur, qui prétend que la validité de la cession des actions de CPP S.A. dépend de son inscription au « *livre registre des actionnaires* », refuse de produire ce document et, de ce fait, n'est pas en mesure de prouver le bien-fondé de ses allégations. En toute hypothèse, l'inscription de

---

[124] Réplique des demanderesses au contre-mémoire de la défenderesse, du 23 février 2003, p. 31.

[125] Transcription de l'audience du 29 octobre 2001, p. 84-85 (Víctor Pey Casado).

[126] Exposé complémentaire sur le fond de l'affaire du 11 septembre 2002, p. 64.

MM. Venegas, González et Carrasco au livre-registre des actionnaires serait sans effet sur la propriété des actions litigieuses du fait que ces personnes n'en ont jamais fait l'acquisition et n'ont jamais été en possession des titres et des formulaires de transfert, contrairement à M. Pey Casado.

177. Le fait que M. Pey Casado n'ait pas utilisé, pour sa part, les formulaires de transfert en blanc qu'il possédait pour procéder à une inscription au livre-registre des actionnaires s'expliquerait, d'une part, par la saisie du livre-registre par l'armée chilienne en septembre 1973, et, d'autre part, par l'absence de délai relatif à l'accomplissement de cette formalité qui, au demeurant, ne constitue pas une obligation puisqu'aucune sanction n'est prévue en cas de non-respect. Selon les demanderesses, la coutume commerciale en vigueur au Chili en 1972 permettait du reste d'attendre la fin des négociations pour apposer le nom de l'attributaire du transfert sur le formulaire et procéder à l'inscription sur le livre-registre des actionnaires. Le livre-registre des actionnaires, en possession de M. Pey Casado avant d'être saisi par l'armée le 11 septembre 1973, n'a toujours pas été restitué à son propriétaire, empêchant ainsi ce dernier d'accomplir la formalité de publicité à laquelle il a toujours été en droit de procéder.

178. A titre subsidiaire, dans l'hypothèse où le Tribunal estimerait que M. Pey Casado n'est pas le propriétaire des actions de la société CPP S.A., les demanderesses indiquent que depuis le mois d'avril 1972, M. Pey Casado exerce un contrôle absolu sur les sociétés CPP S.A. et EPC Ltda, fait que l'Etat défendeur aurait reconnu. Les demanderesses invoquent également la clause de la nation la plus favorisée afin de se voir appliquer l'article 1.2 de l'API Chili-Australie et le protocole de l'API Chili-France qui tous deux reconnaîtraient la notion de contrôle effectif.

2. Conclusions du Tribunal

179. Au vu des éléments exposés et des documents produits par les parties, le Tribunal estime tout d'abord que M. Pey Casado a effectivement procédé à l'acquisition des sociétés CPP S.A. et EPC Ltda, contrairement aux allégations de la défenderesse. Il estime également que cette acquisition doit être considérée comme un investissement au sens de l'article 25 de la Convention CIRDI.

a) M. Pey Casado a fait l'acquisition des sociétés CPP S.A. et EPC Ltda

180. L'époque à laquelle se sont déroulés les faits de la présente affaire est à la fois lointaine et marquée par une situation politique et économique très particulière. Aussi l'établissement des faits s'est-il

293

avéré une tâche difficile et chaque partie s'est employée à défendre une version des faits au moyen de la documentation dont elle pouvait disposer. Après un examen attentif des arguments et des pièces soumises par les parties, le Tribunal, dans l'exercice de son pouvoir d'appréciation des preuves, est parvenu à la conclusion que M. Pey Casado a acheté l'intégralité des actions de la société CPP S.A. au cours de l'année 1972. Cette conclusion repose sur trois éléments principaux que sont la conclusion de ce que les parties appellent les « *Protocoles d'Estoril* », complétés par ce qu'elles appellent le « *Document de Genève* », les versements effectués au profit de M. Darío Sainte Marie pour un montant total de 1,28 million USD et la remise à M. Pey Casado, en plusieurs paquets, des titres de la société accompagnés de leurs formulaires de transfert signés en blanc.

181. Le Tribunal estime qu'il est établi que M. Pey Casado a bien versé à M. Darío Sainte Marie la somme de 500.000 USD le 29 mars 1972, au moyen d'un virement de la banque Manufacturers Trust Co. de Londres sur le compte bancaire de M. Darío Sainte Marie à Madrid.[127] L'annexe 21 à la requête d'arbitrage montre clairement qu'un virement de cette somme a été effectué vers le compte de M. Sainte Marie au *Banco hispano americano*, qui l'a reçu le 4 avril 1972. C'est effectivement ce dont prend acte le contrat intitulé « *Protocoles d'Estoril* », signé le 13 mai 1972, et qui parmi les obligations « *déjà satisfaites* » incluait le « *dépôt antérieur de US$ 500.000* ».[128]

182. Le Tribunal juge crédible la thèse des demanderesses selon laquelle M. Darío Sainte Marie était propriétaire de l'intégralité du capital de CPP S.A. au moment où ont commencé les négociations pour la vente des actions de la société. M. Osvaldo Sainte Marie, frère de Darío Sainte Marie, déclare en effet dans son témoignage qu'aucun des actionnaires n'avait acquis ses titres en dehors de M. Sainte Marie, seul propriétaire de la société CPP S.A.[129] Il est clair pour le Tribunal que M. Darío Sainte Marie et M. Pey Casado ont successivement eu recours à la même pratique consistant à acheter tous les titres de la société, à inscrire au registre des actionnaires un

---

127 V. exposé complémentaire sur la compétence du Tribunal arbitral du 11 septembre 2002, p. 16. Les demanderesses se fondent sur l'annexe 21 à la requête d'arbitrage du 3 novembre 1997 pour établir la preuve du virement.

128 V. exposé complémentaire sur la compétence du Tribunal arbitral du 11 septembre 2002, p. 16 et la copie des Protocoles d'Estoril en annexe C-65.

129 Témoignage d'Osvaldo Sainte Marie du 8 octobre 1975 (annexe C-113). (« Ninguno de los socios, salvo Darío Sainte Marie, aportan nada de su patrimonio. Son acciones de favor que nos regala el propietario del Consorcio », p. 7). V. également la plainte pour délits fiscaux déposée par le directeur du service national des impôts internes le 1er septembre 1975, p. 2 (annexe C-42).

certain nombre d'autres actionnaires et à émettre des titres en leur nom, tout en conservant ces titres avec les formulaires de transfert signés en blanc. L'émission des titres permettait de se conformer à la législation sur le nombre d'actionnaires requis pour éviter la dissolution de la société et de bénéficier de la possibilité de récupérer et/ou céder des titres au moment choisi. Le Tribunal reviendra sur cette pratique plus loin dans ses développements.

183. Comme l'a relevé la défenderesse, 93% des titres émis[130] avant la vente du capital à M. Pey Casado l'étaient au nom de M. Darío Sainte Marie. Les 7% restant avaient été émis au nom de membres de sa famille qui, comme l'a expliqué M. Osvaldo Sainte Marie, n'avaient effectué aucun paiement à cette fin.

184. Le 30 mars 1972, M. Pey Casado est nommé à la présidence du conseil d'administration, confirmant ainsi que l'intéressé prend progressivement le contrôle de la société CPP S.A. Le 6 avril 1972, M. Darío Sainte Marie a consenti à M. Pey Casado devant notaire le pouvoir de céder 50% des droits qu'il détenait dans la société EPC Ltda et d'en fixer le prix. M. Pey Casado affirme avoir reçu à cette même date de M. Sainte Marie un paquet de 25.200 actions, accompagnés de leurs bordereaux de transfert signés en blanc. De l'avis du Tribunal, c'est le mode d'acquisition utilisé par MM. Pey Casado et Sainte Marie, évoqué ci-dessus, qui rend possible et crédible cette version des faits, contrairement à ce que prétend la défenderesse. En effet, M. Pey Casado a soutenu qu'il avait pour ambition de « *consolider la possession du journal par un groupe réduit de personnes qui assureraient, au-delà de ma propre existence, la position indépendante du journal* [...] ».[131] C'est dans cette perspective qu'il a proposé la vente d'un certain nombre d'actions à M. González, puis M. Venegas et enfin M. Carrasco. La situation économique de l'époque ne permettant pas de fixer le prix des titres, M. Pey Casado les a conservés ainsi que les bordereaux de transfert signés par chacun des intéressés, de façon à ce que M. Pey Casado puisse signer à son tour le bordereau de transfert, dans l'hypothèse où il ne serait pas donné suite à la vente à l'un ou l'autre des acheteurs potentiels. Ainsi, en même temps que M. Pey Casado effectuait l'acquisition du capital de la société CPP S.A., des titres étaient émis au nom de MM. González, Venegas et Carrasco dans la perspective d'une éventuelle association avec M. Pey Casado.

185. Le 13 mai 1972, M. Pey Casado et M. Sainte Marie ont signé le document intitulé « *Protocoles d'Estoril* » au Portugal.[132] Les

---

[130]   Ce pourcentage du capital correspond à 37.200 actions.
[131]   V. la transcription de l'audience du 29 octobre 2001, p. 84 (M. Pey).
[132]   V. annexe C-65. Les Protocoles d'Estoril prévoient dans leur partie pertinente :

demanderesses voient dans ce document un contrat de vente de l'intégralité des 40.000 actions de la société CPP S.A. pour la somme de 1,28 million USD. La défenderesse a pour sa part soutenu que les Protocoles d'Estoril ne pouvaient être qualifiés de contrat de vente, ne serait-ce que du fait de son intitulé « *obligations complémentaires à celles déjà satisfaites, acceptées par les deux parties* » qui ne pourrait être celui d'un contrat de vente. Le Tribunal reviendra plus

---

« Obligations complémentaires à celles déjà satisfaites, acceptées par les deux parties

A.   Il sera déposé [au bénéfice de] D.S.M. US\$ 250.000 au même lieu et sous la même forme que le dépôt antérieur de US\$ 500.000 et il sera remis à V.P., qui la conservera par devers lui, une lettre de change, [qui viendra] à échéance dans le délai d'un an à compter de la présente date pour US\$ 250.000 (deux cent cinquante mille dollars), payables en Escudos chiliens au taux de change [pratiqué par] les courtiers, plus les impôts relatifs au règlement des droits d'achat de devises en vigueur au Chili au moment où sera effectué le paiement total.

B.   Les éléphants seront sortis au 31.12.71.

C.   Seront restituées les lettres endossées par DSM qui sont à la présente date en la possession de la Banque d'Etat.

D.   Il sera régularisé un contrat de rente viagère qui permettra à DSM de percevoir 30% (trente pour cent) des revenus que feront apparaître les bilans jusqu'au décès de DSM, moment à partir duquel cette rente viagère sera de 3% (trois pour cent) en faveur de chacune des personnes mentionnées au point G, rentes qui s'éteindront au décès de chacun des bénéficiaires.

E.   Une fois remplies toutes les conditions [exposées] ci-dessus DSM remettra à V P 50% des actions du Consortium que DSM conserve en sa possession, avec les transferts en blanc, il transférera la marque « Clarín » au Consortium et consentira à VP un pouvoir aux fins de transférer la totalité de sa participation dans Clarín Ltée., incluant toutes les prérogatives légales et statutaires, qu'il posséderait à cette date, au prix et aux conditions que VP estimera convenable, prix que DSM donnera pour reçu.

F.   DSM accepte qu'en remplacement de ce qui est stipulé aux points A et D il lui soit déposé US\$ 500.000 (cinq cent mille dollars 0/00) à son nom dans une banque suisse et que soit remis à VP une lettre de change, à son ordre, venant à échéance dans le délai d'un an, pour US\$ 280.000 (deux cent quatre-vingt mille dollars), lettre qui devra être payée en Suisse. En garantie de ce paiement DSM gardera en sa possession 12.000 (douze mille) actions du Consortium. En cas d'acceptation de cette option par VP il est convenu l'élimination des rentes viagères mentionnées au point B.

G.   Les bénéficiaires des rentes viagères au taux de 3% (trois pour cent) chacune, mentionnées au point D sont : CARMEN KAISER LABBE, CARLOS DARÍO SAINTE-MARIE KAISER, CARMEN DOROTEA SAINTE-MARIE KAISER, CARMEN VERONICA SAINTE-MARIE KAISER, CARMEN PAOLA SAINTE-MARIE KAISER ET JUAN PABLO SAINTE-MARIE KAISER, au total six bénéficiaires.

H.   Dans le courant de 1973 seront sortis les éléphants de l'année 1972 ».

en détail sur la méthode d'interprétation qu'il convient d'adopter mais tient d'ores et déjà à préciser que, conformément au principe d'interprétation de l'effet utile, ce document doit être interprété de manière à lui donner un sens, en tenant compte des circonstances qui ont entouré sa conclusion et son exécution.

186. A ce stade, le Tribunal se limitera à indiquer que les Protocoles d'Estoril prévoient effectivement le paiement de 1,28 million USD, si l'on prend en compte le premier « dépôt » de 500.000 USD déjà effectué sur le compte de M. Sainte Marie et la somme de 780.000 USD résultant de la combinaison des clauses A et F. Le contrat prévoit par ailleurs la remise de 50% des actions de CPP S.A., ce qui correspond à 20.000 actions. Les 5200 actions supplémentaires reçues le 6 avril, qui n'apparaissent pas expressément dans les Protocoles, ont pourtant bien été achetées. Les Protocoles d'Estoril précisent en effet qu'ils établissent « des obligations complémentaires à celles déjà satisfaites, acceptées par les deux parties ».[133] La remise des 5.200 actions par Darío Sainte Marie à Víctor Pey Casado, qui a eu lieu avant le 13 mai, doit être rangée dans la catégorie de ces obligations déjà satisfaites et acceptées par les parties. L'obtention de ces actions est du reste confirmée par les documents postérieurs à la vente dans lesquels il est conclu que M. Pey Casado a acquis la totalité des actions de la société CPP S.A.

187. Le 14 juillet 1972, 20.000 titres de la société CPP S.A. ont été émis au nom de M. González et son nom a été inscrit dans le livre-registre des actionnaires de la société. Dans le même temps, M. Pey Casado conservait les titres émis et les bordereaux de transfert en blanc signés par M. González.

188. Le 14 août 1972, 2.800 titres sont émis au nom de M. Darío Sainte Marie. Il s'agit de ceux détenus par les membres de la famille de M. Darío Sainte Marie,[134] remis à M. Pey Casado le 6 avril 1972. Le 6 septembre de la même année, 5.200 titres, auparavant au nom de M. Sainte Marie, sont émis au nom de M. Venegas. Ce sont ces titres,

---

[133] V. également l'explication de M. Pey Casado lors de l'audience du 7 mai 2003: « Tous les accords auxquels nous sommes parvenus ainsi que ceux intervenus avant le Protocole d'Estoril et le Protocole d'Estoril lui même, et aussi l'accord intervenu ultérieurement dans le Document de Genève en octobre 1972, tous ces accords ont toujours été rédigés par moi, de ma propre main. Tous ont été confisqués par les autorités chiliennes et je n'ai pu récupérer que ceux qui ont été gardés à la Huitième Chambre criminelle de Santiago dans la procédure dont on a beaucoup parlé pendant cet arbitrage. Le prix définitif a été fixé à Estoril le 13 mai 1972 » (v. la transcription de l'audience du 7 mai 2003, pp. 533 (M. Pey Casado)).

[134] Il s'agit de MM. Osvaldo Sainte-Marie, Pablo Sainte-Marie, Juan Kaiser Labbé et de Mme Juana Labbé Venegas.

accompagnés des formulaires de transfert en blanc signés par M. Venegas, que M. Pey Casado a conservés.

189. Le 23 septembre 1972, M. Sainte Marie a signé devant le Consul du Chili résidant à Zürich un « *pouvoir spécifique* » conférant à M. Pey Casado le droit de procéder à la vente de tout ou partie des droits de M. Sainte Marie en qualité d'associé d'EPC Ltda ainsi que le droit de vendre à CPP S.A. un éventail de marques commerciales ayant trait au journal *Clarín*.[135] M. Pey Casado a du reste fait usage de ce pouvoir en cédant 3,5% du capital de EPC Ltda à CPP S.A. et le pourcent restant à M. Carrasco.[136]

190. Le 2 octobre 1972, M. Pey Casado rédige un document dit Document de Genève, à l'attention de M. Sainte Marie, afin de compléter les dispositions des Protocoles d'Estoril.[137] M. Pey Casado confirme dans ce document avoir reçu 12.000 actions de la société de CPP S.A. D'après les demanderesses, ces 12.000 actions ont été effectivement remises le lendemain, ainsi que les 2.800 autres actions que détenait M. Sainte Marie. Le fait que ces actions ne soient pas expressément mentionnées dans le document n'enlève rien au fait qu'elles ont été remises à M. Pey Casado. Ainsi que l'a déjà relevé le Tribunal, des documents émanant des autorités chiliennes

---

[135] V. annexe C-80.

[136] V. annexe C-68.

[137] Le Document de Genève prévoit dans sa partie pertinente :
« Monsieur Darío Sainte-Marie
En main propre
Je déclare qu'à la présente date, j'ai reçu de vous douze mille (12.000) actions [relatives à la] propriété du Consortium Publicitaires et Périodique S.A. (Titres 2-4-5 et 6) que je conserverai en ma possession sans les céder ou les transférer à quelque titre que ce soit à quiconque, [qu'il s'agisse] d'une personne physique ou morale, jusqu'à ce que soient remplies chacune des conditions suivantes :
a) Que soit complètement réglée une lettre de change acceptée par moi et tirée en votre faveur, à échéance du 11 septembre 1973 ;
b) Que vous soyez libéré de toute obligation ou sanction fiscale émanant de l'Entreprise Périodique Clarín Ltée et /ou du Consortium Publicitaire et Périodique S.A. relatives aux exercices et bilans annuels jusqu'au 31 décembre 1972 ; et
c) Que vous soyez exonéré de toute obligation, dettes et/ou retraits justifiés sur votre compte personnel ou celui de l'un quelconque des membres de votre famille jusqu'au 30 septembre 1972, tant en [ce qui concerne] l'Entreprise Périodique Clarín Ltée, que le Consortium Publicitaire Périodique S.A.
Si certaines des conditions ci-dessus n'étaient pas remplies je m'engage à vous restituer, avec les transferts correspondants, les douze mille actions du Consortium Publicitaire et Périodique SA, que je conserverai en ma possession en dépôt de garantie de l'accomplissement intégral des stipulations énoncées sous les lettres a, b et c ».

confirment que la totalité des actions a bien été acquise par M. Pey Casado.[138] Ce dernier était du reste en la possession de toutes les actions et des formulaires de transfert correspondants lorsque l'armée les a saisis.

191. En échange de ces actions et des formulaires de transfert, M. Pey Casado a payé la somme de 780.000 USD par le biais de virements et d'une lettre de change au profit de M. Sainte Marie que M. Pey Casado affirme avoir remise en mains propres au vendeur.

192. Les demanderesses ont fourni la preuve que des virements de 500.000 USD[139] et 250.000 USD[140] ont été effectués au profit de M. Sainte Marie à partir du compte en banque n°11.235 à la *Bank für Handel und Effekten* dont M. Pey Casado était le titulaire.[141] Elles ont également apporté la preuve d'un virement de 10.000 USD, qui toutefois ne mentionne pas le nom du destinataire.[142] Elles affirment également que M. Pey Casado a remis à M. Sainte Marie une lettre de change pour un montant de 20.000 USD. Bien que les demanderesses n'aient pas produit de copie de cette lettre de change,[143] le Tribunal estime que ces paiements ont bien été effectués. En effet, des documents émanant des autorités chiliennes de l'époque indiquent de façon tout à fait officielle que le compte n°11.235 de M. Pey Casado avait fait l'objet d'un transfert de 780.000 USD[144] et concluent que M. Pey Casado a effectivement effectué le paiement d'une somme du même montant au profit de M. Sainte Marie.[145]

193. Le 18 octobre 1972, 1.200 titres sont émis au nom de M. Venegas et 1.600 autres titres sont émis au nom de M. Carrasco. Comme dans les cas précédents, M. Pey Casado a conservé ces titres ainsi que les formulaires de transfert en blanc signés par les intéressés.

---

[138] V. le rapport d'expertise des inspecteurs des services des impôts internes du 26 novembre 1975, p. 5, produit en annexe C-43.

[139] V. Ordre de paiement à M. Sainte Marie de 500.000 USD à partir du compte n°11.235, produit en annexe C-67.

[140] Id.

[141] V. attestation de la *Bank für Handel und Effekten* du 22 juillet 1997 produite en annexe 4 au mémoire des demanderesses du 17 mars 1999.

[142] V. Ordre de paiement de 10.000 USD à partir du compte n°11.235, produit en annexe C-161.

[143] Les parties demanderesses se fondent en partie sur l'attestation de M. Osvaldo Sainte Marie, produite en annexes C113 et D19.

[144] V. notamment plainte déposée par le directeur national du service des impôts internes du 19 mars 1976, produit en annexe C-41 et mémorandum du Ministère de l'intérieur du 3 février 1975, produit en annexe C-8.

[145] V. mémorandum du Ministère de l'intérieur du 3 février 1975, produit en annexe C-8.

194. Pour ce qui concerne EPC Ltda, les parties sont d'accord sur le fait que la société CPP S.A. a fini par détenir 99% du capital. Elles s'opposent en revanche sur l'identité du véritable propriétaire du un pourcent restant. Pour la défenderesse, le 1% restant serait la propriété de M. Carrasco que lui aurait vendu M. Sainte Marie. M. Pey Casado soutient au contraire qu'il bénéficiait d'un pouvoir lui permettant de vendre l'intégralité des actions d'EPC Ltda. M. Pey Casado, qui jouissait de la sorte d'un contrôle total sur EPC Ltda, aurait donc pu céder facilement un pourcent du capital à M. Carrasco et faire émettre un titre à son nom pour éviter la dissolution.[146]

195. La seule lecture des pièces ne suffit pas à déterminer l'identité du véritable acquéreur du un pourcent restant du capital de la société EPC Ltda.[147] Néanmoins, confronté à deux présentations des faits contradictoires, le Tribunal est convaincu que la version présentée par M. Pey Casado est la plus vraisemblable car la détention de 1% du capital d'EPC Ltda n'avait pour M. Carrasco, actionnaire captif, aucun intérêt en termes de contrôle de la société. Elle ne pouvait avoir pour but que de satisfaire aux exigences de la loi chilienne sur le nombre d'actionnaires, dans l'intérêt de celui qui contrôlait la société, M. Pey Casado. Ce dernier était donc bien le véritable propriétaire du un pourcent restant.

196. Au vu des éléments qui précèdent, le Tribunal est en mesure de conclure que M. Pey Casado a effectivement fait l'acquisition, pour la somme de 1,28 million USD, de la totalité des titres[148] de la société CPP S.A., qui elle-même possédait l'intégralité du capital de la société EPC Ltda.

---

[146] V. la transcription de l'audience du 5 mai 2003, p. 152 (M. Pey): « Dans le but d'éviter l'extinction de la société limitée, vu que selon la loi du Chili tout le patrimoine ne peut pas résider en une seule personne, j'ai décidé dans un accord commun avec M. Ramon Carrasco qu'il apparaisse nominalement avec 1 pour cent de la société limitée » (souligné par nous).

[147] L'annexe 68 produite par les demanderesses indique simplement que M. Pey Casado a vendu à M. Carrasco, par devant notaire, un pourcent du capital et des droits de la société EPC Ltda. Une autre pièce produite par les demanderesses indique que M. Carrasco se serait ensuite engagé à revendre ses actions d'EPC Ltda (v. mémorandum du Sous-secrétaire d'Etat à l'intérieur du 3 février 1975 (annexe C-8) : « En novembre 1992 Sainte-Marie cédait au même Carrasco Peña 1% de l'Entreprise Périodique "Clarín", ce dernier s'obligeant et promettant de vendre ce 1% au Consortium Publicitaire et Périodique S.A. pour la somme de 1000 escudos »).

[148] Le capital social de CPP S.A. est bien resté de 40.000 actions ainsi qu'en atteste la communication n°01500 de la surintendance des valeurs et des assurances du Chili du 5 mai 1995 (annexe C-79).

197. La conviction du Tribunal est renforcée par le fait que la version des faits activement défendue par l'Etat du Chili n'est étayée par aucune preuve pertinente et n'est pas susceptible d'être conciliée avec l'existence de certains documents jugés probants par le Tribunal.

198. Afin d'étayer la thèse selon laquelle MM. González, Venegas, Carrasco et Sainte Marie auraient été les véritables acquéreurs et propriétaires des actions de CPP S.A., la défenderesse se fonde essentiellement sur les documents suivants :

- les titres en possession desquels se trouvait M. Pey Casado à l'époque et que les demanderesses ont produits ;
- les demandes de décharge effectuées en 1974 par MM. González et Venegas, dans lesquelles ils acceptent la confiscation des titres de CPP S.A. ;
- les déclarations de González, Venegas, Carrasco de 1975 affirmant qu'ils sont les propriétaires des actions litigieuses devant la Huitième Chambre du Tribunal correctionnel de Santiago ;
- les décisions de justice dans lesquelles ces mêmes personnes n'ont pas été condamnées pour fraude fiscale.

199. Le Tribunal constate toutefois que la défenderesse n'a produit aucun contrat de vente des actions auquel l'un ou l'autre des prétendus actionnaires aurait été partie. La défenderesse n'a pas davantage fourni de preuve d'un éventuel paiement émanant de ces personnes.

200. La défenderesse n'a pas non plus fourni d'explication crédible sur l'existence des formulaires de transfert en blanc signés par MM. González, Venegas, Carrasco et Sainte Marie. Selon la défenderesse, il s'agirait simplement d'une anomalie qui ne se prêterait à aucune explication logique. La défenderesse n'apporte pas non plus d'éclaircissement satisfaisant sur les raisons pour lesquelles ces formulaires se trouvaient en possession de M. Pey Casado[149] et non en possession de leurs prétendus propriétaires. L'argument selon lequel M. Pey Casado aurait été mandaté par MM. González, Venegas, Carrasco pour vendre leurs actions n'est fondé que sur de

---

[149] Les autorités chiliennes de l'époque ont écrit à plusieurs reprises que les titres et les formulaires de transfert correspondants se trouvaient en la possession de M. Pey lorsque la saisie a été effectuée. V. par exemple, le rapport du conseil juridique du Ministre de l'intérieur du 16 octobre 1974, le rapport du Conseil de la défense de novembre 1974, communiqués par le Chili le 12 novembre 2002, le mémorandum du Ministère de l'intérieur du 3 février 1975, produit en annexe C-8 et la plainte déposée par le directeur national du service des impôts internes du 19 mars 1976, produit en annexe C-41.

simples affirmations et aucun contrat en ce sens n'a été produit par la défenderesse.

201.   La défenderesse ne parvient pas non plus à concilier sa propre version des faits avec les documents contractuels conclus entre M. Sainte Marie et M. Pey Casado. Elle se contente de décrire M. Pey Casado comme une sorte de mandataire ou d'intermédiaire dans une transaction qui serait sans rapport avec la cession des actions et dont on ne pourrait déterminer précisément la teneur.

202.   Les demanderesses ont pour leur part produit un ensemble de documents qui montrent que les autorités chiliennes ont à plusieurs reprises conclu que M. Pey Casado avait acquis les titres de CPP S.A. et les avaient conservés avec les formulaires de transfert en blanc.

203.   M. Pey Casado a constamment été visé par une série de décrets adoptée peu après la saisie du journal El Clarín. Ainsi, un premier texte, le décret-loi n°77 du 13 octobre 1973, déclare illicites et dissoutes les entités affiliées à la mouvance marxiste[150] et prévoit que les biens des entités dissoutes passeront en pleine propriété de l'Etat.[151] Un décret suprême n°1726 du 3 décembre 1973 est ensuite adopté en vue de l'application de l'article 1 du décret-loi n°77 et prévoit que le Ministre de l'intérieur est chargé d'identifier les entités visées par le décret-loi. S'agissant des personnes physiques, le Ministre de l'intérieur déclarera de la même façon la mise à l'étude de leur situation patrimoniale.[152] C'est le décret exempté n°276 du 21 octobre 1974 qui applique les dispositions du décret-loi n°77 aux sociétés CPP S.A. et EPC Ltda. C'est également dans ce décret qu'apparaît pour la première fois le nom de Víctor Pey Casado. Le décret déclare en effet la mise à l'étude de la situation patrimoniale de MM. Darío Sainte Marie, Osvaldo Sainte Marie, Víctor Pey Casado, Mario Osses González, Emilio González González, Jorge Venegas Venegas et Ramon Carrasco Peña.

204.   A peine quelques jours avant l'adoption du décret n°276, le 16 octobre 1974, le conseiller juridique du Ministre de l'intérieur a écrit à ce dernier pour lui indiquer que les titres de la société CPP S.A. et

---

[150]   Le décret vise dans son article 1 « les partis, entités, groupements, factions ou mouvements [d'affiliation marxiste], […] de même que les associations, sociétés ou entreprises de quelque nature que ce soit, qui directement ou au travers de tierces personnes appartiendraient ou seraient dirigées par l'une d'entre elles ».

[151]   V. décret-loi n°77 du 13 octobre 1973 déclarant illicites et dissolvant les partis politiques indiqués, article 1 (annexe 19 au mémoire des demanderesses, du 17 mars 1999).

[152]   V. décret suprême n°1726 approuvant le règlement en vue de l'application de l'article 1 du décret-loi n°77 de 1973 (annexe 73 au contre-mémoire de la défenderesse, du 3 février 2003).

les formulaires de transfert correspondants avaient été trouvés en la possession de M. Pey Casado et de l'ensemble des éléments examinés, « *[...] il résulterait que c'est Víctor Pey Casado qui a acheté le Consortium Publicitaire et Périodique S.A. et l'Entreprise Périodique Clarín Ltée [...]* ».[153] De même, dans un rapport du Conseil de défense de l'Etat datant de 1974,[154] il est également conclu que « *c'est à Pey que se trouvent ainsi transmis tous les droits dans les sociétés propriétaires de Clarín et de ses bâtiments, machines, fonds, etc* », et ce sur le fondement d'une analyse des Protocoles d'Estoril et de la remise des titres et des formulaires de transfert à M. Pey Casado par MM. González, Venegas et Carrasco.

205. Un mémorandum du 3 février 1975, qui indique avoir été lu en public par le Sous-secrétaire d'Etat à l'intérieur, parvient à une conclusion identique :

> « *Des éléments exposés et compte tenu que tous les titres relatifs aux actions et les transferts en blanc [émanant] des personnes au nom desquelles ces titres figurent, furent trouvés en la possession de Víctor Pey, il résulte que c'est ce dernier qui a acheté le Consortium Publicitaire et Périodique S.A., et l'Entreprise Périodique Clarín, effectuant les paiements correspondants au moyen de US$ 780.000 fournis par la Banque Nationale de Cuba sans préjudice des US$ 500.000 que Sainte Marie avait reçu antérieurement* ».[155]

206. Ce mémorandum confirme également le mode d'acquisition des actions utilisé par M. Pey Casado :

> « *Le titre en faveur de González González régularisé le 14 juillet de cette même année 1972, ne fut pas remis à son bénéficiaire, mais fut conservé par un personnage, Víctor Pey Casado, joint à un transfert blanc signé, naturellement, par González, comme il est attesté d'une manière digne de foi par l'enquête. [...]*
> *En date des 6 septembre et 18 octobre 1972, des transferts de 5.200 et 1.200 actions respectivement furent réalisés en faveur de Jorge Venegas Venegas, la société donnait son agrément au titre correspondant. Toutefois aussi bien les titres que les transferts signés*

---

[153] Annexe produite par le Chili le 12 novembre 2002.
[154] Il est vraisemblable que ce rapport date de 1974 ; il manque la première page de ce rapport produit par le Chili le 12 novembre 2002.
[155] V. mémorandum du Sous-secrétaire d'Etat à l'intérieur du 3 février 1975 (annexe C-8).

> *en blanc par Venegas ont été également trouvés en la possession de Víctor Pey Casado. [...]*
>
> *Le 18 octobre 1972, il est réalisé un nouveau transfert de 1600 actions, propriété de Darío Sainte Marie, en faveur de Ramon Carrasco Peña, qui, comme cela avait été le cas précédemment, n'a pas non plus reçu le titre corrélatif, mais l'a remis à Pey Casado, avec un transfert signé en blanc ».*[156]

207. C'est seulement une semaine après la publication de ce mémorandum qu'est adopté le décret n°165 du 10 février 1975 qui prévoit la confiscation des biens meubles des sociétés CPP S.A. et EPC Ltda et d'un ensemble d'immeubles appartenant à ces mêmes sociétés. Le préambule du décret se réfère expressément au décret n°276 et mentionne spécifiquement M. Pey Casado.[157]

208. Quelques mois plus tard, le décret suprême n°580 du 24 avril 1975 déclare que M. Pey Casado se trouve dans la situation prévue à l'article 1.2 du décret-loi n°77[158] qui lui-même prévoit que « *[les] biens [des partis politiques et des autres entités mentionnées dans les sections précédentes[159]] passeront en pleine propriété à l'Etat [...]* ». Ce décret transfère également à l'Etat la propriété de certains fonds déposés auprès de l'Association d'épargne et de prêts Ahorromet appartenant à M. Pey Casado[160]. Le décret suprême n°1200 du 25 novembre 1977 vient compléter le décret suprême n°580 en déclarant

---

[156] V. annexe C8, pp. 2-3.

[157] V. Décret suprême n°165 du Ministère de l'intérieur du 10 février 1975, para. 5 du préambule (annexe 1 au mémoire des demanderesses, du 17 mars 1999).

[158] Décret suprême n°580 du 24 avril 1975, article 3 (annexe 20 à la requête d'arbitrage, du 3 novembre 1997). Le décret suprême n°580 du 24 avril 1975 modifie également par son article 1 le décret suprême n°165 pour y ajouter un bien immeuble.

[159] Ces entités comprennent notamment « les associations, sociétés ou entreprises de quelque nature que ce soit, qui directement ou au travers de tierces personnes appartiendraient ou seraient par l'une d'entre elles [entités d'affiliation marxiste] » (article 1 du décret n°77).

[160] Décret suprême n°580 du 24 avril 1975, article 4 (annexe 20 à la requête d'arbitrage du 3 novembre 1997). Le décret précise également dans son considérant n°6 que MM. Venegas et González ont formulé des décharges dans lesquelles ils acceptent la confiscation des titres de la société CPP S.A., tout en demandant à jouir de la libre disposition de tous leurs autres biens. De telles décharges ne suffisent pas à prouver que MM. Venegas et González sont les véritables acquéreurs des actions faute de preuve venant conforter cette version des faits. Il est par ailleurs surprenant que MM. Venegas et González aient accepté la confiscation d'un seul de leurs prétendus biens, précisément celui dont l'acquisition est revendiquée par M. Pey Casado et reconnue à maintes reprises par les autorités chiliennes de l'époque.

que « *passent en pleine propriété à l'Etat les biens meubles et immeubles, droits et actions, appartenant audit Pey Casado, et en particulier, la totalité des fonds investis en certificats d'épargne indexés de la Banque centrale du Chili* ».[161]

209. A la fin de l'année 1975, au cours de la procédure pendante devant la Huitième Chambre du Tribunal correctionnel de Santiago, les inspecteurs des services des impôts internes ont présenté un rapport d'expertise qui, une fois encore, concluait que M. Pey Casado avait fait l'acquisition des actions de la société CPP S.A. :

> « *Cela étant, encore que les transferts d'actions aient été effectués aux personnes indiquées dans les paragraphes précédents, ces dernières n'ont pas reçu les titres, ayant signé à leur tour des transferts en blanc en faveur de Víctor Pey Casado, qui du 30 mars au 6 décembre 1972 était président du Directoire de la Société, d'où l'on déduit que ce doit être ce dernier qui a acheté le Consortium Publicitaire et Périodique S.A.* ».[162]

210. Les décisions rendues dans cette affaire par la Huitième Chambre n'ont pas condamné MM. Gonzales, Venegas et Carrasco pour infraction fiscale faute de preuve. M. Pey Casado a quant à lui été déclaré rebelle.[163] La défenderesse en conclut que MM. González, Venegas et Carrasco ont été reconnus par la justice comme étant les véritables propriétaires des actions de la société CPP S.A. Or, au vu des pièces versées au dossier, de la décision de la Huitième Chambre

---

[161] Décret suprême n°1200 du 25 novembre 1977, article 2 (annexe 20 à la requête d'arbitrage du 3 novembre 1997). Ce même décret transfère en outre la propriété de tous les droits et actions de M. Pey Casado dans la société Socomer Ltda et ses filiales (article 2). V. également la communication secrète entre le Ministre des terres et de la colonisation et le Ministre de l'intérieur du 10 novembre 1977 (annexe 20 à la requête d'arbitrage du 3 novembre 1997).

[162] Rapport des inspecteurs des services des impôts internes du 26 novembre 1975, p. 5 (annexe C-43). Les inspecteurs concluent également que le vrai propriétaire des entreprises serait Salvador Allende, Víctor Pey Casado ayant acquis les actions « *sur commission de Salvador Allende Gossens* » (p. 6). On retrouve des conclusions similaires dans une production de documents effectuée par le directeur national du service des impôts internes qui indiquait que « *ces transferts ont été trouvés, de même que les titres auxquels j'ai fait référence précédemment, dans les bureaux de Víctor Pey Casado, qui, pour le compte et sur commission de Salvador Allende, contrôlait les sociétés propriétaires du Quotidien Clarín, les prête-noms Carrasco, Venegas et González apparaissant devant les tiers* » (annexe C-41).

[163] V. décision de la Huitième Chambre du Tribunal correctionnel du 1er septembre 1976 (annexe C-197).

du 29 mai 1995 et des contradictions internes à l'argumentation de la défenderesse, le Tribunal ne peut parvenir à une telle conclusion.

211.   Les décisions des 11 décembre 1975, 11 juin 1976 et 17 janvier 1977 sont particulièrement elliptiques et ne font pas apparaître leur motivation. La décision rendue le 11 décembre 1975 indique simplement qu' « *attendu la valeur probante du dossier il n'y a pas lieu à déclarer d'accusation Jorge Venegas Venegas, Emilio González González et Ramon Carrasco Peña* ».[164] De même, dans sa décision du 11 juin 1976, la Cour d'appel de la Huitième Chambre a rejeté l'appel formé contre la première décision, estimant que les conditions de l'infraction reprochée à MM. González, Venegas et Carrasco n'étaient pas remplies.[165] Enfin, la Huitième Chambre a jugé le 17 janvier 1977 que « *au moyen des différents antécédents réunis dans le dossier n'apparaît pas complètement justifié l'existence du délit prévu et sanctionné à l'art. 97 N°4 du Code des Impôts, imputé à Jorge Venegas, Emilio González et Ramon Carrasco en ce qu'ils auraient indiquée comme prix d'acquisition des actions du Consortium Publicitaire et Périodique S.A. un prix inférieur au [prix] véritable, dans le but d'échapper à l'impôt* ».[166]

212.   La juridiction chilienne s'est donc contentée de constater que l'accusation n'avait pas rassemblé suffisamment de preuve pour établir l'existence d'une infraction fiscale. A aucun moment, la Huitième Chambre n'a affirmé ou reconnu que « *seuls les achats d'actions effectués par [MM. González, Venegas et Carrasco] auprès de CPP SA seraient valables* ».[167] Il n'y a aucun élément dans les pièces fournies par la défenderesse qui aille en ce sens.[168]

213.   Le 1er février 1995, M. Pey Casado a déposé une demande devant la Huitième Chambre du Tribunal correctionnel de Santiago afin d'obtenir la restitution des « *titres et instruments originaux de cession d'actions signés en blanc* » par MM. González, Venegas, Carrasco et Sainte Marie, correspondant aux 40.000 actions de la société CPP S.A. Le requérant précisait dans sa demande qu'il avait pour « *but d'entreprendre des actions destinées à attaquer les*

---

[164]   Annexe 88 au contre-mémoire de la défenderesse du 3 février 2003.
[165]   Annexe 89 au contre-mémoire de la défenderesse du 3 février 2003.
[166]   Annexe 90 au contre-mémoire de la défenderesse du 3 février 2003.
[167]   Réplique de la défenderesse du 4 avril 2003, p. 57.
[168]   Dans leurs déclarations devant la Huitième Chambre, MM. González, Venegas, Carrasco n'ont fait qu'affirmer avoir acheté les actions de CPP S.A. Les attestations postérieures de MM. Venegas et Ovalle ne prouvent pas davantage que les actions de CPP S.A. ont été acquises par MM. González, Venegas, Carrasco.

prétendues expropriations de biens faisant partie du patrimoine de la société Consortium Publicitaire et Périodique S.A. [...] ».[169]

214. La Huitième Chambre a signifié la demande de M. Pey Casado au service des impôts internes qui n'a pas réagi à cette signification. Le 19 mai 1995, le Tribunal correctionnel a demandé à ce que soit « *démontré préalablement la pleine propriété des actions dont la restitution est demandée* ».[170] M. Pey Casado a fait valoir les élément suivants : en vertu de l'article 700 du code civil, le possesseur est réputé propriétaire dès lors que personne d'autre ne justifie de cette qualité ; la qualité de possesseur et propriétaire de M. Pey Casado n'a jamais été contestée ; il n'existe pas de registre public « *qui ferait foi de l'inscription* des *instruments de cessions d'actions, dès lors que tous les antécédents relatifs à cette société furent confisqués de manière illicite ; et la restitution sollicitée a précisément pour objet la reconstitution du livre des actionnaires, avec toutes les formalités et moyens de publicité qu'exigent aussi bien la Loi que le Règlement des Sociétés Anonymes* ».[171]

215. Le 29 mai 1995, au vu « *de la valeur probante des antécédents* », la Huitième Chambre a accepté d'ordonner la restitution des documents demandés. Après examen du dossier, le Tribunal correctionnel a estimé que M. Pey Casado ne pouvait prouver sa qualité de propriétaire qu'à l'aide des éléments du dossier judiciaire qu'il détenait, reconnaissant par là même que M. Pey Casado était effectivement l'acquéreur et le propriétaire des actions.

216. La défenderesse a fait valoir que cette décision était mal fondée. Le Tribunal correctionnel se serait dispensé d'établir au préalable si le requérant avait la qualité de propriétaire et n'aurait pas informé les « *véritables intéressés* » - MM. González, Venegas, Carrasco - du dépôt de la demande de M. Pey Casado.

217. Le Tribunal arbitral constate d'une part que la décision de la Huitième Chambre était publique et qu'elle n'a pas fait l'objet d'un quelconque recours par le service des impôts internes ou par des tiers susceptibles d'être intéressés par l'affaire. Le Tribunal correctionnel s'est par ailleurs prononcé sur le fondement des pièces demandées par le requérant et des arguments qui lui ont été présentées pour accueillir favorablement la demande de restitution de M. Pey Casado. La décision de la juridiction chilienne constitue ainsi un élément supplémentaire permettant de conclure que M. Pey Casado doit être considéré comme l'acquéreur et le propriétaire des titres de CPP S.A.

---

[169] V. annexe 21 à la requête d'arbitrage du 3 novembre 1997.
[170] Exposé complémentaire sur le fond de l'affaire du 11 septembre 2002, p. 51.
[171] Id.

218. En outre, l'argument supplémentaire de la défenderesse selon lequel la décision de la Huitième Chambre ne constituerait pas une reconnaissance judiciaire du droit de propriété de M. Pey Casado sur les actions parce qu'il s'agirait d'une « *pure décision procédurale dérivant simplement de la possession physique des documents de la part du demandeur au moment de leur confiscation* »[172] n'est pas convainquant.

219. Dans le souci d'être complet, le Tribunal examinera en dernier lieu l'argument de défenderesse visant à contester la validité juridique du contrat de vente des actions de CPP S.A.

220. Le Tribunal rappellera que, dans le dernier état de son argumentation, l'Etat défendeur a estimé inutile l'analyse de droit international privé développée par les demanderesses et concentré sa critique sur la qualification du contrat avancée par celles-ci.[173] L'argumentation de la défenderesse revient en réalité à accepter l'analyse de droit international privé des demanderesses et à soutenir que les Protocoles d'Estoril et le Document de Genève ne peuvent être interprétés comme un contrat de vente des actions de CPP S.A., quel que soit le droit applicable. Dans cette perspective, la défenderesse a développé toute une argumentation fondée sur les termes précis employés par les Protocoles d'Estoril et le Document de Genève. En analysant les termes du contrat isolément et de façon littérale, la défenderesse s'est efforcée de montrer que ces documents ne pouvaient, en définitive, avoir aucune signification précise.

221. Le Tribunal relèvera d'emblée que les autorités chiliennes de l'époque ne semblent avoir eu aucune difficulté à qualifier de contrat de vente la transaction conclue entre M. Sainte Marie et M. Pey Casado.

222. En outre, s'il est vrai que l'utilisation de certains termes manque de précision ou paraît inadapté,[174] le Tribunal estime qu'il convient d'adopter une méthode d'interprétation qui confère un effet utile aux documents qui lui sont soumis. En l'espèce, les circonstances entourant la rédaction et la conclusion des Protocoles d'Estoril et du Document de Genève sont décisives et ne peuvent être simplement écartées. M. Pey Casado et M. Sainte Marie, unis par des liens

---

[172] Contre-mémoire de la défenderesse du 3 février 2003, p. 108.

[173] V. la transcription de l'audience du 6 mai 2003, pp. 280-281 (Me Di Rosa): « On a parlé hier du droit applicable, mais en réalité dans ce type d'accord ce qui prévaut c'est le texte même du contrat, mais ni le Document d'Estoril ni le Document de Genève ne font jamais référence à une vente achat d'actions du Consortium CPP ». Pour l'argumentation antérieure, v. contre-mémoire de la défenderesse du 3 février 2003, pp. 293-297.

[174] C'est le cas, par exemple, du terme « *dépôt* » ou, dans un autre registre du terme « *éléphants* » (v. annexe C-65 précitée).

d'amitié, n'ont pas entouré d'un formalisme pointilleux le déroulement de la transaction et la rédaction des documents qui la matérialisent. Il y a toutefois bien un accord sur la chose et sur le prix, sans contrainte de forme, ce qui satisfait les conditions posées par le droit applicable selon l'analyse non contestée des demanderesses lors des audiences de mai 2003.

223. En effet, comme cela résulte de l'examen des faits et des prises de position des autorités chiliennes, M. Pey Casado a bien procédé au paiement, en plusieurs fois, de la somme de 1,28 million de USD et M. Sainte Marie lui a remis, en plusieurs fois également, les 40.000 actions de CPP S.A. Le fait que les Protocoles d'Estoril et le Document de Genève ne soient pas totalement exhaustifs et aient pu être complétés par des accords verbaux entre les parties est tout à fait compatible avec l'application du principe de liberté de forme des contrats.

224. Toutefois, même dans l'hypothèse où il existerait un contrat de vente entre M. Pey Casado et M. Sainte Marie, la défenderesse estime qu'il est nécessaire de distinguer entre le contrat de vente des actions, dont la validité serait établie, et le « *transfert du contrôle des actions concernées* » qui exigerait la satisfaction d'un certain nombre de formalités sous peine de nullité.

225. Les demanderesses estiment pour leur part qu'il était possible et conforme au droit chilien en 1972 d'acquérir des actions nominatives par le biais de la remise des titres émis au nom d'un tiers et du formulaire de transfert en blanc signé par le tiers en question. Il suffisait de procéder ultérieurement aux formalités prévues par la loi pour que les actions figurent au nom de l'acquéreur. Il s'agissait là, selon les demanderesses, d'un usage commercial répandu.

226. Après examen de l'argumentation des parties, le Tribunal considère que s'il existait une pratique courante telle que la décrivent les demanderesses, il était tout de même nécessaire en 1972 de respecter les formalités prescrites par l'article 451 du code de commerce et l'article 37 du règlement sur les sociétés anonymes afin d'acquérir la propriété des actions avec effet *erga omnes*. La demanderesse et le Professeur Guillermo Bruna, qui a donné une consultation à la demanderesse,[175] n'ont pas apporté la preuve de l'existence d'un usage permettant d'acquérir la pleine propriété des actions avec effet *erga omnes* par la remise du titre émis au nom d'un tiers et du formulaire de transfert en blanc signé par ce tiers.

227. En revanche, le Tribunal n'est pas davantage convaincu par la démonstration de la défenderesse sur les conséquences du défaut

---

[175] V. consultation du Professeur Guillermo Bruna du 21 juin 2002 (D17).

d'accomplissement des formalités et, notamment de l'inscription au livre-registre des actionnaires. La défenderesse soutient en effet que le non-respect des formalités entraîne la nullité absolue des actes qui ne s'y conforment pas,[176] sans toutefois documenter son affirmation. Après avoir affirmé la « *primauté incontestable du code de commerce sur le code civil en la matière* », elle ne désigne aucune disposition de ce code prévoyant la sanction de nullité en cas de non respect de l'article 451. La jurisprudence[177] et la doctrine[178] invoquées n'indiquent pas non plus que la nullité devrait sanctionner le défaut d'accomplissement des formalités prévues pour le transfert des actions nominatives. Tout au plus peut-on en conclure que le non-respect des formalités est susceptible de rendre le transfert litigieux inopposable aux tiers et à la société.[179]

228. En l'absence de délai spécifique imposé par la législation en vigueur pour procéder aux formalités requises,[180] M. Pey Casado aurait pu remédier à cette inopposabilité en procédant aux formalités nécessaires, ce dont il a été empêché par la saisie de ses titres. Contrairement à ce que soutient la défenderesse, le fait que M. Pey Casado n'ait pas procédé à l'accomplissement des formalités en question avant la saisie de ses titres ne signifie pas qu'il ne *pouvait* pas le faire. Tout en continuant à se conformer à la réglementation sur le nombre minimal d'actionnaires, M. Pey Casado était bien en mesure de procéder aux formalités requises et avait, de l'avis du Tribunal, très vraisemblablement l'intention d'y procéder dès que la situation politique et économique le permettrait.

229. Le Tribunal conclut que, au moment où a été effectuée la saisie du journal El Clarín, M. Pey Casado devait être considéré comme le seul propriétaire légitime des actions de la société CPP S.A.

230. Il convient à présent de déterminer si l'opération réalisée par M. Pey Casado satisfait la condition d'investissement posée par l'article 25 de la Convention CIRDI.

---

[176] V. consultation du Professeur Sandoval pour la défenderesse du 3 février 2003, p. 25.

[177] V. décision de la Cour suprême du Chili du 15 décembre 1942 (annexe 37) ; décision de la Cour suprême du Chili du 27 novembre 1991, rendue sous l'empire d'une nouvelle législation (annexe 38) ; décision de la Cour d'appel de Valparaiso du 5 novembre 1935 (annexe 39).

[178] V. Julio Olavarria Avila, *Manual de Derecho Comercial*, 1970, pp. 354-357 (annexe 36 du rapport Sandoval).

[179] V. décision de la Cour d'appel de Valparaiso du 5 novembre 1935, considérant n°5 (annexe 39 du rapport Sandoval).

[180] Le délai posé à l'article 37 ne concerne que « les transferts présentés avant la clôture du registre des actionnaires ».

b)　　L'acquisition des sociétés CPP S.A. et EPC Ltda satisfait la condition d'investissement au sens de la Convention CIRDI

231.　Les parties ont fait valoir l'une et l'autre, à juste titre, que la Convention CIRDI ne contient pas de définition de la notion d'investissement. L'examen de la jurisprudence CIRDI fait cependant apparaître qu'il existe au moins deux conceptions de la notion d'investissement au sens de la Convention CIRDI. La première se contente d'identifier un certain nombre de « *caractéristiques* » qui permettraient de conclure à l'existence d'un investissement. Il suffirait, dans cette conception, que certaines de ces « *caractéristiques* » habituelles de l'investissement, pas nécessairement toutes, se rencontrent au cas d'espèce pour que l'on puisse conclure que l'on se trouve en présence d'un investissement. C'est la solution qu'ont retenue les tribunaux arbitraux dans les affaires *Fedax c. Venezuela*[181], *CSOB c. Slovaquie*[182] et, plus récemment, *MCI c. Equateur*[183]. Cette conception peu exigeante de l'investissement est également défendue par certains auteurs.[184] D'autres tribunaux arbitraux retiennent au contraire une véritable définition de l'investissement qui suppose la satisfaction de critères spécifiques. Si l'ensemble de ces critères ne sont pas cumulativement satisfaits, ils en concluent qu'il ne saurait y avoir d'investissement au sens de la Convention CIRDI[185]. Cependant, dans la définition de ces critères, la jurisprudence arbitrale n'est pas totalement uniforme. Certains tribunaux ont jugé qu'il existe un investissement dès lors que sont réunis trois éléments : l'existence d'un apport dans le pays concerné, le fait que cet apport porte sur une certaine durée et qu'il comporte, pour celui qui le fait, un certain risque.[186] D'autres ont

---

[181]　*Fedax N.V. c. Venezuela*, affaire CIRDI n°ARB/96/3, décision sur la compétence du 11 juillet 1997, para. 43.

[182]　*Ceskoslovenska Obchodni Banka c. République slovaque*, affaire CIRDI n°ARB/97/4, décision sur la compétence, 24 mai 1999, para. 90, *in* Emmanuel Gaillard, *La Jurisprudence du CIRDI*, Pédone 2004, p. 577, spéc. p. 598.

[183]　*M.C.I. Power Group L.C. and New Turbine, Inc. c. Equateur*, affaire CIRDI n°ARB/03/6, sentence, 31 juillet 2007, para. 165.

[184]　V. spéc. Christoph H. Schreuer, *The ICSID Convention : a Commentary*, 2001, p. 140, para. 122.

[185]　Sur les différents courants d'interprétation de la notion d'investissement au sens de la Convention CIRDI, v. E. Gaillard, *La jurisprudence du CIRDI*, Pedone, 2004, p. 828, et les obs. sous la décision sur la compétence rendue dans l'affaire *Bayindir* le 14 novembre 2005, JDI 2006.362.

[186]　V. spéc. *Consortium Groupement L.E.S.I.-DIPENTA c. Algérie*, affaire CIRDI n°ARB/03/08, sentence du 10 janvier 2005, para. 13(iv), JDI 2006.237, spéc. pp. 239-240. V. également *L.E.S.I. S.p.A. et ASTALDI S.p.A. c. Algérie*, affaire CIRDI n°ARB/05/3, décision du 12 juillet 2006, para. 72(iv).

estimé, à partir d'une analyse reposant sur le préambule de la Convention CIRDI, que l'existence d'un investissement au sens de la Convention CIRDI reposait sur la réunion de quatre éléments, les trois précédents étant complétés par l'élément de contribution de l'opération litigieuse au développement économique de l'Etat d'accueil.[187] Quelques décisions isolées ont même conclu qu'il ne pouvait y avoir d'investissement si le demandeur ne pouvait établir que l'opération réalisée avait contribué positivement au développement de l'Etat d'accueil.[188]

232.   Le présent Tribunal estime pour sa part qu'il existe bien une définition de l'investissement au sens de la Convention CIRDI et qu'il ne suffit pas de relever la présence de certaines des « *caractéristiques* » habituelles d'un investissement pour que cette condition objective de la compétence du Centre soit satisfaite. Une telle interprétation reviendrait à priver de toute signification certains des termes de l'article 25 de la Convention CIRDI, ce qui ne serait pas compatible avec l'exigence d'interpréter les termes de la Convention en leur donnant un effet utile, comme l'a justement rappelé la sentence rendue dans l'affaire *Joy Mining Machinery Limited c. République arabe d'Egypte* le 6 août 2004.[189] Selon le Tribunal, cette définition ne comprend en revanche que trois éléments. L'exigence d'une contribution au développement de l'Etat d'accueil, difficile à établir, lui paraît en effet relever davantage du fond du litige que de la compétence du Centre. Un investissement peut s'avérer utile ou non pour l'Etat d'accueil sans perdre cette qualité. Il est exact que le préambule de la Convention CIRDI

---

[187]   V. spéc. *Salini Costruttori S.p.A. and Italstrade S.p.A. c. Morocco*, affaire CIRDI n°ARB/00/4, décision sur la compétence du 23 juillet 2001, para. 52, JDI 2002, p. 208 ; *Joy Mining Machinery Limited c. République arabe d'Egypte*, affaire CIRDI n° ARB/03/11, sentence sur la compétence du 6 août 2004, para. 53, JDI 2005.163, p. 168 ; *Jan de Nul N.V. and Dredging International N.V. c. République arabe d'Egypte*, affaire CIRDI n° ARB/04/13, décision sur la compétence du 16 juin 2006, para. 91. Cette dernière décision nuance son analyse en précisant que les quatre éléments énumérés doivent être examinés dans leur globalité. V. également *Helnan International Hotels A/S c. République arabe d'Egypte*, affaire CIRDI n° ARB/05/19, décision sur la compétence du 17 octobre 2006, para. 77 et *Saipem S.p.A. c. La République populaire du Bangladesh*, affaire CIRDI n° ARB/05/07, décision sur la compétence et recommandation sur les mesures provisoires du 21 mars 2007, para. 99.

[188]   *Malaysian Historical Salvors, SDN, BHD c. Malaisie*, affaire CIRDI n° ARB/05/10, sentence du 17 mai 2007, para. 125 et 139. V. également *Patrick Mitchell c. République démocratique du Congo*, affaire CIRDI n° ARB/99/7, décision sur la demande d'annulation du 1er novembre 2006, para. 29.

[189]   Affaire CIRDI n° ARB/03/11, sentence sur la compétence du 6 août 2004 ; paras.49-50, JDI 2005.163, p. 167.

évoque la contribution au développement économique de l'Etat d'accueil. Cette référence est cependant présentée comme une conséquence, non comme une condition de l'investissement : en protégeant les investissements, la Convention favorise le développement de l'Etat d'accueil. Cela ne signifie pas que le développement de l'Etat d'accueil soit un élément constitutif de la notion d'investissement. C'est la raison pour laquelle, comme l'ont relevé certains tribunaux arbitraux, cette quatrième condition est en réalité englobée dans les trois premières.

233. En l'espèce, les trois conditions qui commandent la qualification de l'investissement, l'existence d'un apport, le fait que cet apport porte sur une certaine durée et qu'il comporte, pour celui qui le fait, certains risques, sont à l'évidence satisfaites.

a) M. Pey Casado a en effet apporté ses propres capitaux afin d'acquérir les entreprises CPP S.A. et EPC Ltda. Il leur a également apporté son savoir-faire d'ingénieur et s'est impliqué dans la gestion du journal en assumant les fonctions de président du conseil d'administration de la société CPP S.A.

b) M. Pey Casado a effectué son investissement pour une durée indéterminée, au moins pour plusieurs années. Le fait que les titres des sociétés CPP S.A. et EPC Ltda et leurs biens ait été saisis ne saurait sérieusement être invoquée pour conclure que la condition de durée n'est pas satisfaite en l'espèce.

c) Enfin, l'acquisition et l'exploitation d'un journal, certes largement diffusé,[190] est une opération présentant certains risques, le secteur d'activité étant marquée d'une forte spécificité et le contexte économique et politique de l'époque étant incertain.

234. Bien qu'il estime que la condition de contribution au développement de l'Etat d'accueil n'est pas requise, le Tribunal relève, à titre surabondant, qu'elle serait en toute hypothèse satisfaite en l'espèce. L'acquisition et le développement du journal Clarín, dont le tirage était, selon les acteurs de l'époque, le plus important du pays, a indubitablement participé à l'essor économique, social et culturel du pays.

235. Le Tribunal conclut des développements qui précèdent que la condition d'investissement au sens de l'article 25 de la Convention CIRDI est bien satisfaite en l'espèce.

---

[190] V. par exemple l'article de journal produit en annexe C-84 et les déclarations de Me Garcés et Víctor Pey Casado lors de l'audience du 5 mai 2003 (transcription de l'audience du 5 mai 2003, p. 24 et p. 134 respectivement).

B. La condition de nationalité au sens de la Convention CIRDI

236. La deuxième question contestée concernant la compétence du Tribunal arbitral et du Centre est celle de savoir si M. Pey Casado remplissait ou non la condition d'être le ressortissant d'un Etat autre que l'Etat défendeur, Etat d'accueil de l'investissement.

237. L'article 25 (2) a) de la Convention CIRDI précise que « *ressortissant d'un autre Etat contractant* » signifie :

> « *toute personne physique qui possède la nationalité d'un Etat contractant autre que l'Etat partie au différend à la date à laquelle les parties ont consenti à soumettre le différend à la conciliation ou à l'arbitrage ainsi qu'à la date à laquelle la requête a été enregistré conformément à l'article 28, alinéa (3), ou à l'article 36, alinéa (3), à l'exclusion de toute personne qui, à l'une ou à l'autre de ces dates, possède également la nationalité de l'Etat contractant partie au différend ; »*

238. Le moment pertinent pour apprécier la nationalité de M. Pey Casado est donc celui de la date à laquelle les parties ont consenti à soumettre le différend à l'arbitrage, ainsi que la date à laquelle la requête a été enregistrée. Dans le cas d'espèce, M. Pey Casado a consenti à l'arbitrage du CIRDI, par une déclaration écrite à Santiago, le 2 octobre 1997.[191] La requête d'arbitrage des demanderesses a été enregistrée par le CIRDI le 20 avril 1998.

239. Il n'est pas contesté que M. Pey Casado possédait la nationalité d'un Etat contractant autre que le Chili – en l'occurrence, la nationalité espagnole – à ces deux dates critiques.[192]

240. La question contestée est celle de savoir si M. Pey Casado était, à l'une de ces dates, double national. Une spécificité de la Convention CIRDI est qu'elle exclut expressément, dans son article 25 (2) (a) *in fine*, « *toute personne [physique] qui, à l'une ou l'autre de ces dates [du consentement et de l'enregistrement] possède également la nationalité de l'Etat contractant partie au différend* ».[193]

---

[191] Consentement exprimé à l'exclusion de ce qui concerne le différend concernant la restitution ou l'indemnisation de la presse Goss.

[192] V., par exemple, mémoire en réplique sur l'incompétence du 27 décembre 1999, p. 42 ; contre-mémoire de la défenderesse du 3 février 2003, pp. 211 et ss. V. aussi l'avis de droit du Professeur Pierre-Marie Dupuy, soumis au soutien du contre-mémoire de la défenderesse du 3 février 2003, pp. 3-7.

[193] Bien que le projet préliminaire de la Convention CIRDI ait prévu la règle contraire, l'exclusion des doubles nationaux a été incorporé dans l'article 25 (2) a) de façon très claire. Comme le résume le Rapport des Administrateurs de la Banque : « Il convient de noter qu'en vertu de la clause

241.   Il convient de préciser que, dans ce contexte, la question de savoir si l'une des deux nationalités de la partie demanderesse était sa nationalité effective ou dominante ne semble pas pertinente « *de lege lata* ». Il suffirait pour la défenderesse de montrer que la partie demanderesse possédait la nationalité de l'Etat d'accueil aux moments critiques, que cette nationalité soit effective ou non pour exclure, la compétence du Centre.[194] En d'autres termes, pour que les conditions de la compétence requises par l'article 25 de la Convention CIRDI soient remplies, il ne suffirait pas que la nationalité dominante du demandeur soit celle d'un autre Etat que l'Etat défendeur mais il faudrait encore qu'il ne possède pas la nationalité de cet Etat défendeur. Ce n'est que dans la situation dans laquelle la nationalité de l'Etat d'accueil paraîtrait totalement artificielle ou totalement dépourvue d'effectivité que la question de l'exclusion des doubles nationaux de la compétence du Centre en application de l'article 25 de la Convention CIRDI pourrait se poser, mais cette situation n'est pas celle qui se rencontre dans la présente espèce.

242.   C'est sur le fondement de ces principes que la défenderesse a soutenu que toute compétence du CIRDI et du présent Tribunal arbitral serait exclue, au motif que, à l'une des deux dates critiques, M. Pey Casado aurait été double national car il aurait possédé, outre la nationalité espagnole, la nationalité chilienne depuis 1958.

243.   Quant aux faits, on se bornera à se référer ici, pour éviter des répétitions inutiles, à l'exposé détaillé contenu dans l'exposé des faits de la présente sentence, un autre résumé, au moins provisoire, se trouvant aussi dans la décision du 8 mai 2002.[195] On rappellera néanmoins, pour plus de clarté, les données essentielles suivantes :

(a) de cet alinéa (2), une personne physique possédant la nationalité de l'Etat partie au différend ne sera pas admise à être partie aux procédures établies sous les auspices du Centre, même si elle possède en même temps la nationalité d'un autre Etat. Cette exclusion est absolue et ne peut être écartée même si l'Etat partie au différend y consent ».

[194]   Le Professeur Schreuer indique dans ce contexte que, lors des travaux préparatoires de la Convention CIRDI, « suggestions to admit dual nationals if the host State's nationality was not effective or if that host State has not recognized the foreign nationality specifically failed » et que « the ineligibility of an investor who also possesses the host State's nationality applies irrespective of which of the several nationalities is the effective one ». Christoph H. Schreuer, The ICSID Convention: a Commentary, 2001, p. 271, paras. 442 et 444. V. aussi l'avis de droit du Professeur Pierre-Marie Dupuy, soumis au soutien du contre-mémoire de la défenderesse, du 3 février 2003, pp. 7 & 25 et ss.

[195]   Nos 50 et ss, v. aussi nos 37-39.

244. Né en Espagne en 1915, M. Pey Casado a émigré au Chili en 1939 à l'époque de la défaite de la République espagnole par la rébellion franquiste, et y a vécu jusqu'en 1973. Il a été enregistré pour la première fois au Consulat d'Espagne à Santiago en 1947.

245. Le 24 mai 1958, l'Espagne et le Chili ont signé une <u>Convention bilatérale sur la double nationalité</u> (« *Convention bilatérale sur la double nationalité* »), texte permettant aux ressortissants de l'une des parties contractantes d'acquérir la nationalité de l'autre, sans perdre leur nationalité d'origine. C'est en application de ce texte que M. Pey Casado a sollicité et obtenu la nationalité chilienne.[196]

246. Le préambule de cette Convention bilatérale sur la double nationalité rappelle que les Espagnols et les Chiliens font partie d'une communauté caractérisée par l'identité de traditions, culture et langue, et les Etats contractants considèrent que :

> « *il n'y a aucune objection juridique pour qu'une personne puisse avoir deux nationalités, à condition que seulement l'une d'entre elles aie pleine efficacité, et indique la législation à laquelle elle est soumise* ».

247. L'article 1.1 de la Convention prévoit :

> « *que les Chiliens nés au Chili et réciproquement les Espagnols nés en Espagne, pourront acquérir la nationalité espagnole ou chilienne, respectivement, dans les conditions et de la façon prévue par la législation en vigueur dans chacune des parties contractantes, sans perdre leur nationalité antérieure* ».

248. L'article 2 prévoit notamment que :

> « *les Espagnols qui ont acquis la nationalité chilienne en conservant la nationalité d'origine devront être inscrits dans [...] le Registre chilien de Cartes de Nationalisation* ».

249. Dès cette inscription, les Chiliens en Espagne et les Espagnols au Chili jouiront de la pleine condition juridique des ressortissants de la façon prévue dans cet accord et dans les lois des deux pays. L'article 3 précise que « *l'octroi de passeport, la protection diplomatique et l'exercice des droits civils et politiques se feront par la loi du pays où ils sont domiciliés [...]* ».

250. L'article 3, al. 2, exclut pour les doubles nationaux l'application simultanée des législations des deux Etats et fait prévaloir la loi de

---

[196] Decreto Supremo n°8054 du 11 décembre 1958.

l'Etat du domicile. L'article 4 précise que le domicile est présumé être établi dans l'Etat de la seconde nationalité acquise ; il pose le principe de l'unité de domicile, lequel ne peut être changé qu'avec la résidence habituelle dans l'autre Etat contractant, pour autant que ce changement soit inscrit dans le registre approprié.

251. C'est donc en 1958 que M. Pey Casado est devenu un double national, sa nationalité prépondérante devenant, à cause de son domicile au Chili, la nationalité chilienne, les lois du Chili lui étant applicables dans toutes les matières concernant notamment les passeports, la protection diplomatique et l'exercice des droits civils et politiques.

252. Le fait de l'acquisition par la première partie demanderesse, en décembre 1958, de la nationalité chilienne, et donc de son statut de double national espagnol et chilien, selon la Convention bilatérale sur la double nationalité de 1958, n'est ni contesté ni contestable. Les seules questions décisives en l'espèce sont celles de savoir si, aux dates critiques, il avait conservé la nationalité chilienne, comme le prétend la défenderesse dans son exception d'incompétence, ou si, comme l'opposent les parties demanderesses, il en avait été privé ou y avait renoncé valablement.

253. Avant d'examiner les arguments de la privation et la renonciation de la nationalité chilienne, il convient de rappeler les principes régissant le droit applicable à la question de la nationalité des parties.

1. Le droit applicable à la question de la nationalité

254. Les parties ont plaidé en détail la question du droit applicable à la question de la nationalité des parties demanderesses. La défenderesse a allégué que seul le droit chilien était applicable, la question de la nationalité étant « *une question de l'intérêt de l'Etat [...] qui établit, souverainement, suivant son propre intérêt, les moyens de l'acquérir ou de la perdre [...]* ».[197] Les demanderesses n'ont pas contesté que les règles qui déterminent la nationalité sont du domaine réservé de l'Etat, mais elles ont soutenu que la question serait néanmoins également soumis aux principes du droit international et qu'un

---

[197] Mémoire d'incompétence de la défenderesse du 20 juillet 1999, p. 19 ; mémoire en réplique sur l'incompétence du 27 décembre 1999, p. 36-37 ; contre-mémoire de la défenderesse du 3 février 2003, pp. 217 et ss ; réplique de la défenderesse du 4 avril 2003, p. 8 ; transcription de l'audience du 15 janvier 2007, p. 311, para. 10-40 ; pp. 33-34 (Me Di Rosa). V. aussi l'avis de droit du Professeur Pierre-Marie Dupuy, soumis au soutien du contre-mémoire de la défenderesse, du 3 février 2003, qui conclut « *la dévolution de [la nationalité] ressortit à la compétence exclusive de chaque Etat. En l'occurrence, c'est exclusivement le droit chilien qui détermine l'existence ou la non existence de la nationalité chilienne de M. Pey Casado.* » (p. 3).

« *tribunal international conserve son pouvoir d'appréciation en cette matière* ».[198]

255. Il y a lieu de rappeler les principes et règles du droit international concernant le droit applicable aux questions de la nationalité. Dans son Opinion sur les *Décrets tunisiens et marocains de nationalité*, de 1923, la Cour permanente de Justice internationale[199] a considéré que, vu le caractère essentiellement relatif de ce problème qui dépend de l'évolution des relations internationales, les questions de nationalité appartenaient en principe au domaine réservé. En 1955, la Cour internationale de Justice, dans l'affaire *Nottebohm* a déclaré que « *il appartenait au Liechtenstein, comme à tout Etat souverain, de régler par sa propre législation l'acquisition de sa nationalité, car le droit international laisse à chaque Etat le soin de régler l'attribution de sa propre nationalité* ».[200]

256. Selon la Convention de La Haye de 1930 sur les conflits de lois en matière de nationalité, entrée en vigueur le 1er avril 1937,[201] il appartient à chaque Etat de déterminer, selon sa propre loi, qui sont ses nationaux (art. 1) et que « *any question as to whether a person possesses the nationality of a particular State, shall be determined in accordance with the law of that State* » (art. 2).[202]

257. La Commission du Droit international des Nations Unies a discuté cette matière de manière approfondie et son Rapporteur Spécial a

---

[198]   V. exposé complémentaire sur la compétence du Tribunal arbitral du 11 septembre 2002, pp. 95-96 ; transcription de l'audience du 15 janvier 2007, p. 71, para. 7-11 (Me Garcés). Auparavant, les demanderesses ont soutenu que la nationalité de l'investisseur devrait être déterminée, en premier lieu, conformément au droit espagnol. V. réponse au mémoire soutenant l'incompétence soumis par la défenderesse, du 18 septembre 1999, pp. 72-73 ; réplique à la réponse soumise par la République du Chili au contre-mémoire réfutant le déclinatoire de compétence, du 7 février 2000, p. 12 ; réplique des demanderesses au contre-mémoire de la défenderesse, du 23 février 2003, pp. 210 et ss.

[199]   Cour permanente de Justice internationale, *Décrets tunisiens et marocains de nationalité*, Série B, avis consultatif n°4, 7 février 1923.

[200]   2ème phase – Liechtenstein c. République du Guatémala, jugement du 6 avril 1955, p. 20. Le même arrêt précise que « un Etat ne saurait prétendre que les règles par lui établies devraient être reconnues par un autre Etat que s'il s'est conformé à ce but général de faire concorder le lien juridique de la nationalité avec le rattachement effectif de l'individu à l'Etat qui assume la défense de ses concitoyens, par le moyen de la protection vis-à-vis des autres Etats » (id. p. 23).

[201]   Mais non ratifiée par l'Espagne ou par le Chili, bien que les représentants de ces deux pays aient exprimé leur accord au cours des négociations.

[202]   179 LNTS 89. L'article 3 de la Convention déclare en outre que « a person having two or more nationalities may be regarded as its national by each of the States whose nationality he possesses ».

déclaré que « *in principle, questions of nationalities fall within the domestic jurisdiction of each State* ».[203]

258. Dans l'affaire *Nottebohm*, la Cour internationale de Justice a également évoqué la situation des doubles nationaux :

> « *Lorsqu'un Etat a conféré sa nationalité à une personne et qu'un autre Etat a conféré sa propre nationalité à cette même personne, il arrive que chacun de ces Etats, estimant qu'il a agi dans l'exercice de sa compétence nationale, s'en tient à sa propre conception et se conforme à celle-ci pour son action propre. Chacun de ces Etats reste jusque là dans son ordre juridique propre. Cette situation peut se trouver sur le terrain international et être examinée par un Arbitre international....* »[204]

259. Le plus souvent, l'arbitre international n'a pas eu, à proprement parler, à trancher entre les Etats en cause un conflit de nationalités, mais à déterminer si la nationalité invoquée par l'Etat demandeur était opposable à l'Etat défendeur :

> « *L'arbitre international a tranché de la même façon de nombreux cas de double nationalité où la question se posait à propos de l'exercice de la protection. Il a fait prévaloir la nationalité effective, celle concordant avec la situation de fait, celle reposant sur un lien de fait supérieur entre l'intéressé et l'un des Etats dont la nationalité était en cause. Les éléments pris en considération sont divers et leur importance varie d'un cas à l'autre. Le domicile de l'intéressé y tient une grande place, mais il y a aussi le siège de ses intérêts, ses liens de famille, sa participation à la vie publique, etc.* »[205]

260. Suivant ces règles bien-établies en droit international, le Tribunal arbitral considère que c'est en appliquant le droit chilien que doit être examinée la question de savoir si en l'espèce les autorités chiliennes ont, comme il est allégué par l'intéressé, privé M. Pey Casado de sa nationalité chilienne, ou bien, s'il s'avère que tel n'a pas été le cas, si M. Pey Casado a valablement renoncé à la nationalité chilienne.

---

[203] Yearbook of the International Law Commission A / 2163, 1952, p. 7.
[204] Liechstenstein c. République du Guatémala, jugement du 6 avril 1955, p. 21.
[205] *Id.*, p. 22.

2.   L'argument de la privation de la nationalité chilienne

    a)   Position des parties

261.   Selon M. Pey Casado, il aurait perdu sa nationalité chilienne, en conséquence du coup d'Etat militaire du 11 septembre 1973 au cours duquel le Président Allende fut assassiné. Après un raid des militaires dans les bureaux du journal Clarin, craignant pour sa vie, il s'est réfugié, le 14 septembre 1973, dans l'Ambassade du Venezuela à Santiago. Les autorités chiliennes lui auraient refusé, à une date qui n'était pas précisée par les parties dans la procédure, de renouveler son passeport chilien, dont la validité avait expiré en décembre 1971. Ce refus de passeport ou de renouvellement, est-il prétendu, équivaudrait *de facto* à une « *dénaturalisation* », une « *dénationalisation* » ou une déchéance.[206]

262.   Cependant les autorités chiliennes ont accordé un sauf-conduit, le 27 octobre 1973, à M. Pey Casado, comme à d'autres personnes, grâce auquel il put se rendre au Venezuela, où il établit sa résidence et obtint un passeport d'urgence pour apatride le 8 janvier 1974 et une carte d'identité pour les étrangers en transit le 28 janvier 1974.[207] Il fut considéré dans ce pays comme « *en transit* » (« *transeunte* ») jusqu'à la date du 8 janvier 1975, date à laquelle il obtint une carte d'identité nationale vénézuélienne, comme résident.

263.   La thèse de M. Pey Casado est, en résumé, que, dès septembre 1973 (mois du coup d'Etat militaire) il a perdu la nationalité chilienne, en raison du comportement des autorités militaires, qui lui refusaient les droits protégés par la Convention bilatérale sur la double nationalité,

---

[206]   V. réponse au mémoire soutenant l'incompétence soumis par la défenderesse, du 18 septembre 1999, pp. 59 et ss ; réplique à la réponse soumise par la République du Chili au contre-mémoire réfutant le déclinatoire de compétence du 7 février 2000, p 12 ; exposé complémentaire sur la compétence du Tribunal arbitral du 11 septembre 2002, pp. 100 et ss ; réplique des demanderesses au contre-mémoire de la défenderesse, du 23 février 2003, pp. 186 et ss ; consultation juridique de M. Victor Araya, soumis par les demanderesses au soutien de la réplique des demanderesses au contre-mémoire de la défenderesse, du 23 février 2003 ; transcription de l'audience du 15 janvier 2007, pp. 69-70 (Me Garcés). Selon les demanderesses, l'existence d'une telle « *dénaturalisation* » serait également reconnue par le droit international ; v. réponse au mémoire soutenant l'incompétence soumis par la défenderesse, du 18 septembre 1999, pp. 63-64. V aussi la consultation juridique par le Professeur Fernando M. Mariño, soumis au soutien de la réplique des demanderesses au contre-mémoire de la défenderesse, du 23 février 2003.

[207]   La première partie demanderesse a soutenu que les autorités chiliennes auraient retiré ce sauf-conduit quand M. Pey Casado est monté en avion, le laissant sans aucune pièce d'identification. V. la transcription de l'audience du 15 janvier 2007, p. 69, para. 1-6. (Me Garcés).

refusaient de renouveler son passeport, lui refusaient une protection diplomatique, le déclarait « *rebelle* »,[208] bref, le privaient de son statut de ressortissant chilien au moins *de facto*, par exemple par l'interdiction de rentrer librement au Chili,[209] si bien que dès cette période, il n'était plus qu'un ressortissant espagnol.[210] En fait, on notera que la copie du passeport déposé au dossier montre une validité expirant le 12 décembre 1971.[211] M. Pey Casado a exposé qu'il avait voyagé au Portugal et en Suisse notamment en mai et octobre 1972, respectivement, afin de négocier et de conclure l'achat de la société CPP S.A. que souhaitait vendre M. Dario Sainte-Marie. Quels passeports ont-ils été utilisés au cours de ces voyages n'est pas parfaitement clair, mais il apparaît établi, cependant, que M. Pey Casado s'est rendu au Consulat ou à l'Ambassade du Venezuela pour y trouver refuge et a quitté le Chili pour le Venezuela avec un passeport chilien expiré. Au Venezuela, sa demande d'un passeport chilien fut rejetée à nouveau et il reçut des autorités locales un passeport spécial pour apatride. Le 9 janvier 1974, le Consulat espagnol à Caracas lui octroya un visa de 3 mois pour l'Espagne, où il se rendit le 31 mai 1974.

264. La défenderesse a prétendu à l'appui de son objection d'incompétence que M. Pey Casado avait conservé la nationalité chilienne aux dates critiques.[212] Elle a soutenu qu'une « *dénaturalisation* » n'était pas prévue par le droit chilien comme cause de perte de nationalité et que les actes commis par la dictature en 1973 n'avaient pas entraîné une privation de nationalité des victimes.[213] Selon la défenderesse, en droit chilien, le retrait de la

---

208 Annexe C-197.

209 V. annexe C-257.

210 Les parties demanderesses ont argumenté notamment: « [...] comment soutenir que la privation unilatérale infligée à Monsieur Pey-Casado, de la part de l'Etat chilien, non seulement de toutes les prérogatives liées à la Convention bilatérale du 24 mai 1958, mais au-delà, de celles ressortissant aux droits humains les plus élémentaires, pourrait s'accompagner du maintien – tout aussi unilatéralement imposé – d'une composante particulière de cette même Convention, que nous avons vu violée, foulée aux pieds et anéantie en la personne de l'investisseur espagnol ! », mémoire des demanderesses du 17 mars 1999, pp. 28-29.

211 Annexe C-252.

212 V. mémoire en réplique sur l'incompétence du 27 décembre 1999, pp. 22 et ss.

213 Selon la défenderesse « la dictature a commis ces atrocités avec un grand nombre de Chilien et aucun d'entre eux n'a perdu la nationalité pour ces faits. La dictature, ceci est su de tous, a commis des crimes atroces, mais ceci n'a rien à voir avec cette affaire et encore moins avec la nationalité chilienne de M. Pey. » Mémoire en réplique sur l'incompétence du 27 décembre 1999, p. 22. V. aussi l'avis de droit du Professeur Humberto

nationalité par les autorités chiliennes était assujetti à l'accomplissement de formalités – notamment un « *décret suprême* » - formalités qui n'avaient pas été remplies dans le cas de M. Pey Casado.[214]

b)   Conclusions du Tribunal

265.   En droit, la question se pose de savoir si le comportement des autorités chiliennes a constitué un retrait ou une privation de la nationalité.

266.   M. Pey Casado, à l'instar de nombreux autres citoyens considérés comme ennemis du nouveau régime issu du coup d'Etat militaire, ou rebelles, et publiquement dénoncés comme tels par ledit régime, a été contraint de chercher asile à l'étranger pour protéger sa vie et sa liberté. Il semble même que, compte tenu de sa situation personnelle et patrimoniale éminente, de son influence et de ses liens avec le Président Allende, M. Pey Casado ait été particulièrement menacé et visé par les voies de fait et mesures de la dictature militaire.

267.   La Commission interaméricaine des Droits de l'Homme, dans son rapport de 1985 sur la situation pour le moins troublante des droits de l'homme au Chili, a analysé en détail le droit d'avoir une nationalité et de n'en être pas privé arbitrairement. A en croire ce rapport, il résulterait de l'article 6 de la Constitution chilienne de 1925, en vigueur en 1973,[215] que la nationalité ne pourrait être perdue que dans trois cas : d'abord, en cas de naturalisation dans un pays étranger ; ensuite, en cas d'annulation des documents de naturalisation (décision contre laquelle un recours est possible devant la Cour suprême) ; troisièmement, en cas de services rendus pendant la guerre aux ennemis du Chili ou leurs alliés.[216]

Nogueira Alcalá, soumis à l'appui du contre-mémoire de la défenderesse du 3 février 2003, pp. 28-32 ; v. contre-mémoire de la défenderesse du 3 février 2003, pp. 242 et ss.

[214]   Mémoire en réplique sur l'incompétence du 27 décembre 1999, pp. 25-28.

[215]   Comme le Professeur Cea l'a réitéré lors de l'audience du 15 janvier 2007, la Constitution de 1925 a fait l'objet d'une modification en 1980, puis d'une réforme en 2005. V. la transcription de l'audience du 15 janvier 2007, p. 20, para. 1-4.

[216]   La Constitution chilienne de 1925 a été modifiée, par le Décret 175 du 3 décembre 1973 (postérieur au coup d'Etat militaire). Cette modification ajoute un cas de privation de la nationalité pour le motif suivant : « *En raison d'une attaque sérieuse menée par l'extérieur contre les intérêts essentiels de l'Etat, au cours d'un Etat d'urgence prévu par l'article 72(17) de cette Constitution Politique.* » Il n'a pas été établi que - malgré l'état d'urgence - cette disposition ait été effectivement appliquée par les autorités chiliennes à M. Pey Casado ni que la défenderesse ait soutenu que l'achat par ce dernier des actions du journal Clarín à Estoril et/ou à Genève ait constitué une

268.   Le premier cas est évidemment modifié par la Convention hispano-chilienne sur la double nationalité qui autorise expressément les ressortissants chiliens à conserver leur nationalité, lorsqu'ils obtiennent la nationalité espagnole. Quant aux deux autres hypothèses ci-dessus mentionnées, elles ne paraissent pas être réalisées en l'espèce. Néanmoins, et même si aucune des causes de perte de nationalité prévues par la Constitution chilienne s'applique directement, la question se pose de savoir si les autorités chiliennes auraient, par leurs actes, privé M. Pey Casado de sa nationalité chilienne.

269.   Le Gouvernement du Chili a fourni à la Commission interaméricaine de Droits de l'Homme le nom des personnes privées par l'autorité de la nationalité chilienne et le nom de M. Pey Casado ne figure pas dans cette liste. Mais ce fait, dépendant de la seule initiative et appréciation de l'autorité en question (appréciation fondée sans doute sur son propre intérêt, dans le contexte de ses relations avec ladite Commission inter-américaine) ne peut être tenu pour une preuve décisive. A s'en tenir au droit chilien, qui est en principe applicable selon les principes du droit international rappelés plus haut à la question de la nationalité chilienne de M. Pey Casado et aux éléments figurant au dossier, le comportement des autorités militaires chiliennes, si arbitraire ou choquant qu'il puisse être à l'égard de la première partie demanderesse, ne permet de tirer aucune conclusion quant à la perte de cette nationalité ou à son maintien. Parmi les divers documents déposés au dossier, on ne trouve aucune preuve formelle de la prétendue privation de la nationalité chilienne par un acte d'autorité.

270.   Une autre question est celle de savoir si, comme le prétendent les parties demanderesses,[217] la délivrance d'un sauf-conduit à M. Pey Casado par les autorités chiliennes peut ou doit être interprétée comme comportant reconnaissance formelle, bien qu'implicite, d'une perte de nationalité. La réponse ne peut être que

---

« attaque sérieuse menée par l'extérieur contre les intérêts essentiels de l'Etat ». Si tel avait été le cas, ce qui n'est pas prouvé, il y aurait éventuellement lieu de se demander si le Tribunal arbitral peut tenir compte du décret-loi 175 – à supposer qu'il n'ait pas été annulé et considéré comme de nul effet par la législation chilienne postérieure à la chute du régime militaire. Quoi qu'il en soit, il y a lieu de relever que l'article 2 du décret-loi 175/1973 prévoyait que toutes les pertes de nationalité devaient être déclarées par un décret suprême motivé. Et un décret subséquent (n°355/1974) offrait à un intéressé la possibilité (effective ou théorique) de faire appel à la Cour suprême pour s'opposer à une privation par décret de sa nationalité.

[217]   V. exposé complémentaire sur la compétence du Tribunal arbitral du 11 septembre 2002, pp. 102-103.

négative, sauf circonstances exceptionnelles, car la remise d'un sauf-conduit n'est nullement destinée à des apatrides, mais caractérise une situation de conflit.[218]

271. Quant au Rapport de 1974 sur la situation des droits de l'Homme au Chili, publié par la Commission interaméricaine des Droits de l'Homme, il affirme d'autre part que « *the Chilean Ministry of Foreign Affairs had granted 2945 safe-conduct for Chileans who had taken refuge in diplomatic missions in Santiago, and 547 courtesy safe-conducts for members of the family of those persons* ». Le même Rapport mentionne en outre que le Venezuela avait accepté un total de 249 personnes, chiliennes ou étrangères, comme réfugiées du Chili.

272. Les demanderesses ont soutenu, en se fondant sur une pièce C-1,[219] que, en fait, et contrairement aux affirmations du Gouvernement chilien, « *plusieurs milliers de chiliens ont bel et bien perdu la plupart des droits inhérents à la nationalité [...]* ». Le Rapport précité, par exemple, indique que beaucoup de chiliens étaient expulsés par le Chili, que leurs passeports étaient valides seulement pour sortir du Chili une fois, qu'ils ne pouvaient pas les renouveler et qu'ils étaient parfois obligés de demander un document de voyage à l'agence des Nations Unies pour les réfugiés.[220] A supposer exacte et prouvée cette affirmation, il ne semble pas qu'elle équivaille à la preuve d'une perte juridique de la nationalité elle-même à proprement parler.

273. Quoi qu'il en soit des violations et actes arbitraires commis par le Gouvernement militaire du Chili en 1973, il n'est pas établi qu'ils aient entraîné la privation *de jure* de la nationalité chilienne de M. Pey Casado.[221] De l'avis du Tribunal arbitral, le Professeur

---

[218] C'est ainsi que, par exemple, le Black's Law Dictionary distingue entre passeport et sauf-conduit et définit ce dernier comme un document « conferring permission upon an enemy subject or others to proceed to a particular place for a defined object », Black's Law Dictionary (6ième edition, 1990) p. 1336.

[219] Rapport du Secrétaire général de l'ONU à l'Assemblée générale du 8 octobre 1976, paragraphes 415 – 422.

[220] *Idem*, para. 420.

[221] À ce stade de l'analyse, il y a lieu d'ajouter que les positions ou déclarations des autorités du Venezuela relatives à M. Pey Casado, comme apatride, étranger de passage (« *transeunte* ») notamment sont sans incidence quant à la question du maintien ou de la perte de la nationalité chilienne. Selon la Convention de 1954 sur le statut des apatrides, est sans nationalité « *a person who is not considered as a national by any State under the operations of its law* ». Tel n'était pas le cas de M. Pey Casado, qui était sans doute possible ressortissant de l'Espagne et aussi, probablement, à en croire au moins l'examen auquel il a été procédé jusqu'ici, un ressortissant chilien en 1973. Il

Dupuy a souligné avec raison cette conclusion dans son avis de droit de février 2003 :

> « [...] le fait qu'un Etat n'exerce pas sa protection à l'égard de l'un de ses ressortissants n'a aucune signification quant au maintien ou au retrait par ce même Etat de la nationalité de son ressortissant. Soit qu'il décide de ne pas la lui accorder en application du caractère discrétionnaire de sa compétence pour ce faire, soit qu'il ne l'exerce pas dans le cas d'un double national, son abstention s'explique pour d'autres raisons que celle de vouloir maintenir ou supprimer la nationalité de l'individu concerné. Cela n'a tout simplement rien à voir ; le lien établi entre le non exercice par le Chili de sa protection à l'égard de M. Pey Casado et l'éventuel retrait de sa nationalité chilienne paraît tout simplement dépourvu de pertinence juridique. »[222]

274.   Le Tribunal arbitral constate donc que la première partie demanderesse n'a pas été privée de la nationalité chilienne par ces actes commis en 1973.

3.   <u>La nationalité de M. Pey Casado entre 1974 et 1996</u>

275.   A toutes fins utiles, et avant d'examiner la question de la renonciation volontaire de la nationalité chilienne, il semble opportun de rechercher encore si, depuis 1973-1974, la situation s'est modifiée ou non en ce qui concerne la nationalité de la première partie demanderesse. A ce propos, les parties se sont référées à la Convention bilatérale sur la double nationalité et ont débattu de son application éventuelle à cette dernière question.

276.   Selon l'article 4.3 de ladite Convention, « au cas où une personne qui jouit de la double nationalité change sa résidence au territoire d'un troisième Etat, on comprendra pour domicile, afin de déterminer la dépendance politique et la législation applicable, le dernier domicile qu'il a enregistré dans le territoire d'une des hautes parties contractantes ». Il en résulterait que, selon cette Convention, à l'époque où il s'est établi au Venezuela, M. Pey Casado conservait sa

---

n'était par conséquent pas apatride. De plus, il découle des principes de Droit international public qu'une interprétation par un pays tiers de la situation de M. Pey Casado, ici par le Venezuela, ne peut avoir aucune conséquence quant à une définition de la nationalité chilienne, question appartenant au domaine réservé de cet Etat.

[222]   Avis de droit du Professeur Pierre-Marie Dupuy, soumis au soutien du contre-mémoire de la défenderesse du 3 février 2003, pp. 20-21.

nationalité chilienne, comme sa nationalité « primaire », en même temps qu'il continuait à être un ressortissant espagnol. Selon l'article 4.2 de ce même Convention, un chilien ne peut changer son domicile que s'il transfère sa résidence habituelle en Espagne et s'y enregistre au Registre civil espagnol. Or le 31 mai 1974 M. Pey Casado s'est rendu en Espagne et, le 4 juin 1974, s'y est enregistré au Registre de la Municipalité de Madrid, recevant alors une carte d'identité de nationalité espagnole.[223]

277. L'article 10 de la loi de 1957 sur le Registre civil espagnol déclare que le Registre de l'état civil se compose des registres municipaux, des registres consulaires et d'un registre central.[224] D'après l'article 18 de la même loi, le registre central possède une compétence subsidiaire ou résiduelle pour enregistrer les faits qui ne peuvent être enregistrés autre part. L'article 64 de la même loi prévoit que les questions de nationalité et de domicile sont enregistrées dans le registre pertinent. En outre, l'article 1er des règlements de 1958 sur le registre de l'état civil espagnol prévoit que les divers organes du registre civil ont l'obligation de communiquer entre eux.[225]

278. Il résulte de ce qui précède que, contrairement à la thèse de la défenderesse,[226] l'enregistrement par M. Pey Casado au Registre municipal de Madrid a bel et bien produit ses effets : il en est résulté au moins un changement valable de la nationalité « *primaire* » de M. Pey Casado, au sens de la Convention bilatérale sur la double nationalité. En 1974, par conséquent, en application de ce Traité, la nationalité « *primaire* » de M. Pey Casado est devenue espagnole, alors que sa nationalité « *secondaire* », au sens de ce même Traité, est devenue de nationalité chilienne.

279. Il a été allégué aussi que cet enregistrement au Registre municipal n'avait pas en fait été transcrit dans le Registre approprié et, par conséquent, n'aurait pas été valable à l'époque, ce défaut étant corrigé seulement en 1996. Cet argument est sans portée en l'espèce. En effet, à la supposer établie, cette absence de transcription devrait être considérée comme la simple omission par un fonctionnaire espagnol de la formalité requise. En outre, l'article 64 de la Loi de 1958 sur le Registre civil prévoit expressément que c'est la date de la déclaration, et non pas celle de la transcription, qui doit être considérée comme celle de l'enregistrement. Toute conclusion

---

[223] V. réponse au mémoire soutenant l'incompétence soumis par la défenderesse, du 18 septembre 1999, pp. 58-59.
[224] Annexe C-150.
[225] *Id.*
[226] V., par exemple, contre-mémoire de la défenderesse du 3 février 2003, pp. 24-25.

différente sur ce sujet ne pourrait avoir de conséquences que sur les circonstances permettant de définir la nationalité « *primaire* » et le droit applicable, et non pas la question ici à l'examen, celle de la détention d'une nationalité en tant que telle.

280. Peu après ces événements, le 11 juin 1974, M. Pey Casado obtient un passeport espagnol. Il quitte alors l'Espagne pour revenir au Venezuela et, la même année, il s'enregistre au Consulat espagnol à Caracas.[227] Le 8 janvier 1975, il reçoit une carte d'identité de résident du Venezuela. Le 10 avril 1977, il reçoit un passeport espagnol du Consulat de Caracas (dont la validité expire le 10 mai 1979). Il se rend ensuite du Venezuela au Pérou où, le 24 mai 1977, il s'enregistre au Consulat espagnol de Lima. Ce Consulat lui remet deux passeports : l'un le 25 juin 1979 (date d'expiration le 24.06.1984) et l'autre le 16 janvier 1984 (date d'expiration 15.01.1989). En 1988, il retourne au Venezuela et, le 17 novembre 1988, reçoit un passeport du Consulat espagnol à Caracas (date d'expiration le 16.11.1993). Le 18 janvier 1989, il renouvelle sa carte d'identité espagnole. Enfin, après la chute du régime du Général Pinochet, M. Pey Casado se rend au Chili pour la première fois depuis 1973, le 4 mai 1989.

281. Les parties ont évoqué la question de savoir si, à un moment quelconque entre 1974 et 1989, M. Pey Casado aurait vu modifier sa nationalité. Ceci au regard au regard de la Convention bilatérale sur la double nationalité, laquelle prévoit de manière précise les conditions d'un changement de situation à cet égard. En l'espèce, M. Pey Casado aurait pu changer sa nationalité « *primaire* » par application de l'article 2.2 de ladite Convention mais seulement en transférant son domicile et en s'y enregistrant dans le « *Registre des Cartes de nationalisation* » au Chili. À défaut, sa nationalité « *primaire* » serait demeurée la même quand bien même son domicile aurait été transféré dans un Etat tiers, non contractant (en l'espèce le Venezuela ou le Pérou). En l'espèce, il n'a pas été allégué que M. Pey Casado aurait transporté son domicile d'Espagne au Chili. Il en résulte que pendant toute cette période et jusqu'à 1989, M. Pey Casado aurait continué d'avoir la double nationalité espagnole et chilienne, et que sa nationalité « *primaire* » au sens de la Convention bilatérale hispano-chilienne, aurait continué à être espagnole depuis 1974.

282. Il y a lieu de rechercher maintenant s'il y a eu changement de nationalité après 1989. Le 4 mai 1989, on l'a vu, après la déposition du Général Pinochet, M. Pey Casado se rend au Chili. Selon lui, il s'est agi d'un séjour temporaire, avec le but de se renseigner quant à

---

227   Annexe C-18.

la situation des actions de la société CPP S.A.[228] Selon la défenderesse, en revanche, M. Pey Casado aurait eu l'intention de reprendre une résidence au Chili.[229] Après 1989, se produisent une série de faits ou événements présentant de l'intérêt pour l'examen de la question de la nationalité. Ils comprennent différentes déclarations de M. Pey Casado concernant sa nationalité ainsi que divers faits (plus ou moins clairs et plus ou moins cohérents) résultant de ou accompagnant son retour au Chili.

283. Le premier exemple consiste en la création de la *Fundación Presidente Allende*, fondation dont les actes constitutifs lors de sa création le 16 janvier 1990 en Espagne mentionnent M. Pey Casado, l'un des trois fondateurs, comme un double national espagnol et chilien. Il n'est peut-être pas sans intérêt de rappeler que, par la suite, soit en 1999,[230] les statuts de la Fondation ont été modifiés pour faire disparaître la mention de la nationalité chilienne et indiquer la seule nationalité espagnole comme étant celle de M. Pey Casado.[231]

284. Selon la défenderesse, M. Pey Casado s'est identifié ou décrit lui-même à plusieurs reprises, dès le 2 octobre 1991, comme de nationalité chilienne, et il a requis l'assistance des autorités chiliennes après son retour. Ainsi, par exemple, le 5 janvier 1991, il demande et obtient une carte d'identité chilienne. Le 17 février il s'inscrit au Registre des votants à Vitacura.[232] Le 20 février 1991, toujours au Chili, il constate la perte de son passeport espagnol, et demande un passeport à l'autorité chilienne qui le lui accorde. C'est avec un passeport chilien qu'il se rend au Venezuela et, à en croire la défenderesse, en Europe en 1997. Entre le 20 octobre 1991 et janvier 1997, M. Pey Casado se serait donné à plusieurs reprises comme Chilien,[233] notamment dans ses demandes d'aide au titre du retour des émigrés. Ainsi, le 25 mai 1992, il s'annonce à l'*Oficina Nacional de Retorno* (qui s'occupe des émigrés chiliens de retour). Le premier août 1992, il est identifié comme Chilien dans un contrat de travail avec son frère, ainsi que à diverses reprises à l'aide de sa carte nationale d'identité chilienne en août 1992. En 1993, M. Pey Casado

---

[228] Réponse au mémoire soutenant l'incompétence soumis par la défenderesse, du 18 septembre 1999, pp. 73-74.

[229] Contre-mémoire de la défenderesse du 3 février 2003, pp. 26 et ss.

[230] Annexe 135.

[231] V. à ce sujet les documents suivants: annexe 22 au contre-mémoire de la défenderesse du 3 février 2003 et annexe C-7 des demanderesses, qui concordent en déclarant M. Pey Casado comme double national lors de la création de la Fondation ; v. annexe 135 au contre-mémoire de la défenderesse du 3 février 2003 sur la modification du statut de la Fondation comme décrivant M. Pey Casado avec la seule nationalité espagnole.

[232] Annexe 29 au contre-mémoire de la défenderesse du 3 février 2003.

[233] V. mémoire en réplique sur l'incompétence du 27 décembre 1999, pp. 48-49.

s'inscrit au Registre électoral de La Reina (Chili). Le 23 octobre 1994, il voyage en Bolivie avec son passeport chilien. Il aurait fait de même avec le même passeport le 6 novembre 1994 dans un voyage en Bolivie puis en Espagne, le 25 mai 1997, en passant par les États Unis.[234] Le 28 mai 1997, séjournant alors en Espagne, il obtient à Madrid un passeport espagnol.

285. À ce stade de l'analyse, il y a lieu de conclure, à propos des faits précités, survenus après le retour de M. Pey Casado au Chili après 1989, qu'ils n'ont pas modifié la situation juridique existant précédemment. M. Pey Casado demeurait double national espagnol/chilien jusqu'en 1997.

286. Cela étant, la question qui demeure à examiner est celle de savoir si, comme il l'a allégué, M. Pey Casado a valablement renoncé à sa nationalité chilienne par ses déclarations faites en 1997, ce qui est contesté par l'Etat défendeur.

4. L'argument de la renonciation à la nationalité chilienne

287. Les faits considérés par la première partie demanderesse comme comportant une renonciation à la nationalité chilienne[235] peuvent être résumés de la manière suivante :

288. Le 10 décembre 1996, M. Pey Casado informe le département chilien de l'émigration qu'il a résidé en Espagne depuis 1974 et qu'il n'entendait pas se prévaloir de la Convention hispano-chilienne sur la double nationalité. Il demande à faire inscrire dans le registre chilien des « *cartes de nationalisation* » - seul compétent à cet égard selon un arrêt de la Cour suprême[236] - sa situation de fait depuis qu'en septembre 1973 le Chili lui a dénié les bénéfices de ladite Convention, si bien que sa nationalité exclusive serait la nationalité espagnole.[237]

289. Le 19 décembre 1996, la municipalité de Madrid confirme que la résidence de M. Pey Casado est en Espagne. Le 7 janvier 1997, M. Pey Casado demande au registre civil du consulat espagnol à Santiago de prendre note du fait qu'il ne bénéficie pas de la

---

[234] V. exposé complémentaire sur la compétence du Tribunal arbitral du 11 septembre 2002, p. 112.

[235] V. le résumé présenté par la première partie demanderesse lors de l'audience du 15 janvier 2007, transcription de l'audience du 15 janvier 2007, p. 70 (Me Garcés).

[236] Cf. annexe C-95.

[237] Annexe C-21 ; v. réponse au mémoire soutenant l'incompétence soumis par la défenderesse, du 18 septembre 1999, p. 61 ; réplique à la réponse soumise par la République du Chili au contre-mémoire réfutant le déclinatoire de compétence, du 7 février 2000, pp. 13-14.

Convention bilatérale sur la double nationalité, et, le 5 février 1997, le Consulat d'Espagne à Santiago raye le nom de M. Pey Casado de son registre des citoyens espagnols résidant au Chili après avoir constaté que son domicile légal est situé en Espagne.

290. Le 16 septembre 1997, M. Pey Casado fait une déclaration auprès du Consulat d'Espagne à Mendoza (Argentine) où il répète ce qu'il avait écrit précédemment au Ministère de l'intérieur du Chili, le 10 janvier 1996. Il y précise ce qui suit : « *pour ne laisser place à aucun doute à cet égard, je déclare que la communication du 10 décembre 1996…doit s'entendre de la façon qui convient le mieux en Droit aux fins desquelles elle a été présentée, y compris comme preuve de ma renonciation expresse et solennelle à la nationalité chilienne au cas où serait requise par l'Administration chilienne une renonciation formelle à la nationalité chilienne, ce que j'affirme et à quoi je souscris de nouveau par le présent acte… »*[238] (souligné par nous).

291. Quelques semaines plus tard, le 2 octobre 1997, M. Pey Casado consent à l'arbitrage du CIRDI, à l'exclusion du litige concernant la rotative Goss.

292. Le 20 novembre 1997, le juge du registre espagnol donne suite à la requête de M. Pey Casado tendant à voir confirmer que sa résidence est à Madrid depuis le 4 juin 1974. Le 24 avril 1998, le Conseil de M. Pey Casado demande au Ministère espagnol des affaires étrangères de vérifier le changement de domicile de M. Pey Casado en 1974. Une copie de cette demande est envoyée le 10 juillet 1998 aux autorités chiliennes par l'intermédiaire du Consulat espagnol à Santiago. La lettre est transmise le 24 juillet 1998 au registre chilien où un fonctionnaire public enregistre, le 4 août 1998, la renonciation par M. Pey Casado à sa nationalité chilienne et par conséquent son statut d'étranger. Ce fait est établi et non contesté mais la validité de cet enregistrement, et la compétence dudit fonctionnaire, seront contestés par la suite.[239]

293. Au vu ces faits, la question se pose de savoir si M. Pey Casado a valablement renoncé à sa nationalité chilienne en s'enregistrant et en ayant sa résidence à Madrid depuis juin 1974 (comme l'a confirmé le juge du registre espagnol), en informant, le 10 décembre 1996, le Département chilien de l'émigration de ce fait et du fait qu'il n'entendait pas se prévaloir de la Convention sur la double nationalité

294. En ce qui concerne la convention bilatérale sur la double nationalité, celle-ci prévoit expressément la possibilité pour les ressortissants des

---

[238] V. annexes C-40, C-14 et C-52.
[239] V. la transcription de l'audience du 16 janvier 2007, p. 7 (Me Di Rosa).

deux pays de conserver leur nationalité d'origine. La déclaration de M. Pey Casado de son changement de résidence vers l'Espagne a pour conséquence un changement de la loi qui lui est applicable mais ne le prive nullement de ses deux nationalités. Par ailleurs, la Convention ne prévoit rien quant aux conséquences du fait qu'un ressortissant d'un des deux Etats déclarerait ne pas vouloir se prévaloir de la Convention. Elle prévoit divers avantages spécifiques pour les doubles nationaux mais ne dit rien de ceux qui, après avoir acquis les deux nationalités et bénéficié de leurs avantages, ou de certains d'entre eux, ne désireraient plus s'en prévaloir.

295. La seule question est donc de savoir si la déclaration et les autres actes de M. Pey Casado équivalent à une renonciation à la nationalité chilienne. Or, ainsi qu'on l'a vu plus haut, toutes les questions relatives à cette nationalité relèvent en principe du droit chilien. Il y a donc lieu d'analyser le droit chilien applicable à ce sujet.

296. L'article 11 de la Constitution chilienne indique ce qui suit quant aux causes de perte de la nationalité.

> *1° Par naturalisation dans un pays étranger, sauf dans le cas de ces chiliens compris dans les n°1°, 2° et 3° de l'article antérieur qui auraient obtenu une autre nationalité sans renoncer à leur nationalité chilienne et en accord avec ce établi dans le numéro 4° du même article.*
>
> *La cause de perte de nationalité chilienne signalée précédemment n'aura pas d'effet sur les chiliens qui, en vertu des dispositions constitutionnelles, légales ou administratives de l'Etat sur le territoire duquel ils résident, adoptent la nationalité étrangère comme condition de leur permanence dans celui-ci ou d'égalité juridique dans l'exercice des droits civils avec les ressortissants du pays respectif ;*
>
> *2° Par décret suprême, en cas de prestation de services au cours d'une guerre extérieure aux ennemis du Chili ou à leurs alliés.*
>
> *3° Par sentence judiciaire condamnatoire pour délits contre la dignité de la patrie ou les intérêts essentiels et permanents de l'Etat, ainsi considérés par loi approuvée avec quorum qualifié. Dans ces procès, les faits s'apprécieront toujours en conscience ;*
>
> *4° Par annulation de la carte de naturalisation, et*
>
> *5° Par loi qui révoque la naturalisation concédée par faveur.*

297. La Constitution chilienne ne prévoit donc pas expressément la renonciation comme une cause de perte de la nationalité. La question

a été longuement débattue entre les parties au cours de la procédure, de savoir si l'énumération dans la Constitution du Chili des causes de perte de la nationalité était ou non limitative ou exhaustive, la défenderesse donnant une réponse affirmative, le demandeur répondant, lui, par la négative.

a) Position des parties

298. Les demanderesses ont soutenu, à titre subsidiaire à leur position principale selon laquelle M. Pey Casado aurait été privé de la nationalité chilienne en 1973, que M. Pey Casado « *avait renoncé formellement à la* nationalité *chilienne, laquelle, dans son cas, est une prérogative attachée au bénéfice du Traité bilatéral entre l'Espagne et le Chili du 24 mai 1958* ».[240] D'après les demanderesses, cette renonciation à la nationalité chilienne aurait pris effet à la date de la déclaration de M. Pey Casado, le 10 décembre 1996.[241]

299. Selon les demanderesses, une renonciation volontaire à la nationalité chilienne serait permise par la Constitution chilienne, bien qu'elle ne soit pas énumérée expressément comme cause de perte de nationalité dans l'article 11.[242] Le Tribunal arbitral ne devrait pas s'arrêter aux motifs de perte de nationalité prévus par l'article 11 de la constitution chilienne pour décider de la validité d'une renonciation de la nationalité d'après le droit chilien, mais il devrait analyser d'autres sources de droit chilien, comme la Convention bilatérale sur la double nationalité qui prévoit, en son article 6, des actes concernant la perte et la récupération de la nationalité qui ne seraient pas inclus dans la constitution.[243]

---

[240] Mémoire des demanderesses du 17 mars 1999, p. 26 ; exposé complémentaire sur la compétence du Tribunal arbitral du 11 septembre 2002, pp. 127 et ss ; transcription de l'audience du 15 janvier 2007, pp. 70 et ss (Me Garcés). V. aussi consultation juridique du Professeur Fernando M. Mariño, soumis au soutien de la réplique des demanderesses au contre-mémoire de la défenderesse, du 23 février 2003.

[241] V. réponse au mémoire soutenant l'incompétence soumis par la défenderesse, du 18 septembre 1999, pp. 61-62 ; exposé complémentaire sur la compétence du Tribunal arbitral du 11 septembre 2002, pp. 134 et ss ; transcription de l'audience du 15 janvier 2007, p. 70, paras. 37-38 (Me Garcés). V. aussi la consultation juridique de M. Victor Araya, soumise par les demanderesses au soutien de la réplique des demanderesses au contre-mémoire de la défenderesse, du 23 février 2003, pp. 14 et ss.

[242] Transcription de l'audience du 15 janvier 2007, pp. 75 et ss (Me Garcés). Les demanderesses prétendent qu'une interprétation contraire résulterait en une solution discriminatoire.

[243] Réponse au mémoire soutenant l'incompétence soumis par la défenderesse, du 18 septembre 1999, pp. 69-70 ; transcription de l'audience du 15 janvier 2007, p. 72 (Me Garcés).

300. En outre, les demanderesses ont soutenu que cette solution trouverait appui dans les règles du droit international, qui admettraient la renonciation volontaire de la nationalité.[244]

301. Les demanderesses se sont également fondées sur le cas de M. Witker, arbitre initialement désigné par le Chili dans le présent litige, et qui (selon les déclarations répétées de ce Gouvernement au CIRDI en date du 20 août 1998 et du 21 octobre 1998) a « *renoncé préalablement* » à sa nationalité d'origine - chilienne - pour obtenir la nationalité mexicaine « *en conformité avec la Constitution politique de la République du Chili* ».[245]

302. De son côté, la défenderesse a longuement soutenu l'impossibilité ou l'illégalité, en droit chilien, d'une renonciation volontaire à la nationalité chilienne,[246] principalement au motif que les causes de perte de la nationalité chilienne prévues par l'article 11 de la constitution chilienne n'incluent pas le cas de la renonciation volontaire de la nationalité[247] et que cette disposition devrait être interprétée de manière stricte.[248]

303. Lors de l'audience du 15 janvier 2007, le Tribunal arbitral a entendu l'avis du Professeur Cea, Président de la Cour constitutionnelle du

---

[244] V. réponse au mémoire soutenant l'incompétence soumis par la défenderesse, du 18 septembre 1999, pp. 65-66 ; réplique à la réponse soumise par la République du Chili au contre-mémoire réfutant le déclinatoire de compétence, du 7 février 2000, pp. 12-13.

[245] V. par exemple, contre-mémoire de la défenderesse du 3 février 2003, pp. 245 et ss ; transcription de l'audience du 15 janvier 2007, pp. 76-77 (Me Garces).

[246] Mémoire d'incompétence de la défenderesse du 20 juillet 1999, pp. 21, 36-38 ; mémoire en réplique sur l'incompétence du 27 décembre 1999, pp. 39-40 ; transcription de l'audience du 15 janvier 2007, pp. 33 et ss (Me Di Rosa). V. aussi l'avis de droit du Professeur Pierre-Marie Dupuy, soumis au soutien du contre-mémoire de la défenderesse du 3 février 2003, pp. 22-25 ; l'avis de droit du Professeur Humberto Nogueira Alcalá, soumis au soutien du contre-mémoire de la défenderesse du 3 février 2003, pp. 3-7.

[247] V. mémoire d'incompétence de la défenderesse, du 20 juillet 1999, p. 29 : « Comme il est possible d'observer, la renonciation n'est pas considérée dans les causes de perte de la nationalité chilienne, que contemplent la perte de la nationalité par nationalisation en pays étranger, dans une telle éventualité si la personne involucrée a renoncé à la nationalité chilienne, elle ne perd pas celle-ci du fait de la renonciation, sinon pour avoir obtenu une autre nationalité. »

[248] Le Professeur Cea a expliqué lors de l'audience du 15 janvier 2007 que « tous les motifs de perte de la nationalité chilienne figuraient dans l'article 11 de la Constitution et étaient les cinq motifs suivants. Il s'agissait d'une liste complète ; liste à laquelle on ne pouvait rien changer et qu'on ne pouvait interpréter autrement que dans sa présentation. » (transcription de l'audience du 15 janvier 2007, p. 19).

Chili, sur la question, et notamment sur la récente réforme constitutionnelle au Chili en août 2005 qui aurait porté justement sur la question de la renonciation volontaire de la nationalité.[249] Notamment, l'article V a) de la Loi 20.050 remplacerait le « *I* » de l'article 12 de la Constitution et dispose que :

> « *La nationalité chilienne aujourd'hui se perd de façon impérative pour des raisons qu'il est impossible d'éluder, raisons qui sont obligatoires et, tout d'abord, par la renonciation volontaire manifestée devant les autorités chiliennes compétentes.* »[250]

304. Selon le Professeur Cea, la possibilité de renoncer à la nationalité chilienne n'existait pas avant cette réforme et ce n'était que la loi 20.050 de la réforme constitutionnelle qui l'aurait introduit dans l'ordre juridique chilien. Il a expliqué au Tribunal arbitral que :

> « *La réforme de l'année 2005 a introduit, dans la Constitution chilienne, un nouveau motif de perte de nationalité, qui n'existait pas auparavant dans notre ordre juridique. Il n'y avait aucun de ces motifs invoqués dans la Constitution antérieure, donc moins encore dans les lois et les règlements, vous le comprendrez. Bien sûr, les ressortissants ne pouvaient donc pas, de façon volontaire, rejeter la nationalité.* »[251]

305. Le Professeur Cea précisait que, notamment, l'article 11 de la Constitution en vigueur avant la réforme de 2005 ne pouvait pas être interprété de façon à admettre une renonciation volontaire de la nationalité chilienne, mais qu'il avait un caractère « *énumératif, ferme, complet* ».[252]

306. En faveur de la conclusion que la renonciation volontaire ne constituait pas un motif de perte de la nationalité chilienne avant 2005, la défenderesse a invoqué certaines décisions de tribunaux chiliens, ainsi que la doctrine chilienne sur la question. En ce qui concerne la jurisprudence, la défenderesse a notamment fait référence a la décision de la Cour d'Appel de Valpareiso de mai 2001,

---

[249]   Transcription de l'audience du 15 janvier 2007, pp. 18 et ss (Professeur Cea).
[250]   Transcription de l'audience du 15 janvier 2007, p. 19.
[251]   Transcription de l'audience du 15 janvier 2007, p. 25, para. 28. V. aussi la transcription de l'audience du 16 janvier 2007, pp. 15 et ss (Me Fernandez).
[252]   Transcription de l'audience du 15 janvier 2007, p. 25.

maintenue par la Cour suprême la même année, qui aurait « *rejeté la possibilité de renonciation pure et simple de la nationalité* ».[253]

b)   Conclusions du Tribunal

307.   De l'avis du Tribunal arbitral, la défenderesse n'est pas parvenue à apporter une démonstration convaincante de l'impossibilité ou l'illégalité, en droit chilien, d'une renonciation volontaire à la nationalité chilienne, en l'absence de textes précis et de jurisprudence pertinente. Ainsi, quant aux quelques décisions des tribunaux chiliens en la matière qui ont été évoquées, aucune d'entre elles ne concerne une situation identique à celle du présent litige, si bien qu'il est difficile ou même impossible d'y trouver la preuve du bien fondé de l'une ou l'autre des thèses contraires qui ont été développées sur la renonciation à la nationalité. Il en est ainsi notamment, sans qu'il soit besoin d'une analyse de détail, de la décision *Vásquez Valencia* du 31 octobre 1989[254] ou de la décision *Turbay* du 25 juillet 1988.[255]

308.   Le texte même de l'article 11 de la Constitution chilienne est ambigu sur la question et ne permet nullement d'affirmer ou de postuler un prétendu caractère limitatif des cas énumérés de perte de la nationalité.[256] Ceci étant, le Tribunal arbitral ne voit pas de justification pour une interprétation stricte du droit chilien de manière à interdire une renonciation volontaire à la nationalité chilienne dans le cas d'espèce.

309.   Ce résultat s'applique *a fortiori* en cas de double nationalité, puisque la renonciation à l'une des nationalités ne conduit pas alors à une situation d'apatridie. En droit chilien, la renonciation volontaire n'est pas autorisée ou valable si elle doit entraîner une situation d'apatridie, ainsi que l'a souligné très clairement le Président de la Cour constitutionnelle, le Professeur Cea, devant le Tribunal arbitral.[257] Si tel n'est pas le cas, la renonciation volontaire est donc

---

253   Transcription de l'audience du 15 janvier 2007, p. 24, para. 16-17 (Professeur Cea).

254   Annexe C-92.

255   Annexe C-147 – v. aussi annexe C-28.

256   On remarquera également à ce propos que, en droit constitutionnel comparé, le texte des constitutions est le plus souvent conçu en termes programmatiques ou de principes généraux - que l'interprétation ultérieure et la pratique, au gré de l'évolution politique, ont été appelées à compléter et préciser – si bien que le caractère limitatif ou exhaustif d'un texte constitutionnel précité peut difficilement être présumé.

257   Lors de l'audience du 15 janvier 2007, le Professeur Cea a notamment expliqué que « une personne ne perd sa nationalité que si, de façon simultanée, elle en acquiert une autre et c'est normal. Sauf, bien sûr, les exceptions qui figurent dans le texte pertinent de la Constitution. En 2002, il n'y avait pas de renonciation pure et simple de la nationalité et il est évident

permise par la Constitution et cela, en bonne logique, non seulement si la renonciation doit être <u>suivie</u> de l'acquisition d'une autre nationalité, mais aussi lorsque cette autre nationalité est <u>déjà</u> acquise, comme dans le cas de la double nationalité.

310. La défenderesse a insisté sur le fait qu'une condition essentielle permettant dans le droit chilien la renonciation volontaire à la nationalité était qu'elle ne résulte pas en une apatridie (ainsi dans l'exemple précité de l'arbitre Witker, devenu mexicain). De même, dans un jugement chilien qui a été souvent cité dans le débat, dans une affaire *Castillón*, la renonciation a été liée à, ou conditionnée par, l'acquisition par l'intéressé de la nationalité du Nicaragua.[258]

311. La *ratio legis* comme la simple cohérence et une logique élémentaire imposent cette conclusion. Rien n'a été établi, aucun texte légal ni aucune décision n'ont été produits ni aucun argument allégué qui soit susceptible de justifier, de l'avis du Tribunal arbitral, un régime qui, en matière de renonciation volontaire, serait discriminatoire : permissif en cas d'acquisition d'une autre nationalité, prohibitif en cas d'autre nationalité déjà acquise, soit de double nationalité. Et pareille différence de traitement serait particulièrement difficile à admettre, présumer ou imaginer dans le cas de deux Etats unis par les liens que souligne leur Convention bilatérale sur la double nationalité.[259] De plus, de l'avis du Tribunal arbitral, l'argument de la défenderesse qu'un double national devrait, afin de valablement renoncer à la nationalité chilienne, d'abord acquérir une troisième nationalité,[260] semble peu logique ou convaincante.

312. Le Tribunal arbitral est de l'avis que la réforme de la Constitution chilienne en 2005 ne change rien en ce qui concerne la renonciation volontaire à la nationalité : il a toujours été possible de renoncer à la nationalité chilienne et le nouvel article 11 de la Constitution ne fait

---

[258] que si cela avait été le cas, des situations d'apatridie seraient survenues et des demandes auraient pu être formulées de façon peu légitime. » (transcription de l'audience du 15 janvier 2007, p. 21). V. aussi la transcription de l'audience du 16 janvier 2007, p. 17 (Me Fernandez).
V. la transcription de l'audience du 15 janvier 2007, p. 81 (question du Président).

[259] Le Tribunal arbitral ne peut pas suivre l'argument de la défenderesse sur la base de la Convention hispano-chilienne sur la double nationalité que « *[l]a double nationalité est un privilège une fois invoquée en conformité avec la Convention. Par sa nature de lien juridique et politique on ne peut y renoncer, car une fois exercé le droit il n'est plus question de l'intérêt particulier de celui qui l'a invoqué, sinon aussi celui de l'Etat qui l'a concédée.* » Mémoire d'incompétence de la défenderesse du 20 juillet 1999, p. 30.

[260] V. la transcription de l'audience du 16 janvier 2007, pp. 56-58 (Me Fernandez).

que confirmer et préciser cette possibilité. De manière générale, le Tribunal arbitral ne peut que suivre l'argument des demanderesses que « *l'inscription d'une règle dans la Constitution ne signifie pas que cette règle n'existait pas avant, bien au contraire* ».[261] Comme l'ont soutenu les demanderesses,[262] la réforme de l'article 11 de la Constitution a simplement ajouté une condition pour une renonciation valable à la nationalité chilienne, notamment celle que la renonciation soit notifiée auprès de l'autorité chilienne compétente.

313. Dans ce contexte, le Tribunal arbitral rappellera également les dispositions concernant la renonciation d'une nationalité contenues dans la Convention inter-américaine des droits de l'Homme. Bien que ces règles ne soient pas directement applicables dans le cas d'espèce,[263] il convient néanmoins de souligner – comme les demanderesses l'ont fait dans cette procédure[264] – que l'article 20.3 de cette Convention en disposant que « *nul ne peut être privé du droit de changer de nationalité* »,, s'oppose à ce qu'un Etat puisse interdire la renonciation à une nationalité.[265] Une règle similaire est incluse, comme l'ont rappelé les demanderesses,[266] à l'article 1 de la Convention panaméricaine de Rio de Janeiro de 1906, toujours en vigueur au Chili, qui dispose qu'une personne de double nationalité qui rétablit sa résidence dans son pays d'origine et l'y maintient durant plus de deux ans, abandonne la deuxième nationalité acquise par naturalisation si elle exprime cet abandon.[267]

---

[261] Transcription de l'audience du 15 janvier 2007, p. 77 (Me Garcés).

[262] Transcription de l'audience du 15 janvier 2007, pp. 77-78 (Me Garcés).

[263] La Convention a été ratifiée par le Chili le 21 août 1990, mais elle ne s'applique évidemment pas directement aux ressortissants espagnols. V. aussi l'argumentation de la défenderesse, mémoire en réplique sur l'incompétence, du 27 décembre 1999, p. 41.

[264] Transcription de l'audience du 15 janvier 2007, p. 73- 74 (Me Garcés).

[265] Le Tribunal arbitral ne peut pas suivre l'argument de la défenderesse que le droit de changer la nationalité n'inclut pas le droit de renoncer à la nationalité (v., par exemple, la transcription de l'audience du 16 janvier 2007, p. 55 (Me Fernandez)), au moins dans les cas où la renonciation ne mène pas à l'apatridie de la partie renonçant.

[266] V. réponse au mémoire soutenant l'incompétence soumis par la défenderesse, du 18 septembre 1999, pp. 69-70 ; transcription de l'audience du 15 janvier 2007, p. 79 (Me Garcés).

[267] Annexe C-27. L'article 1 stipule : « Si un citoyen natif de l'un des pays signataires de la Convention et naturalisé dans un autre d'entre eux, rétablissait sa résidence dans son pays d'origine, sans intention de retourner dans celui où il aurait été naturalisé, il sera considéré qu'il reprend sa citoyenneté d'origine, et qu'il renonce à la citoyenneté acquise par ladite naturalisation. […] »

314. De l'avis du Tribunal arbitral, malgré l'opinion contraire de certains auteurs chiliens qui interprètent la décision de la Cour d'Appel de Valparaiso dans un sens opposé, il semble qu'une des raisons pour lesquelles le législateur chilien a expressément inclus le droit de changer de nationalité est de mettre la Constitution chilienne en conformité avec la Convention inter-américaine des droits de l'Homme et d'autres conventions internationales.[268]

315. Au fond, la réforme ne fait que confirmer ce qui a toujours été l'esprit du droit chilien, même avant la révision de la Constitution, à savoir de suivre la Convention inter-américaine des droits de l'Homme et permettre la renonciation volontaire à la nationalité chilienne.

316. La réforme de 2005 de l'article 11 de la Constitution chilienne n'a fait qu'ajouter l'exigence formelle que, pour pouvoir valablement renoncer à la nationalité chilienne, la partie renonçante doit présenter cette renonciation à un fonctionnaire chilien compétent, exigence qui n'existait pas auparavant.[269]

317. On rappellera que, le 16 septembre 1997, M. Pey Casado a procédé expressément auprès du Consulat d'Espagne à Mendoza (Argentine) à une déclaration de renonciation « *au cas où serait requise par l'Administration chilienne une renonciation formelle* ». Le 4 août 1998, M. Pey Casado a été en conséquence inscrit comme étranger dans le Registre chilien de l'état civil - un acte officiel impliquant la reconnaissance de la renonciation par l'Etat du Chili.[270]

---

[268] La défenderesse a confirmé l'impact qu'avaient ces conventions internationales dans le contexte de la réforme constitutionnelle au Chili, sans pour autant être d'accord avec la conclusion que ceci prouverait la validité d'une renonciation de la nationalité chilienne. V. la transcription de l'audience du 16 janvier 2007, p. 55 (Me Fernandez) : « [...] *j'ajoute que le président avait aussi pensé à d'autres traités internationaux auxquels le Chili avait souscrit. En réalité, il a voulu mettre à jour notre Constitution par rapport à ces traités internationaux. Parmi ceux-ci, on trouvait la Convention interaméricaine des droits de l'Homme ou Convention de San-Jose du Costa Rica.* »

[269] V. la plaidoirie des demanderesses, transcription de l'audience du 16 janvier 2007, p. 56 (Me Garcés).

[270] Cette reconnaissance formelle par un officier public du statut d'étranger (non-chilien) de M. Pey Casado (cf. le décret no. 597 du 14 juin 1984 – règlement concernant les étrangers) a paru gêner le Ministère chilien de l'intérieur qui, le 23 juin 1999 - soit pendant le cours de la présente procédure arbitrale - a entrepris des démarches tendant à faire annuler l'inscription, au motif que l'officier d'état civil n'aurait pas été compétent pour y procéder. Comme d'autres démarches ou manipulations auxquelles des parties à l'arbitrage croient devoir ou pouvoir recourir *pendente lite* pour infléchir le cours de la procédure ou influencer le Tribunal arbitral (v., par

338

318. Il n'est pourtant pas certain qu'une reconnaissance par l'Etat défendeur, si significative soit-elle, soit indispensable à sa prise en considération par le Tribunal arbitral. Ce dernier doit certes se fonder d'abord sur le droit public chilien, applicable à la question de nationalité, et c'est précisément ce qu'il a fait, à la lumière des allégations et preuves des parties, pour conclure que ce droit permettait la renonciation volontaire, sauf si une situation d'apatridie devait en résulter.

319. Indépendamment de ce fait, il y a lieu de rappeler que si, en droit international, le droit applicable à la nationalité d'un Etat donné est en principe le droit de cet Etat, le juge ou l'arbitre international détient cependant le pouvoir d'en apprécier le contenu et les effets, comme indiqué par exemple dans la sentence rendue par un Tribunal CIRDI dans l'affaire *Soufraki c. Emirats Arabes Unis* du 7 juillet 2004.[271] Dans la sentence *Soufraki*, le Tribunal arbitral, appelé à trancher comme en l'espèce la question de sa compétence au regard de la nationalité du demandeur, après avoir rappelé que, en droit international, la nationalité relevait du domaine réservé et que la législation de chaque Etat décidait de son acquisition ou de sa perte, a déclaré ce qui suit :

> « *...when, in international arbitral or judicial proceedings, the nationality of a person is challenged, the international tribunal is competent to pass upon that challenge. It will accord great weight to the nationality law of the State in question and to the interpretation and application of that law by its authorities. But it will in the end decide for itself whether, on the facts and law before it, the person whose nationality is at issue was not a national of the State in question and when, and what follows from that finding. Where, as in the instant case, the jurisdiction of the international tribunal turns on an issue of nationality, the international tribunal is empowered, indeed bound, to decide that issue.* »[272]

---

exemple, la Décision n°43 du 28 avril 2000, ou les tentatives faites pour obtenir de Madrid une interprétation favorable et commune d'un traité bilatéral), pareils actes sont de nature à susciter inévitablement le scepticisme des arbitres.

[271] Une demande d'annulation de la décision a été rejetée à la majorité par le Comité *ad hoc* saisi de la question par une décision du 5 juin 2007 (v. *Soufraki c. Emirats arabes unis*, affaire CIRDI n° ARB/02/7, décision du Comité *ad hoc* sur la demande d'annulation de M. Soufraki, 5 juin 2007, para. 139).

[272] *Idem*, para. 55.

320. Ce pouvoir d'appréciation est en outre conforme à l'esprit de la Convention CIRDI et de son article 25(2)(a). Selon le commentaire de Christoph Schreuer, un investisseur ayant une double nationalité ne peut avoir accès au système CIRDI qu'à la condition de renoncer à la nationalité de l'Etat défendeur avant de consentir à la juridiction du CIRDI, la validité de la renonciation étant appréciée en principe au regard de la loi nationale dudit Etat, étant admis toutefois qu'un tribunal international n'est pas lié dans tous les cas par la loi nationale en cause.[273] A propos de l'hypothèse dans laquelle l'Etat d'accueil voudrait imposer sa nationalité à l'investisseur, le Professeur Schreuer écrit notamment :

> « *During the Convention's preparatory work, it was generally acknowledged that nationality would be determined by reference to the law of the State whose nationality is claimed, subject, where appropriate, to the applicable rules of international law (History, vol. II, page 67, 286, 321, 448, 580, 705, 839). In particular, it was pointed out that the Commission or Tribunal would have to deal appropriately with cases where a host State <u>imposed</u> its nationality upon an investor* »[274] (souligné par nous)

---

[273] « [...] an international tribunal is not bound by the national law in question under all circumstances. Situations where nationality provisions of national law may be disregarded include cases of effective nationality lacking a genuine link between the State and the individual [...] » Christoph H. Schreuer, The ICSID Convention: a Commentary, 2001, p. 272, para. 446. Cf. la sentence CIRDI déjà citée, dans l'affaire Soufraki.

[274] *Op. cit.*, p. 267 para. 430. Les parties demanderessses ont rappelé dans ce contexte, à raison, que les rédacteurs de la Convention CIRDI avaient conclu qu'un tribunal arbitral ne devait pas permettre qu'un Etat impose sa nationalité pour échapper au devoir de se soumettre au CIRDI. V. mémoire des demanderesses du 17 mars 1999, p. 26, faisant référence à : History, vol II, pp. 582, 658, 705, 868, 874, 876-877. V. aussi réponse au mémoire soutenant l'incompétence soumis par la défenderesse, du 18 septembre 1999, pp. 66 et ss ; exposé complémentaire sur la compétence du Tribunal arbitral du 11 septembre 2002, p. 96. Voir aussi les observations du Tribunal arbitral dans sa Décision du 8 mai 2002, pp. 38-39. Le Tribunal arbitral note l'avis différent du Professeur Dupuy qui, dans son avis de droit, écrit : « *Il apparaît en effet évident que les travaux préparatoires se préoccupaient du scénario où l'Etat hôte impose sa nationalité à l'investisseur étranger. Les travaux préparatoires ne traitaient pas de la situation observée dans la présente affaire, qui est à l'inverse* [sic]*, puisqu'on y rencontre le ressortissant du pays hôte de l'investissement cherchant à se débarrasser de sa nationalité afin de s'ouvrir le recours à un arbitrage international autrement inaccessible.* » (Avis de droit du Professeur Pierre-Marie Dupuy, soumis au soutien du contre-mémoire de la défenderesse du 3 février 2003, p. 29 ; v.

340

321. Le passage suivant du même auteur est particulièrement significatif ou pertinent. Il démontre que les rédacteurs de la Convention CIRDI ont été conscients du risque qu'un Etat d'accueil utilise son droit interne de la nationalité de manière intéressée ou abusive :

> « *The host State may not impose its nationality on a foreign investor for the purpose of withdrawing its consent. During the Convention's drafting the problem of compulsory granting of nationality was discussed and the opinion was expressed that this would not be a permissible way for a State to evade its obligation to submit a dispute to the Centre (History, vol. II, page 658, 705, 876). But it was decided that this question could be left to the decision of the Conciliation Commission or Arbitral Tribunal.* »[275]

322. Il revient donc au Tribunal arbitral d'apprécier le contenu et les effets du droit chilien sur la nationalité et de l'appliquer au cas d'espèce. Ce faisant, le Tribunal est conduit à conclure de ce qui précède la validité d'une renonciation volontaire à la nationalité chilienne lorsque la partie renonçant est double nationale, renonciation dont la réalité a été prouvée par la première partie demanderesse.

323. Aussi pour les raisons indiquées ci-dessus, le Tribunal arbitral estime n'être pas en mesure d'admettre l'exception d'incompétence fondée sur l'allégation selon laquelle la première partie demanderesse possèderait, à la date pertinente, la nationalité chilienne.

C. La condition de consentement

324. Le consentement de l'Etat à l'arbitrage étant donné par l'API, il convient de vérifier si les conditions d'application de l'API sont réunies.

325. Les parties ont longuement débattu des points suivants : la condition d'investissement au sens de l'API, la condition de nationalité au sens de l'API, la compétence *ratione temporis* au sens de l'API et l'exercice de l'option irrévocable (*fork in the road*) posée par l'API. Le Tribunal examinera chacun de ces points tour à tour.

---

aussi contre-mémoire de la défenderesse du 3 février 2003, pp. 287-288). Le Tribunal arbitral estime au contraire qu'une interdiction de renoncer à une nationalité (dans un cas où une telle renonciation ne mènerait pas à l'apatridie) équivaut à l'imposition par l'Etat de sa nationalité.

[275] Christoph H. Schreuer, *The ICSID Convention : a Commentary*, 2001, p. 272, para. 447.

1. La condition d'investissement au sens de l'API

326. Avant d'exposer son analyse et ses conclusions sur la condition d'investissement au sens de l'API, le Tribunal rappellera la position des parties sur ce sujet.

    a)   Position des parties

    i.   *Position de la défenderesse*

327. La défenderesse estime que l'opération réalisée par M. Pey Casado ne satisfait aucune des conditions relatives à l'investissement posées par l'API, et plus particulièrement l'article 1(2), l'article 2(2) et le préambule du traité, évoqué en tant que moyen d'interprétation des dispositions du traité.

328. Selon l'Etat défendeur, qui s'appuie à cet effet sur la consultation du Professeur Dolzer, « pour qu'un investissement soit protégé par l'APPI Chili-Espagne, le texte de l'APPI Chili-Espagne exige que l'investissement respecte, entre autres, les trois conditions requises suivantes : (1) les actifs qui constituent l'investissement doivent avoir été 'acquis conformément à la législation du pays récepteur de l'investissement' ; (2) l'investissement doit comporter un transfert de capital vers l'État 'récepteur de l'investissement' et (3) l'investissement doit être qualifié d'investissement d'un investisseur de l'une des Parties contractantes ' dans le territoire de l'autre ' ».[276]

329. La première condition, posée par l'article 1(2) de l'API, imposerait le respect de la législation spéciale qui se rapporte aux investissements étrangers, ce que confirmerait l'article 2(2) de l'API en exigeant que l'opération litigieuse constitue un « *investissement étranger* » en vertu de la réglementation chilienne en vigueur en 1972. La seconde condition impliquerait l'existence d'un transfert de capitaux vers l'intérieur de l'Etat récepteur en provenance de l'extérieur.[277] Le procès-verbal des réunions techniques qui ont eu lieu entre les représentants du Chili et de l'Espagne les 29, 30 septembre et le 1er octobre 1998 corroborerait cette analyse en indiquant qu' « *[a]u paragraphe 3 du préambule, l'expression ' investissements ' se réfère au transfert de capitaux vers le pays bénéficiaire de l'investissement, c'est-à-dire que cela suppose une entrée d'actifs sur le territoire de la Partie contractante bénéficiaire de l'investissement* ».[278] La défenderesse ajoute que cette condition

---

[276] Contre-mémoire de la défenderesse du 3 février 2003, pp. 152-153 et consultation du Professeur Dolzer, para. 41.

[277] V. contre-mémoire de la défenderesse du 3 février 2003, pp. 150-151. La défenderesse invoque le préambule de l'API ainsi que les articles 1(2) et 6 à l'appui de son analyse.

[278] V. contre-mémoire de la défenderesse du 3 février 2003, p. 153.

serait fréquemment insérée dans les API auquel le Chili est partie et souvent utilisée comme critère de définition de la notion d'investissement étranger. Enfin, la troisième condition reviendrait simplement à exiger que l'investissement soit un investissement étranger.

330. Etant donné que les fonds transférés par M. Pey Casado ne sont jamais entrés au Chili, il ne pourrait être considéré comme un transfert de capitaux vers l'Etat récepteur de l'investissement. En outre, comme il n'a pas été établi que les fonds ont été transférés par un investisseur de l'autre partie contractante afin d'acheter les actions d'une société chilienne, le prétendu investissement de M. Pey Casado n'aurait pas la qualité d'un investissement d'un investisseur de l'une des parties contractantes « *sur le territoire de l'autre* ».[279]

331. L'argument des demanderesses selon lequel il n'existerait pas au Chili de définition de la notion d'investissement étranger serait inexact. De même, il serait tout aussi erroné d'affirmer, comme le font les demanderesses, que la réglementation qui régissait les investissements étrangers au Chili en 1972 était facultative et que, par voie de conséquence, il pouvait exister des investissements étrangers non enregistrés comme tels auprès des autorités compétentes.

332. Pour la défenderesse, il ne suffit pas qu'un investissement puisse être qualifié d'étranger « *d'une façon ou d'une autre* ». En application des articles 1(2) et 2(2) de l'API, un investissement en 1972 aurait dû être approuvé et enregistré comme investissement étranger conformément à la réglementation pertinente, en l'occurrence la réglementation issue de la Décision n°24 de la Commission de l'Accord de Carthagène (ci-après « *Décision n°24* »), entrée en vigueur au Chili avec les décrets n°482 et 488 de 1971.[280] Les investissements qui, comme celui de M. Pey Casado, n'auraient pas été effectués conformément à la législation sur l'approbation des investissements étrangers, alors en vigueur au Chili, se trouveraient hors du champ d'application de l'API.

333. Selon la défenderesse, la Décision n°24 serait entrée en vigueur au Chili par le décret suprême n°482 en date du 25 juin 1971. Bien que la *Contraloría General de la República*[281] ait annulé ce décret, le président de la République a adopté le décret d'insistance n°488 en date du 29 juin 1971, en vertu d'un pouvoir accordé à l'époque au

---

[279] Id, p. 156.

[280] V. contre-mémoire de la défenderesse du 3 février 2003, p. 165.

[281] La défenderesse définit la Contraloría comme « *l'organisme chargé, selon la Constitution politique, de veiller à la légalité des actes de l'Administration* » (v. contre-mémoire de la défenderesse du 3 février 2003, p. 165).

président de la République et lui permettant de passer outre l'opposition de la *Contraloría*, ce que les demanderesses passeraient sous silence dans leur argumentation. Ce second décret, reprenant le décret n°482, aurait fait entrer en vigueur le 30 juin 1971 le régime commun de traitement des capitaux étrangers et des marques, brevets, licences et privilèges, approuvé par la Décision n°24. Cette dernière aurait ainsi été applicable depuis le 30 juin 1971 jusqu'au 13 juillet 1974 « *au moins* », date à laquelle la nouvelle réglementation mise en place par le décret-loi n°600 serait entrée en vigueur.

334. La défenderesse souligne que la date d'entrée en vigueur de la Décision n°24, par le biais des décrets n°482 et 488, a été confirmée par la presse chilienne, et de nombreux organismes tels que le Conseil de défense de l'Etat, le service des impôts internes, le gouvernement chilien, l'Assemblée de l'Accord de Carthagène et la Commission de l'Accord de Carthagène.

335. La Décision n°24 serait également entrée en vigueur sur le plan international le 13 juillet 1971, lorsque l'Equateur a notifié au Conseil de l'Accord de Carthagène la promulgation du décret d'incorporation de la Décision n°24. L'affirmation selon laquelle la Décision n°24 ne serait entrée en vigueur sur le plan international que le 15 septembre 1973 serait infondée. Le fait que la Cour suprême de Colombie ait annulé le décret d'incorporation de la Décision n°24 ne changerait rien au fait que l'Etat colombien avait rempli les formalités nécessaires à l'entrée en vigueur le 5 juillet 1971.

336. Le décret n°258 du 4 avril 1960 sur le statut de l'investisseur ne serait pas applicable, contrairement à ce que prétendent les demanderesses. L'article 2 du décret n°482 disposait en effet que « *les dispositions de toute nature contraires au régime établi à l'article premier du présent décret ou incompatibles avec celui-ci sont abrogées* »,[282] ce qui permettrait de conclure que « *tous les investissements réalisés en 1972 [...] auraient été régis principalement par la Décision N°24, et non par le Décret N°258* ».[283]

337. Or, selon la défenderesse, l'opération réalisée par M. Pey Casado en 1972 ne satisfait pas les conditions requises par la Décision n°24 pourtant applicable à l'époque.

338. L'investissement étranger direct étant défini comme « *les apports provenant de l'étranger appartenant à des personnes physiques ou des entreprises étrangères [...]* »,[284] M. Pey Casado n'aurait jamais

---

[282] V. contre-mémoire de la défenderesse du 3 février 2003, p. 172 et annexe 9 au rapport de M. Santa María.

[283] V. contre-mémoire de la défenderesse du 3 février 2003, p. 172.

[284] Article 1 de la Décision n°24.

pu effectuer un investissement étranger au sens de la Décision n°24 puisque l'intéressé était à l'époque un ressortissant chilien.[285] La prétention des demanderesses selon laquelle la Décision n°24 ne définirait pas les investissements étrangers serait démentie par le texte même de son article 1.

339. La défenderesse déduit également de cette disposition que la Décision n°24 exigeait un transfert de capitaux de l'étranger vers le territoire chilien. M. Pey Casado ayant réalisé des transferts de fonds en Europe et en dollars américains, le second critère posé par la Décision n°24 ne serait pas davantage satisfait.

340. Enfin, la Décision n°24 met en place un système d'autorisation préalable de l'investissement par l'organisme national compétent[286] et d'enregistrement obligatoire par ce même organisme.[287] Ces obligations seraient liées au plan de participation nationale prévue par la Décision n°24 dans le but d'atteindre « *une participation croissante du capital national dans les entreprises étrangères existantes ou qui venaient s'établir sur le territoire des pays membres* ».[288] La Décision n°24 comporterait également des interdictions spécifiques concernant notamment l'acquisition d'actions, de participations ou de droits de propriété d'investisseurs nationaux et l'investissement dans certains secteurs d'activité économique, tels que la presse, réservés aux entreprises nationales. Pour la défenderesse, c'est à tort que les demanderesses considèrent que le régime commun de traitement applicable aux capitaux étrangers comme un régime facultatif, ainsi que le montreraient de nombreuses dispositions de la Décision n°24.

341. La défenderesse résume l'ensemble des points que le Comité des investissements étrangers (« *organisme national compétent* » voulu

---

[285] V. contre-mémoire de la défenderesse du 3 février 2003, p. 174.

[286] La défenderesse souligne que l'article 2 de la Décision n°24 prévoyait notamment que « tout investisseur étranger qui souhaite investir dans l'un quelconque des pays membres devra présenter sa demande auprès de l'organisme national compétent, lequel, après évaluation, l'autorisera quand celui-ci correspond aux priorités de développement du pays récepteur » (v. contre-mémoire de la défenderesse du 3 février 2003, pp. 175-176).

[287] La défenderesse cite l'article 5 de la Décision n°24 en vertu duquel « tout investissement étranger direct fait l'objet d'un enregistrement auprès de l'organisme national compétent avec la convention déterminant les conditions de l'autorisation. Le montant des investissements est enregistré en monnaie librement convertible » (v. contre-mémoire de la défenderesse du 3 février 2003, p. 176).

[288] V. contre-mémoire de la défenderesse du 3 février 2003, p. 176 et annexe C-100 ou annexe 16 au rapport de M. Sainte Marie. La défenderesse indique que ce plan devait être développé dans la demande d'autorisation présenté par l'investisseur étranger.

par la Décision n°24) doit examiner avant d'autoriser et d'enregistrer un investissement étranger dans les termes suivants :

> « *une fois la demande d'investissement étranger présentée, le Comité des investissements étrangers devait examiner celle-ci et déterminer si l'investissement étranger proposé (i) envisageait les priorités de développement du pays ; (ii) prétendait effectuer une activité qui n'était pas considérée comme déjà convenablement pourvue par des entreprises existantes ; (iii) ne consistait pas en une acquisition d'actions, de participations ou de droits de propriété d'investisseurs nationaux, (iv) prévoyait un régime de participation nationale progressive ; (v) ne pénétrait pas des secteurs d'activité économique que les pays membres avaient réservé aux entreprises nationales, publiques ou privées , comme, par exemple, la propriété de quotidiens, magazines, périodiques, prévus à l'article 5 de la Loi 16.643 sur l'Abus de Publicité et (vi) ne contrevenait pas aux interdictions expresses d'investissement étranger prévues dans la Décision N°24 (dans certaines industries et/ou secteurs, comme les entreprises de transport interne, de publicité, d'émission de radio commerciales, de chaînes de télévision, de journaux, de magazines, etc.) ».[289]*

342. La défenderesse en conclut que « si M. Pey avait présenté en tant qu'étranger une demande pour l'autorisation d'un investissement étranger au Chili, consistant en l'acquisition d'actions de l'entreprise périodique chilienne CPP S.A., celle-ci aurait été rejetée in limine par le Comité des investissements étrangers » car contraire aux articles 3, 38 et 43 de la décision n°24.[290]

343. La défenderesse précise que le Comité des investissements étrangers, organisme chargé de mettre en œuvre les dispositions de la Décision n°24, aurait été désigné par le Président Allende, de façon transitoire, dans une lettre[291] transmise au Conseil de l'Accord de Carthagène.[292]

---

[289] Contre-mémoire de la défenderesse du 3 février 2003, p. 179.

[290] V. contre-mémoire de la défenderesse du 3 février 2003, p. 180.

[291] Cette lettre aurait été conservée par le successeur de l'Assemblée de l'Accord de Carthagène, le Secrétariat général de la Communauté andine (v. la transcription de l'audience du 6 mai 2003) et montrerait que l'organisme national compétent pour appliquer les dispositions de la Décision n°24 a bien été désigné.

[292] V. la transcription de l'audience du 6 mai 2003, pp. 364 et ss. La défenderesse rejette les accusations des demanderesses selon lesquelles elle

344.   La défenderesse soutient par ailleurs que la réglementation cambiaire (le décret n°1272), invoquée par les demanderesses, ne pourrait être applicable à l'opération réalisée par M. Pey Casado, cette réglementation n'étant applicable qu'en cas d'apport de devises au Chili.[293] En toute hypothèse, quand bien même l'opération litigieuse aurait entraîné un apport de devises au Chili, une autorisation expresse du Comité des investissements étrangers aurait été nécessaire, en application de l'article 2 de la Décision n°24. L'obligation d'obtenir cette autorisation serait sans rapport avec l'inscription à la Banque centrale du Chili prévue à l'article 14 de la loi sur le change international, contrairement à ce que prétendent les demanderesses.   Citant l'un des experts qu'elle a consulté, la défenderesse estime qu'« *à partir de l'entrée en vigueur au Chili de la Décision N°24, la Loi sur le change international (Décret 1272) est devenu [sic] inapplicable aux capitaux qui entraient au Chili afin de réaliser un investissement étranger* ».   Elle fait valoir que « *la Décision N°24 était d'application unique et exclusive [aux apports de devises]* » et « *exigeait une autorisation expresse du Comité des*

---

[293]   aurait produit de faux documents et renvoie aux annexes 6 et 7 à la réplique de la défenderesse du 4 avril 2003 pour établir l'authenticité des documents produits (v. également réplique de la défenderesse du 4 avril 2003, pp. 29-31).

V. contre-mémoire de la défenderesse du 3 février 2003, pp. 181-184.   La défenderesse soutient que les statuts du Fond Monétaire International sont sans aucun rapport direct avec la question de l'investissement étranger, contrairement à ce que prétendent les demanderesses (v. *ibid.*, pp. 181-182). Elle explique également que, en dépit du caractère facultatif des dispositions du décret n°258, « *avant la Décision n° 24, il était impossible pour un investisseur d'effectuer un investissement étranger au Chili sans se faire enregistrer soit au titre du décret n° 258, soit à celui du décret n° 1272* » (v. réplique de la défenderesse du 4 avril 2003, p. 36). En toute hypothèse, les demanderesses feraient erreur en invoquant le décret n°1272 car cette réglementation n'a pas un caractère facultatif (la défenderesse renvoie à l'article 3 du décret-loi) et « *ne traite pas des investissements étrangers mais des opérations de change internationales* » (la défenderesse a modifié son argumentation sur ce point : dans son mémoire en réplique sur l'incompétence, du 27 décembre 1999, elle déduisait de l'article 14 du décret n°1272 que « *le transfert de capitaux constituait une exigence fondamentale pour qu'existe un investissement étranger* » (p. 89)).   De l'avis de la défenderesse, « *il est évident que la prétendue acquisition des actions de la société CPP SA ne constituait pas une opération de change international* ». Le décret-loi n°1272 serait donc sans pertinence en l'espèce.   Enfin, si le Tribunal devait conclure que la Décision n°24 était entrée en vigueur en 1972, il lui serait inutile de se pencher sur les décrets-lois n°258 et 1272, la Décision   n°24   excluant   toute   autre   réglementation   en   matière d'investissements étrangers (v. réplique de la défenderesse du 4 avril 2003, p. 37).

investissements étrangers ».[294] Une opération conduite sans autorisation préalable aurait été illicite et sanctionnée par une amende. Jamais il n'aurait été établi par les demanderesses que M. Pey Casado avait obtenu l'autorisation imposée par la réglementation en vigueur.

345. Au total, la défenderesse considère que les demanderesses se trouvent face à un dilemme inextricable : « d'un côté, si en 1972 M. Pey était un étranger, il n'aurait pas pu effectuer le prétendu investissement, ou pour le moins il n'aurait pas pu le faire en conformité avec la législation en vigueur au Chili relative aux investissements étrangers, qui interdisait de tels investissements dans des journaux nationaux (comme l'était El Clarín) ; au contraire, s'il était chilien, nous ne nous trouverions pas non plus face à un investissement étranger, mais (par définition) face à un investissement national ».[295] Dans un cas comme dans l'autre, l'investissement de M. Pey Casado n'aurait pu avoir la qualité d'investissement étranger conformément à la législation chilienne en vigueur en 1972 et se trouverait exclu du champ d'application de l'API.

ii.   *Position des demanderesses*

346. Selon les demanderesses, l'opération réalisée par M. Pey Casado satisferait les conditions posées par l'API, et plus particulièrement ses articles 1(2) et 2(2), et devrait être considérée comme ayant la qualité d'investissement étranger au sens de la législation chilienne en vigueur en 1972.[296]

347. Les demanderesses soutiennent en outre que l'API ne prévoit aucune procédure d'autorisation ou d'enregistrement des investissements. Seul l'article 6 de l'API dispose que chaque partie à l'API accordera à l'autre la possibilité de transférer librement la rémunération reçue par les ressortissants d'un des Etats parties, qui auraient obtenu de l'autre partie les autorisations correspondantes. Aucune restriction semblable n'est prévue pour les transferts de capitaux étrangers.

348. Conformément à la réglementation du FMI, la notion de « *transfert de capitaux* » devrait être comprise comme l'exportation du capital investi vers l'extérieur de l'Etat d'accueil de l'investissement. Les directives de la Banque mondiale retiendraient une définition similaire. Selon les demanderesses, c'est en ce sens qu'il conviendrait d'interpréter les termes « *transferts de capitaux* »

---

[294]   V. contre-mémoire de la défenderesse du 3 février 2003, pp. 182-183.
[295]   *Id.*, pp. 185-186.
[296]   V. mémoire des demanderesses du 22 mars 1999, pp. 31 et ss et réplique à la réponse soumise par la République du Chili au contre-mémoire réfutant le déclinatoire de compétence, du 7 février 2000, p. 29 et ss.

employés dans l'API Espagne-Chili. La notion de « *transfert de capitaux* », d'abord utilisée dans le préambule du traité, serait précisée dans l'article 6 relatif à la possibilité de transférer librement les revenus des investissements réalisés sur le territoire de l'Etat d'accueil. La thèse de l'Etat défendeur, qui consiste à définir le transfert de capitaux, à partir du préambule de l'API, comme l'introduction de capitaux sur le territoire chilien, serait erronée. En toute hypothèse, les articles de l'API devraient prévaloir sur la formulation moins spécifique du préambule.

349. Les demanderesses soulignent également que lorsque l'Etat chilien a souhaité que des restrictions sur les transferts de capitaux soient mises en place, le texte du traité le prévoit expressément, comme dans le cas de l'API Malaisie-Chili. En l'espèce, l'API prévoit simplement à son article 4 un traitement des investisseurs espagnols égal à celui que reçoivent les chiliens. L'obtention du procès-verbal des réunions techniques de septembre-octobre 1998 ne saurait permettre à la défenderesse d'imposer *a posteriori* des limites à l'admission des capitaux étrangers que ne contenaient pas l'API, ce procès-verbal étant sans valeur et, de surcroît, interprété de façon incorrecte par l'Etat défendeur.

350. Les demanderesses estiment également que l'investissement effectué par M. Pey Casado satisfait les conditions relatives au respect de la législation chilienne en vigueur en 1972, prévues aux articles 1(2) et 2(2) de l'API.

351. Selon les demanderesses, il n'existerait en effet aucune définition de l'investissement étranger en droit chilien en 1972, ce qui laissait une grande liberté aux investisseurs. Le caractère « *étranger* » d'un investissement dépendait « *essentiellement de l'origine des devises et du paiement en devises étrangères* »[297] ; en aucun cas la nationalité de l'investisseur n'aurait été une condition nécessaire à l'existence d'un investissement étranger. Ni le décret-loi n°258 du 30 mars 1960, ni le décret-loi n°1272 du 7 septembre 1961, tous deux invoqués par la défenderesse, ne contiendraient de définition de l'investissement étranger. Aucun de ces deux textes n'introduirait de restriction fondée sur la nationalité de l'investisseur. Le décret-loi

---

[297] V. réplique à la réponse soumise par la République du Chili au contre-mémoire réfutant le déclinatoire de compétence, du 7 février 2000, p. 31. V. également réplique des demanderesses au contre-mémoire de la défenderesse, du 23 février 2003, p. 53. Il serait en revanche « *important* » que la contrepartie du capital investi se trouve au Chili (réponse au mémoire soutenant l'incompétence soumis par la défenderesse, du 18 septembre 1999, p. 117).

n°600 de 1974, postérieur à l'investissement de M. Pey Casado, ne définirait pas davantage l'investissement étranger.[298]

352. Aux yeux des demanderesses, la défenderesse chercherait à appliquer à l'investissement de M. Pey Casado des restrictions découlant de la réglementation cambiaire prévue dans les décrets-lois n°258 et 1272. Or, cette interprétation serait incompatible avec les statuts du FMI. Etant donné que le régime du contrôle des changes mis en place par le FMI n'est pas applicable à l'opération réalisée par M. Pey Casado et que l'objectif des décrets-lois n°258 et n°1272 consiste à organiser le contrôle des changes et le transfert de capitaux en conformité avec les statuts du FMI, la défenderesse ne pourrait prétendre que l'investissement effectué par M. Pey Casado aurait violé la réglementation cambiaire et plus particulièrement le décret-loi n°1272 et le décret-loi n°258.

353. En outre, les deux décrets-lois mettraient en place des régimes facultatifs offrant la possibilité à certaines catégories d'investisseurs de bénéficier de franchises relatives au régime de contrôle des changes. La lecture des statuts du FMI indiquerait par ailleurs que la notion de « *transferts de capitaux* » correspond à des « *sorties de capitaux* » de l'Etat d'accueil. Les demanderesses en concluent que les deux décrets-lois chiliens avaient pour objet de réglementer l'offre de franchises relatives au régime du contrôle des changes en vue du transfert des capitaux vers l'extérieur du Chili. Le texte de ces deux décrets-lois montrerait qu'il était facultatif de demander à en bénéficier précisément parce que cette réglementation ne concernait que les demandes d'octroi de franchises, en vue de l'exportation hors du Chili du capital investi dans l'espace économique chilien.

354. Dans le même but d'établir le caractère facultatif des régimes de franchises mis en place par les deux décrets-lois, les demanderesses insistent sur leurs dispositions et plus particulièrement sur l'article 1er du décret-loi n°258 et l'article 14 du décret-loi n°1272. Selon l'expert consulté par les demanderesses sur ce point, « *[l]a rédaction de cet Article [14], non obligatoire, laisse place pour l'investisseur [à l'alternative consistant] à opter ou non pour ladite inscription du capital. En procédant comme il l'a fait l'investisseur espagnol ne se rend pas bénéficiaire des franchises envisagées dans l'Article 14 cité*

---

[298] V. réponse au mémoire soutenant l'incompétence soumis par la défenderesse, du 18 septembre 1999, pp. 118-119. Les demanderesses citent un ouvrage de Roberto Mayorga selon lequel la principale source du droit de l'investissement étranger au Chili est le décret-loi n°600 et la notion d'investissement étranger n'est pas « *expressément conceptualisée dans la législation chilienne* », exception faite des API conclus par le Chili (annexe D10).

plus haut et dans le Décret ayant Force de Loi (DFL) numéro 258 du 30 mars 1960, autre instrument juridique optionnel dont bénéficiaient les Investissements Étrangers à cette époque-là ».[299] Les demanderesses soutiennent en outre que M. Pey Casado et le gérant de la banque centrale de l'époque, Jaime Barrios, auraient échangé des lettres en 1972 indiquant qu'une inscription de l'investissement de M. Pey Casado à la banque centrale n'était pas obligatoire.[300]

355. La défenderesse, dont l'argumentation aurait radicalement changé dans le contre-mémoire du 3 février 2003, reconnaîtrait désormais le caractère facultatif de l'application des décrets-lois n°258 et 1272 mais insisterait en revanche sur le fait que l'investissement de M. Pey Casado ne satisferait pas les critères posés par la Décision n°24 qui devrait être appliquée en l'espèce. Toutefois, l'argument de la défenderesse ne saurait être accueilli au motif que les conditions nécessaires à l'entrée en vigueur et à l'application de la Décision n°24 n'étaient pas satisfaites au moment où M. Pey Casado a réalisé son investissement.

356. Les demanderesses font ainsi valoir que l'application de la Décision n°24 dépendait de son incorporation dans le droit interne de chacun des Etats signataires. La Colombie n'ayant adopté le décret incorporant la Décision n°24 dans son ordre juridique interne que le 15 septembre 1973, la Décision n°24 n'aurait pu être appliquée avant cette date.

357. Les demanderesses soulignent également que la Décision n°24 n'avait été publiée que sous forme de décret le 25 juin 1971. La légalité de ce décret avait été remise en cause par la *Contraloría* qui estimait que l'incorporation de la Décision n°24 en droit chilien nécessitait une loi. L'exécutif aurait passé outre la décision de la *Contraloría « par la voie, légale mais extraordinaire »* du décret en

---

[299] V. exposé complémentaire sur la compétence du Tribunal arbitral du 11 septembre 2002, p. 55 et consultation de M. Alfonso Inostroza Cuevas, Président du directoire et du comité exécutif de la banque centrale du Chili du 5 novembre 1970 au 15 mai 1973, p. 1 (annexe C-44). Les demanderesses soutiennent que « *[d]ans le cas de l'Article 14, concrètement, les franchises consistaient à avoir accès au marché officiel des devises, à acquérir les devises à un taux de change préférentiel et à réexporter tout ou partie du capital apporté ainsi que les intérêts et bénéfices qu'ils produiraient* » (réponse au mémoire soutenant l'incompétence soumis par la défenderesse, du 18 septembre 1999, p. 117).

[300] Les demanderesses ont demandé à l'Etat défendeur de produire ces lettres mais ce dernier n'aurait pas été en mesure de les localiser (v. exposé complémentaire sur la compétence du Tribunal arbitral du 11 septembre 2002, p. 59).

réitération (*decreto de insistencia*).[301] La lecture du décret n°746 indiquerait cependant que ce n'est qu'en 1974 qu'il est mis fin à « *la situation de légalité douteuse du Décret N° 482, du 25 juin 1971, motif pour lequel il n'était pas appliqué pour ce qui concerne les particuliers* ».[302] Les demanderesses invoquent également un compte rendu de session ordinaire de la Commission du Groupe de Carthagène au cours duquel la fragilité juridique du décret de réitération incorporant la Décision n°24 a été critiquée.

358. Le préambule du décret-loi n°600 du 11 juillet 1974, qui ne mentionne pas le décret n°482 du 25 juin 1971 mais vise le décret-loi n°1272 de 1961 et les engagements internationaux valablement obligatoires au Chili, montrerait que le décret n°482 n'était pas applicable au Chili à cette époque et que la mise en application de la Décision n°24 pour les particuliers n'était pas obligatoire. L'article 13 et l'article 2 des articles transitoires seraient la preuve du caractère optionnel du statut mis en place par le décret-loi n°600. L'article 40 du décret-loi n°600, qui abroge le décret n°258 du 4 avril 1960, démontrerait que c'est ce dernier qui était en vigueur en 1972 et non le décret n°482. Le décret-loi n°746 du 6 novembre 1974 serait la première norme ayant force de loi incorporant la Décision n°24 dans l'ordre juridique interne chilien.

359. En toute hypothèse, la doctrine relative à la Décision n°24 et un certain nombre de documents officiels du Groupe de Carthagène indiqueraient que la Décision n°24 n'avait pas été effectivement appliquée avant 1974. L'inapplication de la Décision n°24 au Chili serait du reste corroborée par le fait que l'Etat défendeur, représenté par le Comité des investissements étrangers, n'a pas produit un seul document d'époque montrant que la Décision n°24 était appliquée alors que ces documents devraient se trouver dans les archives de l'organe intéressé, le Comité des investissements étrangers.[303] La lettre dont la défenderesse prétend qu'elle émane de Salvador Allende et qui désigne l'organisme national compétent aux fins de la Décision n°24 ne serait pas un document authentique et ne pourrait donc constituer une preuve crédible de l'application la Décision n°24 au Chili. Les demanderesses insistent notamment sur le fait que les modalités de présentation du document et certains aspects de la rédaction, l'absence de preuve de sa publication officielle au Chili et de sa prise en compte par le Directoire de l'Accord de Carthagène lui

---

[301] V. exposé complémentaire sur la compétence du Tribunal arbitral du 11 septembre 2002, p. 63.

[302] Id.

[303] V. la transcription de l'audience du 5 mai 2003, p. 201-202 et la transcription de l'audience du 7 mai 2003, pp. 474-475 (Me Garcés).

ôteraient tout caractère probant.[304] Les demanderesses en concluent que la Décision n°24 n'aurait pas été effectivement appliquée au Chili avant l'expropriation de M. Pey Casado.

360.   Même si, par extraordinaire, les mesures nécessaires à l'application effective de la Décision n°24 dans l'ordre juridique chilien avaient été adoptées et appliquées, la Décision n°24 n'aurait pas été applicable à l'investissement de M. Pey Casado. En effet, la Décision n°24 introduirait une nouvelle condition dans la législation chilienne en exigeant que l'investisseur soit de nationalité étrangère pour que son investissement soit qualifié d'investissement étranger. Cependant, la Décision n°24, « *par sa nature et par sa finalité, [n'aurait pu] s'appliquer en 1972 à l'investissement au Chili fait par un ressortissant espagnol qui avait la qualité de bénéficiaire de la Convention de double nationalité* ».[305] Selon les demanderesses, « *la caractéristique principale de la « Décision N° 24 » était de permettre que les investisseurs privés ayant la nationalité chilienne (ou d'un autre pays membre du Groupe Andin) prennent progressivement le contrôle de la majorité du capital d'une entreprise primitivement étrangère* ».[306]

361.   Les demanderesses soutiennent par ailleurs que la loi sur les abus de publicité du 17 juillet 1967, qui limitait la participation des actionnaires étrangers dans les entreprises du secteur des médias, ne pourrait être invoquée à l'encontre de M. Pey puisque les autorités chiliennes lui reconnaissaient le bénéfice de la Convention sur la double nationalité. En toute hypothèse, le non-respect des règles de détention du capital n'aurait entraîné que des sanctions purement administratives.

362.   Les demanderesses concluent sur l'état du droit chilien en 1972 que :

> « *[l]a loi chilienne permettait aux chiliens aussi bien qu'aux étrangers*
> • *d'investir au Chili des capitaux internationaux avec une liberté pratiquement totale, sans distinguer entre investisseurs nationaux et étrangers, y compris des chiliens ayant leur résidence au Chili investissant des capitaux internationaux. Les dérogations à cette liberté étaient expresses et exceptionnelles. Le Chili n'a pas rapporté la preuve d'une quelconque*

---

[304]   V. réplique des demanderesses au contre-mémoire de la défenderesse, du 23 février 2003, pp. 59-60 et la transcription de l'audience du 5 mai 2003, pp. 202-204 (Me Garcés).

[305]   Transcription de l'audience du 5 mai 2003, pp. 198-199 (Me Garcés).

[306]   V. exposé complémentaire sur la compétence du Tribunal arbitral du 11 septembre 2002, p. 65.

> *dérogation applicable à un investisseur espagnol qui*
> *en 1972 aurait bénéficié des avantages de la*
> *Convention de double nationalité ;*
> • *de conclure au Chili et/ou à l'étranger un contrat*
> *d'achat et de vente d'actions d'une société localisée au*
> *Chili, dont l'exécution pouvait avoir lieu à l'étranger*
> *et dont la monnaie du contrat et du paiement pouvait*
> *être une devise étrangère ;*
> • *aucune norme interne n'interdisait de convenir à*
> *l'étranger du paiement en devises, également à*
> *l'étranger, en règlement du prix de vente des actions*
> *d'une société chilienne ;*
> • *aucune norme interne ne faisait dépendre la*
> *qualité d'investissement étranger de la destination que*
> *le vendeur aurait pu donner au prix reçu [...] ».*[307]

363. Les demanderesses ajoutent que l'investissement réalisé par M. Pey Casado serait également compatible avec la réglementation actuelle sur les investissements étrangers au Chili. Elles citent en exemple les *American Depositary Receipts*, qui permettent d'acheter et de vendre des actions de sociétés chiliennes sur le marché boursier à New York et prouveraient, contrairement à ce qu'affirme la défenderesse, qu'un investisseur n'a pas pour obligation d'effectuer, aux fins de l'API ou de la législation chilienne en vigueur en 1972, le paiement du prix de son investissement sur le territoire de l'Etat d'accueil.

364. A titre subsidiaire, les demanderesses invoquent la clause de la nation la plus favorisée et l'API Chili-Belgique qui n'exige pas des investissements réalisés antérieurement à l'entrée en vigueur de l'API qu'ils aient la qualité d'investissement étranger au sens de la législation de la partie concernée.

b) Conclusions du Tribunal

365. Avant d'exposer l'analyse et les conclusions du Tribunal, il convient de rappeler les dispositions pertinentes de l'API Espagne-Chili.

366. L'article 1 de l'API définit le terme « *investissements* » dans son deuxième paragraphe :

> « *Par investissements on désigne toute sorte d'avoirs,*
> *tels que biens et droits de toute nature, acquis en*
> *accord avec la législation du pays recevant*
> *l'investissement et en particulier, encore que non-*
> *exclusivement, les suivants :*

---

[307] Exposé complémentaire sur la compétence du Tribunal arbitral du 11 septembre 2002, pp. 48-49.

Actions et autres formes de participation dans les sociétés.

Crédits, valeurs et droits découlant de toute sorte d'apports réalisés dans le but de créer une valeur économique ; y compris expressément tous les prêts consentis à cette fin, qu'ils aient ou non été capitalisés.

Biens meubles et immeubles, ainsi que toute sorte de droits liés à ces derniers.

Les droits de toute sorte relevant du domaine de la propriété intellectuelle, y compris expressément les patentes d'invention et marques commerciales, de même que les licences de fabrication et de "savoir-faire".

Les droits de mise en œuvre d'activités économiques et commerciales consentis par la loi ou en vertu d'un contrat, en particulier ceux liés à la prospection, la culture, l'extraction ou exploitation de ressources naturelles » (traduction libre fournie par les demanderesses).

367. L'article 2 de l'API prévoit dans ses deux premiers paragraphes que :

« 1.Chacune des Parties soutiendra, dans la mesure du possible, les investissements effectués dans son territoire par des investisseurs de l'autre Partie et admettra ses investissements conformément à ses dispositions légales.

2. Le présent Traité s'appliquera aux investissements qui seraient réalisés à partir de son entrée en vigueur par des investisseurs de l'une des Parties contractantes dans le territoire de l'autre. Toutefois, il bénéficiera également aux investissements réalisés antérieurement à son entrée en vigueur et qui, selon la législation de la Partie contractante concernée, auraient la qualité d'investissement étranger » (traduction libre fournie par les demanderesses).

368. La formulation de l'article 1(2) reflète une conception large de la notion d'investissement. Le Tribunal constate d'emblée que l'achat des titres de CPP S.A. et d'EPC Ltda est couvert par la définition de l'investissement établie par l'article 1(2) qui considère comme un investissement les *« actions et autres formes de participation dans les sociétés »*. La seule condition posée par cet article est celle de l'acquisition en conformité au droit de l'Etat d'accueil.

369. L'article 2(2) précise que les investissements effectués antérieurement à l'entrée en vigueur de l'API ne bénéficieront de la protection de l'API que s'ils peuvent être qualifiés d'investissements

étrangers au sens de la législation de l'Etat d'accueil. Le Tribunal estime que la législation à laquelle fait référence l'API est la législation chilienne en vigueur au moment auquel l'investissement est réalisé, c'est-à-dire en 1972.

370. Pour que l'API soit applicable à une opération réalisée en 1972, il est nécessaire que l'opération litigieuse corresponde à la définition de l'investissement établie par l'article 1(2) de l'API et qu'elle ait la qualité d'investissement étranger au sens de la législation chilienne appliquée à l'époque.

371. Invoquant le préambule de l'API, la défenderesse soutient cependant que l'opération doit impliquer un transfert de capitaux en provenance de l'extérieur vers l'intérieur du territoire chilien.

372. Le second paragraphe du préambule est formulé dans les termes suivants :

> « *Se proposant de créer des conditions favorables pour les investissements réalisés par les investisseurs de chacune des parties dans le territoire de l'autre impliquant des transferts de capitaux [...]* »

373. Selon la défenderesse, l'exigence de transfert de capitaux en provenance de l'Etat de l'investisseur vers l'intérieur de l'Etat d'accueil, évoquée par le préambule de l'API, devrait être distinguée de la faculté pour l'investisseur de sortir de l'Etat d'accueil de son investissement les capitaux qu'il y a investis, faculté prévue par l'article 6 de l'API intitulé « *transfert* ».[308] Les demanderesses estiment au contraire que l'article 6 ne fait qu'expliciter le sens du terme « *transfert* » utilisé dans le préambule et que le concept de transfert de capitaux ne peut désigner qu'un transfert vers l'extérieur de l'Etat d'accueil, conformément aux statuts du FMI.[309]

374. L'interprétation du traité avancée par la défenderesse revient à imposer un critère supplémentaire dans la définition du terme « *investissements* » sur le seul fondement du préambule. Or, s'il peut éclairer le sens des dispositions des articles du traité, le préambule ne saurait poser, à lui seul, une condition supplémentaire qui ne figure pas dans le corps du traité.

---

[308] L'article 6 de l'API prévoit dans sa partie pertinente que « chaque partie accordera aux investisseurs de l'autre Partie, pour ce qui concerne les investissements réalisés dans son territoire, la possibilité de transférer librement les revenus de ces investissements et autres versements en rapport avec eux, et en particulier, mais non exclusivement, les suivants [...] ».

[309] Les demanderesses précisent tout de même que l'API peut être « *amené à couvrir d'autres investissements, afin de créer* 'des conditions favorables' » (exposé complémentaire sur la compétence du Tribunal arbitral du 11 septembre 2002, p. 73).

375. En l'espèce, les articles 1(2) et 2(2) ne posent pas de difficultés particulières d'interprétation. Le préambule, composé de trois brefs paragraphes et rédigés en termes très généraux, reflète essentiellement le souhait de créer des conditions favorables à l'investissement entre les deux Etats parties. Il est clair que ces trois paragraphes ne contiennent aucune disposition de fond susceptible de créer des conditions supplémentaires à l'octroi de la protection offerte par l'API. Si le Tribunal acceptait l'interprétation de la défenderesse, il consacrerait une interprétation particulièrement restrictive du terme investissement au sens des articles 1(2) et 2(2) de l'API allant contre la lettre et l'esprit du préambule. Une telle démarche serait de toute évidence contraire à l'article 31 de la Convention de Vienne sur le droit des traités.

376. Le Tribunal tient à préciser que l'interprétation des termes du préambule[310] et de l'article 1(2)[311], consignée dans le procès-verbal des réunions techniques des 29, 30 septembre et 1er octobre 1998 entre l'Espagne et le Chili, organisées à la demande de ce dernier, n'est d'aucun secours pour la défenderesse.

377. En effet, l'initiative de la défenderesse, visant à organiser une rencontre entre les représentants des deux Etats parties au traité afin de s'entendre sur l'interprétation de certains de ses termes, est intervenue après l'introduction de la requête d'arbitrage (3 novembre 1997) et son enregistrement (20 avril 1998). Il s'agit là d'un acte incompatible avec les dispositions de l'article 10.6 de l'API qui imposent aux Etats parties de s'abstenir « *d'échanger, au travers des canaux diplomatiques, des arguments concernant l'arbitrage ou une*

---

[310] « Dans le paragraphe 3 du préambule, l'expression ' Invertions ' [sic] réfère aux transferts de capitaux vers le pays receveur de l'investissement, ceci, suppose une entrée d'actifs sur le territoire de la Partie contratante [sic] receveuse de l'investissement. Dans ce sens là, et suivant ce qu'établit le dit préambule, l'objet principal de l'accord est la protection et le développement des investissements qui impliquent le transfert de capitaux » (transcription des réunions techniques des 29, 30 septembre et 1er octobre 1998 entre l'Espagne et le Chili (annexe 15 au mémoire d'incompétence de la défenderesse du 20 juillet 1999)).

[311] « Dans l'article 1.2, la référence qui indique que, par investissement s'entendent tous types d'avoirs acquis en accord avec la législation du pays receveur, signifie qu'est ce pays [sic] celui qui, conformément à la législation, définit le caractère de l'investissement étranger d'une opération déterminée. Comme conséquence, les uniques avoirs qui peuvent être considérés comme investissements étrangers pour les effets de l'Accord, et qui peuvent bénéficier de sa protection, sont ceux acquis en conformité avec la législation du pays receveur de l'investissement » (transcription des réunions techniques des 29, 30 septembre et 1er octobre 1998 entre l'Espagne et le Chili (annexe 15 au mémoire d'incompétence de la défenderesse, du 20 juillet 1999)).

action judiciaire déjà entamée jusqu'à ce que les procédures correspondantes aient été conclues ». Il est clair que l'interprétation du préambule et de l'article 1(2) de l'API entre dans la catégorie des « *arguments concernant l'arbitrage* » échangés postérieurement à l'introduction de la procédure. En conséquence, le Tribunal ne tiendra pas compte de l'interprétation figurant dans le procès-verbal litigieux, sans pour autant préjuger du bien-fondé de cette dernière.

378. Le Tribunal relève également que l'interprétation des demanderesses consiste à limiter la portée des termes « *transferts de capitaux* » sans pour autant fournir de véritable justification. Au total, le Tribunal ne voit dans l'argumentation des parties aucun motif convaincant qui conduirait à lire dans le préambule une restriction liée au type de transfert de capitaux qu'un investisseur pourrait effectuer. Il ne voit pas davantage de raison d'appliquer une telle restriction aux dispositions de fond du traité et plus particulièrement aux articles 1(2) et 2(2).

379. Il est clair, en revanche, que les articles 1(2) et 2(2) de l'API exigent de l'investisseur qu'il effectue un investissement qui soit conforme à la législation chilienne en vigueur à l'époque et, s'agissant d'investissements existant au moment de l'entrée en vigueur du traité, qui puisse être qualifié d'investissement étranger au sens de cette législation.

380. La défenderesse a concentré son argumentation sur la Décision n°24 dont elle affirme qu'elle est entrée en vigueur au Chili le 30 juin 1971, qu'elle était applicable et effectivement appliquée et qu'elle n'a pas été respectée par l'investissement étranger que M. Pey Casado prétend avoir réalisé en 1972.

381. Ainsi que l'a indiqué la défenderesse, la Décision n°24 trouve son origine dans l'Accord de Carthagène, traité d'intégration subrégional signé par le Chili le 26 mai 1969 et publié au journal officiel chilien le 30 juillet 1969.[312] L'Accord de Carthagène crée une commission, organe supérieur composé de représentants des Etats membres et doté d'un pouvoir de décision,[313] dont le rôle consistera notamment à approuver et à soumettre « *à la considération des pays membres un régime commun de traitement applicable aux capitaux étrangers et, entre autres, sur les marques, patentes, licences et royalties* » le 31

---

[312] V. décret n°428 du 30 juillet 1969 (annexe 8 à la consultation du Professeur Santa María du 3 février 2003). Les autres pays signataires sont la Bolivie, la Colombie, l'Equateur et le Pérou. L'Accord de Carthagène a été conclu dans le but d'appliquer à l'échelon régional le traité de Montevideo sur le marché commun latino-américain (v. consultation du Professeur Santa María du 3 février 2003, p. 9).

[313] V. article 6 de l'Accord de Carthagène (annexe 8 à la consultation du Professeur Santa María du 3 février 2003).

décembre 1970 au plus tard.[314]   En outre, « *les pays membres [s'engageaient] à adopter les mesures nécessaires à l'application pratique de ce régime et ce, dans les six mois suivant l'approbation de celui-ci par la commission* ».[315]

382. Conformément aux dispositions de l'Accord de Carthagène, la commission a approuvé dans sa Décision n°24 du 31 décembre 1970 « *le régime commun de traitement applicable aux capitaux étrangers et sur les marques, patentes, licences et royalties* ».[316]

383. Les demanderesses ont développé deux arguments qui, selon elles, devraient conduire le Tribunal à conclure que la Décision n°24 n'est pas entrée en vigueur.

384. Les demanderesses estiment tout d'abord que les conditions posées à l'article A des dispositions transitoires de la Décision n°24 n'ont pas été respectées, la Colombie n'ayant incorporée la Décision n°24 en droit colombien que le 15 septembre 1973, ce qui aurait empêché la Décision n°24 d'entrer en vigueur avant cette date.

385. Le Tribunal rappellera que l'article A des dispositions transitoires de la Décision n°24 prévoit que « le présent régime entrera en vigueur lorsque tous les pays membres auront déposé auprès du secrétariat du Conseil les instruments par lesquels ils le mettront en pratique sur leurs territoires respectifs, conformément aux dispositions du deuxième alinéa de l'article 27 de l'Accord de Carthagène ».[317]

386. La défenderesse a pour sa part produit une attestation émanant du secrétariat de la Communauté andine indiquant que la Colombie avait adopté un décret n°1299 le 30 juin 1971, notifié à la commission de Carthagène le 5 juillet 1971. Le dernier instrument a été déposé par le Pérou le 13 juillet 1971.[318]

387. Le Tribunal ne peut que constater que les conditions posées par l'article A des dispositions transitoires de la Décision n°24 ont été satisfaites le 13 juillet 1971, une fois que tous les pays membres ont

---

[314] V. article 27 de l'Accord de Carthagène (annexe 8 à la consultation du Professeur Santa María du 3 février 2003).

[315] *Id.*

[316] V. Décision n°24 de la commission de l'Accord de Carthagène adoptée lors de la troisième période de sessions extraordinaires du 14 au 31 décembre 1970 (annexe 10 à la consultation du Professeur Santa María du 3 février 2003).

[317] V. article A des dispositions transitoires de la Décision n°24 de la commission de l'Accord de Carthagène adoptée lors de la troisième période de sessions extraordinaires du 14 au 31 décembre 1970 (annexe 10 à la consultation du Professeur Santa María du 3 février 2003).

[318] V. lettre du secrétariat de la Communauté andine du 26 avril 2000 (annexe 5 à la réplique de la défenderesse du 4 avril 2003).

eu déposé les instruments par lesquels ils mettraient en pratique la Décision n°24. Le fait que l'instrument déposé par la Colombie ait fait l'objet d'un recours postérieurement à son dépôt auprès du secrétariat du Conseil de l'Accord de Carthagène ne peut avoir de conséquences sur l'entrée en vigueur de la Décision n°24 dans les autres Etats membres, la Colombie s'étant déjà engagée vis-à-vis de ces derniers en déposant le décret n°1299 auprès de l'organe compétent de l'Accord de Carthagène. En revanche, l'annulation du décret n°1299 a des effets en droit interne colombien la Décision n°24 demeurant sans application jusqu'à ce que le Gouvernement colombien fasse usage de prérogatives constitutionnelles pour faire entrer en vigueur le régime commun grâce au décret n°1900 du 15 septembre 1973.[319]

388. Le premier argument des demanderesses ne peut donc être accueilli.

389. Les demanderesses soulèvent un second argument qui consiste à mettre en cause la légalité du décret n°482 du 25 juin 1971 incorporant la Décision n°24 en droit chilien.

390. L'incorporation de la Décision n°24 en droit chilien s'est effectuée au moyen de deux décrets. Le premier décret, en date du 25 juin 1971, devait approuver et faire entrer en vigueur le régime mis en place par la Décision n°24.[320] Les deux parties s'accordent cependant sur le fait que ce premier décret a fait l'objet de critiques de la part de la *Contraloría general* qui estimait que la Décision n°24 devait être incorporée dans l'ordre juridique chilien au moyen d'une loi et non d'un décret.[321] Au terme d'une analyse détaillée,[322] la défenderesse a

---

[319] V. rapport du directoire sur les dispositions légales prises par les pays membres en relation avec la Décision n°24 du 8 septembre 1974 (annexe C-100).

[320] V. décret suprême du 25 juin 1971 (annexe 9 à la consultation du Professeur Santa María du 3 février 2003 sur la valeur juridique des décrets d'insistance sous la constitution de 1925 : le cas du décret n°482 de 1971 (mise en vigueur de la Décision n°24 de la commission de l'Accord de Carthagène)).

[321] V. l'ordonnance de renvoi de la *Contraloría general* du 28 juin 1971 (annexe 7 à la consultation du Professeur Santa María du 3 février 2003 sur la valeur juridique des décrets d'insistance sous la constitution de 1925 : le cas du décret n°482 de 1971 (mise en vigueur de la Décision n°24 de la commission de l'Accord de Carthagène)). La *Contraloría general* est un organe autonome qui, au sein de l'administration d'Etat, exerce un contrôle de constitutionalité et de légalité des décrets suprêmes (v. article 1 de la loi n°10.336, annexe 12 à la consultation du Professeur Santa María du 3 février 2003 sur la valeur juridique des décrets d'insistance sous la constitution de 1925 : le cas du décret n°482 de 1971 (mise en vigueur de la Décision n°24 de la commission de l'Accord de Carthagène)).

[322] V. en particulier la consultation du Professeur Santa María du 3 février 2003 sur la valeur juridique des décrets d'insistance sous la constitution de 1925 :

toutefois démontré que le Président de la République du Chili était en droit d'insister sur l'adoption du décret critiqué par la *Contraloría general* s'il est convaincu de sa légalité et s'il réunit la signature de tous les ministres d'Etat. Le 30 juin 1971, le Président de la République du Chili a ainsi adopté un décret d'insistance (ou de réitération), signé de tous les ministres d'Etat, de façon à ce que la Décision n°24 soit incorporée dans le droit chilien.[323]

391.   Le Tribunal estime dès lors que le Président de la République a agi conformément aux pouvoirs qui lui étaient conférés à l'époque et que la Décision n°24 a pu finalement entrer en vigueur par le biais du décret d'insistance du 30 juin 1971. Les demanderesses ont du reste reconnu que le pouvoir exécutif avait eu recours à « *la voie, légale mais extraordinaire, du 'Décret en réitération'* ».[324]

392.   Dans l'hypothèse où la Décision n°24 serait entrée en vigueur, les demanderesses ont toutefois fait valoir que « *l'application pratique* » de la Décision n°24 exigeait l'adoption d'un certain nombre de mesures qui n'ont pas été prises et qu'en conséquence la Décision n°24 n'a jamais été effectivement appliquée.

393.   Les demanderesses insistent particulièrement sur le fait que l'Etat chilien n'a pas nommé l'organisme national compétent chargé de mettre en application les principaux aspects de la Décision n°24. Elles mettent en doute l'authenticité d'un document produit par la défenderesse qui montrerait que le Chili avait désigné le comité des investissements étrangers pour accomplir les fonctions d'organisme national compétent.

394.   Le Tribunal rappellera que l'article D des dispositions transitoires de la Décision n°24 prévoit que « [d]ans les trois mois suivants [sic] l'entrée en vigueur du présent régime, chaque pays membre désignera le ou les organismes compétents en matière d'autorisation, d'enregistrement et de contrôle de l'investissement étranger et du transfert de technologie et informera les autres pays membres et le Conseil à cet égard ».

395.   La défenderesse a produit la copie d'une lettre du Président Salvador Allende et de son ministre des affaires étrangères, adressée aux

---

le cas du décret n°482 de 1971 (mise en vigueur de la Décision n°24 de la commission de l'Accord de Carthagène) produit par la défenderesse.

[323]   V. le décret d'insistance (*decreto de insistencia*) du 30 juin 1971 (annexe 7 à la consultation du Professeur Santa María du 3 février 2003 sur la valeur juridique des décrets d'insistance sous la constitution de 1925 : le cas du décret n°482 de 1971 (mise en vigueur de la Décision n°24 de la commission de l'Accord de Carthagène)).

[324]   Exposé complémentaire sur la compétence du Tribunal arbitral du 11 septembre 2002, p. 63.

membres du comité des investissements étrangers, informant ces derniers que le comité assumerait à titre transitoire le rôle d'organisme national compétent, au sens de la Décision n°24, et « *chargé de l'autorisation, de l'enregistrement et du contrôle des investissements étrangers directs, y compris de ceux déjà existants, tant qu'un organisme différent n'aura pas été affecté à ces fonctions* ». Il est précisé également que « *tous les contrats d'importation de technologie et relatifs aux licences d'exploitation de marques et de patentes d'origine étrangère, y compris ceux déjà conclus, devront être enregistrés auprès de ce même organisme* ».[325]

396. Cette lettre porte deux dates, le 8 septembre 1972 sur la première page et le 13 janvier 1972 sur la seconde. Elle ne mentionne pas, tout au moins expressément, le délai de trois mois prévu à l'article D des dispositions transitoires, délai en toute hypothèse écoulé quelle que soit la date prise en compte dans le courrier du Président Allende. Elle n'indique pas davantage la date à laquelle les nouvelles fonctions du comité des investissements étrangers devront prendre effet, la lettre étant simplement rédigée au futur.

397. Sans qu'il soit nécessaire de se prononcer sur l'authenticité de ce document, le Tribunal constate qu'il s'agit d'une note d'information qui appelle non seulement certaines précisions, telle que la date de prise d'effet des fonctions du comité ou l'articulation des relations du comité avec un certain nombre d'autres organismes,[326] mais également une confirmation officielle. En effet, comme l'ont relevé les demanderesses, le comité des investissements étrangers aura pour mission de mettre en application un ensemble de règles fixées par la commission de l'Accord de Carthagène, organe issu d'un accord d'intégration international. Il serait pour le moins surprenant que la désignation du comité ne fasse pas l'objet d'une publication au journal officiel chilien, ne serait-ce que pour informer les investisseurs intéressés.

398. A supposer toutefois que cette lettre ait été suffisante pour que la désignation prenne effet dans le courant de l'année 1972, la

---

[325]   Lettre du Président Salvador Allende et de son ministre des affaires étrangères aux membres du comité des investissements étrangers en date des 13 janvier et 8 septembre 1972 (annexe 17A à la consultation du Professeur Santa María du 3 février 2003).

[326]   La lettre indique en effet que « [l]e Comité devra agir à ces fins, en étroite collaboration avec les autres services de la Corporation de Développement de la Production ainsi qu'avec la Banque Centrale du Chili et, tout spécialement, en coordination avec le Secrétariat exécutif aux affaires relatives à l'ALALC, le Comité assesseur des crédits extérieurs, la Commission de révision des contrats de royalties de la Banque Centrale, la Commission nationale de la recherche scientifique et technologique et le Bureau de la planification nationale ».

multiplicité des tâches confiées au comité des investissements étrangers, sur laquelle a insisté la défenderesse, promettait une activité intense. Or, comme l'ont souligné les demanderesses, l'Etat défendeur n'a produit aucun document susceptible d'attester de l'accomplissement des fonctions du comité des investissements étrangers. La défenderesse n'a soumis aucun exemplaire d'autorisation[327] ou d'enregistrement[328] demandés ou octroyés en application de la Décision n°24, éléments dont elle n'a pourtant cessé de souligner l'importance. Elle n'a produit aucun document découlant de l'application effective de la Décision n°24 émanant des organismes qui devaient travailler en étroite collaboration avec le comité des investissements étrangers. Enfin, la défenderesse n'a produit aucune des « *providencias* » exigées par l'article 27 de l'Accord de Carthagène pour l'application pratique de la Décision n°24 autres que le décret d'entrée en vigueur au Chili, pas plus qu'elle n'en a montré l'existence.

399. Les demanderesses invoquent pour leur part certains travaux de la doctrine qui concluent à l'absence d'application de la Décision n°24 au Chili. Monsieur Stephen Lau indique dans un ouvrage publié en 1972 que « *[t]he legal force of the Decision 24 in the individual nations is yet unclear* ».[329] Monsieur Peter Schliesser et Madame Sylvie Volnay constatent pour leur part que « *[e]n fait et jusqu'à maintenant, seul le Pérou s'est conformé fidèlement au Code.[330] Quant au Chili, à la Bolivie et à l'Equateur, et bien que le Code soit en vigueur dans ces pays, ceux-ci n'avaient pas, en mai 1972, pris les dernières décisions nécessaires pour que les mesures prévues par le Code puissent être appliquées* »[331]. Monsieur Michel Carraud évoque ce qui ne fut que « *les premières applications* » de la Décision n°24 par les pays andins et le « *revirement brutal [qui] s'est effectué durant l'année 1974* » à la suite de celles-ci et de l'arrivée au pouvoir de la junte militaire au Chili.[332]

400. Un rapport du directoire de l'Accord de Carthagène du 8 septembre 1974 confirme le défaut d'application effective de la Décision n°24

---

[327] V. article 3 et l'annexe 1 de la Décision n°24.

[328] V. article 5 et l'annexe 1 de la Décision n°24.

[329] V. Stephen Lau, *The Chilean Response to Foreign Investment*, 1972, p. 27 (annexe C-116).

[330] Le « *Code* » désigne la Décision n°24.

[331] Peter Schliesser et Sylvie Volnay, Régime des investissements étrangers à l'intérieur du Marché commun andin, JDI, 1972.558, spéc. p. 561.

[332] V. Michel Carraud, *Nature et portée de l'Accord de Carthagène d'intégration sous-régionale andine*, Notes et études documentaires, 21 octobre 1977, n°4421 – 4422 – 4423, p. 53, spéc. p. 64.

dans les pays andins auquel seul le Pérou fait exception.[333] Ce document montre également que jusqu'en 1974, le Chili, tout comme d'autres pays, n'a pas adopté de mesures d'application de la Décision n°24 autres que le décret d'entrée en vigueur (en l'occurrence, le décret suprême n°482). Les représentants de la délégation chilienne, qui défendaient à l'époque l'adoption d'un nouveau décret sur le statut de l'investissement étranger[334] critiqué dans ce rapport pour ses divergences avec la Décision n°24, ont fourni des éléments d'explication sur le défaut d'application de la Décision n°24. Cette dernière étant entrée en vigueur au moyen d'un décret d'insistance et non d'une loi, elle pouvait faire l'objet d'un recours par les justiciables concernés devant les tribunaux. Le rapport précise que le risque de multiplication de recours favorablement accueillis faisait craindre une remise en cause généralisée de la Décision n°24.[335] Cette crainte a donc à la fois contribué au défaut d'application effective de la Décision n°24 et servi d'explication à l'absence de référence expresse à la Décision n°24 dans le décret n°600 du 13 juillet 1974.[336]

---

[333] V. rapport du directoire sur les dispositions légales prises par les pays membres en relation avec la Décision n°24 du 8 septembre 1974 (annexe C-100, également produite par la défenderesse en annexe 14 à la consultation du Professeur Santa María du 3 février 2003).

[334] V. décret n°600 du 13 juillet 1974 (annexe C-104).

[335] Le rapport indique que « [l]e Délégué du Gouvernement chilien a poursuivi en indiquant que le mécanisme au moyen duquel la Décision n°24 a été mise en vigueur dans ce pays 'permettait aux particuliers concernés d'avoir recours à nos tribunaux supérieurs de justice pour soutenir l'illégalité de la Décision n°24 et obtenir un arrêt qui déclarerait nulle son application au Chili dans les matières qui modifieraient la législation interne. Cette mesure, a-t-il ajouté, produirait des effets dans les cas particuliers où ce recours serait introduit, étant donné que les sentences de la Cour Suprême n'ont pas d'effet de caractère général (…)'. Bien qu'il soit vrai que, dans le système chilien, les arrêts de la Cour suprême de Justice qui déclarent démontrée l'exception d'inconstitutionnalité n'ont pas d'effet erga omnes, comme c'est le cas des sentences sur l'inconstitutionnalité rendue par la Cour de Justice de la Colombie, il n'en demeure pas moins qu'une fois cette exception déclarée à l'égard de la Décision 24 dans un cas particulier la voie serait ouverte pour que cette décision se transforme en doctrine et commence à s'appliquer de manière générale » (rapport du directoire sur les dispositions légales prises par les pays membres en relation avec la Décision n°24 du 8 septembre 1974 (annexe C-100)).

[336] Les désaccords entre le Chili et les autres pays membres relatifs à l'application de la Décision n°24 sont devenus tels que le Chili s'est retiré de l'Accord de Carthagène à compter du 30 octobre 1976 (v. procès-verbal final de la XVème période de sessions ordinaires de la commission de l'Accord de Carthagène, du 10 au 14 et du 19 au 20 septembre 1974 (annexe C-101) et

401. Le Tribunal conclut que si les décrets n°482 et 488 ont fait entrer en vigueur au Chili la Décision n°24, celle-ci n'a pas fait l'objet d'une application effective, en l'absence d'adoption des mesures nécessaires à cette fin et ce en raison des risques que cela présentait. Il est donc inutile d'analyser en détail les dispositions de fond de la Décision n°24 concernant les investissements étrangers.

402. La Décision n°24 n'ayant pas été effectivement appliquée au Chili, il convient d'examiner la réglementation à laquelle la Décision n°24 devait se substituer. L'article 2 du décret suprême n°482 prévoyait en effet que « *les dispositions de toute nature contraires ou incompatibles avec le régime visé à l'article premier du présent décret sont abrogées* ».[337]

403. Les parties ont abondamment débattu du sens et de la portée du décret-loi n°258 du 30 mars 1960 sur le statut de l'investisseur et du décret-loi n°1272 du 7 septembre 1961 dit loi sur les opérations de change international.

404. L'examen des écritures permet de constater que les parties s'accordent en définitive sur le fait que le décret-loi n°258 du 30 mars 1960 est d'application facultative. Le Professeur Sainte Marie, consulté par la défenderesse, explique ainsi dans sa consultation du 3 février 2003 que « *la réglementation du décret était facultative puisque seuls les investisseurs qui désiraient recevoir les franchises prévues par le décret avaient pour obligation d'enregistrer leurs investissements et d'obtenir l'approbation du Président de la République* ».[338]

405. C'est effectivement ce qu'indiquent les dispositions des articles 1[339] et 4[340] du décret-loi n°258 qui ne contient pas par ailleurs de véritable

---

procès-verbal final de la XXème période de sessions ordinaires de la commission de l'Accord de Carthagène, 4 août et 30 octobre 1976 (annexe C-102)).

[337] Article 2 des dispositions transitoires du décret suprême n°482 du 25 juin 1971 (annexe 9 au rapport du Professeur Santa María du 3 février 2003). Le service des impôts internes a fait l'analyse suivante : « *Le régime des capitaux étrangers est régi au Chili par les règles du D.S. N°482 de 1971 (la Décision N°24), sans préjudice du maintien en vigueur du D.F.L. (Décret ayant Force de Loi) N°258 de 1960 pour tout ce qui ne lui est pas contraire ou n'est pas incompatible avec celui-ci* » (v. la circulaire n°161 de la Direction des impôts internes du Chili, en date du 22 décembre 1972 (annexe 15 à la consultation du Professeur Santa María du 3 février 2003)).

[338] Consultation du Professeur Santa María du 3 février 2003, p. 8.

[339] L'article 1 prévoyait que « [l]es personnes qui apportent dans le pays de nouveaux capitaux, provenant de l'extérieur, dans le but d'initier, fortifier, élargir, améliorer ou rénover des activités productrices, agricoles, minières, d'industrie de la pêche ou bien d'autres activités qui soient qualifiées comme ayant un intérêt pour l'économie nationale par décret du Président de la

définition de l'investissement étranger. M. Pey Casado n'avait donc aucune obligation de se conformer aux dispositions de ce décret-loi s'il n'avait pas l'intention de demander le bénéfice des franchises prévues par ce texte.

406. Les parties se concentrent également sur différents aspects du décret-loi n°1272. La défenderesse se fonde sur les articles 14, 15 et 16 du décret pour conclure qu'il ne s'applique pas à l'opération réalisée par les demanderesses. Selon la défenderesse, « *il était permis de se référer à ladite norme si des devises étaient introduites dans le pays puisqu'elles devaient être converties en pesos chiliens dans une banque ou dans un organisme chilien avalisé par une loi spécifique. Cette loi, en essence, autorisait le rapatriement du capital et des bénéfices à ceux qui s'y référaient. [...] Il faut souligner que les dispositions du décret n'étaient pas applicables aux transactions qui n'impliquaient pas d'entrée de devises dans le pays* ». Les demanderesses déduisent quant à elles de l'article 14 que le décret met en place un régime optionnel, les investisseurs ayant la possibilité de s'inscrire auprès de la Banque centrale s'ils souhaitent bénéficier de la possibilité de vendre librement les devises introduites au Chili.

407. L'article 14 du décret-loi n°1272 prévoyait que :

> « *[l]es personnes physiques et morales, nationales ou étrangères, qui transfèrent au Chili des capitaux en devises étrangères et qui s'inscrivent à la Banque centrale du Chili, pourront vendre librement ces devises dans la limite indiquée dans l'article antérieur. A cet effet la Banque centrale leur octroiera un certificat d'inscription nominatif et non transférable. Les personnes qui ont adopté cette exception pourront réexporter librement, de forme totale ou partielle, les dits capitaux, avec préalable dévolution du dit certificat d'inscription ou d'annotation sur la remise partielle, suivant le cas [sic]. Ainsi, en accord avec les conditions antérieures et dans le cadre des limitations légales, la Banque centrale du Chili autorisera les*

---

340   République et qui désirent adopter les franchises qui sont établies dans le présent décret faisant force de loi, seront régies par les dispositions suivantes » (article 1 du décret-loi n°258 (annexe C-111)).
L'article 4 disposait que « [l]e Président de la République a seul la faculté d'accepter ou de rejeter les apports de nouveaux capitaux provenant de l'extérieur et qui désirent adhérer au présent DFL, et octroyer ou refuser, en tout ou partie, les franchises envisagées dans celui-ci, conformément aux dispositions du présent DFL » (article 4 du décret-loi n°258 (annexe C-111)).

> *remises correspondantes aux intérêts et bénéfices produits par les dits capitaux »*[341] *(traduction libre des parties demanderesses).*

408. S'il est vrai que l'article 14 offre la possibilité de bénéficier de franchises moyennant le respect de certaines conditions, il est également exact que cet article fait de l'introduction de devises étrangères au Chili une condition d'application du texte. Comme l'a souligné à juste titre la défenderesse, ce décret ne concerne pas directement les investissements étrangers ; il n'en fournit pas davantage de définition générale applicable en droit chilien. En toute hypothèse, M. Pey Casado n'ayant pas effectué de transfert de devises étrangères au Chili, ce texte n'a pas vocation à s'appliquer à son investissement.

409. Il convient en dernier lieu d'examiner les arguments des parties concernant la loi n°16.643 sur l'abus de publicité du 17 juillet 1967.[342] La défenderesse invoque l'article 5 de la loi n°16.643 selon lequel « *le propriétaire de tout journal, revue ou écrit journalistique dont la direction nationale se situe au Chili, ou de toute agence d'informations nationales, et le concessionnaire de toute radio émettrice ou station de télévision devront être chiliens* ». Elle invoque également l'article 6 qui dispose que « *les journaux, les revues, les écrits journalistiques ou les transmission [sic] de stations de radio ou de télévision ne pourront débuter tant qu'ils n'auront pas rempli les conditions de l'article 5 [...]* ».[343] Sur le fondement de ces dispositions, la défenderesse fait valoir que les demanderesses se trouvaient nécessairement face à un dilemme : respecter les dispositions de la loi n°16.643 et ne pas satisfaire le critère de nationalité étrangère posée aux articles 1 et 2 de la Décision n°24 ou satisfaire ce critère et violer les dispositions de la loi n°16.643.

410. Le Tribunal a déjà conclu que la Décision n°24 n'avait en réalité jamais fait l'objet d'une application effective au Chili. Le dilemme mis en évidence par la défenderesse ne s'est donc jamais réellement posé. En 1972, lorsque M. Pey Casado a effectué son investissement, il était titulaire de la double nationalité hispano-chilienne. Résidant au Chili depuis 1947, M. Pey Casado bénéficiait de la Convention sur la double nationalité depuis 1958. La loi n°16.643 ne contenant pas de disposition spécifique relative aux doubles nationaux, la situation de M. Pey Casado était donc tout à fait compatible avec les dispositions de ce texte.

---

[341] Article 14 du Décret-loi n°1272 (annexe 5 à la consultation du Professeur Santa María du 3 février 2003).

[342] V. loi n°16.643 sur l'abus de publicité du 17 juillet 1967 (annexe 21 à la consultation du Professeur Santa María du 3 février 2003).

[343] V. la consultation du Professeur Santa María du 3 février 2003, pp. 24-25.

411.   Au vu de l'ensemble des développements qui précèdent, le Tribunal
       conclut qu'il n'existait pas, dans le droit chilien en vigueur en 1972,
       de définition établie de l'investissement étranger et que l'opération
       réalisée par M. Pey Casado s'est conformée au droit chilien qui lui
       était applicable. En conséquence, le Tribunal considère que
       l'investissement de M. Pey Casado, l'achat d'actions d'une société
       chilienne du secteur de la presse au moyen de paiements en devises
       étrangères effectués sur des comptes bancaires en Europe, satisfait
       les conditions posées par l'API et plus particulièrement par ses
       articles 1(2) et 2(2).

2.   La condition de nationalité au sens de l'API

412.   Afin de bénéficier de la protection de l'API, la première partie
       demanderesse doit remplir les conditions de nationalité prévues par
       cet accord.

413.   L'API définit, dans son article 1ᵉʳ, le terme « *investisseurs* » qui sont
       protégés par les garanties de l'API comme :

> « *...les personnes physiques ou ressortissants
> nationaux, selon le droit de la Partie correspondante,
> et les personnes morales, y compris les compagnies,
> associations de compagnies, sociétés commerciales et
> autres organisations qui se trouveraient constituées
> ou, selon le cas, dûment organisées conformément au
> droit de cette Partie et qui auraient leur siège dans le
> territoire de cette dernière, nonobstant le fait qu'elles
> appartiennent à des personnes physiques ou juridiques
> étrangères.* »

414.   La condition de la nationalité au sens de l'API se distingue de celle
       de la nationalité au sens de l'article 25 de la Convention CIRDI en
       deux aspects fondamentaux. D'abord, contrairement à l'article 25 de
       la Convention CIRDI, l'API ne précise pas le moment de
       l'appréciation de la nationalité de la partie requérante. De l'avis du
       Tribunal, la condition de nationalité au sens de l'API doit être établie
       à la date du consentement de l'investisseur à l'arbitrage. L'offre
       d'arbitrer contenue dans le traité doit en effet exister, ce qui suppose
       que les conditions d'application du traité soient satisfaites, à la date
       du consentement de l'investisseur pour que celui-ci puisse parfaire la
       convention d'arbitrage résultant de l'offre générale d'arbitrer
       contenue dans le traité. Par ailleurs, les conditions d'application du
       traité, dont la condition de nationalité, doivent également être
       satisfaites, en l'absence de précision contraire du traité, à la date de la
       ou des violations alléguées, faute de quoi l'investisseur ne pourrait se
       prévaloir devant le tribunal arbitral mis en place en application du
       traité d'une violation de celui-ci.

415.   Deuxièmement, le traitement des doubles nationaux par l'API est différent dans son champ d'application et son contenu de celui prévu par la Convention CIRDI. Pour remplir la condition de la nationalité au sens de l'API, il suffit pour la partie demanderesse de démontrer qu'elle possède la nationalité de l'autre Etat contractant. Contrairement à ce qui a été soutenu par la défenderesse,[344] le fait que la demanderesse ait une double nationalité, comprenant la nationalité de la défenderesse, ne l'exclut pas du champ de protection de l'API. De l'avis du Tribunal arbitral, il n'existe pas de condition de nationalité « *effective et dominante* » pour les double-nationaux dans ce contexte. Un double-national n'est pas exclu du champ d'application de l'API, même si sa nationalité « *effective et dominante* » est celle de l'Etat de l'investissement (contrairement à ce qui a été soutenu dans l'avis de droit du Professeur Dolzer, produit par la défenderesse).[345] La considération du but même de l'API et sa rédaction excluent au contraire l'idée d'une condition de nationalité effective et dominante. Ainsi que l'a souligné le Professeur Dolzer, l'API accorde sa protection aux « *investisseurs de l'autre Partie* » ou « *investisseur d'une Partie Contractante sur le territoire de l'autre* » (v., par exemple les articles 2(1), 2(2), 3(1), 4(1), 5, 6, 7(1), 8(1), 10(1) de l'API). L'API n'aborde pas expressément la question de savoir si les double-nationaux hispano-chiliens seraient couverts par son champ d'application. De l'avis du Tribunal arbitral, il ne se justifierait pas d'ajouter (sur la base de ce qui a été prétendu être des règles de droit coutumier international) une condition d'application qui ne résulte ni de sa lettre ni de son esprit.[346]

416.   Dans le cas d'espèce, il suffit pour M. Pey Casado de démontrer qu'il possédait la nationalité espagnole au moment de l'acceptation de la compétence du tribunal arbitral sur le fondement de l'API et, pour bénéficier de la protection de fond du traité, au moment de la ou des

---

[344]   V. contre-mémoire de la défenderesse du 3 février 2003, pp. 6-7 ; pp. 123 et ss ; transcription de l'audience du 15 janvier 2007, pp. 45-46 (Me Leurent) ; v. aussi la transcription de l'audience du 6 mai 2003, p. 401 (Me Di Rosa).

[345]   V. spéc. consultation p. 15 et le contre-mémoire de la défenderesse du 3 février 2003, p. 7.

[346]   Le Tribunal arbitral partage à ce propos l'opinion des parties demanderesses, notamment qu'en analysant la condition de la nationalité au sens de l'API, le Tribunal doit partir de l'API et l'analyser « *sans aller rechercher des conditions supplémentaires implicites* » transcription de l'audience du 15 janvier 2007, p. 61 (Me Malinvaud). Les règles concernant le domaine de la protection diplomatique invoquées par la défenderesse (transcription de l'audience du 15 janvier 2007, pp. 46 et 51 (Me Leurent)) ne changent rien à cette conclusion.

violations alléguées de l'API. Comme on l'a vu dans les développements qui précèdent, cette condition est satisfaite.[347]

417. En toute hypothèse, le Tribunal arbitral observera qu'à supposer même que la notion de nationalité effective et dominante soit un élément pertinent dans le cas de double nationalité, aux fins de l'application de l'API bien que celui-ci ne le prévoie pas, cette condition serait remplie dans le cas d'espèce. A partir de 1974, la nationalité « *primaire* » de M. Pey Casado est la nationalité espagnole, cette nationalité étant également sa nationalité d'origine.

418. Pour toutes ces raisons, de l'avis du Tribunal arbitral, la première partie demanderesse remplit la condition de la nationalité au sens de l'API.

3.   La condition d'application *ratione temporis* de l'API

419. Pour que l'acceptation par l'investisseur de l'offre d'arbitrer émise par l'Etat dans l'API puisse parfaire le consentement des parties, il est nécessaire que l'offre d'arbitrer faite par l'Etat couvre les matières que l'investisseur prétend soumettre à l'arbitre. C'est la satisfaction de cette condition, qui dépend des conditions d'application *ratione temporis* de l'API, que le Tribunal se propose d'examiner à présent..

420. L'API Espagne-Chili est entré en vigueur le 29 mars 1994.

421. L'article 10 de l'API Espagne-Chili prévoit la possibilité de recourir à l'arbitrage CIRDI en cas de « *controverse* » relative aux investissements entre l'Etat d'accueil et un investisseur de l'autre Etat partie à l'API :

> « *1.Toute controverse relative aux investissements, au sens du présent Traité, entre une Partie contractante et un investisseur de l'autre Partie contractante sera, dans la mesure du possible, résolue par des discussions amiables entre les deux parties à la controverse.*
> *2. Si la controverse n'a pas pu être résolue au terme de six mois à partir du moment où elle aura été*

---

[347]   L'expert consulté par la défenderesse, le Professeur Dolzer, admet l'application de l'API dans ce cas, et écrit dans son avis de droit du 3 février 2003 : « *[...] il est possible, selon mon opinion, qu'un ' investisseur de l'autre Partie Contractante ' dans le contexte de l'APPI Chili-Espagne soit une personne de double nationalité hispano-chilienne qui investisse au Chili, mais seulement si la nationalité dominante et effective de cette personne est la nationalité espagnole.* » (p. 11).

soulevée par l'une ou l'autre des Parties, elle sera soumise, au choix de l'investisseur :
Soit aux juridictions nationales de la Partie contractante impliquée dans la controverse ;
Soit à un arbitrage international dans les conditions décrites au paragraphe 3.
Une fois que l'investisseur aura soumis la controverse aux juridictions de la Partie contractante impliquée ou à l'arbitrage international, le choix de l'une ou l'autre de ces procédures sera définitive.
3. En cas de recours à l'arbitrage international la controverse pourra être portée devant l'un des organes d'arbitrage désignés ci-après au choix de l'investisseur :

Au Centre International pour le Règlement des Différends Relatifs aux Investissements (CIRDI) créé par la « Convention sur le Règlement des Différends relatifs aux Investissements entre Etats et nationaux d'autres Etats », ouvert à la signature à Washington le 18 mars 1965, si chaque partie au présent Traité y a adhéré. Si cette condition n'est pas remplie, chaque Partie contractante donne son consentement pour que la controverse soit soumise à l'arbitrage en conformité avec le règlement du Mécanisme complémentaire du CIRDI.

A une Cour d'arbitrage « ad hoc » établie en accord avec les règles d'arbitrage de la Commission des Nations Unies pour le Droit Commercial International (CNUDMI) [sic].
4. L'organe arbitral statuera sur la base des dispositions du présent Traité, du droit de la Partie contractante qui serait partie à la controverse – y compris les règles relatives aux conflits de lois – et des termes d'éventuels accords particuliers conclus en rapport avec l'investissement, de même que des principes du droit international en la matière.
5. Les sentences arbitrales seront définitives et contraignantes pour les parties à la controverse.
6. Les Parties contractantes s'abstiendront d'échanger, au travers des canaux diplomatiques, des arguments concernant l'arbitrage ou une action judiciaire déjà entamée jusqu'à ce que les procédures correspondantes aient été conclues ; hormis quant-au fait que les Parties à la controverse n'auraient pas exécuté la décision de la Cour arbitrale ou l'arrêt du

> *Tribunal ordinaire, selon les modalités d'exécution*
> *établies dans la décision ou l'arrêt ».[348]*

422. C'est l'article 2 de l'API qui contient les dispositions relatives à son application dans le temps :

> *« 1.Chacune des Parties soutiendra, dans la mesure du possible, les investissements effectués dans son territoire par des investisseurs de l'autre Partie et admettra ses investissements conformément à ses dispositions légales.*
> *2. Le présent Traité s'appliquera aux investissements qui seraient réalisés à partir de son entrée en vigueur par des investisseurs de l'une des Parties contractantes dans le territoire de l'autre. Toutefois, il bénéficiera également aux investissements réalisés antérieurement à son entrée en vigueur et qui, selon la législation de la Partie contractante concernée, auraient la qualité d'investissement étranger.*
> *3. Il ne s'appliquera pas, néanmoins, aux controverses ou réclamations surgies ou résolues antérieurement à son entrée en vigueur ».[349]*

423. L'application dans le temps du traité soulève deux questions distinctes : celle de la compétence *ratione temporis* du Tribunal arbitral saisi sur le fondement de l'API et celle de l'applicabilité *ratione temporis* des obligations de fond de l'API.

424. Les Tribunaux arbitraux constitués dans les affaires *Salini* et *Impregilo* ont du reste justement souligné cette distinction :

> *« [...] one must distinguish carefully between jurisdiction* ratione temporis *of an ICSID Tribunal and applicability* ratione temporis *of the substantive obligations contained in a BIT ».[350]*

---

[348] Traduction produite par les parties demanderesses en annexe 3 à la requête d'arbitrage, du 3 novembre 1997.

[349] Traduction produite par les parties demanderesses en annexe 3 à la requête d'arbitrage, du 3 novembre 1997.

[350] *Salini Costruttori S.p.A. and Italstrade S.p.A. c. Le Royaume hachémite de Jordanie*, affaire CIRDI n° ARB/02/13, décision sur la compétence, 29 novembre 2004, para. 176, *JDI*, 2005.182, spéc. p. 205. Voir aussi *Impregilo v. Pakistan*, affaire CIRDI n° ARB/03/3, décision sur la compétence, 22 avril 2005, *JDI*, 2006.287, spéc. p. 302 : « *care must be taken to distinguish between (1) the jurisdiction* ratione temporis *of an ICSID tribunal and (2) the applicability* ratione temporis *of the substantive obligations contained in a BIT* » (para. 309).

425. Ainsi que l'observe le Professeur Christoph Schreuer, « [e]ven if jurisdiction is established under a treaty, this does not mean that the treaty's substantive provisions are necessarily applicable to all aspects of the case. The general rule is that the law applicable to acts and events will normally be the law in force at the time they occurred ».[351]

426. Les demanderesses ont indiqué lors des audiences du 15 janvier 2007 que le seul critère à prendre en compte était l'apparition d'une controverse postérieurement à l'entrée en vigueur de l'API. Ce n'est qu'à titre subsidiaire que les demanderesses invoquent l'applicabilité des obligations de fond de l'API, en se fondant cumulativement sur les notions de fait illicite continu et de fait illicite composite.[352] Il s'agit en réalité de deux problèmes distincts qui seront examinés séparément par le Tribunal.

427. En effet, pour que l'Etat chilien puisse voir sa responsabilité engagée en application des dispositions de l'API, il faut d'une part que le Tribunal soit compétent *ratione temporis* et, d'autre part, que les dispositions de fond de l'API soient applicables *ratione temporis* aux violations alléguées.

428. Le Tribunal ne pourra se déclarer compétent *ratione temporis* que si l'investissement des parties demanderesses est couvert par l'API au moment des faits litigieux et si le ou les différends invoqués sont eux-mêmes couverts par l'API.

429. Les dispositions de fond de l'API ne sont quant à elles applicables que si l'API est en vigueur au moment où sont commises les violations alléguées.

430. Il convient tout d'abord de déterminer si l'investissement des parties demanderesses est couvert au sens de l'article 2 de l'API.

---

[351] Christoph H. Schreuer, *Consent to arbitration*, Transnational Dispute Management, vol. 2, n°2, novembre 2005 (article mis à jour le 27 février 2007), p. 33, disponible sur le site www.transational-dispute-management.com.

[352] Transcription de l'audience du 15 janvier 2007, p. 91, (Me Malinvaud). C'était déjà la position des parties demanderesses lors des audiences de mai 2003: « *la première position du demandeur est que la Décision 43 du 28 avril 2000 constitue un acte de dépossession qui est à l'origine d'une nouvelle controverse soulevée par les demanderesses, et que dès lors toute la question de l'application* ratione temporis *du traité n'a plus d'intérêt* » (transcription de l'audience du 5 mai 2003, p. 178 (Me Malinvaud)).

a)   L'investissement effectué en 1972 par M. Pey Casado est-il
couvert par l'API ?

431.   L'article 2.2 de l'API Espagne-Chili prévoit que « [l]e présent Traité
s'appliquera aux investissements qui seraient réalisés à partir de son
entrée en vigueur par des investisseurs de l'une des parties
contractantes dans le territoire de l'autre. Toutefois, il bénéficiera
également aux investissements réalisés antérieurement à son entrée
en vigueur et qui, selon la législation de la Partie contractante
concernée, auraient la qualité d'investissement étranger ».

432.   Le seul objet de l'article 2.2 de l'API Espagne-Chili est de définir les
investissements protégés par le traité. En l'occurrence, il ne fait pas
de doute que les conditions posées par ce texte sont satisfaites.
L'investissement en question, effectué par M. Pey Casado en 1972 et
ayant la qualité d'investissement étranger conformément à la
législation chilienne, est bien couvert par l'API.

433.   Le Tribunal se propose dès lors de déterminer si les différends dont
font état les parties demanderesses sont survenus après l'entrée en
vigueur de l'API Espagne-Chili.

b)   Les différends invoqués par les parties demanderesses sont-ils
couverts par l'API ?

434.   L'article 2.3 de l'API prévoit que celui-ci « ne s'appliquera pas,
néanmoins, aux controverses ou réclamations surgies ou résolues
antérieurement à son entrée en vigueur ». Le Tribunal ne pourra
donc se déclarer compétent ratione temporis que s'il est en présence
de   « controverses »   ou   de   « réclamations »   survenues
postérieurement à l'entrée en vigueur de l'API.

435.   Les termes du paragraphe 2.3 choisis par les Etats parties à l'API,
« *controverses* » et « *réclamations* », laissent penser que les Etats
parties attribuaient à chacun de ces termes une signification distincte.
Si les parties ont tour à tour mis en avant des interprétations
différentes de ces deux notions, c'est sur la définition et la portée du
terme « *controverses* » que le désaccord des parties est le plus net.

436.   Il ressort en effet de l'examen des écritures que les parties ont fini
par   s'entendre   sur   la   signification   à   donner   au   terme
« *réclamations* »,   équivalent   du   terme   anglais   *claims*,   et
correspondant ici à une demande formée par l'une des parties pour
faire valoir ses droits.[353]   Le débat sur la définition du terme

---

[353]   V. par exemple la transcription de l'audience du 29 octobre 2001, p. 110
(intervention du conseil des demanderesses, Me Malinvaud) : « *[...] en ce
qui concerne réclamation, finalement on est assez d'accord, ça se traduirait
en anglais je dirais par ' claim ' » [...] cela suppose une action de réclamer,
donc une action, une demande, une action en droit* » (p. 110) ; v. également

« *controverses* » doit en revanche être tranché : si le terme « *controverses* » est considéré par les deux parties comme synonyme de « *différends* », les parties sont cependant en profond désaccord sur le sens et la portée qui doivent être conférés à ce terme.[354]

437. Les demanderesses invoquent trois différends qu'elles estiment tous trois postérieurs à la date d'entrée en vigueur de l'API : le premier serait survenu en 1995,[355] le deuxième en 2000[356] et le troisième en 2002.[357] Le Tribunal examinera tour à tour chacune de ces prétentions.

i. *Le différend de 1995*

(a) Position des parties

438. Pour la défenderesse, le seul différend qui puisse être identifié dans cette affaire est né bien avant l'entrée en vigueur de l'API. La défenderesse prétend en effet déduire des dispositions de l'API, et notamment de son article 10, que « *la controverse est un conflit ou différend juridique qui n'a pas besoin, selon le TBI, d'être présentée à une partie par l'autre partie* ».[358] Cette interprétation serait confirmée par le procès-verbal des réunions techniques qui ont eu lieu entre les représentants du Chili et de l'Espagne les 29, 30 septembre et le 1er octobre 1998,[359] à l'initiative du Chili, afin de

---

la transcription de l'audience du 4 mai 2000 au cours duquel la défenderesse a traduit les termes litigieux de l'article 2.3 de la façon suivante : « *le Traité ne sera pas applicable à des ' controversias ', différends en français, et ' reclamaciones ', dépôts de demande en français, survenus avant son entrée en vigueur le 29 mars 1994* ».

[354] V. par exemple le mémoire en réplique sur l'incompétence du 27 décembre 1999, pp. 64-71.

[355] Réplique des demanderesses au contre-mémoire de la défenderesse, du 23 février 2003, pp. 240-241 (les parties demanderesses évoquent ainsi « *la première controverse* », p. 240).

[356] Réplique des demanderesses au contre-mémoire de la défenderesse, du 23 février 2003, p. 22.

[357] Réplique des demanderesses au contre-mémoire de la défenderesse, du 23 février 2003, p. 121.

[358] Note de plaidoirie de l'Etat du Chili relative aux audiences des 29 et 30 octobre 2001, p. 72.

[359] Le procès-verbal du 1er octobre 1998 contient une interprétation des termes de l'article 2.3 de l'API: « Les parties accordent que les mots ' controverse ' et ' réclamation ' ne sont pas synonymes, mais qu'ils définissent des situations différentes. Le mot « controverse » devra être interprété comme discussion ou conflits d'intérêts, ce qui laisse constance indubitable, que se soit ou non produite l'action en réclamation. S'entend par « réclamation » l'action ou l'effet de réclamer, ceci est, protester contre une chose, ou s'opposer à celle-ci de mode verbal ou écrit ».

préciser le sens et la portée de certaines dispositions de l'API.[360] Selon la défenderesse, l'article 2.3 de l'API doit être compris comme excluant les controverses et les réclamations nées des actes qui se seraient produits avant l'entrée en vigueur de l'API.[361] Or, en l'espèce, « *le différend juridique, objet du présent arbitrage, [serait] né le 10 février 1975* », date à laquelle a été adopté le décret de confiscation des biens des sociétés CPP S.A. et EPC Ltda. Selon l'Etat défendeur, les demanderesses l'auraient elle-même admis en affirmant que « *le différend juridique exposé ici découle directement de l'investissement de M. Victor Pey Casado, confisqué par le Décret N°165 du 10 février 1975 [...]* ».[362]

439.   Les demanderesses estiment quant à elles que la notion de « controverse » implique nécessairement « la présence de deux versions contraires qui s'opposent »[363] et vise « toutes hypothèses conflictuelles où un minimum d'échanges est intervenu afin de matérialiser la controverse, la contestation ou la discussion ».[364] Il est donc nécessaire, selon les demanderesses, de distinguer la controverse des faits qui en sont à l'origine,[365] distinction dont se dispense l'Etat défendeur.[366] En l'espèce, les demanderesses invitent le Tribunal à faire une distinction entre la confiscation des biens des sociétés CPP S.A. et EPC Ltda, faits qui remontent à 1975, et la première controverse qui n'est survenue qu'en 1995. Selon les demanderesses, « la première controverse est [...] née après l'entrée

---

[360]   V. mémoire d'incompétence de la défenderesse du 20 juillet 1999, pp. 58-59 et la transcription de l'audience du 1er octobre 1998 en annexe 15 à ce mémoire. La défenderesse fait valoir notamment que son initiative est compatible avec l'article 10.6 de l'API puisqu'elle a pris contact le 25 août 1998 avec les autorités espagnoles pour solliciter une réunion relative à l'interprétation de l'API, avant la constitution du Tribunal au mois de septembre 1998 (v. mémoire en réplique sur l'incompétence du 27 décembre 1999, p. 77). Par ailleurs, le fait que Me Banderas, représentant du Chili dans la présente procédure, ait pu conduire la délégation chilienne présente aux réunions techniques des 29, 30 septembre et 1er octobre 1998 n'aurait rien de frauduleux puisque la conduite de ce type de négociation relève des fonctions habituelles de Me Banderas (v. mémoire en réplique sur l'incompétence du 27 décembre 1999, p. 78).

[361]   V. contre-mémoire de la défenderesse du 3 février 2003, p. 144.

[362]   Mémoire en réplique sur l'incompétence du 27 décembre 1999, p. 64. V. également note de plaidoirie de l'Etat du Chili relative aux audiences des 29 et 30 octobre 2001, pp. 74 et ss.

[363]   Dossier de plaidoirie des parties demanderesses relatif aux audiences des 29 et 30 octobre 2001, p. 19.

[364]   Réponse au mémoire soutenant l'incompétence soumis par la défenderesse, du 18 septembre 1999, p. 93.

[365]   Dossier de plaidoirie des parties demanderesses relatif aux audiences des 29 et 30 octobre 2001, p. 19.

[366]   V. la transcription de l'audience du 15 janvier 2007, p. 84 (Me Malinvaud).

en vigueur de l'API, lorsque l'État du Chili a répondu par la négative [le 20 novembre 1995] à la réclamation de M. Pey Casado et de la Fondation espagnole [du 6 septembre 1995] ».[367] Les demanderesses contestent enfin « la valeur » du procès-verbal du 1er octobre 1998 invoqué par la défenderesse au motif que celui-ci serait contraire à l'article 10.6 de l'API[368] et aurait été obtenu frauduleusement par les autorités chiliennes.[369]

(b)   Conclusions du Tribunal

440.   A titre préliminaire, le Tribunal entend se prononcer sur l'interprétation des termes de l'article 2.3 consignée dans le procès-verbal des réunions techniques des 29, 30 septembre et 1er octobre 1998 entre l'Espagne et le Chili, organisées à la demande de ce dernier. L'initiative de l'Etat défendeur, visant à organiser une rencontre entre les représentants des deux Etats parties au traité afin de s'entendre sur l'interprétation de certains de ses termes, est intervenue après l'introduction de la requête d'arbitrage (3 novembre 1997) et son enregistrement (20 avril 1998). Comme il a déjà été indiqué, il s'agit là d'un acte incompatible avec les dispositions de l'article 10.6 de l'API qui imposent aux Etats parties de s'abstenir « *d'échanger, au travers des canaux diplomatiques, des arguments concernant l'arbitrage ou une action judiciaire déjà entamée jusqu'à ce que les procédures correspondantes aient été conclues* ». Il est clair que l'interprétation de l'article 2.3 de l'API entre dans la catégorie des « *arguments concernant l'arbitrage* » échangés postérieurement à l'introduction de la procédure. En conséquence, le Tribunal ne tiendra pas compte de l'interprétation figurant dans le procès-verbal litigieux, sans pour autant préjuger du bien-fondé de cette dernière.

441.   Le Tribunal se propose dès lors d'examiner la notion de « *controverse* » que les parties tiennent pour équivalente à celle de différend. Celle-ci est définie dans la jurisprudence des juridictions internationales comme « *un désaccord sur un point de droit ou de fait, une contradiction, une opposition de thèses juridiques ou d'intérêts entre deux personnes* ».[370] Afin d'établir l'existence d'un

---

[367]   Réplique des demanderesses au contre-mémoire de la défenderesse, du 23 février 2003, p. 241.

[368]   V. réplique à la réponse soumise par la République du Chili au contre-mémoire réfutant le déclinatoire de compétence, du 7 février 2000, pp. 25-26.

[369]   V. réplique à la réponse soumise par la République du Chili au contre-mémoire réfutant le déclinatoire de compétence, du 7 février 2000, pp. 26-27.

[370]   Affaire des *Concessions Mavrommatis en Palestine*, arrêt n°2, 1924, Série A, n°2, pp. 4 et ss, spéc. p. 11. Voir également l'affaire relative au *Timor*

tel différend, « *il faut démontrer que la réclamation de l'une des parties se heurte à l'opposition manifeste de l'autre* ».[371]

442. La position de la jurisprudence CIRDI en la matière n'est pas différente.[372] Dans l'affaire *Maffezini c. Espagne*, le Tribunal arbitral a justement défini la notion de « *dispute* » dans les termes suivants :

> « *[...] there tends to be a natural sequence of events that leads to a dispute. It begins with the expression of a disagreement and the statement of a difference of views. In time these events acquire a precise legal meaning through the formulation of legal claims, their discussion and eventual rejection or lack of response by the other party. The conflict of legal views and interests will only be present in the latter stage, even though the underlying facts predate them. It has also been rightly commented that the existence of the dispute presupposes a minimum of communications between the parties, one party taking up the matter with the other, with the latter opposing the Claimant's position directly or indirectly. This sequence of events has to be taken into account in establishing the critical date for determining when under the BIT a dispute qualifies as one covered by the consent necessary to establish ICSID's jurisdiction* ».[373]

443. Cette définition du différend, qui exige un minimum d'échanges entre les parties, l'une portant le problème à la connaissance de l'autre, cette dernière s'opposant à la position de l'autre partie directement ou indirectement, est également celle retenue par le

---

[371] *oriental*, arrêt, 30 juin 1995, C.I.J. Recueil 1995, pp. 91 et s, spéc. pp. 99-100 (la Cour rappelle la jurisprudence constante de la Cour Permanente de Justice Internationale et de la Cour Internationale de Justice en la matière). Affaire du *Sud-Ouest Africain*, exceptions préliminaires, arrêt, C.I.J. Recueil 1962, p. 328.

[372] V. *Maffezini c. Espagne*, affaire CIRDI n° ARB/97/7, décision sur la compétence du 25 janvier 2000, para. 94 ; *Empresas Lucchetti, S.A. and Lucchetti Peru, S.A. c. Peru*, affaire CIRDI n° ARB/03/4, sentence du 7 février 2005, para. 48 ; *Impregilo S.p.A. c. République islamique du Pakistan*, affaire CIRDI n° ARB/03/3 décision sur la compétence du 22 avril 2005, paras.302 et ss, *JDI*, 2006.287, spéc. p. 302 et ss ; *M.C.I. Power Group L.C. and New Turbine, Inc. c. Equateur*, affaire CIRDI n° ARB/03/6, sentence du 31 juillet 2007, para. 63 ; *Sociedad anónima Eduardo Vieira c. la République du Chili*, affaire CIRDI n° ARB/04/7, sentence du 21 août 2007, para. 245.

[373] V. *Maffezini c. Espagne*, ibid, para. 96.

présent Tribunal.[374] Ainsi que l'a souligné le tribunal arbitral dans l'affaire *Helnan c. Egypte*, « *[The parties' disagreement] crystallizes as a 'dispute' as soon as one of the parties decides to have it solved, whether or not by a third party* ».[375] Ce n'est qu'avec l'expression et la confrontation des points de vue des parties que se cristallise le différend.

444.   En l'espèce, l'API est entré en vigueur le 29 mars 1994. Ce n'est que le 1er février 1995 que M. Pey Casado a saisi la Huitième Chambre du Tribunal correctionnel de Santiago d'une demande en restitution des 40.000 actions de la société Consortium Publicitaire et Périodique S.A.[376] Les parties demanderesses situent ainsi la première controverse après le 29 mai 1995, date à laquelle le juge de la Huitième Chambre du Tribunal correctionnel de Santiago a ordonné la restitution des titres de propriété de CPP S.A., des contrats de cession de ces titres et des justificatifs de paiement du prix.[377] Le 6 septembre 1995, Victor Pey Casado a en effet adressé au Président du Chili une première demande de restitution des « *biens confisqués, et actuellement aux mains du Fisc, appartenant à 'l'Entreprise Périodique Clarín Ltée' et au 'Consortium Publicitaire et Périodique S.A.'* ».[378]

445.   Le différend se cristallise au cours des échanges ultérieurs entre M. Pey Casado et le gouvernement chilien : le 20 novembre 1995, le ministère des biens nationaux informe M. Pey Casado du fait que « *pour le moment, il n'est pas possible d'accéder à ce qui est demandé, dès lors que la loi qui va régler la situation par vous décrite n'a pas encore été promulguée* ».[379] Le 10 janvier 1996, M. Pey Casado réitère sa demande de restitution auprès du Président de la République.[380] L'offre de consultations amiables formulée par M. Pey Casado le 30 avril 1997[381] n'ayant débouché sur aucun accord,

---

[374]   Cette définition a été reprise dans la sentence rendue dans l'affaire *Impregilo c. Pakistan* (*Impregilo S.p.A. c. République islamique du Pakistan*, affaire CIRDI n° ARB/03/3, décision sur la compétence du 22 avril 2005, para. 304, *JDI*, 2006.287, spéc. p. 302 et ss) et l'affaire *Vieira c. Chili* (*Sociedad anónima Eduardo Vieira c. la République du Chili*, affaire CIRDI n° ARB/04/7, sentence du 21 août 2007, para. 237 et para. 249).

[375]   V. *Helnan International Hotels A/S c. République arabe d'Egypte*, affaire CIRDI n° ARB/05/19, décision sur la compétence du 17 octobre 2006, para. 52

[376]   Annexe 21 à la requête d'arbitrage du 3 novembre 1997.

[377]   Exposé complémentaire sur la compétence du Tribunal arbitral du 11 septembre 2002, p. 174.

[378]   Annexe 22 à la requête d'arbitrage du 3 novembre 1997.

[379]   Annexe 23 à la requête d'arbitrage du 3 novembre 1997.

[380]   Annexe 23 à la requête d'arbitrage du 3 novembre 1997.

[381]   Annexe 11 à la requête d'arbitrage du 3 novembre 1997 ; v. également annexe 12 à la requête d'arbitrage.

M. Pey Casado a exprimé son consentement à l'arbitrage par lettre du 2 octobre 1997.[382]

446. Le Tribunal en conclut que le différend est né après l'entrée vigueur du Traité, les parties n'ayant pas exprimé et opposé leurs différences de vues avant l'année 1995. Les demanderesses ont précisé à plusieurs reprises qu'il fallait distinguer le différend et les faits à l'origine du différend.[383] Le Tribunal partage cette analyse. Comme l'a récemment rappelé le tribunal arbitral constitué dans l'affaire *Duke Energy*, « *What is decisive of the Tribunal's jurisdiction* ratione temporis *is the point in time at which the instant legal dispute between the parties arose, not the point in time during which the factual matters on which the dispute is based took place* ».[384]

447. L'argument de la partie adverse selon lequel « *le différend juridique, objet du présent arbitrage, est né le 10 février 1975* », ne tient aucun compte de la distinction entre le moment où survient le différend et celui où se produisent les faits litigieux qui en sont la source.[385] La date invoquée par la défenderesse est celle de l'adoption d'un décret de confiscation qui est certes à l'origine du différend mais n'en est ni la manifestation concrète ni la cristallisation ; l'Etat défendeur ne fait pas état d'une opposition entre M. Pey Casado et le Gouvernement chilien à cette époque qui soit susceptible de refléter l'expression d'un différend. Le premier différend allégué étant postérieur à l'entrée en vigueur de l'API Espagne-Chili, la condition de compétence se trouve satisfaite à son égard.

---

[382] Annexe 10 à la requête d'arbitrage du 3 novembre 1997. La Fondation Président Allende indique quant à elle avoir exprimé son consentement le 6 octobre 1997, par une résolution du conseil des fondateurs de la Fondation (annexe 2 à la requête d'arbitrage du 3 novembre 1997). La requête d'arbitrage est déposée par les parties demanderesses le 3 novembre 1997.

[383] V. par exemple la transcription de l'audience du 4 mai 2000, p. 110 (Me Malinvaud) : « *le Chili fait une confusion entre la controverse et les faits à l'origine de la controverse* » ; v. également la transcription de l'audience du 5 mai 2003, pp. 176-177 (Me Malinvaud) qui distingue les faits à l'origine de la controverse entre 1973 et 1977 et la controverse elle-même, née en 1995-1997 ; v. la transcription de l'audience du 15 janvier 2007, p. 84 (Me Malinvaud) et la transcription de l'audience du 16 janvier 2007, pp. 40-41 (Me Malinvaud).

[384] *Duke Energy International Peru Investments No. 1, Ltd. c. Pérou*, affaire CIRDI n° ARB/03/28 décision sur la compétence, 1er février 2006, para. 148.

[385] Mémoire en réplique sur l'incompétence du 27 décembre 1999, p. 64 ; v. également la transcription de l'audience du 15 janvier 2007, p. 10 et p. 16 : « *le Chili a dit que la controverse a eu lieu quand ont eu lieu les actes d'expropriation [...]* ». V. également la transcription de l'audience du 16 janvier 2007, p. 21 (Me Di Rosa).

ii.   *Le différend de 2000*

(a)   Position des parties

448.   Ayant pris connaissance le 3 avril 2000 de la Décision n°43 du Ministère des biens nationaux, décision qui accorde une indemnisation à des personnes autres que les parties demanderesses pour la confiscation des biens des sociétés CPP S.A. et EPC Ltda, les demanderesses ont prétendu immédiatement que « *la résolution du 28 avril 2000 constitue en soi un nouvel acte de dépossession ou de dénégation de la protection de l'investissement des demandeurs. Et que donc la question de savoir si c'est avant ou après l'entrée en vigueur du traité, que cette controverse a jailli, [...] paraît aujourd'hui un peu hors de propos, puisque le 28 avril dernier, un nouvel acte de cet ordre là a été réalisé* ».[386]

449.   Dès le lendemain, la défenderesse s'est opposée radicalement à cette position : « La Résolution 43, nous dit-on, a un effet de dépossession pour ce qui concerne les propriétaires de ces actions. Rien n'est plus loin de la vérité. C'est bien le contraire. Bien au contraire, cette décision permet de rendre recevable la demande par les propriétaires légitimes de ces actions ».[387]

450.   Pour la partie défenderesse, la Décision n°43 est loin d'être « *à l'origine d'un nouveau litige qui entre dans le champ de l'API* ». Le Tribunal s'est déjà, selon elle, prononcé sur la question pour conclure que « *la Décision n°43 ne se référait qu'à des tiers et non aux Demanderesses, et qu'en tout cas elle n'avait causé aucun préjudice aux Demanderesses compte tenu du fait qu'elle avait simplement donné un avis sur la compensation à des tiers, sans prétendre se prononcer sur un quelconque droit de propriété que pourraient avoir les Demanderesses* ».[388]

451.   Les demanderesses ont conclu à l'opposé que la Décision n°43 « *constitue en tout état de cause, et si nécessaire, un nouvel élément constitutif du différend* »[389]. Elles précisent dans leur mémoire du 23 février 2003 que « *[l]a controverse portant sur la ' Décision N° 43 ' est née les 3 et 4 mai 2000 devant le Tribunal arbitral, lorsque le*

---

[386]   Transcription de l'audience du 4 mai 2000, pp. 99-100 (Me Malinvaud).

[387]   Transcription de l'audience du 5 mai 2000, p. 164 (Me Banderas).

[388]   Contre-mémoire de la défenderesse du 3 février 2003, p. 147. V. également la transcription de l'audience du 16 janvier 2007, p. 22 (Me Di Rosa) : « *Pour ce qui est de la Résolution 43, dès lors qu'elle se réfère au même subject matter - l'expropriation antérieure -, il ne s'agirait pas d'une controverse* ».

[389]   Exposé complémentaire sur la compétence du Tribunal arbitral du 11 septembre 2002, p. 174.

Chili a dévoilé son existence et les demanderesses y ont exprimé leur opposition ».[390]

(b)   Conclusions du Tribunal

452.   Le Tribunal constate que la Décision n°43 a été contestée dès les audiences sur la compétence de mai 2000. A cette occasion, une nette opposition, exprimée en termes juridiques, est apparue immédiatement entre les parties.

453.   Au vu des prétentions respectives des parties exposées ci-dessus, le Tribunal estime sans hésitation que l'opposition qui s'est manifestée entre les parties lors des audiences de mai 2000, dès que les parties demanderesses ont pris connaissance de la Décision n°43, est constitutive d'un différend. Là encore, le différend étant survenu postérieurement à l'entrée en vigueur du traité, la condition de compétence *ratione temporis* est satisfaite.

iii.   *Le différend de 2002*

(a)   Position des parties

454.   Selon les demanderesses, un différend résultant du déni de justice allégué par les demanderesses *« est né après l'entrée en vigueur de l'API Espagne –Chili »*[391]. Les demanderesses font en effet valoir que la procédure engagée en 1995 devant la Première Chambre civile de Santiago pour la restitution de la rotative Goss ou l'indemnisation de sa valeur de remplacement n'a donné lieu à aucune décision sur le fond en sept ans[392]. En outre, dans le cas où la Première Chambre civile de Santiago rendrait une décision au fond dans cette affaire, l'adoption de la Décision n°43 priverait d'effet le jugement de la juridiction chilienne dans la mesure où les bénéficiaires de la Décision n°43 ont déjà été indemnisés pour la rotative en question.[393]

455.   Les demanderesses soulignent également que leurs recours auprès du pouvoir exécutif et du pouvoir judiciaire visant à mettre en cause la compatibilité de la Décision n°43 avec la procédure judiciaire introduite en 1995 ont tous été rejetés.[394] Elles indiquent avoir attiré en vain l'attention du *Contralor general* sur l'incompatibilité de la

---

[390]   Réplique des demanderesses au contre-mémoire de la défenderesse, du 23 février 2003, p. 22. V. également la transcription de l'audience du 5 mai 2003, p. 226 (Me Malinvaud) et la transcription de l'audience du 15 janvier 2007, p. 90 (Me Malinvaud).

[391]   Réplique des demanderesses au contre-mémoire de la défenderesse, du 23 février 2003, p. 121.

[392]   V. réplique des demanderesses au contre-mémoire de la défenderesse, du 23 février 2003, p. 107.

[393]   Demande complémentaire des demanderesses du 4 novembre 2002, p. 6.

[394]   *Id.*, pp. 2-5.

Décision n°43 avec l'action intentée devant la Première Chambre civile de Santiago.[395] Leur demande de rétractation des décrets de paiement de l'indemnisation accordée par la Décision n°43, déposée le 29 juillet 2002, aurait également été rejetée *in limine litis* le 14 octobre 2002.[396] Par ailleurs, la demande de mesures conservatoires des demanderesses déposée auprès de la Première Chambre civile de Santiago à l'encontre de la Décision n°43 a été rejetée le 2 octobre 2001[397] et la requête déposée par les demanderesses auprès de la Cour suprême le 5 juin 2002 arguant d'un conflit de compétence entre le pouvoir exécutif et le pouvoir judiciaire a été déclarée irrecevable[398]. Enfin, les parties demanderesses indiquent que leur recours en protection constitutionnelle pour violation de leur droit de propriété sur la rotative Goss, porté devant la Cour d'appel de Santiago, a lui aussi été déclaré irrecevable et sans fondement par cette dernière le 6 août 2002.[399]

456. Le rejet de l'ensemble de ces recours est constitutif, selon les demanderesses, d'un déni de justice à l'origine d'un différend né après l'entrée en vigueur de l'API, lorsque, d'une part, les parties demanderesses ont déposé un recours en rétractation devant le *Contralor* le 29 juillet 2002 et lorsque, d'autre part, la Première Chambre civile de Santiago a rejeté leur demande de mesures conservatoires le 2 octobre 2001.[400]

457. La défenderesse n'aborde pas directement dans ses écritures la question de l'existence d'un différend relatif au déni de justice allégué par les demanderesses. La défenderesse procède cependant à la description de l'affaire portée devant les juridictions chiliennes le 4 octobre 1995.[401] Elle attire notamment l'attention du Tribunal sur trois décisions, dont les deux premières ont été rendues par la Première Chambre civile de Santiago. La première décision invoquée est celle du 20 décembre 1996 dans laquelle la Première Chambre civile soumet aux parties une série de six questions,[402] accompagnée

---

[395] *Id.*, pp. 2-3 et annexe C-224.
[396] *Id.*, p. 3 et annexes C-220 et C-216.
[397] *Id.*, p. 4 et annexe C-219.
[398] *Id.*, pp. 3-4 et annexe C-218.
[399] *Id.*, p. 5 et annexes C-222 et C-223.
[400] V. Réplique des demanderesses au contre-mémoire de la défenderesse, du 23 février 2003, pp. 121-122.
[401] V. contre-mémoire de la défenderesse du 3 février 2003, pp. 110-115.
[402] Les six questions sont les suivantes :
« M. Pey a-t-il effectivement la capacité d'ester en justice.
Titre au nom duquel M. Pey demande la restitution de la rotative Goss.
Existence d'un contrat de dépôt portant sur la rotative ; origine et modalité dudit contrat.

d'une demande de preuve des faits allégués.[403] Le 26 avril 1999, la Première Chambre civile de Santiago a rejeté la requête de M. Pey Casado visant à ajouter une question à la liste dressée par la juridiction chilienne dans son arrêt du 20 décembre 1996.[404] La défenderesse affirme enfin que M. Pey Casado a fait appel de l'arrêt de la Première Chambre civile du 20 décembre 1996. La Cour d'appel de Santiago aurait rejeté la demande de M. Pey Casado le 4 octobre 2002.[405] La défenderesse avance également que la Première Chambre civile de Santiago aurait rejeté la demande de suspension formulée par M. Pey Casado au moment où les parties demanderesses ont déposé leur demande complémentaire.[406]

458.   La défenderesse conclut que la demande complémentaire du 4 novembre 2002 doit être rejetée, les parties demanderesses ayant fait jouer l'option irrévocable (*fork-in-the-road*) contenue à l'article 10.3 de l'API en introduisant leur demande relative à la rotative Goss devant les juridictions de l'Etat d'accueil.[407]

(b)   Conclusions du Tribunal

459.   Les parties demanderesses ont introduit une procédure judiciaire le 4 octobre 1995 devant la Première Chambre civile de Santiago visant à obtenir la restitution de la rotative Goss.[408] Toutefois, même si certaines décisions concernant des questions d'ordre probatoire ont été rendues dans cette procédure,[409] les pièces produites montrent que

---

Titre en vertu duquel l'État du Chili est en possession de la rotative dont la restitution est réclamée.

Les délais exigés par la loi pour exercer une voie de recours ont-ils effectivement été dépassés.

M. Pey a-t-il effectivement subi des préjudices causés par des actes imputables à l'État chilien ; si oui, quelle est la nature et le montant des dommages? » (V. contre-mémoire de la défenderesse, du 3 février 2003, pp. 112-113).

[403]   V. annexe 102 au contre-mémoire de la défenderesse du 3 février 2003.

[404]   V. contre-mémoire de la défenderesse du 3 février 2003, p. 113 et annexe 104 au contre-mémoire.

[405]   V. contre-mémoire de la défenderesse du 3 février 2003, p. 114 et annexe 109 au contre-mémoire.

[406]   V. contre-mémoire de la défenderesse du 3 février 2003, p. 115.

[407]   V. contre-mémoire de la défenderesse du 3 février 2003, pp. 192 et ss.

[408]   V. annexe 48 au contre-mémoire de la défenderesse du 3 février 2003.

[409]   Selon les parties demanderesses, cette procédure interne, qui vise à obtenir la restitution de la rotative Goss, n'a donné lieu à aucune « *sentence* » (V. Réplique des demanderesses au contre-mémoire de la défenderesse, du 23 février 2003, p. 107). Les décisions invoquées par la défenderesse ne peuvent de fait être qualifiées de jugement sur le fond de l'affaire (V. contre-mémoire de la défenderesse du 3 février 2003, pp. 110 et ss.). Après que le Conseil national de Défense a répondu à la requête du 4 octobre 1995 en invoquant le défaut de qualité pour agir de la partie demanderesse (annexe

la Première Chambre civile ne s'était pas prononcée sur le fond lorsqu'est intervenue la Décision n°43 et lorsque les demanderesses ont déposé leur demande complémentaire devant le Tribunal arbitral le 4 novembre 2002.

460.   Les parties demanderesses ont également tenté en vain de faire reconnaître l'incompatibilité de la Décision n°43 avec cette procédure judiciaire.

---

100 au contre-mémoire de la défenderesse du 3 février 2003), la Première Chambre civile a rendu le 20 décembre 1996 une première décision comportant six questions et demandant aux parties de rassembler des preuves précises au soutien de leurs prétentions, dans un certain délai (décision de la Première Chambre civile de Santiago du 20 décembre 1996 (annexe 102 au contre-mémoire de la défenderesse du 3 février 2003)). Le 31 janvier 1997, le conseil de M. Pey Casado demande à ce que soit substitué un premier élément de preuve, que soit retiré un second élément et ajouté un nouvel élément de preuve proposé par la partie demanderesse (requête de M. Pablo Vermehren Dominguez, au nom de M. Pey Casado, en date du 31 janvier 1997 (annexe 103 au contre-mémoire de la défenderesse du 3 février 2003). L'élément de preuve en question visait à déterminer si la rotative Goss faisait partie de l'inventaire des biens meubles auquel se réfère l'article 4 du décret suprême n° 165 de 1975 (*Ibid.*) ; cette requête est, d'après la défenderesse, rejetée par la Première Chambre civile le 26 avril 1999 (décision de la Première Chambre civile de Santiago du 26 avril 1999 (annexe 104 au contre-mémoire de la défenderesse du 3 février 2003)).
Le 23 juin 1999, M. Pey Casado, par l'intermédiaire de son avocat, informe la Cour de l'existence d'un arbitrage concernant les « *biens et crédits* » de la société CPP S.A., à l'exception de la rotative Goss, objet du litige porté devant la Cour (annexe 105 au contre-mémoire de la défenderesse sur la compétence). A cette même date, l'avocat de M. Pey Casado demande également à la Cour de bien vouloir ordonner au Ministère de la Défense nationale d'indiquer les motifs de l'occupation des locaux du journal Clarin et de produire les documents correspondants (v. *Id.*). Il demande également à la Cour que soit nommé un expert afin d'établir l'état de conservation de la rotative Goss et de déterminer sa valeur de remplacement dans le cas où la restitution serait impossible (requête de M. Pablo Vermehren Dominguez, au nom de M. Pey Casado, en date du 23 juin 1999 (annexe 105 au contre-mémoire de la défenderesse du 3 février 2003)). Le 27 juillet 1999, le Procureur de Santiago fait valoir quant à lui auprès de la Cour que M. Pey Casado n'a pas prouvé qu'il était propriétaire de la rotative Goss ou de la société EPC Ltée (Observations du Procureur de Santiago en date du 27 juillet 1999 (annexe 106 au contre-mémoire de la défenderesse du 3 février 2003)). Les 10 et 13 août 1999, la Première Chambre civile aurait tenté sans succès de localiser la rotative Goss, l'inspection ordonnée s'étant révélée infructueuse (v. contre-mémoire de la défenderesse du 3 février 2003, p. 117).
L'appel formé par M. Pey Casado contre la décision du 20 décembre 1996 a pu être rejeté le 4 octobre 2002 par la Cour d'appel de Santiago (v. contre-mémoire de la défenderesse du 3 février 2003, pp. 117-118 et annexe 109 au contre-mémoire) mais il ne s'agit pas d'une décision sur le fond.

461. Le 2 octobre 2001, la Première Chambre civile de Santiago s'est déclarée incompétente pour juger de l'incompatibilité entre la Décision n°43 et la procédure engagée devant elle depuis le 4 octobre 1995. Seule la Cour suprême serait compétente.[410]

462. Après avoir informé le *Contralor* de l'incompatibilité de la Décision n°43 avec l'action portée devant la Première Chambre civile de Santiago depuis le 4 octobre 1995,[411] les parties demanderesses lui ont reproché d'avoir entériné les 22 et 23 juillet 2002 le paiement d'une indemnisation au profit des bénéficiaires de la Décision n°43, cette indemnisation comprenant notamment le préjudice subi du fait de la confiscation de la rotative Goss.[412]

463. Les parties demanderesses ont ainsi intenté les recours suivants :

- Le 5 juin 2002, M. Pey Casado a introduit une requête devant la Cour suprême sur le fondement d'un conflit de compétence entre le pouvoir exécutif et le pouvoir judiciaire au motif que le pouvoir exécutif ne respectait pas la compétence exclusive de la Première Chambre civile de Santiago ; cette requête a été rejetée le 2 juillet 2002 ;[413]

- Le 6 juillet 2002, M. Pey Casado intente un recours en reconsidération de la décision de rejet du 2 juillet 2002 ; ce recours est rejeté le 26 juillet 2002 par la Cour suprême ;[414]

- Le 29 juillet 2002, une demande de rétractation de la décision du *Contralor* des 22 et 23 juillet 2002 est formée par M. Pey ;[415] le 14 octobre 2002, le *Contralor* a déclaré la demande irrecevable en se référant à l'arrêt de la Cour suprême du 2 juillet 2002 ;[416]

- Le 3 août 2002, M. Pey Casado a formé devant la Cour d'appel de Santiago un recours en protection constitutionnelle relatif à son droit de propriété sur la rotative Goss, droit qui aurait été violé par les décisions du *Contralor* des 22 et 23 juillet 2002 entérinant les décrets de paiement des indemnités accordées dans la Décision n°43 ;[417] le 6 août 2002, la Cour

---

[410] V. annexe C-219.

[411] V. annexe C-224.

[412] V. demande complémentaire des demanderesses du 4 novembre 2002, p. 3.

[413] V. *id.*, pp. 3-4 et annexe C-218.

[414] V. annexe C-217.

[415] V. demande complémentaire des demanderesses du 4 novembre 2002, p. 3 et annexe C-220.

[416] V. demande complémentaire des demanderesses du 4 novembre 2002, p. 3 et annexe C-216.

[417] V. *id.*, p. 5 et annexe C-222.

d'appel de Santiago a déclaré la demande irrecevable pour manque manifeste de fondement.[418]

464. Le Tribunal estime que le dernier différend entre les parties, s'est cristallisé au cours de la période 2002-2003. Avec l'introduction de leur demande complémentaire le 4 novembre 2002, les demanderesses ont, pour la première fois dans cette procédure, reproché à l'Etat chilien un déni de justice et ainsi formulé une réclamation.[419] C'est en demandant au Tribunal arbitral dans son mémoire du 3 février 2003 de rejeter la demande complémentaire des demanderesses que la défenderesse a confirmé l'existence d'un différend sur la question du déni de justice.[420]

465. Au vu de ce qui précède, le Tribunal conclut que les trois différends invoqués par les demanderesses sont bien survenus postérieurement à l'entrée en vigueur de l'API et qu'il est en conséquence compétent *ratione temporis* pour en connaître.

466. Cela ne signifie pas pour autant que les dispositions de fond de l'API sont applicables à l'intégralité des violations alléguées par les demanderesses. En effet, en vertu du principe de non-rétroactivité des traités, l'applicabilité des obligations de fond d'un traité est déterminée, sauf accord contraire des parties que le Tribunal estime ne pas être intervenu en l'espèce, en fonction de la date à laquelle s'est produit le fait illicite et non en fonction du moment où apparaît et se cristallise le différend, critère distinct ne servant qu'à établir la compétence *ratione temporis* du Tribunal. Ce n'est que si la violation alléguée est postérieure à l'entrée en vigueur du traité que les dispositions de fond de ce dernier seront applicables à ladite violation. Cette question sera examinéedans les développements concernant le fond.

4. L'option irrévocable (*fork-in-the-road*)

467. Le consentement de l'Etat à l'arbitrage résultant de l'API n'est donné que pour autant que l'investisseur n'a pas renoncé à se prévaloir des dispositions du Traité en exerçant des voies de droit que le Traité

---

[418] V. *id.*, p. 5 et annexe C-223.

[419] V. *id.*, p. 2 et ss. Dans leur réplique des demanderesses au contre-mémoire de la défenderesse, du 23 février 2003, les parties demanderesses font valoir que « *le Tribunal est compétent* ratione temporis *selon l'art. 2(3) de l'API parce que le différend portant sur les presses GOSS et la Décision N° 43 est né après l'entrée en vigueur de l'API Espagne-Chile* » (p. 121). Selon la défenderesse, « *les Demanderesses ont exercé leur choix unique dans le cadre de l'APPI Espagne-Chili* » et ne peuvent présenter leur demande fondée sur le déni de justice (réplique de la défenderesse du 4 avril 2003, p. 38 et ss).

[420] Contre-mémoire de la défenderesse du 3 février 2003, pp. 196 et ss.

estime, en stipulant une clause d'option irrévocable ou de *fork in the road*, incompatibles avec celles qu'il offre lui-même.

468.   Le Tribunal rappellera les arguments développés par les parties sur l'exercice de l'option irrévocable prévue à l'article 10 de l'API Espagne-Chili avant de formuler les conclusions auxquelles il est parvenu sur la question.

a)   La position des parties

i.   *La position de la défenderesse*

469.   La défenderesse soutient que M. Pey Casado a exercé l'option irrévocable prévue à l'article 10 de l'API « en introduisant une action en justice devant les tribunaux chiliens en ce qui concerne les biens confisqués à CPP S.A. et EPC Ltda ».[421]

470.   La défenderesse déduit en effet de la formulation de la demande introduite par M. Pey Casado le 4 octobre 1995 « que l'intention de [ce dernier] n'était pas à l'origine de chercher uniquement à obtenir la restitution ou l'indemnisation devant des tribunaux chiliens de la rotative Goss mais que cette demande faisait partie d'un plan à plus vaste portée qui comportait une série de demandes contre la République du Chili relatives à divers biens confisqués –tant les biens personnels de M. Pey Casado que ceux appartenant à la société dont il dit être actionnaire majoritaire (c'est-à-dire de CPP S.A.). C'est pour cette raison que M. Pey Casado a affirmé qu'« en premier lieu » il demandait la restitution de la rotative Goss et que « ultérieurement » il introduirait de nouvelles demandes relatives à d'autres biens ».[422] M. Pey Casado n'aurait formulé une réserve sur la possibilité d'un arbitrage CIRDI devant la Première Chambre civile que plusieurs mois plus tard.

471.   La défenderesse invoque par ailleurs les rapports d'activité de la Fondation Président Allende des années 1995, 1996 et 1997 au motif que ceux-ci montreraient que la Fondation considérait elle aussi que « *la demande initiale devant la Première Chambre Civile du Tribunal de Santiago faisait partie d'un plan de réclamations à soumettre aux tribunaux chiliens en ce qui concerne la confiscation de CPP S.A. et EPC Ltda* »[423] et qu'elle n'avait envisagé la possibilité de l'arbitrage CIRDI qu'en 1997.

---

[421]   Contre-mémoire de la défenderesse du 3 février 2003, p. 188 ; mémoire d'incompétence de la défenderesse du 20 juillet 1999, pp. 128-131 ; mémoire en réplique sur l'incompétence du 27 décembre 1999, p. 146 et p. 162 et note de plaidoirie du Chili relative aux audiences des 29 et 30 octobre 2001, p. 108.

[422]   Contre-mémoire de la défenderesse du 3 février 2003, p. 189.

[423]   V. *id.*, p. 191.

472. Après avoir rappelé que la clause d'option irrévocable a pour but d'éviter les procédures dédoublées ou parallèles et le découpage des demandes bien par bien, la défenderesse fait valoir, en se fondant sur une consultation du Professeur R. Dolzer, que l'article 10 ne pourrait permettre d'introduire à la fois une action en justice devant un tribunal étatique avant la fin de la période réservée aux consultations amiables puis une requête d'arbitrage devant un tribunal arbitral ayant le même objet, une fois achevée la période de consultations amiables. La situation dans laquelle se trouve l'Etat défendeur, qui doit mener de front deux procédures, l'une devant les tribunaux chiliens, l'autre devant le présent Tribunal, pour régler la même question de fond, serait précisément celle que l'API a pour but d'éviter.

473. La défenderesse estime que la demande introduite devant les juridictions chiliennes concerne « les dommages causés par la confiscation de CPP S.A. et EPC Ltda » et « a précisément le même objet que sa demande devant le CIRDI ».[424] En outre, « *tant l'affaire GOSS que l'action engagée devant le CIRDI sont fondées sur les mêmes prétendus droits de propriété au regard de la loi chilienne* ».[425] A supposer même que la demande de M. Pey Casado devant les juridictions chiliennes ne concerne que la rotative Goss, ce qui au demeurant ne serait pas le cas, le Tribunal ne pourrait autoriser les demanderesses à diviser leurs demandes comme elles le font et devrait conclure que M. Pey Casado a exercé l'option irrévocable prévue par l'API.

474. Si toutefois le Tribunal refusait de se considérer incompétent au motif que l'option irrévocable n'a pas été exercée du fait de l'action introduite devant les tribunaux chiliens, la défenderesse demande au Tribunal de rejeter la demande complémentaire déposée par les demanderesses le 4 novembre 2002.

475. Selon la défenderesse, « [l]es Parties demanderesses prétendent transférer devant le CIRDI une demande qu'elles avaient intentée au Chili et qu'elles avaient toujours caractérisé comme une demande indépendante et séparée de celle qu'elles avaient intentée devant le CIRDI, en dépit du fait déjà mentionné que cette demande introduit exactement la même question de fond que celle qui doit être décidée dans le présent arbitrage. Les Parties demanderesses ont intenté leur action concernant la presse GOSS au Chili en 1995 (c'est-à-dire après l'entrée en vigueur de l'APPI) et en introduisant leur demande

---

[424]   V. contre-mémoire de la défenderesse du 3 février 2003, p. 188.
[425]   Réplique de la défenderesse du 4 avril 2003, p. 39. Cette identité de fondement priverait les demanderesses de la possibilité d'invoquer la sentence rendue dans l'affaire *Alex Genin c. Estonie*.

devant le CIRDI, elles ont choisi de ne pas retirer l'action qu'elles avaient intentée au Chili ».[426]

476. L'Etat défendeur en conclut que la demande complémentaire est contraire aux dispositions de l'article 10(3) de l'API, à l'article 26 de la Convention CIRDI, à l'article 40(1) du Règlement d'arbitrage du CIRDI ainsi qu'aux « *principes fondamentaux de fair play, préclusion et de justice de procédure* ».[427] Elle ne pourrait donc être accueillie.

477. Enfin, les demanderesses ne sauraient échapper à l'application de la clause d'option irrévocable en invoquant à titre subsidiaire la clause de la nation la plus favorisée. L'examen de la jurisprudence arbitrale CIRDI permettrait de conclure que la clause de la nation la plus favorisée de l'API Espagne-Chili n'est formulée de façon suffisamment large pour être appliquée à la clause de règlement des différends comme le souhaiteraient les demanderesses.

ii.   *La position des demanderesses*

478. Les demanderesses estiment avoir « exclu du consentement à l'arbitrage la controverse relative à la 'restitution pure et simple – ou, à défaut, [paiement] de la valeur de remplacement correspondante – de la machine rotative GOSS', parce que, sur cette question spécifique et cela seulement, il se poursuit, depuis une date antérieure au consentement [à l'arbitrage], un procès devant les tribunaux internes au Chili (Rôle n°3.510-95 de la 1er. Chambre Civile de Santiago, intitulé Pey c. Fisc du Chili) […] ».[428] Invoquant la sentence rendue dans l'affaire Olguín c. Paraguay, les demanderesses insistent sur le fait que la restitution de la rotative Goss ou l'obtention de sa valeur de remplacement est l'unique objet de sa demande devant la Première Chambre civile de Santiago. Elles précisent également que l'action introduite par ailleurs devant la Huitième Chambre du Tribunal correctionnel de Santiago avait pour unique but d'obtenir la restitution des titres de CPP S.A. dont M. Pey Casado est propriétaire. Les lettres adressées au Président de la République du Chili en 1995 et 1996 et au gouvernement chilien en 1997, qui visaient à obtenir une solution amiable du litige ne constituent pas davantage un exercice de l'option irrévocable prévue par l'article 10 de l'API.

---

[426]   V. contre-mémoire de la défenderesse du 3 février 2003, pp. 196-197.

[427]   Contre-mémoire de la défenderesse du 3 février 2003, p. 197.

[428]   Réponse au mémoire soutenant l'incompétence soumis par la défenderesse, du 18 septembre 1999, p. 139. V. également réplique à la réponse soumise par la République du Chili au contre-mémoire réfutant le déclinatoire de compétence, du 7 février 2000, p. 22.

479. A aucun moment la défenderesse n'aurait apporté la preuve que les demanderesses auraient introduit une action devant les juridictions chiliennes ayant le même objet que le présent arbitrage.

480. Selon les demanderesses, la clause d'option irrévocable ne s'applique pas davantage à leur demande complémentaire relative au déni de justice qu'elles prétendent avoir subi dans la procédure introduite devant les tribunaux chiliens pour obtenir la restitution de la rotative Goss.[429] L'exercice de l'option irrévocable serait en effet impossible dans le cas d'un déni de justice car lorsqu'une partie porte un différend devant une juridiction interne et que cette procédure interne débouche sur un déni de justice, par définition imprévisible, alors que par ailleurs la même partie a introduit une procédure d'arbitrage, la demande portée par la suite devant le Tribunal arbitral est nécessairement différente. Le déni de justice dans la procédure introduite en 1995 pour obtenir la restitution de la rotative Goss pourrait donc être porté à la connaissance du Tribunal sans que soit exercée l'option irrévocable.

481. A titre subsidiaire, les demanderesses se fondent sur la clause de la nation la plus favorisée de l'API Espagne-Chili et invoquent notamment les clauses de règlement des différends des API Suisse-Chili,[430] Chili-Allemagne[431] et Chili-Pays-Bas,[432] estimant que la jurisprudence arbitrale permettrait en l'occurrence l'application la clause de la nation la plus favorisée à la clause de règlement des litiges de l'API.

b)   Conclusions du Tribunal

482. L'article 10 de l'API prévoit dans sa partie pertinente que :

> *« Si la controverse n'a pas pu être résolue au terme de six mois à partir du moment où elle aura été soulevée par l'une ou l'autre des Parties, elle sera soumise, au choix de l'investisseur :*
> *Soit aux juridictions nationales de la Partie contractante impliquée dans la controverse ;*

---

[429]   V. réplique des demanderesses au contre-mémoire de la défenderesse, du 23 février 2003, p. 114. V. demande complémentaire des demanderesses, du 4 novembre 2002. Les demanderesses ont élargi le champ du déni de justice dans cette affaire, estimant qu'il découle également d'une *« dénégation abusive de l'accès à l'arbitrage allant dans le sens de pousser le Tribunal arbitral vers le déni de justice »* (transcription de l'audience du 15 janvier 2007, p. 95 (Me Garcés)).

[430]   Les demanderesses invoquent l'article 9(3) de l'API Suisse-Chili.

[431]   Les demanderesses se fondent sur l'article 10(3) de l'API Chili-Allemagne.

[432]   Les demanderesses invoquent la disposition du protocole complétant l'API Chili-Pays-Bas relative à l'article 8 de l'API.

> *Soit à un arbitrage international dans les conditions décrites au paragraphe 3.*
> *Une fois que l'investisseur aura soumis la controverse aux juridictions de la Partie contractante impliquée ou à l'arbitrage international, le choix de l'une ou l'autre de ces procédures sera définitif »* (traduction libre fournie par les demanderesses).

483. L'exercice de l'option irrévocable suppose la réunion de trois conditions. Les demandes portées respectivement devant les juridictions nationales et devant le Tribunal arbitral doivent avoir à la fois le même objet et le même fondement et être présentées par les mêmes parties.

484. Ainsi que l'a rappelé très clairement le Tribunal arbitral constitué dans l'affaire *Occidental Exploration and Production Company c. Equateur*:

> « *[t]o the extent that a dispute might involve the same parties, object and cause of action it might be considered as the same dispute and the 'fork in the road' mechanism would preclude its submission to concurrent tribunals* ».[433]

485. Le Tribunal arbitral dans l'affaire *Azurix c. Argentine*,[434] a justement souligné que l'exigence de la triple identité a été constamment réaffirmée par les tribunaux arbitraux. De même, dans l'affaire *CMS c. Argentine*, le Tribunal arbitral a rappelé qu'une clause d'option irrévocable ne pouvait trouver à s'appliquer lorsque les parties et le fondement de la demande sont différents.[435]

---

[433] *Occidental Exploration and Production Company c. République d'Equateur*, affaire LCIA n° UN3467, sentence finale du 1er juillet 2004, para. 52.

[434] *Azurix Corp. c. La République d'Argentine*, affaire CIRDI n° ARB/01/12, décision sur la compétence du 8 décembre 2003, para. 89, *JDI* 2004.275, spéc. p. 281. Dans cette affaire, le Tribunal s'est référé aux trois critères posés dans l'affaire *Benvenuti c. Congo* - l'identité de parties, d'objet et de fondement - avant de préciser que « *[t]his line of reasoning has been consistently followed by arbitral tribunals in cases involving claims under BITs (...)* » (v. paras.88-89). V. également *Enron Corporation and Ponderosa Asset, LP c. La République d'Argentine*, affaire CIRDI n° ARB/01/3, décision sur la compétence du 4 janvier 2004, para. 97.

[435] CMS Gas Transmission Company c. La République d'Argentine, affaire CIRDI n° ARB/01/8, décision sur la compétence du 17 juillet 2003, para. 80, JDI 2004.236, spéc. pp. 250-251. V. Pan American Energy LLC et BP Argentina Exploration Company c. La République d'Argentine, affaire CIRDI n° ARB/03/13 et BP America Production Co. and Others c. La République d'Argentine, affaire CIRDI n° ARB/04/8, décision sur les objections préliminaires du 27 juillet 2006, para. 157.

486.   Si l'un des trois éléments de la triple identité rappelée ci-dessus fait défaut, la clause d'option irrévocable ne peut être appliquée. Or, cette triple identité n'a jamais existé dans la présente affaire.

    i.   *Exclusion de la rotative Goss du champ des demandes présentées dans l'arbitrage*

487.   Dans la lettre du 2 octobre 1997 par laquelle M. Pey Casado a exprimé son consentement à l'arbitrage, il était précisé que :

> « [...] *le présent consentement inclut dans son champ d'application toutes et chacune des controverses juridiques découlant de la confiscation de mes investissements commerciaux cités [ci-dessus], à la seule exception de celle relative à la restitution pure et simple – ou, à défaut, [paiement] de la valeur de remplacement correspondante – de la machine rotative GOSS, achetée en 1972 et installée au siège du quotidien CLARIN. Le consentement inclut toutefois la controverse juridique relative à tous les préjudices découlant de la mainmise sur ladite rotative, consistant en* damnum emergens, lucrum cessans *et intérêts compensatoires* ».[436]

488.   Le contentieux relatif à la restitution de la rotative Goss a donc été expressément et très clairement exclu du champ de compétence du Tribunal.

489.   Les demanderesses demandaient par ailleurs dans leur demande d'arbitrage que le Tribunal « déclare illégitime et contraire au Droit international la saisie et la confiscation de l'investissement réalisé par le citoyen espagnol M. Victor Pey Casado »[437] et condamne la République du Chili au paiement de dommages-intérêts pour le préjudice subi du fait de la saisie et la confiscation des biens des demanderesses, sur le fondement des dispositions pertinentes de l'API Espagne-Chili.[438] Les demanderesses n'ont jamais cherché par la suite à modifier l'étendue de leur consentement à l'arbitrage en y incluant la rotative Goss, ainsi qu'en attestent leurs écritures postérieures.

490.   Dans la demande déposée devant la Première Chambre civile de Santiago le 4 octobre 1995, M. Pey Casado a fait valoir que la rotative Goss avait été illicitement saisie par l'Etat chilien en 1973 et, sur le fondement des dispositions du code civil chilien, demande que

---

[436]   Lettre de M. Pey Casado du 2 octobre 1997 (annexe 10 à la requête d'arbitrage du 3 novembre 1997).

[437]   Requête d'arbitrage du 3 novembre 1997, p. 10.

[438]   *Id.*, pp. 9-10.

lui soit restituée la rotative en question. Dans le cas où la restitution serait impossible, M. Pey Casado demande une indemnisation correspondant à la valeur de la rotative plus les intérêts et, le cas échéant, une indemnisation pour les éventuels dommages qu'aurait subis la rotative.[439]

491. La requête d'arbitrage et la demande introduite devant le juge chilien ont donc un objet et un fondement distincts. La première consiste à demander réparation du préjudice découlant des actes de saisie et de confiscation relatifs aux sociétés CPP S.A. et EPC Ltda sur le fondement de certaines dispositions de l'API Chili-Espagne, tandis que la seconde vise la restitution d'un bien meuble bien identifié, la rotative Goss, et expressément exclu du champ du consentement à l'arbitrage, en se fondant sur le droit chilien.

492. Le simple fait que M. Pey Casado ait exprimé devant le juge chilien l'intention d'introduire dans le futur de nouvelles demandes concernant d'autres biens appartenant la société CPP S.A., sans pour autant procéder effectivement au dépôt de ces demandes, ne saurait déclencher l'application de la clause d'option irrévocable. Ainsi que l'a rappelé à juste titre le Tribunal arbitral dans l'affaire *Pan American Energy c. Argentine*, les tribunaux ne concluront jamais à la légère que les demandeurs ont choisi de porter leur différend devant les juridictions de l'Etat d'accueil et, de ce fait, exercé l'option irrévocable prévue dans l'API applicable. Cela reviendrait à priver de toute utilité la possibilité de recourir à l'arbitrage international.[440]

493. En l'espèce, les demanderesses ont très clairement distingué l'objet et le fondement de la demande déposée devant la juridiction chilienne de ceux de la requête d'arbitrage. Le Tribunal considère par conséquent que l'option irrévocable prévue à l'article 10(2) de l'API n'avait pas été exercée par M. Pey Casado lorsqu'il a déposé sa requête d'arbitrage.

ii. *La demande fondée sur le déni de justice ne se heurte pas à l'option irrévocable car ce n'est pas, par définition, ce qui était demandé aux juridictions locales*

494. La demande complémentaire des demanderesses du 4 novembre 2002, confirmée par leurs mémoires postérieurs et lors des audiences,

---

[439] Demande de M. Pey Casado devant la Première Chambre civile de la Cour d'appel de Santiago du 4 octobre 1995 (annexe 48 au contre-mémoire de la défenderesse, du 3 février 2003).

[440] V. *Pan American Energy LLC et BP Argentina Exploration Company c. Argentine*, affaire CIRDI n° ARB/03/13 *et BP America Production Co. and Others c. Argentine*, affaire CIRDI n° ARB/04/8, décision sur les objections préliminaires du 27 juillet 2006, para. 155.

consiste à porter devant le Tribunal non pas la demande de restitution de la rotative Goss mais une demande de réparation pour le préjudice découlant du déni de justice subi par M. Pey Casado dans cette procédure interne.

495. Le Tribunal estime que la clause d'option irrévocable contenue dans l'API n'empêche pas les demanderesses de porter leur demande relative au déni de justice devant le Tribunal arbitral. Ainsi que l'explique justement le Professeur Jan Paulsson dans son ouvrage consacré au déni de justice, l'allégation de déni de justice du fait des juridictions nationales est précisément celle qui ne sera pas affectée par la clause d'option irrévocable :

> « *Treaties which require an election of remedies, with the result that a claimant chooses an irreversible direction at a fork in the road, do not preclude claims before an international tribunal with respect to acts or omissions which were not encompassed in the petition made to an initially elected national forum. The most obvious instance would be an allegation of denial of justice in that very forum* »[441].

496. En l'espèce, bien que les parties soient les mêmes, l'objet de la demande complémentaire, qui consiste à demander une indemnisation pour le préjudice subi du fait d'un déni de justice, n'est de toute évidence pas identique à celui de l'action portée devant les tribunaux chiliens pour obtenir la restitution de la rotative Goss. Le fondement est également différent dans chaque affaire : la demande relative au déni de justice est fondée sur l'API ; l'action intentée devant le juge chilien est fondée sur le droit chilien et, plus particulièrement, sur les dispositions du code civil relatives à la restitution.

497. Le Tribunal conclut que l'option irrévocable prévue à l'article 10(2) de l'API n'avait donc pas été exercée lorsque les demanderesses ont déposé devant le Tribunal arbitral leur demande complémentaire relative au déni de justice.

498. Les demanderesses n'ayant pas fait jouer la clause d'option irrévocable, il est inutile de s'interroger sur l'éventuelle application de la clause de la nation la plus favorisée à la clause de règlement des différends de l'API.

---

[441]   J. Paulsson, *Denial of Justice in International Law*, Cambridge University Press, 2005, p. 130.

D.   Conclusion

499.   En résumé, le Tribunal arbitral a constaté qu'il était bien en présence d'un différend d'ordre juridique en relation directe avec un investissement au sens de la Convention CIRDI, et que les parties ont consenti par écrit à soumettre au Centre ce différend. De plus, le Tribunal arbitral est parvenu à la conclusion que, ayant valablement renoncé à sa nationalité chilienne avant son consentement à soumettre le différend à l'arbitrage, M. Pey Casado est bien un « *ressortissant d'un autre Etat contractant* » au sens de l'article 25 (2) (a) de la Convention aux dates critiques.

500.   Dès lors, le Tribunal arbitral ne peut que rejeter l'exception qui a été soulevée par la défenderesse et admettre sa compétence pour statuer sur le fond du litige pour ce qui concerne la première partie demanderesse, M. Pey Casado.

V.   LA COMPETENCE DU CENTRE ET DU TRIBUNAL POUR CONNAITRE DE LA DEMANDE DE LA FONDATION PRESIDENTE ALLENDE

501.   La prochaine question à examiner, compte tenu des exposés et des conclusions respectives des parties, est celle de la compétence du CIRDI et du Tribunal arbitral quant à la deuxième partie demanderesse, la Fundación Presidente Allende (« *Fondation Presidente Allende* » ou « *Fondation* »).[442]

---

[442]   Les demanderesses ont soulevé que la défenderesse n'a fait d'objection à la qualité pour agir de la Fondation Presidente Allende durant les six mois après avoir eu connaissance de la Requête d'arbitrage du 3 novembre 1997, et que cette qualité de la Fondation ne figurait pas parmi les motifs allégués dans la lettre du Chili au Secrétaire général du CIRDI en date du 18 mars 1998, dans laquelle le Chili demandait à ce que le CIRDI n'enregistre pas la Requête pour défaut de la juridiction du Centre (v. réponse au mémoire soutenant l'incompétence soumis par la défenderesse, du 18 septembre 1999, p. 128 ; mémoire des demanderesses du 17 mars 1999, p. 31). En réponse, la défenderesse a soutenu qu'il n'existe pas d'obligation de contester la qualité pour agir dans le délai allégué et que, en tout état de cause, le Chili l'aurait contesté plus tard, par une lettre adressée au CIRDI en date du 5 mai 1998 (v. mémoire en réplique sur l'incompétence du 27 décembre 1999, p. 122). Le Tribunal constate que les demanderesses n'ont pas tiré de conséquences procédurales du délai allégué dans lequel la défenderesse a soulevé l'exception d'incompétence quant à la Fondation Presidente Allende et que, notamment, elle n'a pas conclu à l'irrecevabilité de cette exception sur cette base. En tout état de cause, la qualité pour agir de la Fondation Presidente Allende a été soulevée en détail, au plus tard dans le premier mémoire d'incompétence de la défenderesse, du 20 juillet 1999.

502. Avant d'examiner si les conditions légales de la compétence du CIRDI et du Tribunal arbitral sont remplies, il convient de rappeler brièvement les faits concernant la création[443] ainsi que l'activité de la Fondation Presidente Allende.

A.   Résumé des faits

503. La Fondation Presidente Allende a été crée le 16 janvier 1990 par un acte notarié passé à Madrid. Le notaire, Maître Jaime García Rosado y García mentionne que sont comparus devant lui Monsieur Juan Enrique Garcés Ramón (disposant de pouvoirs conférés à lui par M. Pey Casado le 6 octobre 1989[444] et par Monsieur Gonzalo-Oscar Marten Garcia (Ministre de la Planification Nationale du Chili entre novembre 1970 et septembre 1973) ainsi que Monsieur Oscar Soto Guzman (médecin personnel du Président Allende) aux fins de créer une Fondation Presidente Allende, comme fondation culturelle de droit privé à but non lucratif. La Fondation est domiciliée Calle Alfonso XII à Madrid et a été créée pour une durée indéterminée.[445]

504. Selon l'article 3 des Statuts de la Fondation, son but est « la promotion des libertés et droits culturels, civiques, démocratiques, sociaux et économiques du peuple du Chili et des peuples hispano-américains, conformément aux valeurs et aux idéaux soutenus para [sic] Salvador Allende ».[446]

505. Le capital de la Fondation est composé de divers éléments : un million de pesetas donné par Monsieur Garcés Ramón, cent mille pesetas apportés par Monsieur Martner Garcia et 90% des avoirs de diverses sociétés apportés par M. Pey Casado en tant que « *propriétaire des actions sociales, du patrimoine et des droits de toute nature* » (« *en su condición de proprietario de las acciones sociales del patrimonio y derechos de cualquier naturaleza* »).[447] Ces sociétés sont définies à l'article 11 des Statuts de la façon suivante : « *'Consortium Publicitaire Périodique S.A.', constitué par acte du 3 août 1967 par-devant Me Rafael ZALDIVAR, Notaire à Santiago du Chili, dont le siège est à Santiago du Chili, 'Entreprise Périodique Clarin Limitée', constituée au Chili en 1955, dont le siège est à* »

---

443   Déjà mentionné dans la partie Faits de la présente sentence.

444   M. Pey Casado avait donné pouvoir à Monsieur Marten Garcia, aux fins de créer ladite fondation, le 6 octobre 1989 par devant un notaire de Miami. V. annexe C-7 à la réponse au mémoire soutenant l'incompétence soumis par la défenderesse, du 18 septembre 1999.

445   Annexe C-7 à la réponse au mémoire soutenant l'incompétence soumis par la défenderesse, du 18 septembre 1999.

446   *Id.*

447   *Id.*

Santiago, acquis par l'achat [par M. Pey Casado] *à Monsieur Sainte-Marie Soruco qui a eu lieu en 1972 ».*[448]

506. En ce qui concerne les apports de M. Pey Casado à la Fondation, il apparaît que M. Pey Casado a signé l'acte de transfert et celui d'acceptation par-devant un notaire des États-Unis, le 6 février 1990, agissant en sa double qualité de Président de la Fondation et de ressortissant espagnol.[449] Cet acte a été enregistré mais la donation aurait été acceptée par la Fondation au Ministère espagnol de la Culture le 14 décembre 1994,[450] deux semaines après l'entrée en vigueur de la loi 30/1994[451] exonérant les fondations d'impôts pour les donations en leur faveur (article 65).[452]

507. Une ordonnance ministérielle du 27 avril 1990[453] a approuvé, classé et enregistré la Fondation. Cette ordonnance transcrivait littéralement, conformément à la législation régissant les fondations citées dans l'ordonnance, les données figurant dans les « *écritures portant constitution de la Fondation* » du 11 janvier précédent, dont le capital de la Fondation limité à 1,1 millions de pesetas.

508. Selon la défenderesse, en 1995 et 1996, les activités de la Fondation auraient été consacrées essentiellement à suivre les procédures judiciaires et/ou politiques en cours au Chili, et notamment devant le Parlement chilien, en ce qui concerne la reconnaissance des droits patrimoniaux cédés à la Fondation, ainsi qu'à agir juridiquement en vue d'obtenir du pouvoir judiciaire chilien une indemnisation pour les dommages subis dès 1973.[454]

509. La Fondation a fait valoir aussi les activités multiples, judiciaires, politiques et culturelles qu'elle mène depuis sa création.[455] Les demanderesses ont rappelé que les actions en justice conduites par M. Pey Casado l'avaient été également en défense des intérêts de la Fondation en vertu des accords autorisant aussi bien la Fondation que

---

[448] *Id.*

[449] V. annexe 18 au mémoire des demanderesses du 17 mars 1999.

[450] Annexe 9 à la requête d'arbitrage du 3 novembre 1997.

[451] Journal Officiel du 25 novembre 1994.

[452] V. la table chronologique des faits en relation avec la compétence et le fond de l'affaire, du 11 septembre 2002, p.14.

[453] Publiée au *Journal Officiel* du 6 juillet 1990.

[454] V. contre-mémoire de la défenderesse du 3 février 2003, pp. 191-193, et annexes 118, 119, 120 et 121.

[455] Intervention au Parlement européen, au sujet des confiscations sous le régime militaire à l'occasion de l'examen de l'accord-cadre CEE-Chili ; attribution de bourses d'études aux étudiants chiliens en Espagne ; défense des victimes de toutes nationalités du régime issu du coup d'Etat ; actions en justice en Europe dans l' « *affaire Pinochet* » ; actions auprès du Parlement espagnol, en restitution des biens confisqués ; etc.

M. Pey Casado à agir l'un en faveur de l'autre pour la récupération de leurs biens confisqués.

510. La défenderesse a fait remarquer que, en 1999, les statuts de la Fondation avaient été modifiés sur divers points, comme l'emploi du capital en cas de dissolution, et pour énoncer que M. Pey Casado possédait, non pas une double nationalité comme déclaré précédemment par le mandataire de M. Pey Casado mais la seule nationalité espagnole.[456]

511. À la lumière de ces faits ainsi résumés, il y a lieu d'examiner si le Centre et le Tribunal arbitral sont compétents pour se prononcer sur les demandes de la seconde partie demanderesse, la Fondation Président Allende.

B.   En droit

512. Les conditions légales pour la compétence du CIRDI et du Tribunal arbitral, notamment celles posées par l'article 25 de la Convention CIRDI, on été décrites en détail ci-dessus, dans le contexte de l'analyse de la compétence du CIRDI et du Tribunal arbitral de connaître de la demande de M. Pey Casado.

513. Pour que le Centre et le Tribunal arbitral soient compétents pour connaître de la demande de la Fondation Presidente Allende, cette dernière doit notamment justifier de l'existence d'un différend d'ordre juridique, que ce différend oppose un Etat contractant et le ressortissant d'un autre Etat contractant, que ce différend soit en relation directe avec un investissement et que les parties aient consenti par écrit à soumettre le différend au Centre.

514. Ainsi qu'on l'a vu à propos de la première partie demanderesse, ni la condition relative à l'existence d'un différend d'ordre juridique, ni celle relative à la qualité d'Etat contractant ne font l'objet de contestation de la part de la défenderesse.   En revanche, les parties sont en désaccord sur la condition d'investissement, sur la condition relative à la nationalité de l'investisseur, ainsi que sur la condition de consentement. La majorité des arguments présentés par les parties dans le contexte de la compétence du Centre et du Tribunal arbitral quant à la Fondation Presidente Allende concernent les questions de savoir si M. Pey Casado a valablement cédé la majorité des actions de CPP S.A. et EPC Ltda à la Fondation, et quelle serait la conséquence d'une telle cession sur de droit d'agir de la Fondation et sur la compétence du Centre et du Tribunal arbitral à l'égard de la Fondation.

---

[456]   Annexe 135 au contre-mémoire de la défenderesse du 3 février 2003.

1. **La condition d'investissement au sens de la Convention CIRDI**

515. La première condition de compétence contestée concerne l'investissement au sens de l'article 25 de la Convention CIRDI, et notamment la question de savoir si la Fondation Président Allende peut être considérée comme une partie à un litige qui soit « *en relation directe avec un investissement [...]* ».

516. Si la position de la Fondation était examinée de manière « *indépendante* » et en soi, c'est-à-dire abstraction faite de la cession de droits opérée en sa faveur par M. Pey Casado, il y aurait lieu de se demander si, au moins *prima facie*, elle ait le caractère d'« *investisseur* ». En effet, elle n'a fait que recevoir de M. Pey Casado (et d'autres) une donation (terme utilisé par son Conseil, Me Garcés), ceci abstraction faite de ses buts énoncés dans ses statuts.[457] Il est toutefois superflu d'approfondir cette question à ce stade, dès lors que le débat entre les parties s'est concentré sur la question de la cession d'une partie de ses droits par M. Pey Casado à la Fondation.

517. La question de savoir si la Fondation se qualifie comme « *investisseur* » au sens de l'article 25 de la Convention CIRDI dépend donc de la validité et des effets du transfert de droits dont elle a bénéficié, à titre gratuit, de la part de la première partie demanderesse.[458] Cette question est d'abord une question de droit privé ou de droit international privé, qu'il convient de distinguer de la seconde question à examiner, notamment celle des effets, qu'on pourrait appeler de droit international public, en ce qui concerne plus précisément la compétence du Centre et du Tribunal arbitral et la qualité pour agir de la Fondation.

518. Le Tribunal arbitral examinera successivement la question de la validité de la cession (a) et celle de ses effets (b).

a) La validité de la cession en faveur de la Fondation Presidente Allende

i. *Positions des parties*

519. A titre préliminaire, le Tribunal arbitral rappelle que la défenderesse a soutenu que, pour que la Fondation puisse faire valoir des droits à l'égard de la défenderesse, il faudrait qu'elle ait valablement obtenu

---

[457] Au jour de l'introduction de la demande d'arbitrage, la Fondation paraît n'avoir guère contribué à l'économie chilienne, et ne prétend pas l'avoir fait, encore que l'article 3 de ses Statuts puisse être éventuellement interprété comme lui assignant des objectifs dont le Chili devait normalement obtenir à l'avenir bénéfice, d'ordre essentiellement culturel, social ou juridique. V., par exemple, la transcription du 4 mai 2000, pp. 74-75 (Me Garcés).

[458] V. l'article 11 du Statut de la Fondation, précité.

les droits transférés.[459] Ceci supposerait que M. Pey Casado en ait été titulaire, compte tenu du principe général *nemo plus juris ad alium transferre potest quam ipse habet* (ou *nemo potest facere per alium quod per se non potest*). D'après la défenderesse, « *les réclamants n'ont jamais été propriétaires des bien confisqués* ».[460] Encore lors de l'audience de janvier 2007, la défenderesse a soutenu la thèse que « *M. Pey n'avait aucun droit vis-à-vis d'El Clarin en vertu de l'API qu'il aurait pu transférer à la Fondation Allende* ».[461]

520. Le Tribunal arbitral ayant constaté que, contrairement à la thèse de la défenderesse, M. Pey Casado avait bien établi son titre de propriété, il est superflu de rouvrir ici cette discussion.

521. Le Tribunal doit cependant analyser la question de savoir si M. Pey Casado a valablement cédé les actions en question à la Fondation Presidente Allende. A ce propos, la défenderesse a soutenu que la cession ne pouvait pas être valable vue l'absence du consentement du Chili. D'après la défenderesse, le droit international ne permet pas un tel transfert des intérêts sans le consentement de l'Etat.[462]

522. En outre, la défenderesse a soutenu que la cession des actions des sociétés CPP S.A. et EPC Ltda par M. Pey Casado à la Fondation constituait une «*fraude à la loi*» faite dans le seul but de permettre à une partie étrangère d'invoquer les droits concernant ces sociétés devant un Tribunal CIRDI. En particulier, la défenderesse a argumenté que « *[t]ant les tentatives de dénationalisation que la cession à la Fondation 'Presidente Allende' des éventuels 'droits émanant de la confiscation', ont été effectuées dans le seul but de connecter cette situation avec une nationalité étrangère et donner ainsi, frauduleusement, compétence au Centre* ».[463]

523. Les demanderesses, elles, ont soutenu, (sans pour autant fournir d'analyse complète sur le sujet) que « la donation effectuée par l'investisseur en faveur de la Fondation [était] valable en droit

---

[459] V., par exemple, la transcription des audiences des 3 et 5 mai 2000 et le contre-mémoire de la défenderesse du 3 février 2003, pp. 197 et ss.

[460] Mémoire d'incompétence de la défenderesse du 20 juillet 1999, p. 13.

[461] Transcription de l'audience du 15 janvier 2007, p. 7 (Me Sanchez Castellón).

[462] Contre-mémoire de la défenderesse du 3 février 2003, pp. 198 et ss, 203. La défenderesse a souligné, à l'appui de son argument, que M. Pey Casado n'aurait pas mentionné la cession au Chili et que, par conséquent, la défenderesse n'était même pas au courant de la cession.

[463] Mémoire en réplique sur l'incompétence du 27 décembre 1999, p. 127. V. aussi la transcription de l'audience du 3 mai 2000, pp. 53 et ss (Me Mayorga).

espagnol (et en droit international privé chilien) [...] »[464], qu'une telle transmission de crédit « *a lieu par simple consentement, sans autre formalité que celle qu'impose la nature des opérations qui lui servent de cause* » et que, notamment, « *elle peut se faire valablement sans que le débiteur en ait connaissance préalable, et même contre sa volonté* ».[465]

524. En ce qui concerne l'allégation de « *fraude à la loi* », les demanderesses ont répondu qu'aucune fraude n'avait été prouvée par le Chili et que « *[l]a cession des droits de M. Pey Casado s'est faite en 1989 et 1990 [...], soit antérieurement à la signature du Traité bilatéral de 1991, et s'expliquait par la qualité humaine de M. Pey Casado, son grand âge et son attachement à son pays, l'Espagne. Cette cession a été très manifestement indépendante de la présente instance* ».[466]

ii.   *Conclusions du Tribunal*

525. De l'avis du Tribunal arbitral, la Fondation a démontré qu'elle était en possession de 90% des actions de CPP S.A.,[467] qui lui ont été transmises par M. Pey Casado au moyen d'écritures passées entre le 6 octobre 1989 et le 27 mai 1990.[468] Cette transmission a été parfaite à la date de l'inscription de cette dernière au Registre des Fondations du Ministère espagnol de la Culture, le 27 avril 1990.[469]

526. Comme le Tribunal l'a constaté ci-dessus, c'est le 16 janvier 1990 que, à la suite d'un pouvoir donné par M. Pey Casado le 6 octobre 1989, la « *Fundacíon Presidente Allende* » a été créée selon le droit espagnol et avec son siège en Espagne.[470] Le 6 février 1990, M. Pey Casado a comparu par-devant un notaire à Miami et, agissant au nom de la Fondation espagnole et avec les pleins pouvoirs que l'article 6 de ses statuts confèrent au Président de la Fondation,[471] a passé un

---

[464]   Mémoire des demanderesses du 17 mars 1999, p. 30. V. aussi l'exposé complémentaire sur la compétence du Tribunal arbitral du 11 septembre 2002, pp. 149-150.

[465]   Exposé complémentaire sur la compétence du Tribunal arbitral du 11 septembre 2002, pp. 151-152.

[466]   Réplique à la réponse soumise par la République du Chili au contre-mémoire réfutant le déclinatoire de compétence, du 7 février 2000, p. 21. V. aussi la transcription de l'audience du 4 mai 2000, pp. 97-98 (Me Malinvaud).

[467]   Annexes 6 à 9, 17 et 18 au mémoire des demanderesses du 17 mars 1999.

[468]   Annexe 9 à la requête d'arbitrage, du 3 novembre 1997 ; annexes 17 et 18 mémoire des demanderesses du 17 mars 1999.

[469]   Une condition établie dans les écritures de cession du 6 octobre 1989, annexe 17 au mémoire des demanderesses du 17 mars 1999.

[470]   Annexe 22 au contre-mémoire de la défenderesse du 3 février 2003.

[471]   « Article 6: Le Conseil des Fondateurs et, en son nom, le Président, exercera les compétences dévolues à la Direction, en accord avec ce qui est stipulé à l'Article 9, section 3 de la Réglementation des Fondations Culturelles

contrat de cession irrévocable, d'une part, et d'acceptation de la cession, d'autre part, portant sur le « *patrimoine, les titres, droits et crédits de toute nature découlant des contrats privés d'achat et vente que le cédant a passé en 1972 avec M. Dario Sainte-Marie Soruco, par lesquels ce dernier a vendu, et M. Victor Pey Casado a acheté cent pour cent des actions [de CPP SA et d'EPC Ltée] ».*[472]

527.   D'après l'article 2 du contrat de cession, « [l]a cession décrite à la section précédente comprend les droits de pleine propriété du CEDANT sur quatre-vingt-dix pour cent (90%) des actions des entreprises citées, le CESSIONNAIRE étant subrogé en lieu et place du CEDANT dans le contrat initial. [...] »

528.   De l'avis du Tribunal arbitral, selon le droit applicable à la cession (quel qu'il soit – espagnol, chilien ou autre), le consentement du débiteur cédé n'est pas nécessaire (et le contraire n'a pas été prouvé dans la présente procédure[473]). On notera en passant que la notification de la cession de créances au débiteur n'a d'autre portée que de l'obliger envers le nouveau créancier.[474]

529.   De plus, le Tribunal arbitral n'est pas convaincu par l'allégation de la défenderesse que la cession de droits par M. Pey Casado en faveur de la Fondation Allende aurait constitué une « *fraude à la loi* ». Comme l'ont rappelé les demanderesses, le fait que la cession a été faite en 1989 et 1990, avant l'entrée en vigueur de l'API et sept ans avant l'introduction de la présente instance, indique que la cession n'était pas liée à cette instance. De l'avis du Tribunal arbitral, la défenderesse n'est pas parvenue à prouver que cette transaction avait

---

Privées (Décret 2930/72 du 21 juillet 1972), à partir de la date d'inscription de la Fondation au Registre et tant que n'aura pas été réalisée la désignation et la nomination de la totalité des membres de la Direction ».

[472]   Annexe 18 au mémoire de demanderesse du 17 mars 1999.

[473]   Ceci malgré la position de l'expert consulté par la défenderesse, le Professeur Dolzer, qui, dans son avis de droit du 3 février 2003, affirme que « *unless Chile agreed to the assignment (assuming all jurisdictional requirements were met), the Tribunal cannot have jurisdiction over the claim presented by the President Allende Foundation.* » (p. 45), sans pour autant développer les sources de cette partie de son argumentation.

[474]   V. dans ce contexte, Article 1.527 du Code civil espagnol qui dispose : « *Le débiteur qui, avant d'avoir connaissance de la cession, aurait satisfait le créancier, sera libéré de l'obligation.* » ; article 1.902 du Code civil chilien qui dispose : « *La cession [des droits d'un crédit personnel] ne produit pas d'effet à l'égard du débiteur ni à l'égard de tiers tant qu'elle n'a pas été notifiée par le cessionnaire au débiteur ou acceptée par ce dernier.* » Traduction libre par les demanderesses, cité dans leur exposé complémentaire sur la compétence du Tribunal arbitral du 11 septembre 2002, pp. 151-152.

un caractère frauduleux, ou même qu'elle soit liée à la présente instance.

530. En conclusion, la cession doit être considérée comme valable et opposable à la défenderesse.

b) Les effets de la cession sur la question de la compétence du Centre et du Tribunal arbitral

531. La question se pose dès lors de savoir quels sont les effets de cette cession et notamment si elle établit la qualité d'investisseur de la Fondation Presidente Allende, au sens de l'article 25 de la Convention CIRDI. En d'autres termes, le Tribunal arbitral doit déterminer si le cédant, M. Pey Casado, s'est limité à transférer à la Fondation seulement des droits et intérêts qu'on pourrait appeler « *matériels* » dans les deux sociétés CPP S.A. et EPC. Ltda., par exemple de propriété sur les biens ou intérêts transférés, ou s'il n'a pas transféré aussi, en même temps et par là-même, voire nécessairement, des droits de caractère « *procédural* » contre la République du Chili dont le droit d'agir en justice et en arbitrage.

i. *Positions des parties*

532. Selon les demanderesses, la cession des actions équivaut à une cession de la qualité d'investisseur. Au soutien de cette affirmation, les demanderesses ont renvoyé le Tribunal arbitral à l'affaire *Amco Asia c. Indonésie*, dans lequel le Tribunal a décidé que « *[...]the right to invoke the arbitration clause is transferred by Amco Asia with the shares it transfers, Amco Asia not losing the same right, be it as the initial investor or to the extent to which it keeps partly the shares it possessed originally* ».[475] De plus, elles ont soutenu que « *la doctrine admet l'accès à l'arbitrage du CIRDI dans l'hypothèse d'une cession spontanée de droits de la part d'un investisseur personne physique* ».[476] D'après les demanderesses, « *la donation effectuée par l'investisseur en faveur de la Fondation étant valable en droit espagnol (et en droit international privé chilien) la*

---

[475]   Citée par les demanderesses dans leur réponse au mémoire soutenant l'incompétence soumis par la défenderesse, du 18 septembre 1999, p. 137 ; v. aussi mémoire des demanderesses du 17 mars 1999, p. 37 ; exposé complémentaire sur la compétence du Tribunal arbitral du 11 septembre 2002, pp. 154-155.

[476]   Requête d'arbitrage du 3 novembre 1997, p. 4. V. aussi mémoire des demanderesses du 17 mars 1999, pp. 29-31 ; réponse au mémoire soutenant l'incompétence soumis par la défenderesse du 18 septembre 1999, pp. 53-54, dans lequel les parties demanderesses réfèrent à la sentence CCI dans l'affaire 2626 au soutien de leur thèse que la convention d'arbitrage lie les « *cessionnaires et tous acquéreurs d'obligations.* »

Fondation possède la légitimation active en qualité de titulaire des droits lésés ».[477]

533.   En outre, les demanderesses ont souligné que le droit de la Fondation Presidente Allende d'agir en justice sur la base de violations de l'investissement de M. Pey Casado serait prévu par les documents fondateurs de la Fondation. Le Conseil des Fondateurs de la Fondation Allende aurait décidé le 14 décembre 1994 que toute réclamation relative à l'indemnisation des droits et crédits provenant de l'investissement de 1972 peut être formulée indifféremment par la Fondation elle-même ou par M. Pey Casado.[478] Sur cette base, les demanderesses on argumenté que :

> *« Le Conseil des Fondateurs de la Fondation ' Président Allende ' a résolu, le 14 décembre 1994, que toute réclamation relative à l'indemnisation des droits et crédits découlant de l'investissement de 1972, au sens établi dans l'Accord bilatéral entre l'Espagne et le Chili, pouvait être formulée indistinctement par la Fondation elle-même et M. VICTOR PEY CASADO (voir le document annexe no. 3 à notre communication au Centre datée du 15 décembre 1997) ».*[479]

534.   Répondant aux objections soulevées par la défenderesse que les déclarations du Conseil des Fondateurs de la Fondation Allende constituaient des accords internes qui ne sont pas opposables au Chili,[480] les demanderesses ont soutenu que *« [c]e document n'est pas un acte privé ; il a été enregistré le 29 septembre 1997 sous le n°3.042 aux minutes de M. Luis Sanchez Marco, notaire à Madrid, etc. ».*[481]

535.   La défenderesse, elle, a soutenu que la qualité d'investisseur n'a pas été conférée à la Fondation Presidente Allende en vertu de la cession en sa faveur et que, par conséquent, la Fondation n'a pas effectué d'investissement, n'ayant fait un quelconque paiement en échange des droits qui lui ont été cédés.[482]

---

[477]   Mémoire des demanderesses du 17 mars 1999, p. 30.

[478]   Mémoire des demanderesses, du 17 mars 1999, p. 37 ; réponse au mémoire soutenant l'incompétence soumis par la défenderesse du 18 septembre 1999, p. 127 & 133.

[479]   Réponse au mémoire soutenant l'incompétence soumis par la défenderesse du 18 septembre 1999, p. 127.

[480]   Mémoire en réplique sur l'incompétence du 27 décembre 1999, p. 117-118.

[481]   Réplique à la réponse soumise par la République du Chili au contre-mémoire réfutant le déclinatoire de compétence du 7 février 2000, p. 21.

[482]   Contre-mémoire de la défenderesse du 3 février 2003, p. 203, où la défenderesse soutient : « Il convient en outre de faire remarquer qu'en

536. De plus, d'après la défenderesse, pour que la cession transmette la qualité d'investisseur et le droit d'agir à la Fondation Presidente Allende, M. Pey Casado devrait avoir lui-même rempli les conditions de compétence, et notamment « *si M. Pey ne remplit pas les conditions de nationalité du Traité bilatéral, dès lors il n'a pu transmettre à la Fondation Président Allende que des droits qui n'étaient pas couverts par les protections du Traité bilatéral et il semble qu'il y aurait lieu, là aussi, d'en déduire les conséquences.* »[483] Invoquant le principe de droit *nemo dat quod non habet* (ou *nemo potiorem postest transfere quam ipse habet*), la défenderesse a soutenu que « *en 1990 M. Pey n'avait aucun droit de réclamation au titre de l'APPI Chili-Espagne (et moins encore un droit de demande en vertu de la Convention CIRDI) et en conséquence, il n'aurait pu ni ne pouvait céder à la Fondation Président Allende aucun droit de cette nature* ».[484] La défenderesse a résumé cet argument de manière très succincte lors de l'audience du 29 octobre 2001 : « *Notre position est aussi que ce tribunal n'a pas compétence pour connaître de la requête de M. Pey Casado, alors il n'a pas compétence pour connaître de la requête de la Fondation Président Allende* ».[485]

ii.   *Conclusions du Tribunal*

537. De l'avis du Tribunal arbitral, la Fondation Presidente Allende a obtenu la qualité d'« *investisseur* » en vertu de la cession des actions en sa faveur de la part de la première partie demanderesse, M. Pey Casado.

538. Par la cession des actions qui était valable à la date de l'inscription de cette dernière au Registre des Fondations du Ministère espagnol de la Culture, le 27 avril 1990, une partie des droits découlant de

---

l'absence de qualité d' ' investisseur ' conférée en vertu de la prétendue cession, la Fondation Président Allende n'a pas la qualité d' ' investisseur ' parce qu'elle n'a pas effectué d' ' investissement ' au Chili. Il n'apparaît pas non plus que la Fondation Président Allende ait effectué un quelconque paiement en échange des droits qui lui ont supposément été cédés. Il n'y a pas non plus de preuve d'aucun transfert de capitaux vers le Chili de la part de la Fondation Président Allende. »

[483] Transcription de l'audience du 15 janvier 2007, p. 51, para. 25-28 (Me Leurent).

[484] Contre-mémoire de la défenderesse du 3 février 2003, pp. 197-202 ; v. aussi l'avis de droit du Professeur Rudolf Dolzer, soumis par la défenderesse en appui de son contre-mémoire du 3 février 2003, pp. 42-44.

[485] Transcription de l'audience du 29 octobre 2001, p. 11 (Me Goodman).

l'investissement avait été transmise par M. Pey Casado en faveur de la Fondation.[486]

539.   Le Tribunal arbitral partage le point de vue exprimé par le Tribunal arbitral dans l'affaire *Amco Asio c. Indonésie*, qui, en analysant la compétence du CIRDI et du Tribunal arbitral quant à l'une des défenderesses, *Pan American*, a décidé que cette défenderesse avait obtenu la qualité d'investisseur au sens de l'article 25 de la Convention CIRDI par la cession d'actions de la part de l'investisseur original, *Amco Asia*.   Comme l'ont souligné les demanderesses à plusieurs reprises dans la présente procédure, le Tribunal arbitral dans *Amco Asia* a jugé que :

> « [...] *the right acquired by Amco Asia to invoke the arbitral clause is attached to its investment, represented by its shares in PT Amco, and may be transferred with those shares. [...]*
> *[...] the right to invoke the arbitration clause is transferred by Amco Asia with the shares it transfers, Amco Asia not losing the same right, be it as the initial investor or to the extent to which it keeps partly the shares it possessed originally. As a result, the right to invoke the arbitration clause is transferred with the transferred shares, whether or not the same constitute a controlling block, being it understood that for such a transfer of the right to take place, the government's approval is indispensable* ».[487]

540.   Bien que la compétence du Tribunal CIRDI dans *Amco Asia* ait été fondée sur une convention d'arbitrage classique, et non pas sur un API, le même principe s'applique dans la présente affaire.

541.   Les parties demanderesses se sont, avec raison, également référées à la décision du Tribunal arbitral CIRDI dans l'affaire *FEDAX N.V. v. République du Venezuela*[488] qui s'est déclaré compétent dans un cas où avait eu lieu une cession de titularité de billets à ordre (« *promissory notes* »).   Ayant trouvé que de telles instruments étaient des « *eminently negotiable instruments in the secondary market* », le Tribunal a décidé que :

> « *In such a situation, although the identity of the investor will change with every endorsement, the*

---

[486]   Une condition établie dans les écritures de cession du 6 octobre 1989, annexe 17 au mémoire des demanderesses du 17 mars 1999.

[487]   *Amco Asia Corporation et al. c. Règublique de l'Indonésie*, affaire CIRDI n° ARB/81/1, décision sur la compétence du 25 septembre 1983, 1 ICSID Reports (1993), p. 389, 403 ; *JDI* 202,1986.

[488]   Décision sur la compétence du 11 juillet 1997, *JDI* 278.1999.

> *investment itself will remain constant, while the issuer will enjoy a continuous credit benefit until the time the note becomes due. To the extent that this credit is provided by a foreign holder of the notes, it constitutes a foreign investment which in this case is encompassed by the terms of the Convention and the Agreement.*
> *[...] ».* [489]

542. La défenderesse a objecté que cette règle ne pourrait pas s'appliquer dans le cas d'espèce, vu que, contrairement aux faits dans l'affaire *FEDAX N.V. v. République du Venezuela*, la Fondation Presidente Allende n'a pas effectué de paiement en échange des droits qui lui ont été cédés.[490] De l'avis du Tribunal arbitral, le fait que, dans le cas d'espèce, M. Pey Casado ait cédé les actions en vertu d'une donation ne change rien au fait que la Fondation a obtenu la qualité d'investisseur par cette cession. Tant que la cession d'actions qui constituent l'investissement initial est valable (comme le Tribunal arbitral l'a confirmé dans la présente affaire), elle transmet la qualité d'investisseur au cessionnaire.[491]

543. De plus, contrairement à la position de la défenderesse, le fait que l'API n'était pas encore en vigueur au moment de la cession ne change rien à la conclusion que la Fondation a obtenu la qualité d'« *investisseur* » en vertu de cette cession. La cession d'actions de la part de M. Pey Casado ne constituait pas une cession du « *droit de réclamation* » ou « *droit de demande* » (termes utilisés par la défenderesse), mais de la qualité d'« *investisseur* ». La présente affaire ne soulève pas le problème qui se posait dans l'affaire *Mihaly International Corporation c. Sri Lanka*, invoquée par la défenderesse à l'appui de son exception d'incompétence,[492] dans laquelle, selon le résumé de la défenderesse, « *une entreprise canadienne avait cédé*

---

[489] *Fedax N.V. c. Venezuela*, affaire CIRDI n°ARB/96/3, décision sur la compétence du 11 juillet 1997, annexe D5 à la Réplique, para. 40.

[490] Contre-mémoire de la défenderesse du 3 février 2003, p. 203, note 613 : « C'est là une différence importante en ce qui concerne la situation de Fedax N.V. c. Venezuela, où le Tribunal a qualifié la cession de billets à ordre comme un investissement parce que le cessionnaire avait acquis les billets à ordre pour lesquels il émit ultérieurement une réclamation. »

[491] Dans ce contexte, le Tribunal arbitral note également que, dans le cas d'espèce, le contrat de cession entre M. Pey Casado et la Fondation Allende prévoyait expressément qu'un des objectifs de la cession était de permettre à la Fondation Presidente Allende de présenter des réclamations liées aux confiscations au Chili en septembre 1973. V. annexe 18 au mémoire des demanderesses du 17 mars 1999.

[492] V. contre-mémoire de la défenderesse du 3 février 2003, pp. 198-201. Avis de droit du Professeur Rudolf Dolzer, soumis par la défenderesse au soutien de son contre-mémoire du 3 février 2003, pp. 42-45.

ses droits à une entreprise américaine pour tenter de contourner l'obstacle juridique que représentait le fait que le Canada n'était pas partie à la Convention du CIRDI (alors que les Etats-Unis eux l'étaient). » En effet, le souci du Tribunal arbitral dans l'affaire *Mihaly* était d'éviter une cession d'un droit (incomplet) de réclamation – par une partie qui ne remplissait pas les conditions de compétence CIRDI – à une autre qui les remplissait.[493] Cette problématique n'existe pas dans la présente affaire, M. Pey Casado remplissant les conditions de compétence et n'ayant pas besoin de « *contourner* » une carence à ce sujet en transférant son investissement à la Fondation.

544.   Cela dit, il est exact que, comme l'a soutenu la défenderesse, la cession des actions n'a transmis que la qualité d'investisseur à la Fondation, et non pas de ce fait et nécessairement le droit de réclamation. Pour décider du sort des objections d'incompétence soulevées par la défenderesse à l'égard de la Fondation Président Allende, le Tribunal arbitral doit donc analyser la question de savoir si la Fondation Presidente Allende remplit toutes les autres conditions posées tant par la Convention CIRDI que par l'API quant à la compétence du Tribunal Arbitral. En l'espèce, ceci concerne notamment les conditions de la nationalité au sens de la Convention CIRDI ainsi que le consentement des parties de recourir à l'arbitrage CIRDI pour résoudre leur litige.

2.   La condition de nationalité au sens de la Convention CIRDI

545.   Il n'est pas douteux, quant à la condition de nationalité, que la Fondation possède la nationalité espagnole, et seulement celle-ci. En outre, vu que le Tribunal arbitral est parvenu à la conclusion que M. Pey Casado a valablement renoncé à la nationalité chilienne, les questions de changement de la nationalité de la demanderesse et du

---

[493]   V. Mihaly International Corporation c. Sri Lanka, affaire CIRDI n° ARB/00/2, sentence du 15 mars 2002, para. 24, où le Tribunal arbitral décrit ce qui suit : « […] if Mihaly (Canada) had a claim which was procedurally defective against Sri Lanka before ICSID because Mihaly (Canada)'s inability to invoke the ICSID Convention, Canada not being a Party thereto, this defect could not be perfected vis-à-vis ICSID by its assignment to Mihaly (USA). To allow such an assignment to operate in favour of Mihaly (Canada) would defeat the object and purpose of the ICSID Convention and the sanctity of the privity of international agreements not intended to create rights and obligations for non-Parties. Accordingly, a Canadian claim which was not recoverable, nor compensable or indeed capable of being invoked before ICSID could not have been admissible or able to be entertained under the guise of its assignment. »

principe de la continuité de la nationalité,[494] qui ont été soulevés par les parties,[495] ne se posent pas.

546. Il convient cependant de ne pas s'en tenir à cette seule acceptation mais d'examiner si, de manière plus générale, les conditions concernant la nationalité de la deuxième partie demanderesse requises par l'article 25 de la Convention CIRDI sont satisfaites. L'article 25 (2) dispose que « *ressortissant d'un autre État contractant* » signifie, entre autre :

> *(b) toute personne morale qui possède la nationalité d'un Etat contractant autre que l'Etat partie au différend à la date à laquelle les parties ont consenti à soumettre le différend à la conciliation ou à l'arbitrage et tout personne morale qui possède la nationalité de l'État contractant partie au différend à la même date et que les parties sont convenus, aux fins de la présente Convention, de considérer comme ressortissant d'un autre Etat contractant en raison du contrôle exercé sur elle par des intérêts étrangers. »*

547. La défenderesse a allégué cependant que, si les statuts de la Fondation énoncent clairement que la nationalité de cette personne juridique est espagnole, parmi les trois fondateurs un seul avait la nationalité espagnole (Monsieur Garcés), un second (Monsieur Martner) étant (exclusivement) chilien et le troisième, M. Pey Casado, est décrit comme double national. Quant au capital de la Fondation, il est en partie chilien et en partie étranger au Chili. D'après la défenderesse, il serait donc douteux que la Fondation ait la nationalité espagnole, étant donné que la Fondation est « *contrôlée par un directoire dont les membres sont dans leur majorité des ressortissants chiliens, et que l'objectif déclaré de la Fondation Président Allende est de présenter des demandes relatives à des*

---

[494] En tout état de cause, le Tribunal arbitral est de l'avis que le principe de continuité de la nationalité, ayant son origine dans le droit de la protection diplomatique, ne peut être appliqué ici et dans le contexte d'arbitrages d'investissement.

[495] Pour la position des demanderesses, v, exposé complémentaire sur la compétence du Tribunal arbitral du 11 septembre 2002, pp. 158 et ss. La défenderesse a tiré deux conclusions sur le fondement du principe de la continuité de la nationalité: si la première partie demanderesse, M. Pey Casado, devait être tenu pour ayant eu la nationalité chilienne, la question pourrait se poser de l'opposabilité à la République du Chili du transfert de ses droits et intérêts (y compris les droits procéduraux) à une personne juridique espagnole, la Fondation Président Allende. En revanche, s'il devait être considéré comme n'ayant pas la nationalité chilienne, mais exclusivement la nationalité espagnole, la question d'un changement de la nationalité de la demanderesse ne se poserait évidemment pas.

confiscations présumées du Gouvernement militaire chilien à partir du 11 septembre 1973 et ceci, au bénéfice du peuple chilien ».[496]

548.   La question pourrait donc se poser de savoir quels sont les critères déterminant la « *nationalité* » de la personne juridique, une question dont on sait qu'elle a fait l'objet, dans différents domaines (droit international privé, droit international public, par exemple protection diplomatique, nationalisations, condition des étrangers, etc.) de nombreux écrits, controverses et jurisprudences, etc. Les critères proposés ou retenus pour déterminer cette « *nationalité* » – qui ne sont pas nécessairement les mêmes selon le domaine considéré – sont essentiellement le lieu de l'incorporation et celui du siège statutaire, celui du siège réel ou effectif ou du centre de l'administration, ainsi que (dans certains domaines), celui du contrôle. Dans le domaine de la protection diplomatique – dont on rappellera qu'il est étranger à la question ici examinée, celle du sens de la Convention CIRDI, la Cour Internationale de Justice, dans la célèbre affaire de la *Barcelona Traction, Light & Power, Limited,*[497] a écarté la possibilité de *« percer le voile corporatif »* pour définir la nationalité de la société en prenant en compte celle des actionnaires. En l'espèce un tel « *voile* » n'existe pas. La composition des organes de la Fondation est inscrite au Registre du Ministère espagnol de la Culture, lequel est d'accès public, selon la législation relative aux Fondations soumises à la protection de l'État dont il est fait état dans le dossier.

549.   Le critère de la nationalité a été adopté par l'article 25 (2) (b) de la Convention CIRDI et il a été appliqué, en conséquence, par les Tribunaux arbitraux CIRDI.[498] C'est ainsi que dans l'affaire *SOABI c. Sénégal*, le Tribunal arbitral a considéré que : « *As a general rule, States apply either the head office or the place of incorporation criteria in order to determine nationality* »[499] (et non pas celui de la nationalité des actionnaires, sinon dans des circonstances exceptionnelles). De même, le Tribunal arbitral dans l'affaire *Amco Asia c. Indonésie*[500] a justement retenu que : « *the concept of nationality is there a classical one, based on the law under which the juridical person has been incorporated, the place of incorporation and the place of the social seat...* » tout en notant que les parties

---

[496]   Contre-mémoire de la défenderesse du 3 février 2003, p. 204.

[497]   2ième phase, jugement du 5 février 1970, C.I.J., Recueil 1970.

[498]   Christoph H. Schreuer, « *Commentary* », ICSID Review Foreign Investment Law Journal 1997, 59, p. 82.

[499]   Affaire n° ARB/82/1, Décision sur la compétence du 1er août 1984, ICSID Report 175-2, pp. 180-181.

[500]   Affaire n° ARB/81/1, Décision sur la compétence du 25 septembre 1983, 1 ICSID Report 396 ; cf. Schreuer op. cit., ICSID Review Foreign Investment Law Journal 12, 1997, 59, pp. 120-121.

contractantes peuvent prévoir des exceptions (comme le montre l'article 25 para 2 *in fine* de la Convention CIRDI).

550. Par conséquent, la Fondation Presidente Allende, étant incorporée et ayant son siège en Espagne, remplit à l'évidence la condition de la nationalité au sens de l'article 25 de la Convention CIRDI.

3. La condition de consentement

551. En ce qui concerne la condition de consentement, les demanderesses ont soutenu que, pour le successeur ou le cessionnaire d'un investissement, le consentement écrit à la juridiction du Centre n'est pas nécessaire.[501] L'investisseur ayant accordé son consentement, ce consentement étend au cessionnaire la faculté d'être partie à l'arbitrage. Les demanderesses ont également fait référence à la déclaration de M. Pey Casado en date du 2 octobre 1997,[502] dans lequel M. Pey Casado affirme expressément son consentement pour la Fondation (en tant que président et partie du directoire de la Fondation).[503] De plus, en tout état de cause, et malgré le fait qu'aucun consentement de la part de la Fondation n'aurait été nécessaire, la Fondation aurait donné formellement son consentement le 6 octobre 1997.[504]

552. La défenderesse, elle, a soutenu que le Chili n'avait pas consenti à l'arbitrage concernant la demande de la Fondation Allende. De plus, la Fondation, elle, n'aurait pas donné son consentement selon la forme établie par la Convention CIRDI non plus[505] (il s'agit ici surtout de l'argument concernant l'absence allégué de consultations amiables, argument que le Tribunal arbitral va discuter dans la partie « *Fins de Non-Recevoir* » ci-dessous).

---

[501] Requête d'arbitrage, p. 4 : « La doctrine admet l'accès à l'arbitrage du CIRDI dans l'hypothèse d'une cession spontanée de droits de la part d'un Investisseur personne physique. » ; mémoire des demanderesses du 17 mars 1999, p. 30 ; réponse des demanderesses au mémoire soutenant l'incompétence soumis par la defenderesse du 18 septembre 1999, pp. 127-128 ; réplique à la réponse soumise par la République du Chili au contre-mémoire réfutant le déclinatoire de compétence du 7 février 2000, p. 21 ; transcription de l'audience du 4 mai 2000, pp. 77-78 (Me Garcés).

[502] Annexe 10 à la requête d'arbitrage du 3 novembre 1997.

[503] Réponse des demanderesses au mémoire soutenant l'incompétence soumis par la defenderesse du 18 septembre 1999, pp. 128-129.

[504] Requête d'arbitrage du 3 novembre 1997, p. 4 ; mémoire des demanderesses du 17 mars 1999, p. 36 ; réponse au mémoire soutenant l'incompétence soumis par la défenderesse du 18 septembre 1999, p. 128 ; réplique à la réponse soumise par la République du Chili au contre-mémoire réfutant le déclinatoire de compétence du 7 février 2000, p. 21.

[505] Mémoire en réplique sur l'incompétence du 27 décembre 1999, pp. 117-120.

553. De l'avis du Tribunal arbitral, il est clair que la Fondation Presidente Allende a consenti à l'arbitrage (à l'exclusion de ce qui concernait la rotative Goss) le 6 octobre 1997.[506]

554. Le consentement de la défenderesse à l'arbitrage étant donné par l'API, il convient de vérifier si les conditions d'application de l'API sont réunies.

a) La condition d'investissement au sens de l'API

555. La première question à examiner est celle de savoir si la Fondation Presidente Allende possède la qualité d'investisseur au sens de l'API. Comme l'a affirmé dans cette procédure le Professeur Dolzer :

> « *Unlike a commercial contract, a BIT is a treaty between States containing the host State's* a priori *consent to resolve by international arbitration disputes with a strictly circumscribed group of persons, described in the Chile-Spain BIT as ' l'investisseur de l'autre Partie.' If the claimant does not fall within this group, its claim simply is not covered by the host State's consent* ».[507]

556. Il convient de rappeler que l'article 1.2 de l'API prévoit une notion très large d'« *investissement* » en stipulant :

> « *Par ' investissements' on désigne toutes sortes d'avoirs, tels que biens et droits de toute nature, acquis en accord avec la législation du pays recevant l'investissement et en particulier, encore que non exclusivement, les suivants :*
> *Actions et autres formes de participation dans les sociétés. [...]*»

557. Au regard de cette définition très large, incluant « *toutes sortes d'avoirs* », et vu le fait que l'API stipule expressément que les « *actions et autres formes de participation dans les sociétés* » constituent un « *investissement* », la Fondation Presidente Allende peut, de l'avis du Tribunal arbitral, être considérée comme « *investisseur* » en vertu de l'API, et cela même en examinant la position de la Fondation de manière « *indépendante* » et en soi, c'est-à-dire abstraction faite de la cession de droits opérée en sa faveur par M. Pey Casado. Le seul fait d'être propriétaire des actions des

---

[506] V. annexe 2 à la requête d'arbitrage du 3 novembre 1997.
[507] Avis de droit du Professeur Rudolf Dolzer, soumis par la défenderesse au soutien de son contre-mémoire du 3 février 2003, p. 44.

sociétés CPP S.A. et EPC Ltda justifie la qualité d'investisseur de la Fondation.[508]

558. Cette conclusion est renforcée par le fait que, en tout état de cause, la Fondation Allende a obtenu la qualité d'investisseur par la cession de la part de l'investisseur initial, M. Pey Casado, d'une grande partie de son investissement. A ce propos, les mêmes règles que le Tribunal arbitral a énoncées quant à la notion d'investissement au sens de l'article 25 de la Convention CIRDI s'appliquent. Compte tenu de la rédaction très large de l'API, une interprétation plus stricte ne se justifierait pas. En particulier, l'API ne requiert pas que l'investisseur ait fait l'investissement lui-même, ce qui laisse ouverte la possibilité qu'un investissement (et la qualité d'investisseur) puisse résulter d'une cession de la part de l'investisseur initial.

559. Le Tribunal arbitral note, en passant, qu'une solution très similaire a été appliquée par le Tribunal arbitral dans l'affaire *CME Czech Republic B.V. v. The Czech Republic* qui a trouvé que :

> « *The acquired shares, including all rights and legal entitlements, are protected under the Treaty. Upon the acquisition, the Claimant's predecessor became the owner of the investment in the Czech Republic. The Treaty does not distinguish as to whether the investor made the investment itself or whether the investor acquired the predecessor's investment. In this respect, Article 8 of the Treaty defines an investment dispute as existing if a dispute concerns an investment of the investor. Article 1 of the Treaty clearly spells out than an investment comprises every kind of asset invested either directly or through an investor of a third State, which makes it clear that the investor need not make the investment himself to be protected under the Treaty.* »

---

[508] L'article 1.1 de l'API n'exclut pas de la définition d'investisseur les personnes morales dont les activités ne seraient pas à caractère lucratif, et que les parties demanderesses ont invoqué la clause de la nation la plus favorisée en rapport avec des API ratifiés par le Chili ayant défini les Fondations comme des « *investisseurs* » (par exemple avec l'Allemagne, article 4). Selon cette thèse, la Fondation a au Chili des intérêts à portée économique, culturelle, sociale et humanitaire. Elle aurait donc en elle-même la qualité d'investisseur en vertu de l'article 1er de l'API et, à titre subsidiaire, de la clause de la nation la plus favorisée de l'API Espagne-Chili en rapport avec l'article 1.2.b de l'API Chili-Australie. L'argument ne saurait prospérer, la satisfaction des conditions d'application du traité sur le fondement duquel l'action est introduite devant être constatée avant même que l'investisseur ne puisse se prévaloir de la clause de la nation la plus favorisée.

560. Pour ces raisons, de l'avis du Tribunal arbitral, la deuxième partie demanderesse satisfait la condition d'investissement au sens de l'API.

b)　La condition de nationalité au sens de l'API

561. L'article 1.1 de l'API définit le terme « *investisseur* » comme :

> « *[...] les personnes physiques ou ressortissants nationaux, selon le droit de la Partie correspondante, et les personnes morales, y compris les compagnies, associations de compagnies, sociétés commerciales et autres organisations qui se trouveraient constituées ou, selon le cas, dûment organisées conformément au droit de cette Partie et qui auraient leur siège dans le territoire de cette dernière, nonobstant le fait qu'elles appartiennent à des personnes physiques ou juridiques étrangères.* »

562. L'API Espagne-Chili a donc retenu le double critère de l'incorporation et du siège. Ces critères sont réunis en ce qui concerne la Fondation Presidente Allende.

c)　La condition d'application *ratione temporis* de l'API

563. Le Tribunal arbitral a analysé la question d'applicabilité *ratione temporis* de l'API en détail ci-dessus et il a conclu que les trois différends invoqués par les parties demanderesses sont bien survenus postérieurement à l'entrée en vigueur de l'API. Il est en conséquence compétent *ratione temporis* pour en connaître.

564. Il convient de rappeler brièvement que les trois différends en questions sont : (i) le différend de 1995 concernant la demande en restitution des 40.000 actions de la société CPP S.A. ; (ii) le différend de 2000 concernant la Décision n°43 ; et (iii) le différend de 2002 concernant le déni de justice allégué par les parties demanderesses.

565. Le Tribunal arbitral considère que les conclusions auxquelles il est arrivé ci-dessus quant à sa compétence *ratione temporis* pour connaître des demandes de la première partie demanderesse s'appliquent également aux demandes faites par la seconde partie demanderesse, la Fondation Presidente Allende. Les trois différends en question ont été introduits dans cette instance par les deux parties demanderesses et ils sont nés aux mêmes dates pour la Fondation Allende que pour M. Pey Casado. Cela est évident à propos des différends de 2000 et de 2002, qui sont nés après que la présente instance avait été introduite. En ce qui concerne le différend de 1995, concernant la demande en restitution des 40,000 actions de la société CPP S.A., il convient de rappeler les faits suivants, qui

415

montrent que le différend est bien surgi en même temps pour M. Pey Casado et pour la Fondation Presidente Allende.

566. M. Pey Casado revendiquait le 20 novembre 1995 et le 10 janvier 1996 100% des droits de CPP S.A., ce qui incluait le pourcentage transféré à la Fondation. Ainsi le Ministre des biens nationaux avait répondu le 20 novembre 1995 en tenant compte du fait que la réclamation de M. Pey Casado portait sur la totalité des biens de CPP S.A., M. Pey Casado agissait de la sorte en vertu de l'accord du 20 décembre 1994, intervenu entre lui-même et le Conseil des Fondateurs de la Fondation, accord incorporé aux minutes d'un notaire à Madrid. Cet accord avait été communiqué au Centre le 19 décembre 1997. Le Tribunal arbitral observe que la mise à exécution de cet accord a bien été faite. C'est ainsi que :

- La Requête introduite par M. Pey Casado en 1995 avait été faite <u>avec l'accord de la Fondation</u>, auprès de la Huitième Chambre criminelle de Santiago, pour la restitution de la totalité des 40.000 titres originaux de CPP S.A., de leur transfert signé en blanc et des justificatifs de leur paiement.[509]
- La Requête introduite par M. Pey Casado avait été faite <u>avec l'accord de la Fondation,</u> auprès de la Première Chambre civile de Santiago, en 1995, en réclamation de la restitution de la totalité de la puissante rotative GOSS.[510]

567. Pour ces raisons, le Tribunal estime que les conclusions auxquelles il est arrivé quant à sa compétence *ratione temporis* pour connaître des demandes de M. Pey Casado s'appliquent également aux demandes faites par la Fondation Presidente Allende et qu'il est donc compétent *ratione temporis* pour connaître des trois différends invoqués par la Fondation Presidente Allende.

4. <u>Conclusion</u>

568. En résumé, la seconde partie demanderesse a établi, aux yeux du Tribunal arbitral, qu'elle remplissait bien les conditions posées pour la compétence tant par l'article 25 de la Convention CIRDI que par l'API. Il en résulte dès lors que le Tribunal arbitral est compétent pour statuer sur le fond du litige pour ce qui concerne la deuxième partie demanderesse, la Fondation Presidente Allende.

---

[509] V. annexe 21 à la requête d'arbitrage du 3 novembre 1997.

[510] V. annexes C-105 et C-106, et les extraits de ladite procédure produits par le Chili après la clôture de la procédure orale le 5 mai 2000 et dont la version française a été produite après les audiences des 29 et 30 octobre 2001.

VI. LES FINS DE NON-RECEVOIR - L'ABSENCE ALLEGUEE DE CONSULTATIONS AMIABLES DE LA PART DE LA FONDATION PRESIDENTE ALLENDE

569. Il y a lieu de mentionner brièvement un dernier argument soulevé par la défenderesse, de manière quelque peu subsidiaire, relativement à l'absence alléguée des consultations amiables de la part de la Fondation Presidente Allende, consultations qui, à son avis, auraient dû constituer un préalable au dépôt de la requête d'arbitrage.[511]

570. L'argument de la défenderesse est fondé sur l'article 10 de l'API qui dispose :

> « *1. Toute controverse relative aux investissements, au sens du présent Traité, entre une Partie contractante et un investisseur de l'autre Partie contractante sera, dans la mesure du possible, résolue par des discussions amiables entre les deux parties à la controverse.*
> *2. Si la controverse n'a pas pu être résolue au terme de six mois à partir du moment où elle aura été soulevée par l'une ou l'autre des Parties, elle sera soumise, au choix de l'investisseur :*
> *Soit aux juridictions nationales de la Partie contractante impliquée dans la controverse ;*
> *Soit à un arbitrage international dans les conditions décrites au paragraphe 3. [...] »*

571. De l'avis du Tribunal arbitral, l'objection de la défenderesse ne peut pas être retenue pour deux raisons. En fait et d'abord parce que M. Pey Casado a tenté de diverses manières de telles consultations. La défenderesse a soutenu à ce propos que lesdites tentatives avaient été faites par M. Pey Casado « *à titre exclusivement personnel* » et que les lettres en question « *n'ont en aucune façon agi au nom, ou pour le compte de la Fondation Allende, laquelle n'est même pas mentionnée dans ledit courrier* ».[512] D'après les demanderesses, « *M. Casado a agi non seulement pour lui, mais pour la Fondation Allende, comme il l'a toujours fait depuis que la Fondation a existé et, ceci en vertu d'un pouvoir parfaitement enregistré et connu* ».[513]

---

[511] V., par exemple, mémoire d'incompétence de la défenderesse du 20 juillet 1999, pp. 112-126, 142-143 ; contre-mémoire de la défenderesse du 3 février 2003, pp. 205-208.

[512] Transcription de l'audience du 3 mai 2000, p. 47 (Me Brower).

[513] Transcription du 4 mai 2000, p. 98-99 (Me Malinvaud) ; v. aussi pp. 74-77 (Me Garcés).

572. De l'avis du Tribunal arbitral, les tentatives de consultations ont bien été faites de la part de M. Pey Casado pour les deux parties demanderesses. Il est pourtant superflu d'entrer en cette discussion vu que, en tout état de cause, compte tenu du nombre et de la nature des mesures (de dépossession et autres) prises contre M. Pey Casado et de l'absence de réponse de la Présidence et d'autres autorités chiliennes à ses demandes,[514] compte tenu enfin de la politique générale du Gouvernement chilien à son égard (tant avant qu'après novembre 1997, date du dépôt de la requête), M. Pey Casado et la Fondation Président Allende étaient tous deux en droit de considérer que des consultations amiables n'auraient aucune chance de succès et seraient à l'évidence vouées à l'échec (« *obviously futile* ») (pour transposer ici une formule classique en matière d'épuisement des recours internes).

573. Ensuite, en droit, l'objection de la défenderesse ne peut pas être retenue parce que l'exigence de consultations préalables amiables ou de tentatives de conciliation (selon une formule souvent incluse dans les traités bilatéraux d'investissement comme en maints accords comportant des clauses d'arbitrage) n'a en général et dans le présent litige aucun caractère impératif ou contraignant, mais plutôt et seulement le caractère d'une simple recommandation procédurale, voire d'une clause de style diplomatique.[515]

---

[514] V. aussi à ce sujet la section consacrée au déni de justice et à l'absence de « *traitement juste et équitable* » ci-dessous.

[515] Cf. par exemple la décision du Tribunal CIRDI dans l'affaire SGS Société Générale de Surveillance SA c. Islamic Republic of Pakistan, affaire CIRDI n° ARB/01/03, où il est dit notamment que « compliance with such a requirement is…not seen as amounting to a condition precedent for the vesting of jurisdiction. » V. aussi la sentence dans l'affaire Consortium Groupement L.E.S.I.-DIPENTA c. Algérie, affaire CIRDI n°ARB/03/08, sentence du 10 janvier 2005, para. 32, où il est dit que « […] la condition examinée n'a pas un caractère absolu et […] l'on devrait pouvoir en faire abstraction dans des cas où il apparaîtrait à l'évidence qu'une tentative de conciliation serait d'emblée vouée à l'échec, en raison de l'attitude manifestée de manière définitive par l'autre partie » ; Bayindir Insaat Turizm Ticaret Ve Sanayi S.A. c. Pakistan, affaire CIRDI n° ARB/03/29, décision du 15 novembre 2005, où le Tribunal arbitral « agrees with the view that the notice requirement does not constitute a prerequisite to jurisdiction. Contrary to Pakistan's position, the non-fulfillment of this requirement is not 'fatal to the case of the claimant.' »

VII. RESPONSABILITE DE L'ETAT POUR LES VIOLATIONS DE L'API

574.   Avant d'examiner le bien fondé des violations alléguées par les demanderesses, le Tribunal arbitral doit encore se déterminer sur l'application dans le temps des dispositions de fond de l'API.

A.   Application dans le temps des dispositions de fond de l'API

575.   Bien que les écritures et les explications orales des parties sur ce point n'aient pas toujours été d'une parfaite clarté, le Tribunal constate que les parties s'opposent sur les conditions d'application dans le temps des dispositions de fond de l'API. Les demanderesses soutiennent à titre principal qu'il suffit que la controverse entre les parties soit survenue postérieurement à l'entrée en vigueur de l'API pour que les dispositions de fond de ce dernier soient applicables rétroactivement à des violations antérieures à son entrée en vigueur. Elles prétendent à titre subsidiaire que les violations alléguées antérieures à l'entrée en vigueur du traité constituent un fait illicite continu ou des éléments d'un fait illicite composite dont la durée s'étend au-delà de l'entrée en vigueur du traité et auxquels les dispositions de fond du traité sont applicables.[516]

576.   Le Tribunal examinera tour à tour chacune de ces deux prétentions.

1.   La survenance d'une controverse postérieurement à l'entrée en vigueur de l'API suffit-elle pour que les dispositions de fond de ce dernier s'appliquent rétroactivement à la cause ?

a)   Position des parties

577.   Après avoir rappelé la nécessité de distinguer la compétence *ratione temporis* du Tribunal de l'applicabilité *ratione temporis* des obligations de fond contenues dans l'API, la défenderesse pose en principe que « *tout acte supposé d'expropriation qui serait intervenu avant l'entrée en vigueur de l'API reste hors de l'application de [cet] API, même s'il y a au sein de l'API une [clause] des investissements préexistants [i.e. article 2.2]* ».[517] Elle demande au Tribunal de distinguer « *l'application rétroactive d'un traité* » de ce qu'elle appelle « *l'aspect rétrospectif d'une obligation dans un traité* » et dont relèvent les dispositions de l'article 2.2. La défenderesse estime ainsi que l'article 2.2 n'a pour autre objet que de prévoir que les

---

[516]   V. le résumé de l'argumentation des parties demanderesses présenté lors de l'audience du 15 janvier 2007 (transcription de l'audience du 15 janvier 2007, p. 84 (Me Malinvaud)).

[517]   V. la transcription de l'audience du 15 janvier 2007, pp. 12 et 13 (Me Di Rosa).

investissements réalisés avant l'entrée en vigueur de l'API sont protégés par ce dernier de la même manière que les investissements réalisés postérieurement à l'entrée en vigueur de l'API ; le fait que les conditions de l'article 2.2 puissent être satisfaites ne confère aucun effet rétroactif à l'API.[518] L'emploi du futur dans le traité militerait en outre contre l'application des dispositions de fond à des actes antérieurs à son entrée en vigueur.[519] La défenderesse considère enfin que les dispositions de fond de l'API ne pourraient être applicables à des actes de l'Etat antérieurs à l'entrée en vigueur de l'API que si celui-ci contenait une disposition expresse prévoyant son application rétroactive, ce qui n'est pas le cas en l'espèce.[520]

578.   Selon les demanderesses, l'article 2.2 de l'API constitue une dérogation au principe de non-rétroactivité énoncé par l'article 28 de la Convention de Vienne puisqu'il permet d'appliquer l'API « *aux investissements réalisés antérieurement à son entrée en vigueur* ».[521] L'application combinée des paragraphes 2.2 et 2.3 permettrait de conclure que « *le Traité [l'API] peut s'appliquer à des faits antérieurs à l'entrée en vigueur du Traité* »[522] car l'API ne contient « *aucune date butoir excluant de son champ d'application des faits (actes de dépossession) à l'origine d'une controverse* ».[523] Dès lors qu'une controverse est née entre les parties en 1995, postérieurement à l'entrée en vigueur du traité, les dispositions de fond de ce dernier sont applicables à des faits antérieurs à son entrée en vigueur.[524]

b)   Conclusions du Tribunal

579.   Le paragraphe 2.2 de l'API Espagne-Chili dispose simplement que les investissements antérieurs à l'entrée en vigueur de l'API peuvent

---

[518]   V. contre-mémoire de la défenderesse du 3 février 2003, p. 138 et p. 140. Lors de l'audience du 15 janvier 2007, la défenderesse a fait valoir que l'article 2.2 ne concerne pas en réalité la compétence *ratione temporis* mais plutôt la compétence *ratione materiae* du Tribunal (v. la transcription de l'audience du 15 janvier 2007, p. 9 (Me Di Rosa)).

[519]   V. la transcription de l'audience du 15 janvier 2007, p. 14 (Me Di Rosa).

[520]   V. la transcription de l'audience du 15 janvier 2007, p. 14 et p. 11 (Me Di Rosa). La défenderesse affirme également que « *le Traité ne s'applique pas à des actes de l'Etat antérieurs à l'entrée en vigueur de l'accord* » (transcription de l'audience du 15 janvier 2007, p. 8 (Me Di Rosa)).

[521]   Réplique à la réponse soumise par la République du Chili au contre-mémoire réfutant le déclinatoire de compétence, du 7 février 2000, p. 24. V. également la réplique des demanderesses au contre-mémoire de la défenderesse, du 23 février 2003, p. 237, note 430.

[522]   Réplique à la réponse soumise par la République du Chili au contre-mémoire réfutant le déclinatoire de compétence, du 7 février 2000, p. 24.

[523]   Dossier de plaidoiries des parties demanderesses relatif aux audiences des 29 et 30 octobre 2001, pp. 21-22.

[524]   V. la transcription de l'audience du 15 janvier 2007, p. 84 (Me Malinvaud).

être couverts par ce dernier. Il ne préjuge pas de l'applicabilité des dispositions de fond de l'API aux violations alléguées et ne peut être interpréter comme conférant un effet rétroactif à l'API permettant de l'appliquer aux violations antérieures à son entrée en vigueur.

580.   Ainsi que l'a relevé le Tribunal arbitral constitué dans l'affaire *SGS c. Philippines* :

> « *According to Article II of the BIT, it applies to investments 'made whether prior to or after the entry into force of the Agreement'. Article II does not, however, give the substantive provisions of the BIT any retrospective effect. The normal principle stated in Article 28 of the Vienna Convention on the Law of Treaties applies: the provisions of the BIT 'do not bind a party in relation to any act or fact which took place or any situation which ceased to exist before the date of the entry into force of the treaty'* ».[525]

581.   L'interprétation selon laquelle l'article 2.2 de l'API conférerait un effet rétroactif aux dispositions de fond de l'API serait contraire au principe de non-rétroactivité posé par la Convention de Vienne (art. 28) :

> « *[à] moins qu'une intention différente ne ressorte du traité ou ne soit par ailleurs établie, les dispositions d'un traité ne lient pas une partie en ce qui concerne un acte ou fait antérieur à la date d'entrée en vigueur de ce traité au regard de cette partie ou une situation qui avait cessé d'exister à cette date* ».

582.   Si, conventionnellement, les parties sont autorisées à déroger au principe de non-rétroactivité, cette dérogation ne saurait être présumée. Elle signifie en effet que l'Etat accepte de protéger les investissements postérieurs et antérieurs au traité et surtout que l'Etat s'engage à avoir respecté les obligations du traité vis-à-vis des investissements accomplis sur son territoire, avant même la date

---

[525]   *SGS Société Générale de Surveillance S.A. c. République des Philippines*, affaire CIRDI n° ARB/02/6, décision sur la competence du 29 janvier 2004, para. 166. L'Article II de l'Accord entre la Confédération suisse et la République des Philippines concernant la promotion et la protection réciproque des investissements, intitulé « *Champ d'application* », est rédigé dans les termes suivants : « *Le présent Accord est applicable aux investissements effectués sur le territoire d'une Partie contractante, conformément à ses lois et règlements, par des investisseurs de l'autre Partie contractante, avant ou après son entrée en vigueur* ».

l'entrée en vigueur du traité.[526] Un tel engagement de se reconnaître responsable d'agissements qui ont déjà eu lieu au moment où le traité entre en vigueur ne saurait être présumé.[527]

583.   La partie demanderesse voit pourtant dans l'article 2.3 de l'API « *une dérogation expresse à ce que l'on pourrait appeler une application rétroactive du Traité* ».[528] Le Tribunal ne partage pas cette analyse. Le fait d'affirmer expressément à l'article 2.3 que l'API ne s'applique pas aux *différends* survenus antérieurement à son entrée en vigueur ne signifie pas, même implicitement, que l'API pourrait s'appliquer à toutes les *violations* commises avant son entrée en vigueur. Cela reviendrait à renverser le principe posé à l'article 28 de la Convention de Vienne et constamment réaffirmé en jurisprudence.

584.   Comme l'a justement rappelé le Tribunal constitué dans l'affaire Mondev, « The basic principle is that a State can only be internationally responsible for breach of a treaty obligation if the obligation is in force for that State at the time of the alleged breach. The principle is stated both in the Vienna Convention on the Law of Treaties and in the ILC's Articles on State Responsibility, and has been repeatedly affirmed by international tribunals ».[529] Le Tribunal ne voit en l'espèce aucune raison de déroger à ce principe. La formulation au futur des obligations de fond de l'API[530] est du reste un indice supplémentaire de l'inapplicabilité de ces obligations à des faits survenus lorsqu'elles n'existaient pas.[531]

---

[526]   Le Tribunal relève que l'investisseur ne pouvait pas compter sur la possibilité d'un recours fondé sur un API qui n'existait pas à l'époque de son investissement ni à celle des violations alléguées de 1973-1977. V. la remarque du Tribunal dans l'affaire *Lucchetti* à propos de l'investisseur: « *[The investor] cannot say that it made its investment in reliance on the BIT, for the simple reason that the treaty did not exist until years after Lucchetti had acquired the site, built its factory, and was well into the second year of full production. It cannot conceivably contend that it invested in reliance on the existence of this international remedy* » (*Empresas Lucchetti, S.A. and Lucchetti Peru, S.A. c. Pérou*, affaire CIRDI n° ARB/03/4, sentence du 7 février 2005, para. 61).

[527]   Ainsi que le relève l'auteur du commentaire des articles de la C.D.I. sur la responsabilité de l'Etat pour fait internationalement illicite, « *les cas d'acceptation rétroactive de la responsabilité sont très rares* » (James Crawford, *Les articles de la C.D.I. sur la responsabilité de l'Etat*, Pedone, 2003, p. 159).

[528]   Transcription de l'audience du 15 janvier 2007, p. 84 (Me Malinvaud).

[529]   V. *Mondev International Ltd. c. Etats-Unis d'Amérique*, affaire CIRDI n° ARB(AF)/99/2, sentence finale du 11 octobre 2002, para. 68.

[530]   V. par exemple, les articles 3, 4, 5 et 6 de l'API Espagne-Chili.

[531]   V. *Tradex Hellas S.A. c. Albanie*, affaire CIRDI n° ARB/94/2, décision sur la compétence du 24 décembre 1996, para. 65, *JDI*, 2000.151, spéc. p. 155 et

585. Au total, l'argument de la partie demanderesse ne tient pas compte de la distinction, pourtant essentielle, entre la compétence *ratione temporis* du Tribunal et l'applicabilité *ratione temporis* des dispositions de fond du traité. Ces deux exigences doivent être satisfaites l'une et l'autre pour que la responsabilité internationale de l'Etat puisse être engagée sur le fondement du traité. L'existence d'une controverse postérieure à l'entrée en vigueur de l'API ne peut à elle seule entraîner l'application rétroactive automatique des dispositions de fond de l'API en question. L'API Espagne-Chili ne contient aucun article de nature « *dérogatoire* », susceptible de permettre l'application de ses dispositions de fond à des faits antérieurs à son entrée en vigueur.

586. Les demanderesses font valoir cependant à titre subsidiaire que les violations que l'Etat défendeur aurait commises avant l'entrée en vigueur de l'API ont un caractère continu ou constituent un élément d'un fait composite illicite et se seraient poursuivies au-delà de l'entrée en vigueur. Elles en concluent que les dispositions de fond de l'API seraient applicables au fait illicite continu ou au fait illicite composite allégués.

2. Les violations alléguées antérieures à l'entrée en vigueur de l'API constituent-elles un fait illicite continu ou des éléments d'un fait illicite composite auxquels les dispositions de fond de ce traité sont applicables ?

587. Avant d'exposer la position des parties et les conclusions du Tribunal sur ce point, il convient de procéder à un bref rappel des principaux faits pertinents.

a) Rappel des faits pertinents

588. Le 11 septembre 1973, les biens de M. Pey Casado, y compris les biens des sociétés CPP S.A. et EPC Ltda, sont saisis par les forces armées chiliennes.[532] Une série de décrets est ensuite adoptée sur la période 1973-1977.

589. Ainsi, le décret-loi n°77 du 13 octobre 1973 déclare illicites et dissouts « les partis, entités, groupements, factions ou mouvements [d'affiliation marxiste], de même que les associations, sociétés ou entreprises de quelque nature que ce soit, qui directement ou au travers de tierces personnes appartiendraient ou seraient dirigées par

---

ss. V. également *Técnicas Medioambientales Tecmed, S.A. c. Mexique*, affaire CIRDI n° ARB (AF)/00/2, sentence finale du 29 mai 2003, para. 65.

[532] V. exposé complémentaire sur le fond de l'affaire du 11 septembre 2002, p. 65. V. également la transcription de l'audience du 6 mai 2003, p. 453, Me Di Rosa qui estime que « *la confiscation [et non pas seulement la saisie] a eu lieu en 1973* ».

423

l'une d'entre elles ».[533] Le décret prévoit également que les biens des entités dissoutes passeront en pleine propriété de l'Etat.[534] Un décret suprême n°1726 du 3 décembre 1973 est adopté en vue de l'application de l'article 1 du décret-loi n°77 et prévoit que le Ministre de l'intérieur est chargé d'identifier les entités visées par le décret-loi. S'agissant des personnes physiques, le Ministre de l'intérieur déclarera de la même façon la mise à l'étude de leur situation patrimoniale[535]. C'est le décret exempté n°276 du 21 octobre 1974 qui applique les dispositions du décret-loi n°77 aux sociétés CPP S.A. et EPC Ltda. Il déclare également la mise à l'étude de la situation patrimoniale de MM. Dario Sainte Marie, Osvaldo Sainte Marie, Victor Pey Casado, Mario Osses Gonzalez, Emilio Gonzalez Gonzalez, Jorge Venegas Venegas et Ramon Carrasco Peña.[536]

590. Se référant notamment au décret exempté n°276,[537] le décret suprême n°165 du 10 février 1975 déclare dissoutes les sociétés CPP S.A. et EPC Ltda[538] et prévoit que leurs biens meubles et immeubles, dont une liste est dressée dans le décret, passent en pleine propriété à l'Etat.[539]

591. Le décret suprême n°580 du 24 avril 1975, d'une part, modifie le décret suprême n°165 pour y ajouter un bien immeuble[540] et, d'autre part, déclare que M. Pey Casado se trouve dans la situation prévue à

---

[533] Décret loi n°77 du 8 octobre 1973 déclarant illicites et dissolvant les partis politiques indiqués, article 1 (annexe 17 au mémoire des demanderesses, du 17 mars 1999).

[534] Id.

[535] Décret suprême n°1726 approuvant le règlement en vue de l'application de l'article 1 du décret-loi n°77 de 1973 (annexe 73 au contre-mémoire de la défenderesse du 3 février 2003).

[536] Décret exempté n°276 du 9 novembre 1974 (annexe 74 au contre-mémoire de la défenderesse du 3 février 2003).

[537] Décret suprême n°165 du Ministère de l'intérieur du 10 février 1975, para. 5 du préambule (annexe 1 au mémoire des demanderesses du 17 mars 1999). Le décret suprême n°165 vise également les dispositions des décrets-lois n°1, 77, 128 de 1973 et 527 de 1974.

[538] Décret suprême n°165 du Ministère de l'intérieur du 10 février 1975, article 1 (annexe 1 au mémoire des demanderesses du 17 mars 1999).

[539] Décret suprême n°165 du Ministère de l'Intérieur du 10 février 1975 (annexe 1 au mémoire des demanderesses du 17 mars 1999), articles 2, 3 et 4. Le Tribunal note que l'article 3 prévoit non pas l'expropriation d'un bien immeuble mais celui du droit à indemnisation prévu par le décret-loi n°93 du 20 octobre 1973 pour compenser l'expropriation d'un immeuble qui appartenait à la société CPP S.A. (v. décret-loi n°93 du 20 octobre 1973, articles 3 à 9, annexe 3 au mémoire des demanderesses du 17 mars 1999).

[540] Décret suprême n°580 du 24 avril 1975, article 1 (annexe 20 à la requête d'arbitrage du 3 novembre 1997).

l'article 1.2 du décret-loi n°77.[541] Ce décret transfère également à l'Etat la propriété de certains fonds déposés auprès de l'Association d'épargne et de prêts Ahorromet appartenant à M. Pey Casado.[542]

592. Enfin, le décret suprême n°1200 du 25 novembre 1977 vient compléter le décret suprême n°580 en déclarant que « passent en pleine propriété à l'Etat les biens meubles et immeubles, droits et actions, appartenant audit Pey Casado, et en particulier, la totalité des fonds investis en certificats d'épargne indexés de la Banque centrale du Chili ».[543] Ce même décret transfère en outre la propriété de tous les droits et actions de M. Pey Casado dans la société Socomer Ltda et ses filiales.[544]

593. Le Tribunal relève qu'un certain nombre de ces décrets a été annulé par les juridictions internes chiliennes. Ainsi, dans un jugement du 13 janvier 1997, la 21ème Chambre civile de Santiago a déclaré « *atteints de nullité de droit public* » pour violation de l'article 4 de la Constitution de 1925 le décret exempté n°276 du 9 novembre 1974, le décret suprême n°580 du 24 avril 1975 et le décret suprême n°1200 du 25 novembre 1977.[545] La Cour a en conséquence ordonné la « *restitution au demandeur [M. Pey Casado] des biens qui lui furent pris et mis sous séquestre* ». Ces biens sont distincts de ceux des sociétés CPP S.A. et EPC Ltda. A la connaissance du Tribunal, le décret suprême n°165 est toujours en vigueur.

---

[541] Décret suprême n°580 du 24 avril 1975, article 3 (annexe 20 à la requête d'arbitrage du 3 novembre 1997).

[542] Décret suprême n°580 du 24 avril 1975, article 4 (annexe 20 à la requête d'arbitrage du 3 novembre 1997).

[543] Décret suprême n°1200 du 25 novembre 1977, article 2 (annexe 20 à la requête d'arbitrage du 3 novembre 1997).

[544] Décret suprême n°1200 du 25 novembre 1977, article 2 (annexe 20 à la requête d'arbitrage du 3 novembre 1997). V. également la communication secrète entre le Ministre des terres et de la colonisation et le Ministre de l'intérieur du 10 novembre 1977 (annexe 20 à la requête d'arbitrage du 3 novembre 1997).

[545] Jugement du 13 janvier 1997 de la 21ème Chambre civile de Santiago (Produit avec la communication des parties demanderesses du 19 décembre 1997). Les biens en question sont distincts de ceux des sociétés CPP S.A. et EPC Ltda. Ce jugement a été confirmé par un arrêt de la Cour suprême du Chili du 14 mai 2002 (annexe C-138). La défenderesse remarque que le décret suprême n°16 du 8 janvier 1979 prévoyait déjà que le Décret suprême n°1200 ne produirait dorénavant pas d'effet en ce qui concerne les droits et les actions qui correspondent à Victor Pey Casado dans l'entreprise Socomer Ltda et ses entreprises associées (annexe 78 au contre-mémoire de la défenderesse du 3 février 2003).

594.   M. Pey Casado ayant été contraint de quitter le Chili et n'ayant pu y retourner qu'en 1989[546], il ne formule sa première demande de restitution des biens confisqués qu'en septembre 1995.[547] Le 4 octobre 1995, il se porte par ailleurs devant les tribunaux chiliens pour obtenir la restitution de la rotative Goss.[548] Le 20 novembre 1995, le ministère des biens nationaux informe M. Pey Casado que la loi d'indemnisation qui permettra de traiter les situations comparables à celle de M. Pey Casado n'a pas encore été promulguée.[549] Le 10 janvier 1996, M. Pey Casado réitère sa demande de restitution auprès du Président de la République, sans obtenir de réponse.[550] Le 3 novembre 1997, les demanderesses déposent leur requête d'arbitrage auprès du CIRDI.[551]

595.   Le 25 juin 1998 est promulguée la loi n°19.568 relative à la restitution ou indemnisation pour biens confisqués et acquis par l'Etat à travers les décrets-lois n°12, 77 et 133 de 1973, n°1697 de 1977 et n°2436 de 1978. Les parties demanderesses vont cependant informer le Ministre des biens nationaux par lettre du 24 juin 1999 de leur décision de ne pas recourir à la loi n°19.568, du fait de la requête

---

[546]   V. contre-mémoire de la défenderesse du 3 février 2003, p. 26 : « Le 4 mai 1989, M. Pey revient pour la première fois au Chili depuis son départ en 1973 ».

[547]   Annexe 22 à la requête d'arbitrage du 3 novembre 1997.

[548]   Demande initiale de M. Pey Casado du 4 octobre 1995 devant la 1ère Chambre civile du Tribunal de Santiago (annexe 48 au contre-mémoire de la défenderesse du 3 février 2003). V. *supra* paras.459 et ss.

[549]   Annexe 23 à la requête d'arbitrage du 3 novembre 1997.

[550]   V. requête d'arbitrage du 3 novembre 1997, p. 8 et annexe 23 à la requête d'arbitrage du 3 novembre 1997.

[551]   Après l'échec de l'offre de consultations amiables formulée par M. Pey Casado le 30 avril 1997 (annexes 11 et 12 à la requête d'arbitrage du 3 novembre 1997), M. Pey Casado et la Fondation Président Allende ont exprimé leur consentement à l'arbitrage respectivement le 2 et le 6 octobre 1997 (annexe 10 et 2 à la requête d'arbitrage du 3 novembre 1997). Dans la lettre exprimant son consentement à l'arbitrage, M. Pey a bien précisé que la question relative à la restitution de la rotative était exclue : « *[...] le présent consentement inclut dans son champ d'application toutes et chacune des controverses juridiques découlant de la confiscation de mes investissements commerciaux cités [ci-dessus], à la seule exception de celle relative à la restitution pure et simple – ou, à défaut, [paiement] de la valeur de remplacement correspondante – de la machine rotative GOSS, achetée en 1972 et installée au siège du journal CLARIN. Le consentement inclut toutefois la controverse juridique relative à tous les préjudices découlant de la mainmise sur ladite rotative, consistant en* damnum emergens, lucrum cessans *et intérêts compensatoires* ».

d'arbitrage introduite en 1997 et de la clause d'option irrévocable (*fork-in-the-road*) contenue dans l'API Espagne-Chili.[552]

596. Le 28 avril 2000, Le Ministre des biens nationaux rend la Décision n°43 selon laquelle les dispositions de la loi n°19.568 sont applicables aux biens confisqués aux sociétés CPP S.A. et EPC Ltda.[553] Cette décision accepte cependant d'indemniser des requérants autres que les parties demanderesses pour la confiscation des biens en question. Le Ministre des biens nationaux maintiendra la Décision n°43 que les demanderesses contesteront en vain.[554]

597. Le Tribunal se propose, après ce bref rappel des faits pertinents, d'examiner les prétentions des parties relatives à l'applicabilité des dispositions de fond de l'API.

b)   Position des parties

598. Dans le dernier état de leur argumentation, les demanderesses font valoir que le Tribunal se trouve en présence soit d'un fait illicite continu, soit d'un fait illicite composite et auxquels seraient

---

[552]   Lettre des parties demanderesses au Ministre des biens nationaux du 24 juin 1999 (annexe C-32).

[553]   Le Ministre des biens nationaux a pu considérer que « les biens identifiés ci-dessus furent confisqués à CPP SA, propriétaire à 99% de EPC Ltée., ainsi qu'à cette dernière, en application du D.L. N°77 de 1973 pris par le Ministère de l'Intérieur, lequel a dissous les sociétés considérées prête-noms de partis politiques déterminés qui y étaient spécifiés, et a disposé de leur biens. Ce qui vient d'être exposé est confirmé par la lecture d'une copie des décrets confiscatoires eux-mêmes : N°165 du Ministère de l'Intérieur, en date du 10 février 1975, et N°580 du même Ministère en date du 24 avril, de cette même année, et d'une copie des inscriptions respectives des immeubles indiqués au nom du Fisc du Chili dans le Registre de la Propriété du conservateur des Hypothèques compétent » (décision n°43 du 28 avril 2000, produite avec la communication des parties demanderesses au CIRDI du 11 mai 2000).

[554]   V. la correspondance entre les parties demanderesses, le Ministre des biens nationaux et le *Contralor general*: lettre de J. Garcés au nom de Victor Pey Casado et de la Fondation Président Allende au Ministre des biens nationaux du 24 juin 1999 (annexe C-32), lettre des parties demanderesses au Ministère des biens nationaux et au *Contralor* du 6 mai 2000 (communication des parties demanderesses au CIRDI du 4 janvier 2001), lettre du Ministre des biens nationaux aux parties demanderesses du 14 juillet 2000 relative à la légalité de la décision n°43 (communication des parties demanderesses au CIRDI du 27 avril 2001), lettre des parties demanderesses au Ministre des biens nationaux du 18 juillet 2000 (communication des parties demanderesses au CIRDI du 27 avril 2001), lettre des parties demanderesses au *Contralor* du 25 juillet 2000 (communication des parties demanderesses au CIRDI du 27 avril 2001), et lettre du *Contralor* aux parties demanderesses du 22 novembre 2000 relative à la légalité de la décision n°43 (communication de la défenderesse au CIRDI du 18 décembre 2000).

applicables les dispositions de fond de l'API.[555] Se fondant essentiellement sur des arrêts de la Cour européenne des droits de l'homme, les demanderesses qualifient « *l'expropriation de 1975-1977* »[556] et la Décision n°43[557] de violations continues, contraires notamment à l'article 5 de l'API.[558] Les demanderesses prétendent ainsi que le caractère continu de l'expropriation des biens litigieux résulte de la nullité du décret n°165 adopté en 1975. Le décret litigieux serait nul au regard du droit interne, la Cour suprême ayant elle-même déclaré nuls un certain nombre d'autres décrets de la même époque et relatifs à d'autres biens de M. Pey Casado.[559] Les demanderesses avancent également que le décret n°165 serait contraire au droit international et insistent notamment sur la solution adoptée dans l'arrêt *Loizidou* qu'elles estiment applicable à la présente affaire.[560] Le fait illicite composite allégué engloberait quant à lui « *les décrets de 1975 et 1977* », « *le refus d'indemnisation de 1995* » et la Décision n°43 du 28 avril 2000.[561] Les demanderesses prétendent enfin être victimes d'un déni de justice pour la période

---

[555] V. la transcription de l'audience du 15 janvier 2007, pp. 87 et ss (Me Malinvaud).

[556] V. la transcription de l'audience du 15 janvier 2007, pp. 90-91 (Me Malinvaud). V. réplique des demanderesses au contre-mémoire de la défenderesse, du 23 février 2003, pp. 237 et ss (l'argumentation des parties demanderesses a parfois manqué de clarté : elles ont ainsi invoqué la qualification de « *fait illicite composite continu* »).

[557] Réplique des demanderesses au contre-mémoire de la défenderesse, du 23 février 2003, p. 20. La décision n°43 a également été qualifiée de violation des articles 3, 4 et 5 de l'API par les parties demanderesses : « *Le 28 avril 2000 les articles 3, 4 et 5 de l'API ont été enfreints sous une nouvelle forme, qui s'est ajoutée à la dépossession antérieure* » (exposé complémentaire sur le fond de l'affaire du 11 septembre 2002, p. 125).

[558] V. mémoire des demanderesses du 17 mars 1999, p. 39 et la réplique des demanderesses au contre-mémoire de la défenderesse, du 23 février 2003.

[559] V. exposé complémentaire sur le fond de l'affaire du 11 septembre 2002, p. 77. Il s'agit des décrets n°276 de 1974, n°580 de 1975 et n°1200 de 1977 (v. Jugement du 13 janvier 1997 de la 21ème Chambre Civile de Santiago, produit avec la communication du 19 décembre 1997 et l'arrêt de la Cour suprême du Chili du 14 mai 2002 (annexe C-138)). V. également réponse au mémoire soutenant l'incompétence soumis par la défenderesse, du 18 septembre 1999, pp. 42 et ss.

[560] V. réplique des demanderesses au contre-mémoire de la défenderesse, du 23 février 2003, pp. 236 et ss. V. également la transcription de l'audience du 15 janvier 2007, p. 90 et la transcription de l'audience du 16 janvier 2007, pp. 38-39 (Me Malinvaud).

[561] V. l'argumentation développée à titre subsidiaire par les parties demanderesses dans la transcription de l'audience du 15 janvier 2007, pp. 87-88 (Me Malinvaud).

1995-2002, en violation de l'article 4 de l'API.[562] Lors des audiences de janvier 2007, les demanderesses ont élargi leur demande fondée sur le déni de justice en alléguant que « *c'est à l'ensemble du contentieux soumis au Tribunal arbitral que s'applique, de notre point de vue, le déni de justice subi par M. Pey* ».[563]

599.   Selon la défenderesse, l'expropriation opérée par le décret de 1975 est un acte instantané, antérieur à l'entrée en vigueur du traité, auquel les obligations de fond du traité de l'API ne sont pas applicables.[564] S'appuyant sur la décision du Tribunal du 25 septembre 2001[565], la défenderesse fait également valoir que la Décision n°43 ne peut quant à elle être considérée comme un acte illicite ; elle n'est qu'une conséquence d'une expropriation qui s'est achevée bien avant l'entrée en vigueur de l'API.[566] La défenderesse considère qu'il n'existe pas non plus d'acte composite illicite en l'espèce et qu'en toute hypothèse, seuls les dommages qui auraient été subis après l'entrée en vigueur pourraient être examinés par le Tribunal.[567] Enfin, la défenderesse ne s'est pas prononcée sur l'applicabilité des dispositions de fond de l'API au déni de justice allégué par les demanderesses.[568]

c)   Conclusions du Tribunal

600.   Après examen des faits et des prétentions des parties, le Tribunal est parvenu à la conclusion que l'expropriation résultant du Décret n°165 ne peut être analysée comme un fait illicite continu et ne peut se voir appliquer les dispositions de fond de l'API. En revanche, les dispositions de fond de l'API sont applicables *ratione temporis* à la

---

[562]   V. la transcription de l'audience du 16 janvier 2007, pp. 42 et ss, spéc. p. 45 : « le fondement juridique du déni de justice se trouve à l'évidence dans l'article 4 de l'API Espagne-Chili » (Me Garcés).

[563]   Transcription de l'audience du 16 janvier 2007, p. 46 (Me Garcés). V. également la transcription de l'audience du 16 janvier 2007, p. 47 (Me Malinvaud) : « *le refus répété d'indemnisations à partir de 1995 est bien un déni de justice qui est un fait de l'Etat en réalité distinct de l'expropriation invoquée au titre de l'article 5 du Traité et qui est applicable à toutes les demandes qui sont présentées devant votre Tribunal* ».

[564]   V. la transcription de l'audience du 15 janvier 2007, p. 15 (Me Di Rosa). V. également contre-mémoire de la défenderesse du 3 février 2003, pp. 144-146.

[565]   Décision sur les mesures conservatoires sollicitées par les parties du 25 septembre 2001.

[566]   V. la transcription de l'audience du 15 janvier 2007, p. 16 (Me Di Rosa).

[567]   V. la transcription de l'audience du 16 janvier 2007, pp. 23-24 (Me Di Rosa).

[568]   Contre-mémoire de la défenderesse du 3 février 2003, p. 182 et ss. La défenderesse a formulé une objection aux développements des parties demanderesses sur le déni de justice lors de l'audience du 16 janvier 2007 (v. transcription de l'audience du 16 janvier, p. 45 (Me Goodman)).

violation résultant de la Décision n°43 et au déni de justice allégué par les demanderesses, ces actes étant postérieurs à l'entrée en vigueur du traité.

i. *Les dispositions de fond de l'API ne sont pas applicables ratione temporis à l'expropriation prononcée par le décret n°165 du 10 février 1975*

601. Pour tenter de démontrer que les dispositions de fond de l'API, et notamment celles de l'article 5 relatives à l'expropriation, sont applicables *ratione temporis* à l'expropriation de 1975, les parties demanderesses se fondent sur la prétendue nullité *ab initio* du décret n°165[569] au regard du droit interne et sur la jurisprudence de la Cour européenne des droits de l'homme, pour en déduire le caractère continu de l'acte litigieux. La violation alléguée, bien antérieure à 1994, se serait ainsi poursuivie au-delà de la date d'entrée en vigueur de l'API.

602. En l'espèce, aucun des arguments avancés par les demanderesses ne convainc le Tribunal.

603. L'argumentation développée par les demanderesses sur la nullité du décret n°165 au regard du droit interne ne suffit pas à justifier leur position. En effet, les demanderesses se bornent à inviter le Tribunal à faire une application par analogie de l'arrêt de la Cour suprême du Chili du 14 mai 2002 sans véritablement démontrer en quoi le décret litigieux serait lui-même contraire à l'article 4 de la Constitution de 1925.[570] A la connaissance du Tribunal, la validité du Décret n°165 n'a pas été remise en cause par les juridictions internes et ce décret fait toujours partie de l'ordre juridique interne chilien.

604. Pour tenter d'établir que le décret n°165 constitue une violation à caractère continu au regard du droit international, les demanderesses invoquent certains arrêts de la Cour européenne des droits de l'homme et notamment l'arrêt *Loizidou*.[571]

605. Le Tribunal estime que la jurisprudence invoquée ne trouve pas à s'appliquer en l'espèce et ne peut servir de fondement pour qualifier de fait illicite continu une expropriation qui, en l'espèce, a été condamnée avant l'entrée en vigueur du traité.

---

[569] V. exposé complémentaire sur le fond de l'affaire du 11 septembre 2002, p. 152. V. également réplique des demanderesses au contre-mémoire de la défenderesse, du 23 février 2003, p. 254.

[570] V. exposé complémentaire sur le fond de l'affaire du 11 septembre 2002, pp. 76-78, spéc. p. 77. V. également réplique des demanderesses au contre-mémoire de la défenderesse, du 23 février 2003, p. 237, note 430.

[571] V. réplique des demanderesses au contre-mémoire de la défenderesse, du 23 février 2003, p. 238 et la transcription de l'audience du 15 janvier 2007, p. 90 (Me Malinvaud).

606. En effet, dans l'affaire *Loizidou*, la Cour est parvenue à la conclusion que la Turquie avait commis une violation continue du droit de propriété de la partie demanderesse au motif que la Constitution de la République turque de Chypre nord de 1985, norme antérieure à l'entrée en vigueur de la Convention vis-à-vis de l'Etat défendeur et sur laquelle était fondée le transfert de propriété litigieux, ne pouvait se voir attribuer de validité juridique. En adoptant un raisonnement implicite,[572] la Cour n'a toutefois pas vérifié l'existence des deux composantes du concept de violation continue, à savoir « *un événement critique constituant la violation première, et sa continuation* »,[573] ne distinguant pas notamment une situation d'occupation *de facto* de celle où a lieu un transfert de propriété.[574] La solution retenue par la Cour revêt, aux yeux du présent Tribunal, un caractère exceptionnel[575] que reflète la vigueur des opinions dissidentes sur la question de l'application de la Convention *ratione temporis*.[576] Elle repose sur une interprétation particulièrement large de la notion de violation continue que ne partage pas le présent Tribunal.

607. L'arrêt *Papamichalopoulos*, également invoqué à plusieurs reprises par les demanderesses au soutien de leur thèse sur l'expropriation comme acte continu, doit lui aussi être distingué de la présente affaire. L'arrêt ne concerne pas un transfert de propriété nettement identifié dans le temps mais l'occupation *de facto* de terrains par l'armée au moyen d'actes successifs. Le gouvernement grec n'avait en outre pas soulevé d'exception d'incompétence *ratione temporis* et la Cour a pu se borner « *à noter que les griefs des intéressés ont trait à une situation continue, qui subsiste à l'heure actuelle* ».[577] Les autres affaires citées brièvement par les demanderesses lors des audiences de janvier 2007 (*SGS c. Philippines, Ilascu c. Moldavie et Russie, Broniowski c. Pologne*[578]) ne concernent pas des cas

---

[572]   La Cour n'affirme pas expressément qu'il s'agit d'une violation continue. V. sur ce point les observations de P. Tavernier, *JDI* 1997.273, spéc. p. 274.

[573]   V. *Loizidou c. Turquie*, fond, C.E.D.H., Recueil 1996-VI, opinion dissidente du juge Jambrek, para. 5.

[574]   V. *Loizidou c. Turquie*, fond, C.E.D.H., Recueil 1996-VI, opinion dissidente du juge Baka, pp. 30-31.

[575]   V. James Crawford (ed.), Les articles de la C.D.I. sur la responsabilité de l'Etat, Pedone, 2003, p. 163.

[576]   V. *Loizidou c. Turquie*, fond, C.E.D.H., Recueil 1996-VI, opinions dissidentes des juges Bernhardt, Baka, Jambrek, Pettiti et Gölcüklü.

[577]   *Papamichalopoulos et autres c. Grèce*, C.E.D.H., Série A, n°260-B (1993), para. 40.

[578]   L'affaire *SGS c. Philippines* concernait un simple refus de payer une dette en application d'un contrat (*SGS Société Générale de Surveillance S.A. c. République des Philippines*, affaire CIRDI n° ARB/02/06, décision sur la compétence du 29 janvier 2004) ; l'arrêt *Ilascu* concernait un cas de

d'expropriation et ne permettent pas de conclure que les actes de confiscation commis en l'espèce avant l'entrée en vigueur de l'API sont des actes continus qui se seraient poursuivis au-delà de l'entrée en vigueur de l'API.

608. En l'espèce, l'expropriation litigieuse, qui a débuté avec les saisies effectuées par l'armée en 1973, s'est achevée avec l'entrée en vigueur du décret n°165 du 10 février 1975 qui a prononcé le transfert de propriété des biens des sociétés CPP S.A. et EPC Ltda à l'Etat. A cette date, l'expropriation était consommée, quelle que soit l'appréciation que l'on peut porter sur sa licéité. Aussi le Tribunal considère que l'expropriation dont se plaignent les demanderesses doit être qualifiée d'acte instantané, antérieur à la date d'entrée en vigueur de l'API. Cette analyse est conforme à la position de principe de la Cour européenne des droits de l'homme qui considère l'expropriation comme un acte instantané et qui ne crée pas une situation continue de « *privation d'un droit* ».

609. Dans l'affaire *Malhous*, la Cour a en effet rappelé :

> « *qu'elle ne peut examiner une requête que dans la mesure où elle se rapporte à des événements s'étant produits après l'entrée en vigueur de la Convention à l'égard de la Partie contractante concernée. En l'espèce, les biens du père du requérant ont été expropriés en juin 1949 et attribués à d'autres personnes physiques en 1957, soit bien avant le 18 mars 1992, date à laquelle la Convention est entrée en vigueur à l'égard de la République tchèque (Kuchař et Štis c. République tchèque (déc.), n°37527/97, 23 mai 2000, non publiée). La Cour n'est donc pas compétente* ratione temporis *pour examiner les circonstances de l'expropriation ou les effets continus produits par elle jusqu'à ce jour. A ce propos, elle rappelle et confirme la jurisprudence bien établie de la Commission selon laquelle la privation d'un droit de propriété ou d'un autre droit réel constitue en principe un acte instantané et ne crée pas une situation continue de « privation d'un droit » (voir, par exemple, Mayer et autres c. Allemagne, requêtes n°s 18890/91,*

---

détention illégale, l'expropriation n'ayant pas été discutée (v. paras.404-405) (*Ilascu et autres c. Moldavie et Russie*, C.E.D.H., 8 juillet 2004) ; l'arrêt *Broniowski* portait sur la mise en œuvre d'un droit à une mesure compensatoire que le droit interne avait conféré au demandeur avant la date d'entrée en vigueur de la Convention européenne des droits de l'homme et continué à lui accorder après cette date (*Broniowski c. Pologne*, C.E.D.H., décision sur la recevabilité du 19 décembre 2002).

19048/91, 19342/92 et 19549/92, décision de la
Commission du 4 mars 1996, Décisions et rapports
(DR) 85-B, p. 5, et Brežny c. Slovaquie, requête
n°23131/93, décision de la Commission du 4 mars
1996, DR 85-A, p. 65) ».[579]

610. La Cour a repris ce raisonnement dans sa jurisprudence ultérieure, confirmant, d'une part, que la Convention n'est pas applicable *ratione temporis* à des faits qui sont antérieurs à son entrée en vigueur et, d'autre part, que l'expropriation constitue en principe un acte instantané et qu'elle n'est pas créatrice d'une situation continue.[580] Il en va de même dans la présente affaire : les

---

[579] *Malhous c. République tchèque*, C.E.D.H., décision sur la recevabilité du 13 décembre 2000, p. 16 (B 2° c).

[580] V. par exemple Smoleanu c. Roumanie, C.E.D.H., arrêt du 3 décembre 2002, paras.45-46 : « [...] la Cour rappelle, premièrement, qu'elle ne peut examiner une requête que dans la mesure où elle se rapporte à des événements s'étant produits après l'entrée en vigueur de la Convention à l'égard de la Partie contractante concernée. En l'espèce, la maison de la requérante a été nationalisée en 1950, soit bien avant le 20 juin 1994, date à laquelle la Convention est entrée en vigueur à l'égard de la Roumanie. La Cour n'est donc pas compétente ratione temporis pour examiner les circonstances de la nationalisation ou les effets continus produits par elle jusqu'à ce jour. Elle rappelle et confirme sa jurisprudence bien établie selon laquelle la privation d'un droit de propriété ou d'un autre droit réel constitue en principe un acte instantané et ne crée pas une situation continue de « privation d'un droit » (voir, par exemple, Lupuleţ c. Roumanie, requête no 25497/94, décision de la Commission du 17 mai 1996, Décisions et Rapports (DR) 85-A, p. 126) . V. Bergauer c. République Tchèque, C.E.D.H., décision sur la recevabilité, 13 décembre 2005, p. 10 : « The Court notes that the expropriation of the applicants' or their predecessors' property occurred shortly after the Second World War almost fifty years ago, long before the entry into force of the Convention with respect to the Czech Republic. Moreover, according to the Convention case-law, a deprivation of ownership or other rights in rem is in principle an instantaneous act and does not produce a continuing situation of the "deprivation of a right" (see Malhous v. the Czech Republic (dec.) [GC], no. 33071/96, ECHR 2000-XII, with further references) ». V. également Abbasov c. Azerbaïdjan, C.E.D.H., décision partielle sur la recevabilité du 24 octobre 2006, p. 5, para. 4 : « Assuming that the complaint falls within the ambit of Article 1 of Protocol No. 1 of the Convention, the Court notes that the applicant's property was confiscated prior to 15 April 2002 [date of the Convention's entry into force with respect to Azerbaijan]. According to the Court's case-law, a deprivation of ownership or other rights in rem is in principle an instantaneous act and does not produce a continuing situation of "deprivation of a right" (see Malhous v. the Czech Republic (dec.), no. 33071/96, ECHR 2000-XII, with further references). It follows that this complaint is also incompatible ratione temporis with the provisions of the Convention within the meaning of Article 35 § 3 and must be rejected in accordance with Article 35 § 4 ».

dispositions de fond de l'API ne sont pas applicables *ratione temporis* aux actes d'expropriation commis avant l'entrée en vigueur du traité, ces actes étant achevés et ne pouvant donner naissance à une situation continue.

611. Une fois le traité en vigueur, il n'est toutefois pas interdit au Tribunal de prendre en considération des faits antérieurs à la date d'entrée en vigueur du traité pour examiner le contexte dans lequel sont intervenus les actes que les demanderesses estiment devoir être qualifiés de violations postérieures à l'entrée en vigueur du traité. C'est ce qu'a rappelé le Tribunal arbitral constitué dans l'affaire *MCI c. Ecuador* qui estimait n'être compétent qu'à l'égard des actes postérieurs à l'entrée en vigueur de l'API lorsque ces actes sont présentés comme des violations de l'API :

> « *Prior events may only be considered by the Tribunal for purposes of understanding the background, the causes, or scope of violations of the BIT that occurred after its entry into force* ».[581]

612. En conséquence, même si en l'espèce les dispositions de fond de l'API ne sont pas applicables aux actes d'expropriation antérieurs à son entrée en vigueur, le Tribunal pourra examiner les violations de l'API qui se sont produites après son entrée en vigueur, en prenant en compte au titre du contexte des événements qui ont eu lieu avant cette date. Il convient dès lors de déterminer si les autres violations invoquées par les demanderesses peuvent effectivement se voir appliquer les dispositions de fond de l'API *ratione temporis*.

ii. *Les dispositions de fond de l'API sont applicables à la Décision n°43 du 28 avril 2000*

613. Selon les parties demanderesses, la Décision n°43 du 28 avril 2000 serait en elle-même contraire aux articles 3, 4 et 5 de l'API.[582] La Décision n°43 a été rendue en application de la loi n°19.568, promulguée postérieurement à l'entrée en vigueur de l'API. Cette loi dispose dans son article 1 que « *les personnes physiques ou les personnes morales, incluant les partis politiques, qui [ont] été privé[e]s du domaine de leurs biens par l'application des décrets-lois N°12, 77 et 133, de 1973 ; 1.687, de 1977, et 2.346, de 1978, auront le droit de solliciter leur restitution ou de réclamer le paiement d'une indemnisation, conformément aux normes établies dans cette loi* » (souligné par nous). L'Etat défendeur a ainsi créé un droit à indemnisation, défini et délimité par la loi interne, et ayant

---

[581]   *M.C.I. Power Group L.C. and New Turbine, Inc. c. Equateur*, affaire CIRDI n° ARB/03/6, sentence du 31 juillet 2007, para. 93.
[582]   See footnote 557.

vocation à s'appliquer à des personnes visées par une législation adoptée pendant la période 1973-1978.

614. La Décision n°43, qui autorise l'indemnisation de personnes autres que les parties demanderesses pour l'expropriation des biens des sociétés CPP S.A. et EPC Ltda en application de la loi de 1998, est qualifiée par les parties demanderesses de « *nouvelle dépossession* »[583] contraire aux dispositions de fond de l'API. Cette décision étant intervenue postérieurement à l'entrée en vigueur de l'API, le Tribunal conclut que les dispositions de fond de ce dernier lui sont applicables *ratione temporis*, sans toutefois préjuger à ce stade de sa décision au fond sur la violation alléguée.

615. Le Tribunal estime en revanche que le fait illicite composite invoqué par les parties demanderesses n'existe pas en l'espèce.

616. Le Tribunal rappellera que les demanderesses prétendent regrouper au sein d'un fait composite « *les décrets de 1975 et 1977* », « *le refus d'indemnisation de 1995* » et la Décision n°43 du 28 avril 2000.[584]

617. Or, l'existence d'un fait illicite composite implique la réunion « *d'une série d'actes ou d'omissions, définie dans son ensemble comme illicite* ». La violation d'une obligation internationale par l'État à raison d'une telle série d'actes ou d'omissions, n'a lieu que lorsque se produit « *l'action ou l'omission qui, conjuguée aux autres actions ou omissions, suffit à constituer le fait illicite* ».[585]

618. Le Tribunal rappellera également que l'allégation de fait composite illicite ne permet pas, en toute hypothèse, de s'affranchir du principe de non-rétroactivité. Ainsi, « *[d]ans le cas où l'obligation en question n'existait pas au début de la conduite mais est née par la suite, la « première » des actions ou omissions de la série, aux fins de la responsabilité des Etats, sera la première à s'être produite après la naissance de l'obligation. Cela n'exclut pas pour autant que les tribunaux puissent prendre en considération des actions ou omissions antérieures à d'autres fins (par exemple, pour établir la base factuelle de violations ultérieures ou pour prouver l'intention)* ».[586]

619. De l'avis du Tribunal, la qualification d'acte illicite composite ne peut pas être retenue en l'espèce car les faits litigieux allégués par les

---

[583] V. par exemple la transcription de l'audience du 5 mai 2003, p. 226 (Me Malinvaud).

[584] V. l'argumentation développée à titre subsidiaire par les parties demanderesses dans la transcription de l'audience du 15 janvier 2007, pp. 87-88 (Me Malinvaud).

[585] Article 15 des articles de la C.D.I. sur la responsabilité de l'Etat.

[586] James Crawford (ed.), Les articles de la C.D.I. sur la responsabilité de l'Etat, Pedone, 2003, p. 172.

demanderesses ne correspondent ni à une série d'actes constitutive d'une infraction distincte des manquements invoqués ni à une pratique de l'Etat chilien découlant de l'« *accumulation de manquements de nature identique ou analogue assez nombreux et liés entre eux* ».[587] Il n'y a pas dans la présente affaire de « *système* » ou d'« *ensemble* » d'actes illicites qui, pris de manière globale, apparaîtrait comme un fait illicite.

620. La saisie et le transfert de la propriété à l'Etat des biens des sociétés CPP S.A. et EPC Ltda sont constitutifs d'un fait consommé et distinct des violations postérieures à l'entrée en vigueur de l'API dont font état les demanderesses. Le Tribunal en a conclu que les dispositions de fond de l'API n'étaient pas applicables à l'expropriation des biens des sociétés CPP S.A. et EPC Ltda.

621. Les autres actes présentés par les demanderesses comme éléments du fait composite allégué se sont tous produits postérieurement à l'entrée en vigueur du traité. Il s'agit essentiellement, selon les demanderesses, du refus d'indemnisation opposé à Monsieur Pey Casado en 1995 et de la Décision n°43. Le refus d'indemnisation se rapporte à une expropriation qui a eu lieu dans les années 70, à une époque où l'API n'était pas en vigueur. Ce refus d'indemnisation n'est pas en lui-même contraire au traité, le seul droit d'indemnisation postérieur au traité n'ayant été créé par le législateur chilien qu'en 1998 ; il ne peut davantage être relié à une violation survenue postérieurement à l'entrée en vigueur du traité, l'expropriation ayant eu lieu bien avant cette date. Présenter le refus d'indemnisation comme l'élément d'un fait composite revient à confondre la notion de différend avec les faits qui en sont à l'origine, ce que les demanderesses ont par ailleurs reproché à la défenderesse.

622. La Décision n°43 du 28 avril 2000 revêt quant à elle un caractère différent. Les demanderesses l'ont qualifié de « *nouvelle dépossession* », notamment dans le but d'accréditer la thèse d'un fait composite comprenant une série de manquements identiques et analogues. Il est pourtant impossible d'exproprier deux fois de suite les mêmes biens. Les biens des sociétés CPP S.A. et EPC Ltda ont fait l'objet d'une expropriation définitive en 1975. Sans anticiper sur le traitement de la violation alléguée, le Tribunal observe que la Décision n°43 paraît devoir s'analyser davantage en une application discriminatoire d'une loi postérieure au traité et des droits que celle-ci a créés. Il s'agit d'une question distincte et non pas d'un fait identique à l'expropriation susceptible de former l'un des ingrédients

---

587   *Irlande c. Royaume Uni*, C.E.D.H., Série A, n°25 (1978), p. 64, para. 159 *in* James Crawford (ed.), *Les articles de la C.D.I. sur la responsabilité de l'Etat*, Pedone, 2003, p. 170.

du fait composite allégué. L'argument des demanderesses ne peut donc être retenu par le Tribunal.

623. En réalité, la seule qualification susceptible d'être retenue serait celle d'un acte composite comprenant une série d'atteintes au traitement juste et équitable de l'investissement des parties demanderesses, résidant essentiellement dans la Décision n°43 et le déni de justice allégué qui lui est lié concernant la rotative Goss. Ces faits sont tous postérieurs à l'entrée en vigueur de l'API. Cette hypothèse n'a toutefois pas été présentée par les demanderesses et son éventuel bien-fondé ne changerait pas la position du Tribunal sur la question de l'applicabilité des dispositions de fond de l'API *ratione temporis* que le Tribunal arbitral estime applicables tant à la Décision n° 43 qu'au déni de justice allégué relatif à la rotative Goss. Que ces faits soient envisagés ensemble, en tant qu'éléments d'un acte composite, ou séparément n'est pas de nature à modifier en quoi que ce soit les conclusions du Tribunal arbitral.

iii.   *Les dispositions de fond du traité sont applicables au déni de justice allégué*

624. Les parties demanderesses prétendent être victimes d'un déni de justice qui aurait eu lieu durant une période commençant en 1995 et allant à tout le moins jusqu'en 2002. Le déni de justice allégué comportait initialement deux aspects : l'impossibilité d'obtenir une décision sur le fond en première instance au bout de sept ans de procédure dans l'affaire concernant la restitution de la rotative Goss et l'intervention de la Décision n°43, dont l'incompatibilité avec la procédure judiciaire a été en vain contestée par les demanderesses, présentées comme une violation de l'article 4 de l'API.[588] Lors des audiences de janvier 2007, les demanderesses ont élargi leur demande fondée sur le déni de justice « *à l'ensemble du contentieux soumis au Tribunal arbitral [...]* ».[589]

---

[588]   V. réplique des demanderesses au contre-mémoire de la défenderesse, du 23 février 2003, pp. 103 et ss. V. également la transcription de l'audience du 16 janvier 2007, pp. 42 et ss, spéc. p. 45 : « *le fondement juridique du déni de justice se trouve à l'évidence dans l'article 4 de l'API Espagne-Chili* » (Me Garcés).

[589]   Transcription de l'audience du 16 janvier 2007, p. 46 (Me Garcés). V. également la transcription de l'audience du 16 janvier 2007, p. 47 (Me Malinvaud) : « *le refus répété d'indemnisations à partir de 1995 est bien un déni de justice qui est un fait de l'Etat en réalité distinct de l'expropriation invoquée au titre de l'article 5 du Traité et qui est applicable à toutes les demandes qui sont présentées devant votre Tribunal* ».

625.   La défenderesse n'a pour sa part pas développé d'arguments sur l'éventuelle applicabilité des dispositions de fond de l'API au déni de justice allégué par les demanderesses.[590]

626.   Après examen des faits[591] et des prétentions des parties, il ne fait pas de doute que le déni de justice allégué par les demanderesses s'étend sur une période postérieure à l'entrée en vigueur de l'API. L'article 4 de l'API lui est donc bien applicable *ratione temporis*.

B.   Le bien-fondé des violations alléguées

627.   Ayant constaté que les dispositions de fond de l'API sont applicables à la Décision n°43 du 28 avril 2000 ainsi qu'au déni de justice allégué, le Tribunal doit à présent examiner le bien-fondé des deux violations alléguées.

1.   Rappel des faits

628.   Les faits concernant la Décision n°43 et le déni de justice allégué par les demanderesses ont été résumés en détail dans la partie IV.C.3. de la présente sentence, dans le contexte de la discussion de la compétence *ratione temporis* du Centre et du Tribunal arbitral. Au risque de répétition, il convient néanmoins de rappeler les éléments factuels principaux concernant ces deux violations alléguées, en introduction de la présente partie sur le fond des demandes, sans pour autant répéter les références détaillés au dossier qui se trouvent ci-dessus.

a)   Décision n°43 - Indemnisation de personnes non-propriétaires

629.   La première violation potentielle concerne l'indemnisation de personnes non-propriétaires par le Ministre chilien des biens nationaux par la Décision n°43 du 28 avril 2000.

630.   En septembre 1995, M. Pey Casado a formulé sa première demande de restitution des biens confisqués. Le 20 novembre 1995, le ministère des biens nationaux informe M. Pey Casado que la loi d'indemnisation qui permettra de traiter les situations comparables à celle de M. Pey Casado n'a pas encore été promulguée. Le 10 janvier 1996, M. Pey Casado réitère sa demande de restitution auprès du Président de la République, sans obtenir de réponse. Le 3 novembre 1997, les demanderesses déposent leur requête d'arbitrage auprès du CIRDI.

---

[590]   Contre-mémoire de la défenderesse du 3 février 2003, p. 182 et ss. La défenderesse a formulé une objection aux développements des parties demanderesses sur le déni de justice lors de l'audience du 16 janvier 2007 (v. la transcription de l'audience du 16 janvier 2007, p. 45 (Me Goodman)).

[591]   V. notamment *supra* paras.459 et ss.

631.	Le 25 juin 1998 est promulguée la loi n°19.568 relative à la restitution ou indemnisation pour biens confisqués et acquis par l'Etat à travers les décrets-lois n°12, 77 et 133 de 1973, n°1697 de 1977 et n°2436 de 1978. Les demanderesses vont cependant informer le Ministre des biens nationaux par lettre du 24 juin 1999 de leur décision de ne pas recourir à la loi n°19.568, du fait de la requête d'arbitrage introduite en 1997 et de la clause d'option irrévocable (*fork-in-the-road*) contenue dans l'API Espagne-Chili.

632.	Le 28 avril 2000, Le Ministre des biens nationaux adopte la Décision n°43 selon laquelle les dispositions de la loi n°19.568 sont applicables aux biens confisqués aux sociétés CPP S.A. et EPC Ltda.[592] Cependant, comme le Tribunal l'a expliqué ci-dessus, la Décision n°43 indemnise des requérants autres que les demanderesses pour la confiscation des biens en question et le Ministre des biens nationaux maintiendra cette décision que les demanderesses contesteront en vain.

b)	L'absence de décision concernant la rotative Goss

633.	La deuxième violation potentielle concerne l'absence de décision des tribunaux chiliens concernant la restitution de la rotative Goss.

634.	Les demanderesses ont introduit une procédure judiciaire le 4 octobre 1995 devant la Première Chambre civile de Santiago visant à obtenir la restitution de la rotative Goss. Comme le Tribunal l'a indiqué de manière plus détaillée en plus ci-dessus, même si certaines décisions concernant des questions d'ordre probatoire ont été rendues dans cette procédure, la Première Chambre civile ne s'était pas prononcée sur le fond lorsqu'est intervenue la Décision n°43 et lorsque les demanderesses ont déposé leur demande complémentaire devant le Tribunal arbitral le 4 novembre 2002.

635.	Les demanderesses ont tenté en vain de faire reconnaître l'incompatibilité de la Décision n°43 avec cette procédure judiciaire. Le 2 octobre 2001, la Première Chambre civile de Santiago s'est déclarée incompétente pour juger de l'incompatibilité entre la Décision n°43 et la procédure engagée devant elle depuis le 4 octobre 1995. Seule la Cour suprême serait compétente. Après avoir informé le *Contralor* de l'incompatibilité de la Décision n°43 avec l'action portée devant la Première Chambre civile de Santiago depuis le 4 octobre 1995, les demanderesses lui ont reproché d'avoir entériné les 22 et 23 juillet 2002 le paiement d'une indemnisation au profit des bénéficiaires de la Décision n°43, cette indemnisation

---

[592]	Décision n°43 du 28 avril 2000, produite avec la communication des parties demanderesses au CIRDI du 11 mai 2000.

comprenant notamment le préjudice subi du fait de la confiscation de la rotative Goss.

636. Finalement, comme le Tribunal arbitral a récapitulé ci-dessus, les demanderesses ont intenté des nombreux recours auprès du pouvoir exécutif et du pouvoir judiciaire contre ces décisions en 2002 et visant à mettre en cause la comptabilité de la Décision n°43 avec la procédure judiciaire introduite en 1995, recours qui ont tous été rejetés.

2. Positions des parties

   a) Position des demanderesses

637. En ce qui concerne la Décision n°43, les demanderesses ont soutenu qu'elle « *constitue en tout état de cause [...] un nouvel élément constitutif du différend* ».[593] D'après les demanderesses, la Décision n°43 serait illégale au regard du droit chilien et engagerait la responsabilité de l'Etat chilien en droit interne.[594]

638. De plus, qualifiant la Décision n°43 de « *fait internationalement illicite* », les demanderesses ont soutenu que cette décision constituait « un fait nouveau ayant un effet similaire à une dépossession puisqu'elle a reconnu la propriété des actions de CPP et EPC à des tiers alors même que ces biens font l'objet du présent arbitrage ».[595] D'après les demanderesses, la Décision n°43 violerait trois des garanties inclues dans l'API, notamment dans l'article 3 (protection), l'article 4 (traitement juste et équitable) et l'article 5 (expropriation).[596]

639. Pour ce qui est la rotative Goss, alors que sa restitution avait fait l'objet d'une demande d'indemnisation devant les juridictions chiliennes et avait, en conséquence, été exclue de la requête d'arbitrage du 7 novembre 1997, il n'en allait pas initialement de même pour la demande d'indemnisation pour le manque à gagner. Dans leur demande complémentaire du 4 novembre 2002, les demanderesses ont fourni une demande d'indemnisation tendant à voir réparer la perte de la rotative Goss en alléguant avoir été victimes d'un déni de justice au sens du droit international au motif que, de 1995 à 2002, « *aucune décision n'avait été adoptée au Chili*

---

[593] Exposé complémentaire sur la compétence du Tribunal arbitral du 11 septembre 2002, p. 174.

[594] V. Exposé complémentaire sur le fond de l'affaire du 11 septembre 2002, pp. 112-124.

[595] Réplique des demanderesses au contre-mémoire de la défenderesse du 23 février 2003, p. 18.

[596] V. Exposé complémentaire sur le fond de l'affaire du 11 septembre 2002, pp. 125-130.

par rapport à la valeur de restitution stricto sensu de la rotative ou sa valeur de remplacement ».[597]

640. Les demanderesses ont invoqué à plusieurs reprises la clause de la nation la plus favorisée. Il est pourtant superflu de résumer ces arguments ici étant donné que les demanderesses semblent ne vouloir tirer aucune conséquence précise de cette clause, comme l'a confirmé Me Garcés à l'audience du 16 janvier 2007.[598] En revanche, sa position sur le fond peut être résumée de la manière suivante.

641. Les demanderesses insistent sur le fait que plus de dix ans après la requête originale aux tribunaux civils du Chili concernant la rotative Goss, il n'y a pas eu de résolution en première instance. Sur la base des faits résumés ci-dessus, les demanderesses ont soutenu que le délai important de la procédure devant la Première Chambre civile de Santiago pour la restitution de la rotative Goss ou l'indemnisation de sa valeur de remplacement et l'absence de décision depuis plus de dix ans constituaient un déni de justice la part du Chili.[599]

---

[597] Demande complémentaire des demanderesses du 4 novembre 2002. V. aussi la transcription de l'audience du 15 janvier 2007, p. 92.

[598] V. la transcription de l'audience du 16 janvier 2007, p. 48, où la réponse donnée par Me Garcés à la question du Président du Tribunal arbitral se lit comme suit :
M. Le Président. – Si vous me le permettez, vous estimez – vous venez de le dire – qu'il n'y a pas lieu d'appliquer la clause de la nation la plus favorisée à toutes les questions. Est-ce à dire qu'il est nécessaire, selon vous, de l'appliquer à certaines questions ?
Dr. Juan E. Garcés. – A aucune question, et merci de poser la question. Elle ne doit s'appliquer à aucune question car la seule fois que nous avons évoqué la clause de la nation la plus favorisée, hier, c'était à titre subsidiaire dans l'affaire de la restitution Goss. Pourquoi à titre subsidiaire ? Parce que, de notre point de vue, le déni de justice prévaut.

[599] Les parties demanderesses ont résumé leur position lors de l'audience du 15 janvier comme suit : « En l'espèce, la Chili a commis un acte de déni de justice, d'un côté, par le délai extraordinaire à établir une vraie solution. A l'heure où nous parlons, nous nous situons plus de dix ans après la requête originale et, à ce jour, il n'y a pas eu de résolution en première instance. Le délai de résolution d'un différend porté à la connaissance des cours est en soit un motif de déni de justice si ce délai est irraisonnable. »[599] Transcription de l'audience du 15 janvier 2007, p. 93, para. 10-16 (Me Garcés). V. aussi réplique des demanderesses au contre-mémoire de la défenderesse, du 23 février 2003, p. 107 ; Transcription de l'audience du 16 janvier 2007, p. 47 (Me Malinvaud) : « […] le refus répété d'indemnisations à partir de 1995 est bien un déni de justice qui est un fait de l'Etat en réalité distinct de l'expropriation invoquée au titre de l'article 5 du Traité et qui est applicable à toutes les demandes qui sont présentées devant votre Tribunal. » En outre, selon les demanderesses, dans le cas où la Première Chambre civile de Santiago rendrait une décision au fond dans cette affaire, l'adoption de la

642. En outre, les demanderesses, qui notent au passage que la « *fork-in-the-road* » et le déni de justice sont des notions incompatibles, soulignent que la « *répudiation du droit d'accès au Tribunal arbitral [...]* » est tout-à-fait différente des exceptions d'incompétence prévues dans le Règlement d'arbitrage et la Convention CIRDI.

643. Il s'agirait donc, selon cette argumentation, d'un déni de justice résultant non seulement de l'attitude des juridictions chiliennes sur le traitement de la question de la rotative Goss mais aussi, plus largement, de l'attitude générale des diverses autorités chiliennes à l'égard du CIRDI et à l'égard du présent Tribunal arbitral.[600]

644. C'est ainsi que, parmi plusieurs exemples de cette attitude de refus du « *droit d'accès à l'arbitrage international* », les demanderesses relèvent en particulier :

- 1997 : l'opposition du Chili à l'enregistrement de la requête d'arbitrage ;
- 1998 : la demande chilienne au Gouvernement espagnol tendant à modifier, sous couvert d'interprétation, le contenu de l'API invoqué par la requête d'arbitrage ;
- 1999 : l'ordre donnée par le Ministre de l'Intérieur aux fins de modifier l'inscription qualifiant M. Pey Casado d'étranger dans le registre chilien de l'état civil ;
- 2000 : la Décision no. 43 précitée, prise à la veille d'une audience du Tribunal arbitral et en défaveur des demanderesses ;

---

[600] Décision n°43 priverait d'effet le jugement de la juridiction chilienne dans la mesure où les bénéficiaires de la Décision n°43 ont déjà été indemnisés pour la rotative en question (demande complémentaire des demanderesses, du 4 novembre 2002, p. 6.)
Cette allégation a été appuyée notamment par des références à la décision rendue le 24 janvier 2004 dans l'affaire CIRDI *SGS c. Philippines* et à l'ouvrage du Professeur Jan Paulsson consacré au *Denial of Justice in International Law*, lequel se réfère à son tour aux opinions des juges S. Schwebel et Charles de Visscher (V. Transcription de l'audience du 15 janvier 2007, pp. 92-93). D'après les demanderesses, « *le point central qui nous intéresse ici, dans cette étude, c'est celui de savoir à quel point on peut considérer comme un « déni de justice » le fait qu'un Etat répudie les droits d'un étranger à accéder à un arbitrage qu'il a reconnu dans un Traité international.* » (Transcription de l'audience du 15 janvier 2007, p. 92 (Me Garcés)). V. aussi la transcription du 15 janvier 2007, pp. 58-59 (Me Muñoz) : « *En réalité, tant les mesures internes prises par le Chili, que ses agissements dans le cadre de la présente procédure tendant à s'opposer à la compétence du présent Tribunal et du Centre, ont pour unique objectif de priver M. Pey de toute réparation et si le Chili parvenait à atteindre cet objectif, il commettrait, à l'égard de M. Pey, le délit de déni de justice.* »

- 2002 : la résolution du pouvoir législatif chilien (Chambre des députés) déclarant que le Chili n'exécutera pas une éventuelle décision arbitrale défavorable ;
- le rejet des recours formés par M. Pey Casado.[601]

645.   En résumé, les allégations de « *déni de justice* » semblent bien revêtir des formes diverses et/ou être fondées sur des faits très différents, qu'il s'agisse de l'absence ou de la lenteur de décisions attendues d'autorités (judiciaires et exécutives) chiliennes, ou de violation des articles de l'API concernant l'expropriation ou la nationalisation illicite (article 5 de l'API), ou le comportement procédural de la défenderesse.

b)   Position de la défenderesse

646.   La défenderesse n'a pas jugé nécessaire de développer une analyse très complète des concepts, invoqués par les demanderesses, de déni de justice ou de traitement juste et équitable, ce qui s'explique peut-être par sa position fondamentale, précédemment exposée, quant à la nationalité de M. Pey Casado et son absence prétendue d'investissement et de propriété des biens meubles ou immeubles confisqués par les autorités militaires.

647.   En ce qui concerne la Décision n°43, la défenderesse a soutenu, comme le Tribunal l'a rappelé ci-dessus, que « *les réclamants n'ont jamais été propriétaires des bien confisqués.* »[602] De plus, elles ont suggéré qu'il serait pervers de :

> « *décourager les pays de faire ce qu'a fait le Chili, c'est-à-dire indemniser les personnes qui ont subi un préjudice. Si toutes les personnes qui n'ont pas été indemnisées pour telle et telle raison, avaient accès au CIRDI du fait de la non application du traitement juste et équitable, j'ai l'impression que cela reviendrait à miner le système* ».[603]

648.   Comme le Tribunal arbitral l'a rappelé ci-dessus, pour la partie défenderesse,

> « *la Décision N°43 ne se référait qu'à des tiers et non aux Demanderesses, et qu'en tout cas elle n'avait causé aucun préjudice aux Demanderesses compte tenu du fait qu'elle avait simplement donné un avis sur la compensation à des tiers, sans prétendre se*

---

[601]   V. contre-mémoire de la défenderesse du 3 février 2003, pp. 117-118.
[602]   Mémoire d'incompétence de la défenderesse du 20 juillet 1999, p. 13.
[603]   Transcription de l'audience du 16 janvier 2007, p. 51 (Me Di Rosa).

prononcer sur un quelconque droit de propriété que pourraient avoir les Demanderesses ».[604]

649. En ce qui concerne les demandes relatives au déni de justice, la défenderesse a formulé une objection aux développements des demanderesses lors de l'audience du 16 janvier 2007,[605] sans pour autant développer cette position.

3. Conclusions du Tribunal

650. La requête d'arbitrage et les conclusions prises par les demanderesses – ainsi que, dans une mesure bien moindre, par la défenderesse vu sa position fondamentale sur les faits, la compétence, et sur le fond – ont soulevé, expressément et implicitement, la question juridique de savoir si le Chili avait ou non violé les principes posés par l'API quant à la protection des investissements.

651. En ce qui concerne les fondements juridiques spécifiques de ces violations alléguées, les demanderesses ont conclu que la Décision n°43 du 28 avril 2000 serait contraire aux articles 3, 4, et 5 de l'API,[606] tandis que l'impossibilité d'obtenir une décision sur le fond des tribunaux chiliens dans l'affaire concernant la restitution de la rotative Goss constituerait une violation de l'article 4 de l'API.[607]

652. Comme le Tribunal l'a expliqué ci-dessus, ayant décidé que les biens des sociétés CPP S.A. et EPC Ltda ont fait l'objet d'une expropriation définitive en 1975, et ayant rejeté la thèse d'un fait illicite composite, la Décision n°43 doit s'analyser en une application discriminatoire d'une loi postérieure à l'API et des droits que celle-ci a créés. Par conséquent, il convient pour le Tribunal d'analyser les

---

[604] Contre-mémoire de la défenderesse du 3 février 2003, p. 144. V. aussi la transcription de l'audience du 6 mai 2003, p. 399 (Me Di Rosa).

[605] V. la transcription de l'audience du 16 janvier 2007, p. 45 (Me Goodman).

[606] V. exposé complémentaire sur le fond de l'affaire du 11 septembre 2002, p. 125 : « Le 28 avril 2000, les articles 3, 4 et 5 de l'API ont été enfreints sous une nouvelle forme, qui s'est ajoutée à la dépossession antérieure. »

[607] V. réplique des demanderesses au contre-mémoire de la défenderesse du 23 février 2003, pp. 103 et ss. V. également la transcription de l'audience du 16 janvier 2007, p. 42 et ss, spéc. p. 45 : « *le fondement juridique du déni de justice se trouve à l'évidence dans l'article 4 de l'API Espagne-Chili* » (Me Garcés) : p. 47 (Me Malinvaud), qui a précisé que « *si le Tribunal devait considérer que l'article 4-1 relatif au traitement juste et équitable ne permet pas d'inclure le déni de justice à titre subsidiaire, nous invoquerions, d'une part, l'article 10.4 relatif à l'application du droit international par le Tribunal arbitral dans le cadre du règlement des litiges et, d'autre part, l'article 7.2 qui prévoit que s'il y a des règles plus favorables en droit international liant le Chili en matière de traitement des investissements, elle prévaudront, même sur le Traite lui-même.* »

violations alléguées, au moins en premier lieu, sur la base de l'article 4 de l'API, les articles 3 et 5 ayant été invoqués par les demanderesses dans le cadre de leur thèse de l'acte illicite continu, qui a été rejetée.[608] Le même fondement, l'article 4 de l'API serait applicable au déni de justice allégué des parties demanderesses.

653. La question se pose en particulier de savoir si le comportement des autorités chiliennes, législatives, administratives et judiciaires, peut ou non être considéré comme constituant un « *déni de justice* » et une violation du devoir d'accorder à l'investissement étranger une protection suffisante, soit plus précisément, un « *traitement juste et équitable* » au sens de l'article 4 (1) de l'API ainsi conçu :

> « *Chaque Partie garantira dans son territoire, en accord avec sa législation nationale, un traitement juste et équitable aux investissements réalisés par des investisseurs de l'autre Partie, sous des conditions non moins favorables que pour ses investisseurs nationaux* ».

654. On notera que les deux notions (de « *traitement juste et équitable* » et de « *déni de justice* »), parfois distinguées et parfois confondues dans la doctrine et la jurisprudence, présentent ce caractère commun d'être, sinon indéfinissables, du moins peu susceptibles d'une définition qui fasse l'objet d'un consensus quant à son contenu. Cela bien que la majorité des traités relatifs à la protection des investissements aient jugé inutile de se référer non pas (ou non pas seulement) au standard minimum de droit international mais à l'obligation d'accorder aux investissements couverts par le traité (c'est-à-dire de leurs ressortissants respectifs) un « *traitement juste et équitable* ».

655. Selon une étude récente de l'OCDE :

> « *l'obligation d'accorder un 'traitement juste et équitable' est souvent énoncée concurremment avec d'autres normes visant à assurer la protection de l'investissement direct étranger par les pays d'accueil. Il s'agit d'une norme de caractère 'absolu' et 'non contingent', c'est-à-dire une norme qui définit le traitement qui doit être accordé selon des termes dont le sens exact reste à déterminer en fonction d'un* »

---

[608] L'article 3 de l'API dispose, sous le titre « protection » : « 1. Chacune des Parties protégera dans son territoire les investissements effectués conformément à sa législation, par des investisseurs de l'autre Partie et il n'entravera pas, au moyen de mesures injustifiées ou discriminatoires, la gestion, le maintien, l'utilisation, la jouissance, l'extension la vente ni, le cas échéant, la liquidation de tels investissements. […]. »

contexte spécifique d'application, à l'inverse des normes 'relatives' intégrées dans les principes du 'traitement national' et de 'la nation la plus favorisée' qui définissent le traitement requis eu égard au traitement accordé à d'autres investissements ».[609]

656. Néanmoins, il est clair que, au titre des manifestations des obligations qui sont couvertes par la nécessité de réserver à l'investissement un traitement juste et équitable, figurent incontestablement celle de ne pas commettre un déni de justice. Comme il a récemment été résumé :

> « *The cases on fair and equitable treatment fall into two broad categories. The first set of cases are concerned with the treatment of investors by the courts of the host State. The second, and more numerous, set of cases deal directly with administrative decision-making ».*[610]

657. Par conséquent, des demandes invoquant un déni de justice de la part des tribunaux de l'Etat d'accueil sont, avec raison, faites sur le fondement juridique d'une violation de l'obligation de garantir un « *traitement juste et équitable* ».[611]

---

[609] C. Yannaka-Small, *La norme du traitement juste et équitable dans le droit international des investissements*, document de travail sur l'investissement international, OCDE numéro 2004/3, septembre 2004 .

[610] Campbell McLachlan, Laurence Shore, Matthew Weiniger, *International Investment Arbitration – Substantive Principles*, Oxford University Press, 2007, p. 227.

[611] V., par exemple, *Mondev International Ltd. c. Etats-Unis*, affaire CIRDI n° ARB(AF)/99/2, sentence du 11 Octobre 2002, 6 ICSID Report 181, où le déni de justice allégué de la part du Massachusetts Supreme Judicial Court a été invoqué sur la base de l'article 1105(1) du traité NAFTA qui prévoit : « *Each Party shall accord to investments of investors of another Party treatment in accordance with international law, including fair and equitable treatment and full protection and security.* » De même, dans l'affaire *Loewen Group Inc et al c. Etats-Unis*, affaire CIRDI n° ARB(AF)/98/3, sentence du 26 juin 2003, le tribunal arbitral a trouvé que l'article 1105 du traité NAFTA, comme l'ont résumé McLachlan/Shore/Weiniger, « *informed by customary international law, was concerned with denials of justice in litigation.* » (Campbell McLachlan, Laurence Shore, Matthew Weiniger, *International Investment Arbitration – Substantive Principles*, Oxford University Press, 2007, p. 230.) V. aussi l'affaire *Waste Management Inc. c. Mexique*, affaire CIRDI n° ARB(AF)/00/3, sentence du 30 avril 2004, p. 35, para. 98, où le tribunal arbitral conclut que « *Taken together, the S.D. Myers, Mondev, ADF and Loewen cases suggest that the minimum standard of treatment of fair and equitable treatment is infringed by conduct attributable to the State and harmful to the claimant if the conduct is arbitrary, grossly unfair, unjust or*

658. Dans le contexte spécifique du présent litige, tel qu'il a été résumé dans la présente sentence dans sa partie Faits et dans les considérations juridiques qui précèdent, l'application de la notion de « *déni de justice* » et celle de l'obligation de « *traitement juste et équitable* » n'appellent pas de longue analyse. Elles se laissent résumer à deux questions relativement simples :

- La première est celle de savoir si l'absence de toute décision par les juridictions chiliennes pendant une période de sept années (1995-2002), d'une part, et l'absence de réponse de la Présidence aux requêtes de M. Pey Casado, d'autre part, sont constitutives d'un déni de justice.

- La seconde est celle de savoir si les investissements reconnus par le Tribunal arbitral comme ayant été faits par M. Pey Casado ont bénéficiés du « *traitement juste et équitable* » prescrit par l'API.

659. Sur la première question, la réponse ne peut être que positive, au regard des faits établis et déjà retenus par le Tribunal arbitral, l'absence de toute décision par les tribunaux civils chiliens sur les prétentions de M. Pey Casado s'analysant en un déni de justice. En effet, l'absence de décision en première instance sur le fond des demandes des parties demanderesses pendant sept années, c'est-à-dire entre septembre 1995 et le 4 novembre 2002 (moment de l'introduction de la demande complémentaire dans la présente procédure) doit être qualifié comme un déni de justice de la part des tribunaux chiliens. En fait, des délais procéduraux importants constituent bien une des formes classiques de déni de justice. Ainsi l'a trouvé le tribunal arbitral dans l'affaire *Robert Azinian et al. c. Mexique*, en *obiter dicta* :

> « *A denial of justice could be pleaded if the relevant courts refuse to entertain suit, if they subject it to*

---

idiosyncratic, is discriminatory and exposes the claimant to sectional or racial prejudice, or involves a lack of due process leading to an outcome which offends judicial propriety – as might be the case with a manifest failure of natural justice in judicial proceedings or a complete lack of transparency and candour in an administrative process.. » V. aussi le résumé par Stephan W, Schill, *Fair and Equitable Treatment under Investment Treaties as an Embodiment of the Rule of Law*, International Law and Justice Working Papers, Institute for International Law and Justice, New York University School of Law, 2006, p. 26 : « *The rule of law elements derived from fair and equitable treatment also influence the institutional structure of the host state's judiciary and the procedural law they apply. Fair and equitable treatment requires that host states provide a fair and efficient system of justice, comprising effective judicial dispute settlement procedures for the review of administrative acts and dispute settlement between private parties.* »

> *undue delay, or if they administer justice in a seriously inadequate way. [...] There is a fourth type of denial of justice, namely the clear and malicious misapplication of the law ».*[612]

660. Comme l'a écrit Jan Paulsson, avec raison, : « [...] delays may be 'even more ruinous' than absolute refusal of access [to justice], because in the latter situation the claimant knows where he stands and take action accordingly, whether by seeking diplomatic intervention or exploring avenues of direct legal action ».[613]

661. De même, la Commission des Réclamations Anglo-Mexicaine a considéré que le délai de neuf ans écoulé depuis le dépôt de la demande de compensation devant une juridiction étatique devait être qualifié de déni de justice mettant en cause la responsabilité de l'Etat sur le plan international :

> *« Nine years have elapsed since the Company applied to the Court to which the law directed it, and during all those years no justice has been done. There has been no hearing ; there has been no award. ... [I]t is ... obvious that a period of nine years by far exceeds the limit of the most liberal allowance that may be made. Even those cases of the very highest importance and of the most complicated character can well be decided within such an excessively long time. A claimant who has not, during so many years, received any word or sign that his claim is being dealt with is entitled to the belief that his interests are receiving no attention, and to despair of obtaining justice ».*[614]

---

[612] Robert Azinian, Kenneth Daviatian & Ellen Baca c. The United Mexican States, affaire CIRDI n° ARB(AF)/97/2, sentence du 1er novembre 1999.

[613] Jan Paulsson, *Denial of Justice in International Law*, Cambridge University Press, 2005, p. 177. Paulsson se réfère également à la décision de l'Arbitre unique dans l'arbitrage *Fabiani* entre la France et le Venezuela en 1896, qui a décidé que les délais importants et les reports constants par les tribunaux vénézuéliens dans le cadre de l'exécution d'une sentence arbitrale constituaient bien un déni de justice : « *Upon examining the general principles of international law with regard to denial of justice, that is to say, the rules common to most bodies of law or laid down by doctrine, one finds that denial of justice includes not only the refusal of a judicial authority to exercise his functions and, in particular, to give a decision on the request submitted to him, but also wrongful delays on his part in giving judgment.* » *No.1 (France v. Venezuela)*, Moore, *Arbitrations*, p. 4878.

[614] *El Oro Mining and Railway Company (Limited)* (Great Britain) v. United Mexican States, Décision No. 55, 18 juin 1931, Recueil des sentences arbitrales, Vol. V, 191-199.

662. La Cour européenne des droits de l'homme s'est également prononcée dans le même sens, en estimant que les sept ans que les juridictions étatiques ont mis pour examiner une demande en compensation à la suite d'une expropriation étaient bien supérieurs à un délai raisonnable, ce qui constitue une violation de l'article 6-1 de la Convention européenne des droits de l'homme qui compte, au rang de ces droits fondamentaux, le droit d'être entendu « *dans un délai raisonnable* ».[615]

663. Le déni de justice résultant des délais importants est également envisagé d'une manière expresse par la Convention portant création de l'Agence multilatérale de garantie des investissements qui le classe parmi les risques couverts par l'Agence :

> « *Article 11. Covered Risks*
> *(a) ... the Agency may guarantee eligible investments against a loss resulting from one or ore of the following types of risk : ... (iii) any repudiation or breach by the host government of a contract with the holder of a guarantee, when (a) the holder of a guarantee does not have recourse to a judicial or arbitral forum to determine the claim of repudiation of breach, or (b) a decision by such forum is not rendered within such a reasonable period of time as shall be prescribed in the contracts of guarantee pursuant to the Agency's regulations, or (c) such a decision cannot be enforced ; ...* »[616]

664. Quant aux comportements procéduraux chiliens dont se plaignent les demanderesses, certains relèvent seulement des droits et moyens à la disposition d'une partie défenderesse qui conteste la compétence ; d'autres ne peuvent s'analyser en un déni de justice à proprement parler, quel que puisse être leur caractère discutable ou leur compatibilité avec l'obligation de bonne foi qui s'impose aux Etats parties à la Convention CIRDI de participer à une procédure arbitrale fût-ce en niant la compétence.

665. Sur la seconde question, celle de savoir si les investissements des demanderesses ont bénéficié d'un traitement juste et équitable, une réponse négative s'impose de l'avis du Tribunal arbitral, compte tenu

---

[615] CEDH, *Ruiz-Mateos c. Espagne*, Arrêt de la Cour plénière du 26 juin 1993, Requête n° 12952/87, série A   n° 262.

[616] Convention portant création de l'Agence multilatérale de garantie des investissements, article 11(a)(iii). V. également F. I. Shihata, *MIGA and Foreign Investment*, Martinus Nijhoff Publishers, 1988, pp. 132-134. I. Shihata souligne que les cas évoqués par l'article susvisé « *represent situations which the Regulations correctly group under the term 'denial of justice.'* »

des conclusions auxquelles il est parvenu précédemment aux termes de son appréciation des preuves et de son analyse juridique. En bref, il s'agit de la conclusion selon laquelle M. Pey Casado a bien démontré avoir procédé à des investissements et être propriétaire de biens meubles ou immeubles qui ont été confisqués par l'autorité militaire chilienne.

666. On rappellera à ce propos l'existence d'un jugement chilien reconnaissant la propriété de M. Pey Casado sur les actions confisquées ainsi que le fait que les autorités chiliennes, exécutives et administratives (comme judiciaires) étaient informées des revendications et demandes formulées par les demanderesses.

667. Quant à l'invalidité des confiscations et au devoir d'indemnisation, il y a lieu de rappeler aussi des déclarations parfaitement claires de la défenderesse dans la présente procédure.[617]

668. Après le rétablissement au Chili d'institutions démocratiques et civiles, les nouvelles autorités ont proclamé publiquement leur intention de rétablir la légalité et de réparer les dommages causés par le régime militaire. Comme la défenderesse l'a souligné :

> *«[...] les gouvernements démocratiques qui remplacèrent en 1990, au moyen d'élection libres, le Gouvernement de Pinochet, se sont primordialement préoccupés de réparer les dommages causés par le régime instauré au Chili par le coup d'état du 11 septembre 1973. En effet, le Gouvernement a pris les mesures pour réparer les dommages causés aux victimes dans tous les secteurs. Concrètement, en relation avec les confiscations, a été approuvée une loi qui dispose de la restitution ou indemnisation pour les biens confisqués, loi prise à l'initiative de l'Exécutif».[618]*

669. Le Tribunal arbitral ne peut que prendre note avec satisfaction de telles déclarations, qui font honneur au Gouvernement chilien.

---

[617] V., par exemple, la transcription de l'audience du 6 mai 2003, pp. 262-263 (Me Castillo) : « La République du Chili ne prétend pas justifier ce qui s'est produit pendant cette période turbulente de notre histoire, bien au contraire. Nous avons réparé sur le plan matériel, nous avons essayé aussi de réparer sur le plan moral, les préjugés soufferts par des personnes pendant cette période » ainsi qu'à la page 264 : « Il ne s'agit pas non plus de justifier la légitimité des actes qui ont découlé de la confiscation de bien de CPP S.A. et Clarin Ltée. Bien au contraire, la République du Chili est constante [sic ; devrait dire « consciente »] des dommages causés par ces confiscations et c'est pour cela qu'elle a indemnisé ces titulaires légitimes. »

[618] Mémoire d'incompétence de la défenderesse du 20 juillet 1999, p. 11.

Malheureusement, cette politique ne s'est pas été traduite dans les faits, en ce qui concerne les demanderesses, pour des raisons diverses qui, au moins pour partie, n'ont pas été révélées ou clairement expliquées par les témoignages ou les autres preuves fournies au Tribunal arbitral. Ainsi qu'on a pu le constater, il n'a nullement été établi, ni même rendu vraisemblable, que M. Pey Casado n'aurait joué qu'un rôle d'intermédiaire voire de prête-nom et que MM. Venegas, Gonzalez ou Carrasco auraient été les véritables propriétaires des actions des sociétés CPP S.A. et EPC Ltda. En particulier, les déclarations ou autres affirmations de ces derniers (par exemple quant à l'attribution à une fondation scientifique – avec le concours de Me Ovalle, un proche de la junte militaire – des biens confisqués) laissent subsister de nombreux points obscurs, compte tenu des circonstances de l'époque. Quoi qu'il en soit de la pertinence et de la valeur des éléments qui ont été retenus à cet égard en droit interne chilien, ces éléments ne peuvent prévaloir sur les considérations qui ont conduit le Tribunal arbitral aux conclusions précédemment énoncées, en application des dispositions de l'API.

670. Il est constant dans la jurisprudence internationale et dans la doctrine qu'un traitement discriminatoire de la part d'autorités étatiques envers ses investisseurs étrangers constitue une violation de la garantie de traitement « *juste et équitable* » inclus dans des traités bilatéraux d'investissement. Comme l'a décidé le Tribunal arbitral dans l'affaire *Waste Management v. Mexico* :

> « *fair and equitable treatment is infringed by conduct attributable to the State and harmful to the claimant of the conduct is arbitrary, grossly unfair, unjust or idiosyncratic, is discriminatory and exposes the claimant to sectional or racial prejudice* ».[619]

671. Un comportement discriminatoire sera couvert comme violation du traitement « *juste et équitable* » notamment dans les cas où le traité bilatéral en question ne contient pas de garantie expresse contre des actes arbitraires ou discriminatoires. Comme l'a récemment résumé un commentateur :

> « *The protection of foreign investors against arbitrary and discriminatory treatment also plays a major role in the operation of fair and equitable treatment. While sometimes international investment treaties contain a specific provision prohibiting such treatment, arbitral*

---

[619] *Waste Management Inc. c. Mexique*, affaire CIRDI n° ARB(AF)/00/3, sentence du 30 avril 2004, pp. 35-36.

> *tribunals also ground this aspect in free-standing guarantees of fair and equitable treatment ».*[620]

672.   Même dans les cas où le traité bilatéral contient une interdiction expresse de comportement arbitraire et discriminatoire, les tribunaux arbitraux ont décidé qu'un tel comportement violerait, en même temps, l'obligation de traiter ses investisseurs de manière « juste et équitable ». Par exemple, dans l'affaire *CMS c. Argentine*, le tribunal arbitral a jugé que :

> *« The standard of protection against arbitrariness and discrimination is related to that of fair and equitable treatment. Any measure that might involve arbitrariness or discrimination is in itself contrary to fair and equitable treatment ».*[621]

673.   De même, M. Vasciannie explique :

> *« [...] if there is discrimination on arbitrary grounds, or if the investment has been subject to arbitrary or capricious treatment by the host State, then the fair and equitable standard has been violated. This follows from the idea that fair and equitable treatment inherently precludes arbitrary and capricious actions against investors ».*[622]

674.   Dans le cas d'espèce, en résumé, en accordant des compensations – pour des raisons qui lui sont propres et sont restées inexpliquées – à des personnages qui, de l'avis du Tribunal arbitral, n'étaient pas propriétaires des biens confisqués, en même temps qu'elle paralysait ou rejetait les revendications de M. Pey Casado concernant les biens confisqués, la République du Chili a manifestement commis un déni de justice et refusé de traiter les demanderesses de façon juste et équitable..

VIII.   DOMMAGES

675.   Le Tribunal arbitral a constaté précédemment, outre sa compétence pour statuer sur la demande d'arbitrage formulée auprès du CIRDI

---

[620]   Stephan W, Schill, *Fair and Equitable Treatment under Investment Treaties as an Embodiment of the Rule of Law*, International Law and Justice Working Papers, Institute for International Law and Justice, New York University School of Law, 2006, p. 19.

[621]   *CMS Gas Transmission Company c. La République d'Argentine*, affaire CIRDI n° ARB/01/8, sentence du 12 mai 2005, p. 84.

[622]   S. Vasciannie, The Fair and Equitable Treatment Standard in International Investment Law and Practice, 70 The British Yearbook of International Law 133 (1999).

par la première et par la seconde demanderesse, que, sur le fond, M. Pey Casado était bien le propriétaire des biens confisqués par les autorités chiliennes et que l'investissement n'avait pas fait l'objet du « *traitement juste et équitable* » prescrit par l'API. En d'autres termes, il a constaté que la défenderesse avait commis un déni de justice et violé, avec la Décision n°43 du 28 avril 2000 et son application, l'obligation d'accorder à l'investissement un traitement juste et équitable.

676. On rappellera aussi à ce propos que, dans l'analyse *ratione temporis* de sa compétence et celle de l'applicabilité des dispositions de fond applicables, le Tribunal arbitral est parvenu à la conclusion que l'article 4 API était bien applicable (après son entrée en vigueur) au déni de justice allégué par les demanderesses.

677. On observera enfin, toujours sur le fond, que la réalité des violations alléguées - ou, plus précisément, en son principe, l'illégalité des confiscations opérées par l'autorité militaire chilienne sur les biens litigieux, n'est pas contestée par la défenderesse.[623] Pas plus que cette dernière ne conteste l'obligation d'indemniser les victimes de confiscations contraires au droit. Ce qu'elle conteste en revanche, ainsi qu'on l'a vu, c'est la qualité pour agir des demanderesses, découlant de leur qualité de propriétaire ou d'investisseur.

678. On se référera à ce propos, par exemple, aux déclarations des représentants de la partie chilienne devant le Tribunal arbitral. Celle-ci a expliqué que la Décision n°43 « *est née d'une procédure établie par une loi chilienne de 1998 selon laquelle l'Etat se proposait d'indemniser les personnes qui avaient été expropriées durant la période de la dictature militaire* ». En novembre 1995, l'Etat chilien a indiqué à M. Pey Casado « *qu'une loi était en cours d'élaboration et que celle-ci, une fois votée, permettrait d'indemniser les personnes qui avaient fait l'objet d'une expropriation* ».[624] On notera en passant qu'il s'est abstenu alors d'indiquer à M. Pey Casado s'il entrait ou non dans la catégorie des personnes ainsi visées. Selon les demanderesses, cette législation, inexistante en 1995, « *prendra trois années avant d'être finalement votée* ».[625]

---

[623] V., par exemple, la transcription de l'audience du 6 mai 2003, pp. 262-263 (Me Castillo), cité ci-dessus.

[624] V. la lettre du Ministère des Biens Nationaux du 20 novembre 1995 : « Compte tenu de ce qui vient d'être exposé, je me permets de porter à votre connaissance le fait que, pour le moment, il n'est pas possible d'accéder à ce qui est demandé, dès lors que la loi qui va régler la situation par vous décrite n'a pas encore été promulguée. » (annexe 23 à la requête d'arbitrage du 3 novembre 1997).

[625] V. la transcription de l'audience du 16 janvier 2007, p. 52 et ss (Me Malinvaud).

679. Ces faits ainsi rappelés, et la question de la qualité pour agir des demanderesses ayant été tranchée par le Tribunal arbitral, il reste à ce dernier à tirer les conséquences de ce qui précède, quant à l'obligation d'indemniser, son exécution concrète et le calcul de son montant.

A. Le dommage souffert par les parties demanderesses

680. L'existence même de dommages résultant de la confiscation n'appelle aucune analyse particulière. Cette existence résulte à la fois, à l'évidence, de la nature des choses, d'une part, et de sa reconnaissance par la défenderesse d'autre part, et cela du seul fait des décisions prises en faveur de MM. Gonzalez, Vinegas, Carrasco et Sainte-Marie. On ne conçoit pas, en effet, l'octroi d'une quelconque indemnité par l'autorité chilienne - fût-ce à d'autres que le véritable propriétaire des biens confisqués, par erreur ou intentionnellement - sans l'admission de dommages causés par la confiscation.

681. Et il est superflu d'ajouter que cette constatation élémentaire est indépendante du droit applicable, qu'il soit interne (chilien) ou international. Quelle qu'ait pu être la base juridique retenue par la défenderesse dans sa décision d'indemniser, le Tribunal arbitral, lui, ne peut que se fonder sur le droit international pour constater le déni de justice et le dommage résultant nécessairement du traitement (non *"juste et équitable"*)[626] réservé à l'investissement.

1. Position des demanderesses

682. Dans leurs mémoires et dans la procédure orale, les demanderesses ont exposé (en tenant compte de la décision du Tribunal du 8 mai 2002 joignant les exceptions au fond) les raisons pour lesquelles elles avaient « *droit à réparation conformément aux principes généraux du droit international, aux principes dégagés par la jurisprudence internationale et au droit chilien* ».[627] On notera à ce propos que les demanderesses ont fondé leur réclamation principalement sur la notion d'expropriation et l'article 5 de l'API - alors que le Tribunal arbitral, compte tenu aussi des limites temporelles de sa compétence, a estimé que la base juridique correcte de la réclamation se trouvait (et ne pouvait se trouver que) dans l'article 4 de l'API relatif au traitement juste et équitable. Les demanderesses ont souligné que « *la Décision N° 43 et le mécanisme mis en oeuvre... pour régler la somme d'environ USD 9 millions à des tiers non propriétaires* »

---

[626] V. la transcription de l'audience du 16 janvier 2007, p. 50 et ss (Me Di Rosa).

[627] Exposé complémentaire sur le fond de l'affaire, du 11 septembre 2002, p. 2.

constituaient « *également* » une violation de l'API du 2 octobre 1991.[628]

683. Enfin, elles ont chiffré leur préjudice à USD 52'842'081.-- pour ce qui concerne le *damnum emergens* et à USD 344'505'593.-- pour le *lucrum cessans*, sommes à parfaire et à augmenter, en particulier, de la réparation des dommages moraux infligés à M. Pey Casado.[629] La question des intérêts et de leur calcul sera évoquée plus loin.

2. Position de la défenderesse

684. Ainsi qu'il résulte des faits et de l'exposé qui précède, dès lors qu'elle dénie, pour divers motifs exposés et discutés précédemment, toute légitimité à M. Pey Casado et à son cessionnaire, la Fondation Allende, pour présenter des revendications et pour réclamer réparation, la défenderesse n'a pas jugé nécessaire ou utile de discuter ou de réfuter les thèses des demanderesses quant à l'évaluation d'un préjudice (à son avis inexistant). Elle a cependant contesté fermement les méthodes d'évaluation des dommages et intérêts employées par ses parties adverses. Dans ce contexte, elle a produit un important rapport d'expertise[630] contre le rapport d'évaluation émis par les demanderesses portant sur le groupe d'entreprises « *Clarin* ».[631]

3. Conclusions du Tribunal arbitral

685. Le Tribunal arbitral estime superflu en l'espèce d'entrer dans une discussion de détail de l'argumentation soutenue par les demanderesses quant à l'évaluation des divers préjudices qu'elles allèguent avoir subis, et cela à la fois pour des raisons de fait et de preuve et en raison du comportement de la défenderesse. Il rappellera cependant que des autorités chiliennes avaient reconnu que M. Pey Casado était propriétaire des titres confisqués[632] et que la défenderesse n'ignorait pas la revendication par M. Pey Casado d'une compensation, au moment où elle a décidé d'indemniser

---

[628] *Id.*

[629] *Id.*

[630] Evaluation établie par M. Brent C. Kaczmarek, du 3 février 2003, soumis par la défenderesse au soutien de son contre-mémoire du 3 février 2003.

[631] Rapport émis par « Alejandro Arraez et Associés, S.A. » sur l'évaluation du groupe d'entreprises chilien « Clarín », du 3 septembre 2002 ; rapport complémentaire émis par « Alejandro Arraez et Associés, S.A. » à celui émis le 3 septembre 2002 sur l'évaluation du groupe d'entreprises chilien « Clarín », du 28 octobre 2002 ; et les commentaires sur le rapport en réplique émis par M. Kaczmarek, du 19 février 2003.

[632] V., par exemple, le Décret suprême n°1200 du 25 novembre 1977 (annexe 20 à la requête d'arbitrage du 3 novembre 1997).

d'autres que lui - un acte constituant de l'avis du Tribunal une claire violation du droit à un « *traitement juste et équitable* » prévu par l'API.

686. Il y a lieu de relever d'abord que l'argumentation des demanderesses concernant l'évaluation du dommage (ainsi du reste, par voie de conséquence, que la réfutation esquissée par la défenderesse par exemple avec le rapport de l'expert Kaczmarek) se réfère à l'expropriation intervenue au Chili dans la période 1973-1977, notamment en 1975, et confirmée par la suite.

687. Or le Tribunal arbitral a conclu précédemment que l'expropriation de 1975 ne pouvait « *se voir appliquer les dispositions de fond de l'API* », celles-ci (par exemple en ce qui concerne le « *traitement juste et équitable* ») n'étant applicables qu'aux actes postérieurs à l'entrée en vigueur du traité.

688. L'expropriation survenue avant l'entrée en vigueur du traité ayant été écartée de l'examen du Tribunal arbitral, il en résulte que, pour cette raison déjà, les allégations, discussions et preuves relatives au dommage subi par les demanderesses du fait de l'expropriation,[633] manquent de pertinence et ne peuvent pas être retenues s'agissant d'établir un préjudice, résultant lui d'une autre cause, de fait et de droit, celle du déni de justice et du refus d'un « *traitement juste et équitable* ».

689. Dans l'exercice de son droit et pouvoir d'appréciation des preuves, le Tribunal arbitral ne peut que constater que les demanderesses n'ont pas apporté de preuve, ou de preuve convaincante, ni par pièces, ni par témoignage, ni par expertise, des importants dommages allégués et causés par les faits relevant de la compétence *ratione temporis* du Tribunal arbitral, et cela qu'il s'agisse du *damnum emergens*, du *lucrum cessans*, ou encore d'un dommage moral - la simple vraisemblance d'un dommage dans les circonstances concrètes de l'espèce ne suffisant évidemment pas.

690. Le Tribunal arbitral ne sous-estime pas les difficultés pratiques pouvant confronter les demanderesses, le cas échéant, dans la recherche et l'obtention des preuves, dont la charge leur incombe, des dommages allégués et de leur montant. Il ne saurait pour autant prendre l'initiative de recourir à une ou plusieurs expertises au motif que ces dernières seraient susceptibles d'apporter ou de faciliter les preuves nécessaires, que les demanderesses n'ont pu fournir jusqu'ici.

---

[633] Laquelle était « consommée », de l'avis du Tribunal arbitral, « avec l'entrée en vigueur du décret N° 165 du 10 février 1975 ».

691.   Il est clair aussi, quoi qu'il en soit, que tout recours à une expertise, l'expérience arbitrale le montre, est en soi généralement de nature à augmenter, parfois fortement, la durée et les coûts d'un arbitrage. En tout état de cause, le Tribunal arbitral est conscient de son devoir de mettre un terme, dès que l'état du dossier le permet, à une procédure d'une durée qui, dépassant la moyenne, a été allongée, ainsi qu'on l'a vu, pour des raisons diverses, dont la complexité inhabituelle des questions litigieuses et l'attitude même des parties.

692.   En l'absence de preuves convaincantes apportées par les demanderesses et le recours à une ou plusieurs expertises devant être exclu, le Tribunal arbitral est cependant en mesure de procéder à une évaluation du dommage à l'aide d'éléments objectifs dès lors que, selon les données incontestées résultant du dossier, les autorités chiliennes elles-mêmes, à la suite de la Décision n° 43, ont fixé le montant de la réparation due aux personnes ayant, selon elles, droit à une indemnisation.

693.   Il convient de rappeler dans ce contexte que le préjudice à indemniser n'est pas celui souffert à la suite de l'expropriation (demande qui n'est pas couverte par les dispositions de fond de l'API), mais celui souffert en raison des violations de l'API que le Tribunal arbitral a constatées et à propos desquelles il est compétent pour rendre une décision. Notamment, l'indemnisation doit servir à mettre les demanderesses dans la position dans laquelle elles seraient si les violations en question n'avaient pas eu lieu, c'est-à-dire si, dans la Décision n°43, les autorités chiliennes avaient indemnisé les demanderesses, et non pas des tierces personnes non-propriétaires des biens en question. Dans cette hypothèse, les autorités chiliennes auraient accordé le montant d'indemnisation qu'elles ont accordé en vertu de la Décision n°43 aux demanderesses dans la présente instance, celles-ci étant, le Tribunal arbitral l'a constaté, les véritables propriétaires des actions des sociétés CPP S.A. et EPC Ltda. Par conséquent, c'est le montant payé comme indemnisation en vertu de la Décision n°43 qui correspond au préjudice souffert par les demanderesses.

694.   L'indemnisation décidée par la Décision n°43 du 28 avril 2000 a été alloué par le Ministère des Biens Nationaux en vertu des décrets d'indemnisation n° 76-79, en date du 11 avril 2002. Il s'agit d'un montant global d'indemnisation de USD 10 millions, bien que le montant exact soit contesté entre les parties. .

695.   La demanderesse a communiqué, par une lettre en date du 19 juillet 2007, au Tribunal les documents qui, selon elles, lui permettent de connaître les montants précis alloués aux bénéficiaires de la Décision n°43 adoptée par Ministère chilien des biens nationaux le 28 avril 2000 et des décrets n°76-79.

696. Selon les demanderesses, le montant précis alloué a été de 196.736,603 UTM,[634] montant qui aurait été calculé par des experts nommés par l'administration chilienne comme montant de l'indemnisation, approuvé en tant que tel par l'ordre ministériel n°165 du 2 avril 2002,[635] et inclus dans les décrets d'indemnisation n°76-79 du 11 avril 2002.

697. D'après l'article 13 de la Loi n°19.518, « le montant de l'indemnisation sera exprimé en unités tributaires mensuelle [UTM] et sera payé en cinq quotas annuelles successives ». Les demanderesses expliquent en outre que « l'UTM est une unité de compte interne du Chili mise à jour selon l'inflation » dont la « valeur est publié on-line par la Banque Centrale du Chili ».

698. En ce qui concerne la conversion du montant UTM en Dollars, les demanderesses, se basant sur l'article 8 de la Loi n°19.518 (publiée au Journal Officiel le 23 juillet 1998) portant sur la restitution où l'indemnisation de bien confisqués, ont soutenu que la valeur de biens immobiliers devait être indemnisée « *à la date de la publication de la présente loi.* » D'après les demanderesses, à cette date, soit en juillet 1998, « *l'équivalent des 196.736,603 UTM était de 4.949.105.985 pesos* ».[636] Le cours du dollar à ce jour aurait été de 465,16. Sur cette base, les demanderesses ont prétendu que le montant précis alloué aux bénéficiaires de la Décision n°43 était d'USD 10.639.577,74. De plus, les demanderesses ont remarqué que la contrevaleur des 196.736,603 UTM à la date du 18 octobre 2007 était d'USD 13.264.471,02.

699. La défenderesse a fourni son analyse dans des lettres du 18 octobre 2007 et du 9 novembre 2007. Produisant une lettre de la Trésorerie Générale de la République en date du 17 août 2007, la défenderesse a soutenu que l'indemnisation en question n'aurait pas été faite en unités UTM, mais en une autre unité comptable, notamment l' « *Unidad de Fomento* » (UF ; d'après les demanderesses, il s'agit d'une « *Inflation-Indexed Accounting Unit* »). D'après la défenderesse, le montant de l'indemnisation aurait été de 343.578,61 UF ; l'équivalent des montants en dollars payés pendant les années 2003 à 2007 serait d'USD 10.132.690,18.[637] Par contre, l'équivalent de 343.578,61 UF à la date du 11 avril 2002, date de décrets d'indemnisation, aurait été d'USD 8.674.750,91.

---

[634] V. la lettre des demanderesses du 19 juillet 2007.

[635] V. lettre des demanderesses du 29 octobre 2007.

[636] V. la précision apportée par les demanderesses dans leur courriel du 19 juillet 2007.

[637] V. lettre de la défenderesse du 18 octobre 2007.

700. Les demanderesses ont fourni des remarques supplémentaires dans une lettre en date du 29 octobre 2007, réitérant leur position que la date critique pour la conversion serait le 23 juillet 1998, date de la publication de la Loi n°19.518 portant sur la restitution où l'indemnisation de bien confisqués. A cette date, l'équivalent en dollars de 343.578,61 UF aurait été d'USD 10.607.830,77.

701. La défenderesse, elle, a fourni des commentaires additionnels par lettre reçu le 9 novembre 2007 (mais erronément datée du 18 octobre 2007).

702. Le Tribunal estime qu'il n'a pas à se prononcer sur les modalités des paiements (calculs, taux de conversion entre UTM/UF et USD, etc.) décidés et effectués au Chili par les autorités. Il considère devoir se fonder seulement sur le montant effectivement payé pendant les années 2003 à 2007, dont l'équivalent en Dollars est de USD 10.132.690,18. Le Tribunal arbitral estime que la condamnation de la défenderesse au paiement d'un tel montant est de nature à placer les demanderesses dans la situation dans laquelle elles se seraient retrouvées si elles avaient fait l'objet, après l'entrée en vigueur de l'API, d'un traitement juste et équitable, en l'absence de tout déni de justice.

703. Le déni de justice retenu par le Tribunal arbitral sur la question de la rotative Goss n'entraîne aucune indemnisation supplémentaire. En effet, cette rotative a été la propriété des sociétés dont les titres, appartenant aux demanderesses, ont fait l'objet de l'indemnisation décidée par le Tribunal arbitral.

704. Une explication complémentaire se justifie en ce qui concerne la demande relative au dommage moral. Outre le fait que les demanderesses n'ont pas apporté de preuves permettant l'évaluation d'un tel préjudice le Tribunal arbitral estime que le prononcé de la présente sentence, notamment par sa reconnaissance des droits des demanderesses et du déni de justice dont elles furent victimes, constitue en soi une satisfaction morale substantielle et suffisante.

B. Intérêts

1. Position des parties

705. Dans leur exposé complémentaire sur le fond de l'affaire, les demanderesses ont conclu à ce que le Tribunal arbitral « condamne l'Etat défendeur à payer aux demanderesses des intérêts moratoires à partir de la date du 11 septembre 2002 et jusqu'à son exécution

intégrale ».[638] D'après les demanderesses, le Tribunal arbitral aurait à appliquer des intérêts composés. Au soutien de cet argument, les demanderesses ont fait référence à plusieurs sentences arbitrales, au rapport d'expert de « Alejandro Arráez y Asociados, S.A. », ainsi qu'à de diverses références doctrinales.[639]

706. Quant au moment à partir duquel le paiement d'intérêts serait dû, les demanderesses ont distingué :

- le « *dies a quo des dommage-intérêts compensatoires* », qui serait dû depuis la date de l'évènement dommageable (d'après les demanderesses, celle de la saisi des biens de CPP S.A. et d'EPC Ltda en septembre 1973) et qui est inclut directement dans le calcul des dommages des demanderesses[640] ; et

- le « *dies ad quem des intérêts moratoires* » qui consisterait en les intérêts dûs depuis le 11 septembre 2002 (date du mémoire incluant les conclusions des demanderesses) jusqu'à la date d'exécution de la Décision.[641]

707. Quant au taux d'intérêt à appliquer, les demanderesses ont demandé que le Tribunal arbitral applique un taux de 10%, étant le taux d'intérêt appliqué dans le rapport d'expert « Alejandro Arráez y Asociados, S.A. ». D'après les demanderesses, ce taux serait « *extrêmement raisonnable* » au vu de la pratique suivie dans l'arbitrage international.[642]

708. La défenderesse a conclu sur la question des intérêts comme suit :

> « *Dans le cas où le Tribunal déciderait que des dommages et intérêts sont dus, la République du Chili se réserverait alors le droit d'étudier plus en détail la question du taux d'intérêt et de son calcul, étant donné que ledit taux et son calcul peuvent dépendre des dommages et intérêts octroyés et de la date à partir de laquelle ils le seront. Pour l'information du Tribunal, le montant maximum des dommages s'élevant à 7 002 629 dollars à la date du 31 décembre 2002, tel qu'il a été calculé dans le Rapport Kaczmarek, supposerait un taux d'intérêt maximum de 5,8% basé sur le calcul de rendement de l'actif fourni dans ce même Rapport Kaczmarek. Les dommages maximums s'élevant à 4 852 973 dollars à la date du 31 décembre 2002 (dans*

---

[638] Exposé complémentaire sur le fond de l'affaire du 11 septembre 2002, p. 152,

[639] V. *id.* pp. 148-150.

[640] *Id.*, pp. 145-147.

[641] *Id.*, pp. 147.148.

[642] *Id.*, pp. 150-151.

> *prendre en compte la valeur de la presse d'imprimerie Goss) supposeraient un taux d'intérêt maximum de 4,7%, également basé sur le calcul du rendement de l'actif ».[643]*

2.   Conclusions du Tribunal

709.   De l'avis du Tribunal arbitral, les demanderesses ont droit au paiement d'intérêts composés annuellement sur la somme principale, intérêts courant à partir de la reconnaissance de la créance d'indemnisation par le Chili en vertu des décrets d'indemnisation n° 76-79 des bénéficiaires de la Décision n°43 du 28 avril 2000, soit le 11 avril 2002, jusqu'à la date de la présente sentence.

710.   Le principe même de l'intérêt n'est en effet ni contesté ni contestable.   Comme l'a souligné le Tribunal arbitral dans l'affaire CIRDI *Asian Agricultural Products Ltd. c. Sri Lanka*, « *in accordance with a long established rule of international law expressed since 1872 by the Arbitral Tribunal which adjudicated the Alabama case between the U.K. and U.S.A., 'it is just and reasonable to allow interest at a reasonable rate' ».*[644]

711.   Sur les modalités de ce principe (caractère simple ou composé de l'intérêt, taux, dates à retenir, etc.), ni la Convention CIRDI, ni l'API ne fournissent d'indications. Le Tribunal arbitral ne peut que se référer à des principes généraux, à la coutume, la pratique et la jurisprudence internationale (aucune recherche de droit national applicable ne se justifiant en l'espèce vu la nature présent du litige).

712.   Quant au taux d'intérêt applicable, s'agissant d'un litige international, il apparaît approprié d'appliquer un taux d'intérêt de 5% qui reflète un taux commercial raisonnable pendant la période considérée vu la nature du présent litige.

713.   L'indemnité à accorder aux victimes de la violation, constatée précédemment, de l'obligation internationale liant l'investisseur à l'Etat d'accueil, est-elle due avec des intérêts simples ou des intérêts composés ? Si la première solution paraît dominante dans le domaine des litiges commerciaux, il n'en est pas de même en matière d'investissements internationaux, où la question, d'abord controversée et incertaine, a subi à une époque récente une nette évolution, comme l'atteste la jurisprudence et la doctrine.

---

[643]   Contre-mémoire de la défenderesse du 3 février 2003, p. 406.
[644]   Affaire CIRDI n° ARB/87/3, sentence du 27 juin 1990, para. 112.

714. Ainsi, dans l'affaire *Wena Hotels Limited c. Egypte*, le Tribunal arbitral, se ralliant à la sentence *Metalclad*,[645] a déclaré que l'intérêt composé :

> « *will best 'restore the Claimants to a reasonable approximation of the position in which it would have been if the wrongful act had not taken place.' Although the Metalclad tribunal awarded compound interest without comment, this panel feels that a brief explanation of its decision is warranted. This Tribunal believes that an award of compound (as opposed to simple) interest is generally appropriate in most modern, commercial arbitrations. As Professor Gotanda has observed 'almost all financing and investment vehicles involve compound interest ... If the claimant could have received compound interest merely by placing its money in a readily available and commonly used investment vehicle, it is neither logical not equitable to award the claimant only simple interest.' For similar reasons, Professor Mann has 'submitted that ... compound interest may be and, in absence of special circumstances, should be awarded to the claimant as damages by international tribunals' ».*[646]

715. De même, dans l'affaire Tecnicas Medioambientales Tecmed S.A. c. Mexique, le Tribunal arbitral, citant plusieurs sentences CIRDI dans la même sens, a exprimé l'opinion que « *application of compound interest is justified as part of the integral compensation owed to the Claimant as a result of the loss of its investment* ».[647]

---

[645] *Metalclad Corporation c. Mexique*, affaire CIRDI n° ARB(AF)/97/1, sentence du 30 août 2000, para. 128.

[646] *Wena Hotels Limited c. Egypte*, affaire CIRDI n° ARB/98/4, sentence du 8 décembre 2000, para. 129.

[647] *Tecnicas Medioambientales Tecmed S.A. c. Mexique*, affaire CIRDI n° ARB(AF)/00/2, sentence du 29 mai 2003, para. 196. V. aussi *Azurix Corp. c. République d'Argentine*, affaire CIRDI n° ARB/01/12, sentence du 14 juillet 2006, para. 440 où le Tribunal arbitral a conclu que « *compound interest reflects the reality of financial transactions, and best approximates the value lost by an investor* ». *MTD Equity Sdn. Bhd. & MTD Chile S.A. c. République du Chili*, affaire CIRDI n° ARB/01/7, sentence du 25 mai 2004, para. 251 : « *[...] compound interest is more in accordance with the reality of financial transactions and a closer approximation to the actual value lost by an investor.* », faisant référence à la décision du Tribunal arbitral dans l'affaire *Compañia de Desarrollo de Santa Elena, S.A. c. République du Costa Rica*, affaire CIRDI n° ARB/96/1, sentence du 17 février 2000, para. 104 : « *Where an owner of property has at some earlier time lost the value of*

716. Le Tribunal arbitral partage pleinement cette opinion pour les raisons générales indiquées, et compte tenu des circonstances de la présente espèce.

C.   Conclusion sur les dommages et intérêts

717. Par conséquent, la défenderesse doit payer aux demanderesses un montant total de USD 10.132.690,18, portant intérêt au taux de 5%, composé annuellement, à compter du 11 avril 2002 jusqu'à la date d'envoi de la présente sentence.

718. La République du Chili doit faire ce paiement dans un délai de 90 jours à compter de la date de la date d'envoi de la présente sentence. Si le paiement n'est pas fait dans ce délai, le montant portera intérêts composés annuellement au taux de 5%, à compter de la date d'envoi de la présente sentence jusqu'à celle du parfait paiement.

IX.   COUTS DE LA PROCEDURE

A.   Position des parties

719. En ce qui concerne les coûts de l'arbitrage, les deux parties ont conclu à ce que l'autre soit condamnée au paiement de l'intégralité des coûts de l'arbitrage, y compris les « *frais et honoraires des Membres du Tribunal, les frais relatifs à l'utilisation des installations du CIRDI, les frais de traduction, ainsi que les frais et honoraires de conseils à raison des avocats, experts et autres personnes appelées à comparaître devant le Tribunal ou à lui*

---

his asset but has not received the monetary equivalent than then became due to him, the amount of compensation should reflect, at least in part, the additional sum that his money would have earned, had it, and the income generated by it, been reinvested each year at generally prevailing rates of interest. » V. aussi *Middle East Shipping and Handling Co. S.A. c. Egypte*, affaire CIRDI n° ARB/99/6, sentence du 12 avril 2002, paras. 174-175. Le *Comité ad hoc* dans l'affaire *Wena Hotels Ltd. c. Egypte*, affaire CIRDI n° ARB/98/4, décision du *Comité ad hoc* du 28 janvier 2002, a décidé que, même dans un cas où la demanderesse n'a pas expressément demandé des intérêts composés, « *both parties must have been aware of the possibility that the Tribunal, referring to international practice might consider compound interest as 'appropriate' in the particular case* ». Pour des exemples dans la doctrine, il suffira de rappeler les travaux de G. Arangio Ruiz, Rapporteur spécial de la Commission du Droit international de l'ONU, *State Responsibility*, [1989] 2 Y.B. Int'l Comm'n 1, 29, U.N. Doc. A/CN.4/SER.A/1989/Add.1), et les études du juge S. Schwebel, *Compound Interest in International Law*, Transnational Dispute Management, Vol. 2/5, novembre 2005, et du Professeur J.Y. Gotanda, *Compound Interest in International Disputes*, Oxford University Comparative Law Forum (2004).

soumettre leur opinion ».[648] D'après les demanderesses, devrait être ajoutés à ces coûts les :

> « *frais encourus pour retrouver les titres de propriété de CPP S.A. et EPC Ltée, saisis illégalement dans les bureaux de M. Pey le 11 septembre 1973, ainsi que pour leur récupération par décision de la 8ème Chambre Criminelle de Santiago le 19 mai 1995, sans lesquels il aurait été impossible de saisir la juridiction internationale* ».[649]

720. Selon les demanderesses, la condamnation de la défenderesse aux frais se justifierait en outre par le « manque flagrant de coopération de la défenderesse avec le CIRDI et son obstruction à la formation et au fonctionnement du Tribunal […] ».[650]

721. La défenderesse a conclu à ce que « tous les coûts qu'elle a dû payer lors de l'arbitrage lui sont remboursés par les Demanderesses », y inclus « [l]es vacations et dépenses professionnelles, y compris celles des avocats, des experts, des témoins et du Tribunal, des frais administratifs du CIRDI et des autres coûts administratifs divers dont a dû s'acquitter la République de Chili durant le procès ».[651]

722. Les parties ont soumis leurs coûts par lettres en dates du 23 octobre 2007 (pour les demanderesses) et du 3 novembre 2007 (pour la défenderesse).

723. Les demanderesses ont soutenu que leurs coûts encourus serait d'USD 1.730.000 en tant que comme coûts de procédure ; et de € 8.835.996, plus USD 1.032.253 comme coûts exposés pour sa représentation et les honoraires de ses conseils, experts, etc.[652]

724. La défenderesse a déclaré avoir payé un total d'USD 4.389.111,56, ce qui exclut pourtant les coûts de procédure proprement dit.[653]

725. Dans une lettre en date du 20 novembre 2007, la défenderesse a exprimé ses objections contre la soumission des coûts de la part des demanderesses, concluant à ce que le Tribunal ne prenne pas en compte la documentation fournie par les demanderesses au soutien de leur lettre concernant les coûts. D'après la défenderesse, les demanderesses auraient, *inter alia*, manqué à leur obligation

---

[648] Exposé complémentaire sur le fond de l'affaire du 11 septembre 2002, p. 151.

[649] *Id.*, p. 151.

[650] *Id.*, pp. 151-152.

[651] Contre-mémoire de la défenderesse du 3 février 2003, p. 407.

[652] V. les annexes à la lettre des demanderesses du 23 octobre 2007 et le rectificatif dans la lettre des demanderesses du 7 novembre 2007.

[653] V. lettre de la défenderesse du 3 novembre 2007.

d'expliquer et de prouver les taux de change appliqué entre les différentes monnaies en question, ainsi que les dates auxquelles elles auraient procédé à la conversion. Plus fondamentalement, la défenderesse a soutenu que les coûts allégués par les demanderesses seraient excessifs et que les demanderesses auraient manqué à leur obligation de rapporter la preuve que les coûts allégués étaient des coûts réels, c'est-à-dire que les montants en question ont en fait été payés par les demanderesses.[654]

B. Conclusions du Tribunal

726. Il est constant qu'en fixant les coûts de la procédure ainsi qu'en décidant de leur répartition, en application de l'article 61(2) de la Convention CIRDI,[655] le Tribunal arbitral dispose d'un large pouvoir d'appréciation.[656]

727. Il y a lieu de distinguer les coûts de la procédure arbitrale proprement dite (qui comprennent les frais de l'institution qu'est le Centre et les honoraires et frais des Arbitres) des coûts exposés par chaque partie pour la présentation de sa cause et les honoraires de ses conseils, experts, etc.

728. Pour les premiers, le Tribunal arbitral tiendra compte de l'ensemble des circonstances de l'espèce, de l'issue de la cause ainsi que des attitudes respectives des parties. A cet égard, il est constant que, comme le montrent les analyses et conclusions qui précèdent, les demanderesses ont eu gain de cause pour l'essentiel, qu'il s'agisse de la compétence du Centre et du Tribunal arbitral, du principe de la responsabilité de la République du Chili et de la violation de l'obligation internationale d'accorder à l'investissement un « *traitement juste et équitable* », ainsi que, sur le fond, de leur qualité de propriétaire des investissements visés par les diverses mesures prises par les autorités chiliennes. Cela en dépit de la contestation déterminée opposée dès le début à la compétence internationale et à leurs réclamations. Au regard de ces faits, il apparaît relativement secondaire que le montant de l'indemnisation finalement allouée aux

---

[654] Voir la lettre de la défenderesse du 9 novembre 2007 (datée par erreur du 18 octobre 2007).

[655] « Dans les cas d'une procédure d'arbitrage le Tribunal fixe, sauf accord contraire des parties, le montant des dépenses exposés par elles pour les besoins de la procédure et décide des modalités de répartition et de paiement desdits dépenses, des honoraires et frais des membres du Tribunal et des redevances dues pour l'utilisation des services du Centre. Cette décision fait partie intégrante de la sentence. »

[656] V., par exemple, Consorzio Groupement L.E.S.I. – DIPENTA c. République algérienne démocratique et populaire, affaire CIRDI n° ARB/03/08, sentence du 10 janvier 2005, p. 42.

demanderesses ne représente qu'un faible pourcentage des dommages-intérêts sollicités par elles.

729. En outre, le Tribunal arbitral estime approprié de prendre en considération l'attitude des parties et leur degré de coopération à la procédure et à la mission confiée au Tribunal. De ce point de vue, force est de constater que la durée de la présente procédure, et par conséquent ses coûts pour toutes les parties et pour le Centre, ont été notablement augmentés par la politique adoptée par la défenderesse consistant, au-delà des exceptions usuelles ou « normales » à la compétence, à multiplier objections et incidents parfois incompatibles avec les usages de l'arbitrage international.

730. Cela étant, la solution couramment adoptée par les tribunaux arbitraux internationaux consistant à prescrire à chaque partie de supporter le coût de ses frais et dépens[657] ne serait pas appropriée de l'avis du Tribunal arbitral, pour qui il se justifie de mettre à la charge de la défenderesse une contribution aux frais et dépens exposés par les demanderesses, que le Tribunal arbitral estime approprié de fixer à USD 2.000.000,- (deux millions).

731. Quant aux frais de procédure proprement dit, le Tribunal arbitral estime approprié, compte tenu des circonstances et des observations qui précèdent, qu'ils soient supportés par les parties dans la proportion de : 3/4 du montant total (soit USD 3.136.893,34) pour la défenderesse et 1/4 du montant total (soit USD 1.045.631,11) pour les demanderesses. En conséquence, le Tribunal arbitral ordonne à la défenderesse de payer aux demanderesses la somme de USD 1.045.579,35.[658]

---

[657] Ainsi, par exemple, dans les cas *Maffezini c. Espagne*, affaire CIRDI n° ARB/97/7, sentence du 9 novembre 2000, paras. 98-99 ; *Middle East Shipping and Handling Co. S.A. c. Egypte*, affaire CIRDI n° ARB/99/6, sentence du 12 avril 2002, paras. 176 ; *Metalclad Corporation c. Mexique*, affaire CIRDI n° ARB(AF)/97/1, sentence du 30 août 2000, para. 130.

[658] Le montant total des frais de la procédure (USD 4.182.524,45) contient une estimation des frais d'expédition de la sentence et peut donc être sujet à une variation minime. Un état financier sera émis par le CIRDI lorsque le compte sera clos. En outre, le montant total des frais de la procédure dépasse le montant des avances payées par les parties (USD 4.109.900). La différence est couverte par les intérêts engendrés par le compte de l'affaire, à savoir USD 72.627,97 (montant déterminé à la date d'envoi de la sentence qui pourra accroître jusqu'à la clôture du compte). La somme de USD 1.045.579,35, qui doit être remboursée par la partie défenderesse aux parties demanderesses, est le résultat de la différence entre les 3/4 du montant total des frais de la procédure (USD 3.136.893,34) et les avances effectuées par la partie défenderesse (USD 2.055.000,-) ajoutées à la moitié des intérêts accrus (USD 36.313,99).

732. La République du Chili doit effectuer ces paiements dans un délai de 90 jours à compter de la date de la date d'envoi de la présente sentence. Si ces paiements ne sont pas faits dans ce délai, les montants porteront intérêts composés annuellement au taux de 5%, à compter de la date d'envoi de la présente sentence jusqu'à celle du parfait paiement.

X.   DISPOSITIF

Par ces motifs

Le Tribunal arbitral, à l'unanimité,

1. décide qu'il est compétent pour connaître du litige entre les demanderesses et la République du Chili ;

2. constate que la défenderesse a violé son obligation de faire bénéficier les demanderesses d'un traitement juste et équitable, en ce compris celle de s'abstenir de tout déni de justice ;

3. constate que les demanderesses ont droit à compensation ;

4. ordonne à la République du Chili de payer aux demanderesses le montant de USD 10.132.690,18, portant intérêt au taux de 5%, composé annuellement, à compter du 11 avril 2002 jusqu'à la date d'envoi de la présente sentence ;

5. met à la charge de la défenderesse une contribution aux frais et dépens exposés par les demanderesses, d'un montant de USD 2.000.000,- (deux millions) ;

6. décide que les frais de procédure seront supportés par les parties dans la proportion de : 3/4 du montant total (soit USD 3.136.893,34) pour la défenderesse et 1/4 du montant total (soit 1.045.631,11) pour les demanderesses ; ordonne en conséquence à la défenderesse de payer aux demanderesses la somme de USD 1.045.579,35 ;

7. ordonne à la République du Chili de procéder au paiement dans un délai de 90 jours à compter de la date d'envoi de la présente sentence, des sommes figurant dans le présent dispositif (points 4, 5 et 6), faute de quoi le montant portera intérêts composés annuellement au taux de 5%, à compter de la date d'envoi de la présente sentence jusqu'à celle du parfait paiement ;

8. rejette toutes autres ou plus amples conclusions.

/signé/
Pierre Lalive, Président
Date : 22 avril 2008

/signé/   /signé/
Mohammed Chemloul, Arbitre   Emmanuel Gaillard, Arbitre

Date : 18 avril 2008   Date : 16 avril 2008

ANNEX 4

International Centre for Settlement of Investment Disputes
Washington, D.C.

In the proceedings between

VICTOR PEY CASADO AND THE FOUNDATION
"PRESIDENTE ALLENDE"
(Claimants)

and

The Republic of Chili
(Respondent)

ICSID Case No. ARB/98/2

———————

AWARD

———————

Members of the Tribunal
Professor Pierre Lalive, President
Mohammed Chemloul, Arbitrator
Professor Emmanuel Gaillard, Arbitrator

Secretaries of the Tribunal
Gabriela Alvarez-Avila / Eloïse Obadia

Date of Dispatch to the Parties: May 9, 2008

. . .

IV.   Jurisdiction of the Center and of the Tribunal over Mr. Pey's claim

. . .

119.   Before proceeding to the examination of these conditions [relevant to the existence of an investment and the nationality of the Claimants], the Tribunal wishes to specify that it is not bound by previously rendered ICSID decisions and awards. However, the present Tribunal considers that it must take into consideration the decisions of international tribunals and, in the absence of compelling reasons to the contrary, draw inspiration from the solutions adopted by well-established arbitral case law. While taking into consideration the specific provisions of the applicable treaty and the facts of the dispute, the Tribunal also considers that it must strive to contribute to the harmonious development of investment law, and, in doing so, satisfy the legitimate expectations of the community of States and of investors as regards the predictability of the law on these questions.[94]

. . .

---

[94]   See, in this regard, *Saipem S.p.A. v. The People's Republic of Bangladesh*, ICSID Case No. ARB/05/7, Decision on Jurisdiction and Recommendation on Provisional Measures dated 21 March 2007, para. 67.

ANNEX 5

Statute of the International Court of Justice

...

Article 38

1. The Court, whose function is to decide in accordance with international law such disputes as are submitted to it, shall apply:

a. international conventions, whether general or particular, establishing rules expressly recognized by the contesting states;

b. international custom, as evidence of a general practice accepted as law;

c. the general principles of law recognized by civilized nations;

d. subject to the provisions of Article 59, judicial decisions and the teachings of the most highly qualified publicists of the various nations, as subsidiary means for the determination of rules of law.

2. This provision shall not prejudice the power of the Court to decide a case *ex aequo et bono*, if the parties agree thereto.

...

Article 59

The decision of the Court has no binding force except between the parties and in respect of that particular case.

...

ANNEX 6

CROSS-REFERENCES IN INVESTMENT ARBITRATION CASE LAW:

SALIENT TOPICS *

Although it is common knowledge that arbitral tribunals, particularly in investment arbitration, refer to prior awards in their reasoning, no systematic review of cross-references in arbitral case law seems to have been undertaken. The following table surveys eight salient topics in investment arbitration to expose the extent to which arbitral tribunals make use of prior awards in their reasoning. It also indicates whether arbitral tribunals have *concurred* with the reasoning in prior awards to support their conclusion, *distinguished* from the prior award's reasoning (either on the facts or on the law), or, as is the case for most of the awards included in this survey, simply *considered* prior awards, without indicating what conclusion they draw from such awards. With time, one notices an obvious increase in the number of awards referred to by tribunals in their reasoning, indicating a trend towards the formation of a *jurisprudence constante* in investment arbitration.

---

* Prepared by Tania Steenkamp, Associate, Shearman & Sterling LLP.

I. DEFINITION OF AN INVESTMENT [1]

Fedax N.V. v. The Republic of Venezuela (ARB/96/3), Decision on Jurisdiction dated July 11, 1997

GENERAL

Kaiser Bauxite v. Jamaica, Decision on Jurisdiction, July 6, 1975: 25 (considered)

Alcoa Minerals v. Jamaica Decision on Jurisdiction, July 6, 1975: 25 (considered)

LETCO v. Liberia, Award, March 31, 1986: 25 (considered)

SOABI v. Senegal, Award, February 25, 1988: 25 (considered)

Holiday Inns v. Morocco: 26 (considered)

Amco Asia v. Indonesia, Decision on Annulment, May 16, 1986: 26 (considered)

Tradex Hellas S.A. (Greece) v. Republic of Albania (ARB/94/2), Award dated April 29, 1999

GENERAL

Fedax v. Venezuela, Decision on Jurisdiction, July 11, 1997: 106 (concurred)

Fedax v. Venezuela, Award, March 9, 1998: 106 (concurred)

Ceskoslovenska Obchodni Banka, A.S. v. The Slovak Republic (ARB/97/4), Decision on Jurisdiction dated May 24, 1999

GENERAL

Fedax v. Venezuela, Decision on Jurisdiction, July 11, 1997: 71–72, 76 (concurred)

Consortium R.F.C.C. v. Kingdom of Morocco (ARB/00/6), Decision on Jurisdiction dated July 16, 2001

GENERAL

Fedax v. Venezuela, Award, March 9, 1998: 51, 60 (concurred)

Alcoa Minerals v. Jamaica, Decision on Jurisdiction, July 6, 1975: 60 (concurred)

---

[1]   This topic does not include related issues, such as shareholder rights, the origin of funds or whether the investment was made "in the territory" of a State. It focuses solely on the criteria for an investment.

Salini Costruttori S.P.A. and Italstrade S.P.A. v. Kingdom of Morocco (ARB/00/4), Decision on Jurisdiction dated July 23, 2001

GENERAL

Fedax v. Venezuela, Award, March 9, 1998: 44, 52 (concurred)

Alcoa Minerals v. Jamaica, Decision on Jurisdiction, July 6, 1975: 52 (concurred)

SGS Société Générale de Surveillance S.A. v. Islamic Republic of Pakistan (ARB/01/13), Decision on Jurisdiction dated August 6, 2003

GENERAL

Fedax v. Venezuela, Decision on Jurisdiction, July 11, 1997: 133 (concurred)

Mihaly v. Sri Lanka, Award, March 7, 2002: 137 (distinguished)

PSEG Global Inc., The North American Coal Corporation and Konya Ilgin Elektrik Üretim ve Ticaret Limite Siketi v. The Republic of Turkey (ARB/02/5), Decision on Jurisdiction dated June 4, 2004

GENERAL

Mihaly v. Sri Lanka, Award, March 7, 2002: 81, 103 (distinguished)

Zhinvali v. Georgia, Award, January 24, 2003: 81 (distinguished)

Joy Mining Machinery Limited v. The Arab Republic of Egypt (ARB/03/11), Award on Jurisdiction dated August 6, 2004

GENERAL

Fedax v. Venezuela, Decision on Jurisdiction, July 11, 1997: 47, 51, 60 (distinguished)

Alcoa Minerals v. Jamaica, Decision on Jurisdiction, July 6, 1975: 51 (considered)

Amco Asia v. Indonesia, Decision on Annulment, May 16, 1986: 51 (considered)

CSOB v. Slovakia, Decision on Jurisdiction, May 24, 1999: 51 (considered)

Atlantic Triton v. Guinea, Award, April 21, 1986: 51 (considered)

Salini v. Morocco, Decision on Jurisdiction, July 23, 2001: 51 (considered), 62 (distinguished)

SGS v. Pakistan, Decision on Jurisdiction, August 6, 2003: 51 (considered)

475

SGS v. Philippines, Decision on Jurisdiction, January 29, 2004: 51 (considered)

Consorzio Groupement L.E.S.I. – DIPENTA v. Democratic and Popular Republic of Algeria (ARB/03/08), Award dated January 10, 2005

GENERAL

Salini v. Morocco, Decision on Jurisdiction, July 23, 2001: 13 (considered), 14 (concurred)

Fedax v. Venezuela, Decision on Jurisdiction, July 11, 1997: 13 (considered)

CSOB v. Slovakia, Decision on Jurisdiction, May 24, 1999: 13 (considered)

SGS v. Pakistan, Decision on Jurisdiction, August 6, 2003: 13 (considered)

SGS v. Philippines, Decision on Jurisdiction, January 29, 2004: 13 (considered)

R.F.C.C. v. Morocco, Decision on Jurisdiction, July 16, 2001:14 (concurred)

Autopista v. Venezuela, Decision on Jurisdiction, September 27, 2001: 14 (concurred)

Petrobart Limited v. The Kyrgyz Republic (SCC Arbitration No. 126/2003), Award dated March 29, 2005

Fedax v. Venezuela, Decision on Jurisdiction, July 11, 1997: p. 71 (concurred)

Salini v. Morocco, Decision on Jurisdiction, July 23, 2001: p. 71 (concurred)

SGS v. Pakistan, Decision on Jurisdiction, August 6, 2003: p. 72 (concurred)

Bayindir Insaat Turizm Ticaret Ve Sanayi A.S. v. Islamic Republic of Pakistan (ARB/03/29), Decision on Jurisdiction dated November 14, 2005

GENERAL

Salini v. Morocco, Decision on Jurisdiction, July 23, 2001: 109, 130, 135 (concurred)

Autopista v. Venezuela, Decision on Jurisdiction, September 27, 2001: 128 (concurred)

Impregilo v. Pakistan, Decision on Jurisdiction, April 22, 2005: 129 (considered)

L.E.S.I.-DIPENTA v. Algeria, Award, December 27, 2004: 130, 133, 137 (concurred)

476

Joy Mining v. Egypt, Award on Jurisdiction, August 6, 2004: 130, 132 (concurred)

Jan de Nul N.V. Dredging International N.V. v. Arab Republic of Egypt (ARB/04/13), Decision on Jurisdiction dated June 16, 2006

GENERAL

Salini v. Morocco, Decision on Jurisdiction, July 23, 2001: 91 (concurred)

Bayinder v. Pakistan, Decision on Jurisdiction, November 14, 2005: 91 (concurred)

L.E.S.I.- DIPENTA v. Algeria, Award, January 10, 2005: 91 (concurred)

Joy Mining v. Egypt, Award on Jurisdiction, August 6, 2004: 91 (concurred)

L.E.S.I. S.p.A. – ASTALDI S.p.A. v. Democratic and Popular Republic of Algeria (ARB/05/3), Decision on Jurisdiction dated July 12, 2006

GENERAL

Salini v. Morocco, Decision on Jurisdiction, July 23, 2001: 72 (considered), 73 (concurred)

Fedax v. Venezuela, Decision on Jurisdiction, July 11, 1997: 72 (considered)

CSOB v. Slovakia, Decision on Jurisdiction, May 24, 1999: 72 (considered)

SGS v. Pakistan, Decision on Jurisdiction, August 6, 2003: 72 (considered)

SGS v. Philippines, Decision on Jurisdiction, January 29, 2004: 72 (considered)

R.F.C.C. v. Morocco, Decision on Jurisdiction, July 16, 2001:73 (concurred)

Autopista v. Venezuela, Decision on Jurisdiction, September 27, 2001: 73 (concurred)

Patrick Mitchell v. The Democratic Republic of Congo (ARB/99/7), Decision on the Application for Annulment of the Award dated November 1, 2006

GENERAL

Fedax v. Venezuela, Decision on Jurisdiction, July 11, 1997: 27 (concurred)

CSOB v. Slovakia, Decision on Jurisdiction, May 24, 1999: 27 (concurred)

Salini v. Morocco, Decision on Jurisdiction, July 23, 2001: 27 (concurred)

477

CONTRIBUTION BY THE INVESTOR

Holiday Inns v. Morocco: 27 (concurred)

Amco Asia v. Indonesia, Decision on Annulment, May 16, 1986: 27 (concurred)

Salini v. Morocco, Decision on Jurisdiction, July 23, 2001: 27 (concurred)

CONTRIBUTION TO THE ECONOMIC DEVELOPMENT OF THE HOST STATE

Fedax v. Venezuela, Decision on Jurisdiction, July 11, 1997: 30 (concurred)

CSOB v. Slovakia, Decision on Jurisdiction, May 24, 1999: 30 (concurred)

Salini v. Morocco, Decision on Jurisdiction, July 23, 2001: 30 (concurred)

Alcoa Minerals v. Jamaica, Decision on Jurisdiction, July 6, 1975: 30 (concurred)

Tradex v. Albania, Award, April 29, 1999: 30 (concurred)

SGS v. Pakistan, Decision on Jurisdiction, August 6, 2003: 30 (concurred)

SGS v. Philippines, Decision on Jurisdiction, January 29, 2004: 30 (concurred)

Saipem S.p.A. v. The People's Republic of Bangladesh (ARB/05/07), Decision on Jurisdiction and Recommendation on Provisional Measures dated March 21, 2007

GENERAL

Salini v. Morocco, Decision on Jurisdiction, July 23, 2001: 99 (concurred)

L.E.S.I.-DIPENTA v. Algeria, Decision on Jurisdiciton, July 12, 2006: 99 (concurred)

Waguih Elie George Siag and Clorinda Vecchi v. The Arab Republic of Egypt (ARB/05/15), Decision on Jurisdiction dated April 11, 2007

GENERAL

Fedax v. Venezuela, Decision on Jurisdiction, July 11, 1997: 204 (concurred)

Malaysian Historical Salvors Sdn, Bhd v. The Government of Malyasia (ARB/05/10), Award on Jurisdiction dated May 17, 2007

GENERAL

Alcoa Minerals v. Jamaica, Decision on Jurisdiction, July 6, 1975: 62–63 (distinguished)

Salini v. Morocco, Decision on Jurisdiction, July 23, 2001: 56, 70, 73–83, 102, 106 (considered), 54-55 (concurred)

L.E.S.I.- DIPENTA v. Algeria, Award, January 10, 2005: 56, 89, 103 (considered)

Joy Mining v. Egypt, Award on Jurisdiction, August 6, 2004: 56, 70, 73, 84–88, 106 (considered), 55 (concurred)

Jan de Nul v. Egypt, Decision on Jurisdiction, November 14, 2005: 56, 101–102, 106 (considered)

SGS v. Pakistan, Decision on Jurisdiction, August 6, 2003: 62, 64 (distinguished)

Bayinder v. Pakistan, Decision on Jurisdiction, November 14, 2005: 49, 56, 99–100, 102, 106 (considered)

CSOB v. Slovakia, Decision on Jurisdiction, May 24, 1999: 49, 56, 97–98 (considered), 66, 67 (concurred)

Patrick Mitchell v. DRC, Decision on Annulment, November 1, 2006: 50, 56, 83, 90–96, 106 (considered)

PSEG v. Turkey , Decision on Jurisdiction, June 4, 2005: 52 (considered)

Mihaly v. Sri Lanka, Award, March 7, 2002: 57–61 (distinguished)

REGULARITY OF PROFIT AND RETURN

Joy Mining v. Egypt, Award on Jurisdiction, August 6, 2004: 108 (distinguished)

CONTRIBUTION BY THE INVESTOR

Salini v. Morocco, Decision on Jurisdiction, July 23, 2001: 109 (distinguished)

Bayinder v. Pakistan, Decision on Jurisdiction, November 14, 2005: 109 (distinguished)

Jan de Nul v. Egypt, Decision on Jurisdiction, November 14, 2005: 109 (distinguished)

Joy Mining v. Egypt, Award on Jurisdiction, August 6, 2004: 109 (distinguished)

DURATION OF THE CONTRACT

Salini v. Morocco, Decision on Jurisdiction, July 23, 2001: 110 (concurred)

L.E.S.I.- DIPENTA v. Algeria, Award, January 10, 2005: 111 (concurred)

Bayinder v. Pakistan, Decision on Jurisdiction, November 14, 2005: 111 (concurred)

RISKS ASSUMED UNDER THE CONTRACT

Salini v. Morocco, Decision on Jurisdiction, July 23, 2001: 112 (concurred)

479

CONTRIBUTION TO THE ECONOMIC DEVELOPMENT OF THE HOST STATE

Salini v. Morocco, Decision on Jurisdiction, July 23, 2001: 113 (considered), 131 (distinguished)

L.E.S.I.- DIPENTA v. Algeria, Award, January 10, 2005: 113 (considered)

Joy Mining v. Egypt, Award on Jurisdiction, August 6, 2004: 114, 123 (considered)

Bayinder v. Pakistan, Decision on Jurisdiction, November 14, 2005: 115, 142, (concurred), 143–44 (distinguished)

Jan de Nul v. Egypt, Decision on Jurisdiction, November 14, 2005: 116 (considered), 142 (concurred), 143–44 (distinguished)

CSOB v. Slovakia, Decision on Jurisdiction, May 24, 1999: 117, 125 (considered), 140 (concurred), 143–44 (distinguished)

Patrick Mitchell v. DRC, Decision on Annulment, November 1, 2006: 118, 126–128 (considered)

PSEG v. Turkey, Decision on Jurisdiction, June 4, 2005: 119–122 (considered)

Mihaly v. Sri Lanka, Award, March 7, 2002: 143 (distinguished)

Ioannis Kardassopoulos v. Georgia (ARB/05/18), Decision on Jurisdiction dated July 6, 2007

GENERAL

Fedax v. Venezuela, Decision on Jurisdiction, July 11, 1997: 116 (concurred)

Salini v. Morocco, Decision on Jurisdiction, July 23, 2001: 116, 117 (concurred)

Jan de Nul v. Egypt, Decision on Jurisdiction, November 14, 2005: 117 (concurred)

Victor Pey Casado and Foundation President Allende v. Republic of Chili (ARB/98/2), Award dated May 8, 2008

GENERAL

Fedax v. Venezuela, Decision on Jurisdiction, July 11, 1997: 231 (considered)

CSOB v. Slovakia, Decision on Jurisdiction, May 24, 1999: 231 (considered)

M.C.I. v. Ecuador, Award, July 31, 2007: 231 (considered)

L.E.S.I.- DIPENTA v. Algeria, Award, January 10, 2005: 231 (considered)

L.E.S.I.-ASTALDI v. Algeria, Decision on Jurisdiciton, July 12, 2006: 231 (considered)

Salini v. Morocco, Decision on Jurisdiction, July 23, 2001: 231 (considered)

Joy Mining v. Egypt, Award on Jurisdiction, August 6, 2004: 231, 232 (concurred)

Jan de Nul v. Egypt, Decision on Jurisdiction, November 14, 2005: 231 (considered)

Helnan v. Egypt, Decision on Jurisdiction, October 17, 2006: 231 (considered)

Saipem v. Bangladesh, Decision on Jurisdiction, March 21, 2007: 231 (considered)

Malaysian Historical v. Malaysia, Award, May 17, 2007: 231 (considered)

Patrick Mitchell v. DRC, Decision on Annulment, November 1, 2006: 231 (considered)

II. DEFINITION OF AN INVESTOR UNDER ARTICLE 25 OF THE ICSID CONVENTION: DUAL NATIONALITY

Champion Trading Company et al v. Arab Republic of Egypt (ARB/02/9), Decision on Jurisdiction dated October 21, 2003

Nottebohm case (Lichtenstein v. Guatemala), ICJ, Judgment, April 6, 1955: 285–88 (distinguished)

Case No A/18, IRAN–US Tribunal, Decision, April 6, 1984: 287–88 (distinguished)

Waguih Elie George Siag and Clorinda Vecchi v. the Arab Republic of Egypt (ARB/05/15), Decision on Jurisdiction dated April 11, 2007

Soufraki v. Egypt, Award, July 7, 2004: 143, 150–52 (concurred)

Champion Trading v. Egypt, Decision on Jurisdiciton, October 21, 2003: 197–99 (concurred)

III. FORK IN THE ROAD CLAUSE

Compañía de Aguas del Aconquija, S.A. & Compagnie Générale des Eaux v. Argentine Republic (ARB/97/3), Award dated November 21, 2000

Lanco v. Argentina, Decision on Jurisdiction, December 8, 1998: 53 (considered)

481

CMS Gas Transmission Company v. The Republic of Argentina (ARB/01/8), Decision on Jurisdiction dated July 17, 2003

Aguas v. Argentina, Award, November 21, 2000: 80 (concurred)

Genin v. Estonia, Award, June 25, 2001: 80 (concurred)

Olguin v. Paraguay, Decision on Jurisdiction, August 8, 2000: 80 (concurred)

Azurix Corp. v. The Argentine Republic (ARB/01/12), Decision on Jurisdiction dated December 8, 2003

Benvenuti and Bonfant v. Congo, Award, August 15, 1980: 88 (concurred)

CMS v. Argentina, Decision on Jurisdiction, July 17, 2003: 89 (concurred)

Enron Corporation and Ponderosa Assets, L.P. v. The Argentine Republic (ARB/01/3), Decision on Jurisdiction dated January 14, 2004

Aguas v. Argentina, Award, November 21, 2000: 97 (concurred)

Genin v. Estonia, Award, June 25, 2001: 97 (concurred)

Olguin v. Paraguay, Decision on Jurisdiction, August 8, 2000: 97 (concurred)

Benvenuti and Bonfant v. Congo, Award, August 15, 1980: 97 (concurred)

Occidental Exploration and Production Company v. The Republic of Ecuador (UNCITRAL LCIA Case No. UN 3467), Final Award dated July 1, 2004

Lanco v. Argentina, Decision on Jurisdiction, December 8, 1998: 44 (considered)

Azurix v. Argentina, Decision on Jurisdiction, December 8, 2003: 51 (considered)

Elettronica Sicula (ELSI) (Canada v. Italy), ICJ, July 20, 1989: 49 (considered)

Wena Hotels v. Egypt, Decision on Annulment, February 5, 2002: 50 (concurred)

Lauder v. Czech Republic, Final Award, September 3, 2001: 51, 52 (concurred)

Genin v. Estonia, Award, June 25, 2001: 51 (considered)

Aguas v. Argentina, Award, November 21, 2000: 51, 62 (considered)

CMS v. Argentina, Decision on Jurisdiction, July 17, 2003: 51 (considered)

Vivendi v. Argentina, Decision on Annulment, July 3, 2002: 51, 62 (considered), 52, 53 (concurred)

SGS v. Pakistan , Decision on Jurisdiction, August 6, 2003: 54 (considered)

SGS v. Philippines, Decision on Jurisdiction,, January 29, 2004: 54 (considered)

AES Corporation v. The Argentine Republic (ARB/02/17), Decision on Jurisdiction dated April 26, 2005

CMS v. Argentina, Decision on Jurisdiction, July 17, 2003: 95, 97 (concurred)

Azurix v. Argentina, Decision on Jurisdiction, December 8, 2003: 96, 97 (concurred)

Camuzzi International S.A. v. The Argentine Republic (ARB/03/2), Decision on Jurisdiction dated May 11, 2005

Vivendi v. Argentina, Decision on Annulment, July 3, 2002: 110 (concurred)

MTD v. Chile, Award, May 25, 2004: 112 (considered)

Sempra Energy International v. The Argentine Republic (ARB/02/16), Decision on Jurisdiction dated May 11, 2005

Vivendi v. Argentina, Decision on Annulment, July 3, 2002: 121 (concurred)

MTD v. Chile, Award, May 25, 2004: 123 (considered)

M.C.I. Power Group L.C. and New Turbine, Inc. v. Republic of Ecuador (ARB/03/6), Award dated July 31, 2007

Vivendi v. Argentina, Decision on Annulment, July 3, 2002: 186 (considered)

Victor Pey Casado and Foundation President Allende v. Republic of Chili (ARB/98/2), Award dated May 8, 2008

Occidental v.Ecuador, Final Award, July 1, 2004: 484 (concurred)

CMS v. Argentina, Decision on Jurisdiction, July 17, 2003: 485 (concurred)

Azurix v. Argentina, Decision on Jurisdiction, December 8, 2003: 485 (concurred)

Enron v. Argentina, Decision on Jurisdiction, January 4, 2004: 485 (concurred)

Pan American v. Argentina and BP v. Argentina, Decision on Prelimanry Objections, July 27, 2006: 485,492 (concurred)

483

IV.   MOST-FAVORED-NATION CLAUSE

Emilio Agustín Maffezini v. Kingdom of Spain (ARB/97/7), Decision on Jurisdiction dated January 25, 2000

Anglo-Iranian Oil Company Case, ICJ, Judgment, July 22, 1952: 43, 44 (considered)

Case Concerning Rights of Nationals of the United States of America in Morocco, ICJ, Judgment, August 27, 1952: 43, 47 (considered)

Ambatielos case, ICJ, May 19, 1953: 43, 48 (considered)

Ambatielos case, Commission of Arbitration, Award, March 6, 1956: 43, 49-54 (considered)

The Mavrommatis Palistine Concessions Case (Greece v. UK), PCIJ, August 30, 1924: 63 (distinguished)

Interhandel Case (Switzerland v. USA), ICJ, March 21, 1959: 63 (distinguished)

AAPL v. Sri Lanka, Award, June 27, 1990: 51 (considered)

ADF Group Inc. v. United States of America (ARB(AF)/00/1, Award dated January 9, 2003

Maffezini v. Spain, Decision on Jurisdiction, January 25, 2000: 197 (considered)

Técnicas Medioambientales Tecmed, S.A. v. United Mexican States (ARB(AF)/00/2), Award dated May 29, 2003

Maffezini v. Spain, Decision on Jurisdiction, January 25, 2000: 69 (considered)

Siemens A.G. v. Argentine Republic (ARB/02/8), Decision on Jurisdiction dated August 3, 2004

Anglo-Iranian Oil Company Case, ICJ, Judgment, July 22, 1952: 95-96, 99 (distinguished)

Case concerning the Rights of Nationals of the United States of America in Morocco, ICJ, Judgment, August 27, 1952: : 97-100 (considered)

Ambatielos case, Award, March 6, 1956: 100-102 (considered)

Maffezini v. Spain, Decision on Jurisdiction, January 25, 2000: 103, 109 (concurred)

Salini Construttori S.p.A. and Italstrade S.p.A. v. Hashemite Kingdom of Jordan (ARB/02/13), Decision on Jurisdiction dated November 29, 2004

Anglo-Iranian Oil Company Case, ICJ, Judgment, July 22, 1952: 106 (considered)

Case concerning the Rights of Nationals of the United States of America in Morocco, ICJ, Judgment, August 27, 1952: 106 (considered)

Ambatielos case, Award, March 6, 1956: 106-112, 117 (distinguished)

Maffezini v. Spain, Decision on Jurisdiction, January 25, 2000: 113-119 (distinguished)

Plama Consortium Limited v. Republic of Bulgaria (ARB/03/24), Decision on Jurisdiction dated February 8, 2005

Anglo-Iranian Oil Company Case, ICJ, Judgment, July 22, 1952: 214 (considered)

Case concerning the Rights of Nationals of the United States of America in Morocco, ICJ, Judgment, August 27, 1952: 213 (considered)

Ambatielos case, Award, March 6, 1956: 215 (distinguished)

Maffezini v. Spain, Decision on Jurisdiction, January 25, 2000: 193, 203, 216-224 (distinguished)

Ceskoslovenska v. Slovakia, Decision on Jurisdiction, May 24, 1999: 211 (considered)

Siemens v. Argentina, Decision on Jurisdiction, August 3, 2004: 205, 226 (considered)

Salini v. Jordan, Decision on Jurisdiction, November 9, 2004: 225 (concurred)

Tecmed v. Mexico , Award, May 29, 2003: 226 (considered)

Gas Natural SDG, S.A. v. Argentine Republic (ARB/03/10), Decision on Preliminary Questions on Jurisdiction dated June 17, 2005

Maffezini v. Spain, Decision on Jurisdiction, January 25, 2000: 45-47 (concurred)

Siemens v. Argentina, Decision on Jurisdiction, August 3, 2004: 41-44, 47 (concurred)

Salini v. Jordania, Decision on Jurisdiction, November 9, 2004: 48 (considered)

Berschader v. The Russian Federation (SCC Arbitration Institute Case No. 080/2004), Award dated April 21, 2006

Maffezini v. Spain, Decision on Jurisdiction, January 25, 2000: 163-64 (considered), 184 (concurred)

Siemens v. Argentina, Decision on Jurisdiction, August 3, 2004: 165 (considered)

Gas Natural v. Argentina, Decision on Jurisdiction, June 17, 2005: 166, 181 (distinguished)

Salini v. Jordania, Decision on Jurisdiction, November 9, 2004: 167-69 (considered)

Ambatielos case, Award, March 6, 1956: 200-201 (considered)

Plama v. Bulgaria, Decision on Jurisdiction, February 8, 2005: 170-74, 177-78, 180 (concurred)

Suez, Sociedad General de Aguas de Barcelona S.A., and InterAguas Servicios Integrales del Agua S.A. v. Argentine Republic (ARB/03/17), Decision on Jurisdiction dated May 16, 2006

MTD Equity v. Chile, Award, May 25, 2004: 61 (concurred)

Maffezini v. Spain, Decision on Jurisdiction, January 25, 2000: 60 (concurred)

Siemens v. Argentina, Decision on Jurisdiction, August 3, 2004: 61 (concurred)

Plama v. Bulgaria, Decision on Jurisdiction, February 8, 2005: 62-66 (distinguished)

National Grid plc v. Argentine Republic (UNCITRAL), Decision on Jurisdiction dated June 20, 2006

Case concerning the Rights of Nationals of the United States of America in Morocco, ICJ, Judgment, August 27, 1952: 87, 89 (considered)

Maffezini v. Spain, Decision on Jurisdiction, January 25, 2000: 83, 88, 89, 92 (concurred)

Siemens v. Argentina, Decision on Jurisdiction, August 3, 2004: 85 (considered)

Gas Natural v. Argentina, Decision on Preliminary Questions on Jurisdiction, June 17, 2005: 91 (considered)

Salini v. Jordania, Decision on Jurisdiction, November 9, 2004: 84, 90, 91

(considered)

Ambatielos case, Award, March 6, 1956: 83, 86, 89 (considered)

Plama v. Bulgaria, Decision on Jurisdiction, February 8, 2005: 90, 91-92 (distinguished)

Suez & Vivendi v. The Argentine Republic (ARB/03/19) and AWG Group v. The Argentine Republic (UNCITRAL), Decision on Jurisdiction dated August 3, 2006

MTD Equity v. Chile, Award, May 25, 2004: 63 (concurred)

Maffezini v. Spain, Decision on Jurisdiction, January 25, 2000: 62 (concurred)

Siemens v. Argentina, Decision on Jurisdiction, August 3, 2004: 63 (concurred)

Plama v. Bulgaria, Decision on Jurisdiction, February 8, 2005: 64-68 (distinguished)

Telenor Mobile Communications A.S. v. Republic of Hungary (ARB/04/15), Award dated September 13, 2006

Suez, Sociedad General de Aguas de Barcelona S.A..v. Argentina, Decision on Jurisdiction, May 16, 2006: 88, 98-99 (distinguished)

Maffezini v. Spain, Decision on Jurisdiction, January 25, 2000: 85-87 (considered)

Siemens v. Argentina, Decision on Jurisdiction, August 3, 2004: 85 (considered)

Plama v. Bulgaria, Decision on Jurisdiction, February 8, 2005: 89-90, 93, 98-99 (concurred)

Salini v. Jordania, Decision on Jurisdiction, November 9, 2004: 89 (considered)

Gas Natural v. Argentina, Decision on Preliminary Questions on Jurisdiction, June 17, 2005: 88 (considered)

RosInvestCo UK Ltd. v. Russian Federation (SCC Arbitration Institute Case No. 080/2004), Award on Jurisdiction dated October 2007

Maffezini v. Spain, Decision on Jurisdiction, January 25, 2000: 136 (considered)

Siemens v. Argentina, Decision on Jurisdiction, August 3, 2004: 136 (considered)

Plama v. Bulgaria, Decision on Jurisdiction, February 8, 2005: 136 (considered)

487

Salini v. Jordania, Decision on Jurisdiction, November 9, 2004: 136 (considered)

Gas Natural v. Argentina, Decision on Preliminary Questions on Jurisdiction, June 17, 2005: 136 (considered)

Telenor v. Hungary, Award, September 13, 2006: 136 (considered)

Suez & Vivendi v. Argentina, Decision on Jurisdiction, August 3, 2006: 136 (considered)

National Grid v. Argentina, Decision on Jurisdiction, June 20, 2006: 136 (considered)

Suez, Sociedad General de Aguas de Barcelona v. Argentina, Decision on Jurisdiction, May 16, 2006: 136 (considered)

Berschader v. Russia, Award, April 21, 2006: 136 (considered)

MTD Equity v. Chile, Award, May 25, 2004: 136 (considered)

V. FAIR AND EQUITABLE TREATMENT

SD Myers Inc. v. Government of Canada (NAFTA UNCITRAL Arbitration), Partial Award dated November 13, 2000

USA on behalf of George W. Hopkins v. Mexico (U.S.-Mexico), Decision, March 31, 1926: 260 (concurred)

Wena Hotels Limited v. Arab Republic of Egypt (ARB/98/4), Award dated December 8, 2000

American Manufacturing and Trading v. Zaïre, Award, February 21, 1997: 84 (concurred)

AAPL v. Sri Lanka, Award, June 27, 1990: 84 (concurred)

Pope and Talbot Inc. v. The Government of Canada (NAFTA UNCITRAL Arbitraiton), Award on the Merits of Phase 2 dated April 10, 2001

SD Myers v. Canada, Partial Award, November 13, 2000: 110, 113 (distinguished)

Metalclad v. Mexico, Award, August 25, 2000: 110 (considered)

Loewen v. US, Interim Award, January 5, 2001: 110 (considered)

Mondev International Limited v. United States of America (ARB(AF)/99/2), Award dated October 11, 2002

Shufeldt claim (United States/Guatemala), Decision, July 24, 1930: 98 (concurred)

Norwegian Shipowners' Claims, Award, October 13, 1922: 98 (concurred)

Philips Petroleum v. Iran (Iran – U.S.), Award, 29 June 1989: 98 (concurred)

Neer claim (U.S.-Mexico), Decision, July 23, 2002: 114–17 (distinguished)

Elettronica Sicula (ELSI) (Canada v. Italy), ICJ, July 20, 1989: 127 (concurred)

United Parcel Service of America Inc. v. Government of Canada (NAFTA UNCITRAL), Award on Jurisdiction dated November 22, 2002

Pope & Talbot v. Canada, Award, April 10, 2001: 95 (distinguished)

ADF Group Inc. v. United States of America (ARB(AF)/00/1), Award dated January 9, 2003

Mondev v. USA, Award, October 11, 2002: 180, 183–86 (concurred)

Neer claim (U.S.-Mexico), Decision, July 23, 2002: 179, 181 (distinguished)

Tecnicas Medioambientales Tecmed S.A. v. The United Mexican States (ARB(AF)/00/2), Award dated May 29, 2003

SD Myers v. Canada, Partial Award, November 13, 2000: 153 (concurred)

Mondev v. USA, Award, October 11, 2002: 153 (concurred)

Neer claim (U.S.-Mexico), Decision, July 23, 2002: 154 (concurred)

Elettronica Sicula (ELSI) (Canada v. Italy), ICJ, July 20, 1989: 154 (concurred)

The Loewen Group, Inc. and Raymond L. Loewen v. United States of America (ARB(AF)/98/3), Award dated June 26, 2003

Metalclad v. Mexico, Award, August 25, 2000: 128 (distinguished)

SD Myers v. Canada, Partial Award, November 13, 2000: 128 (distinguished)

Pope & Talbot v. Canada, Award, April 10, 2001: 128 (distinguished)

Pope & Talbot v. Canada, Award, May 31, 2002: 131 (concurred)

Elettronica Sicula (ELSI) (Canada v. Italy), ICJ, July 20, 1989: 131 (concurred)

Mondev v. USA, Award, October 11, 2002: 133 (concurred)

Waste Management, Inc. v. United Mexican States (ARB(AF)/00/3), Award dated April 30, 2004

Mondev v. USA, Award, October 11, 2002: 91, 95, 98 (concurred)

ADF v. USA, Award, 9 January 2003: 91–92, 96, 98 (concurred)

SD Myers v. Canada, Partial Award, November 13, 2000: 94, 98 (concurred)

Loewen v. USA, Award, June 26, 2003: 97, 98 (concurred)

MTD Equity Sdn. Bhd. And MTD Chile S.A. v. Republic of Chile (ARB/01/7), Award dated May 25, 2004

Tecmed v. Mexico, Award, May 29, 2003: 114–15 (concurred)

Waste Management v. Mexico, Award, April 30, 2004: 114 (concurred)

Occidental Exploration and Production Company v. The Republic of Ecuador (LCIA Case No. UN 3467), Final Award dated July 1, 2004

Metalclad v. Mexico, Award, August 25, 2000: 185 (concurred)

Tecmed v. Mexico, Award, May 29, 2003: 185 (concurred)

Gami Investments, Inc. v. The Government of the United Mexican States (NAFTA UNCITRAL Arbitration), Final Award dated November 15, 2004

SD Myers v. Canada, Partial Award, November 13, 2000: 93 (concurred)

Waste Management v. Mexico, Award, April 30, 2004: 95–97, 101 (concurred)

ADF v. USA, Award, 9 January 2003: 95 (concurred)

Neer claim (U.S.-Mexico), Decision, July 23, 2002: 95 (distinguished)

CMS Gas Transmission Company v. The Argentine Republic (ARB/01/8), Award dated May 12, 2005

Genin v. Estonia, Award, June 25, 2001: 276 (concurred)

Metalclad v. Mexico, Award, August 25, 2000: 278 (concurred)

Tecmed v. Mexico, Award, May 29, 2003: 279 (concurred)

Pope & Talbot v. Canada, Award, April 10, 2001: 282 (considered)

Eureko B.V. v. Republic of Poland, *Ad hoc* arbitration, Partial Award dated August 19, 2005

Tecmed v. Mexico, Award, May 29, 2003: 235 (concurred)

International Thunderbird Gaming Corporation v. The United Mexican States (NAFTA UNCITRAL Arbitration), Award dated January 26, 2006

Mondev v. USA, Award, October 11, 2002: 194 (concurred)

ADF v. USA, Award, 9 January 2003: 194 (concurred)

Waste Management v. Mexico, Award, June 2, 2000: 194 (concurred)

Waste Management v. Mexico, Award, April 30, 2004: 194 (concurred)

Neer claim (U.S.-Mexico), Decision, July 23, 2002: 194 (distinguished)

Genin v. Estonia, Award, June 25, 2001: 194 (concurred)

SD Myers v. Canada, Partial Award, November 13, 2000: 194 (concurred)

Azinian v. Mexico, Award, November 1, 1999: 194 (concurred)

Loewen v. USA, Award, June 26, 2003: 194 (concurred)

Elettronica Sicula (ELSI) (Canada v. Italy), ICJ, July 20, 1989: 194 (concurred)

Saluka Investments B.V. (The Netherlands) v. The Czech Republic (UNCITRAL Arbitration), Partial Award dated March 17, 2006

MTD v. Chile, Award, May 25, 2004: 297 (concurred)

SD Myers v. Canada, Partial Award, November 13, 2000: 297 (concurred)

Tecmed v. Mexico, Award, May 29, 2003: 302 (concurred)

CME v. Czech Republic, Award, September 13, 2001: 302 (concurred)

Waste Management v. Mexico, Award, April 30, 2004: 302 (concurred)

Occidental v. Ecuador, Award, July 1, 2004: 303–4 (distinguished)

SD Myers v. Canada, Partial Award, November 13, 2000: 305 (concurred)

Azurix Corp. v. The Argentine Republic (ARB/01/12), Award dated July 14, 2006

Tecmed v. Mexico, Award, May 29, 2003: 361, 371 (concurred)

Neer claim (U.S.-Mexico), Decision, July 23, 2002: 365, 372 (distinguished)

Genin v. Estonia, Award, June 25, 2001: 366–67, 372 (distinguished)

Mondev v. USA, Award, October 11, 2002: 368 (concurred)

ADF v. USA, Award, 9 January 2003: 368 (concurred)

Loewen v. USA, Award, June 26, 2003: 369 (concurred)

Waste Management v. Mexico, Award, April 30, 2004: 370 (concurred)

LG&E Energy Corp., LG&E Capital Corp., LG&E International Inc. v. Argentine Republic (ARB/02/1), Decision on Liability dated October 3, 2006

CMS v. Argentina, Award, May 12, 2005: 125, 127 (concurred)

Occidental v. Ecuador, Award, July 1, 2004: 125, 127, 128, 129 (concurred)

MTD v. Chile, Award, May 25, 2004: 125, 126, 127 (concurred)

Metalclad v. Mexico, Award, August 25, 2000: 125 (concurred)

Mondev v. USA, Award, October 11, 2002: 129 (concurred)

Tecmed v. Mexico, Award, May 29, 2003: 127, 128, 129 (concurred)

Waste Management v. Mexico, Award, April 30, 2004: 128, 129 (concurred)

Genin v. Estonia, Award, June 25, 2001: 129 (concurred)

BG Group Plc. V. Republic of Argentina (*Ad hoc* UNCITRAL Arbitration), Final Award dated December 24, 2007

Waste Management v. Mexico, Award, April 30, 2004: 292, 294, 301 (concurred)

Generation Ukraine v. Ukraine, Award, September 16, 2003: 295 (concurred)

Revere Copper and Brass, Inc. v. Overseas Private Investment Corp, Award, August 25, 1978, 56 ILR 258: 296 (concurred)

LG&E v. Argentina Decision on Liability, October 3, 2006: 297, 301 (concurred)

Saluka v. Czech Republic, Partial Award, March 17, 2006: 298 (concurred)

CMS v. Argentina, Award, May 12, 2005: 299 (concurred)

Genin v. Estonia, Award, June 25, 2001: 301 (concurred)

Mondev v. USA, Award, October 11, 2002: 301 (concurred)

Loewen v. USA, Award, June 26, 2003: 301 (concurred)

Occidental v. Ecuador, Award, July 1, 2004: 301 (concurred)

Tecmed v. Mexico, Award, May 29, 2003: 301 (concurred)

CMS v. Argentina, Award, May 12, 2005: 301 (concurred)

Azurix v. Argentina, Award, July 14, 2006: 301 (concurred)

Siemens AG v. Argentina, Decision on Jurisdiction, August 3, 2004: 301 (concurred)

Thunderbird v. Mexico, Award, January 26, 2006: 302 (concurred)

SD Myers v. Canada, Partial Award, November 13, 2000: 302 (concurred)

VI.   UMBRELLA CLAUSE

SGS Société Générale de Surveillance S.A. v. Republic of the Philippines (ARB/02/6), Decision on Jurisdiction dated January 29, 2004

SGS v. Pakistan, Decision on Jurisdiction, August 6, 2003:   95–97, 119–26 (distinguished)

Vivendi v. Argentina, Decision on Annulment, July 3, 2002: 122 (considered)

Joy Mining Machinery Limited v. Arab Republic of Egypt (ARB/03/11), Award on Jurisdiction dated August 6, 2004

Lauder v. Czech Republic, Final Award, September 3, 2001: 71 (considered)

Genin v. Estonia, Award, June 25, 2001: 71 (considered)

Vivendi v. Argentina, Award, November 21, 2000: 71 (considered)

CMS v. Argentina, Decision on Jurisdiction, July 17, 2003: 71 (considered), 76 (concurred)

Azurix v. Argentina, Decision on Jurisdiction, December 8, 2003: 71 (considered)

Vivendi v. Argentina, Decision on Annulment, July 3, 2002: 71 (considered), 75

(concurred)

Wena Hotels v. Egypt, Decision on Annulment, February 5, 2002: 71 (considered), 74 (concurred)

SGS v. Pakistan , Decision on Jurisdiction, August 6, 2003: 71, 77, 80 (considered)

SGS v. Philippines, Decision on Jurisdiction,, January 29, 2004: 71, 77, 80 (considered)

Salini Construttori S.p.A. and Italstrade S.p.a. v. Hashemite Kingdom of Jordan (ARB/02/13), Decision on Jurisdiction dated November 15, 2004

SGS v. Pakistan , Decision on Jurisdiction, August 6, 2003: 125-26 (distinguished)

SGS v. Philippines, Decision on Jurisdiction, January 29, 2004: 124-25 (distinguished), 130 (considered)

Young hi Oo Trading Pta v. Myanmar (ASEAN I.D. Case No. ARB/01/1), Award, March 31, 2003: 130 (considered)

CMS Gas Transmission Company v. The Argentine Republic (ARB/01/8), Decision on Jurisdiciton dated May 12, 2005

Lauder v. Czech Republic, Final Award, September 3, 2001: 300 (considered)

Genin v. Estonia, Award, June 25, 2001: 300 (considered)

Vivendi v. Argentina, Award, November 21, 2000: 300 (considered)

Azurix v. Argentina, Decision on Jurisdiction, December 8, 2003: 300 (considered)

SGS v. Pakistan, Decision on Jurisdiction, August 6, 2003: 300 (considered)

SGS v. Philippines, Decision on Jurisdiction, January 29, 2004: 300 (considered)

Eureko B.V. v. Republic of Poland (UNCITRAL), Partial Award dated August 19, 2005

Fedax v. Venezuela, Award, March 9, 1998: 252 (considered)

SGS v. Pakistan, Decision on Jurisdiction, August 6, 2003: 253, 257–58 (distinguished)

SGS v. Philippines, Decision on Jurisdiction, January 29, 2004: 255–57 (concurred)

Noble Ventures, Inc. v. Romania (ARB/01/11), Award dated October 12, 2005

SGS v. Pakistan, Decision on Jurisdiction, August 6, 2003: 47, 58 (considered)

SGS v. Philippines, Decision on Jurisdiction, January 29, 2004: 48, 59–60 (concurred)

Salini v. Jordan, Decision on Jurisdiction, November 15, 2004: 49, 57 (concurred)

El Paso Energy International Company v. The Argentine Republic (ARB/03/15), Decision on Jurisdiction dated April 27, 2006

SGS v. Philippines, Decision on Jurisdiction, January 29, 2004: 69, 76–77 (distinguished)

Noble Ventures v. Romania, Award, October 12, 2005: 69 (considered), 77 (distinguished)

SGS v. Pakistan, Decision on Jurisdiction, August 6, 2003: 71–74, 82, 85 (concurred)

Eureko v. Poland, Partial Award, August 19, 2005: 77 (considered)

Salini v. Jordan, Decision on Jurisdiction, November 15, 2004: 78 (considered)

Joy Mining v. Egypt, Award on Jurisdiction, August 6, 2004: 78, 79 (concurred)

Vivendi v. Argentina, Decision on Annulment, July 3, 2002: 79 (concurred)

Pan American Energy LLC, and BP Argentina Exploration Company v. The Argentine Republic (ARB/03/13) and BP America Production Company et. al. v. The Argentine Republic (ARB/04/8), Decision on Preliminary Objections dated July 27, 2006

SGS v. Philippines, Decision on Jurisdiction, January 29, 2004: 98, 104–5 (distinguished)

Noble Ventures v. Romania, Award, October 12, 2005: 98 (considered), 106 (partially distinguished)

SGS v. Pakistan, Decision on Jurisdiction, August 6, 2003: 100–3, 110, 111, 113 (concurred)

Eureko v. Poland, Partial Award, August 19, 2005: 106 (considered)

Salini v. Jordan, Decision on Jurisdiction, November 15, 2004: 107 (considered)

Joy Mining v. Egypt, Award on Jurisdiction, August 6, 2004: 107–9 (concurred)

495

Vivendi v. Argentina, Decision on Annulment, July 3, 2002: 108 (concurred)

LG&E Energy Corp., LG&E Capital Corp. and LG&E International Inc. v. Argentine Republic (ARB/02/1), Decision on Liability dated October 3, 2006

CMS v. Argentina, Decision on Jurisdiction, July 17, 2003: 171 (considered)

SGS v. Philippines, Decision on Jurisdiction, January 29, 2004: 171, 174 (considered)

Siemens A.G. v. The Argentine Republic (ARB/02/8), Award dated February 6, 2007

SGS v. Pakistan, Decision on Jurisdiction, August 6, 2003: 205 (considered)

SGS v. Philippines, Decision on Jurisdiction, January 29, 2004: 205 (considered)

Enron Corporation Ponderosa Assets, L.P. v. Argentine Republic (ARB/01/3), Award dated May 22, 2007

Fedax v. Venezuela, Award, March 9, 1998: 274 (considered)

SGS v. Philippines, Decision on Jurisdiction, January 29, 2004: 274 (considered)

Parkerings-Compagniet AS v. Lithuania (ARB/05/8), Award dated September 11, 2007

SGS v. Philippines, Decision on Jurisdiction, January 29, 2004: 262 (considered)

Vivendi v. Argentina, Decision on Annulment, July 3, 2002: 263 (considered)

Sempra Energy International v. Argentine Republic (ARB/02/16), Award dated September 28, 2007

Fedax v. Venezuela, Award, March 9, 1998: 309 (considered)

SGS v. Philippines, Decision on Jurisdiction, January 29, 2004: 309, 312 (considered), 310 (concurred)

Noble Ventures v. Romania, Award, October 12, 2005: 309 (considered)

SGS v. Pakistan, Decision on Jurisdiction, August 6, 2003: 309 (considered), 310 (concurred)

Joy Mining v. Egypt, Award on Jurisdiction, August 6, 2004: 309 (considered)

Salini v. Jordan, Decision on Jurisdiction, November 15, 2004: 309 (considered)

Impregilo v. Pakistan, Decision on Jurisdiction, April 22, 2005: 309, 310 (considered)

El Paso v. Argentina, Decision on Jurisdiction, April 27, 2006: 309 (considered)

Enron v. Argentina, Award, May 22, 2007: 309 (considered)

VII. CONTRACT CLAIM / TREATY CLAIM

Azurix Corp. v. The Argentine Republic (ARB/01/12), Decision on Jurisdiction dated December 8, 2003

Lanco v. Argentina, Decision on Jurisdiction, December 8, 1998: 78 (considered)

Aguas v. Argentina, Award, November 21, 2000: 78 (considered)

CMS v. Argentina, Decision on Jurisdiction, July 17, 2003: 89 (concurred)

Consortium RFCC v. Kingdom of Morocco (ARB/00/6), Award dated December 22, 2003

Vivendi v. Argentina, Decision on Annulment, July 3, 2002: 41 (concurred)

Genin v. Estonia, Award, June 25, 2001: 41 (concurred)

Azinian v.Mexico, Award, November 1, 1999: 41 (concurred)

Metalclad v. Mexico, Award, August 25, 2000: 42 (considered)

Maffezini v. Spain, Decision on Jurisdiction, January 25, 2000: 42 (considered)

Fedax v. Venezuela, Award, March 9, 1998: 43 (considered)

SGS Société Générale de Surveillance S.A. v. Republic of the Philippines (ARB/02/6), Decision on Jurisdiction dated January 29, 2004

SGS v. Pakistan , Decision on Jurisdiction, August 6, 2003: 133 (distinguished)

Salini v. Morocco, Decision on Jurisdiction, July 23, 2001: 135 (concurred)

497

Joy Mining Machinery Limited v. The Arab Republic of Egypt (ARB/03/11), Award on Jurisdiction dated August 6, 2004

Lauder v. Czech Republic, Final Award, September 3, 2001: 71 (considered)

Genin v. Estonia, Award, June 25, 2001: 71 (considered)

Aguas v. Argentina, Award, November 21, 2000: 71 (considered)

CMS v. Argentina, Decision on Jurisdiction, July 17, 2003: 71, 76 (concurred)

Azurix v. Argentina, Decision on Jurisdiction, December 8, 2003: 71 (considered)

SGS v. Pakistan , Decision on Jurisdiction, August 6, 2003: 71, 77, 80 (considered)

SGS v. Philippines, Decision on Jurisdiction,, January 29, 2004: 71 , 77, 80 (considered)

Wena Hotels v. Egypt, Decision on Annulment, February 5, 2002: 71, 74 (considered)

Vivendi v. Argentina, Decision on Annulment, July 3, 2002: 75 (concurred)

Impregilo SpA v. Islamic Republic of Pakistan (ARB/03/3), Decision on Jurisdiction dated April 22, 2005

Consortium RFCC v. Morocco, Decision on Jurisdiction, July 16, 2001: 215, 259 (concurred)

Cable Television of Nevis v. St. Kitts and Nevis, Award, January 13, 1997: 215 (concurred)

Vivendi v. Argentina, Decision on Annulment, July 3, 2002: 218, 256 (concurred)

Joy Mining v. Egypt, Award on Jurisdiction, August 6, 2004: 261 (concurred)

CMS Gas Transmission Company v. The Argentine Republic (ARB/01/8), Award dated May 12, 2005

Lauder v. Czech Republic, Final Award, September 3, 2001: 300 (considered)

Genin v. Estonia, Award, June 25, 2001: 300 (considered)

Aguas v. Argentina, Award, November 21, 2000: 300 (considered)

Azurix v. Argentina, Decision on Jurisdiction, December 8, 2003: 300 (considered)

SGS v. Pakistan , Decision on Jurisdiction, August 6, 2003: 300, (considered)

498

SGS v. Philippines, Decision on Jurisdiction,, January 29, 2004: 300 , (considered)

Joy Mining v. Egypt, Award on Jurisdiction, August 6, 2004: 300 (considered)

Bayindir Insaat Turizm Ticaret Ve Sanayi A.S. v. Islamic Republic of Pakistan (ARB/03/29), Decision on Jurisdiction dated November 14, 2005

Vivendi v. Argentina, Decision on Annulment, July 3, 2002: 166 (concurred)

Siemens A.G. v. The Argentine Republic (ARB/02/8), Award dated February 6, 2007

Consortium RFCC v. Morocco, Award, December 22, 2003: 248 (concurred)

Waste Management v. Mexico, Award, April 30, 2004: 249 (concurred)

SGS v. Philippines, Decision on Jurisdiction,, January 29, 2004: 250 (considered)

Jalapa Railroad case, US v. Mexico, 1948: 251 (concurred)

Salini v. Jordan, Decision on Jurisdiction, November 9, 2004: 252 (concurred)

VIII. ICSID ANNULMENT MECHANISM

Amco Asia Corporation v. Republic of Indonesia (ARB81/1), Decision on the Application for Annulment dated May 16, 1986 ("Amco I")

ROLE OF THE ANNULMENT MECHANISM

Klöckner v. Cameroon, Decision on Annulment, May 3, 1985: 22 (concurred)

FAILURE TO STATE REASONS

Application for review of Judgment No. 158 of the United Nations Administrative Tribunal 1973 ICJ REP 166: 39 (considered)

Case Concerning the Arbitral Award made by the King of Spain on 23 December 1906 (Honduras v. Nicaragua), Judgment of November 18, 1960, 1960 ICJ REP 192: 41 (considered)

Klöckner v. Cameroon, Decision on Annulment, May 3, 1985: 42, 43 (concurred)

Amco Asia Corporation v. Republic of Indonesia (ARB/81/1), Decision on Annulment dated December 3, 1992 ("Amco II")

MANIFEST EXCESS OF POWERS

Amco v. Indonesia, Decision on Annulment, May 16, 1986: 7.38 (concurred)

FAILURE TO STATE REASONS

Case concerning the Arbitral Award of July 31, 1989 (Guinea-Bissau v. Senegal) 1991 ICJ REP 53: 8.08 (concurred)

SERIOUS DEPARTURE FROM A FUNDAMENTAL RULE OF PROCEDURE

MINE v. Guinea, Decision on Annulment, December 22, 1989: 9.08, 9.09 (concurred)

Wena Hotels Limited v. Arab Republic of Egypt (ARB/98/4), Decision on the Application by the Arab Republic of Egypt for Annulment dated February 5, 2002

ROLE OF THE ANNULMENT MECHANISM

Klöckner v. Cameroon, Decision on Annulment, May 3, 1985: 18 (considered)

Amco v. Indonesia, Decision on Annulment, May 16, 1986: 18 (considered)

MINE v. Guinea, Decision on Annulment, December 22, 1989: 18 (considered)

MANIFEST EXCESS OF POWERS

Klöckner v. Cameroon, Decision on Annulment, May 3, 1985: 22, 38 (considered)

Amco v. Indonesia, Decision on Annulment, May 16, 1986: 22 (considered)

MINE v. Guinea, Decision on Annulment, December 22, 1989: 22 (considered)

SERIOUS DEPARTURE FROM A FUNDAMENTAL RULE OF PROCEDURE

MINE v. Guinea, Decision on Annulment, December 22, 1989: 58 (concurred)

FAILURE TO STATE REASONS

Klöckner v. Cameroon, Decision on Annulment, May 3, 1985: 78 (considered), 79 (concurred)

Amco v. Indonesia, Decision on Annulment, May 16, 1986: 78 (considered)

MINE v. Guinea, Decision on Annulment, December 22, 1989: 78 (considered)

Compañia de Aguas del Aconquija S.A. and Vivendi Universal v. Argentine Republic (ARB/97/3), Decision on Annulment dated July 3, 2002

ROLE OF THE ANNULMENT MECHANISM

MINE v. Guinea, Decision on Annulment, December 22, 1989: 62, 66 (concurred)

CDC Group plc v. Republic of the Seychelles (ARB/02/14), Decision of the Ad Hoc Committee on the Application for Annulment of the Republic of Seychelles dated June 29, 2005

ROLE OF THE ANNULMENT MECHANISM

Klöckner v. Cameroon, Decision on Annulment, May 3, 1985: 35 (distinguished)

Amco v. Indonesia, Decision on Annulment, May 16, 1986: 35 (distinguished)

MINE v. Guinea, Decision on Annulment, December 22, 1989: 35 (concurred)

Vivendi v. Argentina, Decision on Annulment, July 3, 2002: 35, 37 (concurred)

Wena Hotels v. Egypt, Decision on Annulment, February 5, 2002: 35 (concurred)

MANIFEST EXCESS OF POWERS

Amco v. Indonesia, Decision on Jurisdiction, September 25, 1983: 42 (concurred)

MINE v. Guinea, Decision on Annulment, December 22, 1989: 39, 43 (considered)

Wena Hotels v. Egypt, Decision on Annulment, February 5, 2002: 41, 46 (concurred)

SERIOUS DEPARTURE FROM A FUNDAMENTAL RULE OF PROCEDURE

MINE v. Guinea, Decision on Annulment, December 22, 1989: 48, 49 (concurred)

Wena Hotels v. Egypt, Decision on Annulment, February 5, 2002: 48 (considered), 49 (concurred)

FAILURE TO STATE REASONS

Klöckner v. Cameroon, Decision on Annulment, May 3, 1985: 66 (distinguished)

Amco v. Indonesia, Decision on Annulment, May 16, 1986: 66 (distinguished)

MINE v. Guinea, Decision on Annulment, December 22, 1989: 67, 70, 75 (concurred)

Vivendi v. Argentina, Decision on Annulment, July 3, 2002: 68 (considered)

Wena Hotels v. Egypt, Decision on Annulment, February 5, 2002: 69, 70 (considered)

Patrick Mitchell v. the Democratic Republic of Congo (ARB/99/7), Decision on the Application for Annulment dated November 1, 2006

ROLE OF THE ANNULMENT MECHANISM

MINE v. Guinea, Decision on Annulment, December 22, 1989: 19 (concurred)

Vivendi v. Argentina, Decision on Annulment, July 3, 2002: 19 (concurred)

Wena Hotels v. Egypt, Decision on Annulment, February 5, 2002: 19 (concurred)

MANIFEST EXCESS OF POWERS

MINE v. Guinea, Decision on Annulment, December 22, 1989: 56 (concurred)

Wena Hotels v. Egypt, Decision on Annulment, February 5, 2002: 20 (concurred)

FAILURE TO STATE REASONS

MINE v. Guinea, Decision on Annulment, December 22, 1989: 21 (concurred)

Repsol YPF Ecuador, S.A. v. Empresa Estatal Petróleos del Ecuador (Petroecuador) (ARB/01/10), Decision on the Application for Annulment dated January 8, 2007

MANIFEST EXCESS OF POWERS

Klöckner v. Cameroon, Decision on Annulment, May 3, 1985: 39 (concurred)

Amco v. Indonesia, Decision on Annulment, May 16, 1986: 40 (concurred)

MINE v. Guinea, Decision on Annulment, December 22, 1989: 41 (concurred)

Wena Hotels v. Egypt, Decision on Annulment, February 5, 2002: 36, 81 (concurred)

MTD Equity Sdn. Bhd. And MTD Chile S.A. v. Republic of Chile (ARB/01/77), Decision on Annulment dated March 21, 2007

ROLE OF THE ANNULMENT MECHANISM

Klöckner v. Cameroon, Decision on Annulment, May 3, 1985: 52 (concurred), 54

(distinguished)

Amco v. Indonesia, Decision on Annulment, May 16, 1986: 52 (concurred), 54 (distinguished)

MINE v. Guinea, Decision on Annulment, December 22, 1989: 52 (concurred)

Amco v. Indonesia, Decision on Annulment, December 3, 1992: 52 (concurred), 54 (distinguished)

Wena Hotels v. Egypt, Decision on Annulment, February 5, 2002: 52 (concurred)

Vivendi v. Argentina, Decision on Annulment, July 3, 2002: 52 (concurred)

CDC v. Seychelles, Decision on Annulment, June 29, 2005: 52 (concurred)

Patrick Mitchell v. DRC, Decision on Annulment, November 1, 2006: 52 (concurred)

MANIFEST EXCESS OF POWERS

MINE v. Guinea, Decision on Annulment, December 22, 1989: 45, 47 (concurred)

CDC v. Seychelles, Decision on Annulment, June 29, 2005: 45, 47 (concurred)

SERIOUS DEPARTURE FROM A FUNDAMENTAL RULE OF PROCEDURE

Wena Hotels v. Egypt, Decision on Annulment, February 5, 2002: 49 (concurred)

FAILURE TO STATE REASONS

Amco v. Indonesia, Decision on Annulment, May 16, 1986: 50 (concurred)

MINE v. Guinea, Decision on Annulment, December 22, 1989: 50 (concurred)

Amco v. Indonesia, Decision on Annulment, December 3, 1992: 50 (concurred)

Wena Hotels v. Egypt, Decision on Annulment, February 5, 2002: 50 (concurred)

Vivendi v. Argentina, Decision on Annulment, July 3, 2002: 50, 78 (concurred)

CDC v. Seychelles, Decision on Annulment, June 29, 2005: 50 (concurred)

Patrick Mitchell v. DRC, Decision on Annulment, November 1, 2006: 50 (concurred)

COSTS

Klöckner v. Cameroon, Decision on Annulment, May 3, 1985: 111 (concurred)

Amco v. Indonesia, Decision on Annulment, May 16, 1986: 111 (concurred)

Amco v. Indonesia, Decision on Annulment, December 3, 1992: 111 (concurred)

Wena Hotels v. Egypt, Decision on Annulment, February 5, 2002: 111 (concurred)

Vivendi v. Argentina, Decision on Annulment, July 3, 2002: 111 (concurred)

CDC v. Seychelles, Decision on Annulment, June 29, 2005: 111 (concurred)

Patrick Mitchell v. DRC, Decision on Annulment, November 1, 2006: 111 (concurred)

Husein Nuaman Soufraki v. The United Arab Emirates (ARB/02/7) Decision on Annulment dated June 5, 2007

ROLE OF THE ANNULMENT MECHANISM

Klöckner v. Cameroon, Decision on Annulment, May 3, 1985: 21 (concurred), 25 (distinguished)

Amco v. Indonesia, Decision on Annulment, May 16, 1986: 21 (concurred)

MINE v. Guinea, Decision on Annulment, December 22, 1989: 21, 25 (concurred)

Wena Hotels v. Egypt, Decision on Annulment, February 5, 2002: 21 (concurred)

Vivendi v. Argentina, Decision on Annulment, July 3, 2002: 21 (concurred), 26 (considered)

MTD v. Chile, Decision on Annulment, March 21, 2007: 20 (concurred)

MANIFEST EXCESS OF POWERS

Klöckner v. Cameroon, Decision on Annulment, May 3, 1985: 85 (considered)

Amco v. Indonesia, Decision on Annulment, May 16, 1986: 85 (considered)

MINE v. Guinea, Decision on Annulment, December 22, 1989: 101 (concurred)

Wena Hotels v. Egypt, Decision on Annulment, February 5, 2002: 39, 63 (concurred), 111 (considered)

CDC v. Seychelles, Decision on Annulment, June 29, 2005: 39 (concurred)

Vivendi v. Argentina, Decision on Annulment, July 3, 2002: 43 (considered)

MTD v. Chile, Decision on Annulment, March 21, 2007: 94, 118 (concurred)

FAILURE TO STATE REASONS

Klöckner v. Cameroon, Decision on Annulment, May 3, 1985: 123, 125 (concurred)

Amco v. Indonesia, Decision on Annulment, May 16, 1986: 123 (concurred)

MINE v. Guinea, Decision on Annulment, December 22, 1989: 123 (concurred)

Wena Hotels v. Egypt, Decision on Annulment, February 5, 2002: 125 (concurred)

Vivendi v. Argentina, Decision on Annulment, July 3, 2002: 124 (concurred)

CDC v. Seychelles, Decision on Annulment, June 29, 2005: 128 (concurred)

COSTS

Klöckner v. Cameroon, Decision on Annulment, May 3, 1985: 138 (concurred)

Amco v. Indonesia, Decision on Annulment, May 16, 1986: 138 (concurred)

MINE v. Guinea, Decision on Annulment, December 22, 1989: 138 (concurred)

Amco v. Indonesia, Decision on Annulment, December 3, 1992: 138 (concurred)

Wena Hotels v. Egypt, Decision on Annulment, February 5, 2002: 138 (concurred)

Vivendi v. Argentina, Decision on Annulment, July 3, 2002: 138 (concurred)

Patrick Mitchell v. DRC, Decision on Annulment, November 1, 2006: 138 (concurred)

MTD v. Chile, Decision on Annulment, March 21, 2007: 138 (concurred)

Industria Nacional de Alimentos, S.A. and Indalsa Peru, S.A. v. The Republic of Peru (ARB/03/4), Decision on Annulment dated September 5, 2007

FAILURE TO STATE REASONS

MINE v. Guinea, Decision on Annulment, December 22, 1989: 127 (concurred)

Vivendi v. Argentina, Decision on Annulment, July 3, 2002: 128 (concurred)

CMS Gas Transmission Company v. Argentine Republic (ARB/01/8) Decision on Annulment dated September 25, 2007

ROLE OF THE ANNULMENT MECHANISM

Klöckner v. Cameroon, Decision on Annulment, May 3, 1985: 43 (concurred)

Amco v. Indonesia, Decision on Annulment, May 16, 1986: 43 (concurred)

MINE v. Guinea, Decision on Annulment, December 22, 1989: 43 (concurred)

Amco v. Indonesia, Decision on Annulment, December 3, 1992: 43 (concurred)

Wena Hotels v. Egypt, Decision on Annulment, February 5, 2002: 43 (concurred)

Vivendi v. Argentina, Decision on Annulment, July 3, 2002: 43, 99 (concurred)

CDC v. Seychelles, Decision on Annulment, June 29, 2005: 43 (concurred)

Patrick Mitchell v. DRC, Decision on Annulment, November 1, 2006: 43 (concurred)

MTD v. Chile, Decision on Annulment, March 21, 2007: 43, 44 (concurred)

Soufraki v. United Arab Emirates, Decision on Annulment, June 5, 2007: 43 (concurred)

MANIFEST EXCESS OF POWERS

Klöckner v. Cameroon, Decision on Annulment, May 3, 1985: 46 (concurred)

MINE v. Guinea, Decision on Annulment, December 22, 1989: 50 (concurred)

MTD v. Chile, Decision on Annulment, March 21, 2007: 51 (concurred)

FAILURE TO STATE REASONS

Vivendi v. Argentina, Decision on Annulment, July 3, 2002: 54 (concurred)

MINE v. Guinea, Decision on Annulment, December 22, 1989: 55 (concurred)

Wena Hotels v. Egypt, Decision on Annulment, February 5, 2002: 56 (concurred)

COSTS

MTD v. Chile, Decision on Annulment, March 21, 2007: 161 (distinguished)

ANNEX 7

LIST OF PARTICIPANTS

Kamel Achour
Sonatrach

Brooks E. Allen
Sidley Austin LLP

Yas Banifatemi
Shearman & Sterling LLP

John Beechey
Clifford Chance LLP

Pierre-André Beguin
Budin & Associés

Cyrus Benson
Gibson, Dunn & Crutcher LLP

Patrick Bernard
Bernard – Hertz – Béjot

Jean-Georges Betto
Derains & Associés

Emmanuel Bidanda
P3B Avocats

Nigel Blackaby
Freshfields Bruckhaus Deringer

Sylvian Bollée
Université de Reims Champagne-Ardenne

Laurie Achtouk-Spivak
Cleary Gottlieb Steen & Hamilton LLP

Hervé Ascensio
Université Paris I-Panthéon-Sorbonne

Geneviève Bastid-Burdeau
Université Paris I-Panthéon-Sorbonne

Vincent Begle
Norton Rose LLP

Walid Ben Hamida
Université d'Evry

Andrew Berkely
A.W.A. Berkely FCIArb

Sébastien Besson
Python & Peter

Sundip K. Bhundia
Python & Peter

Marion Biniadakis

Karl-Heinz Böckstiegel
University of Cologne

Mireille Bouzols Breton
Technip France

David Branson

Louis-Alexis Bret

Emmanuelle Cabrol
Herbert Smith LLP

Paulo Borba Casella
Casella, Advogados

Philippe Cavalieros
Renault SAS

Mohammed Chemloul

James Claxton

Sandrine Colletier
Clifford Chance LLP

Anna Crevon
Shearman & Sterling LLP

Alberto Croze
Dewey & Leboeuf LLP

Marie Danis
August & Debouzy

Jane Davies-Evans
Freshfields Bruckhaus Deringer

Andrew de Lotbinière McDougall
White & Case LLP

Séverine Brejon de Lavergnée
Total S.A.

Nicolas Brooke
Freshfields Bruckhaus Deringer

Phillip Capper
Lovells LLP

James Castello
Dewey & Leboeuf LLP

Pierre Charreton
France Telecom

Blanche Cheron

Charles Claypoole
Eversheds LLP

James R. Crawford
University of Cambridge

Antonio Crivellaro
*Bonelli Erede Pappalardo Studio
Leglale*

Georges – Albert Dal
Dal & Veldekens

Coralie Darrigade
Shearman & Sterling LLP

Matthieu de Boisséson
Darrois Villey Maillot Brochier

Douis Degos
Eversheds Frere Cholmeley

Jean-Louis Delvolvé
Fleury Quentin Marès Devolvé Rouche

Louis-Christophe Delanoy
Bredin Prat

Stéphane de Navacelle
Debevoise & Plimpton LLP

Antonias Dimolista
A. Dimolista et Associés

Sarah Dookhum
Law Business Research Ltd

Carroll Dorgan
Jones Day

Jennifer Doucleff
Latham & Watkins LLP

Christophe Dugué
Shearman & Sterling LLP

Pierre Duprey
Darrois Villey Maillot Brochier

Phillip Dunham
Dechert

Stuart Dutson
Eversheds LLP

Dominique Falque
Falque et Associés

Raëd Fathallah
Bredin Prat

Julien Fouret
Salans

Sarah François-Poncet
Salans

Laurence Franc-Menget
Gide Loyrette Nouel

Emmanuel Gaillard
Shearman & Sterling LLP

Jean-Yves Garaud
Cleary Gottlieb Steen & Hamilton LLP

José Manuel Garcia Represa
Latham & Watkins LLp

Paul–A. Gelinas

Teresa Giovannini
Lalive

Mattias Göransson
Mannheimer Swartling

Laurent Gouiffes
Allen & Overy LLP

Luc Grellet
Bouloy Grellet & Godin

Jacob Grierson
Jones Day

Sarah Grimmer
Permanent Court of Arbitration

509

Christine Guerrier
Thales

Pierre-Yves Gunter
Python & Peter

Paul B. Hannon

John Heaps
Eversheds LLP

Marc Henry
Lovells LLP

Jean-Christophe Honlet
Salans

Arnaud Ingen-Housz

Charles Jarrosson
Université Paris II-Panthéon-Assas

Anna Joubin-Bret
United Nations Conference on Trade & Development

Jennifer Juvenal
Landwell & Associés

Gabrielle Kaufmann-Kohler
Lévy Kaufmann-Kohler

Laurence Kiffer
Teynier, Pic & Associés

Joachim Knoll
Lalive

Judge Gilbert Guillaume

Lara Hammond
ICC International Court of Arbitration

Christian Hausmann
Hammonds Hausmann

Pierre Heitzmann
Jones Day

Anne Herrmann
Salans

Alexandre Hory
AH Conseil

Laurent Jaeger
Latham & Watkins LLP

Sigvard Jarvin
Jones Day

Patrick Julliard
Université Paris I-Panthéon-Sorbonne

Tamman Kaissi

Elie Kleiman
Freshfields Bruckhause Deringer

François Knoepfler
KGG et Associés

Joachim Kuckenburg
KAB-Kuckenburg-Bureth Associés

Michel Laurendeau

Charles Leben
Université Paris II-Panthéon-Assas

Thorsten Leijonhielm
Mannheimer Swartling

Loretta Malintoppi
Eversheds Frere Cholmeley

Fernando Mantilla-Serrano
Shearman & Sterling LLP

Arthur L. Marriott
Dewey & Leboeuf LLP

Marina Matousekova
Castaldi Mourre & Partners

Mark McNeill
Shearman & Sterling LLP

Marina Mendes Costa
ICC International Court of Arbitration

Isabelle Michou
Herbert Smith LLP

Marie-Joëlle Minoret
Total S.A.

Reza Mohtashami
Freshfields Bruckhause Deringer

Félix J. Montero Muriel
Perez Llorca

Benoît Le Bars
Landwell & Associés

Barton Legum
Debevoise & Plimpton LLP

Bruno Leurent
Winston & Strawn LLP

Sébastien Manciaux
Université de Bourgogne / CREDIMI

Patrick Marès
Fleury Quentin Marès Delvolvé Rouche

David Marteau
Eurotunnel

Pierre Mayer
Dechert

Mélanie Meilhac
ICC International Court of Arbitration

Francis Meyrier
Meyrier Fayout Lacoste

Wendy Miles
Wilmer Cutler Pickering Hale and Dorr LLP

Laurence Mitrovic
Skadden Arps

Frans Mol
Bunge S.A.

Andy Moody
McDermott Will & Emery UK LLP

511

Alexis Mourre
Castaldi Mourre & Partners

Jean-Claude Najar
GE Commercial Finance

Lawrence W. Newman
Baker & McKenzie LLP

Bassam Onaissi

Michael Ottolenghi
Iran-United States Claims Tribunal

François Perret
Université de Genève

Mirèze Philippe
ICC International Court of Arbitration

Michael A. Polkinghorne
White & Case LLP

Tim Portwood
Bredin Prat

Yannick Radi
European University Institute

David Reed
Shearman & Sterling LLP

Benjamin Remy
Université de Poitiers

Claude Reymond
Professeur émérite de l'Université de Lausanne

Charles Nairac
White & Case LLP

Sophie Nappert
Denton Wilde Sapte LLP

Corinne Nguyen
Jones Day

Jérôme Ortscheidt
SCP Vuitton

William W. Park
Boston University Law Faculty

Georgios Petrochilos
Freshfields Bruckhaus Deringer

Philippe Pinsolle
Shearman & Sterling LLP

Charles Poncet
ZPG

Olivier Purcell
Holman Fenwick & Willan

Rupert Reece
Gide Loyrette Nouel

Douglas Reichert

Marie-Estelle Rey
United Nations Conference on Trade & Development

Caroline S. Richard
Freshfields Bruckhause Deringer

José Rosell
Hughes Hubbard & Reed LLP

Jean Rouche
Fleury Quentin Marès Delvolvé Rouche

Deborah Ruff
Dewey & Leboeuf LLP

Anne-Véronique Schaepfer
Schellenberg Wittmer

Franz Schwartz
Wilmer Cutler Pickering Hale and Dorr LLP

David Sellers
Eversheds Frere Cholmeley

Christophe Seraglini
Université de Paris XI

Benjamin Siino
August & Debouzy

Henri-Michel Siraga
Dassault Aviation

Michel Soumrani
Soumrani Lawyers & Legal Counsels

Tania Steenkamp
Shearman & Sterling LLP

Marie Stoyanov
Gide Loyrette Nouel

Peter Rosher
Clifford Chance LLP

Patrick Rothey
Eramet

Youcef Saci
Sonatrach

Michael E. Schneider
Lalive

Eric Schwartz
Dewey & Leboeuf LLP

Christopher R. Seppala
White & Case LLP

Stewart Shackleton
Eversheds LLP

Eduardo Silva Romero
Dechert

Bengt Sjövall
Mannheimer Swartling

Vincenzo Spandri
Benelli Erede Pappalardo Studio Legale

Brigitte Stern
Université Paris I-Panthéon-Sorbonne

Edouard Taÿ Pamart
Holman Fenwick & Willan

Guillaume Tattevin
Permanent Court of Arbitration

William Thomas
Eversheds Frere Cholmeley

Ignacio L. Torterola

Marc van der Haegen
NautaDutilh S.p.r.l.

Ana Vermal
Proskauer Rose LLP

Anne-Pascale Vitale
Champetier de Ribes Spitzer Avocats

Emmanuel Vuillard
Alstom Holdings

Prosper Weil
Professeur émérite de l'Université Paris II-Panthéon Assas

Jane Willems

Matthew Secomb
White & Case LLP

Eric Teynier
Teynier, Pic & Associés

Rachel Thorn
Latham & Watkins LLP

François-Xavier Train
Université de Paris X-Nanterre

Gaëtan Verhoosel
Debevoise & Plimpton LLP

Francisco Victoria-Andreu

Christophe Von Krause
White & Case LLP

Thomas Wälde
Essex Court Chambers

Todd Wetmore
Shearman & Sterling LLP

Roland Ziadé
Cleary Gottlieb Steen & Hamilton LLP

Jean-Pierre Grandjean
Clifford Chance LLP

ANNEX 8

Table of Abbreviations

A.C.	Law Reports, Appeal Cases
All E.R.	All England Law Reports
A.L.R.	Australian Law Reports
AM. J. INT'L L.	American Journal of International Law
AM. REV. INT'L ARB.	American Review of International Arbitration
ARB. INT'L	Arbitration International
ATF	Arrêts du Tribunal fédéral suisse
BRITISH Y.B. INT'L L.	British Yearbook of International Law
BULL. ASA	Bulletin de l'Association Suisse d'Arbitrage
Chron.	Chronique (Dalloz, Petites affiches)
COLUM. L. REV.	Columbia Law Review
F.2d	Federal Reporter 2d Series
F.3d	Federal Reporter 3d Series
FORDHAM INT'L L.J.	Fordham International Law Journal
FORDHAM L. REV.	Fordham Law Review

F.R.D.	Federal Rules Decisions
Gaz. Pal.	Gazette du Palais
HARV. L. REV.	Harvard Law Review
ICC BULL.	ICC International Court of Arbitration Bulletin
I.C.J. REPORTS	International Court of Justice, *Reports of Judgments, Advisory Opinions and Orders*
ICSID REP.	ICSID Reports
ICSID REV.	ICSID Review – Foreign Investment Law Journal
I.L.M.	International Legal Materials
I.L.R.	International Law Reports
INT'L & COMP. L.Q.	International and Comparative Law Quarterly
INT'L ARB. REP.	International Arbitration Report
INT'L CONSTR. L. REV.	International Construction Law Review
INT'L L. REP.	International Law Reports
J. APP. PRAC. & PROCESS	Journal of Appelate Practice & Process
J.D.I.	Journal du droit international (Clunet)
JdT	Journal des tribunaux (Swiss publication)
J. INT'L ARB.	Journal of International Arbitration

J. WORLD INV. / J. WORLD INV. & TRADE	Journal of World Investment / Journal of World Investment & Trade
Lloyd's Rep.	Lloyd's Law Reports
L.Q. REV.	The Law Quarterly Review
P.C.I.J., Series A	Permanent Court of International Justice, Collection of Judgments
REV. ARB.	Revue de l'arbitrage
REV. CRIT. DIP	Revue critique de droit international privé
STOCKHOLM ARB. REP.	Stockholm Arbitration Report
TDM	Transnational Dispute Management
TEXAS INT'L L.J.	Texas International Law Journal
U.C. DAVIS J. INT'L L. & POL'Y	UC Davis Journal of International Law & Policy
U.N.R.I.A.A.	United Nations Reports of International Arbitral Awards
U.N.T.S.	United Nations Treaty Series
W.L.R.	Weekly Law Reports
WORLD TRADE & ARB. M.	World Trade and Arbitration Materials
Y.B. COM. ARB.	Yearbook Commercial Arbitration

ANNEX 9

Table of Authorities [*]

A. INTERNATIONAL DECISIONS

1. Mixed Commissions

Neer Case (United States v. Mexico), 4 U.N.R.I.A.A. 60 (Gen. Cl. Comm'n 1926)	GKK 140

2. Ad Hoc

In the Matter of an Arbitration between Petroleum Dev. (Trucial Coast) Ltd. and the Sheikh of Abu Dhabi, Award, Aug. 28, 1951, 1 INT'L & COMP. L.Q. 247 (1952)	CS 84
Saudi Arabia v. Arabian American Oil Company (ARAMCO), Award, Aug. 23, 1958, 27 INT'L L. REP. 117 (1963); for a French translation, see 1963 REV. CRIT. DIP 272	AM 45
CME Czech Republic B.V. v. Czech Republic (UNCITRAL), Partial Award, Sept. 13, 2001	GKK 141
Pope & Talbot Inc. v. Canada (UNCITRAL (NAFTA) Arbitration), Award in respect of Damages, May 31, 2002, 7 ICSID REP. 148 (2002)	JC 98
Methanex Corporation v. United States of America (NAFTA (UNCITRAL) Arbitration), Final Award, Aug. 3, 2005	TW 120
Eureko B.V. v. Republic of Poland (UNCITRAL), Partial Award, Aug. 19, 2005, 12 ICSID REP. 331 (2005)	JC 103 GKK 141, 142
International Thunderbird Gaming Corporation v. United Mexican States (UNCITRAL (NAFTA) Arbitration), Award, Jan. 26, 2006	JC 102 GKK 141
International Thunderbird Gaming Corporation v. United	TW 114

---

[*] References are made to authors' initials and page numbers.

519

Mexican States (UNCITRAL (NAFTA) Arbitration), Separate Opinion of Thomas Wälde, Jan. 26, 2006	GKK 147
Saluka Investments BV (The Netherlands) v. Czech Republic, Partial Award, Mar. 17, 2006	GKK 141
BG Group Plc. v. Argentine Republic (UNCITRAL), Final Award, Dec. 24, 2007	GKK 143

3. ICC

ICC Case Nos. 3790/3902/4050/4051/4054 (joined cases), 1984 Final award	CS 77
ICC Case No. 4131, Dow Chemical France v. Isover Saint Gobain, Sept. 23, 1982 Interim Award, IX Y.B. COM. ARB. 131, 136 (1984)	AM 45
ICC Case No. 5721, European company v. American and Egyptian parties, 1990 Award, 117 J.D.I. 1020 (1990) (observations by Y. Derains)	AM 45
ICC Case No. 5730, 1988 Award, 117 J.D.I 1029 (1990) (observations by Y. Derains)	AM 45
ICC Case No. 6158	CS 79
ICC Case No. 6519, French Group of Companies v. English company, 1991 Award, 118 J.D.I 1065 (1991) (observations by Y. Derains)	AM 45
ICC Case No. 6673, Licensor v. Licensee, 1992 Award, 119 J.D.I 992 (1992) (observations by D. Hascher)	AM 45
ICC Case No. 7155, Norwegian Company v. Three French Companies, 1993 Award, 123 J.D.I 1037 (1996) (observations by J.-J. Arnaldez)	AM 45

4. ICSID

AES Corporation v. The Argentine Republic (ICSID Case No. ARB/02/17), Decision on Jurisdiction dated April 25, 2005	Annex 1
Azurix Corp. v. Argentine Republic (ICSID Case No.	GKK 139

ARB/01/12), Decision on Jurisdiction, Dec. 8, 2003, 43 I.L.M. 262 (2004); 16:2 WORLD TRADE & ARB. M. 111 (2004); 2004 Bull. ASA 95; for a French translation, see 131 J.D.I. 276 (2004) (excerpts) (observations by E. Gaillard at 282) 131 JDI 282 (2004) (observations)	
Azurix Corp. v. Argentine Republic (ICSID Case No. ARB/01/12), Award, July 14, 2006	GKK 140–41, 141
Bayindir Insaat Turizm Ticaret Ve Sanayi A.S. v. Islamic Republic of Pakistan (ICSID Case No. ARB/03/29), Decision on Jurisdiction, Nov. 14, 2005, 21(1) INT'L ARB. REP. A-1 (2006)	GKK 139
Biwater Gauff (Tanzania) Limited v. United Republic of Tanzania (ICSID Case No. ARB/05/22), Procedural Order No. 3, Sept. 29, 2006	TW 128
BP America Production Company and others v. Argentine Republic (ICSID Case No. ARB/04/8), Decision on Jurisdiction, July 27, 2006	GKK 139
CMS Gas Transmission Company v. Argentine Republic (ICSID Case No. ARB/01/8), Award, May 12, 2005, 44 ILM 1205 (2005)	GKK 139, 140–41, 141, 142, 143
CMS Gas Transmission Company v. Argentine Republic (ICSID Case No. ARB/01/8), Decision of the *ad hoc* committee on the application for annulment of the Argentine Republic, Sept. 25, 2007, 46 I.L.M. 1136 (2007)	JC 103 GKK 142, 143, 146
Compañía de Aguas del Aconquija S.A. and Compagnie Générale des Eaux (Vivendi Universal) v. Argentine Republic (ICSID Case No. ARB/97/3), Award, Nov. 21, 2000, 5 ICSID REP. 299 (2002); 16 ICSID REV. 643 (2001); 40 I.L.M. 426 (2001); XXVI Y.B. COM. ARB. 62 (2001) (excerpts); for a French translation, see 130 J.D.I. 232 (2003) (excerpts)	JC 103
Compañia de Aguas del Aconquija S.A. and Compagnie Générale des Eaux (Vivendi Universal) v. Argentine Republic (ICSID Case No. ARB/97/3), Decision on	JC 103 GKK 139

Annulment, July 3, 2002, 6 ICSID REP. 340 (2004); 19 ICSID REV. 89 (2004); 41 I.L.M. 1135 (2002); 2003 BULL. ASA 346 (excerpts); for a French translation, see 130 JDI 195 (2003) (observations by E. Gaillard at 230)	
Compañia de Aguas del Aconquija S.A. and Compagnie Générale des Eaux (Vivendi Universal) v. Argentine Republic (ICSID Case No. ARB/97/3), Award, Aug. 20, 2007	GKK 139
Consortium R.F.C.C. v. Kingdom of Morocco (ICSID Case No. ARB/00/6), Award, Dec. 22, 2003 [French original], 20 ICSID REV. 391 (2005)	GKK 139
El Paso Energy International Company v. Argentine Republic (ICSID Case No. ARB/03/15), Decision on Jurisdiction, Apr. 27, 2006, 21 ICSID REV. 488 (2006)	JC 103 GKK 142
Enron Corporation and Ponderosa Assets, L.P. v. Argentine Republic (ICSID Case No. ARB/01/3), Award, May 22, 2007	GKK 140–41, 141, 142, 143
Impregilo S.p.A. v. Islamic Republic of Pakistan (ICSID Case No. ARB/03/3), Decision on Jurisdiction, Apr. 22, 2005	GKK 139
Joy Mining Machinery Limited v. Arab Republic of Egypt (ICSID Case No. ARB/03/11), Award, Aug. 6, 2004, 44 I.L.M. 73 (2005); 19 ICSID REV. 486 (2004); for a French translation, see 132 J.D.I. 163 (2005) (excerpts) (observations by E. Gaillard at 177)	GKK 139, 142
Lanco International, Inc. v. Argentine Republic (ICSID Case No. ARB/97/6), Preliminary Decision on Jurisdiction, Dec. 8, 1998, 40 I.L.M. 457 (2001)	GKK 138
LG&E Capital Corp. and LG&E International Inc. v. Argentine Republic (ICSID Case No. ARB/02/1), Decision on Liability, Oct. 3, 2006	GKK 141, 142, 143
Metalclad Corporation v. United Mexican States (ICSID Case No. ARB(AF)/97/1), Award, Aug. 30, 2000, 5 ICSID REP. 212 (2002) ; 16 ICSID REV. 168 (2001); 40 ILM 36 (2001); 119 I.L.R. 618 (2002); XXVI Y.B. COM. ARB. 103 (2001) (excerpts); 16(1) INT'L ARB. REP. A-1	GKK 141

(2001); 13 WORLD TRADE & ARB. M. 47 (2001); for a French translation, see 129 J.D.I. 233 (2002) (excerpts) (observations by E. Gaillard at 190)	
Mondev International Ltd. v. United States of America (ICSID Case No. ARB(AF)/99/2), Award, Oct. 11, 2002, 42 I.L.M. 85 (2003); 6 ICSID REP. 192 (2004); 125 I.L.R. 110 (2004); 15:6 WORLD TRADE & ARB. M. 273 (2003)	GKK 140 JC 98–99
MTD Equity Sdn. Bhd. and MTD Chile S.A. v. Republic of Chile (ICSID Case No. ARB/01/7), Award, May 25, 2004, 12 ICSID REP. 3 (2007); 44 I.L.M. 91(2005)	JC 102 GKK 141
MTD Equity Sdn Bhd. & MTD Chile S.A. v. Republic of Chile (ICSID Case No. ARB/01/7), Decision on Annulment, Mar. 21, 2007	JC 100, 102
Noble Energy Inc. and Machala Power Cía. Ltd. v. Republic of Ecuador and Consejo Nacional de Electricidad (ICSID Case No. ARB/05/12), Decision on Jurisdiction, Mar. 5, 2008	GKK 139
Pan American Energy LLC and BP Argentina Exploration Company v. Argentine Republic (ICSID Case No. ARB/03/13), Decision on Jurisdiction, July 27, 2006	GKK 139, 142
PSEG Global et al. v. Republic of Turkey (ICSID Case No. ARB/02/5), Award, Jan. 19, 2007	GKK 140–41, 141
Saipem S.p.A. v. The People's Republic of Bangladesh (ICSID Case No. ARB/05/07), Decision on Jurisdiction and Recommendation on Provisional Measures, Mar. 21, 2007, 22(4) INT'L ARB. REP. B-4 (2007)	TW 114 Annex 2
Salini Costruttori S.p.A. and Italstrade S.p.A. v. Hashemite Kingdom of Jordan (ICSID Case No. ARB/02/13), Decision on Jurisdiction, Nov. 29, 2004, 44 I.L.M. 569 (2005); 20 ICSID REV. 148 (2005); for a French translation, see 132 J.D.I. 182 (2005) (excerpts) (observations by E. Gaillard at 206)	JC 101
Salini Costruttori S.p.A. and Italstrade S.p.A. v. Kingdom of Morocco (ICSID Case No. ARB/00/4), Decision on	GKK 139

Jurisdiction, July 23, 2001, [French original] 129 J.D.I. 196 (2002) (observations by E. Gaillard at 209); English translation of French original in 6 ICSID REP. 400 (2004); 42 ILM 609 (2003)	
Sempra Energy International v. Argentine Republic (ICSID Case No. ARB/02/16), Award, Sept. 28, 2007	GKK 142, 143
Siemens A.G. v. Argentine Republic (ICSID Case No. ARB/02/08), Award, Feb. 6, 2007	GKK 139, 142
SGS Société Générale de Surveillance S.A. v. Islamic Republic of Pakistan (ICSID Case No. ARB/01/13), Decision on Objections to Jurisdiction, Aug. 6, 2003, 8 ICSID REP. 406 (2005); 18 ICSID REV. 307 (2003); 42 I.L.M. 1290 (2003); 18(9) INT'L ARB. REP. A-1 (2003); for a French translation, see 131 J.D.I. 258 (2004) (excerpts) (observations by E. Gaillard at 270)	JC 101, 103 GKK 139, 142
SGS Société Générale de Surveillance S.A. v. Republic of the Philippines (ICSID Case No. ARB/02/6), Decision on Objections to Jurisdiction, Jan. 29, 2004, 8 ICSID REP. 518 (2005); 19(2) INT'L ARB. REP. C-1 (2004)	AM 52 JC 101, 103 GKK 140, 142
Técnicas Medioambientales Tecmed, S.A. v. United Mexican States (ICSID Case No. ARB(AF)/00/2), Award, May 29, 2003, 43 I.L.M. 133 (2004); 19 ICSID REV. 158 (2004)	JC 102 GKK 140, 141
The Loewen Group, Inc. and Raymond L. Loewen v. United States of America (ICSID Case No. ARB(AF)/98/3), Award, June 26, 2003, 42 I.L.M. 811 (2003); 7 ICSID REP. 442 (2005); 4 J. WORLD INV. 675 (2003); for a French translation, see 131 J.D.I 219 (2004) (excerpts) (observations by E. Gaillard at 230)	GKK 140
Victor Pey Casado and Presidente Allende Foundation v. Republic of Chile (ICSID Case No. ARB/98/2), Award, May 8, 2008 (French original and excerpt translated into English)	Annex 3 Annex 4

5. Permanent Court of International Justice / International Court of Justice

The Case of the S.S. "Lotus" (France v. Turkey), Judgment No. 9 of Sept. 7, 1927, 1927 P.C.I.J., Series A, No. 10	GG 109
Case concerning the Factory at Chorzów (Germany v. Poland), Judgment No. 13 of Sept. 13, 1928, 1928 P.C.I.J., Series A, No. 17	JC 99 GG 109
The Corfu Channel Case (United Kingdom of Great Britain and Northern Ireland v. Albania), Judgment of Apr. 9, 1949, 1949 I.C.J. Reports 4	GG 109
Nottebohm Case (Liechtenstein v. Guatemala), Judgment of Nov. 18, 1953, 1953 I.C.J. Reports 111	GG 109
Nottebohm Case (Liechtenstein v. Guatemala), Judgment of Apr. 6, 1955, 1955 I.C.J. Reports 4	GG 109
Constitution of the Maritime Safety Committee of the Inter-Governmental Maritime Consultative Organization, Advisory Opinion of June 8, 1960, 1960 I.C.J. Reports 150	GG 109
Case concerning the Barcelona Traction, Light and Power Company, Limited (Belgium v. Spain), Judgment of Feb. 5, 1970, 1970 I.C.J. Reports 3	GG 109
Case concerning the Continental shelf (Tunisia/Libyan Arab Jamahiriya), Judgment of Feb. 24, 1982, 1982 I.C.J. Reports 18	GG 110
Case concerning Delimitation of the Maritime Boundary in the Gulf of Maine Area (Canada/United States of America), Judgment of Oct. 12, 1984, 1984 I.C.J. Reports 246	GG 110
Case concerning the Arbitral Award of 31 July 1989 (Guinea-Bissau v. Senegal), Judgment of Nov. 12, 1991, 1991 I.C.J. Reports 53	GG 109–10
Case concerning the Land, Island and Maritime Frontier Dispute (El Salvador v. Honduras: Nicaragua intervening), Judgment of Sept. 11, 1992, 1992 I.C.J.	GG 110

REPORTS 351	
Case concerning Maritime Delimitation in the Area between Greenland and Jan Mayen (Denmark v. Norway), Judgment of June 14, 1993, 1993 I.C.J. REPORTS 38	GG 110
Case concerning the Land and Maritime Boundary between Cameroon and Nigeria (Cameroon v. Nigeria), Judgment of June 11, 1998, 1998 I.C.J. REPORTS 275	GG 107
Case concerning Kasikili/Sedudu Island (Botswana/Namibia), Judgment of Dec. 13, 1999, 1999 I.C.J. REPORTS 1045	GG 110
Case concerning Maritime Delimitation and Territorial Questions between Qatar and Bahrain (Qatar v. Bahrain), Judgment of Mar. 16, 2001, 2001 I.C.J. REPORTS 40	GG 110
Case concerning the Land and Maritime Boundary between Cameroon and Nigeria (Cameroon v. Nigeria: Equatorial Guinea intervening), Judgment of Oct. 10, 2002, 2002 I.C.J. REPORTS 303	GG 111
Case concerning Sovereignty over Pulau Ligitan and Pulau Sipadan (Indonesia/Malaysia), Judgment of Dec. 17, 2002, 2002 I.C.J. REPORTS 625	GG 111
Cases concerning Legality of Use of Force, Preliminary Objections, Judgment of Dec. 15, 2004, Joint Declaration of Vice-President Ranjeva, Judges Guillaume, Higgins, Kooijmans, Al-Khasawneh, Buergenthal and Elaraby, 2004 I.C.J. REPORTS 330, 476, 621, 766, 912, 1061, 1208, 1353	GG 107

B. DOMESTIC DECISIONS

1. France

CA Paris, Oct. 21, 1983, Isover-Saint-Gobain v. Sociétés Dow Chemical France, 1984 REV. ARB. 98 (note by A. Chapelle)	AM 45

CA Paris, Feb. 18, 1986, Aïta v. Ojjeh, 1986 REV. ARB. 583 (note by G. Flécheux)	AM 64
CA Paris, Nov. 30, 1988, Korsnas Marma v. Durand-Auzias, 1989 REV. ARB. 691 (note by P.-Y. Tschanz)	AM 45
Cass. 1e civ., Oct. 22, 1991, Compania Valenciana de Cementos Portland v. Primary Coal Inc., 1992 REV. ARB. 457 (note by P. Lagarde); for an English translation, see 6(12) INT'L ARB. REP. B-1, B-4 (1991)	FP 29
Trib. Com. Paris, Feb. 22, 1999, Publicis v. True North, 2003 REV. ARB. 189	AM 64
CA Paris, Jan. 22, 2004, National Company for Fishing and Marketing "Nafimco" v. Foster Wheeler Trading Company, 2004 REV. ARB. 647 (note by E. Loquin)	AM 64
Cass. 1e civ., June 29, 2007, PT Putrabali Adyamulia v. Rena Holding, 134 2007 REV. ARB. 507 (note by E. Gaillard); J.D.I. 1236 (2007) (note by T. Clay); Petites affiches, No. 192, Chron. 20 (2007) (note by M. de Boisséson); for an English translation, see XXXII Y.B. COM. ARB. 299 (2007)	AM 41

2. Switzerland

Geneva Court of Justice, May 28, 1945, Bälher & Cie v. de Coulanges, ATF 71 I 229	FP 32
Zurich *Kassationsgericht*, Sept. 25, 1947, Iten v. Zurkirchen, ATF 73 I 188	FP 32
Liestal *Präsident des Bezirksgerichtes*, Dec. 14, 1960, Hupfen & Söhne v. Senn & Co., ATF 86 I 269	FP 32
Fed. Trib., Oct. 28, 1988, F. v. R. & R. AG, ATF 114 II 353	FP 32
Fed. Trib., Feb. 22, 1994, B. SA v. L. SA, ATF 120 II 214	FP 32
Fed. Trib., Jan. 22, 1996, ATF 122 III 36	FP 32
Fed. Trib., June 27, 1996, ATF 122 III 426, 1998 JdT	FP 36

171	
Fed. Trib., June 13, 2007, X. v. Réseau hospitalier fribourgeois, ATF 133 III 462	FP 31

3. United Kingdom

Ali Shipping Corp. v. Shipyard Trogir, [1998] 2 All E.R. 136	AM 62
Davis Contractors v. Fareham Urban District Council, [1956] A.C. 696	CS 81
Dolling-Baker v. Merrett, [1990] 1 W.L.R. 1205	AM 62
Hassneh Insurance Co. of Israel and others v. Steuart J. Mew, [1993] 2 Lloyd's Rep. 243 (QB)	AM 62, 65

4. United States

Gulf Petro Trading Co. v. Nigerian National Petroleum Corp., 512 F.3d 742 (5th Cir. 2008) (note by J. Price, for TDM (2008, forthcoming), available at www.transnational-dispute-management.com)	TW 120
Paccon, Inc. v. United States, 399 F.2d. 162 (Ct. Cl. 1968)	CS 77
United States of America v. Panhandle Eastern Corp., 118 F.R.D. 346 (D. Del. 1988)	AM 63

5. Australia

Coppée-Lavalin SA/NV v. Ken-Ren Chemicals and Fertilizers Limited, 1995 REV. ARB. 513 (note by D. Kapeliuk-Klinger)	AM 62
Esso Australia resources Ltd. v. Plowman, [1995] 128 A.L.R. 391	AM 62, 65

6. Sweden

Supreme Court of Sweden, Oct. 27, 2000, Bulgarian Foreign Trade Bank Ltd. v. A.I. Trade Finance Inc.,	AM 63

| 2001 REV. ARB. 821 (note by S. Jarvin and G. Reid) | |

7. Italy

| Italian Supreme Court, 1st Civil Section, Feb. 20, 2004, No. 3370, Emilio Giacomelli, Maria Domenica Mottini v. Fin. Recos S.r.l. | FP 35 |

C. BIBLIOGRAPHY

José E. Alvarez, *The Democratization of the Invisible College*, ASIL Newsletter (Nov. 2007), available at www.asil.org	TW 125
Julio A. Barberis, *La jurisprudencia internacional como fuente de derecho de gentes según la Corte de La Haya*, 1971 ZEITSCHRIFT FÜR AUSLÄNDISCHES ÖFFENTLICHES RECHT AND VÖLKERRECHT 641	GG 108
Henri Batiffol, *La sentence Aramco et le droit international privé*, 1964 REV. CRIT. DIP 647	AM 45
Carl Baudenbacher, *Some Remarks on the Method of Civil Law*, 34 TEXAS INT'L L.J. 333 (1999)	TW 115–16
MAX BAUMANN, DAVID DÜRR, VIKTOR LIEBER, ARNOLD MARTI, BERNHARD SCHNYDER, ZÜRCHER KOMMENTAR – KOMMENTAR ZUM SCHWEIZERISCHES ZIVILGESETZBUCH (Schulthess, 1998)	FP 32–33
Walid Ben Hamida, *The First Arab Investment Court Decision*, 7(4) J. WORLD INV. & TRADE 699 (2006)	TW 131
Klaus Peter Berger, *The International Arbitrators' Application of Precedents*, 9(4) J. INT'L ARB. 5 (1992)	AM 43
Andrea K. Björklund, *Investment Treaty Arbitral Decisions as Jurisprudence Constante, in* INTERNATIONAL ECONOMIC LAW: THE STATE AND FUTURE OF THE DISCIPLINE 265 (C.B. Picker, I.D. Bunn and D.W. Arner eds., Hart Publishing, 2008)	BL 5 GKK 137
Norberto Bobbio, *Ancora sulle norme primarie e norme secondarie*, 59 RIVISTA DI FILOSOFIA 35 (1968)	GKK 145

(translated into French as *Nouvelles réflexions sur les normes primaires et secondaires*, *in* LA RÈGLE DE DROIT 104 (C. Perelman ed., Bruylant, 1971)	
Franco Bonelli, *Acquisizioni di società e di pacchetti azionari di riferimento: le garanzie del venditore*, 21.2 DIRITTO DEL COMMERCIO INTERNAZIONALE 293 (2007)	FP 36
Franco Bonelli and Stefano Rellini, *Effetti della clausola* if and when*: una rassegna ragionata della giurisprudenza italiana e internazionale*, 11.2 DIRITTO DEL COMMERCIO INTERNAZIONALE 239 (1997)	AM 46–47
Stewart Boyd and V.V. Veeder, *Le développement du droit anglais de l'arbitrage depuis la loi de 1979*, 1991 REV. ARB. 209	TW 128–29
PHILLIP L. BRUNER AND PATRICK J. O'CONNOR, BRUNER & O'CONNOR ON CONSTRUCTION LAW (Thomson West, 2002)	CS 84
NAEL BUNNI, THE FIDIC FORMS OF CONTRACT (Blackwell Publishing, 4th ed. 2005)	CS 72
Phillipe Cavalieros, *La confidentialité de l'arbitrage*, III LES CAHIERS DE L'ARBITRAGE 56 (2006)	AM 62
Tai-Heng Cheng, *Precedent and Control in Investment Treaty Arbitration*, 30 FORDHAM INT'L L.J. 1014 (2007)	BL 5 GKK 137
Jacques Chevallier, *L'ordre juridique*, *in* LE DROIT EN PROCÈS 7 (PUF, 1983)	GKK 144
THOMAS CLAY, L'ARBITRE (Dalloz, 2001)	AM 62
Jeffery P. Commission, *Precedents in Investment Treaty Arbitration: a Citation Analysis of a Developing Jurisprudence*, 24 J. INT'L ARB. 129 (2007)	GKK 137, 145
J.P. Commission, *Precedent in Investment Treaty Arbitration: The Empirical Backing*, 4(5) TDM (Sept. 2007), available at www.transnational-dispute-management.com	TW 123
EDWARD C. CORBETT, FIDIC 4TH – A PRACTICAL	CS 72

LEGAL GUIDE (Sweet & Maxwell, 1980)	
RUPERT CROSS AND J.W. HARRIS, PRECEDENT IN ENGLISH LAW (Clarendon Press, 4th ed. 1991)	JC 102
PATRICK DAILLIER AND ALAIN PELLET, DROIT INTERNATIONAL PUBLIC (LGDJ, 7th ed. 2002)	GG 106, 107, 108
Yves Derains, *State Courts and Arbitrators, in* ARBITRATION IN THE NEXT DECADE 27 (ICC Pub. No. 612, 1999)	FP 27 AM 48
Zachary Douglas, *The Hybrid Foundations of Investment Treaty Arbitration*, 74 BRITISH Y.B. INT'L L. 151 (2003)	JC 103
Pierre Duprey, *Do Arbitral Awards Constitute Precedents? Should Commercial Arbitration Be Distinguished in this Regard from Arbitration Based on Investment Treaties, in* IAI INTERNATIONAL ARBITRATION SERIES NO. 3, TOWARDS A UNIFORM INTERNATIONAL ARBITRATION LAW? 251 (A.V. Schlaepfer, P. Pinsolle, L. Degos eds., Juris Publishing, 2005)	TW 114
Sergio Erede, *Durata delle guaranzie e conseguenze della loro violazione, in* ACQUISIZIONI DI SOCIETÀ E DI PACCHETTI AZIONARI DI RIFERIMENTO 199 (F. Bonelli and M. De Andrè eds., Giuffrè, 1990)	FP 35
WILLIAM R. EVERDELL, THE FIRST MODERNS (University of Chicago Press, 1997)	BL 6, 14
Fabrice Fages, *La confidentialité de l'arbitrage à l'épreuve de la transparence financière*, 2003 REV. ARB. 5	AM 65
Richard H. Fallon, *"The Rule of Law" as a Concept in Constitutional Discourse*, 97 COLUM. L. REV. 1 (1997)	GKK 144
FESTI FIORENZO, IL DIVIETO DI "VENIRE CONTRO IL FATTO PROPRIO" (Giuffrè, 2007)	AM 51
MARCEL FONTAINE AND FILIP DE LY, DROIT DES CONTRATS INTERNATIONAUX (Bruylant, 2nd ed. 2003)	AM 47

FOUCHARD GAILLARD GOLDMAN ON INTERNATIONAL COMMERCIAL ARBITRATION (E. Gaillard & J. Savage eds., Kluwer, 1999)	CS 84–85 FP 26, 34
Susan D. Franck, *The Legitimacy Crisis in Investment Treaty Arbitration: Privatizing Public International Law Through Inconsistent Decisions*, 73 FORDHAM L. REV. 1521 (2005)	GKK 143–44
Susan D. Franck, *The Nature and Enforcement of Investor Rights Under Investment Treaties: Do Investment Treaties Have a Bright Future?*, 12 U.C. DAVIS J. INT'L L. & POL'Y 47 (2005)	GKK 143–44
LON L. FULLER, THE MORALITY OF LAW (New Haven, rev. ed. 1969)	GKK 144,
Emmanuel Gaillard, *La distinction des principes généraux du droit et des usages du commerce international, in* ETUDES OFFERTES À PIERRE BELLET 203 (Litec, 1991)	FP 28, 29
Emmanuel Gaillard, *Thirty Years of* Lex Mercatoria: *Towards the Discriminating Application of Transnational Rules, in* ICCA CONGRESS SERIES NO. 7, PLANNING EFFICIENT ARBITRATION PROCEEDINGS: THE LAW APPLICABLE IN INTERNATIONAL ARBITRATION 582 (A.J. van den Berg ed., Kluwer, 1996) (also published in French: *Trente ans de Lex Mercatoria. Pour une application sélective de la méthode des principes généraux du droit*, 122 J.D.I. 5 (1995))	FP 28, 29
Emmanuel Gaillard, *Transnational Law: A Legal System or a Method of Decision Making?*, 17(1) ARB. INT'L 59 (2001)	FP 28, 29
Emmanuel Gaillard, *Le principe de confidentialité de l'arbitrage commercial international*, Dalloz, Chron. 153 (1987)	AM 62
JEREMY GLOVER AND SIMON HUGHES, UNDERSTANDING THE NEW FIDIC RED BOOK (intro. by C. Thomas, Sweet & Maxwell, 2006)	CS 72

Berthold Goldman, *Frontières du droit et "lex mercatoria"*, 9 ARCHIVES DE PHILOSOPHIE DU DROIT 177 (1964)	FP 28
Berthold Goldman, *Nouvelles réflexions sur la* Lex Mercatoria, *in* ETUDES DE DROIT INTERNATIONAL EN L'HONNEUR DE PIERRE LALIVE 241 (C. Dominicé, R. Patry and C. Reymond eds., Helbing & Lichtenhahn, 1993)	FP 28
F.A. HAYEK, THE POLITICAL IDEAL OF THE RULE OF LAW (Cairo, 1955)	TW 116
Guy Horsmans, *Propos insolites sur l'efficacité arbitrale*, III LES CAHIERS DE L'ARBITRAGE 33 (2006)	FP 25–26 AM 52
HUDSON'S BUILDING AND ENGINEERING CONTRACTS (I.D. Wallace ed., Sweet & Maxwell, 11th ed. 2003)	CS 84
Emmanuel Jolivet, *Access to Information and Awards*, 22(2) ARB. INT'L 265 (2006)	AM 49 TW 123
Emmanuel Jolivet, *Les clauses limitatives et élusives de responsabilité dans l'arbitrage CCI*, III LES CAHIERS DE L'ARBITRAGE 254 (2006)	AM 47
Gabrielle Kaufmann-Kohler, *Annulment of ICSID Awards in Contract and Treaty Arbitrations: Are there Differences?*, *in* IAI INTERNATIONAL ARBITRATION SERIES NO. 1, ANNULMENT OF ICSID AWARDS 189 (E. Gaillard & Y. Banifatemi eds., Juris Publishing, 2004)	GKK 147
Gabrielle Kaufmann-Kohler, *Arbitral Precedent: Dream, Necessity or Excuse? – The 2006 Freshfields Lecture*, 23(3) ARB. INT'L 357 (2007)	BL 5, 13 AM 40, 41, 42, 43, 50, 51 TW 114, 123 GKK 137, 144, 145
Gabrielle Kaufmann-Kohler, *In Search of Transparency and Consistency: ICSID Reform Proposal*, 2(5) TDM 5 (2005)	GKK 146

KEATING ON CONSTRUCTION CONTRACTS (V. Ramsey and S. Furst eds., Sweet & Maxwell, 8th ed. 2006)	CS 84
MICHEL VAN DE KERCHOVE AND FRANÇOIS OST, LEGAL SYSTEM BETWEEN ORDER AND DISORDER (I. Stewart trans., Clarendon Press, 1994)	GKK 144
MATTHEW H. KRAMER, IN DEFENSE OF LEGAL POSITIVISM: LAW WITHOUT TRIMMINGS (Oxford University Press, 1999)	GKK 144
MATTHEW H. KRAMER, OBJECTIVITY AND THE RULE OF LAW (Cambridge University Press, 2007)	GKK 143, 144
I. Laird and Rebecca Askew, *Finality versus Consistency: Does Investor-State Arbitration Need an Appellate System?*, 7(2) J. APP. PRAC. & PROCESS 285 (2005)	GKK 143–44, 146
A. DE LAPRADELLE AND N. POLITIS, RECUEIL DES ARBITRAGES INTERNATIONAUX, TOME PREMIER 1798-1855 (A. Pedone, 1905), Foreword by Louis Renault	GG 112
Christian Larroumet, *A propos de la jurisprudence arbitrale*, Gaz. Pal., Dec. 14, 2006, at 5	FP 32, 33 AM 49
ANDRÉ DE LAUBADÈRE, FRANCK MODERNE AND PIERRE DELVOLVÉ, TRAITÉ DES CONTRATS ADMINISTRATIFS, Vol. 2 (LGDJ, 1984)	CS 80, 83
H. Lauterpacht, *Some Observations on Preparatory Work in the Interpretation of Treaties*, 48 HARV. L. REV. 549 (1934-1935)	TW 119, 135
Serge Lazareff, *L'arbitre singe ou comment assassiner l'arbitrage*, *in* GLOBAL REFLECTIONS ON INTERNATIONAL LAW, COMMERCE AND DISPUTE RESOLUTION. LIBER AMICORUM IN HONOUR OF ROBERT BRINER 477 (eds. ICC Publishing, 2005)	FP 31
Julian D.M. Lew, *The case for the publication of arbitration awards*, *in* THE ART OF ARBITRATION – ESSAYS ON INTERNATIONAL ARBITRATION – LIBER AMICORUM PIETER SANDERS 12 SEPTEMBER 1912–1982, at 223 (J.C. Schultsz and A.J. van den Berg eds.,	AM 39, 40

Kluwer, 1982)	
T. Ellis Lewis, *The History of Judicial Precedent*, 48 L.Q. REV. 230 (1932)	TW 121
Humphrey Lloyd, *Book Review (Understanding the New FIDIC Red Book: A Clause-by-Clause Commentary. By Jeremy Glover and Simon Hugues. London: Thompson Sweet & Maxwell, 2006)*, 24 INT'L CONSTR. L. REV. 503, 505 (2007)	CS 73
JOHN LOCKE, THE SECOND TREATISE ON CIVIL GOVERNMENT (1690)	GKK 144
Eric Loquin, *Les obligations de confidentialité dans l'arbitrage*, 2006 REV. ARB. 323	AM 62
CAMPBELL MCLACHLAN, LAURENCE SHORE, MATTHEW WEINIGER, INTERNATIONAL INVESTMENT ARBITRATION: SUBSTANTIVE PRINCIPLES (Oxford University Press, 2007)	JC 103
Giovanni Marini, *Italian Report on Protecting Legitimate Expectations and Estoppel*, in LA CONFIANCE LÉGITIME ET L'*ESTOPPEL* – DROIT PRIVÉ COMPARÉ ET EUROPÉEN VOL. 4, at 295 (B. Fauvarque-Cosson ed., Société de législation comparée, 2007)	AM 51
Pierre Mayer, *Le principe de bonne foi devant les arbitres du commerce international*, in ETUDES DE DROIT INTERNATIONAL EN L'HONNEUR DE PIERRE LALIVE 543 (C. Dominicé, R. Patry and C. Reymond eds., Helbing & Lichtenhahn, 1993)	FP 29
ARTHUR MEIER-HAYOZ, BERNER KOMMENTAR – KOMMENTAR ZUM SCHWEIZERISCHEN PRIVATRECHT	FP 32–33
Joyiyoti Misra and Roman Jordans, *Confidentiality in International Arbitration: An Introspection of the Public Interest Exception*, 23(1) J. INT'L ARB. 39 (2006)	TW 129
JACQUES MONTMERLE, ALBERT CASTON, MARC CABOUCHE, LAURENT DE GABRIELLI AND MICHEL HUET, PASSATION ET EXÉCUTION DES MARCHÉS DE TRAVAUX PRIVÉS (Le Moniteur, 5th ed. 2006)	CS 83

CHRISTOPH MÜLLER, LA PERTE D'UNE CHANCE – ETUDE COMPARATIVE EN VUE DE SON INDEMNISATION EN DROIT SUISSE, NOTAMMENT DANS LA RESPONSABILITÉ MÉDICALE (Staempfli, 2002)	FP 31–32
JÉRÔME ORTSCHEIDT, LA RÉPARATION DU DOMMAGE DANS L'ARBITRAGE COMMERCIAL INTERNATIONAL (Dalloz, 2001)	FP
Jan Paulsson, *International Arbitration and the Generation of Legal Norms: Treaty Arbitration and International Law*, *in* ICCA CONGRESS SERIES No. 13, INTERNATIONAL ARBITRATION 2006: BACK TO BASICS? 879 (A.J. van den Berg ed., Kluwer, 2007); also available at 3(5) TDM (Dec. 2006)	TW 114 GKK 137, 145
Jan Paulsson, *Avoiding Unintended Consequences*, *in* APPEALS MECHANISM IN INTERNATIONAL INVESTMENT DISPUTES 241 (K.P. Sauvant ed., Oxford University Press, 2008)	TW 128, 136 GKK 146
Jan Paulsson, *La Lex Mercatoria dans l'arbitrage C.C.I.*, 1990 REV. ARB. 55	AM 50
Jan Paulsson and Nigel Rawding, *The trouble with confidentiality*, 5(1) ICC BULL. 48 (1994)	AM 64
Jan Paulsson, paper presented at the British Institute of International and Comparative Law's 9th Investment Treaty Forum Public Conference on the topic of "The Emerging Jurisprudence of International Investment Law," held in London on Sept. 14, 2007, *in* INVESTMENT TREATY LAW: CURRENT ISSUES III (A. Bjorklund, I. Laird, S. Ripinsky eds., British Institute of International and Comparative Law, forthcoming 2008)	BL 5
Pascal Pichonnaz, *Le devoir du lésé de diminuer son dommage*, *in* LA FIXATION DE L'INDEMNITÉ 109 (F. Werro ed., Staempfli, 2004)	FP
Andrea Pinna, *La spécificité de la jurisprudence arbitrale*, 16 JUSLETTER 7 (Oct. 2006)	AM 48, 52
Andrea Pinna, *Le concept de jurisprudence arbitrale et son application à la matière sportive*, Gaz. Pal., Oct. 15–	FP 25, 33

17, 2006, at 23	AM 42
Monique Pongracic-Speier, *Confidentiality and the Public Interest Exception*, 3(2) J. WORLD INV. 231 (2002)	TW 128–29
JEAN-FRANCOIS POUDRET AND SÉBASTIEN BESSON, COMPARATIVE LAW OF INTERNATIONAL ARBITRATION (S.V. Berti and A. Ponti trans., Sweet & Maxwell – Schulthess, 2nd ed. 2007)	FP 29 AM 61, 64
ALAN REDFERN AND MARTIN HUNTER WITH NIGEL BLACKABY AND CONSTANTINE PARTASIDES, LAW AND PRACTICE OF INTERNATIONAL ARBITRATION (Sweet & Maxwell, 4th ed. 2004)	CS 83
Gregory Reid, *Confidentiality - an Algorithm*, 2000(1) STOCKHOLM ARB. REP. 53	AM 64
W. Michael Reisman and Eric E. Freedman, *The Plaintiff's Dilemma: Illegally obtained evidence and admissibility in International Adjudication*, 76 AM. J. INT'L L. 737 (1982)	TW 119, 120, 135
NICOLAS ROUILLER, DROIT SUISSE DES OBLIGATIONS ET PRINCIPES DU DROIT EUROPÉEN DES CONTRATS (Cedidac, 2007)	FP 30
SCC ARBITRAL AWARDS 1999 – 2004 (S. Jarvin and A. Magnusson eds., JurisNet, 2006)	AM 54
CHRISTOPH H. SCHREUER, THE ICSID CONVENTION: A COMMENTARY (Cambridge University Press, 2001)	TW 128
Christoph Schreuer and Matthew Weiniger, *Conversations Across Cases – Is there a Doctrine of Precedent in Investment Arbitration?*, *in* THE OXFORD HANDBOOK ON INTERNATIONAL INVESTMENT LAW (P. Muchlinski, F. Ortino, C. Schreuer eds., Oxford University Press, forthcoming 2008) (available at http://univie.ac.at/intlaw/conv_across_90.pdf)	GKK 137, 147
Rolf A. Schütze, *The Precedential Effect of Arbitration Decisions*, 11(3) J. INT'L ARB 69 (1994)	AM 44

Matthew Secomb, *Awards and Orders Dealing with the Advance on Costs in ICC Arbitration : Theoritical Questions and Practical Problems*, 14(1) ICC BULL. 63 (2003)	FP 34
MOHAMMED SHAHABUDDEEN, PRECEDENT IN THE WORLD COURT (Cambridge University Press, 1996)	JC 98 GG 108
Gianluca Sicchiero, *L'interpretazione del contratto ed il principio* nemo contra factum proprium venire potest, *in* CONTRATTO E IMPRESA 507 (CEDAM, 2003)	AM 51
Anthony Sinclair, paper presented at the British Institute of International and Comparative Law's 9th Investment Treaty Forum Public Conference on the topic of "The Emerging Jurisprudence of International Investment Law," held in London on Sept. 14, 2007, *in* INVESTMENT TREATY LAW: CURRENT ISSUES III (A. Bjorklund, I. Laird, S. Ripinsky eds., British Institute of International and Comparative Law, forthcoming 2008)	BL 5
Hans Smit, *Note, Dispute Resolution in Patent Pooling Arrangements: The Arbitration Solution*, 16 AM. REV. INT'L ARB. 547 (2005)	GKK 146
MAX SØRENSEN, LES SOURCES DU DROIT INTERNATIONAL: ÉTUDE SUR LA JURISPRUDENCE DE LE COUR PERMANENTE DE JUSTICE INTERNATIONALE (Einar Munksgaard, 1946)	GG 108
B. STARCK, H. ROLAND, L. BOYER, INTRODUCTION AU DROIT (Litec, 5th ed. 2000)	FP 25, 32
Debra P. Steger, *The Rule of Law or the Rule of Lawyers?*, 3(5) J. WORLD INV. 769 (2002)	TW 129
JUSTIN SWEET AND JONATHAN J. SWEET, SWEET ON CONSTRUCTION INDUSTRY CONTRACTS: MAJOR AIA DOCUMENTS (Aspen Publishers, 4th ed. 2007)	CS 84
BRIAN Z. TAMANAHA, ON THE RULE OF LAW: HISTORY, POLITICS, THEORY (Cambridge University Press, 2004)	TW 116 GKK 144, 145

Kenji Tashiro, *Quest for a Rational and Proper Method for the Publication of Arbitral Awards*, 9(2) J. INT'L ARB. 97 (1992)	AM 60
Alfred, Lord Tennyson, *Aylmer's Field* (1864)	JC 99
PIERRE TERCIER AND CHRISTIAN ROTEN, LA RECHERCHE ET LA RÉDACTION JURIDIQUES (Schulthess, 4th ed. 2003)	FP 37
FRANÇOIS TERRÉ, INTRODUCTION GÉNÉRALE AU DROIT (Dalloz, 6th ed. 2003)	FP 33
THE STATUTE OF THE INTERNATIONAL COURT OF JUSTICE: A COMMENTARY (A. Zimmermann, C. Tomuschat and K. Oellers-Frahm eds., Oxford University Press, 2006)	GG 106, 107
Luc Thévenoz, *La perte d'une chance et sa réparation*, *in* QUELQUES QUESTIONS FONDAMENTALES DU DROIT DE LA RESPONSABILITÉ CIVILE : ACTUALITÉS ET PERSPECTIVES 237 (F. Werro ed., Staempfli, 2002)	FP 31
John B. Tieder, Jr., *The Duty to Schedule and Co-Ordinate on Multi-Prime Contractor Projects—The United States Experience*, 3(2) INT'L CONSTR. L.R. 97 (1986)	CS 76
Silvio Venturi, *Commentaire – Article 197*, *in* COMMENTAIRE ROMAND. CODE DES OBLIGATIONS I, at 1065 (L. Thévenoz and F. Werro eds., Helbing & Lichtenhahn, 2003)	FP 36
R.E. Walck and L.A. Ahee, *Investment Arbitration Update (As of December 31 2007)*, TDM (Feb. 2008), available at www.transnational-dispute-management.com	TW 132
Humphrey Waldock, *General Course on Public International Law*, *in* COLLECTED COURSES OF THE HAGUE ACADEMY OF INTERNATIONAL LAW, Vol. 106-II, Year 1962	GG 108
I.N. DUNCAN WALLACE, THE INTERNATIONAL CIVIL ENGINEERING CONTRACT (Sweet & Maxwell, 1974)	CS 72

I.N. DUNCAN WALLACE, THE INTERNATIONAL CIVIL ENGINEERING CONTRACT: FIRST SUPPLEMENT (Sweet & Maxwell, 1980)	CS 72
Pierre Wessner, *La vente portant sur la totalité ou la majorité des actions d'une société anonyme : la garantie en raison des défauts de la chose*, in MÉLANGES PIERRE ENGEL 459 (Payot, 1989)	FP 36

D. OTHER

European Convention on International Commercial Arbitration, done at Geneva on April 21, 1961, 349 U.N.T.S 374 (1963–1964)	AM 46
United Nations Convention on Contracts for the International Sale of Goods (1980) (available at www.uncitral.org)	AM 47
Statute of the International Court of Justice	PW 95, 96 JC 98, 99 GG 105–08, 111–12 Annex 4
ILC Articles on State Responsibility	JC 100
1985 UNCITRAL Model Law on International Commercial Arbitration (available at www.uncitral.org)	AM 46
Report of the United Nations Commission on International Trade Law on the work of its twenty-first session (New York, 11–20 April 1988), Doc. A/43/17 (available at www.uncitral.org)	AM 57
United Nations Commission on International Trade Law, Case Law on UNCITRAL Texts (CLOUT), User Guide, Doc. A/CN.9/SER.C/GUIDE/1/Rev.1, February 4, 2000 (available at www.uncitral.org)	AM 57
UNTACD, TRANSPARENCY, UNCTAD Series on Issues in International Investment Agreements (2004),	TW 117

540

available at www.unctad.org	
UNIDROIT Principles of International Commercial Contracts	FP 30
Principles of European Contract Law	FP 30, 31
U.K. Housing Grants, Construction and Regeneration Act 1996	AM 46
New Zealand Arbitration Act 1996	AM 61